MANAGING AUSTRALIA'S ENVIRONMENT

Editors

Stephen Dovers and Su Wild River

THE FEDERATION PRESS
2003

Published in Sydney by:
    The Federation Press
    PO Box 45, Annandale, NSW, 2038
    71 John St, Leichhardt, NSW, 2040
    Ph (02) 9552 2200 Fax (02) 9552 1681
    E-mail: info@federationpress.com.au
    Website: http://www.federationpress.com.au

This book is published with the support of Land & Water Australia.
    GPO Box 2182, Canberra, ACT, 2601
    Level 2, UNISYS Building,
    91 Northbourne Avenue, Turner, ACT, 2612
    Ph (02) 6257 3379 Fax (02) 6257 3420
    E-mail: public@lwa.gov.au
    Website: http://www.lwa.gov.au
The opinions expressed in the book represent those of the authors and
not necessarily those of Land & Water Australia and its Board.

National Library of Australia
Cataloguing-in-Publication entry

    Managing Australia's environment

    Bibliography.
    Includes index.
    ISBN 1 86287 447 6

    1.Natural resources – Australia – Management.
    2. Environmental impact analysis – Australia.
    I. Dovers, Stephen. II Wild River, Su.

333.714

© The Federation Press

Typeset by The Federation Press, Leichhardt, NSW.
    Printed by Ligare Pty Ltd, Riverwood, NSW.

MANAGING AUSTRALIA'S ENVIRONMENT

Foreword

A casual browser would be justified in assuming from the title of this book that it purports to provide useful lessons in how to manage Australia's unique environment. They would be right. But a look at the chapter headings reveals no mention of soils, vegetation, wildlife or water ... nothing very practical at all really.

Yet this book is intensely practical, notwithstanding its academic weight and obvious depth of scholarship. Because managing Australia's environment is a big job, far too big for individual landholders or leaseholders or industries or communities. It is a job for all of us. How well we do it impacts on all of us. So we expect governments to take it seriously; we expect legislation to be enacted and government agencies to be responsible for its implementation; we expect research into problems and their solutions; we expect policy statements and funding programs; we expect that a range of organisations, public and private, will play different roles; we expect that science and technology will continually improve our individual and collective capacities to manage Australia's environment.

These are expectations of 'the system' – the institutions, policy processes and management regimes that are the stuff of this book. They are profoundly pervasive and influential in shaping the way resources and environments are managed in Australia. Yet they receive far too little attention, critical or otherwise, compared with farming and forestry practices or the weather.

This timely book fills a big hole, thoroughly and engagingly.

It reviews Australian resource and environmental policy in the broadest sense over the last 30 years. It explores cases and themes across a range of sectors and environmental issues, from forests to oceans, drawing on a range of perspectives from the social sciences. It starts on the premise that we might make more progress in tackling the big environmental and resource management challenges facing Australia if our policies and institutional settings were genuinely adaptive: learning by experience through time and across different sectors; systematically monitoring and evaluating their effectiveness and adjusting accordingly; and giving us clear information about how well we are doing.

This might seem like common sense, but the evidence here suggests that it is far from common. We have been better at announcing new policies, programs and organisations than carefully distilling the lessons from the old ones. We tend to discount the past, to ignore learnings from other sectors, and consequently to repeat our mistakes. We are more comfortable tinkering with little bits than trying to comprehend the whole.

Salutary lessons for our policy makers, administrators and treasuries pepper the pages of this book. It teases out the lessons and 'take home messages' from some of our more notable ventures in environmental policy over three decades. Policy makers rarely make the public spotlight for their impact on the environment in the same way that farmers do. I hope that many will recognise their work through these pages and reflect on what might be done in future to get closer to the principles posited here: *persistence, purposefulness; information-richness and sensitivity; inclusiveness and flexibility.*

In many ways this is an eclectic collection, of both subject matter and contributors. However, consistent themes do inform the stories that emerge throughout. The editorial hand of Dovers and Wild River is light but distinct. The writing is lucid and often pointed. Theories and methodologies don't get in the way of the ideas and insights developed. The three days the authors and project steering committee spent arguing over these issues face-to-face have undoubtedly strengthened the weave. The researchers generally steer clear of prescription, but they generate many useful pointers for improvement and reform in the ways we conceive, develop, implement, analyse, monitor, review and adjust environmental policy and management in Australia.

Managing Australia's Environment is just one output from a research project funded by Land & Water Australia through its Social and Institutional Research Program. This modest research program has done much to underline the importance of social and institutional issues in shaping the way resources are managed in Australia.

Dovers' and Wild River's fine compilation is testament to the practical value and huge further potential of this research. It deserves to be widely read – not just by people interested in environmental policy and sustainability, but by anyone interested in Australian landscapes, lifestyles and livelihoods.

I congratulate the editors and contributors on a great job and commend their work to you.

Andrew Campbell
Executive Director, Land & Water Australia

Contents

Acknowledgements

The research project that led to this book relied totally on the researchers and practitioners who have contributed chapters. For scant reward they have offered much that is of enduring value. Without exception, their insight, generosity and commitment have impressed us enormously.

Land & Water Australia supported the project financially and intellectually; it would not have happened otherwise. In the absence of the sort of core support that research into ecologically sustainable development (ESD) deserves, this body has become the de facto ESD R&D corporation and is world class. It fits well the description of 'adaptive institution', and its impacts substantially exceed its modest budget, small complement of staff and defined charter.

The steering committee for the venture operated with a light yet judicious hand: Richard Price, Warren Musgrave, Onko Kingma, Ronnie Harding, Peter Crabb and Tim Bonyhady. During the course of the project Warren and Onko left government employ and became contributors to the project as well. There is only one steering committee member who has not contributed a chapter in the book, but he was nonetheless central to the initiation of the research, the way in which it proceeded, its outcomes, and to its content of red wine. Richard Price's intellectual and practical contributions to natural resource management in Australia extend far beyond those that might be surmised from his formal office of R&D manager.

Ken Moore and Andrew Campbell made valuable contributions *en route*, bringing fresh perspectives and sharp imperatives. As well as a contributing author and editor, Su Wild River managed the project. Sandra Mitchell assisted with manuscript preparation and Patrick McNamara with proofreading. Clive Hilliker prepared many of the figures. Catherine Mobbs offered many helpful comments while in academia, and along with Christine Ellis at Land & Water Australia assisted with bringing the book to fruition in collaboration with The Federation Press. Margaret Farmer, Chris Holt and Clare Moss at The Federation Press were prepared to entertain and persist with a manuscript of unseemly mass. We trust that readers will understand that the size of this book is in keeping with the magnitude of the task of pursuing a future that is ecologically sustainable and humanly desirable.

S Dovers and S Wild River

Contributors

Nick Abel is working on evolutionary approaches to social-ecological systems, the political economy of institutional change, property rights and the valuation of ecosystem services. His work spans Australian and African rangelands and dryland agriculture. He leads the Ecological and Economic Systems Group at CSIRO Sustainable Ecosystems.

Kate Andrews spent five years assisting the creation and then management of the Lake Eyre Basin Coordinating Group, a community-driven integrated resource management initiative. She is currently with Greening Australia's national office.

Gerry Bates is an environmental law and policy consultant who teaches environmental law at the universities of Sydney and NSW and The Australian National University. He also serves on the Board of the NSW EPA and is author of several texts on environmental law.

Tim Bonyhady is a Professor with The Australian National University's Cross-Cultural Research Centre and Centre for Resource and Environmental Studies, where he traverses environmental history, law and the arts.

Peter Christoff is the Coordinator of Environmental Studies in the School of Anthropology, Geography and Environmental Studies at the University of Melbourne, and is active in research in environmental policy and management.

Peter Crabb is a Visiting Fellow at the Centre for Resource and Environmental Studies, The Australian National University. He has worked extensively on issues of resource and environmental management, especially in the Murray-Darling Basin.

Allan Curtis leads the Social Sciences Program of the Commonwealth's Bureau of Rural Sciences, which operates at the interface between science and policy. Previously, he was Associate Director of the Johnstone Centre at Charles Sturt University, where he now holds an honorary appointment, undertaking research into rural development and resource management. He coordinates social research for CSIRO's Heartlands research program.

John Dore, a researcher from The Australian National University's School of Resources Environment and Society, is presently occupied analysing Mekong Region institutions, governance and new regionalisms based at Chang Mai University in northern Thailand.

Stephen Dovers is a Senior Fellow with the Centre for Resource and Environmental Studies, The Australian National University, where he researches and teaches in policy and institutional dimensions of sustainability, adaptive resource management, science-policy linkages and environmental history.

Robyn Eckersley is a senior lecturer in the Department of Political Science, University of Melbourne where she teaches in global politics, political theory and environmental politics and policy. Her main areas of research are environmental politics and policy.

Sarah Ewing is a geographer and Honorary Fellow of the Department of Civil and Environmental Engineering at the University of Melbourne. She has extensive experience in natural resource management and especially the policy and practice of catchment management. She is a member of the Victorian Catchment Management Council and the Victorian Environmental Assessment Council.

Marcus Haward is Senior Lecturer with the Institute of Antarctic and Southern Ocean Studies and Program Leader in Law, Policy and International Relations at the Antarctic Cooperative Research Centre, University of Tasmania. He has research interests and has published widely in ocean policy and management, fisheries management and integrated coastal zone management.

Clive Hamilton is Executive Director of The Australia Institute, an independent research organisation. He is also a Visiting Fellow with the Graduate Program in Public Policy, The Australian National University, with research interests in environmental policy and economics.

Ronnie Harding is Associate Professor and Director of the Institute of Environmental Studies at the University of NSW where she runs the University-wide Master of Environmental Management Program. She has interests in the application of sustainability principles, especially the precautionary principle, and environmental reporting and education. She has been a member of the NSW State of Environment Advisory Council for the 2000 and 2003 State of Environment reports.

Colma Keating of Dinkum Results is a Perth-based consultant working towards sustainable natural resource management with a strong focus on supporting individuals, groups and organisations to more effectively contribute to discussion, decision and action.

Onko Kingma is Director of the Canberra-based company CapitalAg, providing analysis in agriculture, natural resource management and rural issues, and Visiting Fellow with the Centre for Research and Learning in Regional Australia at the University of Tasmania. He was previously Assistant Secretary with the Commonwealth agency Agriculture, Fisheries and Forestry Australia.

Ian Lowe is Emeritus Professor of Science, Technology and Society at Griffith University, and a prominent analyst of, and commentator on, environmental issues and science policy.

Jennifer McKay is Professor and Director of the Water Policy and Law Research Group at the University of South Australia. She has a national and international reputation for analysis and development of policy instruments for sustainable water management in Australia and India.

Catherine Mobbs manages R&D investments in sustainable natural resource management with Land & Water Australia, having previously undertaken research into the structure and rationality of natural resource management regimes.

Warren Musgrave is a consulting economist working mainly on water related issues. He was Professor of Agricultural Economics at the University of New England from 1971 to 1995, and Special Adviser - Natural Resources, NSW Premier's Department from 1995 to 2000.

Brett Odgers is a Canberra-based consultant in sustainability, regional economics, regulatory systems and environmental planning, with extensive experience in environmental policy and regulation.

Kim Orchard from Orchard's Innovative Consultancy Service has extensive experience in delivery of Indigenous programs within the Commonwealth sphere addressing employment, training, environmental management, cultural heritage protection, the arts and health, and has contributed to the development of policy and legislation in these areas.

Helen Ross is Professor of Rural Community Development at the University of Queensland Gatton. Her work in social dimensions of natural resource management includes social impact assessment and Indigenous environmental management.

Mark Stafford Smith is an systems modeller who has spent 22 years working on Australian rangeland systems from plants and soils, through pastoral herd dynamics and economics, to how whole regions function in an integrated social, economic and environmental sense. He lives and works from Alice Springs.

David Ingle (Dingle) Smith was a Senior Fellow at the Centre for Resource and Environmental Studies, The Australian National University from 1976 until retirement in 1997. His research interests were predominantly in the field of Australian water resources with an emphasis upon the twin hazards of flood and drought. He is currently a Departmental Visitor at the Centre.

Denise Traynor received her PhD from the University of Queensland. She has worked for the Queensland EPA and authored the Inland Waters chapter of that state's 1999 State of Environment report. She is currently taking time out of the workforce to raise two children.

Su Wild River is an academic and environmental consultant based at the Centre for Resource and Environmental Studies, The Australian National University. In recent years she has worked with local governments across Australia developing comparative methods to assess environmental risk and case studies of drivers and constraints to local government delivery of beneficial environmental outcomes.

Jim Woodhill is Head of the Social and Economic Department at the International Agriculture Centre in the Netherlands. Formerly he worked on community-based natural resource management issues in Australia both with Greening Australia and as an academic. He has also worked on environment and development issues in Africa and Asia.

The late **Elspeth Young** was Director of the Environmental Management Program, National Centre for Development Studies, The Australian National University. She was noted for her research bringing Indigenous environmental management aspirations into the public arena, including concerning cattle stations, mobility and community-based planning.

PART I

INTRODUCTION

1

Processes and Institutions for Resource and Environmental Management: Why and How to Analyse?

Stephen Dovers

Centre for Resource and Environmental Studies,
The Australian National University

This chapter introduces the themes and purpose of this book, to explain what is presented, but also to allow the collaborative endeavour that produced it to be better understood, judged, and analysed (see Chapter 23). The book is the result of a nagging suspicion, fed by numerous anecdotal experiences and empirical analyses, that resource and environmental policy and management in Australia suffer from *ad hockery* and amnesia. That is, what we do at a given time often appears uninformed by previous experiences and, often, previous policy and management attempts are not even recognised (Dovers 1995; 1999; Walker 1994).

Amnesia occurs over time, so does *ad hockery*. But forgetfulness is only part of it. Too often, policy and management experiences remain isolated in separate sectors, portfolio areas and jurisdictions, and within small groups concerned largely with one substantive issue, whether that be fisheries, water, biodiversity forests, pollution control, or something else. The modern idea of sustainability – ecologically sustainable development (ESD) in this country – is not about environment but about an intended, integrated policy agenda that is wider and deeper. ESD is about the long term integration of social, ecological and economic imperatives, more precautious approaches to the environment, about including people in policy and management, and creating new institutions and processes. If we are to integrate, then this should not be only in each discrete decision making or policy case, but all the time, across the resource and environmental field. Or, rather, to try and make ESD the coherent and influential *policy field* that it is yet to become. To inform that positive evolution, learning and synthesising across its disparate parts seems a good idea. Such a task could not be pursued alone or even in a small group, but demanded a larger, collaborative venture.

So the project and this book amounts to a broad review of resource and environmental policy over the past three decades. It scans over a variety of issues, jurisdictions, resource sectors, portfolios and institutional forms. It includes the probably obvious and perhaps the unexpected, as chapter topics. The suggestive time period of three decades takes us back to early environmental protection and nature conservation regimes, and to the then emerging organisational and statutory nature conservation provisions. That span allows coverage of some older approaches and issues as well as those that have emerged more recently. It assesses how well we are adapting to the ever-changing demands of managing ourselves in a strange land. Of course some things are missing. As large and rich in variety as the book is, it has not been possible to cover the entire span of resource and environmental management. For example, there is far less focus on urban than on non-urban issues. But the collection is more broad and diverse than anything previously undertaken and should be of interest to anyone even should their particular interest not be covered.

As to 'method', there was not one in the normal academic sense. The subject matter and kind of people involved rendered a defined methodological pathway impossible. And the aim was to bring together a diverse group of qualified thinkers in one venture and let them have their heads, not put them in a straightjacket. Nevertheless, some themes were developed to guide the venture in a few common directions.

Common themes

The participating researchers were given some common themes and topics to address; not strictly, but to guide analysis along comparable lines. Interaction during the course of this research project ensured dialogue between individual researchers and review of emerging analysis and conclusions. A three day meeting in the middle of the project provided opportunity for discussion and could have gone on for three weeks.

The overall framework was that of 'adaptive policy, institutions and management'. This extends the ecological notion of adaptive management to incorporate broader scales of management (regions, catchments, sectors) and to include policy processes and institutional and societal learning dimensions (see Gunderson et al 1995; Dovers and Mobbs 1997; Dovers 1999). Adaptive management originally involved modelling exercises between researchers and managers in relatively bounded ecosystem management situations, to construct management interventions as testable hypotheses, combining the rigour of the scientific method with the contingent realities of politics and management. This is a significant departure from the *ad hoc* and poorly monitored approaches so often evident. In recent years, the approach has expanded to include social and institutional as well as ecological and managerial dimensions. Rather than focusing only on distinct management contexts, we can think more broadly, adding policy processes and institutional arrangements as needing also to be adaptive. This offers an informed, iterative, inclusive and flexible approach to ESD. The features of an adaptive approach are:

- respect for and combination of perspectives from the natural and social sciences;
- recognition of uncertainty, complexity and long time scales;
- construing policy and management interventions as driven by a defined purpose, but *explicitly experimental*, consistently testing understanding and capabilities along the way;

- wide inclusion of stakeholders, in a purposeful and structured fashion; and
- design and maintenance of sophisticated mechanisms (institutions and processes) of feedback and communication between policy and practice and across different situations.

This views 'policy' not as a political and bureaucratic process taking inputs from researchers and other information sources and systems and applying these in decision making, but rather *policy-as-informing-system* in itself. The policy process becomes an iterative system (which it in theory and in much literature is). Not a blinding insight by any means, but not so often evident in practice and too rarely investigated. This will demand political and management humility, accepting that policy disappointment is likely and preparing to learn from this. Adaptiveness represents a departure from the way we often do things, and would be hard to 'do' (see next section). Public policy will always 'muddle through' (Lindblom 1959), but adaptive forms of policy, institutions and management invite a more purposeful muddling through.

The adaptive idea echoes recent political and social theory suggesting 'new' ways of approaching policy and politics (see Eckersley, this volume). Such proposals are described (though less often made operational) by terms and theories of 'civil society', 'dialogic democracy'; 'discursive democracy' and 'communicative rationality'. Certainly, the demand from communities is for more inclusion, the clear need of management is for better information systems, and most people agree that longer-term, learning approaches are needed. The challenge is to integrate these. These complex ideas can be conveniently summarised as 'doing' policy and politics in an iterative, inclusive and mutually informing manner. An adaptive mode seeks to focus such broad notions in the context of ESD. Approaches such as collaborative planning, ecosystem management or integrated catchment management reflect similar principles.

The 'adaptive' framework used here was fleshed out through a series of *checklists* and *themes*. These informed the commissioned studies – not as research prescriptions, as flexibility is required for analysis of very different contexts – but to provide a basis for commonality and comparison. They were intended to focus attention onto the features of processes and institutions supporting (or not) underlying capacities. One aim was to allow a finer resolution of lesson-drawing than is sometimes sought, to inform cross-sectoral learning and communication. The assumption was that there is never complete policy success or failure – all experiences can yield both positive and cautionary lessons. The project was not interested in identifying 'blueprints', where one organisational or institutional model is recommended for relocation in its entirety. The challenge was to identify the *particular features* that contributed to success or failure, so as to inform future activities. To illustrate, a complete 'model' from, say, catchment management or pollution control might not be of generic interest, but the experience with a specific issue or strategy might be, such as regarding participatory planning, research-policy links, statutory design or communication strategies.

The five *core principles* for an adaptive approach were defined as follows:

Persistence: learning and adaptation are more likely to occur if initiatives and processes are properly supported and maintained over time, generally requiring some defensible legal status.

Purposefulness: policy and management need to be driven by widely supported goals and objectives, providing a basis against which progress can be measured and lessons accrued. Although vague and often confusing, ESD principles were viewed as the most appropriate, currently articulated set, given their wide expression in policy and in over 120 Australian statutes (Stein 2000).

Information-richness and -sensitivity: learning depends on close monitoring of the environment and of policy and management experiments, with intensive use and wide ownership of the information produced.

Inclusiveness: policy and management learning and improvement requires the inclusion and participation of those involved and affected (the degree and kind of inclusion being context dependent).

Flexibility: adaptiveness implies a preparedness to learn and change, and the caution that purposefulness should not become rigidity.

Discussion of these principles as research themes recognised the challenge of integrating and exploring tensions between them. However, they were not be interpreted too rigidly or prescriptively. No single analysis was expected to deal with all or even most of these; each contributor here has considered what was relevant to their own area. As well as the five principles, further themes and checklists were used and are summarised below for the record. These detailed the terms *institution* and *policy process*, to encourage isolation of key attributes. In the first, institutional attributes are presented as neutral attributes in the case of analysis of past or existing arrangements, and design parameters in the case of institutional reform. It is likely that a small set of these would be more important in a given case (Dovers and Mobbs 1997):

- extent or limits in geographical space (spatial scale);
- jurisdictional, political and administrative boundaries;
- degree of permanence and longevity;
- intended or actual roles (informational, cultural, legal, economic, etc);
- sectoral or issue coverage/focus;
- nature and source of aims and mandate (in custom, or statute or common law);
- degree of autonomy;
- accountability (how, to whom);
- formality or informality of operation;
- political nature and support (actual, required);
- exclusiveness/inclusiveness (membership, representativeness);
- degree of community awareness and acceptance;
- degree of functional and organisational flexibility;
- resourcing requirements (financial, human, material);

- information requirements (internal, external); and
- reliance on and linkages with other institutions.

The difference between *organisations* and the underlying *institutions* they manifest was recognised but treated according to individual author's preferences. The next checklist represents a view of the elements of policy processes for ESD (from Dovers 1995). This is *not* a model, but a reminder that policy processes have many elements, whether particular or shared with other processes or initiatives, and that one or several elements, whether present or absent, may be crucial. One use of this list is to broaden attention to the pre- and post-conditions necessary to support that very common species, the glossy 'policy statement' (element 10 below). This will be familiar to those acquainted with a policy cycle or system approach, and in that sense is unremarkable, but was constructed specifically for ESD problems:

Problem framing:
1. Discussion and identification of relevant social goals
2. Identification and monitoring of topicality (public concern)
3. Monitoring of relevant natural and human systems and their interactions
4. Identification of problematic environmental change or degradation
5. Isolation of proximate and underlying causes of change or degradation
6. Assessment of risk, uncertainty and ignorance
7. Assessment of existing policy and institutional settings
8. Definition (framing and scaling) of policy problems

Policy framing:
9. Development of guiding policy principles
10. Construction of general policy statement (avowal of intent)
11. Definition of measurable policy goals

Implementation:
12. Selection of policy instruments/options
13. Planning of implementation
14. Provision of statutory, institutional and resourcing requirements
15. Establishment of enforcement/compliance mechanisms
16. Establishment of policy monitoring mechanisms

Monitoring and review:
17. Ongoing policy monitoring
18. Mandated evaluation and review
19. Extension, adaptation or cessation of policy and/or goals
20. Iterative description and explanation of process

Critical general elements, applicable at all stages of a process:
- policy coordination and integration (across and within policy fields)
- public participation and stakeholder involvement
- transparency, accountability and openness
- adequate communication mechanisms (multi-directional, democratically structured)

The next checklist dealt with *problem definition*, or rather the recognition of the attributes of policy problems. These attributes support the claim that policy problems in sustainability may be different in kind and possibly in degree to those in other, more familiar policy fields (Dovers 1997). This encourages more precision as to what peculiar features of a substantive or policy problem make it difficult and/or different (or not):

- broadened, deepened and highly variable spatial and temporal scales;
- the possibility of absolute ecological limits to human activity;
- irreversible impacts, and related policy urgency;
- complexity within and connectivity between problems;
- pervasive risk, uncertainty and ignorance;
- typically cumulative rather than discrete impacts;
- new moral dimensions (eg other species, future generations);
- many environmental assets not traded in markets and thus not valued;
- 'systemic' problem causes, embedded thoroughly in patterns of production, consumption, settlement and governance;
- lack of available, uncontested research methods, policy instruments and management approaches;
- lack of defined policy, management and property rights, roles and responsibilities;
- intense demands (and justification) for increased community participation in both policy formulation and actual management; and
- sheer novelty as a suite of policy problems.

The final checklists concerned policy choice, a critical art but one not always undertaken in a manner suggesting a comprehensive menu of instruments or consistent criteria. Unproductive arguments such as those between advocates of, say, 'market mechanisms' and 'regulation' are a dismal manner of policy choice, denying both the richness of possible instruments and that a mixture will generally be needed. The first checklist provides a basis for identifying the instruments used and inquiring as to the reasons why they were used, why others were not, and why the approach taken did or did not work (from Dovers 1995.) The second proposes ESD-relevant criteria for instrument choice (see Table 1.1 opposite):

Finally, seven further *themes* were proposed to guide the project. These may or may not prove relevant in any particular context, but may emerge as important in considering institutions and processes in terms of adaptive capacity:

Table 1.1: Policy instruments and selection criteria

Instrument class:	Main instruments and approaches:
1. R&D, Monitoring	Increase knowledge generally (basic research) or about a specific matter (applied research); establish a standard; develop technologies or practices; establish socio-economic implications; monitor environmental conditions or policy impact.
2. Communication and Information Flow	Directions: research findings to policy; policy imperatives to research; both to firms, agencies and individuals. Mechanisms: state of the environment reporting; natural resource accounting; community-based monitoring; environmental auditing; fora for consultation or policy debate.
3. Education and Training	Public education (moral suasion); targeted education; formal education (schools, higher ed.); training (skills development); education regarding other instruments.
4. Consultative	Mediation; negotiation; dispute resolution; inclusive institutions and processes.
5. Agreements, Conventions	Intergovernmental agreements/policies (international or within federations); memoranda of understanding; conventions and treaties.
6. Statutory	New statutes or regulations under existing law to: create institutions; establish statutory objects and agency responsibilities; set aside land for particular uses; land use planning; development control; enforce standards; prohibit practices.
7. Common Law	Torts, nuisance, public trust.
8. Covenants	Conservation agreements tied to property title.
9. Assessment procedures	Review of effects; EIA; social impact assessment; cumulative impact assessment; strategic impact assessment; risk assessment; life cycle assessment; statutory monitoring requirements.
10. Self-regulation	Codes of practice, codes of ethics, professional standards.
12. Community Involvement	Participation in policy formulation; community based monitoring; community implementation of programs; cooperative management; community management.
13. Market Mechanisms	Input/output taxes/charges; use charges; subsidies; rebates; penalties; tradeable emission permits/use quotas; tradeable property/resource rights; performance bonds; deposit-refunds.
14. Institutional or Organisational Change	To enable other instruments or policy and management generally, especially over time.
15. Change Other Policies	Distorting subsidies, conflicting policies or statutory objects.
16. Reasoned Inaction	(Where justified by due consideration.)

Criteria for policy instrument choice:

1. *Effectiveness criteria*: information requirements; dependability (re. goals); corrective vs. antidotal focus; flexibility (across contexts, time); gross cost; efficiency (relative to achieving goal); cross-sectoral impacts.

2. *Implementation criteria*: equity impacts; political/social feasibility; legal/constitutional feasibility; institutional feasibility; monitoring requirements; enforcability/avoidability; communicability (to those affected).

Taking account of historical context. If sustainability requires a long view forward, the obvious corollary is for a long view back. Institutions reflect past rather than present or future imperatives and understanding, and the nature of institutions, organisations and processes owe much to historical context. This prospect is discussed in Dovers (2000), and the long history of environmental concern in this country by Bonyhady (2000).

Impacts of globalisation, marketisation and managerialism. These are three interrelated political and policy phenomena. Recent years have seen profound institutional and organisational change driven by neo-liberal political trends. Globalisation of finance, law, markets and information is important and should be recognised as a shaping variable. Marketisation refers to the increased use of market instruments, and to market-oriented reform of institutions and organisations (Dovers and Gullett 1999). Managerialism refers to changes in public administration where generic management skills are valued above specialist ones, and where more rapid change and human movement in institutions has occurred. These phenomena may impact on information systems, community involvement, transparency and accountability, likelihood of regulatory intervention, and the possibility of cross-catchment or whole-of-landscape management.

Role of non-state players. Resource and environmental policy and management have evolved from a regulatory relationship between the state and industry, to a much more complex relationship involving other players. Increasingly, policy is formulated in consultative processes, self-regulatory approaches and community involvement are used, and markets relied upon to achieve policy goals.

Capabilities in policy/management monitoring, evaluation and review. When analysing institutions and processes, it is important to identify whether mechanisms were or are in place to monitor, evaluate and review policy and institutional performance. This is a feature of adaptive approaches and also determines the availability of evidence available for judging institutional or process efficacy.

Information technologies. Many new approaches, instruments and information capacities in ESD are underpinned by increasingly powerful information technologies. These are mostly viewed as enabling better policy and management, but we should be aware of unintended negative impacts such as on community involvement, access to and cost of information, data continuity, policy monitoring, etc.

Coping with risk and uncertainty. Risk and uncertainty pervade ESD issues, and this may or may not be dealt with explicitly by policy processes and institutions. Further, many different approaches and techniques are relevant to decision and policy making under conditions of uncertainty, and the choice to adopt one of these is important in its implications for later policy or management directions (eg. research, cost-benefit analysis, negotiation, quantitative or strategic risk assessment, safe minimum standards, performance bonds, application of the precautionary principle, etc) (Dovers et al

1996). Importantly, risk and uncertainty need to be construed broadly, to include not only quantifiable risk and scientific uncertainty (absence of knowledge) but also such important forms as perceived irrelevance, taboo, distortion and poorly distributed information (Smithson 1989).

The themes and issues above have been influenced heavily by the work of colleagues and myself over the years, but it seems that the basic concern of *ad hockery* and amnesia, if not the more detailed responses to that concern, are shared by many players in resource and environmental management. Anyway, as expected, not all the following chapters deal with the five core principles or other themes in the same manner. All applied their own experience and practical and disciplinary backgrounds to identify other, important themes, which are visited in the final chapter.

Reading this book

The book is broken into only partly arbitrary parts. The first set of chapters – 'sectoral studies' – began as perspectives on current challenges in important resource sectors, used to focus all contributors on current and emerging imperatives and thus avoid any temptation by contributors to prepare only a *post mortem*. They were subsequently rewritten with an eye to the common themes. The following three sections have been organised under the three broad heads of institutions and processes, regulatory and management regimes, and inclusive approaches. The final section contains four added and more reflective perspectives from the standpoints of law, politics, science and economics. The final chapter was meant to be but is not really a 'summary and synthesis'. It attempts that, but can only do so partially and besides is one person's synthesis. The collection should be read and used in its richness and detail. There is no executive summary, because of all people, it is 'executives' who should acquaint themselves with rich detail. Managerialist ignorance of the fine and particular does not suit the challenge of developing adaptive institutions, policy processes and management regimes.

The bulk of research for this book was undertaken over 1999-2001, with updating where necessary in 2002.

References

Bonyhady, T, 2000, Colonial Earth, Melbourne: Meigunyah Press.

Dovers, S, 1995, Information, sustainability, and policy, Australian Journal of Environmental Management 2: 142-156.

Dovers, S, 1997, Sustainability: demands on policy, Journal of Public Policy 16: 303-318.

Dovers, S, 1999, Adaptive policy, institutions and management: challenges for lawyers and others, Griffith Law Review 8: 374-392.

Dovers, S, 2000, On the contribution of environmental history to current debate and policy, Environment and History 6: 131-150.

Dovers, S and Gullett, W, 1999, Policy choice for sustainability: marketization, law and institutions, in Bosselman, K and Richardson, B (eds), Environmental Justice and Market Mechanisms, London: Kluwer Law International.

Dovers, S and Mobbs, C, 1997, An alluring prospect? Ecology, and the requirements of adaptive management, in Klomp, N and Lunt, I (eds), *Frontiers in ecology*, London: Elsevier.

Dovers, S, Norton, T and Handmer, J, 1996, Uncertainty, ecology, sustainability, and policy, *Biodiversity and Conservation* 5: 1143-1167.

Gunderson, L, Holling, C and Light, S (eds), 1995, *Barriers and Bridges to the Renewal of Ecosystems and Institutions*, New York: Columbia University Press.

Lindblom, CE, 1959, The science of muddling through, *Public Administration Review* 19: 79-88.

Smithson, M, 1989, *Ignorance and Uncertainty: Emerging Paradigms*, New York: Springer-Verlag.

Stein, P, 2000, Are decision-makers too cautious with the precautionary principle? *Environmental and Planning Law Journal* 18: 3-23.

Walker, KJ, 1994, *The Political Economy of Environmental Policy: An Australian Introduction*, Sydney: University of NSW Press.

PART II

SECTORAL STUDIES

2

Rangeland Institutions Over Time and Space

Mark Stafford Smith and Nick Abel

CSIRO (Commonwealth Scientific and Industrial Research Organisation)
Sustainable Ecosystems, Alice Springs/Canberra

The rangelands of Australia constitute that large part of the continent that is unsuitable for intensive agriculture or forestry. This 5.5 million km^2 thus approximates the arid and semi-arid interior, plus the lightly settled tropical north, and a few other smaller pockets.

The rangelands are at once the iconic heart and soul of the Australian psyche, and its burden and embarrassment. Although most Australians live on the coast and dream of the surf, it is to the outback that we turn for our more basic identity. This is the land of Uluru, red desert sands, the sheep and the gold upon which Collins Street was built, kangaroos, emus and lizards, millennia of Aboriginal occupation, open spaces, campfires and tall tales.

At the same time it has been the source of political power quite out of proportion to its economic or demographic significance, it has held the shame of Aboriginal mistreatment and of a globally significant loss of biodiversity, and has grabbed the nation's headlines with true anguish over rural decline.

For these reasons and others, implicitly or otherwise, it seems that Australians remain prepared to support and subsidise the management of the rangelands into the future. The question is, can this investment be better targeted and more effective in shaping that future? The following brief points summarise some key features of the rangelands today, on which answers to this question must be founded. Although some of the problems of the range-lands echo those of other rural regions, the rangelands' underlying features of remoteness, low productivity and unpredictability often dramatically alter the way in which they play out.

Rangeland realities

Any discussion of the rangelands must acknowledge the following features, which are drivers or consequences of natural resource management in this vast area of Australia (drawn from, *inter alia*, Morton and Price 1993, Stafford Smith 1994, Abel and Ryan 1996, ANZECC/ARMCANZ 1996).

Biophysical

- Rainfall is highly variable but generally low. This affects all biota and those land uses dependent on them, whether pasture growth for grazing or wildflowers for tourism.
- Soil fertility is generally low, with most nutrients held in the top 2 cm or so, hence easily degraded; but some areas of more fertile and/or more resilient soils occur.
- The low productivity per hectare leading to large management units (paddocks or properties) encompassing much spatial variability. These are therefore hard to monitor for adaptive feedback, and little finance is available to invest in rehabilitation if damage is done.
- The rangelands have lost half their terrestrial mammal species in the past 200 years, At the same time, there has been a major intrusion of feral animals and weeds, and a perception that major land degradation problems have developed (though impacts on fodder and animal production may be less than perceived).
- All these factors vary *greatly* across the rangelands!

Economic

- Falling commodity prices continue to depress conventional industries, especially pastoralism. Wool production has been particularly badly affected over the past decade, despite intermittent respites. These industries were based originally on very low inputs and reasonable outputs, so there are strong limits to potential increases in the efficiency of production.
- Increasing productivity is also affected by increasing costs of required inputs, increasing labour costs, expectations in terms of monitoring health, safety, environmental conditions, etc; in some regions a great increase in inputs could pay off in outputs through intensification (with potential environmental consequences), in others it will not.
- There is still a tendency for the higher investment industries to transfer out much of the money they earn in the rangelands (eg, mining, tourism, where most proceeds are received in cities or overseas).
- The value of production is out of balance with the area of land used:
  - *mining* is worth ca $10bn/year (a trivial area used for production, but more for exploration);
  - *tourism* is worth about $2bn/year but occupies very little land;
  - *grazing* is worth less than $1bn/year, (much less as a profit at full equity figure allowing for a reasonable living wage) but occupying ca 52% of area;
  - *Aboriginal lands* are responsible for substantial social transfers into the rangelands, and increasingly deliver significant non-conventional products to market (eg, art and crafts) from about 22% of the area (but growing most rapidly);
  - *conservation reserves* occupy 7% of the area and are the focus for much of the tourism; however, this does not encompass the range of

variability in soils and vegetation needed for a representative reserve system, and conservation management (as opposed to visitor management) is poorly resourced.

Social

- There is a general trend to an aging and declining non-indigenous population, with decline of smaller and more isolated communities and concentration in larger towns; this general trend is not universal with a few regions showing strong growth.
- Associated with this, there is a small and declining number of community leaders bearing growing burdens of decision-making responsibilities, making them subject to stress-related illness.
- Communities affected by policies made in far-off cities respond with feelings of powerlessness and high suicide rates.
- Population decline is associated with decreasing access to services, although this is somewhat offset by electronic communications.
- At the same time, there is an increasing and younger Aboriginal population, with the older people seeking to return to remote out-stations and the younger component tending to live in towns. A substantial projected rise in work-aged Aboriginal people is associated with high levels of welfare dependency.
- High employee turnover among the providers of most services (especially education, health, many government agencies), coupled with fly-in/fly-out employment structures in many mining operations (and senior management in other activities such as defence, tourism, etc), leading to low institutional memory.
- Regional economies are generally simple, based mainly on the exports of primary products, with a limited number and range of employment opportunities.
- There are unresolved conflicts over native title, land and land use, between pastoralists and Aboriginal people; between Aboriginal people with overlapping land claims; and between pastoralists and conservationists. However, these differ greatly between State jurisdictions.
- An increasing number of regions with economic structural problems are affecting the sustainability of their human communities.
- On the positive side, an increasing diversity of community groups is seeking to control the futures of their regions; and a growing realisation that the attributes of rangelands – remoteness, cultural richness, biodiversity and beautiful landscapes – are growing in value in our increasingly urban and agricultural world.

Institutional

- Land management and use is the responsibility of six State-level jurisdictions (WA, SA, NT, Qld, NSW, Victoria). Each has different legislation, delivery mechanisms, agency policies, regulations and incentives, all of which interacts with federal government, which has its own legislation, policies and agencies.

- Rangelands are the dominant area of land in all but NSW and Victoria, but are the smallest economic force in all, leading to a problem of always being low in priority in each jurisdiction, even though recognised as being of great importance across them all. Hence, a process developing a 'National Strategy for Rangelands Management' has recently been completed, but was devalued by promulgating it as just a set of principles, after a huge effort in community consultation.

- Rangelands are suffering largely from the tyranny of small decisions, with no dramatic inter-jurisdictional catastrophe to precipitate coordinated action (compared to the Murray-Darling Basin, for example); a diversity of major stake-holders lack a community of interest (Table 2.1).

- Aboriginal ownership is increasing through the purchase of leases under the *Aboriginal Land Rights (Northern Territory) Act* (Cth) 1976 and its supporting State and Territory legislation; and under the *Aboriginal and Torres Strait Islander Commission Act* (Cth) 1989. Native Title claims are being laid over extensive areas under the *Native Title Act* 1993, so far with negligible implementation but far-reaching uncertainty. Aboriginal control over land has also increased through joint management arrangements in National Parks.

- Not only are there differences in tenure between jurisdictions but there is also great uncertainty about lease renewals in some jurisdictions (especially WA).

Further background

Stafford Smith et al (2000) analyse some institutional and cultural factors (based on the underlying environment of the rangelands) that may be constraining change. They highlight the differences between regions of the rangelands, and what consequences this could have for uniform policy intervention in rangeland problems. Abel (1999) provides an analysis of rangelands as a complex adaptive system with the implications that this has for perceptions of rangeland problems and solutions. He uses Western NSW to illustrate some of these points for rangelands in the world more generally, and highlights the links (or lack of them) between institutions, stakeholders and research. Additional information supporting the features of the rangelands reported above include recent regional trends (Abel and Ryan 1996; Wilcox and Cunningham in Morton and Price 1993), general statistics (Stafford Smith 1994), legislative diversity (Ledgar in Morton and Price 1993), alternative land uses (Morton and Stafford Smith in Morton and Price 1993), and some indication of the levels of public investment in different regions (Wilcox and Cunningham in Morton and Price 1993).

Core themes

Throughout this paper we use 'institution' to mean the formal and informal rules that humans establish to regulate the behaviour of other humans towards each other and their environment, together with the means of implementing those rules. We therefore include the organisational arrangements, such as a household, a company or a local council, along with the rules under which they operate.

Table 2.1. Political Influences of Stakeholders (based on Abel and Tatnell, 1997)

	Relative Strength Now	Postulated Reasons for Relative Strength	Estimated 20 Year Trend	Reason for Trend
Tourism Industry	Moderate	Good returns to capital Provide employment Urban and international capital	Growing	Growth in demand for diminishing 'wilderness' Perceived as 'non-consumptive'
Conservationists	Moderate	Conservationist paradigm clashes with dominant developmental one Perceived as anti-growth, anti-jobs	Growing	Concerns about sustainability of resource use Species losses Support from urban middle class Support from scientists
Mineral Industry	Strong	Economic importance Provide employment Infrastructure shared with other resource users	Stable	Demand steady Improvements in technology maintain competitiveness
Pastoral Industry	Strong	Iconic status — the self sufficient pioneers Economic importance in the past Uniformity of rural voting Voting systems and electoral boundaries	Weakening	Perceived as damaging the land by urban people Perceived as subsidised Low and diminishing economic importance Decline in relative numbers
Indigenous People	Weak	Loss of land and culture Past policies Low numbers	Growing	Political activism Moral strength of their case Growth in numbers Some urban middle class support

How have rangeland institutions performed in terms of the core themes of this book; persistence, purposefulness, information-richness and sensitivity, inclusiveness and flexibility? A core issue in the foregoing features is the fact that these institutions span seven jurisdictions, as well as several sectoral interests in each, so the answer to this question is clearly variable. However the following generalisations, which are phrased mainly in terms of problems to be solved, are generally applicable.

First, in discussing the history and effectiveness of rangeland institutions, we need to define some issues of scope and scale. From 150 years ago to about the 1980s, perceptions of rangeland use were mainly focused on grazing and mining, with 'management' of the Aboriginal population as the other major policy concern. For the past 40 or so years – but particularly more recently – conservation, tourism and a growing diversity of smaller land uses have gained currency. Policy relating to Aboriginal people has evolved to its current day focus on 'living on the land'. The adjunct concerns of remote area service delivery (health with the Flying Doctor service, education with School of the Air, communications, etc) have expanded to incorporate the Indigenous population and changed in format.

Thus in the past, addressing the institutions that affect resource management in the rangelands meant mainly focusing on grazing. This has recently shifted to a more pluralistic interpretation, with a consequent increase in land use conflicts.

It is also useful to consider a number of different scales. Resource management outcomes affect and are affected by institutions at all scales from the individual manager, through local peer groups, to the regional community and local government, State agency, legislature, national policy and funding framework, and international markets and treaty obligations. We will return to these different scales to discuss institutional constraints to good resource management outcomes at each.

Persistence

At a State government level, institutions intended to oversee rangelands resource management have persisted for almost the entire history of settlement, albeit in different forms in different States. From early on, there have been Lands Boards supported by Departments of Lands or their equivalent in almost all States, aimed at controlling what was mostly leasehold land through a consistent instrument (covenants or lease conditions). The most specialised of these bodies is the Western Lands Commission in New South Wales; in most other States the rangelands areas were dealt with specially but under the same government department as other lands. In most jurisdictions the regulatory role has been supported with some research and extension capacity for most of this history, although the resources dedicated to this have declined markedly in recent years. In all jurisdictions the main tenure instrument has been leasehold land, with some moves towards freehold mainly in Queensland. Of course, there is a difference between active persistence and inertia, and the latter is a considerable element, as indicated in the next section.

At a regional to State level, industry representative bodies have generally persisted, with considerable political clout. Names and allegiances have changed from time to time (eg the recent creation of Agforce in Queensland), and cattle and sheep producers have often gone their own ways, but some form of representation has generally been maintained. The power of this representation is reflected in the remarkable, perhaps lamentable, consistency with which rangeland regions have seen royal commissions and inquiries undertaken into the unhappy condition of one area or another (or the same one again). There has been an endless litany of these since the *Commission appointed to enquire into the state of runs suffering from drought* in South Australia (Northern Runs Commission 1867). Examples such as the *Royal Commission to inquire into the condition of the crown tenants of the Western Division of New South Wales* of 1901 (see Lunney 1994) and the *Royal Commission appointed to inquire into and report upon the financial and economic position of the pastoral industry in the leasehold areas in Western Australia* (Parliament of Western Australia 1940) are echoed by the concerns of today's West 2000 and Gascoyne-Murchison Strategies respectively. Thus the representation has been persistent but, as discussed in the next section, possibly directed by an outdated purpose.

Recently other regional groupings, in particular Landcare groups, are on the rise, but these have their own problems of representativeness and effectiveness in the rangelands as noted below. Community bodies that represent the public interest of conservation management, and bodies of various forms representing Aboriginal lands, have mainly arisen only in the past few decades.

Legislation underpinning land administration and management has been very persistent in WA and NSW. For example, the legislation affecting the NSW rangelands is a complex mixture of ancient and modern. The *Western Lands Act* 1901 (NSW) was established in response to drought, economic recession, land degradation and pastoral poverty. Subsequently, layer upon layer of natural resource legislation has been added. Specific problems have been addressed through *ad hoc* amendments, without fundamental reform. Environmental legislation has been superimposed over outdated sectoral and segmented natural resources law. The consequence is a legislative tangle barely intelligible to the agencies that apply it, let alone the landholders who become ensnared in it. Ledgar (in Morton and Price 1993) describes the diversity of legislation in other States.

Purposefulness

While aspects of institutions have persisted well over the years, their purpose and purposefulness has changed greatly. Holmes (1995) has identified the fact that policy about the rangelands in Australia has moved through three great phases: the first was one of development, the last one of resource conservation, and in between there was an important policy vacuum during which inertia caused significant changes to rangeland institutions. The development phase was marked by a presumption that grazing was an interim step on the path of land use intensification, and that greater and better land uses would eventually colonise the inland. Policy often aimed at avoiding land speculation by enforcing covenants aimed at minimum stocking rates and land development. Short leasehold tenures allowed the State to take back land and subdivide for closer settlement. Land use rights were mostly restricted to grazing.

Around 1940–1950, it began to be apparent that no amount of wishful thinking and realistic economic investment would convert a naturally unreliable and infertile environment into intensive agriculture. For quite a while there was no real policy direction, and in this interregnum the previous institutions persisted through inertia. However, there was little enthusiasm for enforcing convenants, and little by little pastoralists accrued by practice a variety of rights which were never really ceded to them in legislation or regulation. In truth the land tenure instrument became little different to freehold in practice, although it was still very different in law (this has subsequently become particularly important because, unlike freehold title, leasehold may not extinguish native title). This happened at different speeds in different regions, since closer settlement policy was still in vogue in NSW and Queensland as soldiers returned from the Second World War.

During the 1970s, concepts of land conservation provided a new focus for policy. The emphasis was upon the conservation of ecological functions that supported primary production, and conservation of native species for their intrinsic value was not initially considered. A new onus was put on pastoral managers to be seen to be sustainable, and new demands on research to be able to demonstrate this through monitoring, to the extent that failures might actually be taken to court. However, this meant clawing back many of the rights that had accrued to pastoralists in the interregnum, a process that is still very much in progress today. It also meant shifting the focus of legislation to sustainable management rather than infrastructure development. It led to a new approach to drought policy (still being fought by sectoral interests) which emphasised self-reliance rather than industry assistance (see Smith, this volume).

During the past two decades, calls have increased from city-based pressure groups for the conservation of native species for their intrinsic value. This pressure has resulted in legislation to protect rare and endangered species, and native vegetation in general. Legislation for the protection of cultural heritage has likewise been established. Both sets of legislation further restrict the freedoms of leaseholders, in particular in relation to clearing shrubs to increase grass production, and planting opportunity crops.

Many of these trends were paralleled in the mining industry, albeit often much more quickly – in most areas the target for concern is much better defined (a few large companies rather than many 'battlers') and with much greater investment capacity. The same conceptual developments are still occurring in the development of other industries. For example, the 'silver bullet' industry of tourism started off with an environmental *carte blanche*, supported through generous State subsidy purportedly aimed at national park management but really managing tourism impacts. The expectations of this are slowly being clawed back as parks like Uluru and Kakadu start to charge entry fees to assist with management. Similarly, local irrigation schemes in some areas began with hopelessly over-optimistic expectations; although recent

Box 2.1. The National Strategy for Rangelands Management (NSRM)

The NSRM (ANZECC/ARMCANZ 1996) had the potential to be a major force for unifying activity in rangelands, in which the rangelands briefly held the national stage as a stand-alone priority in government; the idea evolved as follows:

1990	First discussions of the need, with a proposal for a Resource Assessment Commission inquiry into rangelands (which never occurred) by then primary industries Minister John Kerin
1992	Formal proposal arising out of Arid Land Administrators Conference
Mar 1993	Prime Minister's Statement on the Environment included a commitment to develop a strategy: approach agreed by governments and working group established; Arid Lands Coalition (formed from conservation groups with an interest in the inland), National Farmers Federation and Indigenous interests provided with some resources to assist participation
Feb 1994	Rangelands issues paper released, requesting comment by Apr 1994. Period of intensive consultations began, with 30 regional and national workshops
1994-1996	Period of detailed drafting based on workshop outcomes, a huge collation of background material (never made public) and 182 formal responses
July 1996	Release of Draft NSRM with 6 month response period
Dec 1996	Responses closed and indication of completion in the near term (ca. 6 months)
July 1997	Final consultations at the Working Group level for submission of drafts to Ministerial Councils later in 1997
1997-1998	Separate SCC/ANZECC/ARMCANZ meetings disjointly debate options for re-writing and/or downgrading the content of final strategy
1998	Two drafts, one very minimalist, another with more of the original
1999	Draft received and accepted by the Councils
Apr 1999	Released as Principles and Guidelines

The NSRM Draft was open to a series of tensions that made it vulnerable. Its ownership was shared between two Ministerial Councils, each with their own committees of officials and sources of advice. While this held out the potential for synergies and broad acceptance of the strategy, lack of coordination between councils led to fragmented decision-making. Meetings of the two councils were not synchronised, and the potential for unilateral modification of group decisions by Ministers was substantial. As a result, some Ministers walked away from the process. There were substantial changes of Ministers and of senior officials during the process. Corporate memory and commitment became important issues, not countered by strong departmental champions. The Working Group comprised officials from the two Ministerial Council committees, landholder interests, the conservation movement, indigenous interests, as well as other experts. Coordination between officials in different government departments was often limited. There was some strong lobbying from stakeholders, principally grazing and conservation interests, but also concerns in relation to land rights.

The draft strategy raised the potential for changes in power and access to resources, issues that could not be resolved in a fragmented environment. Despite the structure and all but a dozen words of the Draft report being agreed among the Working Group, subsequent debate on these tensions downgraded any perception of unanimity. There was a lack of a balanced and synchronised debate on the shape of the final strategy report, which led to Councils being confronted with alternative versions of the document for release to the public. Thus a series of procedural and institutional issues resulted in a context within which significant, but probably not irresolvable, issues downgraded the outcome to a release of *National Principles and Guidelines for Rangelands Management*. The effect of this was to reduce the onus on the various jurisdictions to act, let alone to coordinate, and to disenchant the rangelands public who had committed considerable effort to the process.

developments are more sober, there is still limited application of precautionary assessment. For different ideological reasons there are even parallels on Aboriginal lands, where the creation of development opportunities at all costs is slowly giving way to concerns among the supporters of Indigenous rights for long-term land management.

During the 1990s, an exercise to develop what was finally titled the 'National Guidelines and Principles for Rangelands Management' (ANZECC/ARMCANZ 1999) ought to have provided a consistent purpose for the future of the rangelands. However, the history of their development and downgrading from a binding national management strategy illustrates the fact that as a nation we are still not agreed how this purpose should be implemented (Box 2.1). Although there were other less explicit tensions, the formal major stumbling block in the Draft National Strategy for Rangeland Management occurred between industry and conservation lobbies on exactly what the objectives should be in terms of a 'comprehensive, adequate and representative' reservation system (the only bracketed wording in the draft).

A major problem in all this is that the rangelands encompass so much variation in environmental, economic and social conditions that, at any level better than very broad motherhood statements, a single approach to policy or institutions may well not be useful across the nation (Stafford Smith *et al.* 2000). Added to this is the question of monitoring success across such a vast area, an issue we take up in the next section.

Information-richness and sensitivity

Although research and monitoring effort in rangelands has been by no means trivial, it nonetheless pales into insignificance when compared with the areas concerned. The sheer physical scale of the rangelands, coupled with its natural variability over time and space, has always made monitoring difficult. This applies at the scale of a manager keeping track of how the livestock in one paddock are doing, as much as for land management agencies monitoring performance against covenants on a property, assessing changes in biodiversity, water use in the Great Artesian Basin, mining exploration or marijuana plots. Almost all of these (particularly the last!) have been assisted by recent developments in satellite remote sensing, but remain difficult. Most difficult of all in the environmental domain is separating human-induced change from the massive year-to-year fluctuations in species identity and biomass caused by climatic variability. This makes it genuinely difficult for institutions and individuals to learn from feedback. It should engender support for the precautionary principle in favour of environmental conditions, but equally well provides a shield for a rival precautionary principle based on not missing out on economic gain unnecessarily, where short-term economic risk aversion outweighs environmental risk aversion.

When development-oriented covenants concentrated on such issues as the condition of fences and the sinking of bores, action was taken on defaulters. However, since covenants have begun to address sustainable management of land, very little action has been taken by monitoring authorities.

The rare application of conservation orders in the past 20 years has usually arisen from such blatant abuses where most of the industry was appalled by the actions of the accused and there was a negligible chance of the pseudo-scientific justification being challenged in court. In short, such action depended basically on the overwhelming balance of opinion, which could not be invoked until damage was probably largely irrevocable.

Stafford Smith et al (2000) collate a series of reasons why the difficulty of detecting change, the often long-term nature of such change and the natural tendency of humans to discount the future, add up to inevitable damage in landscapes which are insufficiently resilient for the rate of management errors to be exceeded by the rate of recovery from error.

Perhaps the key problem in this regard is that resource management institutions have presumed that, with sufficient investment, a degree of monitoring information and predictability – equivalent to that in closely settled regions – could be attained. This level of investment has proved impossible to obtain, meaning it has always been possible to blame failure on inadequate information.

But it may be time to face up to the fact that change in certain aspects of certain rangelands simply cannot be monitored in a timely, useful and practical way. This should lead to new 'meta-approaches' to the problem, which may be tailored to the features of different resources, and to the needs of different institutions. The precautionary principle might rate highly among these (eg Stein 2000; Harding and Fisher 1999).

Inclusiveness

In most jurisdictions, pastoral management has been split between a leasehold management agency (usually a Department of Lands) and a development advisory agency (typically a Department of Primary Industries or Agriculture). With the rise of resource conservation, soil conservation responsibilities have sometimes been with another agency, with carriage of soil conservation regulations that sit outside covenant conditions. Responsibilities for cultural heritage and nature conservation are vested in yet other agencies. In most States, soil conservation responsibilities have subsequently been amalgamated with the Lands Department, so the role of 'policing' resource conservation is in one department, development in another, and nature conservation and the protection of cultural heritage are in one or two others again. A similar situation pertains for mining and more recently for tourism.

Typically the departments which identify most closely with each industry (Agriculture, Mining, Tourism) are subject to client capture. The experience of outsiders interacting with these departments is that their view of the industry is often that projected by the industry politically, lagging behind individual industry leaders in the implementation of new ideas. Low population levels and high turnover has resulted in rangelands government agencies being dominated by staff who either stay a long time and who come to identify with their industry community, or who pass through briefly and provide no continuity. There is a fine line between a good extension officer and client capture. The result of all these factors is that the relevant industries are often reasonably well included in decision-making about their own sectors, but this process is largely closed to anyone outside that sector.

This problem has flowed through to Landcare and the scale of regional communities. The Landcare movement was originally predicated on issues of sustainable agriculture, reasonably so in higher rainfall districts. Despite the fact that problems in the rangelands are generally much wider in terms of sustainable habitation and integration across land uses, many rangelands Landcare groups (and pastoral groups generally) have been slow to embrace other stakeholders, probably slower than groups in more closely settled areas. There are exceptions to this, but the apparent legitimacy (not least in access to funding) of Landcare groups yet their reluctance to embrace the broader issues and players has proved a great impediment to community-driven regional planning in rangelands.

A particular argument arises about the legitimacy of the involvement of city-based interests in regional planning in the rangelands. Rural communities are usually uncomfortable with, or even unaware of, the fact that a large portion of rangelands funding flows out from the urban tax base, so that the urban community certainly has some claim on its expenditure. The extent to which this may be justified by the substantial riches that have been removed from the rangelands to create urban wealth in bygone days is a poorly explored issue. The fact that pastoral land is leased from the Crown for specified *pastoral* purposes only weakens the rural case from an urban perspective, but not from a rural one.

Flexibility

The issue of adaptability is somewhat enigmatic in rangelands. Its people are at once hugely adaptable and fundamentally conservative; adaptable does not, of course, necessarily mean purposefully adaptive. However, there is no doubt that among the rangelands population there is an enormous number of experiments going on into finding new ways of surviving economically, and there are certainly rugged individualists genuinely blazing trails into this unknown territory. In an environment with high variability and low predictability, it is a sobering thought that it may in fact pay to be conservative, and operate low risk, low input, low output management strategies. If this is so, then institutional approaches to encouraging innovation and intensification of management may be largely doomed by social selection in response to these environmental characteristics.

It is also true that it takes a long time for the effects of most management activities to be detectable in rangelands. With relatively high levels of turnover and a consequently short institutional memory, it is therefore hard for the adaptive feedback needed for learning to occur. This is especially true in government agencies where remote areas are still regarded as temporary hardship postings in many quarters, but also true among industry participants to a lesser degree. It has taken a very long time for the general policy paradigm in the rangelands to move from development to sustainable living, and the change is not yet complete.

Scale and institutions

It has proved useful to analyse rangelands within the framework of 'complex adaptive systems' (Abel 1999); that is, systems with multiple interacting components in which some components are able to adapt to disturbances, causing the system to change. Such an analysis insists on an emphasis on identifying the scales at which key processes operate in space and time (for example, Table 2.2), as well as the critical times at which control switches between scales in the system hierarchy and when fundamental changes to system resilience may occur.

The hypothetical social contract under which we aim to create some common goals and accept controls on our individual exploitation of our social environment can act at many scales. An important question is to ask at what scale (or integrated scales) institutional structures should operate to have the best chance of the desired outcomes in different environments. In particular, are there special features of the rangelands which imply that different institutional scales may be appropriate here than in other environments?

Humans affect the environment directly mainly at the local scale, albeit often via their agents of change such as livestock, weeds and 4-wheel drive cars (4WD's). Thus it is at this scale that a pastoralist decides on stocking rates or implements some erosion control works; at this scale that a tourist chooses where to drive their 4WD, that a hunter shoots a kangaroo, or a park ranger controls people's access to a site of interest.

However, institutions at broader scales determine how this local activity is implemented and the way in which it is replicated between management units. Thus catchment management plans affect where and how much erosion control work is carried out, regional tourism plans and the road network design affect where tourists go, tax incentives affect whether weed control may be an isolated obsession or a general habit. The questions are: at what scale must an institution act to be effective for different types of resource management questions; does the answer to this question vary across the rangelands; and do we have effective institutions targeted at those scales?

Local land management unit

An individual land management unit may be a paddock, a national park or a tourist site. This resource unit may be affected by an individual pastoralist, a pastoral company, a park ranger system or an ecotourism business. The success of this human management institution can depend greatly on the institutional characteristics – a family providing mutual support can be much more effective than an individual forced to fend for themselves, tax laws affect partnerships differently to companies, some individuals are better skilled than others. At this scale, human management institutions exert very strong control over the individual agents of impact, such as livestock numbers in a paddock, or the construction of car-parks or tracks to manage vehicles, or the driving of the 4WDs themselves. The institutions sometimes manage the environment directly, for example through weed control or ponding banks for erosion. However, there is often a scale mismatch in these cases since many of

Table 2.2. Adaptations originating at (a) local, (b) regional and
(c) national and State scales that can affect resilience of a region.
The contribution to resilience (positive [+] or negative [-]) is subject
to time-scale and spatial boundaries.

(a) Factor	Local scale: adaptation and possible effect on resilience
Biota	[+] drought-adapted forage species and herbivores [+] mixed grazer/browser animal populations increases forage and marketing options, reduces drought risk, and slows shrub encroachment
Diversity – spatial	[+] access to a mix of complementary land systems eg. river channels with heavy soils amid uplands with lighter soils [+] access to grazing in different climatic zones eg. owning properties elsewhere
Diversity – production strategies	[+] diverse enterprises linked to different markets and requiring different weather conditions reduces risk
External resources	[+] access to off-farm jobs and investments
Mental models	[+] smart buying and selling strategies based on accurate perceptions of how landscapes function and of the economic system [-] rate of learning slower than the rate of degradation [-] reluctance to use fire enables shrubs to increase to the detriment of grazing animals [-] short memory of past disturbances means mistakes repeated
Population structure	[-] aging households less able to adapt [+] a relatively large workforce with a mix of sexes and ages expands adaptive opportunities
Savings	[+] savings increase economic options
Scale	[+] a larger land holding yields economies of scale, lower cost per animal, higher profits, lower debt/more savings, better credit rating, more options in responding to disturbances
Technology	[-] paddock layout poorly related to land system boundaries limits production levels and adaptation [-] establishment of permanent water on land systems not adapted to continuous grazing results in deterioration in landscape function

(b) Factor	Regional scales: adaptation and possible effect on resilience
Diversity – spatial	[+] access to diverse land systems that offer a range of opportunities in time and space
Mental models	[-] short cultural memory prevents accumulation of understanding
Population structure	[+] a balanced age structure enhances capacity to respond to disturbances and opportunities [-] aging pastoral population in Australian and US rangelands
Services, infrastructure	[-] immovable infrastructure reduces flexibility [+] high level of services encourages capable people to stay and innovate [+] road network permits the pursuit of protein and energy across the region [+] communication network assists spread of ideas
Social support networks	[+] reciprocal obligations called upon in crises

(c) Factor	National and State scales: adaptation and possible effect on resilience
External resources	[+/-] loans, grants to assist recovery after a disturbance. Can foster dependency instead of adaptation
Institutions and policies	[-] inflexible institutions and policies insensitive to feedback [+] weather- and price-sensitive tax policy spreads benefits and costs across years [+] Landcare etc – community projects that may bring innovative approaches and outside resources [+] decentralised resource management responsive to local changes [-] remoteness of policy making from its local consequences restricts feedback
Mental models	[-] simplified mental models held by agencies stress 'temporal equilibrium' and 'command and control', rather than adaptation to uncertainty [-] short organisational memories lead to repetition of past mistakes
Savings	[+] public savings enable recovery from disturbances, but can foster dependency.

Source: Workshop discussions, Abel et al 2000

these problems are at a catchment scale which crosses management unit boundaries, or are otherwise beyond the resources of a single manager (eg, many weed problems). These types of issues often need to be managed by institutions at another scale.

Industry peer groups and local communities

Unlike rural populations with village elders elsewhere in the world, Australia has historically lacked strong resource management institutions at the local community level. Landcare has begun to fill this gap. However, the sheer geographic area of the rangelands means that the scale of problems that Landcare can tackle elsewhere in a smaller agricultural catchment actually occur within a single pastoral property. Thus Landcare groups in the rangelands are often being encouraged to tackle problems like catchment management while their human catchment is more suited to problems such as regional land use planning. To deal with this, however, different institutional tools are needed which engage the broader community.

Regional communities and local government

As elsewhere in Australia and indeed the world, rangelands regions are being required to take on more self-governance responsibilities. However, they complain widely about receiving responsibilities which are unmatched by rights and resources. Although some regions are struggling towards resolution of these issues (Dale and Bellamy 1998), the rangelands again pose a scale problem. Realistic levels of community interaction for planning require an order of magnitude more travel time than in agricultural areas. The information requirements for the natural resource base and overlying cultural data may be an order of magnitude greater per head of population than elsewhere. The human and financial transaction costs of operating an effective community level institution are generally substantially more per unit of economic output. It would seem that the levels of public investment in equitable regional planning and governance must therefore be greater than in other areas of Australia, unless novel institutions can be found. It is worth noting that *ad hoc* novel systems of governance have been emerging to manage remote pastoral and Aboriginal communities in rangelands in some regions, although these have rarely been formally assessed (see Holmes 1997).

State organisations and government agencies

Industry organisations at the State level, and the State government agencies provide some ability to tailor reactions to the conditions of each State. However, in many cases the differences and similarities are between and across regions rather than within artificial State boundaries. The problems of south-western Queensland and western New South Wales differ far less from each other than from coastal areas of either State, yet it was impossible to create a cross-border regional re-structuring program in the early 1990s. Like the Murray Darling Basin, the problems and opportunities of the Great Artesian Basin and the Lake Eyre Basin transcend State boundaries but do not encompass whole States.

National lobby groups and federal government

Policy emanating from the national level in Australia continues to treat the inland as a single homogeneous blob as far as most policy instruments are concerned, notwithstanding intermittent enthusiasms for regional processes (see Dore et al, this volume). Most interventions, such as tax and transport policy, remain blunt instruments. Yet, with the best of intentions, introducing regional differentiation without a well-structured regional planning process is a vast pork barrel licence, as has been seen time and again with a powerful and heart-tugging rural lobby in times of drought and industry downturn. The pain is real enough, of course, but there is a complex and difficult debate about its significance in comparison with people elsewhere in society and business.

Cross-scale interactions and nested institutions

Processes at each of the scales discussed do not operate in isolation – interactions can occur with broader or finer scales. For example, a government can set national policies that influence land use and management at a local scale (drought policy, for example). Local rural electors, on the other hand, can use their voting power to persuade governments to change policies in their favour. Godden (1997) calls the first 'governing the farm', and the second 'farming the government'. A weakness in current institutional arrangements may be the inability of institutions to perceive or to manage cross-scale processes. Folke et al (1998) discuss the potential for nested institutions with explicit cross scale linkages. Clearly some of our present administrative arrangements already have communications across scales, but whether these are adequate is in doubt. The benefit of any elaboration of the current complexity should exceed the increase in transaction costs.

Temporal scales

For each of the issues related to spatial scale noted above, there is an equally important one in the temporal dimension. At a short time-scale, the irregularity of rangelands seasons and intervention opportunities sits ill with regular budget cycles and market demand. Problems with timeliness of monitoring systems have already been alluded to. Considerable tax policy already attempts to deal with period inequity in time-varying systems, through income averaging, farm management deposits and special drought management instruments; but probably transfers some of the resulting risk from the economic to the environmental management system by doing so. It seems that current resource management institutions at the government level need to be more responsive to annual variability at the local scale than they are, whilst needing to be more stable at the regional to national scale than three year political cycles permit.

However, successful management by institutions at a short time-scale does not necessarily produce good long-term outcomes. The first reason is the understandable desire, mentioned above, to impose stability on systems that are intrinsically unstable. A fine example is that of subsidised feeding of imported fodder to stock during drought, which helps the farmer cope with the short-term impacts of drought at the cost of long-term damage to the land. A common property of unstable rangeland systems is resilience – their capacity to survive disturbances. However, mechanisms that maintain resilience, such as underground storage organs in plants, may be damaged if management imposes stability. Thus resilience may decline under a stable regime, until an extreme disturbance such as a prolonged drought makes the maintenance of stability impossible and the system crashes with heavy mortality of stock and high risk of degradation. The problem arises presumably because of weak feedback from the rangeland system to policy makers, and the inaccuracy of the latter's mental models of the system. Establishment of 'learning organisations' (Senge et al 1994) is an obvious if trite solution.

The second reason why successful management by institutions at a short time-scale does not necessarily produce good long-term outcomes is transaction costs. Tainter (1996) points to the tendency of humans to add social complexity as a means of solving problems of resource allocation and use. Transaction costs thus rise until the marginal benefit of the institutional arrangements may be less than the marginal cost. The case of Western NSW was described earlier: here, around 100 organisations now affect land use. These elaborate arrangements are for the purported benefit of some 52,000 people. Because it is not in the interests of members of institutions that have evolved around problems to offer to sacrifice their own jobs to reduce transaction costs, further elaboration is more likely as new problems arise, rather than simplification. Thus institutions that are beneficial at their inception can become harmful to society and the environment.

Gunderson et al (1995) note a common tendency for resource management institutions to become dysfunctional over time for both reasons above. Measures to address the second category of problems include sunset clauses on legislation, and external reviews of organisations.

We have discussed the nesting of institutions across spatial scales. Folke et al (1998) also note the existence of resource management institutions that are nested in time. The institutional complex contains elements that are invoked only in particular circumstances, so that a graduated response to crises is possible. This concept does appear in Australian rangeland institutions, and, subject to transaction costs, may be worth elaborating.

The design of systems of institutions

Particular institutions have been designed in the past to cope with specific problems, and have subsequently evolved or become maladaptive (Pritchard et al. 1998). Given the lack of feedback from ecological systems to markets, and the proliferation of unintended negative impacts of markets and individual institutions on society and the environment, now is the time to explore the possibility of designing systems of institutions that are nested across temporal and spatial scales. Such a system would need to be sensitive to transaction costs, have built-in infrastructure for learning and adaptation, and be able to contract as well as to grow, and to change direction. As such it will need to address the social conflicts of contraction and resource re-allocation; it is probably to avoid such conflicts that our present approach to social and environmental problems is usually to add new layers of institutional complexity, rarely to shed them.

Conclusion

The rangelands provide a fine example of interactions between institutions and their environmental context. Biophysical characteristics of rangelands, including climatic variability and low productivity, combine to create socio-economic conditions – low population densities, large distances to markets, low investment capacity – which affect institutional needs. Institutional arrangements based on reliable cycles, easy communications, the capacity to recover from mistakes, and physical proximity are stressed to their limits in rangelands environments. Yet these same limitations turn out to be important in less dramatic ways in many other natural resource management issues. Consequently, the rangelands can be a good test bed for examining solutions which are critical there but useful elsewhere.

References

Abel, N, 1999, Resilient rangelands regions, *VIth International Rangelands Congress Proceedings* (vol 1), Townsville, July, pp 21-30.
Abel, N, Ive, J, Langston, A, Tatnell, B, Tongway, D, Walker, B and Walker, P, 2000, Resilience of NSW rangelands: a framework for analysing a complex adaptive

system in Hale, P, Petrie, A Moloney, D and Sattler, P, (eds), *Management for Sustainable Ecosystems*, pp 59-71, Brisbane: Centre for Conservation Biology.

Abel, N and Ryan, S (eds), 1996, *Sustainable Habitation in the Rangelands*, Proceedings of a Fenner Conference on the Environment, October, Canberra: CSIRO.

Abel, N and Tatnell, B, 1997, Rangeland imperatives – a view from Capital Hill, *Australian Rangelands Society Conference*, December, Gatton College, University of Queensland, December.

ANZECC/ARMCANZ Joint Working Group, 1996, *Draft National Strategy for Rangelands Management*, Canberra: Commonwealth of Australia.

ANZECC/ARMCANZ, 1999, *National principles and guidelines for rangeland management*, Canberra: Australian & New Zealand Environment & Conservation Council/Agricultural & Resource Management Council of Australia & New Zealand.

Dale, AP and Bellamy, JA, 1998, *Regional Resource Use Planning: An Australian review.* LWRRDC Occasional Paper 6/98, Canberra: LWRRDC.

Folke, C, Berkes, F and Colding, F, 1998, Ecological practices and social mechanisms for building resilience and sustainability in Berkes, F, and Folke, C (eds), *Linking Social and Ecological Systems: Management Practices and Social Mechanisms for Building Resilience*, pp 414-436,, Cambridge: Cambridge University Press.

Godden, DP, 1997, *Agricultural and Resource Policy: Principles and Practice*, Melbourne: Oxford University Press.

Gundersen, L, Holling, CS, and Light, S, (eds), 1995, *Barriers and Bridges to the Renewal of Ecosystems and Institutions*, Columbia University Press, New York.

Harding, R and Fisher, E, (eds), 1999, *Perspectives on the Precautionary Principle*, Sydney: Federation Press.

Holmes, JH, 1995, Land tenures, property rights and multiple land use: issues for American and Antipodean rangelands, in Cliff, AD, Gould, P, Hoare, AG and Thrift, N (eds), *Diffusing Geography: Essays for Peter Haggett*, pp 262-288, London: Blackwell, London.

Holmes, JH, 1997, Diversity and change in Australia's rangeland regions: translating resource values into regional benefits, *The Rangeland Journal* 19: 3-25.

Lunney, D, 1994, Royal Commission of 1901 on the western lands of New South Wales: an ecologist's summary. in Lunney, D, Hand, S, Reed, P and Butcher, D, (eds), *Future of the Fauna of Western New South Wales*, pp 221-240, Sydney: Royal Zoological Society of New South Wales.

Morton, SR and Price, P (eds), 1993, *R&D for Sustainable Use and Management of Australia's Rangelands.* LWRRDC Occasional Paper No. 06/93, Canberra: Land and Water Resources Research and Development Corporation.

Northern Runs Commission, 1867, *Commission Appointed to Enquire into the State of Runs Suffering from Drought. Report and Minutes of Evidence.* South Australian Parliamentary Papers, vol 2, Government Printer, Adelaide.

O'Meagher, B, Stafford Smith, M and White, DH, 1999, Approaches to integrated drought risk management: Australia's National Drought Policy in Wilhite, DA (ed), *Hazards and Disasters: A Series of Definitive Major Works. Volume II. Drought, a Global Assessment*, pp 115-128, London: Routledge Publishers.

Parliament of Western Australia. 1940, *Report of the Royal Commission Appointed to Inquire into and Report upon the Financial and Economic Position of the Pastoral Industry in the Leasehold areas in Western Australia.* Votes and Proceedings, 3rd Session of Parliament, vol 2, Perth: The Legislative Assembly of Western Australia.

Pritchard, L, Colding, J, Berkes, F, Svedin, U and Folke, C, 1998, *The problem of Fit Between Ecosystems and Institutions*, IHDP Working Paper No 2, Bonn: International Human Dimensions Programme on Global Environmental Change.

Senge, PM, Kleiner, A, Roberts, C, Ross, R.B and Smith, B, 1994, *The Fifth Discipline Fieldbook: Strategies and Tools for Building a Learning Organisation*, London: Nicholas Brealey Publishing.

Stafford Smith, DM, 1994, Sustainable production systems and natural resource management in the rangelands, *Proceedings, ABARE Outlook Conference*, Canberra, February.

Stafford Smith, DM, Morton, SR and Ash, AJ, 2000, Towards sustainable pastoralism in Australia's rangelands, *Australian Journal of Environmental Management* 7: 190-203.

Stein, P, 2000, Are decision-makers too cautious with the precautionary principle, *Environmental and Planning Law Journal* 17: 3-23.

Tainter, JA, 1996, Complexity, problem solving and sustainable societies, from *Getting down to earth: practical applications of ecological economics*, Washington DC: Island Press.

3

The Ocean and Marine Realm

Marcus Haward

Institute of Antarctic and Southern Oceans Studies and Law, Policy and International Relations Program, Antarctic CRC, University of Tasmania

Australia has a significant ocean domain. It has the longest ice-free coastline in the world at 37,000 km and the world's fourth largest offshore Exclusive Economic Zone (EEZ). At approximately 12,000,000 km^2, the EEZ is approximately 50 per cent larger in area than the Australian continental landmass (CSIRO 1998). This EEZ stretches from tropical waters to Australia's sub-Antarctic islands and offshore to the Australian Antarctic Territory (see Figure 3.1). Increased attention to the issues and problems confronting Australia's coastal and ocean environment in the 1990s culminated in the release of *Australia's Oceans Policy* (Commonwealth of Australia 1998a), by the Minister for the Environment, Senator Hill, on 23 December 1998. This policy was released a week before the conclusion of the International Year of the Ocean, making 'Australia the first country in the world to develop a comprehensive, national plan to protect and manage the oceans' (Bateman 1999: 12). This policy follows a number of coastal and ocean management initiatives introduced in the preceding decade (Haward 1995a; Haward and VanderZwaag 1996). While the oceans policy is part of this continuum, it attempts a significant departure from traditional management arrangements and confronts problems and limitations that have been identified in current practices. Institutional arrangements, including those foreshadowed under the *Oceans Policy*, are important in setting the policy space and in developing processes that can accommodate a multiplicity of interests and contending values influencing policy development and implementation.

Australia's ocean domain poses a number of challenges. It includes numerous biogeographic provinces and significant marine environments as well as major marine resources and uses. Ongoing use of coastal and ocean resources by Aboriginal and Torres Strait Islander peoples follows activities undertaken for thousands of years. The majority of the Australian population live on the coast in highly urbanised centres. This area is the location of major industrial centres and transport and other infrastructure. Management of the Australian coast reflects considerable diversity, with legislation and regulatory instruments established by several hundred local governments, six States, two self-governing Territories and the Commonwealth government. An equally diverse range of stakeholders has interests in the coastal zone and offshore Australia. The recognition and management of these differing interests

Figure 3.1. Australia's offshore responsibilities

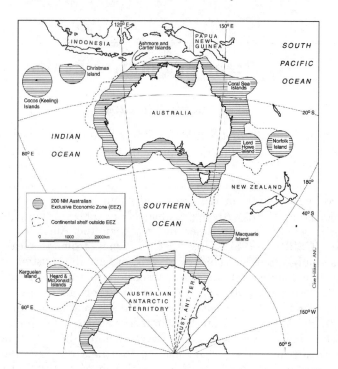

pose distinct challenges to governments in establishing policy frameworks that encourage equitable ecologically sustainable development of coastal and off-shore Australia.

Coastal and oceans management has increased in significance for Australian governments over the past quarter-century. Disputes and struggles over offshore jurisdiction have given way to intergovernmental collaboration, if not full cooperation, in a number of issue areas. Increasing concern to integrate policy responses on coastal and ocean management *within* each sphere of government has paralleled this collaboration. At the same time a range of non-government stakeholders have increased their involvement in coastal and oceans policy. This increased involvement has focused attention on the range of environmental problems facing coastal Australia. Degradation and loss of natural coastal and marine environments, the impacts of point and non-point source land-based pollutants, and uncontrolled urban development have all adversely affected the coastal zone (see RAC 1993). These problems have arisen through neglect, where the ocean was a useful repository of rubbish or a dispersant of waste. Equally many current problems have arisen through what has been termed the 'tyranny of small decisions' (HORSCERA 1991) – simply the focus on single decisions with little attention to their consequences or cumulative impacts on other uses or users and/or the coastal and marine environment.

In federal states such as Australia, ocean policy-like other areas of resource and environmental management-necessarily involves a federal dimension. Ocean and coastal management involves extensive intergovernmental and stakeholder interaction. This policy area is the interface of jurisdiction between all spheres of government in Australia. The jurisdictional question - the responsibility of Commonwealth and State governments - has been a dominant feature of the policy framework. This has led first to the establishment of management regimes that have reflected and reinforced claims for jurisdiction by State governments (including the focus of stakeholder interaction), and, second, to extensive intergovernmental institutions and processes in areas such as fisheries and offshore oil and gas exploitation. These management regimes in different resource use sectors (for example fisheries, offshore oil and gas, marine protected areas) had led, by the later 1990s, to a multiplicity of 'ocean policies', yet with little integration between them. The development of a national oceans policy for Australia in 1997-98 was an ambitious and challenging attempt to set a policy framework that 'integrate[s] oceans management decisions across industry sectors and government jurisdictions' (Commonwealth of Australia 1998a: 10).

The development of oceans policy and management

Government concern with the management of marine resources is longstanding and predates Federation. The States, and local governments, are responsible for a number of activities that directly impact the marine environment. Land use planning and approval for development in the littoral zone is a local government responsibility, subject to State government oversight and, where applicable, Commonwealth investment guidelines. Regulations governing fisheries are, similarly, intergovernmental in character, administered by State and Commonwealth laws. The Commonwealth regulates regulation of dumping and other ship-sourced pollution, although State law governs emissions from pipelines. The regulation of non-point source pollution is equally complex, and at times may involve an intergovernmental dimension.

The Commonwealth has considerable responsibilities affecting the marine environment. Its interest in this area is longstanding, with Commonwealth enacting 'the nation's first anti-pollution law' (Cullen 1985: 8) the *Beaches, Fishing Grounds and Sea Routes Protection Act* (Cth), in 1932. The Commonwealth extended its interests in the post-war period with the *Fisheries Act 1952*, and in the 1960s, in collaboration with the States, developed legislation governing offshore oil and gas developments. In 1975 the Commonwealth enacted the *Great Barrier Reef Marine Park Act 1975* (Cth), seen as one of the 'cornerstones of national environmental policy' (Davis 1991: 147).

Utilisation of Australia's fisheries resources extends back tens of thousands of years, with indigenous peoples around the Australian coastline depending on finfish, shellfish and crustaceans. Dependence on fisheries increased with European settlement, and as pressure on fish stocks increased so too did early attempts to regulate use. Prior to Federation in 1901, fishing was an important activity in each of the 'Australian' colonies, with each colonial legislature enacting various measures to regulate and control the fisheries in adjacent waters following the granting of responsible, but limited, self-government in the 1850s. The Commonwealth's entry into active fisheries management occurred with the proclamation of the *Fisheries Act* 1952 (Cth) in 1955. These legislative instruments provided the base for regulation of fishing activity, usually through controls on fishing through limited entry licensing, controls on gear or vessels, seasonal closures or a combination of these measures. These measures had little effect in containing effort in fisheries, leading to over-exploitation of fisheries with such input controls. The result has been seen as an example of the 'tragedy of the commons' (Hardin 1968) where individual action depletes the resource stock.

Shifts from input to output controls (limiting the level of catch through imposition of quotas or a designated level of catch) have marked a revolution in fisheries management and the activity of fishers in Australian fisheries in the 1990s. This revolution has been accompanied and shaped by wide-ranging administrative and legislative reform. The legislative reforms in Commonwealth fisheries in 1990-91 created a statutory authority, the Australian Fisheries Management Authority (AFMA), to undertake day-to-day management of Commonwealth fisheries and saw statutory management plans established for all Commonwealth fisheries (see Haward 1995a). These management plans gave increased roles and responsibilities to the fishing industry at the same time that industry was provided with statutory based fishing rights and being levied full cost recovery for management costs. Thus these reforms radically changed the traditional regulatory based, input controls and as a result the relationship between government and industry (Haward 1995a). The relationship between industry's increased responsibilities and the move to output controls in fisheries management has been critical in enhancing alternative, more collaborative, approaches to management (Haward and Wilson 1999).

Allocation of 'quota' has altered the legal and economic basis of managing fisheries. Access privileges, (the traditional fishing 'licences') have no property rights attached to them. The licenses may have a significant market value in high-value fisheries governed by limited entry criteria. The introduction of individual transferable quotas (ITQs) in Commonwealth and in some State-controlled fisheries has provided a form of property right for fishers. The introduction of such market instruments has significant effects in terms of the relationships between fishers, between fishers and government and between fishers and other stakeholders. The use of tradeable rights and the creation of quasi-market approaches by such 'trades' in fisheries management has provided an alternative to the traditional regulatory paradigm for both fishers and fisheries managers. In its extreme form this alternative paradigm tackles the 'tragedy of the commons' by creating private property regimes, based on what have been termed 'privatarian' approaches to common pool resources (see, for example, Ferguson 1997). Fisheries quota are, however, allocated within a total allowable catch (TAC) that can be varied according to the viability of the stock.

Jurisdictional disputes between the Commonwealth and State governments over marine resources dominated intergovernmental interaction in the 1960s and early 1970s. These disputes arose as Commonwealth interests came into conflict with established arrangements and activities in which the States played the predominant role. The introduction, by the Whitlam Government (1972-75), of the *Seas and Submerged Lands Act* 1973 (Cth) which declared Commonwealth jurisdiction from the low water mark (LWM), marked the high-tide of this conflict. Prior to the enactment of this legislation, the States had argued that the Commonwealth was only responsible for activities beyond territorial limits which, until November 1990, was three nautical miles from LWM. In response to the Whitlam Government's action the States' mounted a challenge to the legality of the *Seas and Submerged Lands Act* 1973 and actively resisted increased Commonwealth interest in marine resource management. The Commonwealth's legislation, which purported to give effect to international conventions on the Continental Shelf and Territorial Sea, was subject to judicial review by the High Court.

The Offshore Constitutional Settlement

The High Court upheld the legislation in a decision brought down shortly after the Whitlam Government was defeated in an election in December 1975. The newly-elected Fraser Government (1975-83), was confronted by the necessity of accommodating the interests of the States, and taking account of their objections to the *Seas and Submerged Lands Act* 1973, yet maintaining the Commonwealth's obligations (and interests) in the management of Australia's maritime domain and its resources. Negotiations with the States led to an agreement that formalised the responsibilities of both Commonwealth and the States. This intergovernmental arrangement was later termed the Offshore Constitutional Settlement (OCS). The OCS, which neither altered the constitutional division of powers nor reduced intergovernmental tensions offshore, was nonetheless an important and complex intergovernmental agreement. It remans a moot point whether the States fought extremely hard for something the Commonwealth was always prepared to grant. Commonwealth interests were supported by the ongoing developments in the law of the sea, and by the economic benefits of excise revenues from downstream production of oil. The OCS remains, however, the primary arrangement governing the management of marine resources in Australia (Haward 1989). The Howard Government has made it clear that the OCS will not be re-negotiated in the implementation of the oceans policy.

The OCS was concluded after three years of intense intergovernmental negotiations between the Commonwealth and States. During the negotiations with the States it was agreed that to return to the situation pre-*Seas and Submerged Lands Act* 1973 (Cth) whereby the states had jurisdiction from the low water mark to three miles offshore; the Commonwealth from three miles to the edge of national jurisdiction. This was made possible by agreement, in June 1979, on the OCS. The OCS was described as 'a milestone in co-operative federalism' and a major achievement of the Fraser government's new federalism. The OCS remains the only, and therefore the most significant, legacy of the Fraser government's 'new federalism' (see Haward and Smith 1992, 39).

The OCS involved a constitutional mechanism (s 51 xxxviii) never before used. This provision saw each State pass legislation requesting the Commonwealth to pass laws on agreed terms. The Commonwealth then responded by enacting 14 separate pieces of legislation. Two central Acts provide the legislative anchor for the OCS arrangement. The first is the *Coastal Waters (State Powers) Act* 1980 (Cth) which extends the legislative jurisdiction of the states to certain offshore areas. The importance of this Act is that it confers legislative jurisdiction on the states in respect of all matters within coastal waters. The second Act is the *Coastal Waters (State Title) Act* 1980 (Cth) that grants each State the same title to its adjacent seabed as if these areas formed part of the territory of the state.

The OCS established that the States would be responsible for the management of activities in the area from LWM to three nautical miles offshore, with the Commonwealth responsible from this boundary to the edge of national jurisdiction. Australian jurisdiction covers the area within the 200 nautical mile EEZ declared in August 1994. The EEZ coincides with the Australian Fishing Zone (AFZ) declared in November 1979 (see below). The *Coastal Waters (State Titles) Act* 1980, in returning legal ownership to the seabed from LWM to three miles to the States, reduced the chance of the settlement unravelling. Returning title to the States ensured that any future revocation of the OCS would involve constitutional provisions which require adequate compensation for acquisition of State territory, as well as gaining agreement from the State over the revocation of control over the seabed. The OCS included a range of 'agreed arrangements' governing Commonwealth-State relations concerning the management of marine resources. These agreed arrangements were directed at Oil and Gas; Other Sea-Bed Minerals; Fisheries; the Great Barrier Reef Marine Park; Other Marine Parks; Historic Shipwrecks; Ship-Sourced Marine Pollution; Shipping and Navigation; and Crimes at Sea (Haward 1989).

The 'agreed arrangements' led to complementary legislation being passed that ensured the States remained responsible for activities within State waters. The device of complementary legislation, and the spirit of the OCS, established a workable intergovernmental regime for offshore resource management. The OCS enabled the States to undertake activities on behalf of the Commonwealth outside State waters, for example the administration of oil and gas activities, and fisheries enforcement. The OCS also enabled the States to be responsible for management of agreed fisheries to the edge of the 200 mile zone. Equally, the Commonwealth was able to retain control over fisheries such as the southern bluefin tuna, and the Torres Strait fishery that involved international agreements

Developments in the international arena were occurring in parallel with the resolution of domestic institutional arrangements. Australia declared a 200 mile Australian Fishing Zone in 1979, following development in the international law of the sea. In November 1990, Australia announced that it was declaring a 12-mile territorial sea, until then being one of only 11 countries not to take advantage of the provisions of the Law of the Sea

Convention that was concluded in 1982. Australia declared an Exclusive Economic Zone (EEZ) on 1 August 1994 and ratified the Law of the Sea Convention on 5 October 1994. It became an original signatory to this convention that entered force on 16 November 1994. Australia took a lead role in the negotiations at the UN Conference on Straddling Fish Stocks and Highly Migratory Fish Stocks between 1993 and 1995. This conference led to the development of the UN Fish Stocks Agreement that provides a stronger regulatory framework over high seas fishing. The Fish Stocks Agreement entered force on 11 December 2001.

The Law of the Sea Convention provides Australia with the basis for claims over a significant area of ocean and the seabed of the continental shelf. Australia can claim a continental shelf that extends further than 200 miles in certain areas but must lodge its claim to these areas within ten years of ratification of the Convention, that is by 2004. A meeting of States Parties to the Law of the Sea Convention in 2001 agreed to extend the time for lodgement of continental shelf claims and associated data by a further five years. Despite major developments in customary international law of the sea from the 1970s Australia has acted relatively conservatively in relation to offshore claims. Australia extended its territorial sea from three to 12 miles in 1990, well after such an extension had become customary. The declaration of Australia's EEZ was similarly conservative, made just prior to the ratification of the convention. Australia did, however, declare (as noted above) a 200 mile fishing zone in 1979.

Australian governments have also faced the challenges posed by the introduction of sustainable development to the coastal zone. This process may at times felt like 'paralysis by analysis' as at least 16 inquiries or studies were undertaken by the Commonwealth alone between the mid-1960s to the mid-1990s (for a review of these inquiries see Haward 1995a). In 1980 the Commonwealth Parliament released a report, *Australian Coastal Zone Management*, which identified the lack of coordination between Commonwealth, State and local governments as a significant limitation on Australian coastal management (Australia 1980). A further Commonwealth parliamentary report from the House of Representatives Standing Committee on the Environment, Recreation and the Arts (HORSCERA) was released in 1991 (HORSCERA 1991). In recognising the limited success in developing an integrated coastal policy, the HORSCERA report also criticised the lack of effective community-based involvement in coastal management. The HORSCERA inquiry was followed by the Resource Assessment Commission's (RAC) Coastal Zone Inquiry in 1992-93. The RAC inquiry provided an extensive survey of existing policy and practice and, like the previous inquiries, reiterated concerns over the degradation of Australia's coastal zone. In its *Final Report* released in late 1993, the RAC recommended an integrated and strategic focus to Australian coastal management (RAC 1993).

Coastal zone management, as with most land and resource management, is seen as a matter of State jurisdiction. The States have undertaken most coastal zone policy and have an oversight role over local government authorities. Local government has an important, but relatively neglected, role in the management of the coastal zone in terms of land use planning, development approval and maintenance of coastal lands. Local government has the primary, day-to-day, responsibility for much coastal management. As the RAC noted, regulatory instruments such as by-laws or development approval are the principal means of managing the coast. The fragmentation of these instruments and the adoption of different sectoral approaches has led to over 900 regulatory systems being identified in Australia, involving more than 1500 regulatory agents (900 local authorities and 600 state and federal agencies (RAC 1993 58).

Within the State government sphere, in spite of considerable attempts at legislative reform in a number of jurisdictions, coastal zone management remains affected by a legacy of sectorally-based legislation. This contributes to the creation of fragmented and dispersed management arrangements. The States oversee local government control over land use on the coastal margin and regulate industrial development and pollution emissions into the sea. Potential conflicts arise between a local government authority keen to increase its revenue through rates and local charges and a State government concerned at limiting development in coastal areas, particularly those less developed or pristine areas. Each State has a range of agencies with responsibility for aspects of coastal policy and each is moving towards integrated planning in the coastal zone. The development of the *Oceans Policy* by the Commonwealth builds on this previous work, yet also establishes an innovative institutional framework and policy process.

The Oceans Policy

The Oceans Policy is grounded in two key ideas – ecologically sustainable development and multiple use management. The commitment to the development of Australia's Ocean Policy by Commonwealth, State and Territory governments in 1997-98 is a major achievement in ocean management. The Labor Government led by Paul Keating announced its intention to proceed with an oceans policy in December 1995. This proposal did not advance before the Keating Government was defeated in the federal election of February 1996 by the Liberal-National Party Coalition led by John Howard.

The Howard Government's campaign in the 1996 federal election included a commitment to increase funding to environmental projects and policy areas through the creation of the Natural Heritage Trust (NHT) funded by the partial privatisation of Telstra. NHT funds were to be used to fund projects under the Coasts and Clean Seas Initiative, a refocusing of the Coastal Action Program launched by the previous federal government in May 1995. In this way initiatives including Coastcare, a funding program for coastal management under the previous government's Coastal Action Program, were retained under the Coasts and Clean Seas banner.

The policy process

On 3 March 1997 Prime Minister Howard announced his government's intention to proceed with the development of an Oceans Policy grounded on two key principles; ecologically sustainable development and multiple use management. These principles were reinforced in the ocean policy document *New Horizons*, released as a consultation document to encourage public comment, participation and responses (see Sainsbury et al 1997: 8). At the same time, the Prime Minister announced that the Minister for the Environment would have carriage of the policy development process. Environment Australia (EA), the key agency within the broad department or portfolio structure became pivotal in the policy development process. EA commissioned a series of issues and background papers to focus debates and discussion (both within the bureaucracy and with the community) and provided institutional support in organising workshops and fora (O'Connell 1998).

Initially the ocean policy proposals were clearly a Commonwealth initiative, limited to Commonwealth waters outside three nautical miles from the low water mark. While this reflected the reality of Australian jurisdiction offshore, such a focus would clearly limit the practical utility of an integrated approach to marine management. At the same time, however, the Commonwealth and States had maintained close links in the development of coastal zone policies, linkages that had been initiated in the early 1990s.

The publication of Issues and Background Papers from mid- to late-1997 was followed by a focused workshop on a draft policy paper in December 1997. Other initiatives were being pursued in parallel to the release of these papers. The Marine Industry Development Strategy was released in July 1997, and ongoing work was undertaken on marine science and technology. The Minister for the Environment also established a Ministerial Advisory Group (MAG) in September 1997. This 18 member group was chaired by David Connolly, a former shadow Minister for the Environment, and included representatives of key interest groups, academic and research institutions, Aboriginal and Torres Strait Islanders, the Australian Marine Conservation Society and two members from EA.

The MAG was charged with providing advice on the views of a broad range of non-government stakeholders on the development of the Oceans Policy; and any other issue that the advisory group considers relevant to the development of the Oceans Policy (Environment Australia 1998: ii). The MAG provided important information to the Minister for the Environment in a number of key areas, in particular the institutional arrangements to implement the proposed policy. The MAG reported to the Minister in early March 1998 and its report was released publicly by the Commonwealth Minister in May along with the *Australia's Oceans Policy – An Issues Paper* which was essentially a draft policy document (Commonwealth of Australia 1998b).

The Issues Paper

The *Issues Paper* deliberately set out to make the point that it 'does not present a formal position or outcomes agreed by the Commonwealth, State or Territory governments or their agencies or ALGA (the Australian Local Government Association)' (Commonwealth of Australia 1998b: 1). The *Issues Paper* was aimed at focusing public comment, and to this end Environment Australia organised a series of fora around Australia to provide opportunities for the public to get a broad overview of the process and proposal and provide comment. Each forum was in two parts, the first a formal briefing from Environment Australia officials and the second a broader based information session organised with the state branches of the Marine and Coastal Community Network (MCCN). The MCCN provides a coordinating role for the range of community-based organisations and is funded under the Coasts and Clean Seas initiative.

The *Issues Paper* provided a comprehensive survey of key elements and components underpinning an Australian ocean policy, beginning with an opening chapter detailing background information starting with a short discussion on 'why Australia needs an Oceans Policy'. In summary, the *Issues Paper* contained chapters providing key policy frameworks; for example chapters examined 'principles for ecologically sustainable ocean use', 'integrated ocean planning and management', and 'marine industry, science and technology'. Chapter 5 focused on 'principal actions' and involved subsections dealing with 'ocean uses and impacts', 'training and development', 'understanding the oceans', 'protecting the national interests', and 'assessing effectiveness'. Chapter 5 comprises almost two-thirds of the *Issues Paper* and covers activities to be undertaken under the five major categories. These five categories were 'designed to cover development and implementation of Australia's Ocean Policy' (Commonwealth of Australia 1998b: 36). As the *Issues Paper* noted, 'actions in each section may include some that are currently in place; some that may be under active consideration; and new proposals suggested for consideration as components of Australia's Oceans Policy' (Commonwealth of Australia 1998b: 36). These actions include items, which first have no budgetary implications, second are currently funded under existing programs, and third are initiatives which would require new funding.

Funding of the various elements of an oceans policy was one of two clearly central issues emerging from both the *Issues Paper* and the report from the MAG. Funding for the Oceans Policy was announced during the 1998 federal election campaign, as part of the Liberal Party's Environment Policy. This policy launch committed the re-elected government to funding the Oceans Policy as a matter of priority, with A$50 million committed to the policy over three years. A$30 million of this amount would be new funding; the remaining A$20 million would come from NHT funds for both new and ongoing programs (Liberal Party of Australia 1998).

The second and clearly critical issue was the institutional base for policy development, implementation and evaluation. The question of institutional design is important in a federal system like Australia where the States retain significant jurisdiction and responsibilities for coastal and marine management. The Howard Government had clearly stated that its proposed oceans policy would not lead to the development of a Commonwealth agency for ocean management with powers to over-ride State and Territory governments as it saw this as contrary to the cooperative basis of the Offshore Constitutional Settlement. The *Issues Paper* and report of the MAG provided alternative institutional options. These options were:

- Improving consultation processes within existing sectoral arrangements;
- Appointment of an Oceans Policy Advocate with no regulatory powers, but with responsibility to promote cooperative solutions within existing arrangements;
- A focus on particular cross sectoral and cross jurisdictional issues and design specific purpose responses for each case within, where possible, existing mechanisms; or
- A Commonwealth/State ministerial body for managing cross-sectoral issues. This body could either use current sectoral and Commonwealth/State mechanisms or establish regional bodies for assessment and planning.

Australia's Oceans Policy

The release of the *Issues Paper* was followed by a series of fora and public information sessions managed by EA. Public comment was invited following the release of the *Issues Paper*. The drafting of the policy document was undertaken by EA. This emphasised the Commonwealth's commitment but may have enhanced divisions with State governments and agencies over the policy process and outcomes. At the core of the new oceans policy is a commitment to ecosystem based management of the Australian exclusive economic zone, one of the world's largest EEZs. The policy will be implemented through a new regional marine planning process, based on large marine ecosystems. Regional marine plans will integrate sectoral commercial interests and conservation requirements. The involvement of the state and territory governments will be sought in this marine planning process. The Oceans Policy is set out in two volumes, *Australia's Oceans Policy* and *Specific Sectoral Measures* (Commonwealth of Australia 1998a). The first volume is 48 pages in length and contains seven sections and four appendices.

The seven sections are as follows: context for Australia's ocean policy; integrated and ecosystem-based oceans planing and management; implementation arrangements for ocean planning and management; principles for ecologically sustainable use; implementing Australia's ocean policy – some key initial actions; marine science and technology and marine industries; Australia's ocean policy – next steps. The *Sectoral Measures* volume also covers 48 pages and details the major challenges and proposed responses in some 20 areas of oceans planning and management.

Regional Marine Plans (RMPs) will be binding on all Commonwealth agencies. The goals as stated for RMPs are to determine the conservation requirements of each marine region, including the establishment of marine protected areas, prevention of potential conflict between sectors in relation to resource allocation and provision of long term security to all ocean users. The first Regional Marine Plan is being developed for the south eastern region of Australia's EEZ. The South-east region includes waters off the south east of South Australia, Tasmania, Victoria and southeast New South Wales. The region encompasses some 12–15 per cent of the Australian coastline and involves the jurisdictions of the Commonwealth and four States.

Based on the process established in the South-east region, the RMP process involves an initial notification of the planning process. A scoping plan defining boundaries and the key environmental, economic, social and cultural features of the region is then released. The next stage of the process involves a comprehensive assessment of the region's characteristics. The South-east Regional Marine Plan (SERMP) assessment included establishment of six specialised and expert working groups (Ecosystem Function, Bioregionalisation, Management and Institutional, Impacts, Indigenous Uses and Values, and Uses Assessment Reference Group). The membership of each working group varied but included members drawn from Universities, CSIRO, government, Indigenous organisations, industry and community groups. Once the assessment phase is complete objectives and options for the RMP are developed and then negotiated with stakeholders. This leads to the development of a draft plan, and then, after further negotiations, the final plan is released.

The SERMP was initiated in April 2000, with the Scoping Plan released in early 2001. Working groups were established in mid-2001 and their reports (to the South-east Region Steering Committee) completed by the end of 2001. These reports were included in the assessment process. The SERMP is to be released in late 2002. Work has begun on the second RMP – in Northern Australia.

Institutional arrangements

The Oceans Policy established a number of institutions to develop, implement and oversee the policy. A National Oceans Ministerial Board will oversee the implementation of the Oceans Policy. This board comprises the Ministers of Environment and Heritage (chair), Agriculture, Fisheries and Forestry Australia, and Departments of Industry, Tourism and Resources, Transport and Regional Services, and Science.

A National Oceans Office (NOO) has been established to undertake a range of functions, including development of Regional Marine Plans and coordination across government and between governments. A National Oceans Advisory Group has been formed as a key consultative mechanism. Regional Marine Plan Steering Committees, comprising key non-government stakeholders, will be created in each region (see Figure 3.2).

The NOO has been located in Hobart. It is now designated as an Executive Agency under the *Public Service Act* 1999 (Cth) that came into effect in early December 1999. This means that the NOO reports directly to the Minister for Environment and Heritage, and through the Minister to the National Oceans Ministerial Board. The NOO had initially been established within EA, reporting through the Head of the Marine Group to the Minister. The NOO established its work program related to the South East Regional Marine Plan, a process launched with a National Oceans Forum in April 2000.

Figure 3.2. Institutional arrangements: Australian Oceans Policy development and implementation

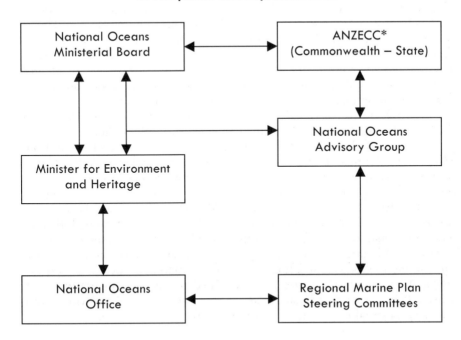

ANZECC ceased to exist as of 2002, see below.
Source: Commonwealth of Australia 1998b.

The National Oceans Advisory Group (NOAG) has played an important part in the development of the Oceans Policy. Many of the members of this body had served on the MAG during the development of the Oceans Policy. NOAG, with 16 members, has representatives of marine industries, conservation, and Indigenous and scientific organisations. NOAG is charged with providing advice to the Ministerial Board on cross-sectoral and inter-jurisdictional issues. It is also expected to provide a forum for the exchange of views and information between the various stakeholders. The NOAG provided support to, and acted as host for, the National Oceans Forum.

Intergovernmental coordination

The Australian and New Zealand Environment and Conservation Council (ANZECC)[1] will facilitate intergovernmental coordination. ANZECC, made up of Environment Ministers from all States, the Commonwealth and Territories as well as New Zealand's Environment Minister, is to be responsible for Commonwealth-State consultations on the implementation of the

---

1   In 2002, ANZECC ceased active intergovernmental cooperation. Its functions have been taken over by the National Environmental Protection Council (NEPC) and the newly established Natural Resources Management Ministerial Council (NRMMC).

Oceans Policy. In addition the Commonwealth expects that members of the National Oceans Board 'who are also members of relevant Commonwealth/State ministerial councils will ensure that linkages are made on matters of mutual interest' (Commonwealth of Australia, 1998a: 17). The key will be in ensuring that these linkages provide an opportunity to overcome current resistance from the states to 'signing on' to the regional marine planning process. Given, too, that ANZECC has responsibilities for environmental matters, rather than marine resources such as fisheries or oil and gas, this coordination may be more difficult than expected.

The release of Australia's Oceans Policy is the first step in the lengthy and complex process involved in implementing this policy. The policy provides for all the critical elements in the broad setting of institutional design and rules that can be used to manage Australia's marine areas. A series of large adjacent ecosystem based multiple use managed areas does provide an unparalleled opportunity for ecologically sustainable development of Australia's EEZ. In a 'Message from the Prime Minister' at the beginning of Australia's Oceans Policy, Prime Minister John Howard claimed that the policy demonstrates 'world leadership by implementing a coherent, strategic planning and management framework for dealing with complex issues confronting the long term future of our oceans' (Commonwealth of Australia 1998a: 1). A number of critical issues related to the implementation of the Oceans Policy remain to be addressed. These issues include resolving current intergovernmental issues and establishing the regional marine plans.

Oceans Policy: institutions, processes and management

Ocean and marine resource management has long been the focus of government attention in Australia. Sophisticated sectorally-based management regimes were established in the 1960s and 1970s. These regimes provided stability for resource users, particularly in the offshore oil and gas sector in relation to royalty arrangements and operating conditions. In fisheries the OCS provided flexibility and allowed diversity in management responses in different States and fisheries. The regime governing oil and gas in offshore Australia was, for example, seen as a model for other federal states such as Canada. It is not until the 1990s, however, that attention to integrating these sectoral management regimes was seriously addressed. As noted elsewhere, until the Oceans Policy was launched, there has been no 'Australian' oceans policy, but rather a multiplicity of policies reflecting the concerns of each of nine Australian governments (see Haward 1996).

Traditionally, ocean and coastal policy has been developed in a fragmented, generally uncoordinated manner by sectoral agencies, either as government departments or statutory authorities. Commonwealth activities and influence increased significantly post World War II, in response to, first, growing international attention to 'law of the sea' issues and, second, in response to perceived limitations to state jurisdiction beyond three miles offshore. The Commonwealth government developed legislation (and therefore had concomitant administrative responsibilities) for fisheries in the 1950s, and oil and gas in the 1960s. The establishment of the Great Barrier Reef Marine Park in the 1970s reflected increased concern with marine environmental protection (Rothwell and Haward 1996). These developments led to increased intergovernmental interaction through ministerial councils and associated standing committees.

The development of collaborative arrangements and formal intergovernmental linkages is clearly an important element in institutional design. So too is the strength of these intergovernmental linkages. In this case such vertical intergovernmental links have considerable importance, being described as 'rods of iron' and contrasted to the 'threads of gossamer' as a metaphor for the much weaker horizontal links between agencies of the same government. The terms 'rods of iron' and 'threads of gossamer' are taken from Warhurst who surveyed 'inter' and 'intra' governmental linkages in Australia (Warhurst 1983). Warhurst's insights are useful in considering the opportunities and limitations in developing integrated policy and management. Gaining agreement within government involving agencies with necessarily different perspectives on the marine and ocean domain may well be more difficult than gaining agreement between governments in, for example, fisheries management or principles for marine protected areas.

Assessing Australian ocean and coastal policy: towards an adaptive approach

The development of Australia's Oceans Policy based on commitments to integrate policy across sectors and jurisdictions is a significant development. The Oceans Policy is both part of a continuum and a departure from existing arrangements. The difficulty will be in ensuring that the core themes of an 'adaptive approach' to policy and institutional development; persistence, purposefulness, information-richness, inclusiveness and flexibility, are able to overcome any rigidity developed over a quarter century of ocean management.

- *Persistence.* The traditional institutional framework governing ocean management has considerable strength. This strength derives from the foundation provided by the OCS, and its related administrative and political arrangements. The Oceans Policy is designed to build on this foundation that resolved the debilitating conflicts over jurisdiction in the 1970s. The challenge is to build on this framework and establish new institutions and processes to deal with the demands of integrated management through an innovative and radical departure from traditional management through regional marine plans. The policy learning that has made the sectoral arrangements 'successful' has been gained over a quarter of a century.

- *Purposefulness.* The Oceans Policy and the regional marine planning process have clearly identified goals, objectives, and a (relatively short three-year) time frame for completion of the first regional plan. These objectives will provide a yardstick for ongoing assessment of performance.

- *Information-richness.* Oceans policy and regional marine planning provide significant challenges in relation to the provision of scientific research to underpin decisions. Integrating different data sets and information is a particular challenge, but critical to the successful implementation of integrated management through the regional marine planning process.

- *Inclusiveness.* A further challenge will be maintaining an inclusive consultative process and providing for broad stakeholder input. Currently the management arrangements within major ocean sectors provide effective input into decision-making by major commercial resource users, but are less effective in providing avenues for input from other stakeholders. Environmental groups, arguing for protection of marine biodiversity, are critical of the traditional emphasis on resource use value. Aboriginal and Torres Strait Islander peoples, while increasingly (but not necessarily fully) involved in resource management decisions in northern Australia have less access to resources or decision-making. Traditional fishing activities by Australia's indigenous peoples raise important management issues such as access to resources and sea claims (see Bergin, 1991, 1993; Exel 1994), and may provide direct conflicts with commercial fishing interests. Broadening stakeholder involvement is important but needs to be a substantive rather than simply a symbolic 'spray-on solution' to organisational failure (see Bryson and Mowbray 1981).

- *Flexibility.* The major challenge is, however, to provide frameworks and processes which can accommodate, and resolve, conflicts between the vast range of interests and values involved in Australia's maritime estate. Adopting adaptive management principles and practices, utilising the dynamics of the process to engage in policy learning, is the task set the NOO and those involved in the regional marine planning process.

Conclusion

It is too soon to provide an evaluation of the Oceans Policy, the NOO or the regional marine planning process. What is apparent is that the NOO is the key institution responsible for the policy and will take the lead in the regional marine planning process. Experience in multiple use planning within the Great Barrier Reef Marine Park as well as terrestrial experiences in forestry through the Regional Forest Agreement (RFA) process emphasises, however, the complexities in such an undertaking. There is obvious opportunity for failure – operationalising the policy through the development of regional marine plans involves significant departures from existing practice, yet at the same time there is an opportunity to advance integrated management of Australia's significant maritime domain. While it is too soon to evaluate the oceans policy, it does not lack advocates or supporters. As in other areas of Australian resource and environmental management it is the interaction between 'individuals, institutions and ideas' (Doern and Phidd 1983) that will contribute to active and adaptive learning over integrated ocean and coastal policy and management.

References

Commonwealth of Australia, 1980, *Management of the coastal zone*, Report of the House of Representatives Standing Committee on the Environment and Conservation, Canberra: AGPS.

Bateman, S, 1999, Australia's oceans policy and the maritime community, *Maritime Studies* 108: 10-17.

Bergin, A, 1991, Aboriginal sea claims in the Northern Territory of Australia, *Ocean and Shoreline Management* 3: 171-204.

Bergin, A 1993, *Aboriginal and Torres Strait Islander interests in the Great Barrier Reef Marine Park*, Townsville: Great Barrier Reef Marine Park Authority.

Bryson, L and Mowbray M, 1981, Community: the spray-on solution, *Australian Journal of Social Issues* 16(4): 255-267.

Commonwealth of Australia, 1998a, *Australia's Ocean Policy – Part 1; Australia's Ocean Policy – Part 2, specific sectoral measures*, Canberra: Environment Australia.

Commonwealth of Australia, 1998b, *Australia's Ocean Policy – an issues paper*, Canberra: AGPS.

CSIRO, 1998, *Facts on Australia's oceans*, Hobart: CSIRO Marine Research.

Cullen, R, 1985, *Australian federalism offshore*, Special Projects Series 1, Melbourne: Law School, University of Melbourne,

Davis, B, 1991, Environmental management, in B, Galligan, O, Hughes and C, Walsh, (eds), *Intergovernmental relations and public policy*, Sydney: Allen and Unwin.

Doern, GB and Phidd, RW, 1983, *Canadian public policy: ideas, structures, process*, Toronto: Methuen.

Environment Australia, 1998, *Report of the Ministerial Advisory Group on Ocean Policy*, Canberra: Environment Australia.

Exel, M, 1994, Australian fisheries management – resource allocation and traditional rights, *ABARE Outlook* 94(2): 231-237.

Ferguson, JR, 1997, The expanses of sustainability and the limits of privatarianism, *Canadian Journal of Political Science* 30(2):285-306.

Hardin, G, 1968, The tragedy of the commons, *Science* 162: 1243-1248.

Haward, M, 1989, The Australian Offshore Constitutional Settlement, *Marine policy* 13(4): 334-348.

Haward, M, 1995a, Institutional design and policy making 'Down Under': developments in Australian and New Zealand Coastal Management. *Ocean and Coastal Management* 26 (2): 73-90.

Haward, M 1995b, The Commonwealth in Australian fisheries management: 1955-1995, *The Australasian Journal of Natural Resources Law and Policy* 2(2): 313-325.

Haward, M, 1996, Institutional framework for Australian ocean and coastal management, *Ocean and Coastal Management* Special Issue: 19-39.

Haward, M and Smith G, 1992, What's new about the new federalism? *Australian Journal of Political Science* 27: 39-51.

Haward, M and VanderZwaag D, 1995, Implementation of Agenda 21 Chapter 17 in Australia and Canada: a comparative analysis', *Ocean and Coastal Management* 29(1-3): 279-295.

Haward, M and Wilson M, 1999, *Co-management and rights based fisheries*, Paper presented at Fish Rights 99 Conference, Freemantle, November, <www.fishrights.99.conf.au>

HORSCERA (House of Representatives Standing Committee on Environment, Recreation and the Arts), 1991, *The injured coastline*, Report of House of Representatives Standing Committee on Environment, Recreation and the Arts, Canberra: AGPS.

Liberal Party of Australia, 1998, *Environment Policy 1998 Federal Election*, Canberra: Liberal Party of Australia.

O'Connell, C, 1998, 'Developing Australia's oceans policy, *ABARE Outlook 98*: 13-18.

RAC (Resource Assessment Commission), 1993, *Coastal Zone Inquiry: final report*, Canberra: AGPS.

Rothwell, DR and Haward, M, 1996, Federal and international perspectives on Australia's maritime claims, *Marine Policy* 20(1): 29-46.

Sainsbury, KM, Haward M, Kriwoken, L, Tsamenyi, M and Ward, T, 1997, *Multiple use management in the Australian marine environment: principles, definitions and elements*, Canberra: AGPS.

Warhurst J, 1983, Intergovernmental managers and cooperative federalism: The Australian case, *Public Administration* 61(3): 308-317.

4

Water Resources Management

Dingle Smith

Centre for Resource and Environmental Studies,
The Australian National University

> The Murray is docile now and the reins are tightening. Its brumby mate, the Darling is being 'broken in' to run in double harness, with the colt of the Snowy River to make a hard-working team never to run away again (Hill 1969: 276).

> They [irrigation developments] paved the way in what has proved to be the most phenomenally successful colonization of waste lands in closer settlement in the Commonwealth's history, an example to Australia, and a vindication of its vast silent spaces that are too lightly dismissed as deserts (Hill 1969: 291).

These quotations from *Water into Gold*, an account of the development of the Murray-Darling Basin by Ernestine Hill, were first written in 1937, commended in a preface from Prime Minister Menzies in 1958, and reprinted in 1969. They are in stark contrast to the following quotation from the Salinity audit (MDBMC 1999: 1):

> The rise of salinity in the landscape is symptomatic of current land uses, which have taken the place of natural systems, resulting in a massive hydrological imbalance that will take up to several hundred years to stabilise.

The quotations also demonstrate equally dramatic shifts in community and governmental perception of aims that underpin national policies related to water resource development. In simple terms the change has been from the control of nature to the need to recognise the merit of living harmoniously with nature. In more sober terminology, from an engineering-dominated paradigm to one that expresses the principles of 'Ecologically Sustainable Development' in legislation at all levels of government (Stein 2000; Bates, this volume).

This chapter traces the history of policy approaches to water resources in Australia, and analyses recent history against the themes of this book. Two appendices to the chapter deal separately with allied and critically important dimensions: monitoring of water resources, and the way we handle extremes of too much and too little water, droughts and floods.

In recent years, water planners have recognised a simple three-step scale to describe the developmental phases of water resources; a worldwide account of water and economic development is given in Falkenmark and Lindh (1993).

The first phase applies to pre-industrial societies where water is regarded as a free gift and easily accessible. The second phase is distinguished by active water exploitation, the construction of dams for hydro-power and irrigation, with inter-basin transfers from better endowed regions to nearby dry regions allowing socio-economic growth of both rural and urban communities. In short, an engineered re-distribution of water in time and space. The final, mature phase has close to maximum attainable level of stream flow regulation in major river basins, the costs of further water resource development and management increase rapidly and attention turns to non-conventional techniques to enhance supply. Even this summary leaves little doubt that parts of Australia, notably the Murray-Darling Basin and the Perth region, have now entered the third and mature phase.

However, for Australia, the arrival and recognition of the mature phase is much more recent than for most countries. This is evidenced by a perusal of *Water in Australia – from myths to reality* (Sewell et al, 1985). The late Derrick Sewell, an internationally recognised authority on national water planning, was surprised by the lack of attention to water planning in Australia in the mid-1980s. This is exemplified by the five myths around which the recommendations in the monograph are based. The myths were:

- water is a free gift;
- water can be managed in isolation;
- the desert can be made to bloom;
- social values will not change; and
- water management is mainly a technical matter.

That challenging these myths was seen as somewhat revolutionary by many of the senior water planners at a workshop held in 1985 is a measure of both a nation yet to recognise its impending move to a mature phase of development and the change in attitudes to water planning that have arisen over the last 15 years or so. In 1985, neither the Commonwealth nor individual States and Territories had formulated comprehensive water or management plans.

The usefulness of recognizing phases of development at national level has however, to be tempered in order to recognise the uniqueness of water resources in individual regions and countries. An outline of Australia's water resources and their use is necessary before we discuss the implications for policy; a recent more detailed account is given in Smith (1998a).

Quantity and use

The key physical features of Australia's water resources are those of the driest (inhabited) continent with a variability of rainfall and runoff only equalled in southern Africa. Notwithstanding the availability of water, a renewable resource, in Australia it will never be a limiting factor in terms of water for direct human use. This is because the average annual discharge (surface water and groundwater recharge) per capita is among the most favourable in the world. The figure for Australia is some 20,000m^3 for each inhabitant. For the Middle East, the countries bordering the Mediterranean, most of Africa and the Indian sub-continent the comparable value is less than 1,000m^3. Urban and domestic water use remain secure because, even if irrigation were to increase, price would see water transfer to higher value uses.

Many of the recurring policy issues in Australia stem from the remarkably uneven spatial and temporal distribution of the resource. An instance of the former is that 58 per cent of divertible water resources are located in the Drainage Divisions of the Timor Sea, Carpentaria and the North-east Coast. These Divisions however, comprise only some 21 per cent of the land area of the continent and 15 per cent of the population. If Tasmania is added to the these northern Drainage Divisions, the corresponding values for the proportion of national divertible annual water is close to 70 per cent. At the other extreme the Western Plateau, which comprises a third of the total land area of the continent, contributes 0.1 per cent of the nation's divertible water. Variability is excellently described in McMahon et al (1992). The coefficient of variation at national level is 0.70 compared to that for Europe at 0.29 with a world figure of 0.47. In more accessible terms, this translates to the need for a dam storage capacity in Australia, for a comparable level of security of supply, to be six times larger than in western Europe.

The availability of water in Australia will never be a limiting factor for supply to the domestic or non-agricultural industrial sectors. However, the situation for growth of irrigated agriculture is a different question. Figure 4.1 summarises the sectorial use of water in Australia, and the spatial variations in use are shown in Figure 4.2. This is dominated by irrigation which accounts for some 70 per cent of average annual use. An alarming statistic is that, of total national water use, some 28 per cent is for irrigation of pasture in the Murray-Darling Basin. This is a region where irrigation results in rising saline water tables with return irrigation flows contributing to the growing river salinity crisis. Of the supply of reticulated water in the capital cities, treated to

Figure 4.1. Sectorial use of water in Australia (from Smith 1998a)

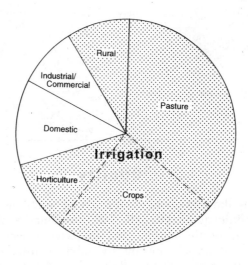

UN water quality drinking water standards, less than 2 per cent is used for human consumption (cooking and drinking) while at least 50 per cent is used for garden watering. Together with the irrigation of pasture, this confirms the national passion for growing exotic grasses that are essentially unsuitable for dry regions with unreliable rainfall patterns.

Figure 4.2. Spatial and sectoral use of water in Australia (from Smith 1998a)

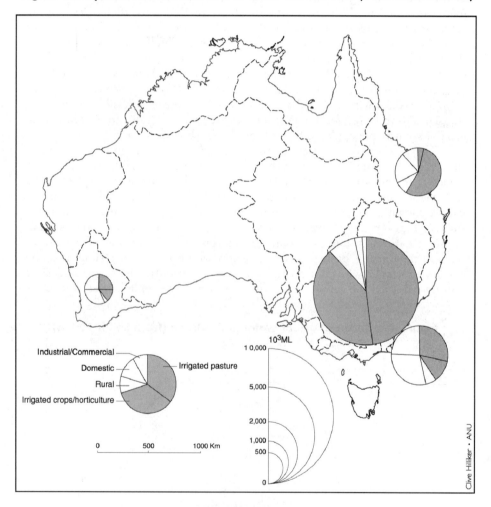

Quality

The most likely limiting factor to the use of water in Australia is that of salinity. The salinity audit (MDBMC 1999), summarises the most recent and reliable estimates of the current and projected extent of salinisation for irrigated areas (wetland salinity) and dryland agricultural catchments (dryland salinity) within the Murray-Darling Basin. Table 4.1 presents the estimates of the extent of current and future areas subject to high and raising watertables. Other areas of Australia show a similar pattern, for instance in south-western Western Australia dryland salinity is increasing at some 18,000 ha per year. The current costs of salinity in the Murray Darling Basin alone are estimated to be some $250m per year, of which half is to the non-farming sector.

Table 4.1. Water table rise in the Murray Darling Basin

State		Estimated Land Area (ha)			
	Area (ha)	Current shallow water tables 1998	Current rising groundwater 1998	Likely water logged 2050	Likely salinity affected 2050
SA	6,900,000	68,000	900,000	112,000	116,000
Victoria	13,050,000	202,000	1,800,000	930,000	840,000
NSW	59,980,000	5,400,000	2,300,000	n.a.	n.a.
Queensland	26,001,000	59,000	n.a.	650,000	n.a.
Total	106,931,000	n.a.	>15,000,000	n.a.	n.a.

Table 4.2. Selection of estimated river salinities, NSW and Queensland

	1998	2020	2050	2100
New South Wales				
Murrumbidgee	250	320	350	400
Lachlan	530	780	1150	1460
Bogan	730	1500	1950	2320
Macquarie	620	1290	1730	2110
Castlereagh	640	760	1100	1230
Namoi	680	1050	1280	1550
Queensland				
Warrego	210	1270	1270	1270
Condamine-Balonne	210	1040	1040	1040
Border Rivers	310	1010	1010	1010

All values in EC units. Note that the estimates are for the downstream end of the rivers. The data are averaged, in some years and for some seasons they would exceed the values given above.

The salinity audit focuses upon estimating salt load and the mobility of salt within the landscape, however for major catchments salinity is also estimated as average salt concentration in river flows. A selection of these is presented in Table 4.2. The salinity values for the rivers are in terms of conductivity. The Murray-Darling Basin Commission suggest that at a value of 800 EC units '… it becomes increasingly difficult to manage irrigation and at this level, damage to tree crops has occurred'. At 1500 EC '… options for consumptive use of water start to become restrictive, irrigation of most leguminous pasture and forage crops is risky. Rice, maize and grain sorghum should not be irrigated at this salinity'. At 1500 EC direct adverse biological effects are likely to occur in river, stream and wetland ecosystems. It is stressed that the data for concentration in Table 4.2 are 'annual average estimates'; for some seasons and some years the values will be in excess of the figures given. In the early-1970s, a number of the catchments in Western Australia upstream of the water supply dams for Perth reached unacceptable levels of salinity. This was due to continued clearing of native vegetation for agricultural purposes that caused a rise in the saline water tables. Restrictions were placed on further activity of this kind and the owners compensated.

A commendable feature of the information presented by the MDBMC is that salinity estimates are presented for time slices into the future. The critical nature of the situation is clear and a Basin Salinity Management Strategy has been developed. However, the severity of the problem was flagged in a consultant report on irrigation salinity prepared for the River Murray Commission in 1970 (GHD, 1970). The estimates at that time, for the year 1985, have proved to be remarkably accurate albeit somewhat conservative. This earlier study was largely ignored; it is hoped that the audit of 1999 will not suffer a similar fate.

History of development

Comprehensive histories of the water development for Victoria, Queensland and Western Australia are available (Powell 1989, 1991, 1998) and a broader national account in Smith (1998a). Smith distinguishes three phases:
- pre-Federation: challenges and response;
- 1901-1945: stops and starts of consolidation; and
- 1945-late 1980s: light on the hill and water in the dam

The pre-Federation phase provided lessons on the problems of adjustment to an unknown climate and, progressively, the emergence of engineering prowess. Instances of the latter are the discovery and initial utilisation of the Great Artesian Basin and the construction of the pipeline from Mundaring, close to Perth, to the water-deprived Kalgoorlie and the Eastern Goldfields. The potential of irrigation was widely lauded and in the early 1890s the Chaffey brothers initiated their acclaimed scheme at Mildura, However, in 1895 the entrepreneurial Canadians had filed for bankruptcy!

From Federation through to the conclusion of World War II saw the emergence of powerful statutory authorities in all the States. These bodies ensured financial backing for the continued growth of water infrastructure. Optimism surrounded the perception of unbounded irrigation that would provide the stimulus for rural settlement aided by waves of soldier settlers. These capital-intensive developments were even more striking given the background of two World Wars separated by prolonged and severe economic depression.

Throughout the earlier phases, irrigation was regarded as the driving force for future expansion in agricultural production. The magnitude of the developments, however, was insignificant compared to those of the 1950s, 1960s and 1970s (Figure 4.3). In these three decades, 75 per cent of the current storage volume was completed, if we include the 1980s the proportion rises to nearly 90 per cent, although many of the 1980s dams were approved and under construction in the 1970s. The storage capacity of dams completed during the 1950s alone, equalled the volumes of all dams built before that date. Mega and multi-purpose schemes were the vogue. The Snowy Mountain Scheme was followed by a series of major Hydro-Electric Commission (HEC) dams in Tasmania and the Ord Dam in Western Australia, with the Burdekin Dam in Queensland representing the last of these massive enterprises.

Figure 4.3. Storage capacities and completion dates for large dams (>100GL) by State, 1901 to mid-1990s (from Smith 1998a)

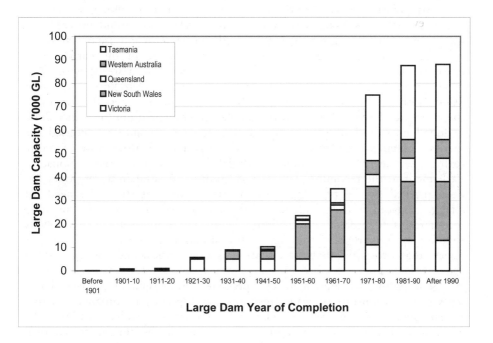

This post-war period of unprecedented expansion was aided by further improvements in engineering techniques and distinguished by the injection of comparatively massive sums of Commonwealth financial assistance, a factor that was not present prior to 1945. There is little doubt that pork-barrelling played a major part in the frenzy of water resource activity. It is not serendipity that the mega-projects each involve a different State! This is confirmed as federal Cabinet papers, with a time lag of 30 years, are released. Those released in 1999 show an initial reluctance to fund the Ord Scheme but this was reversed. The much quoted phrase, coined at that time by Bert Kelly (a Cabinet Minister), and used prior to elections (State or federal) that 'I feel a dam coming on' was fully justified. The 2000 release reveals that the then Minister for National Development, Curley Swartz, tabled a paper that proposed that water '... charges may be more closely related to the real cost of providing water and/or the landholders' capacity to pay for it'. Cabinet resolved that this suggestion be deleted and that '... the Commonwealth should not involve itself in water-charges issues'.

Maturity and economic rationalism

'Maturity', in this context, refers to the third and final phase of water resource development, outlined above. For Australia, this broadly coincides with a worldwide change in thinking to a more rational approach to economic policy of which a user-pays concept is dominant. The two strands match the move in water resource planning from an overwhelmingly demand-driven stance to emphasis on supply. It is difficult to appreciate that less than 15 years ago future water demand was assessed solely on the grounds of population growth and extrapolation of the continued rise in annual water use. Costs of the schemes and prices charged for water were largely ignored and no credence was given to the option of reducing demand by more efficient use of water.

The seeds of change were beginning to emerge in the early 1980s, however they were fanned by a mild zephyr rather than a strong wind. The federal government funded a series of reports, collectively known as *Water 2000*. With the benefit of hindsight, these can be seen as heralding many of the changes of the 1990s. The numerous recommendations in *Water 2000* included measures to combat the adverse impacts of salinity, espoused the merits of changes to water pricing, and stressed the parlous state of monitoring (see the summary volume, DRE 1983). At the time, the response of Parliament to the recommendations was minimal. Australian water policy has been marked by the production of major reviews that stress the need for change to avoid further depletion or degradation of the resource – in more recent terms to protect sustainability. There is typically a blaze of publicity followed by remarkably little action, the situation worsens, there is a new review that proclaims that the situation is now critical and the cycle starts again.

The publication of *Water 2000* pre-dated other seminal changes. These were the relationship of water resource development to broader environmental issues and moves to enhanced community involvement and the growing interest in conflict resolution. For Australia, the impetus for concern of environmental issues was both local and international. The critical issue became the HEC proposal to further expand their building program to include a major dam on the Franklin River. A detailed account is given in Smith and Handmer (1996) but the bare bones were as follows. In late 1981, there was a referendum in Tasmania, which found in favour of the proposal. However, environmental opposition spread to the mainland and, in December 1981, at a federal by-election in Victoria, some 40 per cent of the voters spoiled their ballot papers by writing in 'no dams'. The Commonwealth government became involved when the Fraser administration nominated southwest Tasmania for World Heritage Listing. By the federal election of March 1983, the issue had become of national significance and the victorious Hawke government filed a writ against the government of Tasmania in the High Court of Australia. The significance of these events was not the halting of the Franklin Dam but the realisation that the environmental lobby had become a political entity within the decision-making process at the highest levels. On the international scene the WCED Report (1987) and the subsequent 1992 National Strategy for Ecologically Sustainable Development endorsed by all levels of government in Australia, gave formal recognition to environmental issues many of which were water-related.

The 1980s also witnessed an upsurge in community involvement much of which was also linked to environmental concerns. A contemporary account of these is given in Handmer *et al* (1996). The underlying thrust was to encourage bottom-up planning by involving the community in planning and management decisions. An instance was the Salinity Program in Victoria, introduced in the early 1990s, where traditional bureaucratic processes were discarded to facilitate community-led salinity planning. The Community Working Groups (eventually to number some 400) were provided with technical assistance and were able to involve individual farm households in the planning process. This is described in Stone (1996), the program is no longer in operation, but Sharman Stone is now a senior politician in the Howard administration. Interestingly, the salinity initiative was part of the wider Victorian Landcare program. This name was later used for the national scheme launched by Prime Minister Hawke in July 1989, again a grass roots movement which now has some 4,000 local groups and is regarded internationally as an exemplar of community involvement. This growth in community concern is also associated with the recognition that water cannot be considered in isolation and Landcare, and many similar initiatives (Salt Watch, Water Watch etc), stress the necessity for a holistic view of catchments that link land and water resources. Several commentators, including some in this volume, have recently drawn attention to the problem that community involvement of this kind needs to be followed by a commitment by government to implement the plans that emerge.

Institutional arrangements

It is the contention of this account that change in Australian water policy over the last decade of the 20th century has eclipsed that of the preceding 90 years. This is especially true for the institutional setting although it is impossible to specify a single 'stroke of the pen' decision. There are many pens, State and federal, and change is incremental, but the speed of change is at an unprecedented rate, and with little correlation with the political parties in power.

The powerful statutory bodies that controlled urban and rural water at State level, often with little change since Federation, have all undergone massive reorganisation, in most cases they have been totally restructured. The effects of economic rationalism and marketisation are everywhere apparent. In the mid-1980s it was difficult to name a major water agency that was not headed by an engineer, now it is difficult to find one that is. All State water agencies have moved to adopt corporatisation. This adoption of commercial practices by former statutory bodies can take many forms. The more extreme are better described as franchising, which can be described as public ownership of assets with management leased out for a set period to the private sector. In Australia, the prime example is for metropolitan Adelaide with an overseas consortium, United Water International (UWI), taking over the management from 1 January 1996 for a period of some 15 years. In the public mind and in the media, 'corporatisation' is often misleadingly referred to as 'privatisation', a term that should be restricted to ownership by a private company; that is, the government assets are sold and subsequently traded on the stock market. To date, no government in Australia has undertaken this step although it was proposed by the minority Carnell administration in the ACT but defeated in the Legislative Assembly in early 1999. In the rural sector, a number of State governments have transferred the ownership of irrigation infrastructure, but not the supply dams, to local groups of irrigators. This can be regarded as a form of privatisation.

Although there has been no 'stroke of the pen' sudden change, it is possible to distinguish a series of seminal milestones. These include:
- The National Strategy for Ecologically Sustainable Development, formally adopted by all Heads of Government, December 1992;
- The Hilmer Committee on National Competition Policy, August 1993;
- COAG Strategic Water Resources Policy framework initiated, February 1993; and
- COAG adopts the National Competition Policy, March 1995.

These steps were all initiated by the Commonwealth government and culminated, at the COAG meeting in April 1995, with acceptance by all States of the National Competition Policy. This has a component that presents ' ... a strategic framework for the efficient and sustainable reform of the Australian water industry' (COAG 1995). It was recognised that the water reforms are more difficult than those for energy or transport. The COAG water reforms are linked to three payments, termed 'tranches', from the Commonwealth to the States. These have a timetable and are conditional on the States attaining goals prior to each payment. The final tranche requires the States to '... have fully implemented and continue to observe, all COAG agreements with regard to electricity, gas, water and road transport (COAG 1995).

The COAG reforms require water to be subject to full cost recovery and traded to meet the Hilmer recommendations. A summary of COAG principles (COAGWRTF 1995) is given below:
- That all consumptive and non-consumptive water entitlements be allocated and managed in accordance with comprehensive planning systems and based on full, basin-wide hydrologic assessment of the resource.
- That water entitlements and institutional arrangements be structured so as not to impede the effective operation of water markets and such that, as far as practicable, trading options associated with property rights in water reside with the individual end-users of water.
- That water entitlements be clearly specified in terms of rights and conditions and ownership tenure and share of natural resource being allocated (including probability of occurrence, details of agreed standards of any commercial service to be delivered; constraints to, and rules on, transferability: and constraints of resource use of access).
- That acceptable rules on the holdings of environmental flow entitlements be resolved by jurisdictions, at the same time as

determining the appropriate balance between consumptive and non-consumptive uses of water.

- That where interstate trading of water entitlements is possible, jurisdictions co-operatively develop, on a catchment-by-catchment basis, compatible approaches for planning systems and basin-wide hydrologic assessment methods; water entitlement specifications; pricing and asset valuation arrangements; water entitlement trading arrangements; and provisions for environmental and other instream values.
- That, in implementing and initialising property rights in water, jurisdictions call on water users, interest groups, and the general community to be involved as partners in catchment planning processes that affect the future allocation and management of water entitlements.
- That governments give urgent priority to establishing the administrative and regulatory arrangements that are necessary to implement and support the strategic framework.

The dominance of economic instruments is tempered by the requirement for all States to produce catchment plans that incorporate values for long-term environmental river flows. How to define acceptable environmental flows is complex, with no acceptable code of practice. However, all States have undertaken serious studies of this problem although the approach varies. Different styles may be appropriate given the variations in hydrology and water use across the continent. The unique flow regimes of Australian rivers pose major problems and, in this regard, overseas experience is of limited value. Even prior to human interference, many Australian rivers experienced periods, often of some duration, of zero flow. Thus, strategies based on minimal flows, common in temperate northern hemisphere latitudes, are inapplicable.

The recent inquiry into environmental flow allocations to the Snowy River from the Snowy Mountains Hydro-Electric Scheme is an example of the conflicting issues – economic, political and ecological – that are involved. The inquiry was undertaken as a precursor to the corporatisation of the Snowy Scheme. At present, environmental flows approximate to 1 per cent of average annual flow; the inquiry recommended an increase to 15 per cent with many environmental concerns arguing for at least 25 per cent (Anon 1998). The range of arguments, from irrigation users to environmentalists, are given in Gale et al (1999).

Apart from the vexed question of environmental flows, what they should be and how they are to be costed, other facets of competition policy have made considerable progress. Water trading between users is now accepted by all States, a major change given that the first tentative steps were only introduced in 1983. This has now spread from limited seasonal trading within individual catchments to permanent purchase and extension to trading across State boundaries. An account of these developments is given in Bjorlund and McKay (1998). An accompanying institutional change, that could be considered as exceeding the bounds of incrementalism, is the conversion of water allocations for irrigation by licence to those of full property rights. This again raises the environmental flow issue with the spectre that such arrangements would reduce the current allocations to existing users. A recent study, *Water and the Australian economy* (AATSE 1999) that advances the economic ratio-nalist theme, strongly recommends that any such 'off the top' allocation to the environment should be accompanied by compensation to those who lose; that is, reductions to current licence allocations mainly in the irrigation sector.

So far this account has focused upon what has happened; the tendency with policy reviews is to laud the advantages of the most recently expounded policy and to conclude that this will solve the earlier problems. The COAG reforms have the potential to greatly improve the efficient use of water especially in the irrigation sector and to enhance biodiversity by incorporating environmental flows. However, conflicts between users are apparent, the Snowy Inquiry is but one example. Will the lure of $1.2 billion of payments to the States (indexed and quarantined from assessment by the Commonwealth Grants Commission) for full implementation of the COAG water reforms be sufficient to overcome the potential political consequences? The input of community voices in the COAG agreements was minimal, as were the interests and view of local government. As an example, will local governments in Queensland, who own and manage most local water supply, be happy to see these assets run under the COAG principles? The massive changes via the more extreme forms of corporatisation, let alone privatisation, without wide consultation does not accord well with the growth of community involvement. The recommendations in the AATSE (1999) report draw attention to many matters that need further attention if the COAG principles are to be widely adopted. Among these are the need for much more attention to water quality, especially the costing of the externalities of pollution that are caused by industry, including agriculture. The report also highlights the dearth of good quality data on which to base many of the changes, a deficiency of such impor-tance that a separate review is appended to this chapter. Critical issues that need attention are those of regulatory mechanisms and institutions to control corporatised, franchised and privatised components of the water industry. It is difficult to resolve community involvement with these concepts, and well-resourced government watchdogs are required, as is the case with the priva-tised water industry in Great Britain.

The changes in water policy in Australia in the last decade, especially in the institutional arrangements, are perhaps better described by the term 'sea change' rather than be described as 'incremental'. Such change is not easy in a federal structure and the next decade will likely see much wider community concern, especially at local level, than has been the case to date.

Lessons

What are the lessons from past policy experience and what guidance do they give of adaptive practices? The rapid rate of change in the last decade presents a quandary as to how to compare these to the essentially static policy and institutions prior to the late 1980s. The approach taken here is to summarise policies and their effectiveness for the earlier period and to comment separately on the policies' strengths and weaknesses for those of the last decade. A summary is given in Table 4.3.

Table 4.3. Background to water resource policy – a summary

	Pre late-1980s	Post late-1980s
Persistence	Little change in institutional arrangements, Statutory bodies for irrigation and cities, Local Government Authorities for local services.	Widespread institutional reorganisation and adoption of corporatisation and franchising, Reorganisation of Local Government Authorities.
Purposefulness	Measures distorted by large government schemes, Dictated by demand, almost regardless of cost and externalities.	Marketisation, move to true pricing and trading of water, Use of cost-benefit analysis, Recognition of environmental flows but problems of quality largely ignored.
Information Richness and Sensitivity	Monitoring of quantity, quality, socio-economic and environmental factors have remained inadequate throughout both periods, Little sign of improvement and moves to the more extreme forms of marketisation will hinder progress unless monitoring requirements are specified and overseen by well-resourced regulatory bodies.	
Inclusiveness	State cabinets and statutory bodies made major decisions, Local Government Authorities for local services, Limited range of stakeholders.	Interest in community involvement, Growth of voluntary bodies, Problems of relationship between marketisation and such involvement emerge.
	Water rights of Indigenous people have been ignored through both periods.	
Flexibility	At national level flexibility limited by Constitutional rights of States in resource matters, Commonwealth involvement mainly providing financial assistance.	Moves under Council of Australian Governments to interstate trading of water and adoption of market principles although whether that increases flexibility is questionable.
	Need to encourage adoption of successful Local Government Authorities practices to other States etc.	

Persistence

Pre late-1980s

In detail, organisation of water differed between the States. For discussion, these can be classified into those of water provision (domestic, commercial and irrigation), wastewater management and drainage (mainly urban). Drainage and wastewater management were dominantly a matter for LGAs, domestic and commercial supply varied but for major cities were controlled by statutory authorities and elsewhere by LGAs. Economic regulation of all major developments and price setting, especially for irrigation, were ultimately controlled by State Cabinets.

Water resources and their use were State matters, with the Commonwealth (certainly post-1945) providing financial assistance for major resource developments, especially those involving dams and their associated infrastructure. For many years there had been little change in the statutory bodies, in many cases since Federation. Water had become politicised and the prices charged, especially in the irrigation sector, had little relation to the capital, maintenance and distribution costs.

Post late-1980s

Widespread organisational change is a feature of all water sectors. The driving forces stem from the Hilmer reforms and the associated COAG statements. Thus, competition policy, pricing and economic efficiency are to the fore in all States. The key concept to achieve these aims is corporatisation; that is, the adoption of business practices by government agencies. If and where true pricing is not adopted, the aim is that any exceptions should be made fully transparent. There are however, variations in the degree to which corporatisation is applied. These progress through out-sourcing, the establishment of competing bodies providing the service, to franchising of management for set periods of time. The final stage of privatisation, the selling of assets with private ownership and management, has yet to be followed. The final decision of the pricing of water in all States is still a matter for governments. Public perception of fully privatised water, and its unique problem of monopoly ownership (in contrast to energy), remain barriers to this final step. The various models of corporatisation and competition stem from the COAG reforms. These were initiated by the Commonwealth government, and the carrot of substantial payments to the States for adoption has been the spur to change and innovation.

Purposefulness

Pre late-1980s

The power of statutory bodies and the control of financial outlays and pricing by State governments led to a situation where the concept of measuring progress became progressively distorted. The State and national goals were to develop irrigated agriculture and associated rural settlement with little attention to cost and, with hindsight, to potential adverse environmental effects.

Post late-1980s

The rise of economic rationalism has resulted in improvements to the earlier situation. These include pricing mechanisms that lead to more effective use of water, the irrigation and domestic sectors are excellent examples. Acceptance of systematic analysis of costs and benefits has provided a better measure of purposefulness. There are also moves, so far much less effective, to add environmental factors into the calculus, environmental flow provision is a key example. However, questions of water quality, especially the adverse externalities that arise from many major water users, are still to be addressed.

Corporatisation, franchising and privatisation all require independent and well-resourced regulatory bodies. These apply the rules set by governments within which water enterprises function. These include standards for quality, together with appropriate monitoring, pricing and oversight of a range of agreed community service obligations. The regulatory bodies would oversee a comprehensive range of goals and obligations together with the means to assess them. This regulatory function is widely seen, by both protagonists and critics of such moves, as the Achilles' heel of current moves throughout Australia to implement the Hilmer reforms.

It has to be clearly stated however, that the situation prior to the late 1980s was just as unsatisfactory. The gamekeeper/poacher relationship was overshadowed by the control of powerful statutory authorities and government water agencies who were dedicated to demand-driven goals.

Information-richness and sensitivity

Without doubt, monitoring is the major deficiency of water resource management in Australia, both pre- and post late-1980s. Many reviews limit their criticisms to the shortcomings of the scientific aspects of quantity and quality and stress the particularly lamentable state of the later. However, the assessment of non-scientific parameters is likely worse. Comments on these aspects have become more frequent with the more comprehensive approach to water management of the late 1980s. For instance, AATSE (1999: 119) states that during the study '... it became clear that data systems for integrated economic, environmental and social analysis and management of water development issues are inadequate ... the biggest single deficiency has been the lack of geo-coding of socio-economic data'.

The background to the lamentable state of monitoring is described in Appendix 1 of this chapter. Such basic scientific and social data are essential to assessing even the most rudimentary aspects of purposefulness. The basic questions include how much water is there, what is its quality, where is it, and who uses what, where and for what purpose? Throughout the development phase of Australian water management, the States too often regarded this as a matter for the Commonwealth, or more specifically that the Commonwealth should fund the collection and analysis of such information. The story of collection and analysis of the information necessary for the planning and management of Australia's water resources is one of long-standing and sorrowful neglect.

Inclusiveness

Pre late-1980s

Statutory authorities and State Cabinets, the dominant decision-making bodies, were regarded as representative of the community's wishes – they were, after all, elected! The situation with local government is different; elected members are closer to the issues and non-performance can rapidly lead to change via the ballot box. For local governments, it is the relationships with the upper tiers of government that are of more significance. This is discussed in Appendix 2, within the context of the floodplain management policies and the differences between States (and see Wild River, this volume).

Post late-1980s

During the 1980s, stakeholder involvement became a widely accepted concept. Nowhere was this more apparent than in the environmental field and many of the critical issues were water-related. The willingness of the community, not only environmentalists, to participate voluntarily in water (and land) issues was outstanding with Landcare as a national example. Community input into catchment committees at scales from the Murray-Darling basin down were, and still are, key features.

The acceptance of broad stakeholder involvement is however, at odds with the moves to corporatisation and the potential path to privatisation. It is difficult to see how meaningful input from such a wide range of stakeholders is compatible with these forms of management and ownership. Questions of commercial confidentiality, economic return and the costs and lack of access to basic data are all severe barriers. As an example, the acceptance of environmental flows faces the problems of who will decide on the timing and magnitude of releases and, more fundamentally, who owns the water?

Two other comments are pertinent to inclusiveness. The first is the lack of discussion of Aboriginal water rights, as opposed to land rights, and the other is that the COAG agreements are between the Commonwealth and State governments. Local government had no representation and public debate has been limited, perhaps because of the non-partisan nature of the agreements.

Flexibility

The constitutional responsibility for water resources lies firmly with the States, although the management involves interaction between three tiers of government. This creates a fast-moving series of management styles that can be likened to a national laboratory engaged in active experimentation. There is the opportunity to see what works well and conversely, what does not. However, the advantages of the different approaches by the States and Territories to water resource matters are rarely exploited. There have been some promising innovations in this field that enable local governments to gain from experience elsewhere, some using Internet links. Further exchange of information and experience between local governments of the success, or otherwise, of their approaches to similar problems is a field that could be expanded and could lead to enhanced adaptive management.

Finally, there is a fear that full privatisation of water resources limits future flexibility. Once privatised it is difficult, but not impossible, to return to any other form of ownership or control.

Having reviewed major themes and policy styles in Australian water resource management, we can now turn more specifically to particular issues of obvious import in this country: what we know about water resources (monitoring); and what we do in the face of too much or too little water (drought and flood).

APPENDIX 4.1
The status and role of monitoring

In this account of water research development and policy in Australia, the role of monitoring is described as the Achille's heel. This section is designed to substantiate that statement. Monitoring of water resources is fundamental to their effective management. It is basic to decisions at all spatial scales, from national to small urban catchments. Many of the solutions to Australia's problems of widespread environmental degradation require major changes to land and water use. Governments require information on a range of water resource issues before they are prepared to commit themselves to the massive social change and financial outlays necessary to mitigate these problems. First, it is necessary to understand the different forms of measurement that are required to evaluate the quantity of the resource, its quality and other data and then to review the available monitoring and surveys that are available.

Quantity

The assessment of quantity is based on the knowledge of the various elements of the hydrological cycle. In simple terms, these are precipitation (in Australia overwhelmingly rainfall), and surface and groundwater discharge. Nationally, rainfall is measured daily at several thousand stations; collection and analysis are the responsibility of the Bureau of Meteorology. In contrast, runoff is essentially managed by State agencies who synthesise data from State and local government and a range of other public and private agencies. Recording stations are fewer and more complex and there is a greater need for automatic recorders than for rainfall measurement, because of the need to record peak flood flows from small catchments. Groundwater has separate requirements and is assessed, often poorly, by State agencies.

The situation varies between States but can be illustrated from Western Australia and Queensland (Figure 4.A.1). In WA, a detailed network of gauging stations was not established in the populous south-west until the 1960s and for remoter areas until the 1970s. These phases of expansion were prompted in the south-west by the recognition of an incipient water supply crisis, and in the north by major new industrial (dominantly mining) and agricultural projects (the Ord Scheme). An additional spur was the availability of Commonwealth funding to assist such monitoring.

The major handicap of the late establishment of a recording network is that it is inadequate to provide long-term estimates of runoff, particularly for a continent with the most variable rainfall and runoff in the world. Such information is necessary in order to plan the size of storages and to decide upon secure volumes of irrigation water. A recurring problem is how to assess the costs and benefits of such networks and the provision of the data in an easily accessible form. To meteorologists and hydrologists the value is obvious and of critical importance; to a corporatised or privatised agency the answer is much less clear. There are no agreed methodologies to assess the costs and benefits of the collection of any form of water resource data.

Figure 4.A.1. Stream gauging stations in Western Australia and Queensland (from Institute of Engineers of Australia 1999)

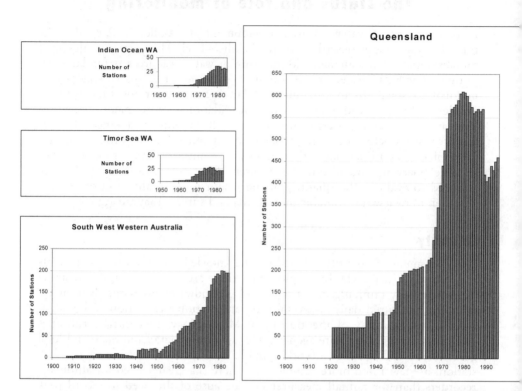

Worldwide, the density of rainfall measuring stations is always greater than for river gauging. However, for Australia with its extreme variability of rainfall and agricultural dominance of irrigation, the development of a river gauging network has always been remarkably inadequate. This was reviewed by Brown (1983) in *Water 2000*. He lists the length of records for each of the 244 Drainage Basins within the 12 Drainage Divisions used to evaluate hydrology at the national level. Only half of the 244 Drainage Basins had 20 years or more of flow records. For the Indian Ocean, Timor Sea and Carpentaria Drainage Divisions, which together account for close to half of the total average annual river discharge for the nation, only three stations had records that exceeded 20 years. This paucity of data, especially for tropical Australia, was a major reason why the estimate of national average annual river discharge for Australian rivers in *Water 2000* was 30 per cent greater than the estimate in the preceding national survey (AWRC 1976). Brown (1983:3) summarises the situation as reflecting '... the still large area of Australia which is not gauged and the relatively short, and in some cases of low accuracy, records available from gauged catchments. This emphasises the need for the continuation and upgrading of the stream gauging programs'.

A feature that emerges from these early national surveys of water quantity is the role of the Commonwealth in promoting and assisting with funding of programs to improve the situation. This commenced in 1963 and provided matching funding for State outlays '... to foster water resource measurement and assessment in areas where deficiencies in information are known to exist ... to be of value for future planning'. Brown comments that Australia differs from most other countries with a federal structure in that there is no central government agency that is responsible for the collection of hydrological data.

From the mid-1960s to the mid-1980s, the Commonwealth provided some 30 per cent of the funding for surface water resource assessment. There is no doubt that the States regarded this funding as integral to the development and maintenance of the networks for surface water assessment. For instance, Brown (1983: 164), in considering future policy options, concludes that '... surface water data collection activities in some States would virtually collapse without any direct assistances from the Commonwealth'. Brown also recommended a firm Commonwealth government commitment to the funding of the hydrological network and stressed the need for this to be '... operated indefinitely because of the high temporal variability of streamflow'. The suggested level of Commonwealth funding was for half of the costs for development and maintenance of the network with additional assistance in northern and arid Australia. The recommendations included a 50 per cent increase in the number of hydrological stations in Queensland and South Australia and the addition of 225 new stations in Western Australia.

Changes to Commonwealth water resource funding in 1986 removed direct assistance for surface water assessment. It is, therefore, of interest to note the comments from the States and Territories as reported in IEA (1999). All acknowledge the critical role of the Commonwealth in establishing hydrological stations in the 1960s and 1970s. There is however, an underlying *crie de coeur*, illustrated by the Tasmanian contribution which states 'from that time [late 1960s] until the 1980s a significant increase in the number of stations occurred, largely as a result of Commonwealth assistance to assess the nation's water resources. Since that time the stream gauging network has contracted due to budget constraints' (IEA 1999: 92).

Growth in the number of river gauging stations for Western Australia and Queensland (see Figure 4.A.1) confirm the increase in the number of recording stations in response to Commonwealth assistance from the 1960s to the 1980s. This is followed by a plateau and the beginning of a downturn. The recommendations in *Water 2000* for increases in the number of stations did not occur, then or since.

Quality

Water quality is much more difficult to asses than quantity. This is because there are a large number of possible water parameters involved and, for some, the analytical methods are complex, time-consuming and expensive. It is common practice to classify quality into physical (eg, pH), particulates (eg, turbidity), and solutes with an additional biological category (eg, bacteria).

A key physical measure in Australia is that of conductivity, a surrogate for salinity.

In Australia, the monitoring of water quality is described in the *State of the Environment 1996* (SEAC 1996) as 'poor and deteriorating'. The damning nature of this comment is re-enforced, as the water quality component of *Water 2000* (Garman 1983) had earlier stressed the lack of data and basic information on this topic. Garman proposed a series of reforms necessary to remedy these deficiencies and these were further addressed in the National Water Quality Management Strategy (NWQMS) in the early 1990s. A review commissioned by the NWQMS identified existing water quality monitoring activities and concluded that half of these were concerned with drinking water, only 5 per cent with monitoring river environments and less than 2 per cent were designed to monitor runoff from agriculture. That the national program of water quality could be described in 1996 as 'deteriorating' is the ultimate condemnation of what has always been a poorly designed and resourced activity. The situation overseas is also far from ideal, but it is inexcusable for Australia in which the major water and land problem of degradation is salinity.

Salinity observations, including continuous recording, are simple and inexpensive. The monitoring required is not a question of instrumented research catchments to investigate details of process but is essential for any policy or management option that aims to lessen the impacts of land and water degradation. The extreme variability of rainfall and runoff, already discussed for quantity, is equally valid for all aspects of quality. As stressed in every textbook on quality, it is imperative to link quality measurements to those of quantity. Water quality programs that rely on monthly readings are of little value for management purposes. This is because the concentration of most water quality parameters vary dramatically with discharge, thus measurements are required at times of flood flow. In practice, this requires the establishment of a network of self-recording or automatic water sampling stations. Such techniques have been available for decades but their use in Australia is still limited.

It is true that decisions upon which water quality parameters should be monitored are difficult, but the paucity of continuous runs of data on salinity (as conductivity) are inexcusable. The Key Sites Program in New South Wales, run by the Department of Land and Water Conservation, is among the best of the State programs. A total of 89 representative sites (associated with long-term river gauging stations) were selected and sampling commenced in July 1992. Detailed accounts of the results are available in the NSW State of the Environment reports for 1995 and 1997 (NSWEPA 1995 and 1997). The major limitation is that the sites are only sampled at monthly intervals. This deficiency is acknowledged in NSWEPA (1997: 224) which states '... it may be necessary to look at a 20-year period to discern trends in water quality above the effects of flow and climate variability and the relatively low sampling frequency of the Key Sites Program (once a month or less)'. At the national scale, it is likely that the only site at which a monthly series of water quality measurements (restricted to conductivity) approaches adequacy is at Morgan on the main stem of the Murray. The record is from 1938 to present, and the data have been analysed on a number of occasions, see Close (1990) and Williamson et al (1997), in order to quantify information on an increasing trend of river salinity.

The NSWEPA (1997) report flags likely changes on how water quality will be assessed in the future. The proposed change is to 'composite indicators', considered to be more relevant to assessing environmental values such as aquatic ecosystems and water supplied for drinking, industry and irrigation. In part, such changes are related to the recent emphasis on environmental river quality and the Water Quality Objectives to be set for all waterways in NSW. How the composite indices are to be defined or measured '... require further investigation'.

The NSW experience illustrates the problem of whether to measure water quality indicators or to focus on the effects of change, perhaps by incorporating biological indicators such as freshwater molluscs. The latter demonstrates changes linked to improving or declining water quality and the former give an indication of which water quality parameters may be responsible for such changes. These are all relevant and difficult issues but the lack of any consistent base line data of any kind remains, and is indicative of the parlous situation of water quality information in Australia. The IEA (1999) review suggests that Victoria and Queensland have also moved to establish water quality networks. However, with commendable honesty, the Tasmanian account states that '... currently Tasmania has no baseline system of water quality monitoring ... government is currently investigating funding mechanisms for the implementation of the system' (IEA 1999: 92).

Socio-economic and environmental monitoring

Until the 1970s, assessment of water resources was restricted to components of the hydrological cycle. Quality was rarely considered and socio-economic and environmental factors were ignored as irrelevant. This accords with the second and active phase of water development outlined in the introduction, a period overwhelmingly concerned with meeting demand but with little attention to restricting the demand. The emergence of the mature phase highlights the need for additional data, such as who uses what and where and, more recently, the requirements to maintain healthy rivers and wetlands.

Australia does have a comprehensive, although rarely quoted, account of national water resource availability and use entitled *1985 Review* (DPIE 1987). This is based on a survey undertaken for the water year 1983-84; there has been no comparable survey since. The variability of rainfall and runoff that bedevil the assessment of hydrological measures of quantity equally apply to water use data. The DPIE review makes a case, rather unconvincingly, that '... for much of Australia, the period was equivalent to a normal year in which water use was about average'. The report presents water resource data in terms of 'divertible flows', essentially a measure of the mean annual flows that could be abstracted in respect to effective storages. It is pertinent to note that these do not take into account 'environmental flows', a concept that had yet to emerge in water resource planning. The data for the water year 1983-84 remain the only national water use study ever undertaken for Australia. A national water audit, likely using different criteria, was in progress at the time of writing as a component of the National Heritage Program.

Quantity and quality are poorly monitored, but the monitoring of any form of use (especially on a spatial base) is dramatically worse. Information on agricultural crops and water use is regularly collected by Commonwealth agencies (such as the Australian Bureau of Statistics) but these lack spatial definition. There are local and regional studies of use, although these are inconsistent in style and content. Detailed analysis of use is integral to more efficient use of water, whether for crop type and irrigation techniques in agriculture or the evaluation of the components of use for domestic supply. An excellent example of the latter is the study of water strategy options for Perth (Stokes et al 1995).

Australia, in common with other nations, has yet to seriously address wider social factors that are relevant to water use. There is need and scope for price and demand studies, and more attention to aspects such as community perception and attitudes to water use. Adaptive approaches to management and policy rely on enhanced monitoring - without it progress will be severely hampered.

APPENDIX 4.2
Intergovernmental policy for extremes: drought and flood

Justifiably, drought and flood have a special place in Australia's psyche and it is no surprise that governments, at all levels, have acted to alleviate the effects of these natural hazards. They provide lessons of interest to those concerned with intergovernmental relations.

Drought

The National Drought Policy was published in 1990 (DPRTF 1990) and accepted by the Commonwealth, State and Territory governments in 1992. The salient objectives are to:

- encourage primary producers of rural Australia to adopt self-reliant approaches to managing for climatic variability;
- maintain and protect Australia's agricultural and environmental resource base during periods of extreme climatic stress; and
- ensure early recovery of agriculture and rural industries, consistent with long term sustainable levels.

Drought was totally removed for any form of federal government assistance under the long-standing Natural Disaster Relief Arrangements (NDRA). The new policy emphasised risk management and stressed that climate variability was a factor that should be integrated into farm management. The Commonwealth government, however, funded a range of research and development projects to assist these aims. These included studies into drought forecasting and strategies to increase farmer awareness of drought risk and planning (eg, Munro and Lembit 1997).

Problems with drought policy

The new policy represented a major change and was applauded by both scientists and economists in Australia and overseas. There were, however, two shortcomings. These were self-reliance and protection of the environment, and assistance under calamitous (later termed 'exceptional') circumstances.

It is difficult to see how an emphasis upon self-reliance matched the aim of protecting the resource base from degradation. The earlier NDRA had many failings but did provide limited assistance to move stock away from drought areas therefore providing some encouragement to destock and lessen the problems of soil degradation. Secondly, the three-volume report of the Drought Task Force contained a single sentence that has subsequently caused major problems. This states that '... drought policy should provide assistance to producers in those calamitous circumstances where government action is required as a measure of last resort' (DPRTF 1990: vol 2, 53).

Initially it was envisaged that the new drought policy would support restructuring of the rural sector; that is, to assist viable farmers and provide funds for those not in that category to leave the industry. This led to links between drought relief, under calamitous circumstances, and the newly introduced Rural Adjustment Scheme (RAS). The Farm Household Support Scheme was introduced, designed to provide financial assistance to farmers unable to meet day-to-day living expenses during drought and also to provide financial incentives for such farmers to leave the industry.

The problems of exceptional drought became the subject of intense media pressure during the major drought that began in 1992-93 and which spread to cover large areas of eastern Australia in 1994 and 1995. In September 1994, Prime Minister Keating, after a visit to drought-stricken central Queensland, announced a new program of Drought Relief Payments (DRP). This removed the link for payments to farmers with long-term prospects and those without. This question is essentially one of welfare payments related to difficulties on how to provide social security to self-employed farmers whose asset base creates problems for assistance. There have been further changes in this area, with this form of payment now known as Exceptional Circumstances Relief Payments, but Botterill (1999) in a review of this problem of farm welfare concludes that current farm welfare policies still focus on the dual role of structural adjustment and ' ... devising schemes to circumvent the assets test which apply to standard social security safety net'.

The second element of Exceptional Circumstances Relief Payments is for business support. This is defined as 'interest subsidies for carry-on finance, debt restructuring and productivity improvements to farm businesses with prospects of viability in the long term, but whose future is at risk because of exceptional circumstances' (AFFA 1999). The interest subsidies were at 100 per cent for the year 1998-99 but will be reduced in subsequent years to a 50 per cent subsidy in 2001-02. The Commonwealth payments related to drought from the period 1976 to 1996 are given in Figure 4.A.2.

Figure 4.A.2 clearly shows that assistance formerly paid under the NDRA has been replaced by payments mainly under the headings of Drought Relief Payments and Rural Adjustment Exceptional Circumstances Interest Subsidies. In addition, some States (notably Queensland) have continued to make payments under schemes similar to those prior to 1990 with the NDRA, and there is a small contribution from the States to some of the Commonwealth measures. The detail is presented in Munro and Lembit (1997). The payments for drought, in terms of present net worth, are very similar to those that existed under the NDRA for drought prior to the National Drought Policy, except that the Commonwealth contribution is now very much larger! The annual reports for the Rural Adjustment Scheme Advisory Council present further detail on these payments; the value for 1997-98 was some $65 million. The overall sum spent on the various forms of drought relief and exceptional payments since the payments were removed from the NDRA is likely about $600 million, the majority from the Commonwealth. Notwithstanding the episodic nature of drought occurrence, financial assistance is now at a level at least comparable to that before the National Drought Policy was introduced.

**Figure 4.A.2 Commonwealth drought payments 1981-1996
(based on Munro and Lembit 1997)**

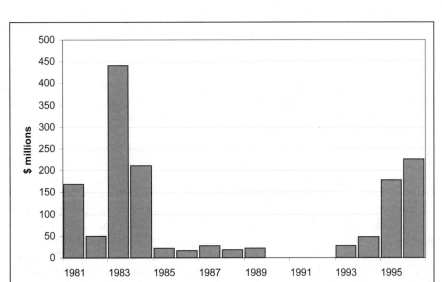

One of the merits of the 1992 National Drought Policy was that it removed the necessity to define 'drought', internationally a stumbling block for drought relief payments. The emergence of exceptional drought payments in 1994 required this question to again be considered, a problem made more difficult because payments were promised, but there was no definition of 'exceptional drought'. Considerable resources have been allocated to this problem; these are reviewed in White and Karssies (1999). A number of factors ranging from analyses of long-term rainfall frequencies to net farm income are included in the definition, the bottom line being that 'exceptional' is an event that would '... occur in average only once in every twenty to twenty five years and have a duration of at least 12 months'. Even more difficult is the question of when to remove the forms of drought assistance. This of course, raises many of the problems inherent in any definition of drought, among the most contentious issues are the problem of 'lines on maps' and the patchy nature of local thunderstorm rains.

This outline of drought policy over the last 30 years indicates that it remains widely regarded in the farming sector, and via the media in the wider community, as an exceptional event and not an integral feature of the variability of Australia's rainfall and runoff. The NDRA remained largely unchanged for two decades and, especially compared to relief arrangements overseas, the farming community were aware of what form the assistance would take. In retrospect, government maintained a firm stance in not changing the rules as severe droughts continued to develop. However, research and development to assist farmers to better plan for drought were scant. The sums provided by governments for relief were small compared to the losses experienced in drought years. Overall the NDRA did little to improve drought response and the distribution of funds were inequitable between States, different forms of farming and, in the opinion of most commentators, propped up inefficient farmers at the expense of good managers. A detailed account of the problems of the former NDRA and associated relief payments in given in Smith et al (1992).

The report of the Drought Policy Review Task Force represented a new approach. This was based on self-reliance and stressed the need for the use of risk management to incorporate drought into farm planning. After about three years, the let-out clause in the policy that referred to 'calamitous circumstances' was invoked. The policy contained no guidance whatsoever on definitions of such events; it is hard to think of a more pertinent example of making policy on the run. 'Calamitous' was quickly changed to 'exceptional' with an ever-evolving set of rules, the basis of which are exceptional circumstances relate to an event with a frequency of about 1 in 20 or 25 years and that the event must last for at least 12 months. Further complications have arisen as other hazards have also been included, such as frost and hail. This does not accord with the original discussion of drought policy that compared the adverse outcomes to those of exchange rates or world commodity prices and concluded that climatic problems were of a similar kind and therefore, did not warrant government interference or relief (subsidies). The outcome is that government assistance for drought now equals that prior to the introduction of the new policy. This is excused in government publications because the farming community did not have time to adjust to the change in policy and to adopt risk management procedures. The removal of the post-1994 forms of assistance will clearly be difficult to achieve.

Under the National Drought Policy, and as a response to the need to define exceptional circumstances, the Commonwealth government has expended large sums on research and development. However, among the voluminous published works on these topics, especially on those related to climatic variability and potential climate change, it is difficult to find any that attempt to analyse the use and usefulness (real or perceived) of the science to farmers. The impression throughout the debate of drought policy and relief is one of top-down policy development whether the 'top' is seen as politicians, economists or scientists.

Throughout the debate, concern for the environment is always prominent. However, it is difficult to see how adherence to self-reliance or the form of the drought relief that is currently available helps to achieve these aims. For instance, a key problem is that of over-stocking at time of drought with all the associated effects on soil erosion, biodiversity and the like. This problem of how to construct drought policy so as to avoid detrimental environmental impacts is worldwide. There is one notable exception; the drought policy introduced in South Africa for areas of stock grazing in the early 1990s, in a climatic environment that has a comparable variability to Australia. There, drought assistance is only available to farmers who agree to abide by government defined stocking rates. Detailed maps for the whole of country are available that define sustainable stocking rates for all forms of livestock. These are based on long-term experimental work from government funded agricultural research stations. A significant by-product of these maps is that they are widely used by rural banks to assess loan applications from farmers. The South African policy is reviewed by Smith (1993) who opined that they provided lessons from which Australia could profit. Spatial information on stocking rates of this kind is unavailable in Australia and is a barrier to encouraging farmers to farm in a sustainable way.

Government assistance for drought-stricken agriculture is now dominantly funded by the Commonwealth and is available to those in the private sector (ie, farming). This, as outlined below, is in contrast to assistance for flood hazard. The original recommendations of the National Drought Task Force have now been ' watered down' to the level where relief is now similar to that of the preceding and discredited policy. It is difficult to discern in the policy any measures that are designed to reduce environmental degradation.

Flood

All agree that the aim of effective floodplain management is to restrict new developments in areas subject to flood. This raises the definitional problem of what is 'flood prone'? The ideal approach, which is gaining momentum, is to employ risk management techniques. This means that the losses from all floods to the level of the probable maximum flood, the worst case scenario, would be considered in assessing new developments. The evaluation could include likely damages expressed as average annual damage and safety of the residents. In practice, flood prone (especially for the residential sector) is commonly defined in terms of the level achieved by the 1 in 100 year flood event. This is far from ideal in terms of economic or scientific criteria but even if such a level were adopted it would provide a useful, albeit imperfect, standard. Detailed technical backgrounds of urban floodplain management are available, see Smith (1991, 1998b).

Why then, are such planning restrictions not implemented throughout Australia? The reasons are complex but stem from the reluctance of councils to impose regulations that are often regarded as counter to local development. In part, this is because existing developments, constructed at earlier times in flood prone locations, would be subject to the new regulations. If floods have not occurred in recent years the community is reluctant to accept that there is a risk. Decisions to implement a planning flood level and related controls, are favoured by Commonwealth and State governments on the grounds of risks to life and property. The two higher tiers of government are, with exceptions outlined below, willing to assist LGAs to implement acceptable floodplain management and separately, to provide disaster relief (under the NDRA).

Flood policy is an excellent example of the relationships between the three tiers of Australian government. In all States the legislation that controls local planning is complex and, in practice, the responsibility for zoning is dominantly a matter for LGAs. The concerns of the Commonwealth are with the safety of its citizens and to lessen its contribution to disaster payments. However, States jealously protect their control over this component of water resources. They too, are concerned with safety and with disaster payments, however they are closer to the political pressures from flood prone communities. At LGA level, controls are perceived as restricting local development and often as inappropriate to local circumstances. Flood zoning is always a controversial local issue and can have adverse impacts on the outcomes of local elections for its proponents.

The problem resolves itself into how can higher tiers of government persuade the third tier to adopt effective floodplain management? Such problems are not unique to Australia and the results of a comparative study involving the USA, New Zealand and New South Wales are available in May et al (1996). The policy style adopted by higher tiers of government can be regarded as representing a continuum, with the extremes termed 'coercive' and 'cooperative' (see also May and Handmer 1992). The former represents a firm stance by higher levels of government, in Australia and the USA represented by States, to actions undertaken by local government authorities – the lowest tier. Among the distinguishing features of a coercive approach are the setting of State or nationwide goals and penalties for non-compliance or tardiness in meeting deadlines. The penalties can be fines, the withholding of State funding or replacing elected local representatives with State-appointed administrators. This approach is widely used in the USA and Florida, a State with major risks from flooding and storm surge, is a specific example. In addition, the federal government in the USA succeeded, many years ago, in introducing a national 1-in-100-year flood standard for new developments. This was linked to the federal subsidy to flood insurance, a key component of the Federal Flood Insurance Program. In order to meet the objectives of such coercive policies, higher tiers of government are prepared to provide technical and financial assistance. This highlights the need for the third tier to have the capacity to undertake the studies necessary to achieve acceptable floodplain management. A further problem with such a coercive approach is that of commitment at the local level. For instance, the setting of a State or national flood standard makes no allowance for the large variations in the degree of hydrological risk from place to place. Such a standardised approach to flood mitigation acts to stifle local community initiatives. This is delightfully termed, in American texts, as a 'cookie cutter' approach. Policies with a large coercive element equate to top-down planning with restricted opportunity for local involvement.

At the other extreme, with a cooperative approach, the higher tiers of government provide broad policy guidelines and encourage local involvement to adapt the overall goals to best suit local circumstances. Co-operative policies are not cheap alternatives; neither coercive nor cooperative styles will achieve the goal of improved floodplain management unless LGAs have the necessary resources and capacity. This requires technical and financial assistance from the higher tiers. May et al (1996) show that a cooperative style can result in enhanced commitment at local level. The problem with truly cooperative policies is that communities may decide not to participate at all. Bottom-up planning and decision-making receive much favourable comment, but a case can be made that planning for hazards that involve risk to life and property are exceptions. In blunt terms, can LGAs be trusted to practice acceptable risk management for hazards without a degree of coercion from the higher tiers?

Floodplain management in Australia

The terms coercive and cooperative, together with the concepts of capacity and commitment, form a useful framework within which to discuss policy and resource issues with multi-tiered governance. This account will restrict detailed comment to New South Wales and Queensland. These two States have markedly different policy styles with similar numbers of flood prone buildings, and together they account for some 85 per cent of the floodplain dwellings in Australia.

New South Wales

New South Wales has pursued the goal of effective floodplain management over some thirty years with more vigour and allocation of resources than any other State. A further feature of significance to policy analysis is that, prior to the mid-1980s, the policy style was markedly coercive prior to a major policy shift to a more adaptive and cooperative style. The latter is termed the 'merits' approach. A summary of the contrasts between the two policy styles is illustrated in Table 4.A.1.

Table 4.A.1. New South Wales flood policies (from May et al 1996)

Components	Flood-prone land policy (1977-84)	Flood 'merits' policy (1985-present)
Inter-governmental Policy	Prescriptive and coercive	Cooperative
Sustainability Concept	Environmental sustainability	Ecologically sustainable development
Policy Prescriptions Procedural Substantive	Restrictive and extensive Restrictive and extensive	Flexible Flexible but limited
Sanctions (*vis-à-vis* Local Government Authorities)	Strong	Weak
Incentives Grants and Subsidies Technical Assistance	High High (mapping)	High High (flood studies)

The coerciveness and inflexibility of the pre-1985 policy is encapsulated in the following extract from a State planning circular in 1982 (NSWDEP, 1982). The policy '... promotes the removal of urban development from flood prone areas wherever this is practicable and appropriate and aims to clear floodways of unnecessary obstructions'. Floodplains were defined by the 1 in 100 year flood and floodways by the 1-in-20-year flood. These were applied uniformly across the State, ignoring local hydrological variability and vulnerability and also the reality that many regional centres were totally located within the limits of the 1-in-100-year flood event. The sticks used by State government to attain compliance were the possible loss of State subsidies for a range of local services, the spectre of legal liability for councils' decisions on land use zoning and the potential for the State to assume local planning powers. LGAs responded with begrudging compliance but clogged up the systems of approvals by referring numerous planning applications to the Land and Environment Court, in part to avoid legal liability.

The touchstone for policy change was the release for public comment of the draft floodplain map (which portrayed the 1-in-100 and 1-in-20-year flood lines) for Fairfield. This was first such map released within the Sydney conurbation although perhaps as many as 50 similar maps had been issued for other parts of New South Wales. Fairfield Council duly informed all individual property owners, by letter, of their flood risk. This caused a massive public backlash, action groups were formed and public meetings attracted in excess of a thousand angry residents. In part this adverse response was because the maps were regarded as wrong, as the area had not experienced major flooding for some decades, but more significant were the perceived effects on house prices and in obtaining housing finance. Flooding became a major issue at a State election called for March 1984. The opposition circulated leaflets to every household stating '... once the Labor Government has mapped your area, the value of your house could be reduced by 50% ... you will not be able to sell or extend your house, you will not be able to borrow on the security of your house'. The Premier, Neville Wran, immediately responded by announcing that all flood maps throughout the State would be withdrawn (this is still the case) and that a new policy would be introduced. Wran was re-elected in December 1984, and a new policy was announced. This is termed the 'merits' approach and represented a policy shift from coercive to cooperative. In 1986 a floodplain manual was released (NSWWD 1986). This is an excellent document outlining the broad policy objectives and the procedures to be followed by Councils. It has attracted much interest as a model for other States.

The merits approach is based upon flexible and negotiated outcomes. The State government continued to provide financial and technical assistance, aided by partnership funding from the Commonwealth. The pattern of funding from these three sources, for the financial years 1969-70 to present, is shown in Figure 4.A.3. For much of this time the contribution from State government and councils exceeded the pattern of 2:2:1 for Commonwealth funding. However, the level of payments from the Commonwealth influences the contributions from the other two partners and hence, the total expenditure. Figure 4.A.3 also show the increase in overall expenditure once the new merits policy became established.

Many, but not all, of the larger Councils with major urban flood problems followed the procedures outlined in the manual and incorporated land use zoning and other regulations into the local planning regulations. Fairfield Council, which experienced near 1-in-100-year floods in 1986 and again in 1988, now has among the best local floodplain management in Australia. The key members of the original action groups were included in the planning process and one has subsequently served a term as mayor. The complete about face of the Fairfield Council and community was not only motivated by the change in State policy but by the powerful stimulus of extreme

Figure 4.A.3: New South Wales urban floodplain expenditure, 1969-70 to 1999-2000 (Data supplied by NSW Department of Land and Water Conservation)

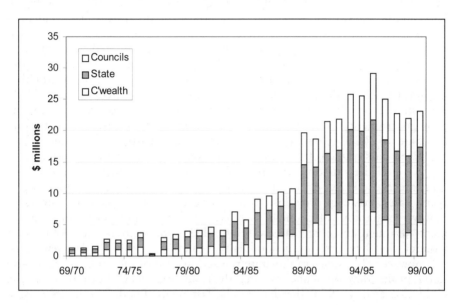

and damaging floods. Over the last decade, Fairfield Council has resumed and demolished over 50 houses located in floodways and has assisted many more householders to raise their dwellings above the 1-in-100 year line. The costs of house raising were provided by the council with assistance from State and federal funds.

Councils that followed the merits procedures undertook detailed studies of hydrology, vulnerability and economic assessment before finally incorporating the agreed floodplain management plan into local planning regulations. LGAs who completed this path according to the manual were granted indemnity from duty of care for flood-related land use decisions. This indemnity is enshrined in New South Wales legislation and was a key factor in gaining the acceptance of councils.

Shortcomings of the merits policy include the reluctance of some councils to undertake floodplain management that follow the methodology outlined in the manual; it is not mandatory. One example is for Liverpool, a neighbour of Fairfield. It is difficult to quantitatively evaluate the outcomes of the merits policy, but building-by-building surveys of a selection of councils that have adopted the merits approach demonstrate that the control of new developments below the 1-in-100-year flood line, and implementation of other flood mitigation measures to existing buildings, have significantly reduced the average annual flood losses (see May 1996: 182). This contrasts to the other councils in the survey that had not adopted the new policy. Despite these measures, overall flood losses at State level, for reasons that are not clear, continue to increase. There is little doubt that, at State level, the co-operative style of policy has lead to major improvements in floodplain management and a much greater awareness and commitment by LGAs.

Queensland

The number of flood prone buildings in Queensland is very similar to that in New South Wales (Smith 1998b). State policy for floodplain management is however very different; indeed there is no State government policy. This is because, traditionally, governance in Queensland has allocated much more of the decision-making role to local councils, floodplain management is a matter for LGAs. The problem is that the State government has never provided either technical (such as floodplain mapping) or financial resources to assist LGAs with studies or with the funding of flood mitigation measures. Worse, the State government has not been prepared, except for minor exceptions, to fund its share of 2:2:1 (Commonwealth, State, local) partnership finance. This effectively bars councils from any Commonwealth government assistance.

Overall the situation with floodplain management is one of neglect and inaction. Most LGAs do not have effective land use zoning for flood or, in many cases, basic information from which to assess flood risk. There are however, a handful of councils that have evolved sound floodplain management although these are largely self-funded. One such is the Gold Coast Council that has introduced floodplain regulations within the last few years; this however also serves to illustrate the seriousness of the problem. Extensive flood prone developments, dominantly residential, have been built in the Gold Coast since 1974, the date of the last major flood. The limits of that flood were mapped, one of the few examples of State agencies undertaking studies of flood hydrology, but that did not stop the construction of at least 10,000 dwellings in the post-1974 period. The need for a change of policy by the council was in response to changed community perception of the flood risk and the possible legal liability of the council for past planning approvals.

Table 4.A.2. Commonwealth assistance to States and Territories for floodplain management and flood relief, 1983-84 to 1992-93 (from Smith 1998c)

	New South Wales	Queensland	All States and Territories
Floodplain Management (FWRAP)	$42.1m	$8.2m	$77.5m
Flood Relief (NDRA)	$133.2m	$229.0m	$379.6m

There is no question that urban flood risk in Queensland continues to increase, by an unknown amount, each year. It is difficult to show this quantitatively but Table 4.A.2 gives a comparison of the Commonwealth contributions for the period 1983-84 to 1992-93, to flood studies and mitigation in Queensland and New South Wales, together with the amount contributed in flood disaster assistance. The contrasts between the two States are clear; what are the policy lessons that stem from this three-tiered government approach?

Policy lessons

There is a need to restrict developments in flood-prone locations. It can be argued that decisions to locate in such hazardous sites are a calculated risk based on decisions by the owners. For commercial enterprises, this is similar to the approach taken by the national policy for drought, and (unlike drought or flood cover for private dwellings) flood insurance is generally available. Problems arise because of the risks to life and the expectation that there will be government assistance to offset part of the tangible losses to householders and to State and LGA infrastructure. Superficially, government floodplain management programs emphasise the residential sector, but the bulk of the assistance under the NDRA is for payments to restore State and local government assets. For example, for the period 1992-93 to 1998-99, some 90 per cent of the total of $195 million of Commonwealth disaster flood assistance to New South Wales was to these two categories. In Queensland, the combined State and Commonwealth disaster payments, dominantly for flood, from 1988-89 to 1998-99, totalled $569 million of which 94 per cent were to State and local government.

The goal of urban floodplain management is to restrict new developments, especially those of a residential nature, in areas at risk from flood. This is widely accepted worldwide, but is difficult to attain. A key factor is that zoning regulations are dominantly a matter for councils and that they are perceived as affecting property values for existing flood prone developments. Local governments are therefore reluctant to introduce zoning of this kind that usually results in adverse community reaction, reflected in local ballot boxes. Equally problematic is the need to undertake studies of flood hydrology and vulnerability that are basic to any form of floodplain management. This highlights the problem of capacity, both technical and financial, required to define risk and to implement appropriate mitigation.

The issue becomes how far are Commonwealth and State governments prepared to go in order to cajole LGAs into undertaking the appropriate studies and adopting acceptable floodplain management? There are a number of sticks and carrots. The sticks are to withhold funding, to point out the possibility of liability under duty of care and/or to take over local planning powers. Carrots are to provide assistance to increase capacity to attain the goal of acceptable floodplain management, to make relief payments conditional on the improvements and/or to grant indemnity for liability for planning decisions if appropriate planning regulations are in place.

The Commonwealth government has taken the initiative in linking relief payments to a separately administered program for assistance with improved floodplain management and mitigation. The current conditions for Commonwealth NDRA require as prerequisites, '... that natural disaster mitigation strategies are in place in respect of likely or recurring disasters or that a commitment is made to develop and implement such a strategy within a reasonable timeframe'. These are sensible conditions but it will be a brave government that first refuses funding to a local or State government agency in the wake of a major damaging flood. The media outcry alone will make it difficult not to provide assistance to repair damaged water supply and sewage systems.

The Australian situation is typical of the cat and mouse, bluff and counter-bluff moves that frequently occur in multi-tiered governance.

Commonwealth NDRA and assistance for flood mitigation are administered in partnership with the States. Surprisingly, State Treasuries have been slow to realise that poor floodplain management results in considerable costs in relief payments, especially as the contribution of States to the NDRA generally exceeds that from federal sources. LGAs make no direct contributions to such disaster aid. It is likely that Queensland will take its approach to a State floodplain management policy more seriously if and when, that State's Treasury decides to reduce such assistance. This could come about if the Commonwealth refused aid because of the lack of floodplain management, leaving the State to either also refuse or to fund the total relief payments.

As mentioned above, the bulk of NDRA payments, State or federal, are to restore local and State infrastructure after flooding; only about 5 per cent goes to relieving personal hardship and distress. A problem with local and State assets is that in many cases it is not possible to make them flood proof. This is especially the case for thousands of kilometres of unsurfaced roads in the remote western shires of Queensland and New South Wales. The low rate base means that for some of these councils, over the long term, the major source of income for maintenance is from relief funds to restore such assets. In this case funding from higher tiers will remain a necessity; for other local government assets the prospect of unquestioned restoration funds is not a good incentive to improve flood reduction measures. It is worth noting that in New Zealand, local governments are required to insure their assets against hazard on the insurance market.

Sticks and carrots, capacity and commitment are all components in the search for effective floodplain management in a multi-tiered government scene. However, policy style is also crucial to success. The cooperative merits-based approach in New South Wales based on inputs from the local community is recommended, but ideally with an element of coercion to include recalcitrant councils. It may well be that the merits approach to policy is sensible for gaining wide acceptance and that it could be followed at a later date by coercion to bring in the stragglers. The concern is for the safety of residents in existing areas with a high hazard risk and the need to regulate new developments in such locations. The hope is that this does not require the stimulus of a major catastrophe, with loss of life, as a spur for action.

References

AASTE (Australian Academy of Technological Sciences and Engineering). 1999, *Water and the Australian economy*. Joint study project of the Australian Academy of Technological Sciences and Engineering and the Institution of Engineers, Australia, Canberra: IEA.

AFFA (Department of Agriculture, Fisheries and Forestry - Australia), 1999, unpublished draft, *Australia's approach to agricultural risk management*, Brief to State of Paraiba, Brazil, August.

Anon, 1998, *Snowy water inquiry final report*, Sydney: Snowy Water Inquiry.

AWRC (Australian Water Resources Council), 1976, *Review of Australia's water resources 1975*, Canberra: AGPS.

Bjornland, H, and McKay, J, 1998, Factors affecting water prices in a rural market: a South Australian experience, *Water Resources Research* 34(6):1563-1570.

Brown, JAH, 1983, *Australia's surface water resources*, Water 2000 Consultants' Report No 1, Canberra: AGPS.

Close, A, 1990, River salinity, in Mackay, N, and Eastburn, E, (eds) *The Murray Basin*, Canberra: Murray Darling Basin Commission.

COAG (Council of Australian Governments), 1995, *Communique for the meeting of 11 April 1995*, Canberra: Council of Australian Governments.

COAGWRTF (Council of Australian Governments Water Reform Task Force), 1995, *Water allocation and entitlements: a national framework for the implementation of property rights in water*, Occasional paper No 1, Canberra: Agricultural and Resource Management Council of Australia and New Zealand.

DPIE (Department of Primary Industries and Energy), 1987, *1985 Review of Australia's water resources and water use*, 2 vols, Canberra: AGPS.

DRE (Department of Resources and Energy), 1983, *Water 2000: a perspective on Australia's water resources to the year 2000*, Canberra: AGPS.

DPRTF (Drought Policy Review Task Force), 1990, *National drought policy*, 3 vols, Canberra: AGPS.

Falkenmark, M, and Lindh, G, 1993, Water and economic development, in Gleick, PH (ed), *Water in crisis: a guide to the world's freshwater resources*, pp 80-113, New York: Oxford University Press..

Gale, SJ and others,1999, The Snowy water inquiry, *Australian Geographical Studies* 37(3): 300-342.

GHD (Gutteridge, Haskins and Davey), 1970, *Murray Valley Salinity Investigation*, 3 vols, Canberra: River Murray Commission.

Garman, DEJ, 1983, *Water quality issues*, Water 2000 Consultant's Report No 7, Department of Resource and Energy, Canberra: AGPS.

Handmer, JW, Dorcey, AHJ and Smith, DI (eds), 1996, *Negotiating water: conflict resolution in Australian water management*, Canberra: Centre for Resource and Environmental Studies, Australian National University.

Hill, E, 1969, *Water into gold*, Sydney: Walkabout Pocketbooks (1st edn, 1937, Melbourne: Mullens and Roberston).

IEA (The Institution of Engineers Australia), 1999, *A century of water resources development in Australia, 1900-1999*, Canberra: IEA.

MDBMC 1999, *The salinity audit*, Canberra: Murray-Darling Basin Ministerial Council.

MDBC (The Murray-Darling Basin Commission), 1999, *Salinity and drainage strategy*, Canberra: MDC.

McMahon, TA, Finlayson, BL, Haines, AT and Srikanthan, R 1992, *Global runoff – continental comparisons of annual flows and peak discharges*, Catena, Cremlingen-Destedt.

May, PJ and Handmer, JW, 1992, Regulatory policy design: co-operative versus deterrent mandates, *Australian Journal of Public Administration* 51(1): 43-53.

May, PJ, Burby, RJ, Ericksen, NJ, Handmer, JW, Dixon, JE, Michaels, S and Smith, DI, 1996, *Environmental management and governance: intergovernmental approaches to hazards and sustainability*, London: Routledge.

Munro, RK and Lembit, MJ 1997 *Climate prediction for agricultural and resource management*, Australian Academy of Science Conference, Canberra, 6-8 May 1997, Canberra: Bureau of Resource Sciences.

Munro, RK and Lembit, MJ (eds),1997, Managing climate variability in the national interest: needs and objectives, in Munro, RK and Lembit, MJ, (eds) *Climate prediction for agricultural and resource management*, Australian Academy of Science Conference Proceedings, 6-8 May 1997, Canberra: Bureau of Resource Sciences.

NSWDEP (New South Wales Department of Environment and Planning), 1982, *Zoning of flood prone land*, Circular No 31, Sydney: NSWDEP.

NSWEPA (New South Wales Environment Protection Agency), 1995, *New South Wales State of the Environment 1995*, Sydney: NSWEPA.

NSWEPA, 1997, *New South Wales State of the Environment 1997*, Sydney: NSWEPA.

NSWPWD (New South Wales Public Works Department), 1986, *Floodplain development manual*, Public Works Department, Report No 86010, Sydney: NSWPWD.

O'Meagher, B, Stafford Smith, M, & White, DK, 2000, 'Approaches to integrated drought risk management: Australia's national drought policy', in White DK (ed) *Hazards and disaster: a series of definitive major works*, Vol 2 Drought, a global assessment, London: Routledge.

Powell, JM, 1989, *Watering the garden state*, Sydney: Allen and Unwin.

Powell, JM, 1991, *Plains of promise, rivers of destiny: water management and the development of Queensland, 1824-1990*, Bowen Hill, Queensland: Boolarong Publications.

Powell, JM, 1998, *Watering the western third: land and community in Western Australia*, Perth: Water and Rivers Commission.

SEAC (State of the Environment Advisory Council), 1996, *State of the environment Australia 1996*, Melbourne: CSIRO.

Sewell, WRD, Handmer, JW and Smith, DI (eds), 1985, *Water planning in Australia: from myths to reality*, Centre for Resource and Environmental studies, Canberra: Australian National University.

Smith, DI, 1991, Extreme floods and dam failure inundation; implications for loss assessment, in Britton, NR and Oliver, J (eds), *Natural and technological hazards: implications for the insurance industry*, pp 149-166, Armidale: University of New England.

Smith, DI, 1993, Drought policy and sustainability: lessons from South Africa, *Search* 24(10): 149-156.

Smith, DI, 1998a, *Water in Australia: resources and management*, Melbourne: Oxford University Press.

Smith, DI, 1998b, *Urban flooding in Queensland*, Brisbane: Department of Natural Resources.

Smith, DI, 1998c, Floodplain management: definitions, solutions and policy, in King, D, and Berry, L, (eds,), *Disaster management: crisis and opportunity*, pp 35-45, Conference Proceedings, 1 November, Centre for Disaster Studies, Cairns: James Cook University.

Smith, DI and Handmer, JW, 1996, Water conflict and resolution: an example from Tasmania, in Handmer, JW, Dorcey, AHJ, and Smith, DI (eds), *Negotiating water: conflict resolution in Australian water management*, Canberra: Centre for Resource and Environmental Studies, Australian National University.

Smith, DI, Hutchinson, MF and McArthur, RJ, 1992, *Climatic and agricultural drought: payments and policy*, CRES Paper no 7, Centre for Resource and Environmental Studies, Canberra: Australian National University.

Smith, DI, Handmer, JW, McKay, JA, Switzer, MA and Williams, RJ, 1996, *Issues in floodplain management: a discussion paper*, National Land Care Program, Canberra: Department of Primary Industries and Energy.

Stokes, RA, Beckwith, JA, Pound, IR, Store, RR, Coghlen, PC and Ng, R, 1995, *A water strategy for Perth and Mandurah*, Publication no WP12, Perth: Water Authority of Western Australia.

Stone, S 1996, Community led land and water use planning: some Victorian experiences, in Handmer, JW, Dorcey, AHJ and Smith, DI (eds), *Negotiating water: conflict resolution in Australian water management*, pp 21-236, Canberra: Centre for Resource and Environmental Studies, Australian National University.

WCED (World Commission on Environment and Development), 1987, *Our common future*, Oxford: Oxford University Press.

White, DK and Karssies, L, 1999, Australia's national drought policy; aims, analyses and implementation, *Water International* 24(1): 2-9.

Williamson, DR, Gates, GWB, Robinson, G, Linke, GK, Seker, MP and Evans, WR,1997, *Historic trends in salt concentration and salt load of streamflow to the Murray-Darling: Report for Salt Action*, Canberra: Murray-Darling Basin Commission.

5

National Forest Policy and Regional Forest Agreements

Catherine Mobbs

Land & Water Australia

[The] forests of Australia are scanty and are not properly protected throughout ... They are subject to constant nibbling under political pressure, and have been in the past most recklessly abused (from *Save Australia: a plea for the right use of our flora and fauna*, J Barrett 1925, p 5).

Concern over the use of forests is hardly new it would seem. Native forests and the forest sector generally have been a defining feature of environmentalism and resource allocation in Australia for decades, with over 70 inquiries carried out, countless local and national political contests, seemingly irreconcilable values held by opposing policy actors, and recurring headaches for policy makers charged with resolving the issues. The draft report of the ESD Working Group on Ecologically Sustainable Forest Use states that past attempts to resolve conflicts have been relatively unsuccessful because of their *ad hoc* nature and tendency 'to address single point conflicts with short term solutions, rather than develop broad regional forest use strategies with ecologically sustainable development objectives' (CoA 1991: 25). In 1992, a year after the working group's report, a National Forest Policy Statement (NFPS) set out for the first time a national framework for the ecologically sustainable management of Australia's forests (CoA 1992).

The NFPS, endorsed by the Commonwealth and all State and territory governments (with Tasmania signing in 1995), was developed by the Australian Forestry Council and the Australia and New Zealand Environment and Conservation Council with the input of other stakeholders. It is an umbrella agreement in which the governments express a commitment to strengthen the integration of their decision-making and to promote cooperative planning for forests. The pathway suggested in the NFPS was the use of a framework of inter-governmental regional forest agreements (RFAs) that protect environmental values and at the same time maintain a vigorous and internationally competitive wood products industry.

This paper considers some lessons for natural resource management (NRM) institutional arrangements arising from the RFA process. At the outset, it must be said that this process is internationally remarkable at least in stated intent and scope. Nothing in NRM policy in this country comes close to the several years of effort and investigation and policy discussion and hundreds of millions of dollars invested. Whatever the failings (whether in process or eventual outcomes), this should be remembered. The following analysis is partial, and draws on a longer study (Mobbs 2000). First, the notion of rationality in policy analysis and planning is introduced. This provides a useful ordering principle to discuss the RFA process and the policy themes underpinning this project. Then, a brief overview of the forest policy context is provided. This is followed by a description of key aspects of one RFA and the final section presents conclusions.

Rationality in policy and planning

A useful analytical perspective with a long history of application in areas of public policy-making and planning is the nature of rationality underlying choices about decisions and approaches; that is, how knowledge is transformed into action.[1] Broadly, rationality or rational behaviour means to exercise sound judgment or good sense. Following trends in wider society, the past 50 years in policy analysis and planning has been dominated by a view that science and technology are the only means to exercise sound judgment in structuring and solving complex problems (Dunn 1994; Sager 1994). This is called instrumental rationality. It assumes that goals are given in advance of inquiry, and relies strongly on means-end analytical techniques to identify the best alternative. Within this broad world-view may be located economic rationality, that is, making choices based solely on their efficiency (using tools such as cost-benefit analyses). While scholars have identified multiple rational bases for choosing alternatives, the dominance of instrumental rationality and its cohorts have been seen as both a cause and a consequence of Western society's dominating and controlling relationship to nature (Wright 1992), and, likewise, our evident difficulties in following ecologically sustainable NRM in Australia (Carden 1992; Walker 1992).

Two critiques of instrumental rationality have gathered strength since the 1980s, interpenetrating discussions of the meaning of sustainability. First, some scholars have argued that our policy and planning processes need to be imbued with, indeed driven by, *ecological* rationality (Bartlett 1986; Dryzek 1987). Broadly, ecologically rational behaviour is concerned with the preservation and maintenance of the 'capacity, diversity and resilience of the biotic community, its long-term life support capability' (Bartlett 1986: 234). The fundamental argument is that healthy biophysical systems underpin healthy human systems. Practical development of such ideas may be found in the literature on adaptive management and ecosystem management (see further Holling 1978; Lee 1993; Gunderson et al 1995; Dovers and Mobbs 1997). The second critique is framed in terms of the need for *communicative* rationality (Habermas 1984, 1987; Sager 1994; Healey 1997). This type of rationality emphasises public discourse, mutual understanding and the

---

1   There is an enormous literature concerning rationality generally, and its delineation in policy and planning specifically. Apart from the literature cited in the text, Simon (1955) and Diesing (1962) are foundation texts. See also Dryzek (1990), Eckersley (1992; this volume) and Saul (1993).

democratisation of policy and planning processes through, for instance, increased attention to public participation. The fundamental argument is that the development and maintenance of healthy human relations has intrinsic value and underpins our capacity 'to find not only common ground but new and higher ground' (Dukes 1996: 125). Practical development of such ideas may be found in the literature on conflict resolution, collaborative planning and management, and public participation (see further Crowfoot and Wondolleck 1990; Gray 1989; Buchy and Hoverman 1999).

Clearly, the ecological and communicative critiques are related in complex ways. Given the constraints of a short paper however, it is sufficient to note their distinctive emphases. The issue for many observers is how, and to what effect, features of ecological and communicative rationality are penetrating our NRM institutions and processes. This paper takes a preliminary look at this issue in the RFA process, focussing on communicative rationality but also making mention of ecological rationality. This approach means that certain of the five principles of persistence, purposefulness, information-richness, inclusiveness and flexibility that have been suggested as core to an adaptive approach to NRM (Dovers, this volume) are pursued in greater depth than others. Specifically, the principle of inclusiveness is a major theme in the description of the RFA case.

The native forest sector

Before we consider the forest policy context, some background to the forest sector is necessary. This sector is well described in Carron (1985), RAC (1992a, 1992b) and Dargavel (1995), and only core features are presented here. Australian forests are dominated by the genera *Eucalyptus* and comprise just over 5 per cent of Australia's land area. Forests are mostly located in an arc around the eastern, south-eastern and south-western margins of the continent and large areas of Tasmania (RAC 1992a). This represents just over half of the area under forests before Europeans came to Australia, with clearing for agriculture being the primary cause of deforestation (Bolton 1981).

Australian forests contain evidence of past Aboriginal use and links to the land, and many areas remain of great significance to present-day Aboriginal people. The forests also contain places and sites of significance for other local through to international cultural and natural heritage values. For instance, east coast temperate and subtropical rainforests are listed as World Heritage areas. Many Australian forests are also valued as high quality wilderness areas (RCA 1992a, 1992b). Australian forests are described as megadiverse in terms of biological diversity and are also notable for a high proportion of endemic species. While hundreds of forest ecosystems and thousands of forest species have been described, it is considered likely that most forest biodiversity in Australia remains unknown.

After Federation in 1901, the State governments retained ownership of virtually all natural resources and power over issues such as forestry. Today, most native forests remain in public ownership, totalling approximately 30 million hectares. About 11 million hectares of native forests are privately owned and thus are the responsibility of the owner within the legal and other obligations set by all three spheres of government. The Commonwealth government has responsibilities for forest allocation and use under various heads of power in the Constitution. For example, the Commonwealth has used the trade and commerce power (s 51(i)) to control or halt State government export of products such as woodchips, and the external affairs power (s 51(xxix)) to intervene with State governments on issues involving international obligations such as those contained within the World Heritage Convention (Jaensch 1997). The Commonwealth has also exercised influence on forest issues through national environmental legislation (eg, *Environmental Protection (Impact of Proposals) Act* 1974). Political differences between the Commonwealth and a State government have frequently determined whether the Commonwealth has used the powers it holds to intervene in forestry decisions.

The public forest estate is broadly divided into three land tenures: (i) State forest, which refers to land managed for multiple uses, but primarily timber production; (ii) other crown land, which refers to other public forest, either unoccupied or occupied under lease, on which timber harvesting occurs but without specific management for timber production; and (iii) conservation reserves, which refer to public forests reserved primarily for conservation and/or recreation (RAC 1992b: G10). The latter tenure includes 'national parks' which are, in most cases, State government administered reserves in Australia. Plantation forests (mostly softwoods and some hardwoods and eucalypts) in public or private ownership are an increasingly significant component of the Australian forest sector.

In 1998, 62,600 people were employed in forest products (including wood and paper) industries. The value of turnover in forest product industries was $11,498 million and, while Australia is a net importer of forest products, export trade was worth $1,297 million (ABARE 1999).

This discussion, as does the RFA process described below, focuses on public native forests, as opposed to plantations or private native forests. Unless otherwise qualified, the term 'forest' from here on is used to refer to native forests in public ownership.

Features of the policy context

There is also a long contextual history to contemporary forest policy and the nature of forest conflicts (see further Routley and Routley 1973; Mercer 1991; Carron 1993). Broadly, forest conflicts have centred on demands to governments to alter or cease timber logging practices in State forests and/or to declare national parks, both as mechanisms to conserve forest values. While processes of re-allocation from timber production to conservation have occurred, conservation interests continue to argue that such decisions have been inadequate and lagged behind changing community values for forests, and that forest harvesting practices are unsustainable. In recent years, timber-dependent rural communities and timber workers have mobilised against conservation interests, arguing the unequal economic impacts that past and projected re-allocation decisions have had on vulnerable individuals and communities (Dargavel et al 1995). In addition, management of privately-owned forests has come under increasing scrutiny with recognition of continuing high rates of vegetation clearance in parts of Australia alongside the interest of some private property owners in plantation development.

Contemporary forest policy has evolved in response to these contrasting agendas. The NFPS sets out 11 national goals and a number of specific policies in the context of twin objectives, (i) to protect environment and heritage values of forests (in part through the establishment of a national system of forest conservation reserves) and, (ii) to provide a sustainable basis for an internationally competitive forest products industry. It committed governments to implementation through Regional Forest Agreements (RFAs) – 20-year binding agreements on forest use and management negotiated between the Commonwealth and relevant State governments. This approach is broadly premised on the desire for long term security or certainty for both conservation and development values, as the following explanation drawn from a Commonwealth government position paper on RFAs indicates:

> The regional forest agreement process is designed to contribute to predictable and stable conditions for land use planning, commercial investment in new and existing forest-based industries, short- and long-term timber harvesting, recreation management, and conservation planning. A regional forest agreement can be used to provide land use boundaries, environmental protection and wood availability that remain fixed for the duration of the agreement (CoA 1995:2).

Despite government commitments to regional implementation of the NFPS, the RFA process languished with little government action to further the approach until a series of heated political debates in 1994 and 1995. These debates concerned Commonwealth ministerial approval of expert woodchip licenses and conflicts over the implementation of interim forest protection measures pending RFA development.[2] Different stakeholders disputed the bases on which areas were designated as 'high conservation value', with protests culminating in a blockade of Parliament House in Canberra by scores of logging trucks and hundreds of timber industry supporters. In December 1994, then Prime Minister Keating announced the phase-out, by 1 January 2000, of 'woodchips exported from native forests that are not covered by, or where there has not been significant progress made toward, a regional forest agreement incorporating a comprehensive, adequate and representative forest reserve system' (CoA 1995: 2). The intent of this was simply that with RFAs in place, the protection of environment and heritage values could be deemed secure, and Commonwealth export controls on woodchips could be lifted. The Keating government's RFA commitments received bipartisan support, and were upheld by the Coalition government which replaced the Keating Labor government in 1996.

---

2   The Commonwealth is responsible for the approval of export licences for unprocessed timber exports such as woodchips. This has been an important and contentious lever applied by the Commonwealth when it chose to intervene in State government forestry decisions. See further Toyne (1994) and Dargavel (1995, 1998).

According to many observers of the RFA process, the impetus for this commitment by the Commonwealth government was not their policy commitment to the development of an ecologically sustainable forest sector, rather it was their desire to remove themselves from forest conflicts and the embarrassment of fights between Commonwealth ministers and bureaucracies over export woodchip licences. In effect, it was hoped that in a post-RFA environment, resolution of future forest conflicts would be the sole responsibility of State governments (who had, after all, long been demanding that the Commonwealth stop interfering in 'their' land use management issues). And so the RFAs commenced. There were 12 RFA processes in Australia (see Figure 5.1). They commenced in 1996 and eleven were completed by April 2001 (an extension to the original cut-off date for completion).

Environmental objectives for biodiversity conservation and reserve decisions were given effect through a related policy development at the time of RFA commencement. The National Strategy for Conservation of Australia's Biological Diversity (CoA 1996) was translated into a set of Commonwealth/ State government agreed criteria for establishing a national comprehensive, adequate and representative (CAR) forest reserve system (JANIS 1997). These criteria are called JANIS criteria after the committee that developed them. The criteria interpret and set out quantitative and qualitative requirements that must be achieved in order to meet biodiversity, old-growth and wilderness conservation objectives, reserve design objectives, and CAR principles. The criteria that received most attention in the process were quantitative targets for reserving areas of forests, 'as far as possible and practicable' in dedicated reserves (JANIS 1997: 11). These targets represent the first time that quantitative measures for the reservation of biodiversity have been agreed on by both Commonwealth and State governments in Australia. The targets include: 15 per cent of the distribution of each forest ecosystem that existed prior to Europeans arriving in Australia; 60 per cent or more if rare or depleted, of existing old growth forest; 90 per cent or more of high quality wilderness; and, all remaining occurrences of rare and endangered forest ecosystems including old growth. While definitions of ecosystem, old growth, wilderness, rare, and so on, were subsequently the subject of much debate in the process, the setting of targets was widely supported. For instance targets were seen to support a nationally consistent approach among different State governments with variable levels of commitment to biodiversity conservation; they offered the potential to bound the previous debilitating forest conservation debates; and, hopefully, they could serve as ecological bottom-lines or constraints on human activities.

A key component of all RFAs is to provide additional certainty to industry, given the recognition that, with the establishment of a CAR reserve system, there may be requirements for industry restructuring. Industry certainty was in large part given effect through specifying and securing quantities of wood resources and access arrangements for forest-based industries for the 20-year term of each agreement. In addition, the Commonwealth and States established the Forest Industry Structural Adjustment Program (FISAP) for Business Exit Assistance and Industry Development Assistance. Most RFAs include specific funding commitments for structural adjustment from either the FISAP program or other sources. Related industry policy developments include the Wood and Paper Industry Strategy which commenced in 1996, and Plantations for Australia: the 2020 Vision (Plantation 2020 Vision Implementation Committee 1997). Funding for the RFA program is based on a matching basis between the Commonwealth and the States. While the overall budget is difficult to determine due to the in-kind components of the budgets in each jurisdiction, the cost of the RFA process in Australia has been estimated at approximately $0.5 billion over five years. This includes structural adjustment assistance to the timber industry, and the cost of conducting assessments, administering the overall program and negotiating the final agreements.

In sum, the National Forest Policy Statement and related policy commitments contained a set of broadly agreed ESD objectives that were to be given practical effect within a limited time period and with the agreement of both the Commonwealth government and the relevant State government. The issues under debate were technically complex, involved significant value conflicts, unequal policy impacts and high degrees of uncertainty, and affected numerous actors across government and non-government sectors. These attributes (which are not atypical of NRM settings) highlight the significance of inclusiveness, that is, the conditions promoting or hindering communicative rationality in the process.

The description following focuses on one RFA process in the State of New South Wales (NSW). Unlike many RFAs in other States, the NSW government attempted from the outset to implement a *partnership* model of participation. The process of joint government assessment of expert advice and scientific studies was extended to non-governmental actors – most notably to representatives from a small number of non-government organisations (NGOs). Herein was an opportunity to achieve multi-stakeholder consensus on decisions that would provide longer-term security for both conservation and production values of forests. Although the theme of inclusiveness is stressed throughout, it is evident that the themes of persistence, purposefulness, information-richness, and flexibility are also closely intertwined. I comment briefly on these additional issues in concluding this case study. First, the main elements of the process and structure are outlined.

Process and structures in brief

All RFAs have five key stages, as set out in Box 5.1 (p 98). Within NSW, RFAs began in four regions – Upper North East, Lower North East, Southern and Eden (located north to south on Figure 5.1). The Upper and Lower North East regions were subsequently completed as one RFA. The information presented later in this case study mostly concerns the RFA process in the Upper North East region.

Figure 5.1. Location of Regional Forest Agreements in Australia

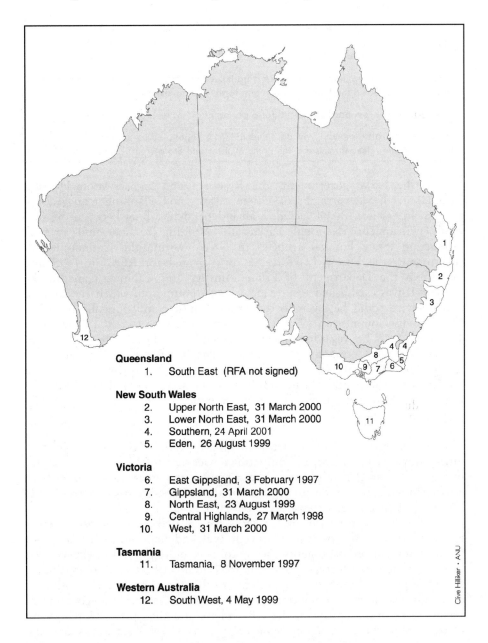

Queensland
1.   South East (RFA not signed)

New South Wales
2.   Upper North East, 31 March 2000
3.   Lower North East, 31 March 2000
4.   Southern, 24 April 2001
5.   Eden, 26 August 1999

Victoria
6.   East Gippsland, 3 February 1997
7.   Gippsland, 31 March 2000
8.   North East, 23 August 1999
9.   Central Highlands, 27 March 1998
10. West, 31 March 2000

Tasmania
11. Tasmania, 8 November 1997

Western Australia
12. South West, 4 May 1999

Clive Hilliker · ANU

Box 5.1. Overview of stages in an RFA process

Scoping agreement. The governments sign a scoping agreement on administrative and operational arrangements.

Comprehensive Regional Assessment (CRA). Assessments of the natural, cultural, social, resource and economic values of the region's forests are undertaken. CRA reports are produced for the consideration of governments and public comment.

Negotiation or 'options development'. CRA data is used to define option/s for forest use and conservation, including land use allocation and forest management systems.

Display. An option/s report is released for a period of public review and comment.

Agreement. A draft regional forest agreement (RFA) is negotiated by governments and submitted to the relevant Ministers. The Prime Minister and State Premier sign a final RFA.

Within the NSW government, the Resource and Conservation Division (RACD) in the Department of Urban Affairs and Planning managed the process. In essence, RACD acted as an independent arbiter between the relevant environment (National Parks and Wildlife Service) and primary production (State Forests) agencies in NSW. Within the Commonwealth government, the Forest Taskforce, a unit created for RFAs in 1995 and located in the Department of Prime Minister and Cabinet, managed the process. It was established to provide a single point from which coordinated policy advice could be given to the Prime Minister and portfolio ministers (Productivity Commission 1999: 175). In similar fashion to RACD, the Forest Taskforce may be regarded as an independent arbiter between relevant agencies in the Commonwealth environment (Environment Australia) and production (Agriculture, Fisheries and Forestry) portfolios. In both jurisdictions, these intended neutral institutions were essential to manage the intra-governmental dynamics of the forest policy process. Conservation and production agencies have developed very different 'epistemic communities' around forest policy issues – that is, communities of knowledge that share technical expertise and principled beliefs (Haas 1992). The agencies in both jurisdictions have a history of conflicting advice and roles in natural resource management in Australia, and like agencies in other fields have been associated with the notion of 'capture' by the interest groups they regulate (a feature of Westminster systems, see Davis et al 1993).

Consultation mechanisms for RFAs have varied widely across different States. They ranged from fairly conventional and limited opportunities for public comment on assessments and options, to more innovative experiments in consultation (see further Coakes 1998; Butterworth et al 1999) including the NSW partnership model. The essence of this model was the establishment of multi-stakeholder committees and opportunities for non-government stakeholders to participate in the CRA phase and the options development phase. Other consultation mechanisms such as stakeholder workshops and print and internet-based newsletters are not discussed here (see for example, <ww.racac.nsw.gov.au>)

There were three types of multi-stakeholder committees in the NSW RFA process – a steering committee, four technical committees (environment/

heritage, social/economic, forest management, and timber resource inventory) and four regional community-based consultative committees. The most striking feature of the committee structure, particularly in comparison to all other RFA processes, with the exception of Queensland,[3] was the initial inclusion of non-governmental actors as full members of the steering and technical committees. (As discussed below, non-governmental actors were eventually removed from the steering committee.) These committees were State-wide project management and decision-making committees and the members commanded the resources of the process. The steering committee was charged with implementing a formal Commonwealth-State agreement and as such was the principle decision-making body for NSW RFAs. Its role included providing policy direction for other committees, approving budgets, time-lines, technical committee recommendations, and ensuring statutory requirements of both governments were met. The role of technical committees was to make decisions about scientific and technical aspects of regional assessments, including methodologies, and to recommend projects for steering committee approval. In both committee structures, the position of Chair rotated between governments and the government members comprised officials (with policy and/or technical backgrounds) drawn mostly from con-servation and production agencies in each government. Independent scientists were not members but were brought in for advice or to undertake assessments. Decision-making was by consensus.

Through RACD, the NSW government facilitated public participation in these committees with the payment of an annual stipend (around $50, 000) to each of what they termed 'core stakeholder groups'. The groups supported in this way were the Nature Conservation Council, the Forest Products Asso-ciation, the Construction, Forestry, Mining and Energy Union, and the NSW Aboriginal Land Council. In addition to the annual stipend, RACD provided data access and familiarisation and training in computerised resource analysis and allocation systems for representatives from the above groups, while all non-government representatives were reimbursed for basic costs associated with meeting attendance.

The regional community-based committees, termed Regional Forest Forums, are consistent with the notion of citizen advisory committees (see Byrne and Davis 1998: 25). One was established in each of the four RFA regions in NSW. The governments' view on the Forums' role in RFAs was set out in terms of providing a local consultative focus and serving 'as a voice or communication channel between the steering committee and regional communities' (NSW CRA/RFA Steering Committee 1997: 1).

The chairperson of each Forum was nominated by the steering com-mittee (in three forums, a high profile member of the community, eg, local mayor, and in the fourth, a professor of forestry). The Forums were more inclusive bodies than the other committees, with around 18 interest groups represented. For instance, local government, catchment management, and

---

3   In Queensland, a Reference Panel of peak non-government and government organisations was established which had a similar role to that of Regional Forest Forums in NSW. Two NGO stakeholders (one conservation, one industry) represented the panel on the Steering Committee. They also attended technical committee meetings on an *ex officio* basis.

bushwalking groups were represented and industries other than the timber industry (apiary, tourism, and more broadly, regional development). All the non-government groups represented on the steering and technical committees were also represented on Forums, although by different individuals. In addition, each Forum had four government members (one local, two State, and one Commonwealth).

In sum, the initial NSW partnership model increased both the range of opportunities for citizen involvement and the range of forest interests at the table, addressing to a greater extent than previous forest policy and planning processes the demand for non-government involvement in decision-making.[4] From here on, the term NGO is used to refer to any non-government actor or group in the process.

Process dynamics – participant reflections on constraints to the partnership model

Perhaps we could anticipate from the background of forest conflicts that the Commonwealth/State/NGO partnership model would not be easy to implement. Indeed, the history of the Upper North East NSW RFA portrays disintegrating relationships rather than cooperative capacities. This is partly illustrated in Box 5.2 (see statements in italics in particular) which provides a summary of some relevant events in the process from late 1997 through to early 1999. This period has most relevance to Eden and the two northern regions, covering the assessment phase, the options development phase, and finally the announcement by the NSW government of forest decisions for these three regions. The latter decision pre-empted formal Commonwealth/ State RFAs by legislating major resource use allocation outcomes and changes to forest management practices.

A comprehensive discussion would need to consider the reasons for and impacts of each of the events in Box 5.2 and other events across RFAs in NSW, and also trace later developments in the process, particularly those relevant to the Southern RFA. Indeed, it should be noted that the later Southern RFA process was quite different in many ways to other NSW RFAs, not least because government and non-government actors sought to apply lessons from other RFA experiences. However discussion needs to be constrained to something more manageable here. The approach is to focus on three key aspects of the process identified in Box 5.2, illustrative of problematic 'moments' in the partnership model:

- The dissolution of the steering committee in late 1997. It was replaced with a pre-existing Commonwealth/State officials group from which NGOs were excluded.

---

4   However the nature of that role was not necessarily agreed. When questioned about the role of NGO stakeholders in such committees, government representatives tended to emphasise 'transparency' and 'communication channel' roles while NGO representatives tended to emphasise an 'influence' role.

- The failure of formal negotiations among NGO stakeholders to try and develop an RFA option/s for the Upper North East RFA region and the subsequent NSW government retreat to an imposed political solution to the impasse.
- The limited role of the Regional Forest Forum in contributing to the Upper North East RFA.

Box 5.2. Relevant events in NSW RFA process, late 1997 – March 1999

Throughout 1997 and 1998	Ongoing disagreements (eg. regarding policy objective interpretations, data, methods and results of projects) within the steering committee and technical committees. Many assessments are delayed. Members of Upper North East Forum (established in May 1997) are increasingly frustrated by lack of transparency regarding process decisions, delays and assessment findings, and also conflicting messages from governments regarding Forum input and role in options development phase.
December 1997	Joint government discussions on NSW RFAs (and the Eden RFA in particular) collapse. *NGOs are effectively removed from high level decision-making with the dissolution of the steering committee.* It is replaced with a Senior Officials Group, comprised of Commonwealth and State government officials.
March 1998	Talks between governments resume. Eden RFA remains unsigned.
August 1998	At their 11th meeting, the Forum presents a consensus request to governments that the options development process for the Upper North East RFA takes place in their region (not outside the region in Sydney), in order to maximise regional relevance and access. Governments refuse but invite Forum members to provide issues for consideration. Members do not respond. After this meeting, the Forum is never reconvened (although no-one knew this would be the case at the time). *The Forum ceases to have any formal existence and role in the RFA process in the region.*
August 1998	NSW government affirms intention to negotiate options for the northern regions and legislate RFAs by the end of 1998 (i.e. prior to State election in March 1999). Several technical projects remain incomplete. Technical committees have released few reports. The Commonwealth government argues against NSW's timetable (the Commonwealth does not want decisions before a Federal election in late 1998).
September – October 1998	Core NGO stakeholders accept an invitation from NSW Premier Carr to participate in an assisted 'stakeholder negotiation' to try and develop an agreed option for the two northern regions. NSW agencies are directed to also negotiate an option ('agency negotiation') – this takes place in a separate process behind closed doors. An October Federal election date is announced and the Commonwealth government becomes a caretaker government, restricting its ability to make decisions with budget implications. *The Commonwealth government refuses to participate in NSW's options development process and refuses to provide social and economic data it holds. RFA discussions between the two governments break down.*
October 1998	*The stakeholder negotiations collapse without agreement on an option or options.* NGOs lobby NSW agencies and Ministers directly for their preferred outcomes. Negotiations continue between NSW agencies and Ministers.

November – December 1998	Premier Carr announces 'NSW Forest Agreements' for the northern and Eden regions, and decisions are legislated (cf. NSW 1999). He gains the support of a timber industry group (Forest Products Association) for the general outcome if not some of the details. Conservation groups reject the outcome and immediately begin protests, blockades in State forests and campaign against the re-election of some State government parliamentarians. The NSW decisions effectively pre-empt Commonwealth/State RFAs by declaring CAR reserve systems, twenty-year timber commitments to industry, and changes to forest management practices. *The NSW Forest Agreements are implemented without any opportunity for public comment or consultation on proposed outcomes.*
March 1999	Despite protests from many quarters, in particular conservation interests, the stability of the outcomes are assured in the short term with the re-election of the NSW Labor government with an increased majority. Talks between governments on joint RFAs for NSW resume. (Eden is eventually signed in August 1999, and a combined northern region RFA is signed in March 2000 (see CoA/NSW 2000). The Southern RFA is not signed until April 2001.)

I asked a number of participants from both governments and a number of NGOs to reflect on these three aspects in particular and to identify the core constraints or tensions that affected the fulsome achievement of the intended partnership model in the Upper North East RFA. Their responses (and divergences of opinion) are summarised in the following points.

Deteriorating inter-governmental relationship compounded by election issues

The relationship between the Commonwealth and NSW government had progressively deteriorated from late 1997 through 1998. Given that different parties were in power in the two jurisdictions, this inter-governmental relationship had never been easy. In the RFA process, these governments had ideological differences about processes and outcomes, and unresolved disagreements about budgets, time-lines and boundaries in the northern regions. The relationship became worse under the pressure of looming elections for both governments. Both governments had good reason to pursue an RFA path at odds, and importantly, *seen to be at odds* in the electorate with the other. This is a 'symbolic use of politics' in Edelman's (1964) terms. These issues affected the willingness and ability of officials on the steering committee to resolve numerous outstanding issues. In effect, officials representing different agencies and different governments became overt protagonists, not neutral partners as the policy model espoused.

Another thread in this story concerns shifting alliances between governments and NGOs. Several participants observed that conservation organisations had declining access to and influence on Commonwealth government decision-making throughout the 1990s (see further Hutton and Connors 1999). Moreover, following the 1998 Federal election and the re-election of the Coalition, a new Minister for Forestry and Conservation was appointed to oversee RFA completion. The minister, the Hon Wilson Tuckey, became the Chair of the RFA Ministerial Group (ie, the Environment minister, and the senior and junior ministers of the Agriculture, Fisheries and Forestry Department). Minister Tuckey publicly re-articulated Commonwealth government policy on RFAs in terms that favoured the timber industry and, in every RFA under development during his tenure, he argued for an industry-sympathetic outcome.

In the NSW RFA process, conservation organisations accordingly targeted their lobbying to the NSW Labor Government on the basis of this government's previously sympathetic conservation decisions and policy commitments. But their influence here also waned as the electoral repercussions of a potential rural/regional backlash on forest decisions became apparent. That is, votes mattered more than the previous alliance.

Two heads of power in a polarised setting

Decision-making in the steering committee was dysfunctional in part because the decision-making structure answered to two heads of power. The role of Chair in the steering and technical committees rotated between a NSW official (from RACD) and a Commonwealth official (from the Forest Taskforce) and, given the circumstances noted above, neither official could exercise sufficient political will or power to force all government and non-government parties to negotiate. Further, despite the efforts of RACD and the Forest Taskforce, 'whole of government' positions in either or both jurisdictions were often difficult to reach. Both dynamics made it much harder to achieve consensus.

Different ideologies of public participation

The two governments advanced different ideologies of public participation. The NSW government espoused a 'strong' participation model, and paid specific attention to the politically active core stakeholder groups (noted above) and their active engagement in key aspects of the process. The Commonwealth government espoused a more traditional consultation model consistent with the administrative procedures of the *Environment Protection (Impact of Proposals) Act* 1974. Their emphasis accordingly was on the release of information and opportunities for public comment on assessments and options. Ideally the two models would complement each other but it seems that neither government could accept the premises of the other model. Rather than balance, many participants believe that the outcome was unsatisfactory in both directions. NGO representatives felt betrayed by the NSW government's unilateral declaration of NSW Forest Agreements and there were limited opportunities for broad public consultation on forest assessments and *no* opportunity for public comment on a draft agreement. (The subsequent process through late 1999 and early 2000 to reach a Commonwealth/State RFA for the region required opportunity for public submissions. This was widely perceived by stakeholders to be window dressing, core resource allocation decisions having been already made by the NSW government.)

Rigid positions

Even before confirmation came from technical assessments, most participants understood that it would be impossible to meet objectives for both biodiversity conservation and timber industry interests in the Upper North East NSW region. Indeed, the JANIS biodiversity criteria document asserted the need for 'flexibility' in applying the criteria for this and other reasons (JANIS 1997: 8-9). There simply wasn't enough high value forest left on public lands to deliver a win-win outcome. To generalise, these objectives on the one hand were to meet biodiversity targets in a (preferably) national park-based reserve system, and on the other, to sustain 'least cost' to the timber industry and communities; that is, no job losses and long term security of the industry resource base for continued development. In part due to the 20-year basis for the agreement, both sides (and here I refer to conservation and industry interests broadly) saw the RFA as a last chance to achieve their preferred outcome and had little incentive to negotiate mutually acceptable trade-offs. In addition, several participants noted that willingness to negotiate trade-offs depended on mutual trust and in this case such trust was not evident.

Insufficient conflict resolution mechanisms and unclear procedural guidelines

In the context of the dynamics portrayed above, government participants added that joint government and NGO consensus, while certainly desirable, was unrealistic. In particular, NGO involvement in steering committee deliberations served to intensify debates (many of which were carried over from technical committees) and lead to delays and impasses. Similar dynamics afflicted options development processes. In conflict situations, consensus decision-making was also constrained by the different types of authority of government and NGO members. For example, government participants in committees and options development processes were obliged to adhere to bureaucratic and political strictures such as budgets and time-lines, and getting approval from 'higher-up' on certain issues. They were also obliged to make decisions before consensus resolutions could be achieved (either because there was insufficient time to allow the consensus process to work, or because consensus was simply unobtainable). NGO members could not be required or depended upon to adhere to the same sort of strictures and were comparatively free to press for different approaches, adopt different interpretations of policy objectives, make demands of the process, go to the media, and/or outside the process by lobbying Ministers directly. From governments' perspective, the only way to move forward at the steering committee level and subsequently in options development was to limit NGO access and resolve governmental conflicts internally, rather than 'on display'.

It is not surprising that NGO members did not view some of these procedural difficulties in the same light as government members. In general, they acknowledged that NGO involvement is time-consuming and demanding. But these members argued that, for sustainability strategies to gain public trust and goodwill, *greater* not less participation and transparency was not only desirable but also essential. Moreover they argued that bureaucrats were as likely as NGOs to behave strategically rather than in good faith. In the minds of NGO members, problems stemmed from both governments and included unwillingness to accept the legitimacy of citizen involvement in decision-making, unwillingness or inability to reach agreement between governments and to demonstrate leadership and direction, and generally poor management of the overall administrative process.

Unresolved regional-centre and holistic-narrow tensions

Constraints on the involvement of the Regional Forest Forum in the Upper North East were different to those that confronted the core NGO groups. Some problems were simply due to 'cascading effects' from dysfunction at higher levels of the process. For example, the abrupt and untimely cessation of the Forum before it could fulfil a role as a 'regional voice' in options development was catalysed by a series of political dynamics noted above. But there were also a number of basic weaknesses in the organisational setting of the Forum. Members identified two related issues in particular: conflicting messages from governments about the role of the community-based Forum, and poor communication.

In retrospect, government officials acknowledge that insufficient attention had been paid to the function and practicality of encouraging regional input to the highly centralised, sectoral and technically complex process. The expectations of Forum members were unreasonably raised, leading to inevitable dissatisfaction with the actual level of access and influence possible in a time-limited process. In addition, many Forum members noted dislocation between their concerns and the intensifying focus of the process on resource allocation between national parks and State forests. Concerns of members which lacked purchase on the process included the role of private property forests in a reserve system and in industry development, likewise the role of local government in guiding such decision-making, Native Title and other Aboriginal community interests, community/regional development, and, the role and potential of other economic uses of native forests apart from the timber industry (eg, tourism, mining, apiary).

Poor communication between the steering and technical committees and the Forum further alienated Forum members. For example, the Forum regarded access to the technical information that would be used to develop and justify an option as essential to their role of representing and encouraging a regional perspective. But very little of this information was ready for public distribution before options development. And even so, the broader issue of capacity building to facilitate the Forum's understanding of technical issues had been neglected, or at least submerged by political events.

Discussion

All of the preceding observations may be seen as contingent dynamics of a particular planning process. However they also invite reflection on the types of rationality and the five policy attributes that have been suggested as the core of an adaptive approach to NRM (Dovers, this volume).

To frame the following discussion, it can first be noted that the RFA process was established in terms of a conventional instrumentally rational planning process; that is, centralised, managerialist, and government-driven, framed in terms of a means-end schema with decisions to be made on the basis of scientific assessments and analyses of different options to achieve pre-set objectives. At the same time, it is clear that demands to embed ecological and communicative forms of rationality in NRM decision-making are challenging the instrumental orientation. The nature of these challenges are drawn out in discussion of adaptive policy attributes.

Purposefulness

The underlying instrumental rationality of the RFA framework has provided a reasonably fertile bed for a purposeful approach to planning. ESD policy objectives were established, agreed, worked through and implemented in a public process. Although many stakeholders were disappointed with the extent of change, the process in NSW and elsewhere in Australia has secured a wide range of improvements to the management systems of both forest conservation and production State agencies, and, to some extent at least, to forest management on private property.

The pre-set goal orientation and the privileging of the products of science have also supported ecological rationality. When RFAs commenced, the problem of how to define and measure sustainability of forest biodiversity had matured to an extent not previously evident in forest policy. This is primarily reflected in the JANIS objectives and associated criteria, quantitative and qualitative targets, and decision-making principles for developing a CAR reserve system. Also significant for ecological rationality is the explicit policy commitment to biodiversity conservation. The JANIS criteria affirm that decisions to protect biodiversity are not simply rear-guard actions in response to development proposals but valid in their own right, economic values notwithstanding. Such criteria are one way that we can systematically evaluate the ecological systems upon which we depend, and so direct our institutions away from damaging them. In this respect it should be acknowledged that the RFA process in Australia has resulted in around 2.5 million hectares of reserves (formal and informal) being added to the reserve system (a 39% increase), including 850,000 hectares of old-growth (a 42% increase in old-growth protection). In addition, over 90 per cent of recognised high quality wilderness forest areas has been reserved. In the Upper North East region of NSW, gains were even more dramatic with over 180 per cent increase in the area of forest reserved.

Nonetheless, it must be understood that the focus of RFAs was on minimising conflicts over public native forests and progress on this front required narrowing the set of issues under debate to essentially the question of resource allocation between national parks and State forests, and, to a lesser extent, issues of ecologically sustainable forest management. On the latter point, one issue on which many observers express concern is their perception that the expansion of the national park estate has only been achieved through intensification of logging regimes in State forests and future commitments to plantation expansion on public and private property. Critics argue that in neither case have the demands of ecologically sustainable forest management been taken into account. In addition, progress on the twin objectives of the RFA process has come at the expense of deep and careful consideration of other equally pressing issues. Among these, as noted above, are the wide range of issues raised by members of the Regional Forest Forum.

Persistence

This is difficult to judge from the distance of a few months but the question of what do we want to 'persist' should be posed. The *outcome* of an RFA – the 20-year governmental agreement on a reserve system and timber allocations? Even though many politically active stakeholders already reject RFA decisions and have vowed to destroy them? Even though community and political attitudes and understandings change and what was once deemed pragmatic is later viewed as unrealistic or even morally repugnant? Arguably, persistence of an RFA as such seems unlikely given the rapidity with which such changes (including environmental) can occur, and also the evident failure in northern NSW to develop cooperative relationships among the different interested parties. More positively, it is important to acknowledge that the 20-year framework for RFAs reflects increased attention to the demands for longer term perspectives on ESD policy implementation (Productivity Commission 1999: 74).

A deeper question, yet to be answered, is to what extent the RFA framework as an innovative *process* of ESD policy and institutional development can accommodate and respond adaptively to changed internal and external circumstances. In this respect, and from the perspective of support for both ecological and communicative rationality, monitoring and evaluation mechanisms are critical. This issue is taken up in the discussion of information-richness and inclusiveness.

Flexibility

This is clearly related to the two previous policy attributes. In terms of ecological rationality, some stakeholders have noted the value of measurable policy targets (eg, for biodiversity objectives), but also concerns that such targets may be applied too rigidly by decision-makers. For instance, measurable targets can invite the response that 'We've done RFAs, what's next?' But the setting and meeting of targets does not do away with the uncertainties underlying such complex NRM issues. A general lesson is to avoid situations where pre-set objectives or targets are framed in such a way as to resist re-definition in the light of new information or understanding.

In terms of communicative rationality, a further lesson from the RFA case is that social flexibility depends on 'both the possibility and the willingness to make concessions' (Sager 1994: 183). If actors perceive they are engaged in a win-lose or lose-lose end-game, rigid behaviour is ensured. In such circumstances, phased or transitional policies and arrangements become particularly significant. That is, acknowledging that some issues must be left until the political environment is more amenable to their progress, but, importantly, being in a better position to inform that debate when it occurs.

This also highlights the importance of gaining broad public support for phased progress towards policy goals. Such a strategy may get us further faster than the big picture comprehensive policy process – a process that, when political realities bite, may only succeed in entrenching marginal change to the status quo.

Information-richness

The RFA case survives a simple test of information-richness – the generation and use of vast quantities of information. Indeed, the purpose of the CRA phase was information assembly and it involved extensive research, synthesis and the integration of different bodies of knowledge. While more funds have been allocated to information gathering in this process than to any previous NRM planning process in Australia, many stakeholders complained about poor data quality and coverage. Perhaps this is inevitable, but other NRM planning processes in Australia would do well to consider whether they have made appropriate accounting for information costs.

As noted above, richness of information is particularly relevant to our capacity to adapt to future change. Advocates of ecological rationality urge close and sustained attention to monitoring processes designed such that we can act to detect and correct problems before irreversible and/or undesirable changes occur. In this respect, critical components of the overall policy frame-work are RFA commitments to five-yearly reviews and monitoring mechanisms, both linked to international Montreal Process criteria and indicators for the conservation and sustainable management of temperate and boreal forests (Montreal Process 1995; MIG 1997) and to State and national State of the Environment and State of the Forest reports. It is not possible here to evaluate the quality of RFA monitoring and review frameworks. Indeed, the specifics of these requirements were not major foci during RFA processes with all final RFAs stating that they required further development. Clearly there are some serious problems to be addressed before we might rely upon them in an adaptive sense. One assessment report for the NSW RFA process notes, 'Monitoring is the single most neglected aspect of environmental management for the delivery of ecolo-gically sustainable forest management in New South Wales' (IEWG 1998: 119). Similar conclusions and identification of the range of organisational, social and political factors that severely constrain monitoring at the regional scale and over the long term are drawn in RFA reports for other States in Australia, indicating the systemic nature of monitoring problems. Richness of information also has important implications when applied to the communicative aspects of the RFA process. These are elaborated in discussion of inclusiveness.

Inclusiveness

An adaptive system fosters greater involvement of all interested parties in policy processes including scientific and technical dimensions. As outlined in the description of the RFA process in NSW, inclusiveness has been evident in principle but limited in practice. Some NGOs gained access to previously closed decision-making structures but later found their access denied and/or their role apparently irrelevant. For their part, many members of the Regional Forest Forum felt geographically, practically and politically remote from every aspect of the process. The lack of government attention to communicating the outcomes of assessments beyond core NGO representatives and their constituencies was a particularly notable failure of the partnership approach. Such conditions of disempowerment and remoteness likewise constrain fulsome expression of communicative rationality (Plumwood 1998).

Bonyhady (2000, and this volume) also puts the NSW government's oft-repeated claim to openness in resource and environmental decision-making in a less than positive light. His examination of the 1995 and 1997 amendments to the *Environmental Planning and Assessment Act* 1979 (NSW) shows a clear trend to increasingly restrictive public participation opportunities. The trend continues with the removal of third-party enforcement rights in respect of relevant forestry operations, as established in the legislation underpinning Forest Agreements (*Forestry and National Parks Estate Act* 1998 (NSW)). It seems a statutory basis for public participation cannot be relied on to protect public rights of objection and appeal. These trends do not augur well for the future of inclusive approaches to NRM planning.

Nonetheless, there were also some worthy innovations in this aspect of the NSW RFA process. While these should not have come at the expense of broader communication, they represent points of departure for future efforts:

- Financial support for NGOs and capacity building for NGO members to engage more effectively in technical aspects of the process;
- Providing a role for NGOs in technical committees, thereby fostering NGO access to and contribution of information, collective analysis, and encouraging debate and argument about the assumptions of both experts and non-experts; and
- Providing a role for NGOs in negotiating outcomes thereby fostering the potential for mutually acceptable outcomes and commitment to implementation.

A further dimension of an adaptive system concerns learning from experience about how best to institutionalise participatory structures and processes. The Southern Regional Forest Forum, for instance, has recognised the need for continuing dialogue beyond RFA completion. The Forum has called on the NSW government to provide a continuing role for such a broadly-based consultative body on forest issues in the future (P Kanowski, pers comm, 7 April 2000). The NSW government response remains unclear. No role is articulated in NSW Forest Agreements, nor in the RFAs for that State. We can only hope that the nascent multi-stakeholder partnerships reflected in the Forums do receive the opportunity to continue their role of critique, robust debate, learning and relationship-building as RFAs begin to take effect, and, that others might learn from their experiences. This hope may be too optimistic. In a review of participation and NSW policy processes (excluding the RFA process), Byrne and Davis make the important point that:

> There is almost no evidence available about the utility of NSW participation processes ... There is no process at present for the NSW government to learn from agency experience with participation. Each

participation exercise tends to be 'one-off'. Few participation processes are evaluated (Byrne and Davis 1998:45).

This observation appears relevant to the RFA process, as a national consultative process and as State-based consultative processes with significant differences among approaches within and between States. For example, although all RFAs contain commitments to public consultation and reporting mechanisms over the 20-year life of the plan, the learning dimension is unclear. At this stage, there is no evidence of intent to document, evaluate or critically reflect on the efficiency and effectiveness of participation in development or implementation of any RFA process.

In closing, I return to the theme of conflict with which I began this paper. The RFA process has grappled with some of the longest-standing and divisive debates over the use of natural resources in Australia. This context alone should invite close analysis of its successes and failings, whether in process or outcomes, for some time to come. Too often, however, lessons from sectoral or 'one-off' policy processes are not considered applicable to other sectors or settings. This is a mistake, especially in the evolving context of sustainability which clearly demands openness to new and untested ways of doing things. Lesson-drawing may be assisted by considering the expression of basic or fundamental principles such as those that underpin this volume, and the notions of communicative and ecological rationality that also inform this paper. But it is also important to be aware that such principles are not always either supportive of each other nor easily combined in practice. What are the implications of pursuing certain principles more vigorously than others, when the nature of sustainability problems would suggest equal attention is crucial? This is one area we need to think about more fully.

Postscript

Will forest conflicts ever be as heated as in the past? Cracks in the RFA edifice are certainly emerging. In 2002, there is no RFA for Queensland as the two governments could not reach agreement on a draft RFA (see Brown 2001). In February 2002, the Victorian and Western Australian governments reduced the area available for logging in native forests in their respective States. The Victorian decision followed an independent assessment of the forest resource inventory and yield forecasts which found that logging in native forests across the State needed to be reduced by one-third in order to achieve sustainable yield. The Western Australian decision followed from its announcement in 2001 that logging in all old growth forests in the State would cease (a response to intense public pressure on the issue). The issue of compensation to the timber industry is a State government issue in each case. Commonwealth legislation (the Regional Forest Agreements Bill 2002) was eventually passed on 14 March 2002, four years after debate on the legislation began in the Senate. The Bill gives legislative effect to certain provisions of the Commonwealth-State Regional Forest Agreements – particularly provisions on exclusion of specified Commonwealth laws, and on compensation to the timber industry. However compensation provisions relate only to Commonwealth government actions. The forest story, of course, continues.

Acknowledgments

The author is grateful to the many participants and observers of the RFA process who have contributed their insights and views to this study, and to fellow contributors to this volume who commented upon an early draft of this paper. Any errors of fact or interpretation are regretted and are of course my responsibility. This study was supported by a Land & Water Resources Research and Development Corporation student scholarship.

References

ABARE (Australian Bureau of Agriculture and Resource Economics), 1999, *Australian commodity statistics 1999*, Canberra: ABARE.

Barrett, J (ed), 1925, *Save Australia: a plea for the right use of our flora and fauna*, Melbourne: Macmillan,.

Bartlett, RV, 1986, Ecological rationality: reason and environmental policy, *Environmental Ethics* 8: 221-239.

Bingham, G, 1986, *Resolving environmental disputes: a decade of experience*, Washington, DC: The Conservation Foundation.

Bonyhady, T, 2000, Driving a Carr through the environment, *Sydney Morning Herald*, 29 January, p 6.

Brown, AJ, 2001, Beyond public native forest logging: National Forest Policy and Regional Forest Agreements after South East Queensland', *Environmental and Planning Law Journal* 18(1): 71-92.

Buchy, M, and Hoverman, S, 1999, *Understanding public participation in forest planning in Australia: how can we learn from each other?* Forestry Occasional Paper 99.2, Canberra: Australian National University.

Butterworth, J, Casella, F, and Nabben, T, 1999, Seeing the parts in the whole, a 'one of the parts; view of the WA Regional Forest Agreement, in Murray-Prior R and Marsh S, (eds), *Evolving systems – challenged minds, proceedings of the National Forum Australasia Pacific Extension Network, 11-12 November 1999*, Perth: APEN.

Byrne, J and Davis, G, 1998, *Participation and the NSW policy process – a discussion paper for The Cabinet Office, New South Wales*, The Cabinet Office, NSW, Sydney.

Carden, MF, 1992, 'Land degradation on the Darling Downs' in KJ Walker (ed), *Australian environmental policy: ten case studies*, Sydney: UNSW Press.

Carron, LT, 1985, *A history of forestry in Australia*, Sydney: Pergamon-ANU Press.

Carron, LT, 1993, Changing nature of federal-State relations in forestry, in Dargavel J and Feary S (eds), *Australia's ever-changing forests II* – Proceedings of the Second National Conference on Australian Forest History, pp 207-239, Canberra: Centre for Resource and Environmental Studies, Australian National University.

Christensen, NL, Bartuska, AM, Brown JH, Carpenter, S, D'Antonio, C, Francis, R, MacMahon, JA, Noss, RF, Parsons, DJ, Peterson, CH, Turner, MG and Woodmansee, RG, 1996, The report of the Ecological Society of America committee on the scientific basis for ecosystem management, *Ecological Applications* 6(3): 665-691.

CoA (Commonwealth of Australia), 1991, *Ecologically sustainable development working groups, Draft report: ecologically sustainable forest use*, Canberra: AGPS.

CoA (Commonwealth of Australia), 1992, *National forest policy statement, a new focus for Australia's forests*, Canberra: AGPS.

CoA (Commonwealth of Australia), 1995, *Regional forest agreements: the Commonwealth position*, Canberra: AGPS.

CoA/NSW (Commonwealth of Australia and State Government of New South Wales), 2000, *Regional forest agreement for North East New South Wales (Upper North East and Lower North East regions) between the Commonwealth of Australia and the State of New South Wales*.

Coakes, S, 1998, Valuing the social dimension: social assessment in the RFA process', *Australian Journal of Environmental Management* 5: 47-54.

Crowfoot, JE and Wondolleck, JM (eds), 1990, *Environmental disputes: community involvement in conflict resolution*, Washington, DC: Island Press.

Dargavel, J, 1995, *Fashioning Australia's forests*, Melbourne: Oxford University Press.

Dargavel, J, 1998, Politics, policy and process in the forests, *Australian Journal of Environmental Management* 5: 25-30.

Dargavel, J, Jackson, G, and Tracey, J, 1995, 'Environmental events in the forests of northern New South Wales: a second order', *Australian Journal of Environmental Management* 2: 224-233.

Davis, G, Wanna, J, Warhurst, J, and Weller, P (eds), 1993, *Public policy in Australia*, 2nd edn, Sydney: Allen & Unwin.

Diesing, P, 1962, *Reason in society: five types of decisions and their social conditions*, Urbana: University of Illinois Press.

Dovers, SR, and Mobbs, CD 1997, An alluring prospect? Ecology and the requirements of adaptive management, in Klomp N, and Lunt I, (eds), *Frontiers in ecology: building the links*, pp 39-52, London: Elsevier.

Dryzek, JS 1987, *Rational ecology: environment and political economy*, New York: Basil Blackwell.

Dryzek, JS 1990, *Discursive democracy – politics, policy, and political science*, Melbourne: Cambridge University Press.

Dukes, EF, 1996, *Resolving public conflict: transforming community and governance*, Manchester: Manchester University Press.

Dunn, WN, 1994, *Public policy analysis: an introduction*, Upper Saddle River, New Jersey: Prentice Hall.

Eckersley, R, 1992, *Environmentalism and political theory: towards an ecocentric approach*, London: State University of New York Press.

Edelman, M, 1964, *The symbolic uses of politics*, Urbana: University of Illinois Press.

Gray, B, 1989, *Collaborating: finding common ground for multiparty problems*, San Francisco: Jossey-Bass.

Gunderson, LH, Holling, CS, and Light, SS (eds), 1995, *Barriers and bridges to the renewal of ecosystems and institutions*, New York: Columbia University Press.

Haas, P, 1992, 'Obtaining international environmental protection through epistemic consensus' in Rowlands, IH, and Greene M (eds), *Global environmental change and international relations*, Basingstoke: Macmillan.

Habermas, J, 1984, *The theory of communicative action, Volume I: Reason and the rationalisation of society*, Boston: Beacon.

Habermas, J, 1987, *The theory of communicative action, Volume II: Lifeworld and system: a critique of functionalist reason*, Boston: Beacon.

Healey, P, 1997, *Collaborative planning: shaping places in fragmented societies*, London: Macmillan Press.

Holling, CS (ed), 1978, *Adaptive environmental assessment and management*, London: John Wiley and Sons,.

Hutton, D and Connors, L 1999, *A history of the Australian environment movement*, Melbourne: Cambridge University Press.

IEWG (Independent Expert Working Group on behalf of the NSW ESFM Group), 1998, *Assessment of management systems and processes for achieving ecologically sustainable forest management in New South Wales*, A report undertaken for the NSW CRA/RFA Steering Committee (Number NA 18/ESFM).

Jaensch, D, 1997, *The politics of Australia*, 2nd edn, Melbourne: Macmillan.

JANIS (Joint ANZECC/MCFAA National Forest Policy Statement Implementation Sub-committee), 1997, *Nationally agreed criteria for the establishment of a comprehensive, adequate and representative reserve system for forests in Australia*, Canberra: ANZECC.

Lee, KN, 1993, *Compass and gyroscope: integrating science and politics for the environment*, Washington, DC: Island Press.

Mercer, D, 1991, '*A question of balance': natural resources conflict issues in Australia*, 2nd edn, Sydney: Federation Press.

MIG (Montreal Process Implementation Group for Australia), 1997, *A framework of regional sub-national level criteria and indicators of sustainable forest management in Australia*, Canberra: Commonwealth of Australia.

Mobbs, CD, 2000, *Regional planning for sustainability: towards adaptive and collaborative perspectives*, unpublished PhD thesis, Australian National University.

Montreal Process, 1995, *Criteria and indicators for the conservation and sustainable management of temperate and boreal forests*, Quebec: Canadian Forest Service, Natural Resources Canada.

NSW (State Government of New South Wales), 1999, *Forest Agreement for Upper North East Region*.

NSW CRA/RFA Steering Committee, 1997, Guidelines for Regional Forest Forums, Memorandum.

Plantation 2020 Vision Implementation Committee, 1997, *Plantations for Australia: the 2020 Vision*, Ministerial Council on Forestry, Fisheries and Aquaculture, Standing Committee on Forestry, Plantations Australia, Australian Forest Growers and National Association of Forest Industries, Canberra.

Plumwood, V, 1998, Inequality, ecojustice, and ecological rationality, in Dryzek JS and Schlosberg D (eds), *Debating the earth: the environmental politics reader*, pp 559-583, Oxford: Oxford University Press.

Productivity Commission, 1999, *Implementation of ecologically sustainable development by Commonwealth departments and agencies*, Canberra: Ausinfo.

RAC (Resource Assessment Commission), 1992a, *Forest and timber inquiry, final report*, vol 1, Canberra: AGPS.

RAC (Resource Assessment Commission), 1992b, *Forest and timber inquiry, final report*, vol 2A, Canberra: AGPS.

Renn, O, Webler, T, and Wiedemann, P (eds), 1996, *Fairness and competence in citizen participation: evaluating models for environmental discourse*, Dordrecht: Kluwer Academic.

Routley, R and Routley, V, 1975, *The fight for the forests: the takeover of Australian forests for pines, wood chips and intensive forestry*, 3rd edn, Research School of Social Sciences, Canberra: The Australian National University.

Sager, T, 1994, *Communicative Planning Theory*, Aldershot: Avebury.

Saul, JR, 1993, *Voltaire's bastards: the dictatorship of reason in the West*, Melbourne: Penguin.

Simon, HA, 1955, A behavioral model of rational choice, *Quarterly Journal of Economics* 69(1): 99-118.

Toyne, P 1994, *The reluctant nation: environment, law and politics in Australia*, Sydney: ABC Books.

Walker, KJ, 1992, The neglect of ecology: the case of the Ord river scheme, in Walker KJ (ed), *Australian environmental policy: ten case studies*, pp 183-202, Sydney: UNSW Press.

Watson, I, 1990, *Fighting over the forests*, Sydney: Allen & Unwin.

Wright, W, 1992, *Wild knowledge: science, language, and social life in a fragile environment*, Minneapolis: University of Minnesota Press.

PART III

PROCESSES AND INSTITUTIONS

6

The Resource Assessment Commission: Lessons in the Venality of Modern Politics

Clive Hamilton

The Australia Institute

Genesis of the RAC

The 1980s were marked by a series of acrimonious and politically difficult environmental disputes, including heritage listing of the Gordon-below-Franklin, the logging of the Queensland wet tropics and Fraser Island, and the proposed Wesley Vale pulp mill. These disputes were especially difficult for the Hawke Government both because the ALP's electoral strategy relied on support from environmental groups and because the Prime Minister placed great emphasis on resolution through negotiated outcomes. The Commonwealth came into direct conflict with several conservative State governments, which took a more developmentalist approach, and was forced to use Commonwealth powers to over-ride the States' traditional resource management responsibilities. Disputes were often settled only after long campaigns, frequently conducted through the media, in which conservationists found they could win broad public support through powerful images and appeals to deep and increasingly influential ethical norms. This occurred at a time when, in other areas of policy, economic rationalism was reaching its zenith in Canberra and State capitals.

The federal government came under pressure from powerful industry groups – notably the mining and forest industries but also the peak business bodies – to develop a better process. At the end of 1988, Prime Minister Hawke announced a package of measures designed to reorient consideration of issues affecting natural resource use and the environment. The package included measures to improve the effectiveness of the Australian Heritage Commission, new consultative procedures between the Commonwealth and the States, negotiation of a forest accord and the establishment of the Resource Assessment Commission (RAC).

Purpose

The *Resource Assessment Commission Act 1989* (Cth) established a new inquiry body modelled on the Industries Assistance Commission (subsequently the Industry Commission and now the Productivity Commission). The objectives of the new body were set out with clarity in the second reading speech by the Minister for Primary Industries and Energy, Mr John Kerin, who had been a champion of the RAC from its inception. The speech was often consulted by the staff of the Commission as a guide to the government's intentions, and it is therefore worth quoting and commenting on at some length.[1] The Minister, perhaps the most enlightened resources minister ever to sit on the front benches, began by saying that the Commission:

> will inquire into, and report on, the environmental, cultural, social, industrial, economic or other aspects of resources and their uses.

Although apparently innocuous, this statement (also reflected in the Act itself) was of exceptional importance for the work of the Commission. In contrast to the inquiries of the Industry Commission (IC) (formed from the Industries Assistance Commission in 1990), which focused almost exclusively on the economic and employment effects of policy changes, the RAC was required to gather information on and evaluate the range of impacts. In other words, it was made clear from the outset that decisions over resource use would not be determined by economic analysis alone.[2] Some parties to disputes were subsequently to be disappointed that the Commission could not apply the unifying framework of economics to generate the 'best solution'. The Minister went on to state:

> the Commission will be required to be guided by ... three policy principles ... first, there should be an integrated approach to conservation and development by taking both aspects into account at an early stage; secondly, resource use decisions should seek to optimise the net benefits to the community from the nation's resources, having regard to efficiency of resource use, environmental considerations, and an equitable distribution of the return on resources; and thirdly, Commonwealth decisions, policies and management regimes may provide for additional uses that are compatible with the primary purpose values of the area ...

While commonplace now, the affirmation that both conservation and development should be taken into account on an equal footing was a significant step, for industry groups in 1989 continued to regard environmental considerations as marginal issues that should be accommodated only when necessary, and certainly should never provide grounds to stop development. The Minister's use of economic language – the need to 'optimise the net benefits' – did not negate the clear intention to give due weight to issues that in their nature fall outside of the economic domain.

The exhortation to take an 'integrated approach' exerted a powerful influence on the work of the Commission in its three inquiries, stimulating sustained attempts to experiment with new analytical methods, to apply techniques that could accommodate differing impacts, and to explore the limitations of these analytical methods. Above all, the Commission took the view that merely providing the government with a list of impacts divided into economic, environmental and social would be a mark of failure; it should

---

1   See House of Representatives, Hansard, 3 May 1989.
2   Although one of the commissioners continued through the course of an inquiry to look for an economic solution to the issue.

attempt to integrate the effects into a framework, albeit a conceptual one that lent itself only to verbal explication. It was this process that led the Commissioners to adopt the 'options approach' in its Kakadu inquiry, an approach that formed the basis for subsequent reports.

The bitter environmental disputes that marked the 1980s were centred on particular development or resource-use proposals, so that the forest dispute, for example, took the form of a series of conflagrations over patches of high conservation value forests in various States. The primary purpose of the RAC was to conduct inquiries into broad resource use issues in order to provide government with an approach to management that would avoid the grass fires that continued to break out. As the Minister said:

> ... RAC inquiries are expected to relate to industries, regions or issues, in contrast to the processes of the Environment Protection (Impact of Proposals) Act which generally apply to a specific project proposal. Inquiries almost always will be into major, complex and contentious resource use issues. They are likely to deal with the resource industries that are of great significance for the economy and the environment.

The Hawke Government was criticised at the time for referring to the Commission the issue of mining at Coronation Hill in Kakadu National Park because the latter was seen to be a specific proposal rather than a broad issue such as 'reconciling mining and the environment'. As events unfolded, the government was further chastised for saddling the Commission with an issue that would bring the wrath of industry down on its head, thereby jeopardising the future of the Commission.

However, in his second reading speech, the Minister foreshadowed the possibility that the government may refer to the Commission smaller-scale inquiries for assessment within a tight time frame. In addition, although the Kakadu inquiry dealt with only one relatively small mining proposal, it was a test case with much wider ramifications not just for the mining industry but for how environmental conflicts would be understood and resolved. Indeed, the Coronation Hill inquiry, and the subsequent decision, had enormous implications for the broader debate in Australia, sending an unambiguous signal to the mining industry that it could no longer assume that developments would be approved in all circumstances, and delivering an extremely important psychological victory to disempowered Aboriginal groups.

Inquiry process

The government appointed a permanent full-time chair of the Commission, Justice Donald Stewart, who presided over each of the three inquiries before the Commission had its 'functions terminated' in 1993. The inquiries were 'to assemble all reasonably attainable information and advice and do what analysis can reasonably be done within the time limits set by the Government'.[3] Its inquiry processes were designed to be similar to those of the IC, in

---

3   Kerin, House of Representatives, Hansard, 3 May 1989

particular providing for open and extensive consultation with all interested parties, including collection and analysis of submissions. Public hearings were to be informal and legal representation 'discouraged', a process of 'evidence' collection that Stewart, with a background in criminal law, struggled with. The consultation processes, however, were extensive and professional, and reflected a genuine desire to hear the views of the various parties. In marked contrast to the consultations of the IC and its successors, well-argued and supported submissions by interested parties were taken seriously by the Commission and influenced its deliberations. A survey of attitudes of interested parties to the work of the Commission undertaken towards the end of its life indicated that those involved were satisfied with the consultation process, although many said that more effort could have been devoted to public information.

Each inquiry was conducted by three commissioners, the chair and two commissioners appointed specifically to each inquiry. In each case the government appointed a biological scientist and an economist to assist the chair. The Commissioners were supported by a secretariat, with each inquiry assigned a branch. There were two additional branches, an administrative branch and a research branch. The purpose of the research branch was to carry out analyses to assist the inquiry branches and in particular to develop and apply new methods of assessment.[4] The formation of the secretariat attracted some of the best and brightest researchers from universities and other parts of the public service. There was a sense that the Commission was engaged in a bold and path-breaking experiment, a sense reinforced by frequent visits by overseas delegations keen to see how this new approach to environment policy worked. Early in 1990, an open day attracted hundreds of visitors to the Commission's offices in Canberra's East Block. Rooms overflowed and talks by Commission staff had to be repeated.

In each of its inquiries, the Commission investigated the issues in their complexity through its own research, commissioned reports and public submissions. It sifted through the evidence, formulated a view about the options and their various implications and wrote a report to the Prime Minister.[5] The Commission was from the outset sensitive to the potentially

---

4   A dispute developed within the Commission over whether the Research Branch had any function other than carrying out specific pieces of research requested by the inquiries. Justice Stewart insisted that it did not, despite the fact that the government had made it clear at the outset that one of its functions was to investigate the application of new techniques of analysis. It became necessary to ask Minister Kerin to write to Justice Stewart reminding him of the government's intention.

5   Economou (1996) claims that business support for the Commission ultimately collapsed because it was located in the Prime Minister's portfolio and reported to the Prime Minister rather than the resources portfolio and resources minister, and that this represented a strategic victory for environmentalists. This is hard to credit, as the alternative location would have meant that the Commission would never have won the cooperation of the environment movement. The proposal to locate the RAC in the resources portfolio was never taken seriously as it contradicted the very purpose of the Commission. On the other hand, location in the Prime Minister's portfolio can hardly be seen as a victory for environmentalists. While senior officers in the Department of Prime Minister and Cabinet were committed to Prime Minster Hawke's consultative style, there were no environmentalists among them. Quite the reverse; they were for the most part economists from Treasury and Finance who were ardent economic rationalists.

disaffecting nature of formal inquiry processes, especially, but not exclusively, with respect to Indigenous people. While industry and environment organisations are familiar with the subtleties of formulating a consistent position backed by evidence and setting it down on paper in a formal submission, Indigenous groups can find this approach rigid, alien and open to misinterpretation. It was recognised that the views of the latter may evolve over the course of an inquiry as consultation and consideration among affected parties proceeded. The role of senior custodians is not the same as the leadership of an industry or environment group; duties and responsibilities and the relationships to members of an affected people are often complex, subtle and not for public display.

Recognising this – particularly with the guidance of Dan Gillespie, the head of the Kakadu inquiry branch of the secretariat – the Commissioners adopted a different approach to gathering the views of Indigenous people. In the case of the Jawoyn people, the traditional owners of the Kakadu Conservation Zone, the Commissioners travelled to their principal settlements first to explain who they were and what they were doing. They listened to a range of views, meeting separately with the men and the women, and attempted to understand and accommodate the cultural sensitivities and ambiguities in some of the arguments, while acknowledging the special position of the senior custodians.

This approach was necessary in order to form a proper view about the impact on Indigenous people of various uses of a resource. It also points to the fact that more or less importance can be attached by decision makers to impacts on Indigenous people – some will accord them a central place, others will accord none. But whatever the decision it is taken on the basis of explicit or implicit value judgments. Minister Kerin observed in his second reading speech:

> We will sometimes face unpalatable choices between conflicting goals on the basis of limited knowledge. The Commission's job will be to assemble all reasonably available information, acknowledge those areas where uncertainties remain, take relevant viewpoints into account and advise the Government on the options it can adopt within a reasonable time frame.

This statement, reflecting the legislation, took on great significance, for it declared something critical about the role of the Commission that was consistently misunderstood by some of the industry groups. The role of the Commission was to advise the government as to the *options* available to it and the likely implications of each of those options. Since resource use decisions inevitably involve value judgments, a recommendation by the Commission as to what the government should do would reflect the Commissioners' own values. While a case could be made that the presentation of options and the organisation and emphasis given to evidence cannot but reflect the preferences and worldview of the Commissioners, it was accepted both by the government and the Commission that decisions must always be political even when based on the best information available.

It was not only industry that failed to understand the role of the Commission, some academic commentators have not grasped its explicit purpose and *modus operandi*. Economou, for example, writes as if the Commission were just another part of the Canberra bureaucracy, referring to 'its own contributions to its demise, via the Coronation Hill finding and its failure to maintain its position in the push and shove of Canberra's competitive bureaucratic politics' (Economou 1996). This misunderstands the vital point, so laboured at the time, that the Commission's role was to assess and advise the government of the options open to it. It did not make any recommendation on what to do with Coronation Hill. It did uncover a large amount of new information, which no doubt informed the public and political debate; but that was its job, it could not do otherwise.[6]

The inquiry process stipulated in the RAC legislation was explicitly modelled on that of the Industry Commission, but its operation in practice could not have been more different. The IC paid lip service to the collection of views and evidence from the public inquiry process.[7] Its views on almost every issue referred to it were formed on the basis of a well-defined and all-encompassing ideology, that of neo-classical economics and its policy interpretation known as economic rationalism.[8] Its worldview was supported by the results of formal economic analysis using a model that had the IC's assumptions about the world built in to it. Unlike the RAC, the outcomes of IC inquiries were entirely predictable, for the IC substituted a clearly articulated ideology for systematic assessment of evidence on the impacts of policy changes. The IC included a branch known within the Commission as the 'thought police' whose acknowledged task was to weed out any deviant ideas.[9] The ideology promoted by the Commission conformed to the political predisposition of government in Canberra.

There is a lesson here. While the RAC assiduously pursued its charter to seek the range of views and carefully sift through the evidence, it lasted less than four years. The IC wrote report after report reflecting its own internal ideology, yet has survived and prospered. It has even absorbed other parts of the bureaucracy – in 1997, as the Productivity Commission, it swallowed the Bureau of Industry Economics and the Economic Planning Advisory Commission. The lesson is that the answers given to government matter much more than the integrity of the process of forming the answers. In the end, the integrity of the RAC process counted for very little.

---

6   Economou (1996) also suggests that 'the opportunities for allowing environmentalists to participate in the decision making process as insiders were clearly irresistible'. If this is meant to imply that environmental leaders played any formal role within the Commission then it is entirely inaccurate. Like business leaders, other government agencies and the general public, environmental leaders could influence the work of the Commission only through their participation in the Commission's public submission and hearing processes.

7   It is reported that standard practice at the Industry Commission was that while submissions were being prepared by interested parties a report based on the Commission's worldview would be drafted with gaps left in the text to be filled by the appropriate quotation carefully culled from the public submissions.

8   There are a number of accounts of how the IC operated. See, for example, the paper by former IC Commissioner Tor Hundloe, 'ESD and the Industry Commission', in C Hamilton and D Throsby (eds), *The ESD Process: Evaluating a Policy Experiment* (Academy of Social Sciences in Australia, Canberra, 1998).

9   One visiting economist from another part of the bureaucracy was allegedly sprayed with water from an atomizer kept under the desk when he put forward a view that was considered 'wet'.

The Kakadu inquiry

Many of the principles of operation and the political currents that swirled around the Commission can be illustrated by an analysis of the inquiry into the proposal to mine Coronation Hill in Kakadu National Park, an inquiry that resulted in the Commission's first and most controversial report (RAC 1991). The inquiry has continuing relevance not least because of the later controversy over the proposed uranium mine at Jabiluka, also within the boundaries of Kakadu National Park (Hamilton 1996). It is also a useful illustration because the Coronation Hill inquiry demonstrated some of the limitations of technical analysis, both ecological and economic, and the impossibility of separating the technical analysis from values and interests.

The principal concern that led to the RAC Inquiry was the potential impact of the proposed mine at Coronation Hill on the natural environment of the Conservation Zone and the Park as a whole. The concerns related to disturbance at the site itself, dust from mining operations, sediment finding its way into the South Alligator River system, seepage or water release from the dams, and transport accidents involving diesel fuel and toxic chemicals. There was concern about the impacts of these on ecosystem processes and on certain rare and endangered species found in the area, especially the pig-nosed turtle. Against the potential environmental impacts of the project was the economic value of the gold mine (also producing platinum and palladium). ABARE estimated the net economic benefits of the mine at $52 million (RAC 1991).[10]

The Inquiry undertook extensive assessment of the environmental values of the Conservation Zone and the likely impacts of the proposed mine on them, and arrived at the following conclusion:

> ... the existing evidence suggests that a single mine development, properly managed and monitored, would have a very small impact on the known biological resources, archaeological values, and the recreation and tourism values of the Zone. There remain, however, a number of environmental issues that the Inquiry believes would be of concern if a single mine were permitted.[11]

These remaining environmental issues are then described in the Report, although they are not straightforward in meaning or interpretation. They are:

- the impact of a mine on future World Heritage listing;
- the incompleteness of biological information on the Zone; and
- the small but non-zero threat posed by the mine development to the aquatic ecosystems of the South Alligator River.

There was one additional environmental issue, and it was probably the most significant of all. The Commission grappled with it, wrote about it, but

---

10   Economou (1996) argues that industry was alienated by the RAC's finding that the Coronation Hill project would not 'reap any major economic bonanza'. In fact, the RAC simply reported an analysis by ABARE (seen then, as now, to be close to the mining industry) to the effect that the net economic benefits of the mine were small.

11   This and subsequent quotations are from RAC (1991), pp 242, xxii, 186.

ultimately could not satisfactorily define it. It is stated most clearly in the Report in the following terms:

> The existence of the Ranger uranium mine in the northern part of Kakadu notwithstanding, many would perceive the commencement of mining in the Conservation Zone as challenging the notion of ecological integrity and preservation that underlies the concept of national parks, and Kakadu National Park in particular.

The idea of the integrity of the Park underlay much of the deliberation. It was argued by several parties that the integrity of the Park would be compromised by any mining in the Conservation Zone, even if it could be shown that any specific ecological impact would be very small. The notion of the integrity of the Park is something that cannot be measured or proved one way or another; as the quotation above indicates it is a 'perception' that some people have. Constrained by a somewhat mechanistic approach to the question, the Commission decided to interpret it as 'ecological integrity', a concept that focuses on the complexity of physical interrelationships within ecosystems. But the concept of the integrity of the Park is more of an ethical one than a scientific one, although scientific demonstration of ecosystem integrity may contribute to some people's perceptions of ethical integrity. It therefore involved judgment rather than scientific facts.

Indigenous issues were regarded as a second-order issue at the start of the inquiry - indeed, it was some weeks into the inquiry before Justice Stewart became aware that Coronation Hill was a sacred site registered under Northern Territory law – but they quickly became critical to the investigation. It is probably true to say that as the inquiry proceeded the accumulation of scientific evidence suggested that the environmental risks of mining, while significant, could be accommodated, while the accumulation of anthropological and cultural evidence indicated that there was no way that mining could be reconciled with the interests of the Jawoyn people. At the start of the inquiry, no-one expected this. The Commissioners' views changed markedly through the course of the inquiry, and so did those of many in the secretariat. Two meetings between the Commissioners and the traditional owners at Waterfall Creek and Eva Valley in late 1990 appear to have been critical moments. It was not that the Commissioners decided that mining should not proceed, but that mining would have a significant effect on the economic, environmental, social and cultural circumstances of the traditional owners. As it transpired, the decision to ban mining – taken unilaterally by Prime Minister Hawke, and announced during a visit to a Catholic girls school the day before the cabinet meeting scheduled to make the decision – was based on the Prime Minister's deep concern for the spiritual beliefs of a marginalised and dispossessed group. After exhaustive investigation of the issues, the Commission came to the following conclusions about the implications of the proposed mine for the Jawoyn people:

> If mining proceeds in the Zone it will be against the wishes of the senior Jawoyn men, who are supported in their view by many Jawoyn people and other senior Aboriginal people in the Region; further, mining will adversely affect the ability of Jawoyn people, particularly

the senior men, to sustain cultural and religious values, beliefs and practices that are important to them.

The Commission attached considerable significance to the social implications of a decision to allow mining that would arise from the statement of opposition to the mine by the senior custodians.

> If mining were to proceed, one of the impacts would be that these men [the three custodians] will lose face in the Aboriginal community. Their perceived inability to carry out the responsibilities bestowed on them by their fathers and by the Aboriginal community, or to sustain the associated beliefs and practices, could be a source of profound personal grief, self-recrimination and harsh judgment by other Aboriginal people.

This statement has considerable relevance to the uranium mine at Jabiluka.

The Conservation Zone clearly had a multiplicity of values; economic, ecological and spiritual. While the Commissioners recognised the irreducibility of these values, some economists saw the situation as one in which extended cost-benefit analysis could provide an answer to the question of how to maximise social welfare from the use of the resource. This way of posing the question reflects an economic view of the world.

As we have seen, in establishing the RAC, the government expressed the view that the Commission should explore the use of innovative techniques for assessing the values of various uses of resources, especially ones that try to integrate the various values of a resource. The Commission was not as adventurous in this task as it could have been, but it did apply a number of little-known methods. The most controversial was the application of the contingent valuation (CV) method to the assessment of the environmental values of Coronation Hill in Kakadu National Park (Imber et al 1991).

The Kakadu CV study brought to public attention the existence of non-market valuation techniques, the hallmark of environmental economics. They are explicit attempts to reduce environmental values to economic ones through the notion of willingness to pay. In so doing they characterise citizens as consumers and attempt to reduce social values and political judgments to purchasing preferences. For many (including the author), despite its technical excellence, the CV study pointed to the distortions inherent in applying economic thinking to complex environmental problems.

As it turned out, the results of the survey were highly damaging to the mining case, as they showed a large majority of Australians were opposed to the mine, even when the expected impacts were described in terms sympathetic to the mining company's case.[12] Although the Commissioners rejected

---

12   By way of anecdote, the Commission employed the services of Professor Richard Carson to provide advice on the formulation, development and interpretation of the Kakadu CV study. A professor at the University of California San Diego, Carson was the author of the 'bible' of contingent valuation, and did most of his consulting work for large corporations. At their first meeting with Carson, the study authors described the situation in Kakadu that was to be valued by the CV study – a mine in an area surrounded by national park, a sacred site disturbed and some possibly endangered species that could be threatened. After half an hour, Professor Carson observed: 'I don't think the mining company is going to like the results of this study'.

the results of the study – with Justice Stewart branding it 'voodoo economics' – the political significance of the results was not lost on the Hawke Government.

Given the Commission's explicit acknowledgement of the need to assess social values, and indeed its legislated requirement to do so, it was important to uncover public attitudes to the issues as an essential component of evaluating the options. Here, the RAC Inquiry revealed a great deal of valuable information. The Inquiry commissioned AGB-McNair to carry out a thorough assessment of public opinion concerning the environment and mining in national parks, information that bears directly on the question of the integrity of national parks (Imber et al 1991, Table 5.10). In fact, this formed part of the CV survey, but the questions asked were of more than passing interest for what they revealed about the nature of values. Some of the results were as follows.

- When asked whether mining in national parks greatly reduces their value, 61 per cent agreed or strongly agreed while 23 per cent disagreed or strongly disagreed.

- When asked whether development should be allowed to proceed where environmental damage from activities such as mining is possible but very unlikely, 46 per cent disagreed or strongly disagreed while 33 per cent agreed or strongly agreed.

- When asked whether jobs are the most important consideration in deciding how to use natural resources, only 23 per cent agreed or strongly agreed, while 51 per cent disagreed or strongly disagreed. This response was all the more remarkable because the survey was carried out at the bottom of a recession.

- Finally, when asked whether, in deciding how to use areas like Kakadu, their importance to local Aboriginal people should be a major factor, 57 per cent agreed or strongly agreed while 20 per cent disagreed or strongly disagreed.

The decision by the Hawke Government to prohibit mining at Coronation Hill had strong public support and the Prime Minister was well aware of the results of the survey.

The Kakadu Commissioners recognised early on that their role was to explore the implications of the various options available to the government and not to make a recommendation as to whether mining should proceed or not. The report was careful to avoid anything that could be construed as a recommendation to mine or to preserve. Nevertheless, many believed that the Commission recommended against mining. A newspaper recently reported that the RAC recommended a mining ban at Coronation Hill. It is a matter of some irony that the mining industry and business groups, which had complained about environmental issues being settled through media campaigns, embarked on a vigorous, and at times vicious,[13] media campaign

---

13   For some illustrations of the viciousness of the attacks on the Jawoyn people see Hamilton (1996).

that reached a crescendo as the Cabinet meeting approached. Writing in the *Mining Review*, the eminent law professor Colin Howard insisted that the interpretation given by the Commission to Jawoyn views would, if accepted by the government, 'set a potentially disastrous precedent' and that the process by which Jawoyn claims were assessed by the Inquiry 'could extend fairly rapidly to every corner of Australia, making a mockery of our concepts of property' (Howard 1991). Mr Hugh Morgan, Managing Director of Western Mining Corporation, addressed the Adam Smith Club in the following terms:

> The decision on Coronation Hill is not merely bizarre, it is resonant with foreboding. ... [T]his decision will undermine the moral basis of our legitimacy as a nation, and lead to such divisiveness as to bring about political paralysis. ... The implications of it will, inevitably, permeate through the entire body politic, and cause, imperceptibly, like some cancerous intrusion, a terminal disability. ... Like the fall of Singapore in 1942, Coronation Hill was a shocking defeat (Morgan 1991).

Mr Morgan went on to observe that, by attaching importance to the Jawoyn people's spiritual beliefs, the Prime Minister, Mr Hawke, 'seeks to impose his own religious, neo-pagan obsessions on the whole nation' and called for a counter attack on the religious crazies and green antinomians 'who threaten our prosperity and eventually our survival'. Ten years later, evidence of moral decay, political paralysis and terminal disablement of the Australian body politic is still to emerge (although the Howard Government retained sufficient confidence in Mr Morgan's forecasting abilities to appoint him to the Board of the Reserve Bank). In view of the hysterical reaction of the mining industry to the Coronation Hill decision, it is hard to believe that the industry was genuine in its desire to see the creation of an impartial body charged with the task of rationally assessing the costs and benefits of resource uses.

While mining interests and industry generally were incensed at the government's decision, and blamed the Commission for a defeat akin to the fall of Singapore, it is uncertain whether this hostility affected the Commission's further inquiries. However, the report on the forest and timber industries was widely seen as a victory for the timber industry. Although the forests inquiry generated an enormous amount of invaluable data and analysis – data and analysis that have been frequently used since – the forests inquiry failed on several counts. The government was taking major decisions while the two-year inquiry was progressing, yet the Commission did not participate and was side-lined. Methodologically, the final report lacked elegance and appeared contradictory, especially in contrast to the superior draft report, and consequently it was difficult for decision makers to interpret the arguments. Overall, although accumulating a huge amount of new information over a two-year period, the report did not make a major contribution to resolving the forestry dispute.

The RAC legacy

The RAC experiment made a number of significant contributions to understanding the process of decision-making about resource uses. They can be summarised as follows:

- It was recognised in its establishment and its operation that use of resources involves social, cultural and environmental values as well as economic ones, and that the former cannot be reduced to the latter. While seemingly trite, this recognition was a critical foundation for the RAC because it averred, at the height of the influence of economic rationalism, that economics can provide only some of the information required to assess environmental issues.

- This meant that when weighing up the various values of each use of a resource, judgments must enter into the decision and that these judgment should reflect society's valuations. The multiplicity of values, some of which are inherently social beliefs, means that competing values can only be decided by expressions of preferences by the community based on deliberation. This in turn implies that the best use of a resource cannot be decided by technical analysis by experts or measurement techniques, even though such analysis may provide vital information in the formation of community views.

- In consequence, the Commission could make recommendations to the government about the best way of using a resource only if the Commissioners applied their own value judgments to the relative importance of the various social, cultural, environmental and economic impacts. Recognising this, the Commission confined itself to exploring and presenting to the government the various feasible options and pointing out the implications of each one.

Each of these may seem self-evident now. But they were the subject of intense debate in and around the RAC. After all, many hoped that the Commission would take the heat out of disputes by providing cool, dispassionate technical analysis.

Reasons for the demise of the RAC

After operating for less than four years, the Keating Labor Government decided to withdraw funding for the RAC and after submission of its third report, on coastal zone management, it ceased to exist at the end of 1993. Analysing the reasons for the demise of the Commission sheds light on the changing state of the environmental debate and, more significantly, the political process. The government stated that the emergence of a number of other consultative and inquiry processes and resource use strategies made the Commission redundant,[14] but few believed that this was any more than face-saving.

---

14   Senator Gareth Evans, Senate Hansard, 1993.

Donald Stewart and Greg McColl, respectively the Chair of the Commission and a commissioner on the Kakadu and coastal zone inquiries, have argued that the Commission was killed off for three reasons: a view that the RAC did not get on well with the States; that it did not recommend that mining at Coronation Hill should proceed and gave too much attention to Indigenous issues; and that an independent body presented too much of a threat to bureaucrats in Canberra (Stewart and McColl 1994). They suggest that the last-mentioned reason was the most important. Dovers and Lindenmayer agree that bureaucratic jealousies and dissatisfaction with the fact that the Commission did not make definite recommendations were significant factors, and add 'impatience with detailed and reasoned analysis' (Dovers and Lindenmayer 1997).

All of these factors were significant. In the end it came down to the fact that the political process was, and remains, too immature to deal properly with reasoned and detailed analysis of issues. Industry was willing to support the process only as long as the Commission leant in its direction, and showed that it was willing to ruthlessly attack the independent arbiter when its expectations were not fulfilled. Many bureaucrats were motivated by territoriality rather than a desire to achieve the best outcome from resource use. In addition, Prime Minister Hawke's consensus style grated on the 'hard-heads' in Cabinet who were products of an industry worldview in which development must prevail. Many of these factors converged on the change of leadership, and it was Keating's accession that was critical in the end. Determined to extirpate all vestiges of the man he defeated, the RAC was too closely associated with Hawke's vision and Hawke's style. Moreover, Keating soon revealed his deep antipathy to the environment movement – he referred to objections to old-growth logging as 'the usual incantations of environmentalists' – and the RAC as an institution designed to attempt to integrate environmental concerns systematically into decision-making was an obvious and easy target.

Industry had strongly supported the formation of the Commission. Mark Raynor, president of the Australian Mining Industry Council declared in 1989: 'It is in large part due to the persistent and continual advocacy of the industry that the RAC is being set up'. The mining industry said that it hoped that competing claims over the environment and resource use would be tested rigorously by the Commission, thereby avoiding decisions by way of 'media battle and ad hoc political decisions'.[15] The forest industries also provided strong support. However, resource industry groups, and the organised business community generally, became increasingly hostile to the RAC and eventually won the ear of the Keating Government.[16]

---

15   Quoted in Stewart and McColl (1994).
16   In this context, Economou (1996) makes a number of misconceived claims about the Commission's role. He argues that the Commission lost industry support in part because of its 'complicity' in the Coronation Hill outcome and its 'propensity to publish' reports that alienated both sides. This wholly misconstrues the role of the Commission. It was not 'complicit' in any decisions, nor did it have a propensity one way or another.

This raises a puzzling question: Why did the resource industries believe that more thorough investigation of the economic, environmental and social impacts of resource uses would advance its case? In the late 1980s, environmentalism was relatively new as a political force and the resource industries found it hard to accept that environmentalism was a permanent feature of the political landscape. It believed that if people could be persuaded to 'see reason' then the 'emotional' claims of environmentalists would be exposed. This was a serious miscalculation. The broader Australian community no longer shared the value system of the resource industries, one in which 'development' takes priority over everything else. Moreover, it is apparent now, if it was not then, that as a general rule the more the workings of ecosystems are investigated, the more complex, diverse and delicate they appear to be. It is therefore true to say that an impartial body charged with investigating the impacts of resource use would almost certainly expose non-economic values as being of greater significance than previously thought. This was true of the ecological values, but also of the depth of community concern for environmental protection, a fact revealed in a range of studies of community attitudes and preferences undertaken by the Commission. It is also true that when, from a state of ignorance, men and women of good will begin to investigate the condition of Australia's Indigenous people they frequently become firm advocates for greater Indigenous rights and protection.

Some concluding comments

The RAC was a bold experiment that undoubtedly advanced the way in which environmental debates are carried out in Australia. There is now a greater emphasis on analysis and, perhaps sometimes, a more careful statement of views. However, apart from internal problems, the Commission was in part a victim of the expectations that were imposed on it. Too many people, caught up in the Enlightenment belief that the 'facts' will provide the solutions, expected the Commission to resolve deep conflicts by rational scientific and economic analysis. Although analysis is essential for exploring the implications of various positions, ultimately environmental conflicts arise out of fundamental differences in value systems, differences that no amount of rational analysis can bridge.

At another level, the RAC did not fail. It was an institution that bridged the gap between two eras, one in which the development mentality struggled to hold back the tide of popular environmentalism and one in which environmental concerns take their place at the centre of policy development. The RAC exposed in the most dramatic way the unwillingness of developers to put aside commercial interests so that the national interest could be fully and properly assessed. As for its inquiries, the mode of its inquiry into Coronation Hill, like the Ranger inquiry before it, gave respectful attention to the claims of traditional owners, and the decision by the government to ban mining based on the information uncovered by the Commission was a watershed in the protection of indigenous interests. The forestry inquiry was in many respects a failure because the Commission refused to recognise that the nature and terms of the debate were changing rapidly during the course of the inquiry. The coastal zone inquiry was a mixed success; many of its arguments have been accepted and adopted by the States, but it suffered from obscurity and the vacuum left by the RAC's demise.

There were other valuable lessons. It became more apparent that information and analysis matter, but that parties that argue for rational assessment are likely to revert to more primitive forms of battle when they start to lose the argument. As the *Australian Financial Review* editorialised in January 1994:

> The RAC had effectively corralled industry and the environmentalists into a rational decision making framework. Whoever lost the argument before the RAC would lose the public debate, and ultimately, the political struggle.[17]

For an organisation like the RAC, set apart from the bureaucratic mainstream, political support is crucial for survival and this translates into having the strong support of powerful cabinet ministers. When this support evaporated the RAC was condemned to an early death.

If the executive is threatened by new bodies with independent charters then why does it set them up in the first place? This question could be asked not only of the RAC, but also of the ESD process and the RFA process (see Dovers; Mobbs, this volume). Is it naivety grounded in the hope that independent analysis will give the government of the day the answers it wants? Or are we asking the wrong question? Perhaps the purpose of establishing these bodies lies not in their outputs, but simply in their short-term ability to displace conflict. In that case, the purpose of bodies like the RAC is not to resolve environmental disputes but to resolve, at least for a time, intractable political problems. If so, then they are doomed to failure because to succeed they must have the strong support of the executive, an executive committed to the process of inquiry and report. The case of the Industry Commission suggests that the process is largely irrelevant as long as the answers are consistent with expectations. In the end, the RAC took its legislated purpose too seriously to become a long-term survivor in the prevailing policy environment. In my judgment, a noble death was preferable.

---

17   AFR Editorial, 12 January 1994, quoted in Stewart and McColl (1994).

References

Dovers, S and Lindenmayer, D, 1997, 'Managing the environment: rhetoric, policy and reality, *Australian Journal of Public Administration* 56: 65-80.

Economou, N, 1996, Australian environmental policy making in transition: the rise and fall of the Resource Assessment Commission, *Australian Journal of Public Administration* 55: 12-22.

Hamilton, C, 1996, *Mining in Kakadu: lessons from Coronation Hill*, Australia Institute Discussion Paper No 9, Canberra: AI.

Howard, C, 1991, Fundamental flaws in the decision on Coronation Hill, *Mining Review* 15(4): 15.

Hundloe, T, 1998, ESD and the Industry Commission, in Hamilton C and Throsby D (eds), *The ESD process: evaluating a policy experiment*, Canberra: Academy of Social Sciences in Australia.

Imber, D, Stevenson, G and Wilks, L, 1991, A *contingent valuation survey of the Kakadu Conservation Zone*, Resource Assessment Commission Research Paper No 3, Canberra: AGPS.

Morgan, H, 1991, The dire implications of Coronation Hill, *IPA Review*, vol 44 no 4, Melbourne: Institute of Public Affairs.

Resource Assessment Commission, 1991, *Kakadu Conservation Zone Inquiry, Final report*, vol 1, Canberra: AGPS.

Stewart, D and McColl, G, 1994, The Resource Assessment Commission: an inside assessment, *Australian Journal of Environmental Management* 1: 12-23.

7

Discrete, Consultative Policy Processes: Lessons from the National Conservation Strategy for Australia and National Strategy for Ecologically Sustainable Development

Stephen Dovers

Centre for Resource and Environmental Studies, The Australian National University

This chapter deals with discrete, consultative policy processes within the policy fields of ecologically sustainable development (ESD) and natural resource management (NRM).[1] While invariably and deeply embedded in and connected to the ongoing policy and institutional landscape, such processes are: targeted at a defined issue or suite of issues; bounded in time; have a stated process (which may change *en route*); produce recognisable policy products; and although public policy mechanisms 'run' by governments, involve non-government stakeholders in a consultative fashion. In Australia such processes, if they deal with an issue of any significance and complexity, will involve federal, State and sometimes local government within the evolving framework of Federation.

Discrete, time-bounded policy processes are by definition *ad hoc* – indeed, that is their rationale. This book is predicated on the idea that *ad hockery* is not a good thing, but recognises the need for persistence to be tempered with flexibility. This chapter explores the policy system's ability to rise to contingencies and eruptions of concern, while still playing a coherent longer-term game. The following discussion will look at examples of discrete policy processes in themselves, but also how well they embed within the longer term evolution of sustainability policy. In placing *ad hoc* processes in such a context, we will take on Davis' (1993: 15) warning that 'apparent [policy] volatility can become, in retrospect, the stately march of consistent underlying change'. Maybe so.

This chapter is not a detailed analysis, but establishes some themes and uses those to identify elements of the Australian experience over the past two decades. Two cases are examined: the National Conservation Strategy for Australia (NCSA) in the early 1980s; and the ESD process in the early 1990s

---

1   There is a large, complex, evolving and inconclusive literature on policy processes more generally that will not be dealt with here; for overviews see Davis et al 1993; Considine 1994; Howlett and Ramesh 1995.

and subsequent policy development.[2] These span the period from the emergence of the modern idea of sustainability as a policy problem in Australia up to the present. As related processes, they offer the opportunity to track the role of discrete policy processes in maintaining discourse (or not) and driving policy development (or not) over time. The analysis of regional forest agreements by Mobbs (this volume) deals with a related process in the late 1990s. Elsewhere in this volume, Haward deals with the encouraging oceans policy, whilst Stafford Smith and Abel discuss the disappointing rangelands policy. This chapter's two subjects differ in being non-sectoral.

Sustainability: an historical trajectory

The two cases address a more integrated agenda than simply 'the environment' – that of sustainability. The modern idea of sustainability might be dated (a little conveniently) from circa Boulding's (1966) famous 'spaceship earth' essay. The modern sustainability debate can be dated from 1972: the UN's Stockholm conference and the publication of *Limits to growth* (Meadows et al 1972). The modern policy agenda dates from the report *Our common future*, by the World Commission on Environment and Development (WCED 1987), and the translation of this into policy principles and plans at the 1992 UN Conference on Environment and Development (UNCED) and the instruments arising from that meeting.[3] However, the component concerns of and debates about the long run sustainability of human societies have a far deeper past in classical economics, energy analysis, development, renewable resource management, and the like. This is an important point: sustainability (or in Australian parlance, ESD) is not a simple and new idea. It is emergent from a long history of worsening problems, evidently failed policy responses, and increasing recognition of linkages across policy problems and fields. The policy processes dealt with in this paper are Australian responses to international developments in sustainability policy, and seek to some extent to integrate different environmental issues on a more whole agenda, and to integrate environmental with social and economic policy.

Problems such as climate change, integrated land and water management, settlement policy, biodiversity conservation and the like are particularly difficult. Indeed, on the basis of the attributes of sustainability problems (see Chapter 1), they are different in kind and degree to problems in 'traditional' policy fields such as service delivery or economic development (Dovers 1997a). Such problem attributes, especially in combination, suggest particular demands on policy, and the five principles of persistence, purposefulness, information-richness, inclusiveness and flexibility respond to these demands. Through those principles, the analysis of the two processes in this chapter will assess how well such attributes were catered for, or whether reliance on traditional forms of public policy process meant that they were not.

---

2   The author, as well as having research interests in policy processes in general, was a local government representative at the NCSA 1983 drafting conference, and an adviser to ESD working groups and to one Commonwealth Department over the period 1989-92.

3   The Rio Declaration, Agenda 21, Convention on Biological Diversity, Framework Convention on Climate Change, statement of principles on forests, and desertification convention.

Discrete policy processes in the policy landscape

Public policy is a constant, with many permanent or at least reasonably persistent institutional arrangements and organisations. Many policy matters are foreseeable and are dealt with in a routine fashion using familiar processes. However, issues that arise unexpectedly, change in nature or intensify in a political sense often require some special structure or process. An existing institutional or organisational structure may in fact cater well for emergent issues – for example, parliamentary committees, Royal Commissions, commissions of inquiry, or a dedicated body such as the Productivity Commission or the RAC (see Hamilton, this volume). For some issues, however, a government (often under pressure from outside) initiates a dedicated process. Such processes will not be without precedent in a political or public policy sense, but are 'one-offs' in significant ways. Various configurations of policy actors (within a government, intergovermental, non-government, etc) might be engaged in discrete processes depending on the specific problem and the proclivities of the government concerning participation.

The NCSA and ESD processes are examples of one-off processes involving not only government but other players as well. Why they could not be or were not handled in some way other than inventing a unique process is complicated. Reasons include novelty and hence a lack of suitable, existing policy formulation processes, the fact that formulation of general policy approaches and goals were involved rather than just applied problem solving, and various pressures from international and non-governmental sources. Discrete policy processes are nonetheless embedded within the broader policy setting, and are in fact an important arena where existing policy institutions, interests and actors interact most intensively. To identify this broader setting, the following summarises a view of the constituent elements of a comprehensive policy process for ESD or NRM problems (Dovers 1995). This is not a blueprint for policy making, but rather a checklist of important pre- and post conditions surrounding the 'policy statement', that avowal of intent that too often is all that people view as constituting policy.

- *Problem framing*: discussion and identification of social goals; monitoring of topicality; monitoring of natural-human system interactions; identification of problematic environmental change; isolation of proximate and underlying causes of change; assessment of uncertainty; assessment of existing policy and institutional settings; definition of the policy problem(s).
- *Policy framing*: development of guiding policy principles; construction of general policy statement; definition of policy goals.
- *Policy implementation*: selection of instruments and options; planning of implementation; provision of statutory, institutional and resource requirements; establishment of compliance/enforcement mechanisms; establishment of policy monitoring mechanisms.
- *Policy monitoring and review*: ongoing monitoring; mandated evaluation and review; extension, adaptation or cessation of policy.

- *General elements, required at all stages:* iterative description and explanation of process; transparency and accountability; public participation and stakeholder involvement; policy coordination (cross-
  problem and cross-field); communication mechanisms.

  NB: the requisite and all-important linkages and feedbacks between
  elements are not described here.

Quite properly, discrete policy processes may deal with different arrays of
these elements. The NCSA and ESD processes did involve discussion of broad
social goals; whereas other more focused processes such the RFA or oceans
processes (Mobbs, Haward, this volume) do not, but deal with implementation issues and information requirements that the other two did not.
However, we can use the checklist above as a heuristic device to assess the
efficacy of each process within its own limits, and the extent to which it
allowed for connection to other elements and thus was informed by earlier
policy efforts or informed later ones. The dangers of policy *ad hockery* and
amnesia are particularly acute for discrete policy processes, simply because
what is not connected to the more permanent institutions of public policy
and administration will be more easily lost, forgotten or come adrift.

Adaptability and learning from policy

The notion of adaptability underpinning this study embodies a tension that
has run through policy analysis and planning for decades, and which is also
evident in contemporary sustainability debates. In policy analysis, it is that
between rational-comprehensive approaches to policy analysis and prescription *versus* an incremental or political realist approach (or, synoptic and anti-
synoptic). Characterised simply, the first construes policy making in a mechanistic vein, where rational and 'scientific' models can explain and design
policy choices. The second says that this is not realistic, and that policy is an
incremental and messier process, where improvements are negotiated and
achieved in small steps, in fits and starts. Critics of 'lists' and 'models' such as
Jenkins-Smith and Sabatier (1994) would likely view the checklist given above
as a dreaded 'stages heuristic', but it represents a halfway compromise between
the two extremes – a more purposeful incrementalism. Another manifestation
of the tension is between rational planning theories and approaches and those
termed communicative planning (Sager 1994; Healey 1997; see also Mobbs,
Eckersley, this volume). The former is linear, centralised, expertise-dependent
and oriented toward the end product of a 'policy' or 'plan', whereas the latter
is more discursive, process-oriented and inclusive. Advocates of either
extreme, as all extreme advocates do, both have a point and miss the point. A
mix of 'rationalities' – ecological, communicative, social, economic, political,
scientific, etc – underlie policy choices (Diesing 1962). However the mix that
informs analysis and prescription will need to change according to the relative
strength of different problem attributes (eg, relative uncertainty or urgency).
The search for an appropriate mixture is nowhere more clearly displayed than
in sustainability policy.

One promising approach to NRM issues, adaptive management, was more rationalistic in its early conceptualisation, not surprisingly as it was scientists and natural system managers who developed the approach. But more recent work and practice has moved toward adaptation based not only on science, experimentation and information feedback, but also on institutional change, discourse amongst stakeholders, and societal learning. Adaptiveness as it is used in this study reflects a halfway point between a scientific rationality and a communicative one. Hopefully it can meld the rigours of the scientific method and the indispensable role of science with the contingent realities of policy and politics (Lee 1993; Gunderson et al 1995; Dovers and Mobbs 1997). Adaptive approaches to both analysis and prescription have some promise of properly emphasising both process and product. Recent critical and political theory emphasises more inclusive, discursive and mutually informing ways of doing politics and policy, and such thinking would appear to be congruent in some ways to emerging participatory approaches to environmental policy. But sustainability theory and policy are also driven by the scientific approaches to uncertainty and complexity. Much of what is interesting in recent resource and environmental management – off-reserve biodiversity conservation, integrated catchment management and bioregional planning, landcare, 'beyond regulation' approaches to environmental protection, etc – are superb testing grounds for ideas about discursive approaches to policy as well as meeting grounds for community, science and policy.

Testing grounds are for learning, and the operational use of past experience requires some thought as to the nature of policy learning. Policy learning and evolution are notions central to this study, and it could hardly be contested that we should wish to benefit from policy lessons, whether positive or negative ones. Yet, 'policy learning is a concept that is advocated but not adequately conceptualised' (May 1992: 350). From the experience of policy *ad hockery* and amnesia, it is infrequent in practice. In seeking to draw lessons from decades of policy processes, we need to address the how, why, who and what of policy learning. On how we learn, there is a difference between trial-and-error and the active designing in of learning mechanisms in public policy arrangements. Both are part of the adaptive idea, but are different. Trial-and-error is central to Lindblom's (1959) famous incremental recipe for 'muddling through', will always be important given inevitable uncertainty and surprise, but is insufficient in itself. Policy failure does not automatically yield lessons, just as the presence of books does not guarantee reading. Policy failure may, rather, induce fatigue, denial or concealment. Actively designing in learning raises the question of the institutional arrangements to support the accrual of lessons and communication of these. This invites a focus on institutional and organisational longevity and memory, arrangements designed to enhance information and communication of policy experiences, non-government networks and professional groupings, and in the context of this chapter, the strategies used (or not) to ensure connection between discrete policy processes and what comes before and after them. An heuristic such as the checklist above assists in this regard, especially in emphasising testable policy goals and monitoring and evaluation.

Simple mimicry is a poor form of learning because it may not lead to improved understanding (May 1992). This is important when policy lessons are sought in a relatively new policy field cutting across a variety of sectors, such as ESD/NRM. It is also important in avoiding the unthinking transfer of models or approaches that have proved successful in one NRM context as 'blueprints' to other NRM contexts where variation in key conditions may demand different approaches. With respect to who learns, what they learn and to what effect, Bennett and Howlett (1992) and May (1992) inform the following simple categorisation, first of *what* and to what effect:

- instrumental learning, about program implementation, organisational issues and specific policy instruments;

- process learning, about successful or unsuccessful processes for policy formulation and implementation; and

- strategic or political learning, about the nature of policy and political systems and how they may be influenced.

And, second, of who might learn:

- government officials concerned with program design and implementation;

- policy communities and networks, comprising government and non-government groups and individuals engaged in policy debates; and

- individuals or groups marginal to or outside policy networks and communities.

Combinations of these might be evident in the two cases dealt with here. The issue of learning begs a much larger discussion. The few points raised above do not include important considerations such as using uncertainty and (mis)information as active political strategies (eg, Smithson 1989; Walker 1994). But it will suffice for the current purpose. In particular, the focus on who learns what and to what effect will be revisited at the end of this paper to provide some leverage on the question of what has occurred in the past two decades. We now turn to the two studies of discrete policy processes.

National Conservation Strategy for Australia

The early 1980s saw the first attempt at an integrated grand plan for the environment. Following the global example of the World Conservation Strategy (WCS), Australia developed the National Conservation Strategy for Australia (NCSA) (Australia 1983). The NCSA was seen, internationally, as 'an exemplary response to the World Conservation Strategy' (Selman 1987). The NCSA was initiated by the conservative Fraser Government, but was in the final stages strongly influenced by the consensus approach favoured by the new Labor Prime Minister, Bob Hawke, a style which also underpinned the ESD process he later initiated. It enjoyed bipartisan political support. The core elements of the process were: Commonwealth endorsement of the WCS in 1980; a Commonwealth/State Steering Committee, a Consultative Group comprising industry and environmental interests, and a small taskforce in the Commonwealth Department of Home Affairs and Environment; a national seminar in 1981, its 1982 proceedings, and a discussion paper arising; public comment on the latter document; a 1982 draft strategy; and a final conference in June 1983, which arrived at the final Strategy (see Erskine 1987; Selman 1987; Mercer 1991: 55).

The NCSA consisted of objectives, principles, and priority national requirements and actions. The objectives were the three used in the WCS: to maintain essential ecological processes and life-support systems; to preserve genetic diversity; and to ensure the sustainable utilisation of species and ecosystems. A fourth aim was added, to maintain and enhance environmental qualities (Australia 1983: 13). The principles were, in summary, to: integrate conservation and development; retain options for future use; focus on causes as well as symptoms; accumulate knowledge for future application; and educate the community (Australia 1983: 15-16). Sixty 'priority national actions' covered the areas of education and training; research; legislation and regulation; international aspects; reserves and habitat protection; controlling pollution; wastes and hazardous materials; using living resources; and conserving soils and water. These were not really 'actions', but general and thus contestable statements of intent to act in specific areas.

Nonetheless, the general direction of the NCSA and its recommendations reflected a more integrated approach to the environment. The idea of an overall 'national strategy' was in itself an advance, as was the practice of drafting national environment policy through the involvement of stakeholders (McEachern 1993). Some recommendations reflected new thinking that is now widespread, such as integrated catchment management. The future of the Strategy, though, was the subject of one loosely worded sentence. Unlike the WCS, which was updated and enlarged upon after a decade (IUCN et al 1991), the Australian Strategy was not revisited, and various recommendations for measures to advance and implement the Strategy were not pursued (Erskine 1987). An Interim Committee reported to the federal Minister for the Environment in August 1985 on implementation of the NCSA but little transpired, and it was not until 1988 that broad guidelines for government decision making to support the Strategy were adopted (Emmery 1993). By this time, the Strategy was as good as dead and about to be overtaken by events and new understanding.

One value of the NCSA consensus-summit approach was the debate amongst interest groups traditionally in conflict, but the content of the final document leaned toward lowest common denominator outcomes: vague and acceptable but not operational.[4] Mercer (1991: 54) said of the Strategy that 'no clear timetable for action was outlined and no targets were set. And, of course, most significantly, there was no legislative backing'. Erskine (1987) identified constraints on implementing the Strategy and subsequent State strategies as including poor institutional arrangements, lack of action plans, tactics and time frames, and lack of relevant information for decision makers. Carew-Reid et al (1994) identified a failure to move quickly from broad to specific policy

---

4   Much was made at the time and later of the consensus approach but the author recalls that
     this consensus was endangered at the final drafting conference by deep tensions over issues
     such as proposals by conservation delegates for a widening of legal standing in environmental
     law (for some irony on this, see Bonyhady, this volume).

objectives. The NCSA may have raised awareness, and its influence is still being felt in local conservation strategies, but it can be concluded that it had no great influence on the broad pattern of production and consumption in Australia. The recognition that it is that broad pattern which needs addressing is the hallmark of sustainability, in rhetoric if not in practice. One substantial initiative that flowed from the NCSA was the idea of state of the environment reporting (SoE), based on the premise that an overall picture of environmental condition was essential to better policy. The Commonwealth began a national SoE process in 1984, which produced two reports before being discontinued soon after (eg, Australia, Department of Arts, Heritage and Environment 1987), only to be resurrected, post-ESD, five years later. Another potentially substantive flow-on was a conservation strategy for the Australian Antarctic Territory but, inexplicably and unforgivably, this strategy lapsed after much work, consultation and even a draft document (Wilder and Handmer 1999).

The NCSA was about environmental protection and resource management; a partial response to the global imperative presented by the WCS. By the time the NCSA was 'up and running', the global scene was about to be changed by the WCED's *Our common future* and the new construct of sustainable development. In terms of persistence, the NCSA has little to recommend it as a model. In terms of purposefulness, the principles developed were not particularly clear or operational or accepted. In terms of information-richness, judgment may be unfair, as the process never pretended to do other than consider summary forms of existing knowledge. In terms of inclusiveness, the process was impressive in that the approach of a drafting conference was progressive at the time, and the beginning of a brief era of more open policy formulation. Given the nature of the process, flexibility is probably not a relevant principle. One may view the NCSA as a failed process, or as a necessary, faltering step early in the process of our coming to grips with the modern idea of sustainability. On balance, while a worthwhile first step, it left little of substance behind.

There was, however, an interregnum between the fading of the NCSA and Australia's response to the WCED in 1990. This was filled by a major Prime Ministerial statement – *Our country, our future* – on the environment (Hawke 1989). Prompts for this statement, as well as the WCED report, were electoral imperatives resulting from the increasingly apparent power of environmental groups, perhaps a realisation that further integration was desirable, and, most importantly, an historic alliance between the Australian Conservation Foundation (ACF) and the National Farmers Federation (NFF) on the issue of land degradation (Campbell 1994: 30-31). This was the first such statement on the environment by an Australian prime minister, referred in passing to the WCED, and was the first Australian statement of the goal and principles of 'ecologically sustainable development' (Hawke 1989: 4). But it was not an integrated package, nor was it the product of a recognisable policy development process. Major elements were initiatives on land degradation (based on the ACF-NFF proposals), including the Decade of Landcare, tree planting, water quality, endangered species, climate change, and ozone depleting substances. The print had hardly dried on the 1989 statement before the Australian government found itself having to respond more fully, in 1990, to the WCED's 1987 report.

The ESD process

The ESD process was the most intensive and broad policy process concerning the environment in Australia to date, and has been applauded internationally as an exemplar for national responses to the global sustainable development agenda. The process is well enough described in the literature to simply note its main features and key strengths and weaknesses; detailed analyses are available elsewhere (Hare 1990; Diesendorf and Hamilton 1997; Hamilton and Throsby 1998; Dovers 1999a; Productivity Commission 1999). ESD was Australia's response to the 1987 WCED report, and its preparation for the 1992 UNCED conference. The key elements of the process were:

- a December 1989 meeting between government and stakeholder representatives, which called for a discussion paper;
- a 1990 Commonwealth discussion paper (CoA 1990);
- nine sectoral working groups (NGOs, government, unions, industry) under three chairs (a scientist and two economists);[5]
- nine working group and two chairs' reports (on intersectoral issues and greenhouse) (ESDWG and ESDWG Chairs 1991);
- a draft strategy drawn from these by a federal-State bureaucratic committee;
- a final National Strategy for Ecologically Sustainable Development (NSESD), accepted by the Council of Australian Governments in December 1992 (CoA 1992a).

Completing the 'meta-policy' setting along with the NSESD were a National Greenhouse Response Strategy and the 1992 Intergovernmental Agreement on the Environment (IGAE), the latter seeking to coordinate and better define the role of the different levels of government. The Strategy was also accompanied by a compendium which listed the working group recommendations and the Strategy's adoption, amendment or otherwise of these (CoA 1992b). The intent of the NSESD and related policies are stated in the Strategy as (pp 8-9):

> *Goal*: Development that improves the total quality of life, both now and in the future, in a way that maintains the ecological processes on which life depends.
>
> *Core objectives*: to enhance individual and community well-being and welfare by following a path of economic development that safeguards the welfare of future generation; to provide for equity within and between generations; to protect biological diversity and maintain essential ecological processes and life-support systems.
>
> *Guiding principles*:
>
> - decision making processes should effectively integrate both long and short-term economic, environmental, social and equity dimensions;

---

5   The ESD Working Groups were: agriculture; energy production; energy use; fisheries; forests; manufacturing; mining; tourism, and transport.

- where there are threats of serious or irreversible environmental damage, lack of full scientific certainty should not be used as a reason for postponing measures to prevent environmental degradation (the precautionary principle);

- the global dimension of environmental impacts of actions and policies should be recognised and considered;

- the need to develop a strong, growing and diversified economy which can enhance the capacity for environmental protection should be recognised;

- the need to maintain and enhance international competitiveness in an environmentally sound manner should be recognised;

- cost effective and flexible policy instruments should be adopted, such as improved valuation, pricing and incentive mechanisms;

- decisions and actions should provide for broad community involvement on issues which affect them.

Many other policies can be viewed as coming under the ESD umbrella. Doubtless, some would have been developed without an ESD process, but were strongly influenced by the ESD discourse and the ensuing Strategy. Others were already in train, but were similarly influenced. Many of these explicitly embody ESD principles, and most were formulated in a similar fashion – that is, discrete processes entailing intergovernmental and stakeholder negotiations. Although there is not space to consider these, they should be included in any consideration of the ESD process. At the national level, this set of subsidiary policies includes the National Strategy for the Conservation of Australia's Biological Diversity (see Williams et al 2002), Oceans Policy (Haward, this volume), Commonwealth Wetlands Policy, National Forest Policy Statement (Mobbs, this volume), National Recreational Fishing Policy, National Strategy for Rangeland Management (Stafford Smith and Abel, this volume), and so on. While there is not space here to do so, these bear analyses in their own right.

Strengths and weaknesses of the ESD process

To limit the scope of the discussion, we will note some matters judged to have been missing from or poorly attended in the process, and then deal in a summary fashion with ESD's strengths and weaknesses under the five principles of persistence, purposefulness, information-richness, inclusiveness and flexibility. The background to the judgments and arguments in what follows can be found in the references provided above. In terms of matters not sufficiently covered by the process, it should be said that the 1990-92 time frame was very tight and that there were limits to what could be achieved. For the record, the following have been stated as issues poorly handled:

- the meaning and possible application of ESD principles;
- the relative merits of different policy instruments and the issue of how to choose policy instruments under different conditions;

- prioritisation or at least differentiated problem definition across the suite of issues dealt with (which were defined largely by traditional economic sectors and portfolio divisions);
- local government (regrettably, and as usual);
- indigenous, migrant and gender issues;
- population issues;[6]
- the role and differentiation of economic growth;
- demand (consumption) as opposed to supply (production) perspectives; and
- the household sector (this was advocated as a sector both by social advocates interested in health and welfare and by some economists interested in better analysis of patterns of production and consumption).

Persistence

Persistence has most often been behind criticisms of the ESD process. The bureaucratic process used to draft the Strategy instantly undermined the unprecedented working group process and the remarkable level of consensus supporting their recommendations. Later implementation has fallen below expectations and stakeholder hopes. The working group discourse and the emerging wider debate was stifled, and nothing was put in place to continue the discourse let alone widen it (as the working groups recommended). And no institutional or organisational mechanism to carry forward ESD survives. An Intergovernmental Committee for ESD had the role of reviewing NSESD implementation, reported once to the Council of Australian Governments (COAG)[7], and was disbanded in 1997.

One interesting outcome was the publication of a compendium of working group recommendations and the response of governments to those via the NSESD. This was an admirable move, and a rare one, to construct such a potential petard. Across the five hundred or so recommendations, the translation of the working groups' report to the Strategy was recorded as (terminology from the Compendium, authors' count): 34 per cent 'accepted'; 46 per cent 'accepted in the following manner' (ie, amended); 16 per cent 'under consideration'; and 4 per cent 'not accepted'. Often, it was put that an existing government policy was sufficient, an interpretation often not agreed with by working group members. Unfortunately, given the poverty of review and evaluation mechanisms, less value has accrued from the detail of the

---

6   Population was in fact being handled by a separate investigation by the broadly based (and soon to become defunct) National Population Council, but its report and indeed the whole issue was ignored by the ESD process. See Population Issues Committee 1991; Dovers et al 1992; Dovers 1997b.

7   The nature and role of COAG deserves attention. A rather undemocratic and opaque body, it has had a variable but at time strong influence in the resource and environmental field in the past decade, via ESD policy and especially in the water sector, where as part of National Competition Policy it has driven policy and institutional reform (see Smith, McKay, this volume).

Compendium than might have been the case. The strength and clarity of policy recommendations across the nine sectors varied. In general, fisheries, agriculture, energy use and tourism moved the policy agenda further, in part at least because of previous policy discussions and development of consensus amongst the main interests.[8]

On the positive side, the influence of the ESD process afterwards was affected particularly through uptake and expression of the ESD principles. This is discussed next under purposefulness. Also, the promulgation of related and subsidiary policies served to continue discourse and policy development at least where those were formulated in some inclusive manner, such as national policies on oceans and biodiversity. However, other policies, such as energy and greenhouse, have not been formulated in as participatory a fashion.

Purposefulness

This is where ESD comes out better; the development (or, rather, adaptation from the international sphere) of core goals and principles and the uptake of these. Unlike many of the specific recommendations, the principles survived the few years after 1992. This is not to say that the ESD principles (see above) are well understood, clear, operational or without internal conflict as a set – on the contrary. But they were stated, are useful and had the endorsement of the main policy groups and interests. Almost unnoticed by many commentators, they have been expressed or referred to in hundreds of policies and programs, and now in more than 120 Australian laws as statutory objects (eg, s 3, *Environment Protection and Biodiversity Conservation Act* 1999) (Stein 2000). The clarity of these statutory expressions and their usefulness in instructing decision makers tends to be inadequate, but the pervasiveness of expression is important. A small but growing number of legal judgments explore these principles, especially the precautionary principle. While adversarial courts of law may be viewed as an unfortunate place for informing policy, they are an appropriate venue for reasoned evolution of the more precise, operational meanings that the consultative policy process could not provide. At least judges expose and struggle with the vagueness of principles that in policy discourse may be tolerated as expedient or comforting. Also, regarding purposefulness and persistence, the fact that the Department of Prime Minister and Cabinet was core to the process was significant and positive, if rather unsettling for the departments traditionally dominating resource and environmental policy. This combined well with the use of three independent chairs and their reporting to a Cabinet sub-committee. The irony is that this attention to whole-of-government and cross-sectoral coordination was abandoned afterwards.

Information-richness

Positively, the working group reports were important compendiums and in some cases unprecedented sources of information. This was remarkable given

---

8   In the case of forests, the working group report suffered from the refusal of environmental NGOs to take part (due to other government policy actions at the time) and the concurrent running of the Resource Assessment Commission inquiry (see Hamilton, this volume).

the time constraints. Unfortunately, the working group reports were limited in the production run, not 'sold' as information compilations, and moreover were produced as unnecessarily weighty documents. Further, the process did allow for some information generation where there were particular needs, such as with alternative energy models. The recommendation for state of the environment reporting has taken effect, with five-yearly SoE reports beginning in 1996 and that process being given a statutory basis in 1999.[9] Given the discrete nature of the process, many of the information deficiencies can be forgiven. However, some recommendations arising from ESD and associated strategies have not eventuated, such as a national approach to long term biodiversity monitoring or a national ESD research advisory council.

Inclusiveness

The ESD process was at once innovative and limited in terms of inclusion of stakeholders. The 'community' was mostly engaged via representatives of selected, major interest groups and lobbying organisations – more corporatism than participatory democracy, but a great advance on traditional, tightly controlled green paper-white paper processes. The use of broadly based working groups was a major innovation, and one fundamental to the successes of the process. Funding was made available to key conservation groups to resource their involvement; this was necessary, innovative and set a precedent. An important quality of the process was the inclusion of interests, sectors and portfolios that had not previously had much to do with 'environmental' policy and certainly not with the emerging sustainability debate. These included health, transport, manufacturing, tourism and consumer affairs. This both reflected the nature of the ESD problem set – cross-sectoral and whole-of-government – and enriched the process with information and different perspectives.[10]

However, there were criticisms of the composition of the groups, in that industry or economic oriented government departments and industry groups 'had the numbers'. They did, but whether this biased the membership depends on whether one views departmental officials as captured by their constituent industry or not. Inexplicably, local government was not explicitly represented, nor were Indigenous people. General community input into the process was too limited and too late in the process to be properly effective. Polling in 1993 indicated that community awareness of the process was very low, but the public meetings that were held attracted considerable interest. Although not often commented on, disciplinary or R&D-based expertise was not a criterion for working group membership. Most of the scientists or academics involved were there as Chairs or as community group representatives rather than in their own right. Explanations of this at the time were

---

9   At the first meeting of an SoE advisory committee in 1992, many government officials were surprised to be informed that national state of environment reporting had been tried and abandoned only five years before, and most did not think that learning from the previous experience was an interesting prospect.

10   Significant examples of this were inputs by the National Health and Medical Research Council and the Public Health Association, and the inclusion of Australian Consumer Association representatives in the process.

various: that 'experts' would dominate the discussion; that expert input could be gained in other ways; and that government officials could provide the expertise required. The deepest criticism on inclusiveness was the active failure (not oversight) to continue the discourse between key stakeholders through some ongoing mechanism. With very well defined policy problems, this would not matter so much. But with a complex and novel policy field like sustainability, ongoing discourse is crucial.

Flexibility

This is a difficult principle to apply to *ad hoc* processes. In part, these processes provide for flexibility and ongoing yet adaptable impact through purposefulness, and the ESD process, as noted above, did this reasonably well through the establishment and partial entrenchment of principles. Within the 1989-92 process itself, flexibility was evident in the taking on of intersectoral issues and greenhouse *en route*, the ability and willingness to engage in research as the need arose, and the attention paid to ongoing institutional and R&D needs (although the latter were largely ignored by government in the implementation stage). The adequate resourcing of the process was part reason for this, along with the mandate and authority and ability of the three chairs to adapt the process, and the exploratory nature of the working group discourse.

Beyond these comments regarding the five principles, there is a further and crucial observation. It is arguable that many of the weaknesses identified in the NSESD and its aftermath are explicable given the nature of the problems being addressed. Problem attributes identified earlier – such as novelty, complexity and connectivity, uncertainty and temporal scale – clearly made the task of the ESD process difficult. The ESD processes attempted to squeeze into a constrained process the issue of deep, structural inconsistencies between human and natural systems, and must be viewed as only one step. Weaknesses become understandable deficiencies and potential learning experiences when addressing a new and complex problem.

But not all the weaknesses can be so excused. Two aspects stand out. First, lack of institutional reform falls into this category. The ESD working groups and Chairs offered recommendations on institutionalisation, and reasonable institutional reforms that might have (and still could) be made have been proposed elsewhere (Dovers 1999a; 2001). Such suggestions include: arrangements for R&D;[11] offices of ESD in first ministers' departments; an ESD commissioner, commission or council; policy advisory and development fora; resurrection of the RAC, and so on. Second and more disturbing was the Productivity Commission's (1999) finding that a key problem in implementation was the failure of agencies to adhere to normal standards of policy making. For this there is no excuse emerging from the particular attributes of the problems. Recognising some of the more excusable

---

11   The advent of the R&D corporations from 1989 is important but not covered here (see Lovett 1997). In many ways, the Land & Water Resources Research and Development Corporation, now Land & Water Australia, became the *de facto* ESD R&D corporation, but with a mandate limited to rural lands. This is laudable, but highlights the lack of broader ESD arrangements.

reasons for tardy implementation, the PC's Presiding Commissioner put it thus (Byron 1999: 2-3):

> The Commission also found that progress had been poor largely due to a failure to adopt existing (and accepted) 'good practice' policy making processes and that, in fact, good practice policy making and promotion of sustainable development are synonymous.

What Byron then outlines as the essentials of good practice is not dissimilar to what introductory policy texts tell first year students, what sound public administration should be about, and what the checklist of policy process elements provided above suggests (ie, start with problem definition and end with monitoring, evaluation and feedback). This is elementary policy failure. Why would ESD have not been subject to normal public administration standards? Were the institutional arrangements and organisational capacities simply insufficient? Or was ESD subject to a more 'active' campaign of inactivity? Implementation by non-core (ie, outside environment and resources) portfolios was a particular problem.[12] Were the core portfolios so weak, or too divided and adversarial, and unable to drive whole-of-government policy change? Did ESD not have enough support? Certainly parts of the bureaucracy have been portrayed as having undermined the process, both during the discourse and in watering down the strategy (this charge was laid not only by green groups but also professional and some industry groups). And the Hawke-Keating prime ministerial change did not help. But such fundamental implementation failure is not explained only by this.

All these questions aside, the real test of a 'meta-policy' as broad as ESD lies in the transfer of its intent through subsidiary policies. It is through these that avowals of intent and general principles can be made operational. The mass of associated and subsequent policy development is, on the face of it, impressive, although the implementation story varies.

Discussion

To bring this chapter to a conclusion, we can consider some of the questions raised in the introductory sections, and revisit the principles in a broader sense. Who has learned what? What have governments learned? Many individual officials have learned a good deal, and the ESD/NRM field is now more networked. But it still remains fragmented and incoherent as a policy field; across sectors, jurisdictions, disciplines and professions. Consideration of specific instruments and approaches have advanced, but are still very far from broad agreement and trustworthy models (eg, design of community-based programs, use of market mechanisms, regulatory compliance). Recent changes to the public sector (downsizing, managerialism, mobility) mean that lack of institutional memory and technical expertise is more and more a problem. Governments more broadly seem to not have settled on a coherent basis for when to use particular styles of policy formulation, and even seem

---

12 The famous and not apocryphal statement in 1994 by a senior officer from one such portfolio: 'ESD? We've done that.'

distinctly bipolar when it comes to controlled versus participatory policy processes. So, in terms of how to run discrete processes, many lessons or at least many experiences from which they could be drawn are there, but we do not appear to avail ourselves of them. In most cases, processes are invented as if for the first time.

Outside of government, non-government policy actors (environmentalists, farmers, industry) have in the past 20 years become much more sophisticated in their participation in and use of discrete processes. This applies both in their role in having such processes established and funded and their role within them. This is healthy for an inclusive, adaptive approach to policy, even if some in government may regret opening the door and creating expectations of both access and resources. Sometimes, the cynicism of government officials is understandable. Too often, non-government policy actors retain the option of leaving a consensus process if it fails to deliver their preferred outcome and return to conventional bargaining and lobbying. Are they unreasonable and expedient, or are the processes poor and thus the governments who construct them to blame?

Turning to the scientific community, Noble (1994) documents the travails of scientists engaging in policy processes, from his experience in the ESD process and with the RAC forests inquiry. He considers the challenges of scientists thus engaged being faced with the realities of a extended peer community, and the poor performance of scientists generally in communicating their knowledge in an ever more crowded market place of ideas, opinions, data and demands. Scientists are still learning to master the challenge of engagement with policy processes. But science, in the form of 'epistemic communities', can at times have considerable influence (Haas 1992; Walker 2001).

And to what effect have we learned? There are two aspects to this. First, at a more specific level, there has been much policy change and program implementation arising from the ESD process. Much of the judgment as to the efficacy of subsequent or subsidiary policy must wait, as it is still early days – positive change in the environment or human use of it is rare so far, but may come. There are strengths and weaknesses evident in the design and implementation thus far of many policies. For example, biodiversity and land degradation have been better attended (through legislative reform and a plethora of programs respectively) than, say, energy and greenhouse. Given the much more 'systemic' nature of energy issues (Dovers 1994), this is not surprising. In one sector, water, profound change has been driven not by ESD considerations but more by an economic rationality embodied in national competition policy (Dovers and Gullett 1999; Smith, McKay, this volume). Against this can be held the criticisms of the ESD process: watering down of the working group recommendations, implementation failure, and resistance to proper institutionalisation. The RFA case analysed by Mobbs (this volume) shows positives and negatives of the more detailed design and implementation of ESD-inspired sectoral policy, the gains that can be made, the difficulties still encountered in participatory modes of interaction between players, and the sheer effort and expense required. Haward (this volume) portrays an encouraging beginning with oceans policy. Little arose from the NCSA, due to vagueness and implementation failure.

Second, how well did the two processes connect to the broader, ongoing policy setting discussed and characterised earlier in this chapter? This requires that we step back from the particulars of such connections, to attempt a longer term understanding of the evolution of sustainability policy. The 'typology' of learning sketched earlier and structuring the preceding discussion may invite consideration only of separately defined policy actors learning about separately defined aspects of policy. While necessary and certainly very useful, such scattered learning may not even equal the sum of its parts. Ideally, the different players (governments, officials, stakeholders) will learn about things (program design, instruments, processes, social goals) in a mutually informing fashion – that is, together, at the same time, and over time. This leads us back to the nature of sustainability policy in the broader sense regarding a range of issues and longer time frames as policy and under-standing co-evolve. The five principles give us some purchase on this, and we can conclude by summarising what seem to be key points and lessons arising.

Persistence. It is apparent that 'proofing' processes against changes of government (or of Minister) is necessary, while still respecting the rights of new governments to pursue policy change. The most obvious strategy here, although one not guaranteed of success, is to develop bipartisan political and wide stakeholder support for initiatives. Also, institutionalisation beyond the rather ephemeral status of 'policy initiative' is desirable if the policy agenda is one expected to be around for a while. This will require political will and a generosity of spirit, and not just on the part of governments. The role of statute law in providing a mandate, driving improvement through expectation of repeat efforts, guaranteeing participation and ensuring transparency is crucial in this regard, but too little recognised (Dovers 1999b; Bonyhady, this volume). In terms of implementation, persistence would be helped by clear allocation of responsibility, mandated and properly resourced reviews set in place early on, and, in the Productivity Commission's words, plain 'good policy practice'. The three broad dimensions of persistence – administrative (implementation), institutional (process oriented) and discursive (maintaining inclusion) – require considerably more attention than given here.

Purposefulness. Underpinning policy with principles that both appeal to the majority of stakeholders and are operational is both difficult and supremely important. Clear recognition of the potential of agreed principles to ease future conflicts is required. So is the need to recognise that principles such as those generated by the ESD process will attract ongoing debate and redefinition – desires to turn off discussion of such central notions as inter-generational equity and precaution like a tap should be resisted. The ability of principles to be expressed in a manner enabling application and later evaluation is in tension with the need to be succinct and the convenience of gaining consensus through vagueness. The equivalence in precision and thus parity in policy development and implementation between (broadly) ecolo-gical, social and economic imperative needs consideration – those goals quantitatively expressed will usually be advantaged in policy debates over those that are not (eg, the JANIS criteria discussed by Mobbs, this volume).

Information-richness. Discrete processes have limited ability to generate new information, except where this is an express purpose. However, even compilations of existing information from often inaccessible sources are valuable. Recognising this and planning communication pathways accordingly and from the outset is advisable (eg. the ESD working group reports).

Inclusiveness. The two cases show the value and the pitfalls of more participatory processes. Participation of course must be genuine, both at the outset and later. If governments engage people, then they should be willing to accord validity to community views and be open to these views having an impact. It is essential that the purpose of participation is well defined, that extra time and resources are provided, and appropriate fora for dialogue established (eg, with a range of value systems and expertise present and rules to facilitate bounded debate). Appreciating the purpose of participation requires a political and bureaucratic literacy on the part of all concerned – a consultative forum must understand that, for example, the Minister is the legal entity who makes the decision, and the Minister should not pretend otherwise. And if there is a need for ongoing discourse, this should be catered for in the spirit of mutually informing adaptiveness. Deciding when to begin or cease participation, to change the nature of it or institutionalise it in the long term is something we seem not well skilled at.[13]

Flexibility. Flexibility within discrete processes is important, but the scope is by definition limited. Flexibility within a process can be enhanced by sufficient time and resources, and by a mandate to adapt the process (eg. objectives and the array of acceptable solutions may need revision) and to seek new information along the way. More significant is that discrete processes are themselves a flexibility mechanism in public policy, allowing the handling of the new, reconstructed or unexpected. This requires accepting *ad hoc* processes as necessarily near term political strategies, but also as part of the ongoing, adaptive endeavour. The core issues are the connections with previous initiatives and with later policy development. For the first, explicit instruction to examine previous policy processes, inquiries, information sources, etc should yield benefits. For the second, policy implementation and institutionalisation appeal – that is, allocating implementation and review explicitly to extant agencies, and/or creating new organisational and institutional arrangements if existing mechanisms are unsuitable. More structured attention to the art and craft of discrete processes as public policy mechanism is needed, even to the extent of promulgating standards or best practice models (eg. building on Byrne and Davis 1998).

Last of all, is there evidence that our evolving policy capacities have been informed by particular attributes of policy problems in sustainability? Have we adapted policy processes to these unusual demands? The very existence of the two cases dealt with here, and many others, shows at least a grappling with some of these attributes.

Generally, the increased advocacy and somewhat lesser application of market mechanisms may show appreciation of systemic causes. Alternatively it

---

13   A discussion of the many kinds and purposes of participation, and the crucial issue of political
      trust, is given in Dovers (2000). See also Mobbs, Curtis, Ewing, Orchard, et al and Eckersley,
      this volume.

may simply be a side effect of a fixation with economic rationality (Dovers and Gullet 1999). Participatory approaches have increased massively at the program level (EverythingCare and EverythingWatch), and in more formal policy and management arrangements in the States (eg, Victoria's Catchment Management Authorities, vegetation committees in various jurisdictions, NSW's Environmental Education Council and Resource and Conservation Assessment Council). Yet there has been evidence of moving away from the (corporatist) participatory model of broad policy formulation at the Common-wealth level, and a tendency to remove independence and even participation from statutory agencies (eg. demise of the Resource Assessment Commission and the Bureau of Immigration, Population and Multicultural Research, regrettable changes to Victoria's Land Conservation Council, partial depart-mentalisation of the Great Barrier Reef Marine Park Authority). The loss of the brief intersectoral focus achieved in the ESD process does not bode well for dealing with cross-problem connections. And the failure to properly institutionalise ESD as a significant policy field embodies two discouraging messages: longer term imperatives and ongoing uncertainty have not been adequately catered for, and ESD is still a marginal player in the game of public policy and administration. The signs are mixed.

References

Australia, Department of Arts, Heritage and Environment, 1987, *State of the environment in Australia 1986*, Canberra: AGPS.

Australia, Department of Home Affairs and Environment,1983, *National Conservation Strategy for Australia*, Canberra: AGPS.

Bennett, CJ and Howlett, M, 1992, The lessons of learning: reconciling theories of policy learning and policy change, *Policy Sciences* 25: 275-294.

Boulding, K, 1966, 'The economics of the coming spaceship earth' in: Jarratt, H (ed), *Environmental quality in a growing economy*, Baltimore: Johns Hopkins University Press.

Byrne, J and Davis, G, 1998, *Participation and the NSW policy process*, Sydney: Cabinet Office, New South Wales.

Byron, N 1999, Economic and environmental policies: grapple or embrace? *Proceedings, 18th National Environmental Law Association Conference*, 8-10 September, Sydney.

Campbell, A, 1994, *Landcare: communities shaping the land and the future*, Sydney: Allen and Unwin.

Carew-Reid, J, Prescott-Allen, R, Bass, S and Dalal-Clayton, B, 1994, *Strategies for national sustainable development: a handbook for their planning and implementation*, London: Earthscan.

CoA (Commonwealth of Australia), 1990, *Ecologically sustainable development: a Commonwealth discussion paper*, Canberra: AGPS.

CoA (Commonwealth of Australia), 1992a, National strategy for ecologically sustainable development, Canberra: AGPS.

CoA (Commonwealth of Australia), 1992b, *Compendium of ecologically sustainable development recommendations*, Canberra: AGPS.

CoA (Commonwealth of Australia), 1992c, *National forest policy statement: a new focus for Australia's forests*, Canberra: AGPS.

CoA (Commonwealth of Australia), 1996, *National strategy for the conservation of Australia's biological diversity*, Canberra: AGPS.

Considine, M, 1994, *Public policy: a critical approach* Melbourne: Macmillan.

Davis, G, 1993, Introduction: public policy in the 1990s, in: Hede, A and Prasser, S (eds), *Policy-making in volatile times*, Sydney: Hale and Iremonger.

Davis, G, Wanna, J, Warhurst, J and Weller, P, 1993, *Public policy in Australia*, Sydney: Allen and Unwin.

Diesing, P, 1962, *Reason and society*, Urbana: University of Illinois Press.

Dovers, S, 1994, Introduction: the issue of energy, in Dovers, S (ed), *Sustainable energy systems*, Melbourne: Cambridge University Press.

Dovers, S, 1995, Information, sustainability and policy, *Australian Journal of Environmental Management* 2: 142-156.

Dovers, S, 1997a, Sustainability: demands on policy, *Journal of Public Policy* 16: 303-318.

Dovers, S, 1997b, Dimensions of the Australian population-environment debate, *Development Bulletin*: 41: 50-53.

Dovers, S, 1999a, Institutionalising ecologically sustainable development: problems, promises and prospects, in Walker, K and Crowley, K (eds), *Australian environmental policy 2: studies in decline and devolution*, Sydney: University of NSW Press.

Dovers, S, 1999b, 'Adaptive policy, institutions and management: challenges for lawyers and others', *Griffith Law Review* 81: 374-393

Dovers, S, 2000, 'Beyond EverythingCare and EverythingWatch: public policy, public participation and participating publics', *Proceedings, International Landcare 2000 Conference*, Melbourne, 2-5 March 2000, Melbourne: Department of Natural Resources and Environment.

Dovers, S, 2001, *Institutions for sustainability*, Tela paper 7, Melbourne: Australian Conservation Foundation.

Dovers, S and Gullett, W, 1999, Policy choice for sustainability: marketisation, law and institutions, in Bosselmann, K and Richardson, B (eds), *Environmental justice and market mechanisms*, London: Kluwer Law International.

Dovers, S and Mobbs, C, 1997, An alluring prospect? Ecology, and the requirements of adaptive management, in Klomp, N and Lunt, I (eds), *Frontiers in ecology: building the links*, London: Elsevier.

Dovers, S, Norton, T, Hughes, I and Day, L, 1992, *Population growth and Australian regional environments*, Canberra: AGPS.

Emmery, M, 1993, *Ecologically sustainable development processes in Australia 1990-1992*, Background paper 3/93, Canberra: Parliamentary Research Service.

Erskine, JM, 1987, *Integration of conservation and development: towards implementing the national conservation strategy for Australia*, Working paper 1987/19, Canberra: Centre for Resource and Environmental Studies, Australian National University, Canberra.

ESD Working Groups, 1991, *Final reports*, 9 vols, Canberra: AGPS.

ESD Working Group Chairs, 1991a, *Intersectoral issues report*, AGPS, Canberra.

ESD Working Group Chairs, 1991b, *Greenhouse report*, AGPS Canberra.

Gunderson, L, Holling, CS and Light, SS, 1995, *Barriers and bridges to the renewal of ecosystems and institutions*, New York: Columbia University Press.

Haas, P, 1992, Obtaining international protection through epistemic consensus, in Rowlands, IH and Greene, M (eds). *Global environmental change and international relations*, Basingstoke: Macmillan.

Hare, WL (ed), 1991, *Ecologically sustainable development: assessment of the ESD working group reports*, Melbourne: Australian Conservation Foundation.

Hawke, RJL, 1989, *Our country, our future. Statement on the environment, The Hon RJL Hawke, Prime Minister of Australia, July 1989*, Canberra: AGPS.

Healey, P 1997, *Collaborative planning: shaping places in fragmented societies*. Basingstoke: Macmillan.

Hilborn, R and Mangel, M 1997, *The ecological detective: confronting models with data*. Princeton: Princeton University Press.

Howlett, M and Ramesh, M 1995, *Studying public policy: policy cycles and policy subsystems*, Oxford: Oxford University Press.

Hutton, D and Connors, L 1999, *A history of the Australian environment movement*, Melbourne: Cambridge University Press.

IUCN (International Union for the Conservation of Nature and Natural Resources). 1991, *Caring for the earth: a strategy for sustainable living*, Gland: IUCN.

Jenkins-Smith, HC and Sabatier, PA 1994, Evaluating the advocacy coalition framework. *Journal of Public Policy*, 14: 175-203.

Lee, KN 1993, *Compass and gyroscope: integrating science and politics for the environment*, Washington DC: Island Press.

Lindblom, CE 1959, The science of muddling through. *Public Administration Review*, 19: 79-88.

Lovett, S 1997, *Revitalising rural research and development in Australia ... the story so far*, Canberra: Land & Water Resources R&D Corporation.

May, P, 1992, Policy learning and policy failure, *Journal of Public Policy* 12: 331-354.

Meadows, DH, Meadows, DL, Randers, J and Behrens, WW, 1972, *The limits to growth*, New York: Universal Books.

Mercer, D, 1991, *A question of balance: natural resources conflict issues in Australia*, Sydney: Federation Press.

McEachern, D, 1993, Environmental policy in Australia 1981-1991: a form of corporatism? *Australian Journal of Public Administration* 52: 173-186.

Noble, I, 1994, Science, bureaucracy, politics and ecologically sustainable development, in Norton, T and Dovers, S (eds), *Ecology and sustainability of southern temperate ecosystems*, Melbourne: CSIRO.

Population Issues Committee, National Population Council, 1991, *Population issues and Australia's future: environment, economy and society*, Canberra: AGPS.

Productivity Commission, 1999, *Implementation of ecologically sustainable development by Commonwealth departments and agencies*, Canberra: AusInfo.

Stein, Justice P, 2000, Are decision-makers too cautious with the precautionary principle? *Environmental and Planning Law Journal* 17: 3-23.

Sager, T, 1994, *Communicative planning theory*, Aldershot: Ashgate.

Selman, P, 1987, *Implementation of the national conservation strategy for Australia*, Working paper 1987/13, Canberra: Centre for Resource and Environmental Studies, Australian National University.

Smithson, M, 1989, *Ignorance and uncertainty: emerging paradigms*, New York: Springer-Verlag.

Walker, KJ, 1994, *The political economy of environmental policy*, UNSW Press, Sydney.

Walker, KJ, 2001, 'Uncertainty, epistemic communities and public policy' in: Handmer, J, Norton, T and Dovers, S (eds), *Ecology, uncertainty and policy: managing ecosystems for sustainability*, Prentice-Hall, Harlow.

Wilder, M and Handmer, J, 'The fate of Australia's Antarctic conservation strategy', (1999) 6 *Australian Journal of Environmental Management* 177.

Williams, J, Read, C, Norton, T, Dovers, S, Burgman, M, Proctor, W and Anderson, H, 2002, *Biodiversity: State of Environment 2001: Theme report*, Melbourne: CSIRO Publishing.

World Commission on Environment and Development, 1987, *Our common future*, Oxford: Oxford University Press.

8

Sustainable Regional Development: Lessons from Australian Efforts

John Dore, The Australian National University, Canberra
Jim Woodhill, International Agriculture Centre, Wageningen, The Netherlands
Kate Andrews, Greening Australia, Canberra
Colma Keating, Dinkum Results, Perth

This chapter explores Australian regional organisations (ROs) and processes, particularly efforts to better manage Australia's natural resources and wider environment within a framework of sustainable development. For our purposes we have adopted the umbrella term of sustainable regional development (SRD) ensuring a range of relevant institutions and initiatives are considered. By SRD we simply mean ecologically sustainable development (ESD) principles applied at the regional scale and by SRD initiatives we mean processes working to improve outcomes for the regional community, economy and environment, in an integrated way.[1] Our discussion draws upon the learning from numerous efforts in all Australian States and Territories which, depending upon their origin, may at different times be tagged as: regional or sub-regional natural resources management (NRM); integrated NRM; integrated catchment management; regional development; regional economic development; regional resource use planning; or 'regional governance' or SRD.

We commence with an exploration of context. Brief reference is made to important global and Australian trends, often forgotten in the hurly burly of domestic politicking. Likewise reference to the recent Australian past is often omitted. This is addressed by considering the Australian history of 'regional development' policies between 1950-2000, noting the different philosophical perspectives that have driven successive initiatives. It serves as a reminder that current regional tensions relating to Australia's federal system of government, far from being completely new, are in many cases modern versions of older stories.

---

1   This chapter draws on lessons learnt during a study of Australian regional initiatives between 1997-2000, which produced various reports and a resource kit on Sustainable Regional Development (see references). This study, involving many people, was undertaken by Greening Australia, supervised by Environment Australia and funded by the Commonwealth Department of Transport and Regional Services.

Figure 8.1 Sustainable Regional Development (SRD)

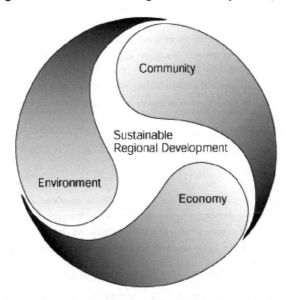

To illustrate the breadth of SRD efforts around Australia, a range of initiatives are introduced. Some of the initiatives are briefly commented upon to give an indication of the types of issues which arise in implementation. An SRD effort focused upon the Lake Eyre Basin receives particular attention.

We have then attempted to distill (at least some of) the lessons from the large number of regional experiments being undertaken around Australia which relate to principles, process, analytical themes and critical issues. A comprehensive set of underpinning principles for SRD initiatives are proposed. An SRD process model is presented for consideration. A checklist of desirable characteristics for these processes is also introduced. A recent review of SRD initiatives undertaken by the authors identified a series of standout themes and critical issues for SRD. It seems obvious that if Australia is to maintain the present, huge community effort to address sustainability issues at the regional scale, or to aid this effort to capture its full potential, there is an urgent need to address these issues. The chapter concludes with some particular recommendations for policymakers interested in learning from the present and the past.

Context

Decisions about the future shape of regional approaches to development in Australia are not removed from the bigger picture of global and national change. As society changes, so too do our institutions, whether leading or following. It is useful to remind ourselves of the larger context, within which we are operating. Following is an opinion of noticeable trends influencing the shape of our own nation.

Table 8.1. Global and Australian trends

Global trends:

Increasing extent of globalisation (impacting on economic sovereignty of nations?)

Rise of capitalist democracies and neo-liberalism (although unfettered neo-liberalism is being widely challenged)

Increasing degrees of human-created risk (eg, mega-cities, war, climate change)

Declining relevance of traditional political structures and ideologies (Left, Right → Third Way?)

Emerging focus on civil society, social capital and democratic participation

Emerging focus on sustainable development (particularly in 'developed' countries)

Australian trends:

Corporatisation and privatisation of government service provision and utilities (though not necessarily a shrinking of the public sector)

Public and private sector out-sourcing of services (reduction in 'non-core' functions)

Exploration of cost-sharing using concepts of: market failure, beneficiary pays, public vs private good

Commonwealth/State/Territory government agency reform

Local government reform and increasingly a transfer to them of new responsibilities

Increased *community participation* and *stakeholder consultation* (both loaded terms!)

Formation of regional organisations (ROs) (whether 'regionalisation' or 'regionalism' can be debated!)

It is an increasingly obvious trend in Australia for 'stakeholders' and the wider community to be increasingly involved in policy formulation and implementation. This reflects a devolutionary trend by governments increasingly wishing to persuade communities and business to undertake, mostly on a voluntary basis, tasks previously seen as the responsibility of government via the public sector. However, it also reflects a genuinely recognised need for substantial, or at least sufficient, consensus and support by key stakeholder groups for government policy to be accepted and implemented within our federal system of government, and more broadly in our Australian systems of governance.

Regional governance is now well and truly on the agenda of Australia's governments and civil society. By this we mean the aggregate of the many ways individuals, organisations and institutions – public and private – manage (or attempt to manage) affairs of wide interest to society. This includes both *formal* institutions empowered (to a greater or lesser extent) to make decisions, plan and implement strategies, enforce compliance; and *informal* arrangements that people and institutions either have agreed to or perceive to be in their common interest. This chapter focuses on the formal regional institutions and associated organisations and processes.

But just what is a region anyway? Regions are often described as being 'communities of common interest', and despite the differences in where the lines may be drawn on maps, many regions have a broadly understood 'fuzzy' border within which people identify with the Pilbara, or the Eyre Peninsula, or the Mallee, or the Riverina etc ... All parts of Australia are in one or other region – both metropolitan and rural. Also, due to various types of 'common interest' some places can legitimately claim to be in more than one region. For our purposes, a suitably broad definition is required, such as '... a sizeable division of territory separated from other areas by a mixture of tangible characteristics which simultaneously sets it apart from neighbouring areas and declares a degree of commonality, or shared identity, among the physical features and/or the inhabitants of that division.' (Powell 1993).

Table 8.2. Different ways regions have been defined

Aggregations of Local government units

Administrative/electoral divisions of an individual State/Territory

Administrative/electoral divisions of the Commonwealth

Statistical districts

Areas with common industrial or economic linkages

Areas with common social or ethnic linkages

Areas separated by clear physical borders such as rivers or roads

Agro-ecological areas differentiated on the basis of their agriculture potential

Areas able to be distinguished on the basis of biotypes, such as dominant native vegetation

Aggregations of natural resource units, such as water catchments

Two regional concepts are of particular importance. Firstly, *regionalism* which we use as referring to regional communities having greater influence over and participating more directly in the decision making that impacts on their region and their futures; the phenomena of increased attention to the regional scale and consequent regional initiatives, and the aforementioned trend of increased participation and consultation, often resulting in partnerships between the community, industry and government. Secondly, *regionalisation* which is a quite different concept referring to the process of government or industry creating administrative regions for more efficient program management, with powers devolved to a greater or lesser extent, from central administration to regional managers (Campbell 1996). Many of the ways in which regions have been 'operationalised' have been to serve some regionalisation purpose. However, the SRD initiatives with which this paper is principally concerned, while perhaps having origins rooted in regionalisation, are essentially characterised by a close connection with regionalism.

At this point it may be useful to reflect on three points in relation to Australia's regional experiences. First, it is plain that 'regional planning' as SRD approaches are often and (hopefully) narrowly described is anything but a new concept. There had been sufficient activity by 1949 for the Commonwealth Department of Post-War Reconstruction, in conjunction with the State departments responsible for regional planning in each State, to produce a document charting the 'history of progress' in regional planning throughout the nation (Commonwealth Department of Post-War Reconstruction 1949). In 1943:

the Prime Minister drew the attention of the Premiers to a marked tendency for local authorities to associate themselves in regional organisations in order to advance proposals for the development of their regions, and expressed the view that regional organisations might be found very useful after the war in advising State and Commonwealth governments regarding the effective development of resources in particular areas, the coordination of administrative services at the local level and outstanding regional problems which would need the attention of the State and Commonwealth authorities.

The same report confirmed that consideration of the environmental dimension is not new by recording the realisation that 'each region presents its own problems and difficulties which are directly related to the particular natural resources and the economic and social structure within the region'. Despite 50 years of stop-start effort, we are still battling with trying to get it right. For example, early guidelines for the Natural Heritage Trust – the high-profile Commonwealth-State NRM funding vehicle introduced by the Howard Government in the late 1990s – called for Regional Management Plans to be a central feature. Even at the beginning it was acknowledged that it could take several years to achieve generally high standard strategic NRM planning and investment (Commonwealth of Australia 1996). They were right. And so, what happened in between 1943-1996, what has happened since, and what are some ideas about what should be happening? In seeking examples of the various government policies which have prevailed, we shall restrict ourselves to a discussion of Commonwealth government policies. In so doing, we acknowledge this limits the inquiry, and we also recognise that there have been many State, Territory and local government regional policies which are also worthy of investigating.

The regional policy of the Commonwealth government, and the nature of the varying policy advice which has been provided to it, during the period from the 1940s until now is much more easily interpreted if the underpinning conceptualising of regions is briefly considered. At different times regions have been considered as some varying combination of: the aforementioned administrative subsets of the nation; willingly coalescing combinations of local communities; inherently disadvantaged places; individually less important than the nation; each a cherished unique component of Australia; and finally, non-metropolitan places. These different conceptions have had a substantial influence on the shape of national policy.

The Australian experience during World War II demonstrated clearly to the Commonwealth that regional government service delivery was required to meet strategic and defence needs effectively. There was a genuine perceived need for *regionalisation*, and a recognition of the tendency for *regionalism*. Consequently the Commonwealth energised a formal meeting process with the States designed to delineate regions, survey resources, aggregate resource information, encourage planning for conservation and natural resources management on a regional scale, and decentralise regional planning, while ensuring that it related to State and national plans. To a large extent, these were rational regional planning efforts, indicative of the era. Nevertheless, the immediately apparent problems identified in 1949 resonate strongly with similar complaints 50 years later, these being the likelihood of: conflict between Commonwealth and/or State initiated regional organisations (ROs) and local government; conflict between the Commonwealth and the States, particularly if the Commonwealth was desirous of a direct relationship between itself and ROs; difficulties in defining and aligning 'development and decentralisation boundaries' with existing administrative boundaries; and finding a middle path between aggregating resource surveys useful for national objectives, and still having them at a scale useful to regions.

The few years of effort by the Curtin-Chifley Labor Commonwealth governments to coordinate and foster a national grid of regions, primarily to foster *economic development*, appears to have been politely tolerated by the States, but rapidly disappeared off the agenda through the 1950s and 1960s with the advent of Liberal/Country party government. Returning to the regional concepts discussion, it should be noted that lack of interest in regional planning in no way equated to lack of interest in rural Australia. During this period, regional planning was an entirely separate concept from supporting rural areas. A mid 1990s resurgence of Commonwealth intervention in regional economic development – but called regional development – by the Keating government resulted in a new Regional Development Program, to be delivered via new ROs that were created or transformed into Commonwealth-approved Regional Economic Development Organisations (REDOs). Support for the REDOs was withdrawn by the incoming Howard government in 1996, however various other forms of Commonwealth support for regional economic development continued.

During the 1970s, Commonwealth regional policy effectively equated to policy for either 'disadvantaged areas' or decentralisation. This revival is now historically associated with the New Cities Program and the Area Assistance Program of the Whitlam government. Prominent in implementation was to be the Department of Urban Affairs and Regional Development, cynically described as being 'a byword for grandiose ideas and wasted expenditure' (Sorenson 1994). However, others have reviewed this episode more favourably, recognising that it displayed a strong *social equity* ethic (Gibson-Graham 1994).[2] A more restrained version of this policy remained under the Fraser government in the form of the Decentralisation Advisory Board, which administered the Commonwealth Decentralised Development Program (DDP), created in 1977[3]. More recent regional approaches with an underpinning social justice paradigm include the regionalised delivery of Commonwealth health, housing and other community services. In addition, there is a strong social theme evident in the formation of the Aboriginal and Torres Strait

---

2   Sorenson (1994) also has sympathy for the underpinning social ethical dimension but argues, not against this, but rather that 'place-specific policies' usually fail and that the Commonwealth government 'should not try and pick winners' but rather focus on macroeconomic policy settings, leaving the rest to the market. Such a view would appear to closely parallel that of the Howard government in the late 1990s.

3   The DDP was very soon rebadged as the Commonwealth Regional Development Program which had a short life prior to being wound up in 1981 with the usual explanation by the Decentralisation Advisory Board (1981), that 'regional development is more properly a matter for State governments'.

Islander Commission (ATSIC), its constituent regional councils, and regional agreements attempting to reconcile the wishes of Aboriginal traditional owners with other forces interested in resource use and development.

In addition to the 'economic' and 'social', there have increasingly been national approaches to regional management of 'the environment'. It has been rightly pointed out that 'all three themes developed independently of one another, despite the interdependence of economic, social and environmental aspects of regional development' (Dale and Bellamy 1998).[4] Regional initiatives focused on the conservation and/or protection of environmental treasures – or assets, depending on your outlook – have also been increasingly prominent. Most recently there has been an enormous spate of regionalisation around Australia creating and jiggling with institutions focused on natural resources management (NRM). These regional NRM institutions are just one 'type' of RO, of the many which have been established for various purposes.

In summary, within Australia a large array of ROs have survived, emerged or evolved to assist in the guiding, planning and activities associated with the ongoing processes of regional planning, development and management. Some of these organisations are simple examples of administrative regionalisation, while many are recently emerged examples of regionalism. These ROs have been sponsored or encouraged by all three spheres of government, as well as by local and regional communities.

Table 8.3. Examples of Regional Organisations (ROs)

Commonwealth and/or State/Territory and/or local government–supported regional development boards. These have different names, structures and funding in various States/Territories and have usually had an economic focus. For example: WA Regional Development Commissions (State), SA Regional Development Boards (State/local).

Regional natural resources management organisations which again have different names, structures and funding in various States/Territories. For example, SA Catchment Water Management Boards, Vic Catchment Management Authorities, NSW Catchment Management Trusts and Catchment Management Committees.

Regional coalitions of local governments, some types of which have adopted the title 'Voluntary Regional Organisations of Councils'. However, there are many forms of coalition, some of which are, in essence, economic development organisations or environmental management groups.

Regional employment and training organisations, such as the Commonwealth-funded Area Consultative Committees.

Organisations with a mandate to assist Aboriginal and Torres Strait Islander people, such as the ATSIC Regional Councils and Land Councils.

Hybrids of the previously mentioned organisations, or new organisations with a specific focus on multi-dimensional 'sustainable regional development'. For example, Cape York Regional Advisory Group (Qld), Lake Eyre Basin Coordinating Group (Qld/NT/SA/NSW), Team*West* Steering Group (NSW).

---

4   This CSIRO work identified important issues and learnings to aid in the design of regional resource planning for Australia's rangelands.

SRD initiatives

Regionalism, often with strong catalytic support from various parts of government, has also spawned a huge range of difficult-to-classify institutions confronting, as best they can, the challenges of putting sustainable development principles into action. We call these SRD hybrids. Within this group there is huge diversity of approach, organisation structure, powers and resources. These hybrids have provided institutional support for initiatives such as: Northern Rivers Framework for a Sustainable Future and TeamWest in Greater Western Sydney (Toomey 1997; Gooding 1999). Many of these recent and ongoing Australian regional activities go at least some way towards qualifying as SRD initiatives: that is, they have an explicit or evolving focus on sustainability at the regional scale. Collectively, they represent a huge public, private, community and government investment in a sustainability quest where the stakes are obviously high. SRD initiatives are potentially very important vehicles for enabling Australia's regions to improve their futures. Each of them has made a substantial contribution to regional human and environmental wellbeing, but participants in all would acknowledge they have been far from perfect.

An SRD initiative generally has a set of particular characteristics. Firstly, it is associated with an identifiable region with some common economic, environmental and social characteristics with which the 'regional community' can identify – although the physical regional boundaries may be quite loosely defined. Next, it involves some coalition of regional stakeholders who have concerns about current environmental, economic and social circumstance, some vision for a preferred future and the motivation to invest in the sustainable development of their region. There are also usually relationships with some combination of local, State/Territory and Commonwealth governments that provide a mixture of funding, government agency expertise and support, institutional legitimacy and policy guidance. Inevitably, there is some form of planning process that aims to identify issues and opportunities for the region and which aims to develop strategies for improving the environment, economy and community of the region. Such planning processes generally aim to be highly consultative with the regional community, consistent with the view that success depends on a high level of community understanding and ownership. Sometimes there is a subsequent investment or funding strategy that enables priority sustainable development actions to be undertaken. A lead RO, ideally representative of all regional interests, generally has responsibility for facilitating and coordinating the initiative and managing the financial resources. Having said all that, it must still be recognised that just within Australia there is a huge diversity of SRD initiatives in terms of their approach, organisational structure, powers and resources. Improving on them by sharing experiences, suggestions, challenges and analyses makes economic, social and environmental sense.

Lake Eyre Basin

In order to enrich and make more tangible the discussion of the evolution and challenges of SRD, we present here the tale (thus far) of the Lake Eyre Basin (LEB) regional initiative[5]. The LEB covers 1.14 million km^2 of central Australia, which is about one sixth of the continent, and equivalent in area to the much more publicised Murray Darling Basin. It encompasses parts of South Australia, Queensland, New South Wales and the Northern Territory. The spatial scale, the small human population and the multiple administrative jurisdictions of various spheres of government, in combination pose powerful challenges to an aspiring integrated SRD initiative. The agreed aim of participants is to work for the sustainable natural resources management and regional development of the Lake Eyre Basin, explicitly acknowledging the links between environment, economy and community. There are, however, understandably diverse opinions about the means by which this should or could be achieved.

The LEB initiative began in 1995 at a public meeting held in Birdsville, convened by the South Australian National Parks Far North Consultative Committee. Members were concerned about the conflict between different groups and the uncertainty about the implications of any decision taken to pursue World Heritage listing (LEBSG 1997). A broad cross-section of stakeholders were invited and many different interest groups, government officers and community members attended. Much work went into making the contacts, encouraging attendance, employing a professional facilitator and planning the meeting. This preparation ensured that participants were able to move on to a next stage if they chose – which they did by forming the LEB Steering Group (with a two-year sunset clause) and preparing its terms of reference. Key components of the terms of reference were to produce an LEB Issues Paper and explore future management options, particularly with regard to catchment management. As an indication of their commitment various groups contributed start-up funds. Subsequent funding was provided from the Natural Heritage Trust and the South Australian and Queensland State governments.

As the first meeting was organised by LEB community members (albeit with government agency support), the elected Steering Group and the subsequent consultation process was less frequently seen as an imposition from 'outside' or government. Having the Steering Group comprised of the various stakeholders created ownership and within-region credibility, encouraging diverse stakeholders to support, rather than undermine, the process. Individuals and various interest groups had a chance to be involved in listening, learning, and determining the outcomes. Building on this ownership theme, the employment of the initial project officer by the Steering Group – not a government agency – further assisted in building community trust and support. This position was based in Longreach, located within an independent

---

5   The case study draws on the experience of by Kate Andrews who has had the privilege of being the project coordinator and later Chief Executive of the process for its inception phase from 1996-2000.

Table 8.4. Example locations of SRD initiatives

Albury-Wodonga, NSW & Vic (Whitlam Growth Centre)
Australian Capital Region, NSW & ACT (Regional SoE)
Blackwood Basin, WA
Brisbane River and Moreton Bay, Qld
Cape York Peninsula, Qld (CYPLUS)
Central Highlands, Qld (CH Regional Resource Use Planning project – CHRRUPP)
Dawson Valley, Qld
Dorset Shire, Tas (Dorset Sustainable Development Strategy)
Eyre Peninsula, SA (Developing an Eyre of Prosperity ...)
Far North Queensland (FNQ2010)
Gascoyne-Murchison, WA
Great Barrier Reef, Qld (Keeping it Great!) [marine region]
Greater Western Sydney, NSW (TeamWest) [metropolitan region]
Hawkesbury-Nepean, NSW
Lake Eyre Basin; Qld, NT, SA, NSW
Launceston Tamar, Tas
Liverpool Plains, NSW
Mount Lofty Ranges, SA
Murray Irrigation (Murray Valley Voice)
Murray-Darling Basin Initiative; Qld, NSW, ACT, Vic, SA
North Eastern Goldfields, WA (Rangeways)
Northern Rivers, NSW (Framework for a Sustainable Future)
Regional Forest Agreements; WA, Tas, Vic, NSW, Qld
Shepparton Irrigation, Vic
South Coast, WA (Southern Prospects)
South East Queensland (SEQ2001)
Southern Adelaide, SA (Regional Environment Strategy)
Sunraysia Irrigation, Vic & NSW (SunRISE21)
Western Division, NSW (Rangelands in the 21st Century)
Wet Tropics, Qld (World Heritage and NQ Joint Board)

organisation. The project officer was not 'from the government' and was accountable to the various stakeholders and communities via the Steering Group.

Numerous and diverse drivers or motivators led to the original decision to explore management options and then to establish a regional management framework. These drivers were both reactive, seeking an alternative to World Heritage listing, and proactive, pre-empting problems so as not to 'end up like the Murray Darling Basin'. Throughout the consultation process, people expressed passion and commitment to the land and rivers, their culture and lifestyles. Retired drovers spoke about the ravaged Murray Darling system and the need to avoid making similar mistakes with resource development; locals discussed with respect the unpredictability of the floods, even after a lifetime of living with and watching the rivers; people worried about their futures and lack of economic viability; and participants discussed the arbitrariness of State/Territory borders in managing a biophysical system.

The first step in the consultation process that followed was to ask what issues were important in the LEB, a precursor to deciding whether there was a need to set up a regional framework to manage them. A wide range of issues were raised – environmental (eg, weeds), economic (eg, viability) and social (eg, security of land tenure). Some of the issues were basin-wide (eg, sustainable grazing systems) while others were local (eg, small town sewage systems).

After discussing catchment management and examples from elsewhere, participants were asked to consider the pros and cons of establishing some form of regional management framework in the LEB. What benefits could it offer? The diverse responses included establishing a community-owned management structure, working together across State-Territory borders and between groups and stakeholders, improving planning, and providing an opportunity to educate people 'outside' about the Basin and its people. Perceived potential problems ranged from duplication with other processes, the time and commitment required by participants, the possibility of it being dominated by one group, and the scale and diversity of the area and stakeholders. For some the LEB natural 'watershed/river basin' boundary seemed irrelevant as they preferred to define regions by other criteria.

It was then possible for participants to design options for management frameworks that took these factors into account, ensuring that opportunities were maximised and potential problems minimised. The framework finalised and endorsed at a large 1997 public meeting is a two-tiered model comprising catchment management committees or equivalents and a Lake Eyre Basin Coordinating Group (LEBCG). A formal Agreement on the management of the Queensland and South Australian portions of the LEB has been signed by Queensland, South Australian and Commonwealth Ministers. The LEBCG was invited to be the community advisory committee to a regular Ministerial Forum and is now fulfilling this role This has created a formal and concrete link between the regional community structure and the political decision making process, an element that participants requested in their design of the LEB framework.

The *SRD Process Model* (Figure 8.2) provides a useful guide in overviewing the progress of the initiative and considering its future (the model is explicated in Dore et al 2000). Each of the listed components of the *Setting up* phase have been essential in the LEB process, although it is important to note that they are linked and often undertaken simultaneously. The model should not be interpreted as suggesting a linear process. At the time of writing, the LEB initiative has completed the *Setting up* and *Planning strategically* phase and has moved on to the *Implementing & managing* and *Learning & adapting* phases. Of course large challenges remain, however, commitment is high.

Another way of analysing the LEB initiative is to use principles suggested as essential for any adaptive institutional management approach involving complex systems and diverse stakeholders (see Chapter 1). The following sections discuss these principles (purposefulness; information-richness

Figure 8.2 SRD Process Model

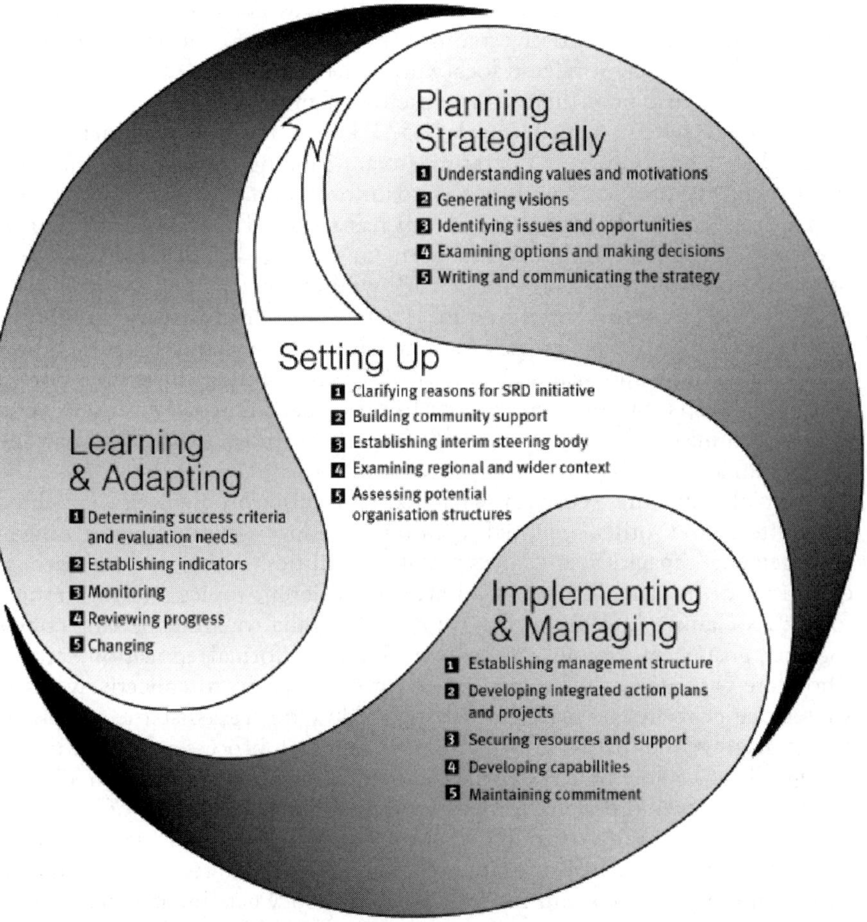

Planning Strategically
1 Understanding values and motivations
2 Generating visions
3 Identifying issues and opportunities
4 Examining options and making decisions
5 Writing and communicating the strategy

Setting Up
1 Clarifying reasons for SRD initiative
2 Building community support
3 Establishing interim steering body
4 Examining regional and wider context
5 Assessing potential organisation structures

Learning & Adapting
1 Determining success criteria and evaluation needs
2 Establishing indicators
3 Monitoring
4 Reviewing progress
5 Changing

Implementing & Managing
1 Establishing management structure
2 Developing integrated action plans and projects
3 Securing resources and support
4 Developing capabilities
5 Maintaining commitment

and sensitivity; inclusiveness; flexibility; persistence) within the practical context of the LEB.

The process of developing a shared purpose is crucial to the success of an organisation made up of diverse stakeholders. An SRD initiative such as the LEB requires an overall purpose that has been developed by all of those involved – a common purpose – in addition to those aspirations individuals or their organisations/constituents may hold. Strategic planning can be used to develop common purpose at all levels, from the most general 'shared vision', through to specific actions. The LEB initiative has found it most effective to start with high priority but non-controversial issues to help people learn how to work together. It was considered that tackling controversial issues too early could be counter-productive, and indeed destructive.

The LEB initiative is indicative of the vastly different levels and types (social, economic, biophysical, 'scientific', cultural, 'local', Indigenous, national, global) of information which are required if regional communities and policymakers are to be informed and informing an SRD process. It is obvious that in order to develop a regional strategy for the whole LEB and subregional (catchment) strategies for areas such as the Cooper and Georgina-Diamantina, the LEB initiative requires information for decision-making. An accessible base of scientific and local knowledge is needed.

In many instances there is an absence of information. For example, the Cooper river system, which travels 1,523 km and has a catchment area of 306,000 km² has only four operating stream gauging stations. In other situations there are problems with access to information. For example, accessing data from some States (eg, Queensland) has required the negotiation of data licensing agreements and this has been far from easy. Moreover, there has been no previously-existing framework within which to do cross-border projects with government agencies. Each State or Territory holds some information about 'their portion' of the LEB, such as land systems, however the classifications and scales are often different, creating difficulties for integrating data sets. Subsequent standardising of data is resource intensive and time consuming. In some cases information only exists for particular jurisdictions.

Finally, making sense of what exists is also problematic. Catchment committees and other regional planning groups – with a wide range of management capacities and interpretative abilities – are dealing with vast quantities of information about an array of different topics and in a range of forms. As Campbell (1996) said, 'All over Australia we are expecting cobbled-together groups of people with varying levels of formal education, many of whom are part-time or voluntary, all of whom are busy, to collectively develop strategic approaches to managing change'. How do we assist the people who are managing and using information in regional processes obtain/improve their skills to be able to do so? This can be only be achieved through allocating resources to develop people's capacity to handle large quantities of diverse and complex material and through ensuring that information is available in accessible forms. The LEB initiative is working to create research partnerships with community groups and individuals so that they can participate, learn and help to direct outputs which are relevant to, and able to be used by, land managers and natural resource management groups.

The LEB initiative also provides an example for the ways in which different social groups have been enabled (or not) to participate in regional processes. Fundamental to the LEBCG is the continued, and increasing, involvement of a wide range of communities and stakeholders in planning and decision-making. Often 'catchment management' has only acknowledged land managers and government agencies as stakeholders and also addressed natural resources in isolation (eg, Burton 1974; Cunningham 1986). There is now increasing recognition of the need for and validity of involving a wider range of stakeholders and of more explicitly addressing the links between the environment, natural resource use, economic and social issues (Mitchell and Hollick 1993; Syme et al 1993). 'Integrated catchment management' theory now expounds the merits of encompassing diversity – of stakeholders, of values and of resource use requirements – and of dealing with the conflict this may generate. This is a major challenge not yet met in practice.

Attempting to embrace this new, more pluralistic view of planning, the LEB initiative encourages flexibility and negotiation by providing a framework that brings together a diversity of stakeholders, values and issues. It does not seek to represent a single line or dominant opinion. This is a difficult role for people to understand as it moves away from the convention where one view or outcome predominates. The role regularly requires explanation to people outside the process who ask 'What is your position on ... ?' and creates a steep learning curve for those in the process. The LEB regional initiative was itself established without any voting, either within the steering group, coordinating group, catchment committees or public meetings and workshops. And the guidelines of the existing catchment (subregional) committees include agreement to rely upon consensus decision-making with voting to be used only as a last resort.

At the public meetings to form the sub-regional committees three major aims emerged for the way the committees should function (ie, their guidelines). These were inclusiveness, accountability, and outcomes. It is essential that a community process engages people across the whole spectrum of possible involvement (not just those who are willing or able to sit on a committee which is what we see occur in many ROs). People can contribute to the process in a multitude of ways and a truly grass roots organisation will create opportunities to allow and encourage this. These may include regular public fora in different places, sub-group meetings based on issues that involve more than just committee members, a regular basin-wide conference; and others. The LEB initiative is providing opportunities for people with varying levels of interest and varying capacity for involvement due to their circumstances (eg, women home-schooling her children on a property or people intimidated by speaking in public).

People should be able to participate, whether it is by chairing a committee or ringing up to raise/discuss an issue once a year. As peoples' interest or circumstances change they should be able to become involved to a greater or lesser degree. It is important to note that people can be actively involved without sitting on a committee. For example, they may have a particular concern with an issue and initiate a project to address it. This does require a major shift in attitudes and culture as, at present in the LEB, people equate involvement with membership of a committee.

It will be interesting to see how the LEB initiative is able to evolve (or not), expanding or limiting its role and structure through adaptive processes as necessary. The funding mechanism of the NHT has allowed for flexibility but will not provide continuity. An SRD initiative needs to be flexible in the scale at which it addresses issues, in the types of partnerships it establishes, the boundaries it defines (particularly sub-regional), its operational arrangements and the process it runs. The LEB initiative is learning to operate at many different scales according to the issue, and also to work with different partners at each of these scales, from landholders and local groups, to major industries and the Commonwealth government.

LEBCG is working with people of 'the basin' not yet involved to find the most appropriate way to enable them to participate. To be truly inclusive the initiative needs to continually learn from its successes and failures and adapt its ways of engaging with stakeholders. For example, Indigenous involvement in the process so far has been minimal. Conventional fora for public consultation have not attracted wide Indigenous participation for a variety of reasons. One reason is that it is not culturally appropriate for representatives of one Indigenous group to speak for another's country. Therefore participation on a committee that covers huge areas can be problematic. At the time of writing the LEBCG was working with Indigenous communities and consultants to find satisfactory ways to establish representation and to more fully involve Indigenous people in the LEB SRD process.

With regard to the need for flexibility, it should also be acknowledged that while there is general agreement between stakeholders of the 'general objectives' related to many LEB issues, this is not always the case. Issues such as: possible industry restructure and 'adjustment'; land and mineral resource rights and tenure, water resources development, biodiversity conservation, etc – all require negotiation between parties with different views. In cases where there are irreconcilable differences of opinion, negotiation can not always replace regulatory measures and government decision-making. Some situations can only be win/lose and in these cases elected decision-makers may have to make the hard calls. However, a non-adversarial and flexible approach in an RO such as the LEBCG assists in unpacking issues and enhancing understanding. This hopefully contributes to more equitable and informed decision-making.

Persistence or lack thereof, has underpinned or undermined many regional efforts. It is a 'given' that an SRD initiative, such as in LEB, needs to persist and endure if it is to achieve desired outcomes. This is particularly the case for a community organisation addressing the difficult long-term challenges associated with maintaining viability, ecosystem protection and sustainable use of natural resources. The start up time for any organisation involving diverse stakeholders is substantial – optimistically at least a couple of years – but this is vital if a foundation of trust is to be built. Without this trust between the stakeholders 'success' is highly unlikely.

Persistence encourages further involvement and commitment from people. Those who have hesitated to become involved for fear of their efforts being ignored or otherwise ineffective are encouraged by longevity and the related capacity to achieve outcomes.

So what are the aspects that need to persist? The structure itself need not persist but should adapt and change as required. Some continuity of staff is important however. If the turnover of staff is too frequent trust can not develop, and acquired knowledge, networks and skills are lost to the region.

Funding support and continuity is also obviously important to the survival of an SRD initiative. The LEB effort received start-up funding direct from the Commonwealth, and also from the Queensland and South Australian governments via various NHT State/Commonwealth partnership arrangements. It has also relied heavily upon in-kind contributions from stakeholders and participants.

Most important is that the principles of an SRD initiative persist as these form the basis of the purpose and 'social contract' with stakeholders which should underpin it. These principles, elaborated upon by others in this book and elsewhere, include commitments to: sustainability, equity, inclusiveness and participation, accountability, effectiveness and efficiency.

Political support is also essential for persistence. Recognising this, LEB participants requested the formation of the Ministerial Forum. This request could (correctly) be interpreted as a request for the political legitimacy required to receive external support and access to policy formulation and decision-making processes of those with legislative powers. The LEBCG has no statutory basis – political support and 'legitimacy' ensures that it can have some influence. A regional process such as this relies upon the goodwill of governments. It does not and can not operate in isolation from the formal spheres of government – despite the occasional community member wanting this to be the case! Obviously legitimacy is also required more broadly. Without obtaining, and retaining, the support and participation of a wide range of stakeholders, a regional initiative such as the LEBCG will become meaningless and useless. It will not be able to achieve change or outcomes and will quickly lose credibility with governments and communities.

Establishing the LEB initiative has taken several years. Those involved hope that the quality and strength of the foundation created has made the investment of time and resources worthwhile. The most crucial outcome is not the design of the framework but the ownership people have of it. Through participating in the process people have developed a greater understanding of the potential and workings of a regional organisation. In forming and reviewing committees people have had to grapple with the nature of an RO. Is it another layer of government? How can it be democratic? How can consensus work and is decision-making with this method fair? What should be the roles and responsibilities of the LEBCG and how does that fit in with governments? Not everyone has participated or is happy with the results to date. To some the LEB initiative represents a threat to the established order (or disorder) while others just wish to be left alone to do their own thing, without interference. Nevertheless, this initiative shows significant promise in fostering genuine community/multi-government approaches to SRD.

Some other SRD initiatives

In order to appreciate the breadth of SRD initiatives, and the range of issues which have emerged, we will briefly illustrate a few more, drawing largely on Dore and Woodhill (1999) and Dovers and Dore (1999).

In the 1990s the *Cape York Peninsula* in Far North Queensland was one of the most photographed, studied and documented regions in Australia. This was due to land rights decisions, the sensitivity of environmental issues and the Cape York Peninsula Land Use Strategy (CYPLUS) process (see CYRAG 1997; Mobbs 2000; Mobbs and Woodhill 1999). Depending on your definition, the region is 137,000 km^2 and home to 18,000 people. CYPLUS was always intended to be a three-stage process: Stage 1 (completed) was essentially about information gathering; Stage 2 (completed 1997) developed recommendations for the future of the region; and Stage 3 (1999+) is the implementation phase. While articulating a clear vision, with well-defined goals, the mandate of the Cape York Regional Advisory Group – which oversaw Stage 2 – was regularly contested and contradicted by governments (Commonwealth and State) whose political support for the process has at various times sharply risen and fallen, and not in a synchronous fashion. Nevertheless, CYPLUS has been sufficiently long-lived to learn from early mistakes. While extraordinarily well resourced in the Stage 1 information-gathering phase, community trust was lost. A refocused Stage 2 was necessary in order to gain or regain the support and input of many local-regional groups.

Stage 2 developed ESD-focused recommendations for the region in a way which was genuinely inclusive of the many different social groupings in the broader Cape York community. Stage 2 developed the goals and strategies necessary to meet the overall vision and the individual visions that have been developed for the subject areas of: Conservation (four strategies; for example, ecosystem management); Cultural (six strategies; for example, maintenance and practice of multiple cultures); Economic (seven strategies; for example, commercial fishing); Lifestyle and Social (seven strategies; for example, housing); Infrastructure (six strategies; for example, regional road links); and Land Tenure. Stage 2 was quite independent, but independence comes at a price if resourcing is dependent on the aforementioned fluctuating political support, which tells us much about our Federal system which has the unenviable task of hearing and juggling the views of conservationists, pastoralists, miners, Indigenous people, tourism operators and local governments, different State agencies as well as Commonwealth departments. The CYRAG members were particularly proud of what was termed by some as a 'values based' approach to planning. This meant that the process enabled different interest groups to explain and understand each other's values as a basis for finding common ground. A spin off of this process was the much lauded Cape York Heads of Agreement that illustrated the potential for cooperative approaches to overcoming land rights conflicts. CYPLUS is considered one of the better examples of a comprehensive Australian SRD strategic planning process. After an enforced 18 month hiatus, CYRAG was reformed in 1999 to re-enter the political maelstrom and aid the Stage 3 implementation phase. The success of this phase will (or should) determine how the initiative will be judged overall.

Another evolving SRD initiative story is from the *Blackwood River basin* of south-west Western Australia which spans an area of 28,000 km^2, includes all or part of 19 local government areas and is home to 40,000 people. The resident community has been participating in a regional group since 1990 (Reid 1999). Originally they focused on the state of the Blackwood River, but their interests have evolved to now focus on the social and economic aspects of sustainability, in addition to their initial charter of addressing land and water management issues. While the Blackwood Basin Group has received significant support from various sources, at the end of the day it has tremendous accumulated knowledge and experience but no statutory backing and (though this may soon change) very limited core funding support. While independent, it is relatively powerless. This is not said to demean its considerable achievements or to deny its present, ongoing value. Despite the constant efforts of many unpaid people, and a very few paid, without political support, obtaining resources to survive and be effective is a constant struggle.

Another initiative, while not as yet having longevity, has clearly demonstrated it is willing to compare with other regions and experiment. The *Queensland Central Highlands* Regional Resource Use Planning Project, is targeting equitable and sustainable resource use and involves the community and their five local governments, State agencies, CSIRO, the University of Central Queensland and Land & Water Australia. A real effort has been made to learn from the successes and failures from other experiences around Australia (Dale and Bellamy 1998). This learning has been actively factored into the process – a rare attribute, due in this case in large part to the social science approaches informing the project.

The *Great Barrier Reef* is the largest coral reef system in the world, stretching more than 2,000 km along the Queensland coast. There has been a long history of jousting between the Commonwealth and Queensland governments which eventually lead to the creation of the Great Barrier Reef Marine Park Authority, which is variously supporting, controlling or serving other parts of 'the institution' including advisory groups and a Ministerial Council (Bowen 1994). The initiative has produced a 25-year plan, released in 1994 (GBRMPA 1994), which is an excellent example of clearly expressed objectives and strategies. It is also a good example of an institution which is necessarily multi-functional as research, planning and management are all required to inform new policy. In recent times its previously perceived independence has been somewhat bridled, but nevertheless it serves as another important experimenting and itself experimental institution.

The *Murray-Darling Basin* (MDB) initiative now involves six of Australia's nine parliamentary jurisdictions (for a history, see Powell 1993). At the direction of the Ministerial Council, the Murray-Darling Basin Commission has, since 1987, coordinated what is undoubtedly one of the spatially largest integrated catchment management efforts anywhere. The MDB initiative is clearly demonstrating some of the desirable attributes of our targeted adaptive institutions. While there are always rumblings, in general the initiative has received consistent multilateral support by participating governments. The initiative has been properly resourced and allowed to develop and learn. Milestones have included the 1988 Salinity and Drainage Strategy, 1989 Natural Resource Management Strategy, 1995 Water Audit, 1996 Basin Sustainability Plan, 1999 Salinity Audit, 2001 Integrated Catchment Management Policy, 2001 Basin Salinity Management Plan, and recent garnering of support for the introduction of environmental flows (see Crabb, this volume) and the expected Basin Salinity Management Strategy 2000+ (see Crabb, this volume). Important leadership is being shown, dependent on continued support by member jurisdictions, in areas such as the development of market mechanisms for water trading, capping of water diversions, comprehensive research into issues such as the extent of salinity, and development of more appropriate institutional arrangements. How many of the previously mentioned institutions have had the same opportunity – via longevity, proper resourcing, statutory underpinning, a measure of independence and political support – to compile a list of similar achievements? Lessons have emerged which are relevant to any analysis of our Federal system, such as: the need for and value in coordinated, inter-government decision-making; the need for occasional 'bullet-biting' (eg, 'the Cap' on water abstractions) given the scale of resource problems; or suggesting new designs for institutional arrangements.

Lessons from regional experiments

The jury is still out on regionalism and the effectiveness of SRD initiatives and their associated ROs. We believe that the focus at this point in time should be on learning how to improve the effectiveness of regional initiatives and organisations, and on creating a more supportive institutional environment rather than prematurely judging 'success' or 'failure'. In this section we have attempted to distil some of the lessons from the large number of regional experiments being undertaken around Australia. There has been much learnt from the experiments of the past 50 years and we can not hope to do justice to it all. However, we offer for debate our opinions about important SRD principles, the SRD process, desirable characteristics of SRD processes and SRD critical issues.

Table 8.5. Principles which should underpin SRD institutional arrangements (Dore et al 2000)

Striving for ...	Explanation ...
Sustainability	as a central goal, including taking a precautionary approach so as not to diminish opportunities for future generations; also recognising the pre-eminent importance of ecological processes upon which communities and economies ultimately depend
Equity	for its own sake, but also as a means of reducing conflict
Inclusiveness and participation	encouraging a high level of diverse stakeholder representation, involvement and ownership; participatory process that is clear, genuine, predictable and maintained over time — recognising that 'participation' is a highly complex matter
Accountability	of all empowered participants to their constituents: ie, to whom is the institution accountable? In practice, how is this accountability evidenced?
Effectiveness	of the processes to really make a difference: ie, does the capacity match the intent?
Efficiency	of the processes: ie, do the ends (outcomes) justify the means (costs, trade-offs, time, dollars)? Also, has there been, or is there, unnecessary duplication?
Durability	relative to short-lived or ad hoc initiatives: ie, has the institution had, or is likely to have, sufficient longevity to persist, experiment, learn and adapt?

Principles

Let us first consider principles. Our work – and that of many others – has lead us to support regional leaders advocating a list of seven (7) principles which we feel should underpin SRD institutional arrangements.[6] While not specific to 'regional institutions' they nevertheless are integral and should not be assumed or skipped over.

Process

The next suggestions relate to the process by which regional arrangements are often created and implemented. The SRD process model is a guide developed with many regional practitioners, intended to highlight the various phases which should collectively comprise an SRD process.

Moreover, it seems that for SRD initiatives to fulfil their potential it is necessary for them to exhibit (at least most of) a long list of desirable characteristics. These are the elements which, if present, are more likely to lead to successful outcomes from SRD processes.

Critical issues

SRD is a complex business and the difficulties encountered, if followed through, quickly begin to challenge – or at least raise questions – about the beliefs, assumptions and structures of modern society. From what we have seen happening in regional Australia – and from the dedication, enthusiasm and passion with which so many people are engaging with the difficulties and opportunities of our times – we are convinced that SRD initiatives have enormous potential. However, this potential will only be realised if the deeper structural causes of the current constraints to SRD are confronted. The starting point is to begin by asking the right questions about our current situation and our aspirations. We have identified what we call *Critical Issues for SRD*. These issues can be seen either as the current 'problems' or as the 'opportunities for improvement', thereby capitalising on the learning from present and past regional efforts. The considerable diversity of efforts around the country must be recognised. For each issue there are places where the situation is excellent and others where an issue is a major impediment to better results.

Understanding the implications of sustainable development: SRD should be paramount to the overarching thinking that drives our regional management and development, plans, initiatives and decisions. There is a need for greater awareness and appreciation of unsustainable practices and systems. Some dominant assumptions, mindsets and paradigms need to be challenged. There is a need for a deeper understanding about sustainability and, as this happens, a need to keep clarifying the vision and direction of SRD initiatives.

---

6   This list is taken from the SRD Kit. It is an adaptation of other 'tests' or 'criteria' promoted in various Australian fora by Munro 1994; Dale and Bellamy 1998; Dovers 1999.

Table 8.6. Desirable characteristics of SRD processes (Dore and Woodhill 1999)

Characteristic	Explanation
Purposeful	Clear reasons for why a process is being employed
Visionary	Based on a well-developed, widely-shared, long-term vision
Informed and informing	Utilises and shares the best available information and builds the knowledge and research base
Holistic	Takes an integrated or 'holistic' view of issues, taking account of social, cultural, economic and ecological issues, their actions and their interdependencies
Integrated	Integrates with other processes, plans, strategies and initiatives, including, where appropriate, indirect or direct links with statutory planning schemes
Appropriate scale	Supports action where it is needed, whether regional, sub-regional or local
Institutional backing	Supported by appropriate, empowered and resourced organisations
Focused	Clearly identifies the key issues for the region
Options evaluated	Assesses positive and negative impacts of alternative options
Costed	Identifies monetary and non-monetary costs and benefits of the options
Prioritised	Prioritises, in a transparent and equitable way, the importance and/or logical order of activities
Action and outcome oriented	Designed to produce action and be held accountable against its outcomes record
Responsibilities clarified	Well-defined and articulated responsibilities and roles for all stakeholders
Negotiated	Negotiated agreements about implementation
Monitored, evaluated	Adequate and coherent framework for monitoring and evaluation
Learns and adapts	Mechanisms in place for learning from the monitoring and evaluation and adapting as required
Communicative and credible	Effectively communicates high-quality, honest information

Developing and maintaining supportive institutional arrangements: All three spheres of government have a significant interest and stake in regional-scale initiatives. However, the allocation of roles and responsibilities both between the different spheres of government and between government and ROs is often unclear, leading to tension and conflict that undermine the potential for improved cooperation. There is a need for an enhanced understanding by regional communities of our federal system of government and a more comprehensive 'whole of government' policy regarding regionalism. This necessitates further reshaping of our institutions and a concomitant clarification of powers, functions and linkages to make our system more compatible with SRD aspirations.

Devolving responsibility and power: Often, governments devolve responsibilities to ROs without devolving the authority or budgets that would empower the ROs to successfully discharge those responsibilities. There is a significant difference between devolving responsibility and truly devolving power. RO and the communities they represent are often surprised when they realise they have less real implementation power than they had thought. Governments and ROs need to be quite clear about their respective responsibilities and the extent of powers (if any) devolved to ROs so that there is no misunderstanding.

Enhancing the capacity of ROs: Many ROs lack the capacity to meet the demands and challenges of SRD. This is largely because they often have an ambiguous, contested mandate within the current structures of government. Where necessary, capacity should be enhanced by professional development and by a more adequate resourcing in terms of people, finance, facilities and time. Continuity of efforts can only be assured by maintaining resources for at least a reasonable period, thereby avoiding the disillusionment and energy drain associated with start–stop initiatives.

Improving coordination: There remains a problem in many places with poor coordination between the different spheres of government, between different government agencies and between different ROs. This is widely seen as wasteful of resources, frustrating, and a major impediment to the attainment of the community, economic and environmental goals of SRD. We need to improve coordination to enable greater efficiency and integration.

Enabling participation: Participation is widely championed, but some fundamental questions need to be constantly re-examined. Which individuals and groups are included in our definition of 'the stakeholders' and 'the community'? And what do we mean by 'participation'? It should be acknowledged that different people and groups have more or less confidence, capacity and power. Participation processes are often unclear and questionable. Does your definition of 'participation' mean consultation, 'insultation', tokenism or true empowerment of all stakeholders to participate meaningfully in an SRD process? Structures and resources are not always in place to enable equitable and informed participation by all. Also, active participation in SRD initiatives can have a high cost for people with many other family, business and community responsibilities. Respecting these other responsibilities is very important.

Improving knowledge systems: Decision-making for SRD is highly dependent on quality social, economic and environmental information. It is necessary to integrate knowledge derived from many diverse, valid sources (local and non-local community/academic/scientific/cultural) and to keep participants well-informed. Often, current systems of research, information gathering and analysis do not adequately meet these requirements. We need to improve our systems for assembling, accessing and synthesising high-quality, current knowledge to inform our regional processes.

Improving processes of adaptive management and social learning: In general, a great deal has been learned about strategic regional planning and decision-making, community participation, program implementation and evaluation. However, the understanding and sophistication of these processes still fall short of what is required to match the complexity and conflicts of SRD. Clearly, successful SRD initiatives require an appreciation of the overarching goal, smart thinking, quality facilitation, and time. Specific attention needs to be given to developing improved processes of adaptive management and ensuring that people in ROs and governments have the opportunity and skill to learn from their experience.

The findings of the research by the authors which identified these critical issues for SRD, were broadly in line with some excellent work by CSIRO which proceeded in parallel (Dale and Bellamy 1998). To add another critical issue from their work would perhaps best be done by noting and appreciating their bargaining concept. In their view, to deliver effective outcomes 'regional resource use planning' must encourage use of approaches which facilitate equitable negotiations among regional stakeholders.

> This [equitable negotiating] requires regional resource use planning that incorporates at least three primary elements: (i) the application of technically sound and innovative social, economic and environmental assessment methods to underpin negotiations; (ii) clear mechanisms to enhance the appropriate institutional and support arrangements to facilitate the negotiation; (iii) clear mechanisms to enhance the participation in the negotiations of as many as possible of the constituents of the stakeholder groups represented in the regional planning arena.

Under a banner of SRD, many existing regional efforts – particularly those which were created to address regional NRM problems or regional economy expansion – can 'cast aside their practical and technocentric heritage and focus' (Woodhill 1999). However, this can only be done by a new acceptance of methodological pluralism, by which we mean 'the capacity to develop and utilise a diversity of methodologies that may range from highly reductionist basic scientific research at one extreme, through to creative artistic expression as a means of developing community understanding at the other' (Woodhill 1999). There have been, and remain, various initiatives trying to do just that. Very different methodologies are required for dealing with the challenges of, for example: community development, job creation, environmental and economic risk assessment and knowledge integration. Underpinning values need to be understood to appreciate different perspectives, to seek cooperation, and to realise the likely limits of acceptable trade-offs. In our view, there remains a significant gap between the general endorsement of the need for varied types of participation, and putting of it into practice, assisted by appropriately prepared facilitators and coordinators with the necessary breadth of skills to appreciate community, scientific and economic perspectives. Nevertheless, as bureaucratic and (other) stakeholders switch to an SRD focus, the likelihood increases of an acceptance of the need to develop the capacity for diverse methodologies to support regional initiatives.

Moreover, both Dale and Bellamy (1998) and Woodhill (1999) are alert to the 'problem', at least partly characterised by ineffectiveness, whereby many previous and current regional efforts have focused on instrumental planning and implementation activities, without also appreciating that there is integral value in messier, participatory arenas which value negotiating and social learning within a more open democratic process which encourages exploration and bounded conflict. It is the latter processes that characterise the contemporary flagships of regionalism closer to the heart of what we would consider to be closer to 'ideal type' SRD initiatives.

Conclusions

It is our contention that the critical issues outlined earlier need to be addressed in order to move forward. This final section suggests ways to produce far more effective return from the 'regional effort'. First, while there is a need to develop and maintain supportive institutional arrangements, governments need to be particularly careful about imposing new institutions, in particular ROs, on regions without due consideration of existing arrangements. With SRD there is usually merit in allowing effective regional institutional arrangements to evolve from regions, often from coalitions or adaptations of pre-existing institutions. Ideally this should occur with the impetus and involvement of stakeholders and local communities.

With regard to devolving responsibility and power, it is clear that there needs to be, when supporting the establishment of regional initiatives, much more effort put into aligning expectations, objectives and responsibilities with mandates, resources, capacities and powers. Lack of thought about these matters has led to considerable frustration and conflict. However, as is well-recognised by many regional leaders, there are advantages and disadvantages in ROs having statutory power. Having limited powers can enable ROs to take a non-threatening, coordinating role with the many different regional stakeholders from government, industry and the wider community.

Enhancing the capacity of regional leaders has also been highlighted as necessary. Embedding a learning culture in ROs is essential. Intra- and inter-regional thinktanks and personnel exchange can help but professional development also requires provision of some practical or heuristic tools.

While coordination of government is a worthwhile ideal and an important issue, failure to reach an 'ideal type' should not be allowed to distract regional efforts. By its very nature, our democracy can be somewhat messy and preferred pathways will often be contested and pit against each other differing philosophies which may be temporarily in vogue with one or other sphere of government. Nevertheless, various factors should be considered, such as: whether there is simply insufficient knowledge of the complex context within which a particular RO or SRD initiative is operating; turf protection by existing organisations/agencies which negatively impacts on regional efforts; and/or being hampered by chains of command from Canberra or State capitals which decrease flexibility.

When addressing participation issues, promoters of SRD must recognise that the effectiveness of regional processes is highly dependent on many different forms of participation by a variety of individuals and groups. This participation must be actively supported. It is a responsibility of regional leaders, facilitators and organisations to create equitable processes and to counter the constraints on different individuals and groups, which can greatly influence their capacity to participate.

With regard to improving knowledge systems, there are several possibilities worthy of consideration. At the very least there is a need to promote trans-disciplinary and inter-disciplinary R&D and to ensure an ongoing process of reviewing, learning and disseminating the experiences of researchers, ROs and SRD initiatives. It is also important that there be ongoing efforts to ascertain the needs for environmental and socioeconomic information and, where appropriate, Geographic Information System (GIS) requirements, to enhance the prospects for improved integrated regional planning. Improving the availability and access to such information by regional people – by which we mean all Australians – is a challenge.

SRD is a long-term process and many regional efforts have only been supported (thus far) on a short-term basis. SRD requires time, patience and some degree of continuity. It takes time to build community trust and support, to develop a strategic approach and to put in place processes and structures to achieve results. Short-term and inconsistent support, if coupled with programs and policies which interfere rather than support, make it exceedingly difficult for SRD efforts to achieve their objectives. Regional organisations do, however, need to learn to be adaptive to changing circumstances. This tension between the need for patience and continuity on one hand, and responsiveness to the changing institutional landscape and community expectation on the other, is unquestionably a challenge for SRD.

In closing, and encompassing most of the identified critical issues for SRD, there is a need to create a way forward through improving our processes of adaptive management and social learning. This will not happen by chance. We need to give more attention to developing reflective, learning and evaluative cultures within our organisations and regions. SRD initiatives present both a suite of challenges and a golden opportunity. An SRD focus challenges the way the Australian democracy functions and the way society deals with complex rapidly changing problems that often bring core values into conflict. A learning response is essential. There is an opportunity to put the rhetoric of ecologically sustainable development (ESD) into practice drawing upon the regional advantages of: appropriate scale to deal with environmental issues; the potential of a community of common interest; and a 'space' complementary to existing spheres of government, which is ripe for continued institutional innovation. This is not to say that SRD initiatives can, of themselves, resolve the larger challenges associated with global trends. However, they are a place where many more Australians can engage in ESD and actively participate in exciting new forms of social learning and democracy.

References

Bowen, J, 1994, 'The Great Barrier Reef: towards conservation and management' in Dovers, S (ed), *Australian environmental history: essays and cases*, Melbourne: Oxford University Press.

Burton, JR, 1974, Water, land and people – the valley region concept as a basis for the management of natural resource systems. Proceedings, Appendix C, 14th Annual Conference of Flood Mitigation Authorities, Maitland.

Campbell, A, 1996, *Regionalism, regionalisation, and natural resource management*, Working paper 96/3, Centre for Resource and Environmental Studies, Australian National University, Canberra.

Commonwealth Department of Post-War Reconstruction, 1949, *Regional planning in Australia: A history of progress and review of regional planning activities through the Commonwealth*, Canberra: Commonwealth of Australia.

Commonwealth of Australia, 1996, *Guidelines for implementation of the Natural Heritage Trust: discussion Paper*, Canberra: Environment Australia.

Cunningham, GM, 1986, Total catchment management – resource management for the future, *Journal of Soil Conservation* 42: 1.

CYRAG (Cape York Regional Advisory Group). 1997, *Cape York Peninsula Land Use Strategy – our land, our future: a strategy for sustainable land use and economic and social development*, Brisbane and Canberra: Queensland Department of Local Government and Planning and Commonwealth Department of Environment.

Dale, A and Bellamy, J (eds), 1998, *Regional resource use planning in rangelands: an Australian overview*, Canberra: Land & Water Resources Research and Development Corporation.

Decentralisation Advisory Board, 1981, *Final report 1 July 1980-30 April 1981*, Canberra: Australian Government Publishing Service.

Dore, J, Keating, C, Woodhill, J and Ellis, K, 2000, Sustainable regional development kit: a resource for improving the community, economy and environment of your region (booklet and CD), Canberra: Greening Australia.

Dore, J and Woodhill, J, 1999, *Sustainable regional development: Vol 1: Executive Summary, Vol 2 Final Report*, Canberra: Greening Australia.

Dovers, S, 1999, Public policy and institutional R&D for natural resources management: issues and directions for LWRRDC, in Mobbs, C and Dovers S (eds), *Social, economic, legal, policy and institutional R&D for natural resource management: issues and directions for LWRRDC*, Occasional paper 01/99, Canberra: Land & Water Resources Research and Development Corporation.

Dovers, S and Dore, J, 1999, Adaptive institutions, organisations and policy processes for river basin and catchment management, Paper for 2nd International River Management Symposium, 29 September-2 October 1999,Brisbane.

GBRMPA (Great Barrier Reef Marine Park Authority), 1994, *The Great Barrier Reef: keeping it great, a 25 year strategic plan for the Great Barrier Reef World Heritage Area.* Townsville: Great Barrier Reef Marine Park Authority.

Gibson-Graham, JK, 1994, Reflections on regions: the white paper and a new class of politics of distribution, *Australian Geographer* 25: 148-153.

Gooding, A, 1999, 'Greater Western Sydney and the TeamWest Project' in Dore, J and Woodhill, J (eds), *Sustainable regional development: final report*, Canberra: Greening Australia.

LEBSG (Lake Eyre Bason Steering Group),1997, *Draft catchment management options paper: collated from the suggestions of people in, and interested in, the Lake Eyre Basin*, Longreach: Lake Eyre Basin Steering Group.

Mitchell, B and Hollick, M, 1993, Integrated catchment management in Western Australia: transition from concept to implementation, *Environmental Management* 17(6): 735-743.

Mobbs, C, 2000, *Regional planning for sustainability: towards adaptive and collaborative approaches*, PhD Thesis, Australian National University.

Mobbs, C and Woodhill, J, 1999, Lessons from CYPLUS in Cape York: An external perspective' in Dore, J and Woodhill, J (eds), *Sustainable regional development: final report*, Canberra: Greening Australia.

Munro, A, 1994, *Getting regions to work: a community based approach to integrated regional development* Melbourne: Local Planning Pty Ltd.

Petrich, J, 1999, The Cape York Regional Initiative – CYPLUS: An insider's perspective, in Dore, J and Woodhill, J (eds), *Sustainable regional development: final report*, Canberra: Greening Australia.

Powell J, 1993, *The emergence of bioregionalism in the Murray-Darling Basin*, Canberra: Murray-Darling Basin Commission.

Reid, D, 1999, The Blackwood catchment initiative: a Chairman's reflections, in Dore, J and Woodhill, J (eds), *Sustainable regional development: final report*, Canberra: Greening Australia.

Sorensen, T, 1994, The folly of regional policy, *Agenda* 1: 33-44.

Syme, GJ, Butterworth, JE and Nancarrow, BE 1993, *National whole catchment management: a review and analysis of processes*, Consultancy report 93/30, Australian Research Centre for Water in Society, Perth: CSIRO.

Toomey, F, 1997, A qualitative approach to regional development: applying sustainability principles in the Northern Rivers Region of New South Wales, Paper presented at the Australia and New Zealand Regional Science Association Inc Conference, 8-12 December 1997, Wellington.

Woodhill, J, 1999, *Sustaining rural Australia*, PhD thesis, Australian National University.

9

Informing ESD:
State of the Environment Reporting

Ronnie Harding and Denise Traynor

Institute of Environmental Studies, University of New South Wales

During the 1990s 'sustainable development' or, in Australia, 'ecologically sustainable development' (ESD) became institutionalised through international agreements and national legislation and policy as a key objective of nations and the accepted framework for environmental protection around the world. The World Commission on Environment and Development (1987) through its report *Our Common Future*, played a leading role in putting sustainable development on the agenda. The 1992 United Nations Conference on Environment and Development (UNCED, or Earth Summit) furthered the process of institutionalisation of sustainable development primarily through the adoption of a 'blueprint for the 21st century' – Agenda 21 – which was adopted by the countries in attendance, including Australia.

In 1992 Australian Commonwealth and State governments endorsed the *National Strategy for Ecologically Sustainable Development*, defining ESD as (Council of Australian Governments 1992: 6):

> ... using, conserving and enhancing the community's resources so that
> ecological processes, on which life depends, are maintained, and the
> total quality of life, now and in the future, can be increased.

The *National Strategy* and May 1992 *Intergovernmental Agreement on the Environment* (Heads of Government in Australia 1992) placed ESD firmly on the legislative and policy agendas for the three levels of government in Australia. Since that time Australian governments and their agencies, conservation groups, academic institutions and the business community have increasingly adopted ESD as a central tenet for their operations and have worked towards finding means for the application of the principles of ESD. Although to date rhetoric has been stronger than on-the-ground ESD outcomes, interest is now developing in how we can *measure progress* towards ESD in Australia.[1]

Introduction

This chapter is concerned with means for 'informing' ESD through institutionalised reporting processes including State of the Environment (SoE)

---

1   See for example recent publications by Brown (2000), Venning and Higgins (2001), Yencken (2001), Public Accounts and Estimates Committee, Parliament of Victoria (2002).

reporting by governments, as well as corporate environmental reporting (CER). It will review the evolution of environmental reporting in Australia and will evaluate the success of environmental reporting mechanisms against the goal of informing ESD. The main emphasis is on SoE reporting by State and National governments, with less detailed consideration of local government and CER. To carry out this evaluation the following questions need to be addressed, reflecting the core themes of this book:

- Is there a mechanism that ensures continuity of reporting, and are the stated goals consistent between reports? In other words, does '*persistence*' characterise the process?

- Has ESD been defined by the reporters? Is measuring progress towards ESD a stated goal of the reporters? Have ESD 'targets' been set, and is data available to measure progress towards these? Is the data appropriate to 'inform' ESD? In other words, is informing progress towards ESD a clearly defined *purpose* of the reporting and have ESD goals been set to report against?

- Is the reporting process formally and meaningfully linked back into policy setting, planning and management actions by appropriate institutions and stakeholders? In other words does the reporting process *richly inform* action in a broad planning and management cycle? And, is the information received used *sensitively* to *adapt* planning and management to achieve set goals.

- Who determines what is included in environmental/sustainability reports? Who determines what data are collected, how and how often? Who determines how those data are interpreted? Who has access to the data? Who determines what indicators are used? Who determines the process for responding to the information in reports and who participates in that process? Who is involved in evaluating the entire planning, management and reporting cycle? In other words, how *inclusive* is the reporting process within a broad management cycle?

- How adaptable is the reporting process to developments in data availability, indicator design and changing needs of users? In other words, how *flexible* is the process? How well is the tension between *flexibility* and *purposefulness* resolved?

This chapter can provide only a preliminary assessment in response to most of these questions. SoE is a fairly new endeavour starting in Australia in the late 1980s but with most activity from the mid-1990s. Corporate Environmental Reporting is even newer with the first stand-alone CER in Australia dating from 1996. In relation to most of these questions, it is still too early for clear trends to be evident.

SoE reporting: international background

Calls for reporting on the state of the environment go back to the early 1970s. In 1972 the first United Nations Conference on the Human Environment (held in Stockholm) called for 'reports on the state of, and outlook for, the environment' (cited in Parris 2000: 3). The United Nations Environment Programme (UNEP) published its first annual SoE report in 1974, to be followed by an analytical, comprehensive SoE report every fifth year. In 1972 the UNEP declared that all countries should be encouraged to report annually on the state of their living resources.[2] In 1979 the Organisation for Economic Development (OECD) prepared its first review of the state of the environment of OECD Member countries. It concluded that Member countries should (OECD 1979):

- reinforce cooperation within the OECD to improve environmental information and environmental reporting;
- intensify efforts to improve scientific knowledge, information, statistics and indicators on the state of the environment in order to contribute to the evaluation of the state of the environment, activities that have an impact on the environment and of environmental policies themselves, with an emphasis on areas in which comparable and practicable indicators could be defined; and
- prepare periodic national reports on the state of the environment and its changes over time.

By the early 1980s many countries around the world, including the USA, Japan, the Philippines, Canada, Denmark, the Netherlands and France were preparing SoE reports (Lloyd 1996).

Work on development of indicators and composite indices to report on trends in particular environmental media such as water or air quality was prolific in the 1970s, especially in North America (Harding and Eckstein 1996). The OECD re-invigorated indicator work for the broader SoE reporting framework and published core indicator sets for this purpose (OECD 1991, 1994, 1998a, 2001), a set of core indicators and a smaller set of ten 'key environmental indicators' aimed at reporting on 'sustainability' (OECD 2001a). In 1993 the OECD introduced a framework for environmental reporting based on a concept of causality (OECD 1993, cited in DEST 1994): human activities exert *pressures* on the environment and change its quality and the quantity of natural resources – their *state*. Society responds to these changes through environmental, general economic and sectoral policies – *response*. This has become known as the pressure-state-response (PSR) model and has been adopted, in some form, by most SoE reporting systems worldwide. Several modifications of the PSR model exist. Some of the most prominent are summarised below:

- condition–pressure–response (CPR) – analogous to human health, where one first inquires about the condition of a person, what pressures may be affecting their condition, and their response to the condition (ACT Office of the Commissioner for the Environment 1997);
- driving force–state–response (DSR) – includes the addition of social, economic and institutional indicators as driving forces affecting 'state' (United Nations Conference on Human Settlements 1996);

---

2 United Nations Resolution 2997 (XXVII), Institutional and Financial Arrangements for International Environmental Co-operation, Dec 1972.

- pressure–state–impact–response (PSIR) – an additional category refers to impacts due to ambient consequences (Environmental Systems Program, Harvard University 1996); and

- pressure–condition–response–implications (PCRI)[3] – looks at the implications of the environment's condition.

Today reporting is occurring at a wide range of levels across the world, from supra-national reports, such as those of UNEP, the World Resources Institute and the European Community (see Parris 2000), to national, state, regional and local, as well as for sectors such as forestry and agriculture and for organisations/corporations.

SoE reporting: Australian background

Within Australia, governments at every level have adopted State of the Environment (SoE) reporting to provide government, industry and the public with information about environmental performance. At the National level, in most States, and at the local government level in New South Wales, SoE reports are required under environmental legislation. Developments at each of these levels are discussed below and also see Table 9.1.

Some organisations have also started to produce public environmental reports to provide their management, staff and the public with information about their environmental performance. These include both private and public sector organisations. See the brief discussion on Corporate Environmental Reporting (CER) below.

In 1992, the Prime Minister announced that agreement had been reached between Commonwealth, State, Territory and local governments on how they would interact on issues dealing with the environment (Heads of Government in Australia 1992). This *Intergovernmental Agreement on the Environment* (IGAE) included a broad set of principles to guide the development of environment policies and set out cooperative arrangements on a range of specific issues, including environmental data collection and handling. Through the IGAE governments agreed that the concept of ecologically sustainable development (ESD) should be used in the assessment of natural resources, land use decisions and approval processes.

Also in 1992 the Council of Australian Governments endorsed the *National Strategy for Ecologically Sustainable Development*. The Council agreed that the future development of all relevant policies and programs should take place within the framework of the ESD Strategy and the IGAE (Council of Australian Governments 1992: 14). One of the recommendations adopted was that governments would establish a decision-making framework for the development, enhancement and management of natural resource data systems. To accomplish this recommendation governments agreed to introduce regular state of the environment reporting to enhance the quality, accessibility and relevance of data relating to ecologically sustainable development. They also

---

3   Commonwealth SoE Advisory Council for the 1996 SoE Report, Ian Lowe (pers comm).

Table 9.1: Review of Australian environment reporting by National, State and Territory governments

Govt	Report type	Agency	Scope	Reasons	Legislation	Model	NCI	ESD	Report cycle	Dates
Common-wealth	SoE	Department of Arts, Heritage and Environment	compilation of publicly available information on environmental sectors	to meet a general need for an overview of environmental conditions	no	condition-pressure-response	no		discontinued after 1987	1986, 1987
Common-wealth	SoE	State of the Environment Advisory Council	comprehensive review of Australian land and marine territory within 200 mile nautical limit	to meet the need for environmental information and satisfy international reporting commitments	no	condition-pressure-response	some overlap	G C	5 years	1996
Common-wealth	SoE	Australian State of the Environment Committee	an independent assessment of the condition of Australia's environment in the year 2001	• provide accurate, up-to-date and accessible information about environmental conditions, and where possible, trends for the Australian continent, surrounding seas and Australia's external territories • increase public understanding of issues related to the Australian environment • provide an early warning of potential problems • report on the effectiveness of policies and programs designed to respond to environmental change.	*Environment Protection and Biodiversity Conservation Act* 1999	condition - pressure - response	yes	G	5 years	2001

Govt	Report type	Agency	Scope	Reasons	Legislation	Model	NCI	ESD	Report cycle	Dates
NSW	SoE	NSWEPA	the latest report contains a central report with core indicators plus five 'Backgrounders' to provide a comprehensive introduction to each of the Report's environmental themes	a tool for raising awareness and providing a sound basis for better informed decisions	*Protection of the Environment Administration Act* 1991	pressure-state-response	Compatible	G C I	3 years (previously 2 years)	1993, 1995, 1997, 2000
Queensland	SoE	QEPA	comprehensive review of environmental and natural resource data across State	to establish a continuing information base for developing sound environmental strategies and management and for assessing the sustainability of development	*Environmental Protection Act* 1994	pressure-state-response	Compatible	G		4 years	1999
Victoria	SoE	Office of the Commissioner for the Environment	reports dealt with a specific theme: inland waters; agriculture				no			discontinued after 1991	1987, 1991
Victoria	Air quality indicators and monitoring	Office of the Commissioner for the Environment									

Govt	Report type	Agency	Scope	Reasons	Legislation	Model	NCI	ESD	Report cycle	Dates
Victoria	Air Monitoring Data	VicEPA	monitoring data for the Port Phillip and Latrobe Valley air quality control regions	to determine compliance with the State environment protection policy for air					annually	1992 – 1996
Victoria	Know Your Catchments, Victoria 1997: an assessment of catchment condition using interim indicators	NRE, CALP, VicEPA	collection of maps of catchment condition indicators on a statewide basis	L and to meet future monitoring requirements for SoE and the NLWRA	Catchment and Land Protection Act 1994					
Victoria	Environmental Health of Streams in the Western Port Catchment, April 1998	VicEPA	a study of the ecological health of streams in the Western Port catchment	to identify environmental 'hot-spots' that need management action to improve river health					ongoing	1998
Victoria	Victoria's Biodiversity Strategy	NRE		L and fulfils commitments in the national Strategy for the Conservation of Biodiversity	Flora and Fauna Guarantee Act 1998		some overlap		one-off	1997
Victoria	Water quality trends in fresh waters (1984–1996)	VicEPA	an assessment of selected water quality parameters in inland waters	feedback on the effectiveness of current and past management practices, and to help determine the need for change	no	exploratory data analysis and linear modelling	some overlap			1996

Govt	Report type	Agency	Scope	Reasons	Legislation	Model	NCI	ESD	Report cycle	Dates
South Australia	SoE	1998 SAEPA with cooperation of NRC and DEHAA	key environmental indicators	to provide credible, quantifiable and repeatable information about the quality of the environment and quality and quantity of natural resources	*Environment Protection Act 1993*	pressure-state-response	some overlap		5 years	1988, 1993, 1998
Tasmania	SoE	Sustainable Development Advisory Council, Resource Planning and Development Committee	summary indicators to describe environmental conditions and trends	a means to assess progress towards defined sustainable development objectives	*State Policies and Projects Act* 1993	pressure-state-response	some overlap	G	5 years	1996/7, due 2002
Western Australia	SoE	State of the Environment Reference Group (1998)	priority environmental issues affecting WA	to inform decision makers within government and the broader community	no	condition-pressure-response	some overlap	G C I	3-4 years	1992, 1998, draft due 2002, final 2003

Govt	Report type	Agency	Scope	Reasons	Legislation	Model	NCI	ESD	Report cycle	Dates
Northern Territory	Bioregions in the Northern Territory: conservation values, reservation status and information gaps	Parks and Wildlife Commission of the Northern Territory	satisfy reporting agreement with ANCA	information used to guide priorities for future conservation planning within and between bioregions			some overlap			1996
ACT	SoE	Office of the Commissioner for the Environment, ACT	key indicators of greatest environmental concern	to provide information, increase public understanding, satisfy reporting requirements and report on the effectiveness of policies and programs towards achieving environmental standards and targets	*Commissioner for the Environment Act* 1993	condition-pressure-response	Compatible	C	3 years (previously annual)	1997, 2000

KEY:

Agency – name of agency that prepared report
Report type – name of report
Scope – purpose of report
Reasons – reasons for reporting:
    L = required by legislation
    P = agency policy
Legislation – if required under legislation, the name
Included – what must be included in report
Model – indicator category
NCI – adoption of national core indicators in some form
ESD: (G) does the report focus on ESD through stated goals,
    (C) a chapter devoted to sustainability, or
    (I) contains sustainability indicators

Dates – years of published environmental reports
NRC – Natural Resources Council, South Australia
NRE – Department of Natural Resources and Environment, Victoria
CALP – Victorian Catchment and Land Protection Council
VicEPA – Victorian Environment Protection Agency
NSWEPA – NSW Environment Protection Authority
WAEPA – WA Department of Environmental Protection
QEPA – Queensland Environmental Protection Agency
SAEPA – SA Environment Protection Agency
NLWRA – the Land and Water Audit
DEST – Department of Environment Sport and Territories
DEHAA – Department of Environment Heritage and Aboriginal Affairs
ANCA – Australian Nature Conservation Agency

agreed to cooperate in developing analysis/information technologies and systems for optimising the use of natural resource databases and using them in pursuit of ESD (Council of Australian Governments 1992: 63).

Commonwealth

In 1981, the Australian House of Representatives Standing Committee on Environment and Conservation recommended that national state of the environment reports be prepared at regular intervals. Australia's first national SoE report was published five years later (Commonwealth of Australia 1986). It was intended to establish a 'benchmark' from which future environmental changes could be reported and indicate environmental conditions that might be expected without further improvement in planning and management. The report was also designed to satisfy Australia's obligation to report on global environmental matters to the OECD and the UNEP, and stimulate more detailed environmental reporting by the States. That process soon lapsed.

In 1992, the Commonwealth Environment Protection Agency released a discussion paper inviting public comment on options for a national State of the Environment reporting system (Commonwealth Environment Protection Agency 1992). It proposed a system that would compile data on indicators of ambient environmental quality plus information on natural resource stocks and the conservation status of ecosystems. Following a public consultation process, the Australian government released a strategic framework to guide the development of state of the Australian environment reporting and a nationally agreed set of environmental indicators (DEST 1994). The framework outlined the purpose of the reporting system, provided principles and objectives to guide its development, and proposed a mechanism for regular evaluation. It formally adopted the PSR model for national state of the environment reporting and set the interval between reports at four years. In May 1996 Australia released its first independent and comprehensive SoE report (State of the Environment Advisory Council 1996). This 1996 report followed ten years after the 1986 national report on the environment which was intended to provide a benchmark for tracking change in the Australian environment and which was billed as the first of a regular series of national SoE reports.

One of the stated functions of the 1996 SoE report was to assess progress towards the goal of ecological sustainability (State of the Environment Advisory Council 1996: ES-5). It identified the key threats to sustainability for its major themes: human settlements, biodiversity, atmosphere, land resources, inland waters, estuaries and the sea, and natural and cultural heritage. An additional chapter titled 'Towards Ecological Sustainability' identified two of the guiding principles in the *National Strategy for Ecologically Sustainable Development* as central to the report:

- decision making processes should effectively integrate both long and short-term economic environmental, social and equity considerations; and
- where there are threats of serious or irreversible environmental damage, lack of full scientific certainty should not be used as a reason for postponing measures to prevent environmental degradation.

The report concluded that:

> Despite the adoption of national strategies for ecologically sustainable development and conservation of biological diversity, there is little evidence that this broader approach and commitment to sustainability has been fully integrated into decision-making. (p ES-9)

Notably there are no clearly defined ESD goals or targets in the 1996 report. The 'key threats to sustainability' identified for each theme in the report, are in reality broad evidence of 'unsustainable' trends in key areas. There is no clearly defined and institutionalised means for using the information in the National SoE Report to inform ESD through government actions and responses. A Productivity Commission report on implementation of ESD by the Commonwealth found that implementation was constrained by inadequate information, namely a lack of regular, long-term monitoring and review of policies and programs related to ESD objectives (Productivity Commission 1999).

The *Environment Protection and Biodiversity Conservation Act* 1999 (Cth) now requires the production of an Australian SoE report every five years. Following the procedure with the 1996 report, an independent Australian State of Environment Committee was appointed to oversee the production of the 2001 Australian SoE. The 2001 SoE is a much slimmer volume than its 1996 predecessor. It draws on seven commissioned theme reports, as did the 1996 report, except that the theme reports are published as separate volumes in 2001. Lead authors, from both the public and private sectors, were chosen by tender to author these reports. They reported to the SoE Committee and each was assisted by an Expert Reference group established for their theme, and the theme reports were each peer reviewed (Australian State of the Environment Committee 2001; Australian State of the Environment Reporting 2000). The 2001 report claims that while it followed a similar conceptual structure, using the Pressure-State-Response model, to the 1996 report, it placed more emphasis on *implications* of conditions, pressures and responses.

States and Territories

SoE reporting in the States and Territories is primarily an activity of the 1990s, and for most the late 1990s. The exception is South Australia which first produced a SoE report in 1988. New South Wales, Queensland, South Australia, Tasmania and the ACT each have a legislatively-based requirement for regular state of the environment reporting (Table 9.1). Although Western Australia has no legislative requirement to report, it has produced two reports, and as discussed further below is currently (mid 2002) undertaking discussions on the future place of SoE reporting within the overall activities of government set in a 'sustainability' framework. Victoria has been reporting on aspects of the environment since 1988. Victorian legislation requires environmental reporting for selected topics (air quality monitoring, catchment condition reports) in relation to monitoring progress towards objectives set in State Environment Protection Policies (SEPPs) (Environment Protection Authority 1996) but does not require a broad SoE report. However, as discussed below, following an election commitment by the Bracks Government, regular SoE reporting has been recommended for Victoria (Public Accounts and Estimates Committee, Parliament of Victoria 2002). The Northern Territory has not yet produced a comprehensive environmental report, but publishes smaller, targeted reports based on specific reporting requirements.

Table 9.1 summarises the SoE reporting activity around Australia at Commonwealth, State and Territory levels, and the following discussion provides an outline of the key features of SoE reporting in each of the States and Territories.

NSW

New South Wales has produced four SoE Reports. The Reports were prepared by the EPA with advice from a stakeholder representative 'Reading Committee' for the first two reports, a 'Reference Committee' for the 1997 Report and a more closely involved 'State of the Environment Advisory Council' for the 2000 Report. Nevertheless, in each case responsibility for the Report rests clearly with the EPA. The aims of SoE reporting in NSW were outlined in a discussion paper released in 1996 (NSW EPA 1996):

- *communicate useable information* to decision-makers to improve management of the environment and assist in the achievement of ecologically sustainable development;
- *provide benchmark environmental data* for the assessment of the cumulative impacts of environmental policies, programs and actions over time and regions;
- *identify issues* that need to be addressed, important information gaps and emerging environmental problems; and
- *raise public awareness* of environmental issues by providing information in a readily understandable style and format.

The comprehensive reports have been arranged according to broad environmental themes (eg, air quality, land, biodiversity) with the 1993 and 1995 reports giving equal emphasis to examining SoE through sectors or issues such as transport, urbanisation, agriculture, forestry. An 'add-on' chapter 'Towards sustainability' was included in 1993, 1997 and 2000. The 1993 and 1995 Reports have broadly similar chapter headings for the environmental themes and sectors covered, but the 1997 Report contains just five chapters, four on environmental themes and the fifth on sustainability. The 2000 Report has six chapters, four on environmental themes, one on human settlements and one on 'Towards environmental sustainability'. The 2000 Report also differed from the 1997 in being supplemented by five SoE 'Backgrounder' volumes covering the four environmental themes and human settlements, and in using an expanded set of some 60 indicators (compared with 23 in 1997) drawn from the ANZECC list of core indicators for environmental reporting (ANZECC 2000). The purpose of these Backgrounders is to 'capture much of the descriptive background material related to these issues' (NSW EPA 2000: 10), so that the Report itself can concentrate on status of environmental issues and trends. This changing content does not make for ready comparison of the State of the Environment and associated pressures and responses, between the reports. While the reports use the pressure-state-response framework, and hence response indicators are included, there is no clear evidence of any institutionalised linking of the reporting process back into government policy.

In the 1997 NSW SoE report ecologically sustainable development (ESD) occupied a prominent position. The 'Introduction' describes ESD as the chief objective of environment protection in NSW and the report as attempting 'to present its issues in the context of that overall objective' outlining the ways it has attempted to do this through the Report as a whole (NSW EPA 1997a: 11). In a 'Towards sustainability' chapter prominent issues for sustainability in NSW were identified and discussed, including, resource consumption, waste, energy, urbanisation and transport. Core indicators from the previous chapters were traced from 1986-1996 to provide an assessment of broad environmental trends. However, the chapter stresses that the complexity of environmental systems and lack of understanding of cause-effect relationships mean that it is not possible 'for most areas to define limits of sustainable resource use, what pollution levels can be assimilated, or even the limits of change that will safeguard ecosystem function and integrity' (p 359), and hence for most areas 'robust indicators or benchmarks against which progress can be explicitly measured still need to be developed' (p 359).

The 1997 SoE Report clearly acknowledges that economic, social and environmental matters need to be integrated for reporting on sustainability, and notes that 'While it may not yet be possible to measure sustainable develop-ment in absolute terms, it is possible to measure progress...in establishing the processes for supporting it' (NSW EPA 1997a: 441). The section concludes that while the framework for sustainable decision-making has been slowly assembled in NSW, a clearer understanding of what ESD means in practice is needed. The 1997 Report makes a start in addressing reporting for ESD, but as discussed below it could be argued that it is not a very 'brave' start when benchmarked against some international endeavours. The 2000 chapter is no braver. Signifi-cantly, it is titled 'Towards *environmental* sustainability', acknowledging that it is not attempting to deal with the social and economic aspects of sustainability. It is briefer than the 1997 chapter and does not attempt to discuss the key environmental themes (such as wastes and energy) with respect to sustainability, but rather talks broadly about 'key determinants' and considers actions and roles of government, the market and the community in implementing ESD. Importantly, the letter from the NSW State of the Environment Advisory Council at the front of the 2000 report notes that SoE reporting is an evolving process, with international trends moving towards use of broader sustainability indicators, and suggests that 'to keep NSW at the forefront, it may be useful to consider incorporating more comprehensive social and economic data within SoE to enhance sustainability reporting' (NSW EPA 2000).

Queensland

Queensland has produced only one SoE Report to date (Environmental Protection Agency Queensland 1999). The Report was prepared by the Envi-ronmental Protection Agency with the assistance of sectoral working groups. The Queensland SoE report 'aims to establish a continuing information base for developing sound environmental strategies and management and for assessing the sustainability of development in Queensland'. The Report is divided into eight chapters: atmosphere, land, inland waters, coastal zone, energy resources, biodiversity, human settlements and cultural heritage. These are discussed within a pressure-state-response framework.

State of the environment reporting for Queensland is seen as an integral part of a four-phase planning and management cycle to ensure accountability of environmental strategies to achieve the object of the *Environmental Protection Act* 1994 (Qld), namely ecologically sustainable development (Environmental Protection Agency, Queensland 1999). These four phases are:

- establishing the state of the environment and defining environmental objectives;
- developing effective environmental strategies;
- implementing environmental strategies and integrating them into efficient resource management; and
- ensuring accountability of environmental strategies.

Following the launch of the 1999 Report, the Queensland Cabinet indicated that government agencies should identify priority issues requiring attention and develop recommended remedial actions, reporting back to Cabinet. An interdepartmental committee to carry out these tasks was developed in 2000. However, the Report itself does not include recommendations for action and may be best regarded as serving to provide a comprehensive overview to better inform decisions rather than being the primary agent for policy change.[4]

Victoria

Victoria produced SoE Reports in 1987 and 1991 but the process was discontinued after 1991. However, since then Victoria has produced a number of thematic environmental reports. The *Environment Protection Act* 1970 (Vic) enables the EPA in Victoria to recommend State Environment Protection Policies (SEPPs) to the Governor. These express in law the community's expectations, needs and priorities for protecting the environment and set a clear statutory basis which guides the EPA's controls and other programs. Each SEPP (Environment Protection Authority, Victoria 1996: 8):

- outlines the particular segment or element of the environment to which it applies (eg, a water catchment);
- outlines the beneficial uses of that environment;
- sets environmental quality objectives to ensure that all agreed beneficial uses of the environment are protected;
- defines indicators of environmental quality used to monitor whether objectives are being met; and
- sets out a broad program for attaining the objectives.

---

4   Pers Comm, Kathryn Adams, Director, Environmental Policy and Economics, Environmental Protection Agency, Queensland, 16 May 2000.

The development and review of SEPPs involves wide stakeholder consultation involving Policy Impact Assessment (PIA) which identifies and explains the key environmental, social and financial implications of the proposed SEPP. The PIA is the 'key mechanism by which environmental reporting data is used in the development of environmental policy'.[5] As shown in Table 9.1, there have been a range of reports in Victoria dealing with specific aspects of the environment and/or specific regions.

Re-introduction of SoE reporting for Victoria was an election commitment of the Bracks Government. The Public Accounts and Estimates Committee of the Parliament of Victoria (2002) in its *Final Report on Environmental Accounting and Reporting* notes that 'The Government will reintroduce SoE reporting in Victoria' (p 85), and recommends that SoE reporting be the responsibility of a Commissioner for Ecologically Sustainable Development. Among other matters, the Committee also recommended that a draft SoE report be released for public comment over three months, that the reporting cycle be five years, and that the government be required to respond to each statewide SoE Report within six months of the Report being tabled in Parliament. These recommendations are clearly significant moves for planning, not only to reintroduce statewide SoE reporting for Victoria, but in doing so within an overall ESD framework and with significant potential for public input and requirement for government response.

South Australia

South Australia has produced three SoE Reports at five year intervals from 1988. Notably, the reports have had different responsible authors and the first Report was produced without legislative requirement to do so. The 1988 and 1993 SoE reports were comprehensive reports covering, with minor exceptions, the same set of environmental and sectoral themes. The 1993 report was an update and review of the 1988 report that aimed to concentrate on those issues highlighted in the previous report and consider (Department of Environment and Land Management 1993: x):

- What has been done during the intervening period (since 1988) to address these issues;
- The effectiveness of the actions; and
- Future strategies for addressing those issues that are not being adequately addressed.

The 1993 Report noted that future reports would differ in format to 'provide a more directed means of evaluating the condition of the environment and the policies and strategies adopted to ensure ecologically sustainable development' (Department of Environment and Land Management 1993: x). The 1998 report provided a comprehensive cover of seven environmental themes and used key environmental indicators, reporting on quantifiable changes in these. It summarised progress against 13 priorities for action identified in the 1993 report and made 18 recommendations aimed at promoting ESD. The reports

---

5   Pers Comm, Terry A'Hearn, Manager, Policy Coordination, Victorian EPA, 19 June 2000.

do not set targets for performance nor do they address ESD other than from the perspective of tracing environmental change.

In 1999 the Department for Environment, Heritage and Aboriginal Affairs produced a position paper on *Environmental Performance Measures* for public discussion. This document revised the list of key environmental indicators used in the 1998 Report to, among other things, bring these into line with the ANZECC proposed set of national environmental indicators (ANZECC 1998). Importantly, it also chose a set of 25 measures from the key environmental indicators, to provide a basis for more regular reporting on environmental performance. For many of these indicators targets have been set at the international level (eg, Montreal Protocol) and national levels (eg, ANZECC water quality guidelines) and these were adopted in the Discussion Paper.[6] Where there were no agreed targets, performance measures were set in accordance with the principles of sustainability (Department for Environment, Heritage and Aboriginal Affairs 1999). The Discussion Paper noted that the 'establishment of environmental performance measures provides links with the financial reporting cycle and enables environmental outcomes to be reviewed against expenditure and provides a mechanism to allocate appropriate levels of resourcing for environmental management programs' (p 12). The Discussion Paper further drew attention to the potential for benchmarking environmental performance across jurisdictions by adoption of standardised environmental information.

Tasmania

Tasmania produced its first SoE Report in 1996 (Sustainable Development Advisory Council 1996). This Report was the legislative responsibility of the Sustainable Development Advisory Council, a body which includes representatives of the community, conservation, industry and government groups. Seven Scientific Reference Groups were formed to advise on the seven environmental themes covered in the Report. The Report also included eight economic sectors (eg, mining, forestry, tourism). Volume 2 of the *State of the Environment, Tasmania*, was published in 1997 and comprised the Council's recommendations to government on the environmental management issues that arose as a result of the state of the environment reporting process (Sustainable Development Advisory Council 1997). These recommendations were based on the information set out in Volume 1 of the SoE Report and public comment on a draft Volume 2 (suggested actions).

In Tasmania, State of the Environment Reporting is used to provide a means to assess progress towards sustainable development objectives outlined in legislation. These include (Sustainable Development Advisory Council 1996):

- to promote the sustainable development of natural and physical resources and the maintenance of ecological processes and genetic diversity; and
- to provide for the fair, orderly and sustainable use and development of air, land and water.

---

6   This was only a draft paper and no formal agreement was reached as to exact targets. The issue of targets is being re-visited (at mid-2002).

In 1998 the Sustainable Development Advisory Council ceased to exist with the establishment of the Resource Planning and Development Commission (RPDC) under the *Resource Planning and Development Commission Act* 1997 (Tas). Among other roles, the independent Commission comprising five Commissioners, took on responsibility for SoE reporting. While the RPDC is responsible for recommendations to government flowing from the SoE reporting process, as a statutory authority it clearly is not able to implement these recommendations, although part of its role is to review responses to the recommendations.

Western Australia

Western Australia produced its first SoE Report in 1992 (Government of Western Australia 1992). This was a comprehensive report covering nine environmental themes, ten regional summaries and 13 'human activities' (eg, forestry, water supply, waste). It has been described as 'a rather bland Government orientated report which achieved little in the way of environmental outcomes' (Higham 2000).

The SoE program was abandoned in 1993-4. Higham (2000) has described how the present SoE program in WA was redesigned from 1995 to put in place an 'environmental policy planning' process which he suggests provides for 'policy feedback, environmental performance monitoring and reporting, and policy learning' and which 'encompasses the function of state of the environment reporting' (p 2). Instead of being set within a pressure-state response framework as is typical for SoE reporting, this new endeavour led to development of a framework which merged the P-S-R model with an adaptive management and a strategic planning model.

A State of the Environment Reference Group was established to steer the process and included representatives from relevant government agencies as well as from major community catchment management groups. A regional approach was taken to reporting with government and community representatives working together to identify environmental issues, and suggest responses, for each of 23 bio-regions in the State (Government of Western Australia 1997a; Higham 2000). One aim was to integrate scientific and local environmental knowledge. This resulted in a set of Working Papers covering 22 environmental issues (Government of Western Australia 1997b) which was then condensed into a Draft SoE Report (Government of Western Australia 1997a) and released for public comment. This was the first time in Australia a SoE Report had been released for public comment. Following the submission period and review the 1998 SoE Report was released (Government of Western Australia 1998).

The Report combined a thematic approach covering identified environmental issues (and their relative regional significance), each of which was given a ranking in terms of environmental status, priority for action, and progress towards ESD in the main natural resource sectors of agriculture, energy, fisheries, forestry, mining and petroleum production, tourism and water supply. As well as the priority ranking, each environmental issue was addressed through indicators, broad environmental objectives for the issue, suggested responses (= recommendations), and a concluding statement from the SoE Reference Group. Discussion on each of the seven natural resource sectors also included 'suggested responses' as well as an assessment of 'challenges to ESD'.

These recommendations to government went to a set of Working Groups comprising representatives of government agencies, which was charged with costing the achievement of the recommendations. In turn this led to Western Australia's first 'Environmental Policy Plan' (Government of Western Australia 1999a). This Plan outlined (Higham 2000):

- the future of environmental policy planning in Western Australia;
- principles of Environmental Policy that will be used throughout the State Government; and
- 180 actions that the government has committed to undertake over the period 2000-2002.

During 2000 the establishment of an Environmental Action Council, comprising environmental leaders in the community and business, was proposed to oversee the future process for environmental policy planning. This was to include (Higham 2000):

- 2002 – release of a Draft SoE Report for public comment;
- 2003 – release of the final SoE Report;
- 2003 – performance audit of the environmental policy plan released in 1999; and
- 2004 – release of the next environmental policy plan to be implemented between 2005- 2008.

However, following the change in government in February 2001 these plans were under review as the government considers a 'sustainability strategy' for the State, and among other things, the place of SoE reporting within this. Meanwhile, the Minister has asked the Environmental Protection Authority (an independent statutory authority) to take responsibility for SoE.

In the late 1990s Western Australia seemed to be making a brave start at integrating SoE reporting into a broad cycle of environmental policy planning and management. It will be interesting to see what the future role of SoE reporting will be within the new 'sustainability agenda' for the State.

Australian Capital Territory

The ACT has produced three SoE Reports. The 1994 and 1995 Reports were in accordance with the *Commissioner for the Environment Act* 1993 (ACT) that required annual reports. Amendments to this Act now require that the SoE reporting period must not be more than four years but allows for more frequent reports. The Reports cover a comprehensive range of environmental themes – atmosphere, land, biodiversity, water and human settlement. The 1997 Report includes both actions for the Office of the Commissioner as well as prioritised recommendations for government.

ACT reporting is independent of any constraints from the Minister or government agencies and is the legislative responsibility of the ACT

Commissioner for the Environment (ACT Office of the Commissioner for the Environment 1997).

Under the Act the Minister is required to present a statement to the Legislative Assembly, six months after the release of the SoE Report, setting out the government's response to the Report. In his annual report (Commissioner for the Environment 1999) the Commissioner for the Environment comments on progress in implementation of SoE Report recommendations that he considered not to have been fully implemented during the year following release of the SoE Report. He also noted his aim to have actions arising from recommendations from SoE Reports incorporated into the budget and output reporting processes, 'so that the link between SoE Reports and management is transparent to all' (p 10). As noted below, the ACT SoE reporting information is also part of a wider regional SoE report.

Regional

A detailed coverage of regional SoE reporting activity is beyond the scope of this chapter. Nevertheless, it is important to draw attention to the extent of activities at this scale and their relative importance in management for sustainability. Alexandra et al (1998: 6) in a report commissioned by Environment Australia, note that:

> Many important decisions about the environment are made at regional (ie, sub-national, generally sub-State/Territory) scales, and the 'region' has become the preferred scale for much national program delivery. This is especially so for coastal, inland water, land and biodiversity programs, reflecting the current arrangements for investing in integrated catchment management, Landcare and related programs.

Alexandra et al (1998) worked with six pilot regions around Australia to develop appropriate indicators for SoE reporting to meet local needs. They also examined the links between the regionally useful indicators and those used at national scale, encouraging use of common indicators where possible. They drew attention to the complexity of regional environmental management, with a range of organisations involved, some focussing within the region concerned and others focussing more broadly (eg, State and Commonwealth agencies and industry or sector-based organisations). At the same time there has been a trend towards development of coordinating structures, such as Regional Organisations of Councils or Catchment Management Authorities (see Wild River, Ewing, Dore et al, this volume).

Reporting along bioregional lines has clear relevance for sustainably managing important catchments and other such regions. At the same time it will be necessary to integrate this reporting with relevant political and socio-economic boundaries. Alexandra et al (1998) identified a range of constraints and opportunities for using indicators to track environmental progress at this level, for aggregating information across spatial scales to feed information into State or national reporting programs and for involving communities in environmental monitoring. Nevertheless, they indicate there is much work to be done to address overlaps and gaps in responsibilities and conclude that 'an orderly process is required to negotiate the demarcation of these responsibilities'.

As one example of the complexity which may affect regional reporting, a SoE reporting period must not be more than four years for the ACT (as a Territory) under the *Commissioner for the Environment Act* 1993, while the 17 NSW Local Governments that join with the ACT to report for the Australian Capital Region, are required to produce a comprehensive SoE report in the first financial year following a council election under the *Local Government Act* (NSW) 1993 (Office of the Commissioner for the Environment, pers comm 2002). In 1997 a regional SoE Report was produced for this Australian Capital Region as an interactive CD-ROM (Sims 2000). This first regional SoE report in Australia was produced in response to the following needs/opportunities (Australian Capital Region Leaders Forum 1997):

- much of the information needed for wise management of the environment is held by Commonwealth or State agencies in a regional form;
- enhanced satellite images are best accessed on a regional basis;
- one collective request to an agency for information is better than 18 separate requests for the same or similar information; and
- the 1995 NSW EPA guidelines for Local Government Authorities advised Councils to draw on environmental data related to the larger ecological context, particularly with respect to water catchments, groundwater aquifers and airsheds and to share data where appropriate.

Comprehensive regional reporting appears to be developing rapidly at present. In addition to the Australian Capital region, the Hunter Region released in September 2000 a set of 15 'Hunter Region Sustainability Indicators'.[7] Eleven of the 15 are socio-economic indicators and the remainder bio-physical. Seventeen local councils in the Northern Rivers and North Coast region of NSW have agreed on a set of 21 indicators for annual local SoE reporting. This will allow for observation of environmental trends across the region and effective management responses (Luckie 2000). Other Regional Organisations of Councils (ROCs) in NSW, including the Eastern and Western ROCs (Jurmann 2000) are also examining regional reporting.[8]

Local government

There are over 700 local governments in Australia. SoE reporting is carried out by a number of these local governments, but is mandatory only in NSW. The *Local Government Act* 1993 (NSW) requires local government authorities in New South Wales to produce annual state of the environment reports. The first SoE report for the year ending after each election of councillors in a local

---

7   Pers Comm, Donna Farragher, Pathways to Sustainability Coordinator, Hunter Regional Organisation of Councils, 1 September 2000.

8   Pers Comm, Helen Sims, Office of the Commissioner for the Environment, ACT, September 2000.

area, must be a *comprehensive* SoE which addresses the eight environmental sectors of land, air, water, biodiversity, waste, noise, Aboriginal heritage and non-Aboriginal heritage. All major environmental impacts have to be reported on as well as related activities including management plans and special Council projects relating to the environment, and the environmental impact of Council activities. *Supplementary* SoE reports must be prepared in the intervening years. These need to identify any new environmental impacts since the last SoE report and update trends in environment indicators that are important to each environmental sector activities (NSW Government 1999).

It is probably fair to say that SoE reporting at local level has not, in most situations to date, fulfilled its proposed roles. In particular there seems to have been a failure to use the SoE information to drive policy and management change and to address ESD. There are however signs that legislative amendments put in place, at least in NSW, may cause changes to fill this gap.

The importance of linking SoE reporting at Local Government level into management planning by Councils is emphasised in two relatively recent documents. One is the December 1999 *Environmental Guidelines: State of the Environment Reporting by Local Government. Promoting Ecologically Sustainable Development* (NSW Government 1999). The other is the February 2000 *Management Planning for NSW Local Government: Guidelines* (NSW Department of Local Government 2000). Amendments to the NSW *Local Government Act* in 1997 put more emphasis on ESD and on linking the SoE reporting process to the overall management planning of Councils. The legislation requires Councils to be well-informed about the environmental circumstances of their areas and to apply the principles of ESD in a fully integrated way through their strategic management cycle (NSW Government 1999).

The *Environmental Guidelines* for Councils in NSW give considerable attention to ESD and provide examples for applying ESD principles at this level. They also encourage SoE reporting at the regional level and provide a list of core indicators, recommended for use by all Councils, as well as encouraging use of supplementary indicators of special relevance to each local area. The indicator list has been designed to align closely with indicators used for SoE reporting at State level in NSW and with those developed nationally through the ANZECC process (NSW Government 1999). NSW Councils are required by law to produce Management Plans and these must contain (among other things) 'activities to manage, develop, protect, restore, enhance and conserve the environment, consistent with the principles of ecologically sustainable development' (NSW Department of Local Government 2000: 49).

The ACT has supported local reporting within the Australian Capital Region, and more broadly, by developing a web-based template for SoE reporting (ACT Commissioner for the Environment, undated). A further resource for local Councils in preparing their SoEs is a NSW EPA web site called 'SoE direct' <http://soedirect.nsw.gov.au/app/index.jsp>. This site provides online access to several NSW EPA data resources relevant to SoE reporting. Councils are able to select an area and the type of information required (eg, about atmosphere, land, water).

Indicators for SoE reporting

Much work on developing indicator sets for SoE reporting has occurred in Australia since the late 1990s. In 1998 the Australian and New Zealand Environment and Conservation Council (ANZECC) released a draft set of core indicators for public comment (ANZECC State of the Environment Reporting Task Force 1998). The national set of core indicators was designed to assist the Commonwealth and State governments to further develop their environmental monitoring, and to help build a national picture of trends and the condition of Australia's environment. During the same period Environment Australia commissioned reports recommending indicators for each of the seven major themes around which Commonwealth State of the Environment reporting is based. This activity was planned as a follow-up development to the release of the 1996 *Australia: State of the Environment Report*. Consultants were commissioned to develop core indicators in the seven sectoral areas as follows: human settlements (Newton et al 1998), biodiversity (Saunders et al 1998), the atmosphere (Manton and Jasper 1998), the land (Hamblin 1998), inland waters (Fairweather and Napier 1998), estuaries and the sea (Ward et al 1998), and natural and cultural heritage (Pearson et al 1998). The consultants were asked to recommend a comprehensive set of indicators and were not to be constrained by current environmental monitoring. Hence these reports were aimed at providing a good scientific basis for longer term planning of environmental monitoring but may be difficult to implement in the shorter term due to lack of data (Alexandra et al 1998: iii). An eighth report deals with the use of indicators by local or regional environmental managers and the role of the community in environment monitoring (Alexandra et al 1998).

In March 2000 ANZECC released their final set of core indicators (ANZECC State of the Environment Reporting Task Force 2000), mentioning the considerable work towards development of indicators in Australia in the late 1990s, including the seven reports from Environment Australia, and the more than one hundred public submissions on their draft core indicator set of 1998. ANZECC described the March 2000 report as a 'further phase in the development of environmental indicators by introducing a set of 'core' indicators ... chosen on the basis that they can be used to report on the state of the environment across jurisdictions within Australia' (p 1). The core set covers six of the themes in the National SoE report, the exception being natural and cultural heritage, which ANZECC say 'will be developed through a separate process'.

The latest development in this sequence of indicator development activity was the release (in August 2000) by ANZECC of a proposed set of 'headline sustainability indicators' for public discussion. The set has been developed through a process managed by a Commonwealth inter-departmental committee chaired jointly by Environment Australia and the Agriculture, Fisheries and Forestry Australia. Twenty-two 'headline indicators of sustainable development' are described as collectively representing 'a way of assessing, over time, whether we are maintaining and enhancing the economic and social services and institutions which Australians, as a community, most value while, at the same time, maintaining the ecological systems on which all life depends' (Commonwealth of Australia 2000). The report stresses that the indicators need to be read as a set, since none of the indicators read in isolation tell us much about sustainability. The sustainability indicators have been selected to address the three core objectives of the *National Strategy for Ecologically Sustainable Development*:

- to enhance individual and community well-being and welfare by following a path of economic development that safeguards the welfare of future generations;
- to provide for equity within and between generations; and
- to protect biological diversity and maintain essential ecological process and life-support.

The paper notes the need to develop indicators relating to social cohesion and community infrastructure in order to complete this set. This latest development is no doubt driven by the OECD interest in 'headline' indicators defined as 'sets of broad indicators which, taken together, can track progress in the direction of ecological sustainability' and sectoral sustainability indicators as providing 'a measure of progress for a particular sector or activity, for example, agriculture or fisheries' (Australian State of the Environment Reporting 2000: 9). The first report against these headline sustainability indicators has recently been released (Environment Australia 2001).

Interestingly, the Australian Bureau of Statistics (ABS) has moved in a similar direction, working since mid-2000 with assistance from an external reference group, to develop a set of 15 integrated indicators to 'Measure Australia's Progress' (MAP). The ABS released its first report against these indicators in April 2002 (Australian Bureau of Statistics 2002).

The move to a common set of core indicators, supplemented where necessary by locally or regionally specific indicators, is important in providing scope for both vertical and horizontal integration of SoE reporting in Australia. As well, the development of 'headline sustainability indicators' (with the environmental indicators drawn from the ANZECC core set) is a necessary move if SoE reporting is to 'inform' sustainability. However, the current sets of indicators which have emerged from ANZECC seem to fall short of producing a means to 'inform sustainability'. A key failing at present is the lack of targets associated with these indicators. Environment Australia in reporting on development of the headline sustainability indicators said that 'to be meaningful, sets of sustainability indicators need to be derived from, or directly related to, authoritative policies for sustainability' (State of the Environment Reporting 2000: 9). The ANZECC set is structured around the three objectives of the *National Strategy for Ecologically Sustainable Development*, but these are so broad as to do little more than focus overall reporting on a fewer number of specified indicators. Until 'sustainability goals' are developed and specific targets are put in place there really is no means of judging progress to sustainability.

At a more fundamental level it could be argued that most of the 'indicators' in the ANZECC sets are in reality selections of 'data' rather than indicators. Take for example some sample 'indicators' from the ANZECC core set (ANZECC State of the Environment Reporting Task Force 2000):

- E + S 2: Area of marine habitat subject to: (a) trawling, (b) anchorage sites, (c) dredging (including dredge spoil dump sites), (d) navigation channels, (e) exploration, and (f) mining.
- IW 9: Incidence of freshwater algal blooms.
- BD 1 Rate of clearing, in hectares per annum, of terrestrial native vegetation types, by clearing activity.

In contrast the international literature on indicators suggests that indicators are not merely raw data or statistics; turning statistics or data into indicators involves some manipulation to give additional features, generally comparison with some reference value. Following from this view of indicators, Bakkes et al (1994: 5) describe an indicator as 'a piece of information which is a part of a specific management process and can be compared with the objectives of that management process and has been assigned a significance beyond its face value'. They further suggest that indicators belong within a specific management context and stress that this is a key point because it means that an indicator must be tailored to a specific process or task and hence, 'there is no such thing as a universal set of environmental indicators' (Bakkes et al 1994: 2-3). Rather, indicators need to be developed specifically for different purposes. Higham (2000: 60) makes an important point in this regard:

> In Western Australia, as in other States of Australia, there has been a tendency to develop indicators in isolation from environmental management and policy systems. We have been driven by the need to report, rather than the need to inform policy and management. The development of indicators out of a need to report will be very costly, both in terms of effective environmental management and the efficiency of environmental monitoring systems.

The reference value against which indicators are compared can take on a number of forms. It may be a legal standard of international or local significance, or a standard defined by government policy or a goal set by a community. Indicators may also be normalised by a temporal comparison; that is, by comparing against the level of a parameter in a particular year. Standards are increasingly likely to be set to represent 'sustainability'. While such sustainability standards remain difficult to define both for scientific and socially-based reasons, this should not prevent either use of targets based on provisional scientific information, or on a 'visioning' process. The Netherlands has defined 'sustainability' targets for its national SoE reporting and there is growing activity at a range of levels in use of 'visioning a sustainable future state' to set targets. It is this comparison with a reference value, which may correspond to the difference between a desired and an actual value, which is crucial to the role of indicators since it steers human action (Bakkes et al 1994).

Data for deriving indicators

The availability of scientifically credible data which are suitable for developing management-relevant indicators is critical for effective SoE reporting. This is a key challenge in a country as large and sparsely populated as Australia. This need has been endorsed by many and the 1996 SoE report for Australia made it clear that, at that time, we lacked an appropriate data base for SoE reporting (State of the Environment Advisory Council 1996). The 2001 Report (Australian State of the Environment Committee 2001: 10) noted the changes since:

> Since 1996, there has been a significant improvement in the data available for SoE reporting involving many organizations ... However, major problems of access to data and consistency of standards and methods of data compilation still exist. Development of adequate and effective responses to environmental challenges is often hampered by the lack of data and information with which to portray accurately how the Australian environment is changing over time.

The need for good data has been reiterated by many recent commentators on SoE (eg, ACT Office of the Commissioner for the Environment 1997; Department for Environment, Heritage and Aboriginal Affairs 1999; Higham 2000; NSW State of the Environment Advisory Council;[9] Public Accounts and Estimates Committee, Parliament of Victoria 2002) as has the need for long-term monitoring to enable time-series information (Australian Capital Region Leaders Forum 1997; Department for Environment, Heritage and Aboriginal Affairs 1999).

One way of increasing monitoring and data collection across Australia is through use of data collected by the large number of 'Watches' or community environmental monitoring (CEM) groups (eg, Streamwatch, Saltwatch, Frogwatch) which have proliferated in recent years. Alexandra et al (1996) have documented these groups and their monitoring activities. It is clear that the monitoring by these groups serves an important educational and motivational role in relation to environmental awareness and care, but the quality of the data collected has often been questioned. Alexandra et al (1998) concluded that CEM groups, and monitoring programs generally, vary greatly in the quality of data collected. Some CEM groups, and especially the larger coordinated monitoring networks such as Waterwatch, can provide reliable data that can be integrated to SoE reporting at higher spatial levels. They further concluded that 'In some cases CEM groups may be the only means of obtaining the geographical coverage and spatial density of data required to support indicators' (Alexandra et al 1998: 50).

There has been much activity in the past five years at both National and State levels in setting up data bases accessible through the web.[10] Nevertheless, access to date remains a key issue. For example, Higham (2000: 59) notes that in Western Australia 'government agencies have been selective in the information made available' and 'Environmental performance auditing will continue to be compromised if access to data is constrained by the interpretation that may be placed on that data'. Higham (2000: 59) reiterated the

---

9   In the Council's letter to the Minister regarding the NSW 2000 SoE report (NSW EPA 2000).
10   See for example CANRI (Community Access to Natural Resources Information) <http://www. canri.nsw.gov.au/>and SoE Direct <http://soedirect.nsw.gov.au/ pp/index.jsp>on the NSW EPA web site.

1997 recommendation of the Commonwealth State of the Environment Advisory Council for legislation to facilitate access to data.

Corporate Environmental Reporting (CER)

CER, as the name suggests, refers to environmental (or, as is now emerging, sustainability) reporting by organisations or corporations. It 'is the voluntary public disclosure of information about an organisation's impacts on the environment, its performance in managing those impacts and its contribution to ecologically sustainable development' (NSW EPA, 1997b). In the early 1990s both the International Chamber of Commerce and *Agenda 21* called on business and industry to report regularly on their environmental performance. In 1992 the Commonwealth Public Accounts Committee recommended that statutory authorities and government business enterprises should include statements concerning their actions in relation to their environmental responsibilities. This is now a requirement under the s 16A(6) of the *Environment Protection and Biodiversity Conservation Act* 1999 (Cth) which states that the annual reports of all Commonwealth Authorities, companies and agencies must:

- include a report on how the actions of, and the administration (if any) of legislation by, the reporter during the period accorded with the principles of ecologically sustainable development; and
- identify how the outcomes (if any) specified for the reporter ... contribute to ecologically sustainable development; and
- document the effect of the reporter's actions on the environment; and
- identify any measures the reporter is taking to minimise the impact of actions by the reporter on the environment; and
- identify the mechanisms (if any) for reviewing and increasing the effectiveness of those measures.

Since July 1998, s 299 (1)(f) of the *Corporations Law* requires that the annual directors' report must contain ... 'if the entity's operations are subject to any particular and significant environmental regulation under a law of the Commonwealth or of a State or Territory – details of the entity's performance in relation to environmental regulation'. This provision remains unchanged under the *Corporations Act* 2001, which replaced the *Corporations Law*. The Institute of Chartered Accountants in Australia, Environmental Accounting Task Force (1998: 8) recommended that 'environmental impacts, whether quantifiable in monetary terms or not, warrant some form of disclosure to the extent that the environmental implications are deemed significant'.

The push both internationally and within Australia for environmental and/or sustainability reporting by organisations, both public and private, is growing. Organisations started by reporting on environmental performance and/or associated liabilities originally as part of their annual report. Recently, this has moved to stand-alone environmental reports, and for some, sustainability reports, with Australia lagging behind the international move to this form of reporting. The first stand-alone CER in Australia, by Western Mining Corporation, dates from 1996.

A 1996 review of environmental reporting in Australia found that while only 24 per cent disclosed environmental information within the annual report, 68 per cent of annual report users sought disclosure of environmental information (Rankin 1996). In 1998 it was estimated that the number of Australian listed corporations that provided some form of environmental disclosure within annual reports had grown to 40 per cent, but the demand for environmental performance information was still not being met (Institute of Chartered Accountants in Australia, Environmental Accounting Task Force 1998). Several reviews of corporate environmental reporting in Australia have concluded that Australia's corporations have not kept up with their international counterparts. For example (Newson and Deegan 1996):

> Australian environmental reporting practices are well behind world 'best practice'. It would appear that the current role of Australian environmental reporting is to bolster and promote public image, rather than providing information that will enable an accurate assessment of an organisation's environmental performance.

In addition, a study of environmental reports released by Australian corporations in 1997 found that the standard of environmental reporting in Australia was generally below the global standard and that only a relatively small number of organisations undertake public environmental reporting compared to in the United States and Europe (Jeyaretnam 1999). A guide produced under Environment Australia's Business of Sustainable Development (BSD) initiative to help promote environmental and social performance of Australian business said the following:

> Public environmental reporting is one of the most important elements of environmental performance used by investors and other stakeholders use to judge a company's social responsibility. (Deni Green Consulting 2001)

While comprehensive corporate environmental reporting is not presently required by law in Australia, pressure is building to promote the disclosure of environmental information by private corporations. Three mandatory reporting requirements currently exist for Australian corporations:

- National Pollutant Inventory for emissions of selected pollutants;
- Greenhouse Challenge Program requires mandatory reporting on greenhouse gas emissions for signatories to the Program; and
- The Corporations Act 2001 requires mandatory reporting within annual directors' reports if a company's operations fall under environmental regulation.

A significant move during 2002 was the introduction of the Financial Services Reform Act (FSRA) which came into effect on 11 March and requires all issuers of financial services products to supply a product disclosure statement (PDS) that must state the extent to which labour standards, environmental, social or ethical considerations are taken into account in the selection, retention or realisation of an investment.[11]

Governments in Australia and international industry umbrella organisations (such as the World Business Council for Sustainable Development 1999) have been encouraging voluntary environmental and/or sustainability reporting by corporations. The NSW EPA produced guidelines for CER in 1997 outlining a range of reasons for corporations to report on environmental matters (NSW EPA 1997b):

- satisfy the community's right to know – the community has a fundamental right to have access to information on emissions, including the risks they pose for public health and amenity and their impact on the environment;

- create market opportunities – to promote the corporation as clean and green, possibly commanding a price premium;

- to gain access to funds and insurance – to tap the increasing 'ethical investment fund' market and provide a more accurate assessment of a corporation's risk profile and management;

- raise staff commitment – public environmental reporting can inform staff and the surrounding community of the importance the corporation places on its environmental performance; and

- strengthen the corporation's negotiating powers with regulators and community – public environmental reporting can increase the confidence of regulatory bodies and the community about the corporation's openness and sincerity about improving environmental performance.

Recently, the Commonwealth has produced *A Framework for Public Environmental Reporting* (Environment Australia 2000) with the Minister for the Environment stating in his Foreword:

> Widespread voluntary public environmental reporting will contribute to improved environmental and economic outcomes by adding to the impetus for organisations to continually seek out and implement eco-efficiency gains. I hope that within Australia both private and public sector organisations will see it as in their best interests to start, or continue, reporting on their environmental performance.

At the international level there has been emphasis by many major corporations on 'sustainability reporting' rather than simply environmental reporting. This has typically been within the discourse of the 'triple bottom line' – the business interpretation of sustainability, emphasising social and environmental as well as economic returns. For example, the Global Reporting Initiative (GRI) was established in 1997 and includes corporations, non-government organisations, international organisations/UN agencies, consultants, accountancy firms and a range of other stakeholders around the world. The GRI was

---

11   From *Ethical Investor* <http://www.ethicalinvestor.com.au/default.asp 16 May 2002>.

established with the mission of designing globally applicable guidelines for preparing enterprise-level sustainability reports. Following an extensive process of consultation, in June 2000 the GRI produced Guidelines for sustainability reporting for organisations (Global Reporting Initiative 2000).

The Draft 2002 Sustainability Reporting Guidelines <www.global reporting.org> report that:

> In the two years that have elapsed since publication of its first *Sustainability Reporting Guidelines* in June 2000, the forces that catalysed the formation of GRI in 1997 have continued unabated and, in most cases, have intensified. Globalisation, governance, accountability, citizenship – powerful forces at the close of the 20th century that spurred the GRI process in its early years – now have moved to the mainstream of policy and management debates. The turbulent first years of the new century underscore the cornerstone of GRI's rapid expansion – higher standards of accountability and dependence on networks of relationships will form part of the fabric of organizational practice in the 21st century.
>
> The mission of creating a new, generally accepted disclosure framework for sustainability reporting continues to garner widespread support in civil society, business, government, and labour. GRI's rapid evolution in just a few years from a bold vision to a new permanent global institution reflects the imperative and the value that various constituencies assign to such a disclosure framework. The modus operandi of the GRI process, rooted in inclusiveness, transparency, neutrality, and continuous enhancement, has enabled GRI to become a leading contributor to giving concrete expression to this new level of accountability.

An updated version of these guidelines was released in late 2002.

The Commonwealth guidelines are about *environmental* reporting, but *sustainability* reporting is discussed under 'Future Reporting Trends' and the important point made that (Environment Australia 2000: 40):

> A sustainability report ... is more than the sum of environmental, social and economic information. It must also seek to integrate this information to allow readers to understand the inter-relations and balance between the three dimensions from the standpoint of both process (how decisions are made) and outcome (the results of decisions).

An important issue is how to link CER into the broader reporting framework at local, regional, State or national levels. At present there is no ready mechanism for this, although reporting on aspects of a corporation's environmental performance, such as greenhouse gas emissions or emissions of selected pollutants, may enter the wider reporting frameworks through the National Pollutant Inventory or the National Greenhouse Gas Inventory. However, this raises the further question as to how well these inventories are integrated into SoE reporting, with the most likely answer at present being, 'not well'.

How well do SoE reporting and CER 'Inform ESD'?

To evaluate the success of SoE and corporate environmental reporting mechanisms against the goal of informing ESD we will now draw on the background information given above to address each of the questions posed earlier in this chapter, reflecting the core themes of this book.

1. *Is there a mechanism that ensures continuity of reporting, and are the stated goals consistent between reports? In other words, does 'persistence' characterise the process?*

To provide some assurance of continuity, a legislative basis for environmental reporting is necessary. Most States and Territories in Australia now have legislated SoE reporting. The exceptions are Western Australia, Victoria and the Northern Territory. The discontinuation of SoE reporting in both the Commonwealth (after 1986) and Victoria (after 1991) highlights the importance of a firmly institutionalised basis for SoE reporting. Higham (2000: 61) notes that 'A simple amendment to the *Environment Protection Act 1986* (WA) similar to that included in s 516B of the *Environmental Protection and Biodiversity Conservation Act 1999* (Cth) [which legislated for five-yearly national SoE reporting] would provide the longevity required for the environmental policy planning program, without constraining the flexibility desirable for innovation'.

At the local level SoE reporting has a legislative basis only in NSW. SoE reporting at the local level has ranged widely in standard under this mandatory requirement. In the early days of local SoE the effectiveness of such mandatory reporting for a number of Councils may be regarded as doubtful, when the reporting may have been of a poor standard and lacking integration into the overall management process. While the 1997 amendments to the *Local Government Act* have put more pressure on Councils to carry out an effective reporting program that is linked to overall management, significant challenges in achieving integrated management planning and SoE reporting remain (Griffiths 2000). Similar reservations regarding mandatory reporting have typified discussion on corporate environmental reporting although many stakeholders have called for mandatory CER (eg, OECD 1998b). Today, at least with the 'bigger players', CER seems to be strongly driven by community demands for transparency and accountability, and for these organisations, this pressure alone is likely to drive regular reporting, at least in the short term.

There is always the risk that mandatory reporting will lead to a 'rubber stamp' exercise of poor quality and little utility, but so long as community and/or regulatory demands and standards are kept at a high level, a legislative basis for reporting must be seen as an advantage. However, to be effective such demands must lead to meaningful feedback on the reporting process with the power to drive high standards.

Where SoE reporting is required by legislation, that legislation outlines what should be included in the report. This is an important safeguard but also may act to hinder desirable change. For example, the legislation requiring SoE reporting by the Commonwealth, States and ACT typically requires assessment of the state of the major environmental resources and values and in many cases also requires review of programs or policies concerned with environ-mental protection (see Table 9.1 for legislation). The legislation at present does not require reporting on progress towards ESD, though ESD is typically mentioned in the overarching objectives of the Acts. It could be argued that this has led to a tension in the reporting process with reporting agencies simultaneously responding to the requirements of the SoE legislation and some also trying to 'move with the times' by including ESD in their SoE Reports. In those situations (such as NSW) where the environment is inter-preted almost solely in biophysical terms, reporting on progress towards ESD (which by definition involves the integration of environmental, social and economic goals) is necessarily doomed to failure. The approach has generally been to add a chapter entitled 'Towards ESD' which in the worst cases is little more than a dumping ground for items that do not readily fit elsewhere in the report, coupled with some 'educational' comments on ESD.

This tension is also evident for local government SoE reporting in NSW. Amendments to the *Local Government Act* (NSW) in 1997 incorporated the ESD principles and require Councils to 'manage their regulatory and service functions in an ecologically sustainable manner' (NSW Government 1999: 1). They also say that 'SoE reporting is a key mechanism for assessing progress towards sustainability' and that 'In effect the legislation requires the council to be well informed about the environmental circumstances of its area and to apply the principles of ESD in a fully integrated way through the council's strategic management cycle of direction, action and accountability' (p 1). In reporting on management plans relating to the environment, council projects and the environmental impact of council activities, 'the reporting would cover, among other things, the application by the council of the principles of ESD throughout its activities' (p 15). However, under the *Local Government Act* the issues on which the councils must report in the SoE are the eight environ-mental themes. The difference since the 1997 amendment is that now councils must also report in the SoE on management plans relating to the environment and its *annual report* should also 'indicate the manner and degree to which the council has been successful in applying the principles of ESD throughout all of its activities' (NSW Government 1999: 8). It seems that both the annual report and the SoE report are expected to play a role in informing ESD. Notably, however, despite the primarily bio-physical emphasis in the eight themes councils must report on in the SoE, much local reporting emphasises socio-economic issues, potentially bringing it closer to 'informing ESD'.

SoE reporting is in its infancy in Australia but is evolving fast. The challenge is to provide legislatively-based requirements to ensure continuity in reporting, both in terms of regularity of the production of reports, and also in their contents (so that trends can be discerned), and at the same time to provide sufficient flexibility for reporting to evolve, learning by experience and moving towards informing ESD, rather than just informing some *environmental* aspects relevant to ESD.

2. *Has ESD been defined by the reporters? Is measuring progress towards ESD a stated goal of the reporters? Have ESD 'targets' been set, and is data available to measure progress towards these? Is the data appropriate to 'inform' ESD? In other words, is*

informing progress towards ESD a clearly defined 'purpose' of the reporting and have ESD goals been set to report against?

To answer these questions it is necessary to consider what is really meant by 'measuring progress towards ESD'. As signatories to the *Intergovernmental Agreement on the Environment* (1992) all levels of government in Australia have agreed to carry out their activities in accordance with the principles of ESD. This has meant that as new legislation or policy is enacted the *National Strategy for ESD* definition of ESD and/or its principles are included. These are broad and widely open to interpretation. Typically the result has been little more than a 'lip-service' response, no matter whether the ESD requirements are included just in the objectives of an Act, or more substantively in the body of an Act. The Productivity Commission recognised this in its 1999 Report where it recommended that the development of performance indicators against clearly stated objectives should be mandatory early in the policy development phase of government departments and agencies to monitor their ESD related policies, programs and regulations.

As we have seen above, reporting on progress to ESD through setting of ESD goals is not presently part of legislative requirements for SoE reporting. Rather ESD is typically part of the broad objectives of the legislation and hence forms the framework for SoE reporting. Through the 1997 amendments to the *Local Government Act*, local government in NSW perhaps comes closest to requiring 'informing of ESD-related matters' within the SoE report.

However, supposing that due attention is paid to a requirement to take account of ESD – what might that mean? ESD is a concept that draws on both science and values for its interpretation and application. It cannot be uniquely defined for any particular situation. While ESD necessarily incorporates integrated social, economic and ecological parameters, to assist in application we can 'unpack' the concept, defining 'components' of ESD. Examples may include specific scientific parameters for water quality, air contaminants, biodiversity and socio-economic parameters relating to employment, urban safety, etc. Both scientific information and social values need to be combined to derive ESD goals or targets for each component. A way of incorporating social values which has been used by a number of communities is to undertake 'visioning' exercises of a desirable future state for a community and then use science and social science data to work back and derive targets for individual components.[12]

Present endeavours in Australia at informing ESD through SoE reporting are at such a 'component' level (but typically without the targets). For example the draft 'National headline sustainability indicators' are no more than a selection of 22 quite separate economic, social and environmental indicators. There is no suggestion that targets will be set to report against and it could be unkindly suggested that the best these can do is provide an 'after-the-event' record of progress towards what turns out to be 'unsustainability'. It should be acknowledged however, that the set is prefaced by the comment that 'The

---

12   See for example <http://www.envcomm.act.gov.au/Soe2000/ACT/Prelims/Towards sustainability. htm> which describes the ACT's concept of visioning towards sustainability.

indicators should be read as a set ... none of the indicators, read in isolation, tells us much about sustainability ... Only read together, and particularly over time, will they tell us whether the things we need and value are being sustained without eroding other things we need or value' (Commonwealth of Australia 2000: 1).

To really 'inform ESD', it is necessary to find appropriate means to bring all these component parameters together to make a 'whole sustainability vision' which recognises interlinkages between the components and which is greater than the sum of the parts. This remains a key challenge for both theorists and practitioners. This challenge importantly includes defining means to measure not only the components but also progress towards the integrated whole. How this might be done is currently a key topic of investigation world-wide at all levels from the corporate to the national. Included at this higher level of integration should be the policies, legislation and administrative arrangements that act to facilitate or hinder the achievement of the 'ESD components'. Considerations at this level may include: economic instruments including tax systems; means for making linkages between sectors and administrative areas to cross-check implications of policy change for sustainability outcomes; means for feeding information from monitoring (technical, scientific and socio-economic) back into decision-making processes to inform sustainability.

In sum, judged by these criteria, informing ESD is not a clearly defined purpose of SoE reporting in Australia. A start would be to set targets for ESD 'components' and report against these. However, we seem presently unwilling to do this, although the Position Paper on *Environmental Performance Measures* for South Australian SoE reporting (Department for Environment, Heritage and Aboriginal Affairs 1999) is an encouraging sign of change, and there have recently been calls for use of targets from other commentators. These include Higgins and Venning (2001: 15) who see goals and targets set within an adaptive management framework as part of an 'emerging system' that will meet the information needs of a sustainable society, and Yencken and Wilkinson (2000: 320) who suggest that:

> for the achievement of ecological sustainability we need:
> * an overall goal;
> * a set of principles which define what is needed to achieve that goal;
> * general targets; and
> * backcasting to help us achieve the goals and targets.

3. *Is the reporting process formally and meaningfully linked back into policy setting, planning and management actions by appropriate institutions and stakeholders? In other words does the reporting process 'richly inform' action in a broad planning and management cycle? And, is the information received used 'sensitively' to 'adapt' planning and management to achieve set goals.*

The brief answer is 'no, but there are welcome signs of change'. The lack of integration of SoE reporting into policy and management cycles has been a constant criticism, with SoE reporting seen as an end in itself rather than as a means to inform better environmental management or, more recently, to inform ESD. The Productivity Commission (1999) noted that:

> Monitoring the effectiveness of policies and programs aimed at implementing ESD does not appear to be undertaken routinely by departments and agencies. Further, there appear to be even fewer examples where the results of monitoring activities are incorporated into policy or program revisions via feedback mechanisms ...

However, there are signs that change may be occurring in this direction in some jurisdictions. These include the following actions and recommendations:

- the 1997 amendments to the *Local Government Act* in NSW requiring linking of the SoE reporting process to the overall management planning of Councils;
- the linking of SoE reporting to management in the ACT, with the Minister required to outline, to the Legislative Assembly, the government's response to SoE report recommendations, and the independent Commissioner for the Environment then commenting on progress in implementation of government's responses;
- the comment by the NSW State of the Environment Advisory Council for the 2000 SoE Report, in its letter to the Minister reproduced in the Report (NSW EPA 2000), that 'SEAC feels strongly that the outcomes revealed in *SoE 2000* should be integrated more formally in environmental decision- and policy-making in this State .... Moreover, it would seem appropriate to formalise within the government process a mechanism where the follow-up to SoE outcomes takes place';
- proposals for Victoria by the Public Accounts and Estimates Committee (2002), outlined above; and
- the environmental policy planning process in Western Australia as at 2000.[13] However, Higham (2000) reported that the evaluation of the first WA cycle found that 'environmental policy planning has not yet resulted in significant policy or program change within the Western Australian Government despite the broad scope of recommendations in the 1998 SoE Report'.

Higham (2000) noted that the WA developments up to 2001 were consistent with those internationally, such as the framework outlined by the United Nations Environment Programme in *Global Environmental Outlook 2000* (UNEP 1999). He also made some useful observations in discussing the Western Australian situation, including (Higham 2000):

- the need for legislation to facilitate access to data and unconstrained use of that data;
- the need for resources to establish a comprehensive database available across Government;

---

13 However, as noted above, the change of Government in Western Australia in February 2001 has brought change and the new arrangements are not yet clear.

- the need to develop indicators as part of environmental management and policy systems;[14]
- the need to explicitly report on *implications* of environmental trends in order to increase the relevance to decision-makers;
- the need to maximise independence when auditing environmental performance;
- the importance of a guiding body for SoE reporting that is independent of government;
- the need for targets;
- the benefits of public participation in the process and the need to develop partnerships between the government, business and community groups to improve policy implementation in WA; and
- the need for a State strategy for ESD and integration of this with the policy planning process.

4. *Who determines what is included in environmental/sustainability reports? Who determines what data is collected, how and how often? Who determines how that data is interpreted? Who has access to that data? Who determines what indicators are used? Who determines the process for responding to the information in reports and who participates in that process? Who is involved in evaluating the entire planning, management and reporting cycle? In other words, how 'inclusive' is the reporting process within a broad management cycle?*

It is important to distinguish here between *topics/issues* to be covered and the *detailed content* of the reports. As just discussed, where reporting is a legislative requirement, the *topics* to be addressed are primarily determined by the regulatory requirements. There may of course be additional matters reported upon which are not strictly required by law. A further important consideration is whether the SoE reporting process is under the control of an independent committee or a government agency. At the State/Territory/ National/Local levels most reporting is presently carried out by government agencies/local councils. There are, however, a few exceptions, as follow. At Commonwealth level an independent Australian State of the Environment Committee is responsible. Among the States, Tasmania had a Sustainable Development Advisory Council, comprising representatives of community, conservation, industry and government groups, with responsibility for compilation of the Report under s 29 of the *State Policies and Projects Act 1993* (Tas). The first SoE Report for Tasmania, released in 1997, was prepared under this Council. In late 1997, the responsibilities of a number of statutory authorities in relation to public land management, planning, resource management and state of the

---

14   In contrast, Higham (2000: 60) notes that 'there has been a tendency to develop indicators in isolation from environmental management and policy systems. We have been driven by the need to report, rather than the need to inform policy and management. The development of indicators out of a need to report will be very costly, both in terms of effective environmental management and the efficiency of environmental monitoring systems'.

environment reporting were aggregated under a single statutory authority, the Resource Planning and Development Commission.

In the ACT SoE reporting is the legislative responsibility of the independent ACT Commissioner for the Environment. Among other States and at the local level there may be public input but the reporting exercise is essentially a government or agency function. Western Australia introduced a broadly participatory process in the late 1990s within a framework of government agency responsibility for reporting, but as outlined above, this process is under review. NSW presently has a non-government SoE Advisory Council, but its influence is limited. Local councils have a legislative requirement to 'involve the community (including environmental groups) in monitoring changes to the environment over time' (NSW Government 1999: 16). The recommendations of the Public Accounts and Estimates Committee (2002) for Victoria, would, if implemented, put SoE reporting in the hands of a Commissioner for ESD.[15] The need for independence was emphasised in the 1997 evaluation of the Commonwealth SoE reporting system (State of the Environment Advisory Council 1997) – 'All reviews have highlighted the critical importance of having a guiding body that is independent of government'. This was seen as important in regard to the acceptance, objectivity and scientific credibility of the outputs.

In terms of choice of indicators used in reporting, the production of the ANZECC Core Set in March 2000 (ANZECC 2000), will no doubt mean a move towards use of common indicators at least at national, State and regional levels, though with scope to use additional location-specific indicators as well. At local level in NSW a draft set of core indicators has been developed (NSW Government 1999) based on the core indicators developed at national, State and regional levels. Councils are encouraged to use indicators from this core set, supplemented by locally relevant indicators where appropriate.

Data

Availability of appropriate data is a key issue for SoE reporting in Australia and has received much comment from a range of sources. For example, the OECD review of Australia's environmental performance (OECD 1998b) found that:

> Despite progress in reporting on the state of the environment, environmental monitoring and environmental data in Australia are often inadequate in terms of coverage and consistency. This weakens the capacity to track environmental progress, formulate cost-effective policies and measure environmental performance. Better environmental data, indicators, monitoring and reporting are necessary so the public and decision makers can better understand the situation and address the most pressing problems.

---

15   The recommendations suggest the Commissioner be a statutory officer appointed for five years, and reporting to Parliament through the Premier or other responsible Minister.

The Productivity Commission (1999) listed inadequate information as a contributor to a general failure for government departments to implement ESD. It acknowledged that:

> some aspects of ESD implementation are highly information and data intensive – particularly in relation to the environment. However, there appears to be little long term commitment to information gathering and reporting in relation to the environmental dimensions of ESD. Different agencies collect data and information, particularly in relation to the environment and natural resource management, and there is limited coordination between these agencies.

And suggested that:

> To build an adequate information base, government may have a role in coordinating existing sources of information (or at least not impeding the flow of information and the linkages between relevant databases) and in developing, and implementing, a strategic approach to fill information gaps and minimise duplication of effort in data collection. Adequate long term funding of data collection (including research and development) is also necessary.

The 1996 National SoE Report noted that 'Australia lacks an integrated national system for measurement of environmental quality, a national database of sufficient calibre to assess and manage environmental quality, and appropriate national baseline data to evaluate the effectiveness of strategies' (State of the Environment Advisory Council 1996: 10-24). The Australian State of the Environment Committee for the 2001 Report noted that while there has been significant improvements in data availability, major problems of access to data and consistency of standards and methods of data compilation still exist and hamper our responses to environmental challenges.

Numerous others have drawn attention to this 'data problem' including the NSW State of the Environment Advisory Council for 2000 SoE Report (NSW EPA 2000) and Hamblin (1998) in her Report on indicators for National SoE reporting on 'the land'. Hamblin (1998: 103) noted that:

> A number of indicators have been proposed that are hard to achieve currently because of the lack of baseline values and the piecemeal nature of past and current research required to bring the indicator to the level of operational reporting.

Hamblin further noted the need for funding to support research into 'operationalising' proposed indicators for SoE reporting, including support for coordination of monitoring by voluntary groups that can feed into indicators that require detailed local knowledge that is 'beyond the capacity of under-resourced government agencies to obtain'.

The Department of the Environment and Heritage (undated) in a submission to the Productivity Commission Inquiry noted constraints on the development of national environmental data:

- environmental data tend to be scattered and decentralised, with every State and every agency tending to maintain its own systems for its own immediate purposes (eg, fisheries, minerals, threatened species, air quality, water quality, etc). There is little consistency among data to allow for aggregation into a national picture and even comparisons between States can be very difficult; and

- access to data is often restricted either because of fears that they may be used for political purposes (eg, forests or contamination of seafood) or increasingly because of cost recovery policies. Even where data exist and are available freely it takes resources to extract them, put them into useable form, and analyse and interpret them.

With regard to the latter point, the OECD (1998b) in its review of SoE in Australia, noted that 'the potential remains to increase public access to environmental information ... There is also scope for expanding reporting from companies on their environmental performance and the impact of their activities'. A 1996 study on the availability and use of environmental statistics in Australia revealed various levels of dissatisfaction with environmental data as follows (Hamilton and Attwater 1996). Many of the following points are based on anecdotal evidence, gathered through discussions with officers in various government departments who have personal experience in state of the environment reporting. The points were:

- Environmental indicators may be defined without specific data sets in mind. These indicators were described as a 'wish list' by one officer. Even when the monitoring is seen to be relevant and useful, funding may simply not be available to provide the required resources. This is particularly true in the biodiversity area. A general lack of qualified taxonomists makes the field work that would be required to catalogue the many different unsurveyed species and ecosystems not physically possible.

- The vast size of Australia and its urbanised population means that thorough environmental monitoring across the entire continent is not possible. Accordingly there is little baseline data on pristine sites for many of the different ecosystems found in Australia. Much of the data collected tends to be in or near population centres where the environment is impacted by human activities to varying degrees.

- No examples were found where monitoring was performed to supply information for SoE reports or indicators; the data that is used was often reanalysed from studies where data was collected for other purposes.

- By the time some government reports reach the public the data they contain may be several years old.

- Users do not know where to access data or did not have knowledge or equipment to access electronic data.

- In order to aggregate local data to State, national and global scales it must be of comparable quality, use comparable units, be collected on compatible time scales and with compatible methodologies.

- Information requested from private corporations may be suppressed under the guise of commercial-in-confidence.

- Releasing environmental data can be difficult for government agencies with the dual responsibilities of developing and managing natural resources. This was recognised by the Chair of the National SoE Advisory Council when he said (Lowe 1996):

  The collection of data needed to assess some important aspects of environmental quality is the responsibility of various areas of government: departments with responsibility for forestry, mining, transport, fisheries and agriculture are obvious examples. In some cases, those departments are reluctant to make available data that would allow independent assessment of their environmental management.

- User-pays policies of government agencies and the need to use specialised electronic equipment or software to access the data make it very expensive. This was summarised by one officer as 'taxpayers are paying for data twice, once to collect it and then again to use it.'

- Much of the data collected prior to the mass introduction of personal computers has not been put into databases due to differences in the methods used to collect and/or analyse the data, or simply due to a lack of appropriate staff to digitise the data.

Much has happened to improve accessibility to environmental data over the past few years. There has been rapid growth in a range of interlinked web-based data systems which offer broad access. These have been established at national and State levels. Of course these will only be as useful as the data that is placed in them, but at least the potential to bring together a vast large amounts of data and make availability clear to a wide range of users, is a considerable advance. It is vital however, that such systems are institutionalised in a manner that will ensure their continuity. Reliable and on-going funding is a necessary prerequisite.

The availability and accessibility of quality environmental information depends to a large degree on the topic of interest. Several major data projects are currently underway in Australia covering perceived priority areas. To take just two examples:

The National Land and Water Resources Audit (NLWRA) was funded to produce a comprehensive national appraisal of Australia's natural (land and water) resource base. These assessments are to serve as a baseline or benchmark for future trend analysis. Two objectives that will benefit the SoE process directly are:

- the development of a national information system of compatible and readily accessible land and water data; and

- a framework for monitoring Australia's land and water resources in an ongoing and structured way.

This will include recommendations on institutional arrangements and processes to ensure the ongoing monitoring of land, vegetation and water resources, and the production of guidelines for the ongoing maintenance and updating of data sets. The Australian Natural Resources Data Library provides a facility to search for and download data made available from the National Land and Water Resources Audit's assessments. A broad range of data sets can be accessed through the web pages found at <http://audit.ea.gov.au/ANRA/docs/data_lib.cfm>

A review of coastal vegetation and landform data was commissioned by the Commonwealth State of the Environment Reporting Unit for use in the 2001 SoE report (Sinclair Knight Merz 1998). Two hundred and twenty three relevant data sets were identified The next phase would be to coordinate a continuous national data set at various scales with a nationally agreed classification scheme for coastal vegetation and landforms.

5. *How adaptable is the reporting process to developments in data availability, indicator design and changing needs of users? In other words, how flexible is the process? How well is the tension between 'flexibility' and 'purposefulness' resolved?*

In the discussion above, the need for a strongly institutionalised base for SoE reporting has been argued. The reason is to provide continuity in reporting and in the indicators used for this so that trends and progress can be tracked over time. The possible down-side to this is that such institutionalisation will hamper the development of SoE reporting into modes which can truly 'inform ESD'. As well, as our values and information bases change it is likely that we will want to modify the indicators we use. It is important to remember that our choice of indicators is not 'value-free'; we 'measure what we treasure' (Van Dieren 1995: 157) and community values are bound to change over time. At present we do not appear to have a means to maintain purposefulness in SoE reporting while simultaneously enabling the flexibility necessary to facilitate improvements or respond to changing values.

For example, the discourse of environmental management has shifted to management for sustainability over the past few years. However, SoE reporting is still firmly lodged in the discourse of environmental management and in many cases this is supported by the legislative requirements for that reporting. As outlined earlier in this chapter, this has led to as yet unresolved tension in the reporting process. We aspire to 'inform ESD' but presently lack both the will and the tools to do so. It may be argued that our current systems of SoE reporting, still institutionalised in the *environment* discourse, are hampering any move to reporting to inform ESD. This is clearly a critical area that needs much research to seek ways of maintaining both the continuity of SoE reporting with a flexibility that will enable improvements to be made and response to changing needs.

Conclusions

Environmental reporting is relatively new to Australia. The first National SoE report was released in 1986. South Australia released its first SoE report in 1988. Major changes to format, structure and content have occurred in subsequent reports, with most reports now adopting the OECD pressure-state-response model, some with minor modifications. Corporate reporting (CER) is even newer with the first stand-alone CER dating from 1996.

Environmental reporting is seen to be in an experimental stage by most government departments. The 1996 National report describes the selection of a 'first generation' set of environmental indicators, that provide a good foundation for future development (State of the Environment Advisory Council 1996). The first Queensland and Tasmanian SoE reports include questionnaires inviting suggestions for improvements from readers for future reports (State of the Environment Queensland 1999; Sustainable Development Advisory Council 1996). The 1997 NSW SoE report (NSW EPA 1997a) discusses improvements to its structure and content, based on previous experience and upon comments received on a public discussion paper released prior to the third report. The 2000 NSW report (NSW EPA 2000) discusses future directions in environmental reporting and the NSW State of the Environment 2003 Advisory Council has as one of its roles to provide 'advice which contributes to the development of SoE reporting beyond 2003'.[16]

In 1996 a seminar was sponsored by the South Australian Department of Environment and Natural Resources to provide opportunities for collaboration between government agencies and other interested groups on the development of environmental indicators (Department of Environment and Natural Resources, South Australia 1996). The preface states that:

> at the current stage in the development of environmental indicators nearly all the measures identified ... are simple indicators relating to a single aspect of the environment. One of the few composite or aggregate measures referred to ... is greenhouse gas emissions ... This clearly demonstrates that work on environmental indicators is still in its infancy when compared with the development and application of economic and social indicators.

While work on environmental indicators may well be still in its infancy it has evolved rapidly in the last four years. In that time a National Core Indicator set has been produced and considerable work has gone into refining indicators for the range of issues typically included in SoE Reports. Five years ago we seemed in danger of repeating the 'colonial railway system'[17] experience with development of indicators heading in different directions across the country. Much has been achieved in bringing about coordination in indicator development, and this has to be useful in terms of comparison of performance and vertical and horizontal integration of reporting.

However, we are still a very long way from 'informing ESD' through SoE reporting. At one level this is due to a lack of relevant data and a lack of understanding of cause-effect relationships in ecosystems. At another level it is due to our inability to define ESD in either scientific or values terms. At yet another level it is because we are trying to inform ESD, which is a complex tri-partite concept involving social, environmental and economic parameters, with tools which are at a primitive stage for reporting just on the environment part of this concept. We will not succeed in informing ESD until we acknowledge that to do so requires a very different approach to informing environmental management. Nor will we inform either environmental management or ESD until we set in place targets against which to judge progress and until we ensure that the reporting

---

16   Letter from the Minister, The Hon Bob Debus, to Chair of the Advisory Council, 2 April 2002.

17   With different railway track gauges in different colonies (States).

process is fully integrated into an overall process of planning, policy development and management.

There are some interesting developments around the country in SoE reporting that can provide experience for others to build upon and it is to be hoped that these 'experiments' are carefully monitored and analysed so that learning takes place. At the same time we should watch carefully developments in corporate reporting, where there may be more scope for experimentation as a result of fewer constraints imposed by an institutionalised framework for reporting, and where there are already interesting experiments in sustainability reporting underway, particularly at the international level. There are many tensions to be worked through as we attempt to move towards reporting to inform ESD; tensions between the need for continuity and strong institutionalisation and the need for flexibility to allow experiment. Resolving these tensions warrants our urgent attention.

References

ACT Commissioner for the Environment, Undated, State of the environment reporting, SOE Author, <http://www.envcomm.act.gov.au/Soe2000/Indicator Descriptions/Indicatorlist.htm>, accessed 6 September 2000.

ACT (ACT) Office of the Commissioner for the Environment, 1997, State of the environment report 1997 ACT, <http://www.EnvComm.act.gov.au/SOE1997/General/SoE/ActAbout.htm>, accessed 1 September 2000.

Alexandra, J, Haffenden, S and White, T, 1996, *Listening to the land. A directory of community environmental monitoring groups*, Melbourne: Australian Conservation Foundation.

Alexandra J, Higgins, J and White, T, 1998, *Environmental indicators for national state of the environment reporting – local and community uses*, Australia: state of the environment, Environmental indicator reports, Canberra: Department of the Environment.

ANZECC (Australian and New Zealand Environment and Conservation Council), State of the Environment Reporting Task Force, 1998, *Core environmental indicators for reporting on the state of the environment*, Discussion paper for public comment, Canberra: ANZECC.

ANZECC (Australian and New Zealand Environment and Conservation Council), State of the Environment Reporting Task Force, 2000, *Core environmental indicators for reporting on the state of the environment*, Canberra: ANZECC.

Australian Bureau of Statistics, 2002, *Measuring Australia's progress*, Publication number 1370.0 2002, Canberra: ABS.

Australian Capital Region Leaders Forum, 1997, State of the environment report 1997, Australian Capital Region, <http://www.EnvComm.act.gov.au/SoE1997/Thm_Lga/region.htm>, accessed 4 September 2000.

Australian State of the Environment Committee, 2001, *Australian State of the Environment 2001*, Independent Report to the Commonwealth Minister for the Environment and Heritage, CSIRO Publishing on behalf of the Department of Environment and Heritage, Canberra.

Australian State of the Environment Reporting, 2000, *State of the Environment Australia Statements*, No 10, April 2000.

Bakkes, JA, van den Born, GJ, Helder, JC, Swart, RJ, Hope, CW and Parker, JDE, 1994, *An overview of environmental indicators: state of the art and perspectives*, National Institute of Public Health and Environment Protection (RIVM), the Netherlands, in cooperation with the University of Cambridge, Study commissioned by UNEP.

Brown, V, 2000, 'Creating a network not a grid: establishing a future-oriented, integrated State of the Region reporting system for the long haul', *SoE 2000, Working Towards Sustainable Communities. Proceedings of the Inaugural National State of the Environment 2000 Conference.*, 3-5 May, Coffs Harbour.

Commissioner for the Environment, 1999, *Commissioner for the Environment: annual report 1998-99*, Australian Capital Territory Government, Canberra.

Commonwealth Environment Protection Agency (CEPA), 1992, *Development of a national state of the environment reporting system – discussion paper*, Canberra: CEPA.

Commonwealth of Australia, 1986, *State of the environment in Australia*, Canberra: Department of Arts, Heritage and Environment.

Commonwealth of Australia, 2000, National headline sustainability indicators – draft paper for discussion.

Commonwealth Public Accounts Committee, 1992, *Social responsibilities of Commonwealth statutory authorities and government business enterprises*, Report 315, Canberra: AGPS.

Council of Australian Governments, 1992, *National strategy for ecologically sustainable development*, Canberra: AGPS.

Deni Green Consulting with Standards Australia and Ethical Investment Services August 2001, A Capital Idea <http://www.ea.gov./industry/sustainable/finance/pubs/capital-idea.pdf>.

Department of the Environment and Heritage, Undated, Submission to the Productivity Commission inquiry into the implementation of ecologically sustainable development by Commonwealth departments and agencies, accessed at <http://www.pc.gov.au/inquiry/esd/subs/sub021.pdf>

Department of Environment and Natural Resources, South Australia, 1996, *Indicators for better environmental management*, Proceedings of a seminar, 9 February. Adelaide: DENR.

Department for Environment, Heritage and Aboriginal Affairs, 1999, *State of the environment reporting in South Australia, Environmental performance measures: signposts to the future*, Position paper for public comment, Department for Environment, Heritage and Aboriginal Affairs, Adelaide: Government of South Australia.

Department of Environment and Land Management. 1993, *State of the environment report: South Australia*, Adelaide: Department of Environment and Land Management, South Australia.

Department of the Environment, Sport and Territories (DEST), 1994, *State of the environment reporting: framework for Australia*, Canberra: DEST.

Environment Australia, 2000, A *framework for public environmental reporting: an Australian approach*, March, Commonwealth of Australia.

Environment Australia, 2001, *Are we sustaining Australia? A report against headline sustainability indicators for Australia*, Environment Australia, Canberra.

Environmental Protection Agency, Queensland, 1999, *State of the environment Queensland*, Brisbane: Queensland Government.

Environment Protection Authority (EPA), Victoria, 1996, *The Environment Protection Act 1970: 25 Years of making a difference*, Publication No 492, EPA, Melbourne: Victoria.

Environmental Systems Program, Harvard University, 1996, *Environmental indicators and indices – draft final report*, (TA 5542-Reg), sponsored by the Asian Development Bank and the Government of Norway.

Fairweather P and Napier, G, 1998, *Environmental indicators for national state of the environment reporting – inland waters*, Australia: state of the environment, Environmental indicator reports, Canberra: Department of the Environment.

Global Reporting Initiative. 2000, <www.globalreporting.org.htm>, accessed September 2000.

Government of Western Australia, 1992, *State of the environment report*, Perth: Government of Western Australia.

Government of Western Australia, 1997a, *Environment Western Australia: 1997 draft state of the environment report*, draft report for public discussion, Perth: Government of Western Australia.

Government of Western Australia. 1997b, *State of the environment reporting group working papers*, Perth: Government of Western Australia.

Government of Western Australia, 1998, *Environment Western Australia: 1998, state of the environment report*, Perth: Government of Western Australia.

Government of Western Australia, 1999a, *Environmental action: government's response to the state of the environment report*, Perth: Government of Western Australia.

Griffiths, E, 2000, 'Integrating management planning and SoE reporting – possible or impossible?', *SoE 2000, Working Towards Sustainable Communities, Proceedings of the Inaugural National State of the Environment 2000 Conference*, 3-5 May, Coffs Harbour.

Hamblin, A, 1998, *Environmental indicators for national state of the environment reporting – the land*, Australia: state of the environment, Environmental indicator reports, Canberra: Department of the Environment.

Hamilton, C and Attwater, R, 1996, 'Measuring the Environment – The Availability and Use of Environmental Statistics in Australia' in: Australian Academy of Science Fenner Conference on the Environment, *Tracking Progress: Linking Environment and Economy through Indciators and Accounting Systems*, Insitute of Environmental Studies, University of New South Wales, Sydney.

Harding, R and Eckstein, D, 1996, 'A preliminary discussion paper on the development of composite indices for state of the environment reporting in NSW', prepared for the NSW EPA by the Institute of Environmental Studies, University of New South Wales, Sydney.

Heads of Government in Australia, 1992, *Intergovernmental agreement on the environment*, Canberra: COAG.

Higgins, J and Venning, J, 2001, 'Introduction', in: Venning, J and Higgins, J (eds), *Towards sustainability, emerging systems for informing sustainable development*, Sydney: UNSW Press.

Higham, A 2000, 'SoE reporting and environmental policy planning in Western Australia'. *SoE 2000, Working Towards Sustainable Communities, Proceedings of the Inaugural National State of the Environment 2000 Conference*, 3-5 May, Coffs Harbour.

Institute of Chartered Accountants in Australia, Environmental Accounting Task Force, 1998, *The impact of environmental matters on the accountancy profession*, discussion paper.

Jeyaretnam, T, 1999, *Public environmental reporting: where does Australia stand?* Victoria: Snowy Mountains Engineering Corporation.

Jurmann, Jacky 2000, 'SoE of Western Sydney: preparing a four-yearly regional integrated report', *SoE 2000, Working Towards Sustainable Communities, Proceedings of the Inaugural National State of the Environment 2000 Conference*, 3-5 May, Coffs Harbour.

Lloyd, B, 1996, 'State of environment reporting in Australia', *Australian Journal of Environmental Management* 3: 151-162.

Lowe, I, 1996, 'National overview of state of the environment reporting in Australia – challenges in developing an integrated system', in Australian Academy of Science Fenner Conference on the Environment, *Tracking progress: linking environment and economy through indicators and accounting systems*, Institute of Environmental Studies, University of New South Wales, Sydney.

Luckie, K, 2000, 'Linking indicators, monitoring, government and community: a regional SoE reporting process', *SoE 2000, Working Towards Sustainable*

Communities, Proceedings of the Inaugural National State of the Environment 2000 Conference, 3-5 May, Coffs Harbour.

Manton M and Jasper J, 1998, Environmental indicators for national state of the environment reporting – atmosphere, Australia: state of the environment, Environmental indicator reports, Canberra: Department of the Environment.

Newson, M and Deegan, C, 1996, Environmental performance evaluation and reporting for private and public organisations, in *Report and Recommendations for the Environment Protection Authority, and State and Regional Development New South Wales*, Report No 650015, Sydney.

Newton P, Flood, J, Berry, M, Bhatia, K, Brown, S, Cabelli, A, Gomboso, J, Higgins, J, Richardson, T, and Ritchie, V, 1998, Environmental indicators for national state of the environment reporting – human settlements, Australia: state of the environment, Environmental indicator reports, Canberra: Department of the Environment.

NSW Department of Local Government, 2000, Management planning for NSW local government: guidelines, February 2000, <www.dlg.nsw.gov.au/otherdoc.htm> accessed on 7 August 2000.

NSW EPA (New South Wales Environment Protection Authority), 1996, *The future of NSW state of the environment reporting: discussion paper*, Sydney: NSW EPA.

NSW EPA, 1997a, *New South Wales state of the environment report 1997*, Sydney: EPA NSW.

NSW EPA, 1997b, *Corporate environmental reporting. Why and how?* Sydney: NSW EPA.

NSW EPA, 2000, *New South Wales State of the Environment 2000 Report*, Sydney: EPA NSW.

NSW Government, 1999, Environmental guidelines. State of the environment reporting by local government. promoting ecologically sustainable development, <www.dlg.nsw.gov.au/otherdoc.htm> accessed 5 August 2000.

OECD (Organisation for Economic Co-operation and Development), 1979, *The state of the environment in OECD member countries*, Paris: OECD.

OECD, 1991, *Environmental indicators – a preliminary set*, Paris: OECD.

OECD, 1994, *Environmental indicators – OECD core set*, Paris: OECD.

OECD, 1998a, Towards sustainable development – environmental indicators, <http://www.oecd.org/env/indicators/index.htm> Accessed 3 August 2000.

OECD, 1998b, *OECD performance reviews – Australia*, Paris: OECD.

OECD, 2001, *OECD Environmental Indicators: Towards Sustainable Development 2001*, Paris: OECD.

OECD, 2001a, *Key Environmental Indicators*, Paris: OECD.

Parris, TM, 2000, Tracking down state of the environment reports, *Environment* 42(3): 3-4.

Pearson M, Johnston, D, Lennon, J, McBryde, I, Marshall, D, Nash, D and Wellington, B, 1998, Environmental indicators for national state of the environment reporting – natural and cultural heritage, Australia: state of the environment, Environmental indicator reports, Canberra: Department of the Environment.

Productivity Commission, 1999, *Inquiry into Implementation of Ecologically Sustainable Development by Commonwealth Agencies and Departments Final Report*, Canberra: AGPS.

Public Accounts and Estimates Committee, Parliament of Victoria, 2002, *Final Report on Environmental Accounting and Reporting*, 46th Report to Parliament, March 2002, Melbourne: Government Printer.

Rankin, M, 1996, *Corporate reporting of environmental information: a survey of Australian annual report users and preparers*, prepared for the Environmental Accounting Task Force of The Institute of Chartered Accountants in Australia.

Saunders D, Margules, C and Hill, B, 1998, *Environmental indicators for national state of the environment reporting – biodiversity,* Australia: state of the environment, Environmental indicator reports, Canberra: Department of the Environment.

Sims, H, 2000, 'Advancing assessment of sustainability and SoE in the ACT', *SoE 2000, Working Towards Sustainable Communities, Proceedings of the Inaugural National State of the Environment 2000 Conference,* 3-5 May, Coffs Harbour.

Sinclair Knight Merz, 1998, *Review of coastal vegetation and geomorphological data,* Report prepared for state of the environment reporting unit, Environment Australia.

State of the Environment Advisory Council, 1996, *Australia: state of the environment 1996,* Melbourne: CSIRO Publishing.

State of the Environment Advisory Council, 1997, *Evaluation of the commonwealth state of the environment reporting system,* Canberra: Environment Australia.

State of the Environment Reporting, 2000, Current trends in indicator work in the OECD and OECD countries, *State of the Environment Australia Statements* 10: 9.

Sustainable Development Advisory Council, 1996, *State of the environment. Tasmania. Volume 1: conditions and trends,* Tasmania: Sustainable Development Advisory Council.

Sustainable Development Advisory Council, 1997, *State of the environment. Tasmania. Volume 2: recommendations,* Tasmania: Sustainable Development Advisory Council.

United Nations Conference on Human Settlements, 1996, *Housing and Urban Indicators: Report of the Secretary–General,* A/CONF.165/CRP.2, New York: UN.

United Nations Environment Programme (UNEP), 1999, *Global environmental outlook 2000,* London: Earthwatch.

Van Dieren, W, 1995, 'Indicators for measuring welfare' in Van Dieren, W (ed), *Taking nature into account,* New York: Copernicus/Springer-Verlag.

Venning, J and Higgins, J (eds), 2001, *Towards sustainability, emerging systems for informing sustainable development,* Sydney: UNSW Press.

Ward T, Butler, E and Hill, B, 1998, *Environmental indicators for national state of the environment reporting – estuaries and the sea,* Australia: state of the environment, Environmental indicator reports, Department of the Environment, Canberra.

World Business Council for Sustainable Development, 1999, Meeting changing expectations: corporate social responsibility, <http://www.wbcsd.ch/ publications/ csrpub.htm> accessed 9 May 2000.

World Commission on Environment and Development, 1987, *Our common future.* Oxford: Oxford University Press.

Yencken, D, 2001, *Where are we going: comprehensive social, cultural, environmental and economic reporting,* Melbourne: The Australian Collaboration.

Yencken, D and Wilkinson, D, 2000, *Resetting the compass. Australia's journey towards sustainability,* Melbourne: CSIRO Publishing.

PART IV

MANAGING, REGULATING AND MOTIVATING

10

Straddling Boundaries: Inter-governmental Arrangements for Managing Natural Resources

Peter Crabb

Visiting Fellow, Centre for Resource and Environmental Studies,
The Australian National University

Human beings create all kinds of boundaries. Even those relevant to the relatively limited topic of this chapter are numerous. There are the boundaries between nation states. Within nation states, they exist between different levels of government or jurisdiction, especially within federal nations. Within any one jurisdiction, there are the boundaries between different agencies or areas of administration. In many respects, they are essential in terms of organisation and good government, but they also create problems. Such agencies usually have narrow and compartmentalised views and mandates that bring both benefits and costs (Barrie 1992: 2):

> From an organisational perspective, clear demarcation lines must be drawn not only to ensure efficiency, but also in the interests of accountability ... However, in addition to splitting problems into manageable pieces, decomposition splinters the wider perspective.

There is another problem and that is the lack of coincidence between the human boundaries and those of the natural world. Natural resources and ecosystems span administrative boundaries both within and between jurisdictions. Their management highlights the need for co-operation and co-ordination (as well as other 'co-' words). If the boundaries have to stay for all their positive benefits, in many instances the attitudes to them have to change. In the words of the Brundtland report (WCED 1987: 9):

> The real world of interlocked economic and ecological systems will not change: the policies and institutions concerned must.

Such issues are particularly evident in the case of inter-jurisdictional river basins and their water, land and other natural resources. They are the classic examples of 'straddling boundaries' and all the associated problems. They are particularly evident at the international level, and perhaps only marginally less complex within some of the world's federal nations, where constitutional responsibilities are split between two or more levels of government, such as Australia, Canada, India and the United States. There is much to learn from these situations. Managing such resources, especially their waters, has a long history of special arrangements, at both international and intra-national levels (Crabb 1995). Such concerns are no longer confined to surface waters, but extend to groundwater, certain land and environmental resources, and particular fauna.

The focus of this chapter is Australia's Murray-Darling Basin (MDB) and the arrangements that have been made for the management of its complex inter-jurisdictional natural resources, especially its waters and lands. By way of an introduction to the discussion and in order to give it a context, some other matters are briefly considered. The second main part of the chapter considers these arrangements in the context of an adaptive approach to resource and environmental management and what can be learned from them.[1]

Inter-jurisdictional river basins

In addition to the Murray-Darling, there are eight other inter-jurisdictional river basins in Australia, namely Lake Eyre (Qld-SA-NT-NSW), Bulloo-Bancannia (Qld-NSW), Ord and Keep rivers (WA-NT), Genoa River (NSW-Vic), Snowy River (NSW-Vic), Glenelg River (Vic-SA), Nicholson River (Qld-NT), and Settlement Creek (Qld-NT) (Figure 10.1).

While the MDB is the most important of Australia's inter-jurisdictional river basins and the one with the longest history of joint management arrangements (Crabb 1997), few of the others have any formal arrangements for their management. However, some have been gaining increasing attention, not least because of the demands being made on their water resources. In an innovative step, the community-based Lake Eyre Basin Coordinating Group was established at the same time as work was being undertaken on the Lake Eyre Basin Agreement by the South Australian, Queensland and Commonwealth governments (see Chapter 8). Any proposal for the expansion of the Ord River Irrigation Scheme would likely renew concerns for the management of the Ord and Keep rivers catchments, not least those that drain to Lake Argyle. The diversion of most of the Snowy River's water by the Snowy Mountains Scheme inextricably links it to the MDB, but also makes it one of the most complex inter-jurisdictional water management issues (Snowy Water Inquiry 1998). What the future holds for these river basins, only time will tell, but perhaps the issue did merit more attention than it was given by the 1988 Constitutional Commission (CC 1988).

Inter-jurisdictional resource management issues are not confined to surface waters. Many groundwater resources span more than one jurisdiction, but apart from the arrangements that have been put in place for the Great Artesian Basin and parts of the Murray and Otway basins (see below), no others have joint management arrangements. Land-based resource issues that are not catchment-based may gain attention as the need for and benefits of joint action become evident, as illustrated by the Australian Alps national parks and Mallee Lands (see below). Tackling the problem of plague locusts

---

1   The chapter raises many issues that can only be touched on, as they are really outside its scope, certainly as far as detailed consideration is concerned. Policy issues and state matters are cases in point, as are such issues as environmental flows and land clearing within the Murray-Darling Basin. Also, it is not the chapter's purpose to provide a comprehensive assessment of all aspects of the various inter-jurisdictional arrangements that are examined. The purpose is to examine the arrangements and their processes to deal with current and future challenges.

Figure 10.1. Inter-jurisdictional river basins in Australia and locations of inter-governmental arrangements for natural resource management in the Murray-Darling Basin

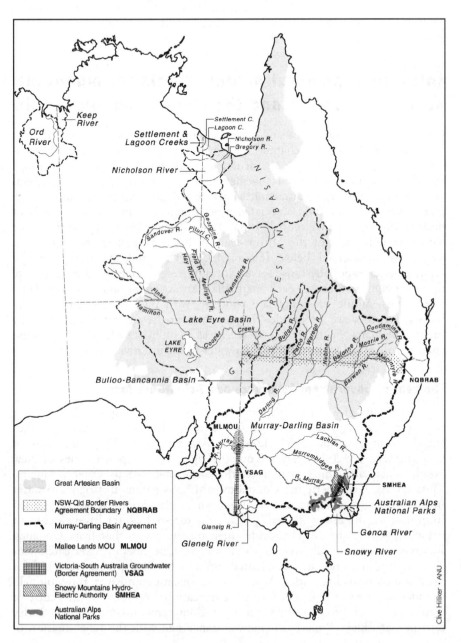

provides another illustration of the need for and benefits of joint action in dealing with a resource issue. Established in 1974, without any formal legis- lative measures, the Australian Plague Locust Commission involves the Commonwealth, NSW, Victoria, Queensland and South Australia and is particularly concerned with outbreaks that are likely to cross State borders (Wettenhall 1985; APLC 1999).

Inter-governmental arrangements for managing natural resources and the Murray-Darling Basin

Coping with the numerous and varied administrative boundaries that have been indicated in this chapter has given rise to many types of inter- governmental arrangements. In turn, many different kinds of 'institutions' have been set up to put the arrangements into operation. These have all been outside the familiar departmental structures of government administration and include statutory and associated arrangements, quangos, memoranda of understanding, etc. (Wettenhall 1983, 1985; Painter 1998). Those that exist within various parts of the Murray-Darling Basin as well as the Basin as a whole are considered below (Figure 10.1). They indicate the variety of arrangements, especially those set up in more recent times, and demonstrate the changing nature of each particular arrangement and its associated institutions. While most pre-date concerns with natural resource sustaina- bility *per se*, they are a reminder that concern for the environment, especially catchment management, is not as recent as is often stated. A number were and are concerned with far more than water in quantitative terms.[2]

The Seat of Government Severance and Acceptance Acts

The availability of water played a major role in the selection of a location for the Australian Capital Territory (ACT) and for the site of Canberra within the Territory (Pegrum 1983: 124-149). Among other things, the Seat of Government Acts 1908-1909 set out the rights and responsibilities of New South Wales and the Commonwealth concerning various water resources. Thus the ACT (formerly the Commonwealth) has paramount rights to water in the Molonglo and Queanbeyan rivers, which New South Wales is required to protect for the use of the ACT. While the forested Cotter River catchment (which is within the ACT) provides high quality water, that from Googong Reservoir has to be fully treated, as most of its Queanbeyan River catchment is in agricultural and rural residential use and the reservoir is also used for various recreational activities. As well as the Queanbeyan River, the Molonglo supplies water to Lake Burley Griffin, a recreational resource in the centre of Canberra. From 1965 to 1998, the joint Commonwealth-NSW Lake Burley Griffin Catchment Project Scheme was concerned with the rehabilitation of

---

2   To the best of knowledge of the author, the arrangements outlined in this chapter are correct as at August 2002.

the catchment and the minimisation of sediment moving into the Lake (NSWDLWC 2000).

Just as NSW has responsibilities to the ACT in terms of catchment management for water supply, so the ACT (as well as NSW) is required to protect the rights of downstream users of Murrumbidgee River waters. It is for this reason that the sophisticated Lower Molonglo Water Quality Control Centre was built to serve the whole of the ACT. However, it does not cater for general urban and stormwater runoff, which can carry high loads of nutrients and other pollutants. Especially during periods of low flow in the Murrumbidgee, this is a matter of concern to water users within and downstream of the ACT.

There are no formal arrangements to co-ordinate water management in the region of the ACT and adjoining NSW. However, *ad hoc* arrangements have been made to deal with particular issues, such as the construction of Googong Reservoir, pollution from mine waste tailings at Captains Flat on the Molonglo River, and water quality in the Murrumbidgee River. As regards the current situation, Starr (1999: 11) has observed in respect of the management of the Googong catchment that 'It is unlikely that there was [or is] any formal agreement or memorandum of understanding'.

In 1989, a NSW-ACT Consultative Forum was established to formalise ACT-NSW liaison arrangements regarding cross-border issues, but it is not known if this has dealt with any water resource issues. The situation is further complicated by Commonwealth involvement stemming from the *Seat of Government Acts* and the fact that many current issues are ones for 'local government', another level of government that does not appear to be involved. However, negotiations have taken place between a number of ACT and NSW government agencies regarding the co-operative management of the region's water resources.

The New South Wales-Queensland Border Rivers Act

A significant stretch of the eastern New South Wales-Queensland border coincides with sections of the Severn, Dumaresq, Macintyre and Barwon rivers. The desire for greater security of irrigation water supplies along the Dumaresq was the driving force for the original 1946 New South Wales-Queensland Border Rivers Agreement. It provided for the conservation and equal sharing of the waters of the Dumaresq River upstream of Mingoola (the point where the tributaries useful for storage converge) and for the regulation of the Border Rivers downstream of Mingoola (i.e. for the supply of water from storages along the rivers which form the border). Amendments to the Agreement in 1968 made provision for the construction of Glenlyon Dam and regulation of flow of the Border River. They also extended the Agreement's coverage to include the equitable distribution of the waters of the 'intersecting streams', which cross the border further west. These are the Moonie, Narran, Bokhara, Ballandool, Birrie, Culgoa, Nebine, Warrego and Paroo, and some small creeks, as well as the Bulloo-Bancania further to the west and beyond the MDB. Except for the Moonie, Nebine, Warrego, Paroo and Bulloo-Bancania, they are distributaries of the Balonne River. These streams 'would not have been considered important at the time of the original agreement' (Morwood nd). The Agreement also provides for the determination of the quantities of groundwater in cross-border aquifers available to each State.

The Agreement set up the Dumaresq-Barwon Border Rivers Commission, generally known as the Border Rivers Commission (BRC). This is the decision-making body for the management of water resources which flow along and across the border and the construction and management authority for works to regulate the flow of water along the border (Dumaresq-Barwon) and for relatively minor works on other rivers. The BRC comprises three Commissioners, one from each State and the third, the Chair person, who is nominated in turn for a term of five years (traditionally a retired officer of that State's bureaucracy). Each State may also appoint a Deputy Commissioner. The State Commissioners are normally senior bureaucrats from each State's department responsible for water resources. The Commission has no staff of its own, its work being undertaken on a part-time basis by officers from the State Departments. A Management Committee made up of staff from the two Departments provides the links with the State Departments (Figure 10.2).

The duties of the BRC include the measurement and studies of flows in the rivers, the investigation of proposals for better conservation, regulation and distribution of flows, the construction and maintenance of the dams, weirs and other works for storage, regulation and distribution of flows, water quality monitoring, the investigation, monitoring and use of groundwater resources associated with the border rivers area, and undertaking river improvement works on the border rivers. With regard to the intersecting streams, the main task of the BRC is 'determining the proportions or quantities of water which should be available to each State from the rivers' (Morwood nd).

Community consultation is undertaken with Border Rivers Food and Fibre, which represents water users interests along the Border Rivers, and the Intersecting Streams Advisory Committee. Meetings with these groups provide advice to the BRC on 'water resource matters such as environmental aspects, water quality, floodplain management and beneficial flooding, and on the sharing of water resources' (DBBRC 1998: 16).

East of Mungindi, the Agreement has worked well as a surface water management and apportionment agreement. However, problems continue with respect to the intersecting streams and the 'equitable distribution' of their waters. Among current issues being considered are a Border Rivers flow management plan, water management plans for the intersecting streams, a management plan for Border Rivers groundwater, and the management of flood flows on the Balonne and Warrego (DBBRC 2001). Consideration has also been given to the management of flows on flood plains, even though these are not covered by the Agreement, illustrating the fact that the Commission has provided a forum for interstate liaison and collaboration on water management and related issues.

Figure 10.2. Border Rivers Commission Structure

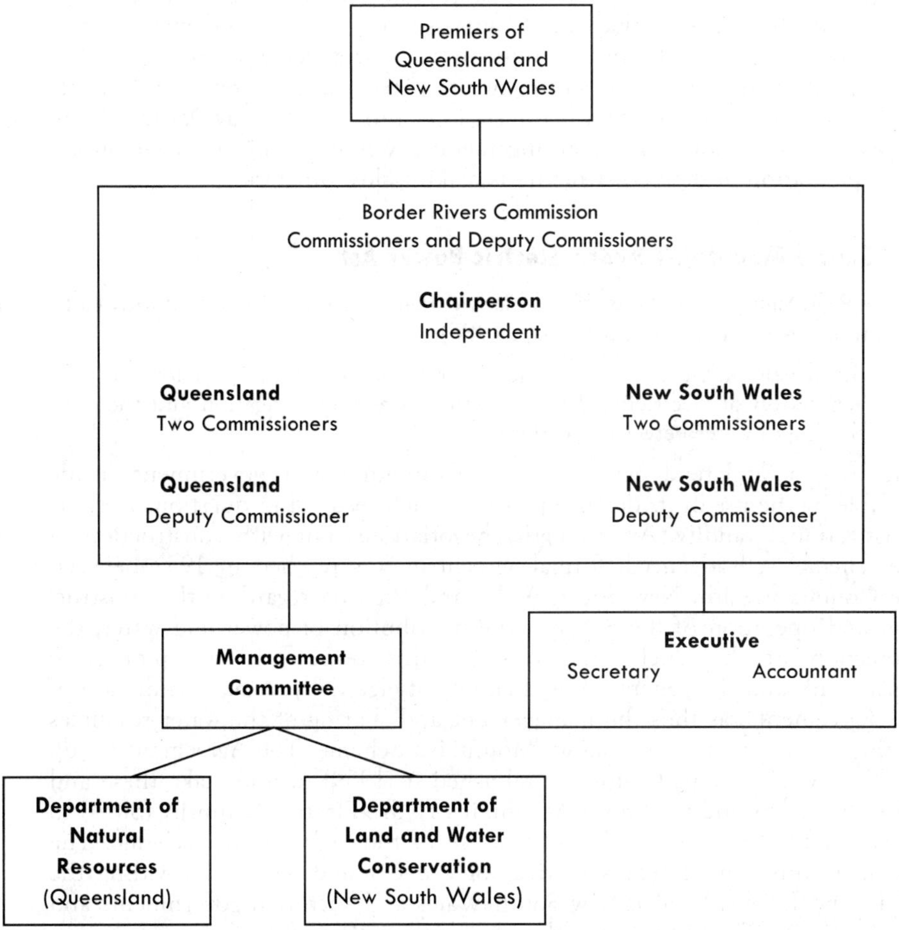

```
                    ┌─────────────────────────┐
                    │    Premiers of          │
                    │    Queensland and       │
                    │    New South Wales      │
                    └─────────────────────────┘
                                 │
┌──────────────────────────────────────────────────────────────────┐
│                    Border Rivers Commission                        │
│           Commissioners and Deputy Commissioners                   │
│                                                                    │
│                         Chairperson                                │
│                         Independent                                │
│                                                                    │
│     Queensland                          New South Wales            │
│   Two Commissioners                   Two Commissioners            │
│                                                                    │
│     Queensland                          New South Wales            │
│   Deputy Commissioner                 Deputy Commissioner          │
└──────────────────────────────────────────────────────────────────┘
            │                                    │
┌───────────────────────┐          ┌────────────────────────────┐
│     Management         │          │         Executive          │
│     Committee          │          │  Secretary      Accountant │
└───────────────────────┘          └────────────────────────────┘
     │            │
┌──────────────┐  ┌──────────────────┐
│ Department of│  │  Department of   │
│   Natural    │  │  Land and Water  │
│  Resources   │  │  Conservation    │
│ (Queensland) │  │ (New South Wales)│
└──────────────┘  └──────────────────┘
```

In response to national water industry reforms, action has been taken to separate the Commission's two major functions, namely water supply and resource management (DBBRC 1999: 15). Under the terms of the Border Catchments Memorandum of Understanding, signed by the NSW and Queensland premiers in September 2000, the DBBRC will focus its attention on the water supply infrastructure and the commercial supply of water in the Border Rivers region. The new Border Catchments Forum, made up of ministers responsible for water resources and environmental portfolios, will be responsible for 'the coordinated management of the water and related resources of the Border Catchments consistent with the principles of ecologically sustainable development'. It will also be responsible for sharing the waters of all the border and trans-border rivers. The Forum will meet at least twice a year in the Border Rivers region and its decisions will not be inconsistent with those of the Murray-Darling Basin Ministerial Council (see below). It is assisted by the Border Catchments Standing Committee comprising representatives of the water resources management and environment portfolios, 'preferably being Commissioners or Deputy Commissioners of the Murray-Darling Basin Commission'. The arrangements are regarded as interim and will be reviewed within two to three years, the review to include 'consideration of their formal translation into the Murray-Darling Basin Ministerial and Commission arrangements'. While a start has been made, implementation of the new structure is making slow progress.

The Snowy Mountains Hydro-Electric Power Act

The 1949 *Snowy Mountains Hydro-Electric Power Act* of the Commonwealth Parliament made provision for (SMA 1986):

> the development and use of the water resources of the area for the generation of electricity, the provision of water for irrigation and the sharing of water between the States.

This was a unilateral action of the Commonwealth government, made possible by the use of its defence powers, which resulted in questions as to its constitutional validity. After lengthy negotiations, but with construction of the scheme well advanced, formal agreement was reached in 1957 between the Commonwealth, New South Wales and Victoria regarding the construction and operation of the Scheme, the distribution of power and water, the protection of the catchment areas (in this respect, it was pioneering legislation), and the generation and supply of electricity. A major function of the Agreement was thus the management and sharing of the water resources of the area covered by the Snowy Mountains Scheme. The Agreement set up the Snowy Mountains Council (established in 1959) to undertake these and other functions and the Snowy Mountains Hydro-Electric Authority (SMA) to carry out the operation and maintenance of the hydro-electric scheme. The Council consisted of representatives of the Commonwealth (providing the Chair and Deputy Chair), New South Wales and Victorian governments and the Authority. The SMA operated under the direction of the Council.

The Snowy Mountains Scheme has two major and tension-creating tasks, namely the generation of electricity (especially in winter) and the storage and provision (in summer) of water for irrigation in the Murray and Murrumbidgee valleys. Because of the former, the Council's membership was dominated by people from the States' electricity industries; because of the latter, when necessary, irrigation has had prior claim to the Scheme's water resources.

In 1997, the *Snowy Hydro Corporatisation Act* was passed, changing the SMA to Snowy Hydro Ltd (which is owned 58% by NSW, 29% by Victoria and 13% by the Commonwealth, a division that reflects the pre-existing ratio of entitlements to electricity supplies). Snowy Hydro was incorporated in June 2001, but the Act did not come into effect until 28 June 2002, following agreement on the return of minimum flows to the Snowy River (Fisher 2000; ISR 2000).[3] Following corporatisation, Snowy Hydro is now

> a single entity operating within a competitive electricity market, supplying regulated releases of water for irrigation and the environment (SMA 1998: 20).

With the removal of the Snowy Mountains Council, Snowy Hydro is in sole charge of its activities, earning income from the sale of electricity and related services. Water is not an asset of Snowy Hydro, its water licence specifying its rights to use, collect, divert, store and release water. It remains to be seen how Snowy Hydro will cope with the on-going tensions between electricity generation and irrigation. For example, while Snowy Hydro is not able to sell water to irrigators, should it be expected to store water for irrigators, on their terms, without making a charge to them?

The Victoria-South Australia Groundwater (Border Agreement) Acts

The Victoria-South Australia border region is dependent for its water supplies on groundwater from two geological systems, the Murray and Otway basins. Their unconfined and confined aquifers provide the only reliable sources of water. The increasing demands and competition for water and their impacts on established users on the South Australian side of the border led to the establishment of the Mallee Proclaimed Region in 1983, which required licences for the use of groundwater for irrigation and marked the start of a monitoring program. With developments in one State having the potential to impact on the other and an inquiry recommendation for joint management (SADME 1982), the Victoria-South Australia Groundwater (Border Agreement) Acts (1985) were passed (BGA 2002: 3):

> The Agreement provides that the available groundwater shall be shared equitably between the States and that it applies to all existing and future bores within the Designated Area, except domestic and stock bores.

The Designated Area is 20 km wide on each side of the full length of the border and is divided into 22 management zones, 11 in each State. The Agreement is operated by the Border Groundwaters Agreement Review Committee, which comprises two members from each State, these being officers of the relevant State government agencies. Regular five-yearly reviews of the Agreement are undertaken by the Committee.

The strategy for groundwater management is based on three principles, namely sustainability of the resource in terms of quantity and quality, equitable sharing of the resource, and economic efficiency in its use (BGA 1996: 8). Permissable Annual Volumes for total withdrawal are set for each Zone. These have changed over time as more has been learned about the

---

3   In late August, 2002, a start was made on increasing the minimum flow in the Snowy River from the prevailing one per cent of the original flow to six per cent. The objective is a flow of 28 per cent of the original flow.

hydrogeology and groundwater movements, recharge rates, and salinity. Considerable research is undertaken by the Committee.

Thus far, the Agreement has worked well, in spite of the fact that the Designated Area and Zones do not accord with the hydrogeology. In seeking to address this, the Committee is working towards consistent management of the aquifers within and beyond the Designated Area, and providing a separate Permissable Annual Volume for each aquifer in each Zone. There are increasing total water demands on the aquifers, with land clearing, irrigation developments and the expansion of forestry affecting recharge rates and contributing to rising groundwater salinity levels (BGA 2000: 4; BGA 2002: 14-15). This has implications for water supplies in the long-term, as well as impacting on established users. While progress is being made towards the placing of meters on all bores, the fact that this is not yet the case raises questions as to how much water is being extracted and, therefore, if users are staying within the set limits.

The Australian Alps National Parks Memorandum of Understanding

The Australian Alps constitute a unique environment. This is reflected in a long history of measures for their protection, as well as their use for a variety of winter and summer recreational pursuits. It is seen in the establishment of a number of national parks and other forms of reserves in Victoria, New South Wales and the ACT. But until recently, the park and jurisdictional boundaries prevented a unified approach to the management of this area of national significance.

Beginning in 1985, a series of meetings brought together people from the (then) Australian National Parks and Wildlife Service and the responsible authorities in NSW, Victoria and the ACT to discuss strategies for the co-operative management of the national parks and other reserves in the Australian Alps. In 1986, the four governments signed a *Memorandum of Understanding in Relation to the Co-operative Management of the Australian Alps National Parks* (MOU). This is a co-operative management program, not an institution. Among the benefits of co-operative management are sharing of knowledge and skills between the agencies, improved overall management of the area's resources, greater public involvement in planning and management, interstate trails, and better public information and education programs. In particular, the Memorandum imposes an obligation on the agencies to adopt complementary management practices. A number of revisions have been made to the MOU, the most recent in 1998.[4] Its objectives are to co-operate to achieve protection of the landscape; protection of native plants and animals and cultural values; protection of the mountain catchments; and provision of outdoor recreation opportunities to encourage enjoyment and understanding of the alpine environment.

---

4   A further review of the MOU is under active consideration, with signing planned for November 2002.

Figure 10.3. Australian Alps Cooperative Management Program Structure

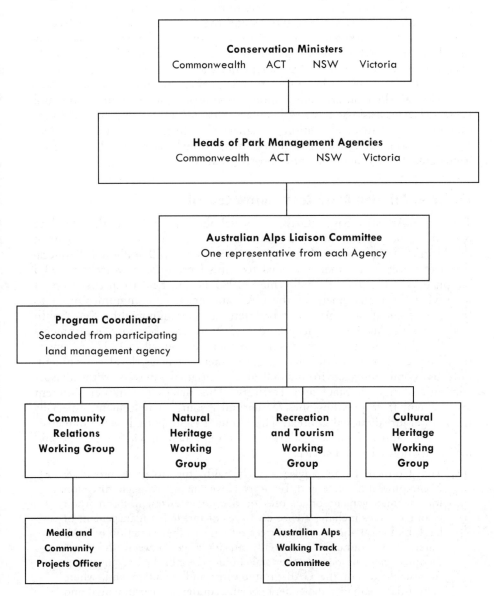

The Memorandum also established the Australian Alps Liaison Committee (AALC), comprising one member from each jurisdiction, administrative support from Environment Australia, and a Program Coordinator (appointed from one of the agencies). The AALC's function is (AALC 1989: 1):

> to co-ordinate the development and implementation of co-operative works programs and other arrangements made under the MOU in relation to co-operative management of the Australian Alps National Parks.

The Committee members are senior managers with direct responsibility for implementing the projects and outcomes of the program. Much of the AALC's work is undertaken by working groups and the Program Coordinator (Figure 10.3). With the help of a Strategic Plan, the Australian Alps are now recognised and managed as one biogeographical unit and a start has been made towards a more consistent and complementary approach to management planning for all of the Alps parks and reserves. For some, the objective is one park.

The World Conservation Union Commission on National Parks and Protected Areas assessed the Australian Alps MOU as 'one of the finest examples of effective cooperation in management in the world' (AALC 1996: 1). The Australian Alps are recognised internationally as world's best practice in the cross-border management of protected areas.

The Great Artesian Basin Consultative Council

The Great Artesian Basin (GAB) covers about 1.7 million km², extending beneath 22 per cent of Australia and including most of the northern half of the Murray-Darling Basin. It stores an estimated 8,700 million ML (megalitres) of water, water that is crucial to annual production worth over $3.5 billion (GABCC 1998: 4). Following a 1995 Forum held to discuss ways of improving the management of the GAB and ensuring community input to that management, an agreement between the Commonwealth, New South Wales, South Australia, Queensland and Northern Territory governments established the Great Artesian Basin Consultative Council in 1997. It is made up of representatives from relevant government agencies, local government, industry, community, environmental and Aboriginal interests, with advisory committees in each State and Territory. This makes it a rather different arrangement from previous ones for natural resource management, especially in an inter-jurisdictional context. The Council is supported by a number of committees and a Technical Working Group, which provides scientific and technical knowledge and advice.

> The Council is an advisory body with the role of providing Commonwealth, State and Territory Governments strategic direction for the management of all uses of the Great Artesian Basin water resources. This includes advice on issues of integrated management of land, biological and water resources relevant to the extraction of GAB water. The Council is essentially an interface between five jurisdictions, water users and other stakeholders, established to encourage sustainable use of the GAB groundwater and maintain and, where appropriate, enhance dependent social, economic, environmental and heritage values (GABCC 2001).

The Council's major concerns are the wastage and over-extraction of groundwater from uncontrolled bores and inefficient water distribution systems, as well as the poor condition of many bores. These are resulting in reduced natural pressures in the aquifers causing declining natural flows and the drying up of many mound springs and other springs. Many bores have ceased to flow.

In 2000, the Council launched its Strategic Management Plan, 'a strategic framework for responsible groundwater and related natural resources management in the Great Artesian Basin' (GABCC 2000, 3). The 15-year Plan has commenced with a $60 million five-year Sustainability Initiative to cap flowing bores and replace open drains with pipelines. The Council is facilitating research and the advancement of knowledge of the Basin, the GABFLOW groundwater model of the major aquifer being of particular importance.

Murray Mallee Partnership Memorandum of Understanding

The Murray Mallee Partnership covers the parks and other conservation reserves in the Murray Mallee areas of NSW, Victoria and South Australia. It started with informal meetings of on-ground agencies' staff, who were doing similar things and seeking to do them better. Though there are significant differences, the Australian Alps provided a model for a formalised arrangement, the terms being set out in a Memorandum of Understanding signed by South Australia, Victoria, New South Wales and the Commonwealth in 1999. The Partnership is seen as 'Conservation without Borders', through the growth and enhancement of co-operative management. The work of the Partnership is undertaken by a Steering Committee and Operations Committee, members being drawn from relevant government agencies and the community-based Bookmark Biosphere Trust, with an executive officer to organise Partnership activities, including regular workshops to increase field staff skills.[5]

The Murray-Darling Basin Agreement

The Murray-Darling Basin Agreement was the response to increasing environmental and resource management problems throughout the MDB and especially the inability of the existing River Murray Waters Agreement (RMWA) and the River Murray Commission (RMC) to cope with the problems of the Murray. In 1915, the RMWA was a pioneering document and the RMC a unique inter-governmental institution. For over 70 years, they regulated water in the main stream of the Murray to ensure that each of the three riparian States, and especially South Australia, received its agreed share of Murray water. Over that time, various amendments were made to the Agreement, reflecting shifts in community values and changes in economic conditions. By no means were all of the changes free of conflict, a comment that also applied to some actions of the Commission, in particular the abandonment of the Chowilla Dam proposal and the construction of Dartmouth Dam. The powers of the RMC were gradually extended, but its prime concern remained with water quantity. However, with the increasing evidence that the successful management of the Murray's river systems was directly related to land use throughout the catchment, further amendments to the Agreement in

---

5   The Alps model has also provided the basis for moves towards integrated management of Booderee National Park, Jervis Bay Marine Park and other reserves in and around the Territory of Jervis Bay, on the NSW South Coast.

1984 enhanced the Commission's environmental responsibilities (Clark 1983; Crabb 1988; Paterson 1987; Powell 1993). But they were not enough. It was soon realised that, through no fault of their own, the RMWA and RMC were unable to meet the needs of the Murray's and the larger MDB's management and growing resource and environmental problems.

The initial Murray-Darling Basin Agreement was signed in 1987 by the Commonwealth, New South Wales, Victoria, and South Australia governments. It was an amendment – the final one – to the RMWA. Five years later, in 1992, a totally new Murray-Darling Basin Agreement was signed, replacing the RMWA. Queensland was also a signatory of the new Agreement. The ACT also now participates by way of a memorandum of understanding. The Agreement was given full legal status by the *Murray-Darling Basin Act 1993* (Cth) passed by all the contracting governments. It finally put into effect a recommendation of a 1902 Interstate Royal Commission on the Murray, namely that 'the river and its tributaries must be looked on as one'.

The purpose of the Agreement is 'to promote and co-ordinate effective planning and management for the equitable efficient and sustainable use of the water, land and other environmental resources of the Murray-Darling Basin'. To achieve this, the Agreement established new institutions at the political, bureaucratic and community levels, namely the Murray-Darling Basin Ministerial Council (MDBMC), the Murray-Darling Basin Commission (MDBC), and the Community Advisory Committee (CAC) (Figure 10.4). These institutions and the activities that give effect to the Agreement are generally termed the MDB Initiative. The MDBMC consists of a maximum of three ministers responsible for land, water and environmental resources from each of the signatory governments and a non-voting member from the ACT. The Council's main functions are:

> to consider and determine major policy issues concerning the use of the Basin's land, water, and other environmental resources and to develop, consider and authorise (as appropriate) measures to achieve the purpose of the Agreement (MDBC 2000, 8).

Being a political forum, it has the power to make decisions for the Basin as a whole. Decisions are reached by consensus and must be unanimous. Once reached, they carry considerable political and moral weight. The CAC is made up of an independent chairperson, 21 representatives chosen on a catchment/regional basis, representatives of four special interest 'peak organisations', and an Aboriginal representative. Its main tasks are to advise the Ministerial Council and Commission on natural resource management issues referred to it and to communicate to the Council and Commission the views of the Basin's communities on matters identified by the CAC as being of concern. The CAC has the difficult task of being a two-way means of communication between the Ministerial Council and the residents of the Basin.

The MDBC is the executive arm of the Ministerial Council. It consists of an independent President, two Commissioners from each of the contracting governments (normally chief executives of the agencies responsible for water, land and environmental resources), and a non-voting representative from the ACT. In addition to its responsibilities for managing the River Murray

Figure 10.4 Structure of the Murray-Darling Basin Initiative

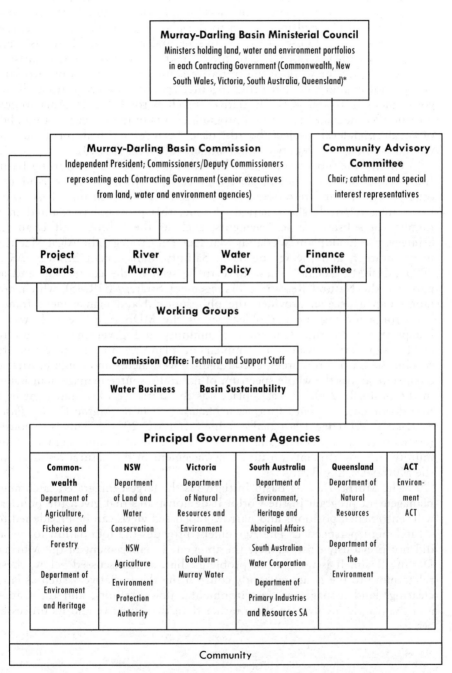

* Participation by the Australian Capital Territory is via a memorandum of understanding.

(undertaken by River Murray Water, an internal business division of the Commission and separate from its resource management and policy functions), the main functions of the Commission are to advise and assist the Ministerial Council in relation to the planning, development, management and sustainable use of the Basin's natural resources. These tasks are undertaken with the assistance of the permanent staff of the Commission Office. Much of the work of the Initiative is undertaken by various working groups and committees that bring together specialist expertise from all the governments involved in the Initiative as well as the CAC. In order to give direction to the major policy and program efforts of the Initiative, a number of small high-level project boards have been established, made up of Commissioners and Deputy-Commissioners (MDBC 2000: 13).

One of the most important achievements of the Murray-Darling Basin Initiative is that it has put in place a process by which the water, land and other environmental resources can be effectively managed on a basin-wide basis. In a relatively short period of time, this process has resulted in a number of substantive achievements, such as the Salinity and Drainage Strategy, the Floodplain Wetlands Management Strategy, the Algal Management Strategy, and the recent Basin Salinity Management Strategy 2001-2005 (MDBMC 2001a). These have to be seen in the context of, and as parts of, the Natural Resources Management Strategy (NRMS), which, for more than a decade, provided the philosophical and management framework for achieving the key objectives of the MDB Agreement. It was a blueprint for co-ordinated, joint community and government action to tackle degradation issues and implement planning and management to sustain the Basin's resources, encouraging governments and communities to co-operate across the whole spectrum of natural resource management issues in the Basin. In 2001, it was replaced as the Initiative's key statement by a new document, *Integrated Catchment Management in the Murray-Darling Basin 2001-2010: delivering a sustainable future* (MDBMC 2001b). This is variously termed a policy statement and 'a draft statement of commitment by community and governments on future management of the natural resources of the Murray-Darling Basin'.[6]

The Murray-Darling Basin Initiative is the largest integrated catchment management program in the world. It demonstrates that given the political will, entrenched positions and narrowly focussed views can be broadened to a catchment perspective. The Agreement provides the foundation for what did not previously exist, namely the integrated management of the Murray-Darling Basin. It is not free of problems, but, as is discussed below, these relate more to the issues currently confronting the Initiative – such as land clearing, land management, environmental flows, salinity, and the Cap – and the people involved in them rather than the Initiative and its processes *per se*.

---

6   The rather sudden appearance of this document without any advance notice, such as in the Commission's annual reports, is a matter that perhaps merits explanation.

An assessment: what can be learned?

In the documentation for this project, it is stated that:

> An adaptive approach has been chosen here because of: its explicit recognition of complexity and uncertainty and thus a need for explicit experimentation; its shared roots in both the natural and social sciences; its recognition of the need for participation; its convergence with other concepts; and its evident appeal to a range of policy and stakeholder groups in Australian natural resource management.

In broad terms, these observations are applicable to all of the inter-governmental arrangements considered in this chapter. To varying degrees, they all demonstrate experimentation, learning and adaptation. Specifically, they demonstrate the five principles that have been identified as the core of an 'adaptive' approach to natural resource management. The following are some illustrations.

Persistence

As indicated by the periods over which they have operated, the inter-governmental arrangements considered in this chapter provide many examples of persistence, the MDB Initiative and its predecessors being quite remarkable examples. Though there have been some 'ups and downs', they have been supported by the governments involved, both politically and in terms of resources. There could always be more of the latter and, at times, the former has not always been consistent. In many cases, the support has simply been by way of letting the arrangements and institutions do the work they were set up to do, without active political involvement or interference. For example, the Victoria-South Australia Groundwater Agreement has operated successfully for over 17 years without political involvement or any change. Their persistence has given them long-term learning and long-term knowledge. The arrangements also demonstrate their persistence by looking to the future, as with the development of new strategies by the GABCC and the AALC, in the latter case in spite of the withdrawal of Commonwealth financial support. While the MDB Initiative's Salinity Management Strategy looks 15 years ahead, the Salinity Audit took a 100 years' view, the associated CSIRO study indicating the long term changes that are needed to farming practices within the Basin (MDBMC 1999, MDBMC 2001a, Walker et al 1999).

A number of the arrangements owe their existence to the persistence of individuals or small groups of people, in the political, bureaucratic and private sectors. The contribution of John Seccombe to the establishment of the GABCC is one of the best examples. Others have played key parts at particular times, such as Gareth Evans, John Kerin, Evan Walker and Joan Kirner in the establishment of the Murray-Darling Basin Agreement and Ian Causley as the first non-Labor member of the MDBMC. Champions are especially important as governments' capacities are reduced. Natural resource management issues are now being increasingly identified by community members.

Persistence, however, can be easily thwarted in many ways. While the inter-jurisdictional arrangements may have been persistent, this has not been true of their constituent State agencies and their personnel. This is particularly evident in terms of membership of the MDBMC and MDBC, especially over recent years. The frequent changes mean a serious loss of both political and corporate knowledge. The same observation applies to the countless changes of personnel in all of the government agencies that are involved, including the MDBC office. Further, just as the various arrangements have had their champions, some have had – and still have – their internal and external detractors.

Purposefulness

All of the arrangements have clear goals and objectives; their institutions have clear purposes. However, there is frequently a gap between statements of intent and actual achievements. It is often not possible to measure progress towards achieving goals and objectives in other than general terms. Being able to do so, being accountable, and thus being able to clearly justify their existence are essential requirements. Purposefulness is demonstrated in constant learning and applying the learning, as with the Victoria-South Australia Groundwater Agreement and beyond the Designated Area, especially in the development of groundwater techniques.

Purposefulness is aided by the ability to make decisions with respect to achieving an arrangement's goals. This is most evident in the case of the MDBMC, the Basin's pre-eminent political forum, but also with the Victoria-South Australia Border Groundwater Agreement Committee and the AALC. It has been noted that 'The success of the [AALC] is dependent on the capacity of members to make decisions on behalf of their agency' (Mackay 1996).

Purposefulness also acknowledges the need for continuing improvements. An independent review of the AALC indicated that it should adopt a more strategic role. Working towards a more consistent and complementary approach to management planning for the Alps parks as a whole can be seen as a positive response. The Border Rivers Commission has not really got to grips with issues on the intersecting streams, especially in terms of rights of established users (flood plain graziers and the environment) and cross-border flows to NSW. While most of the arrangements involve strong networks amongst those involved, these need to be improved, especially beyond those directly involved, as has been acknowledged in the case of the AALC (Mackay 1996). Purposefulness is aided by keeping the structures clearly focussed and as simple as possible to do the tasks required and then exploring them to the maximum, only making changes when they are clearly needed. Will some of the other arrangements have to follow the path of the MDB Initiative in terms of complexity of structures with increasing complexity of tasks? Or is there merit in moving to simpler structures such as the AALC?

Purposefulness can also be thwarted by those involved in the arrangements, especially in the more complex ones, where 'States' rights' and 'turf wars' (within as well as between jurisdictions) often prevail over the wider good and to the detriment of agreed objectives. Apart from the small administrative office of the GABCC, the MDB Initiative is the only arrangement with a separate independent office, which is often the object of 'turf wars' by those outside. By comparison, the other arrangements are non-threatening.

Information-richness and sensitivity

Whatever the topic, learning involves new information or seeing existing information in a new light. In spite of the continued growth in the availability of information, much that is needed is not available and important data sets are not kept up-to-date because monitoring and data collection are not done. Existing knowledge is ignored, much is being lost, even though there is much to learn from it. Studies are commissioned, research is supported, but the reports are not completed or the results are often not put to use. Better data are needed. Increasingly, there is a real need for socio-economic data as well as those of a scientific and technical nature.

The Victoria-South Australia Groundwater Agreement demonstrates the value of shared learning. Quite clearly, much more is learned than the simple sum of each agency's learning. This is also very evident in the activities of the MDB Initiative, where there is a very strong emphasis on each of the governments being the owner and provider of the information, with the MDBC providing the co-ordination and agreed direction. Agreement on data and their validity is fundamental. Learning and information also come from project monitoring and evaluation. A review of the AALC indicated that this was an area that needed to be strengthened (AACM 1997), an observation that applies to other institutions, especially where tasks are outsourced. Also relevant is the importance of people, especially senior bureaucrats and politicians, seeing things for themselves. This can often result in a significant improvement in information-richness and sensitivity.

There are two further aspects to the need for information. Firstly, information needs to be communicated to those who need it in a form that they can understand. This is often not the case, resulting in confusion and dispute, to the detriment of what the arrangements are trying to achieve. The Cap on water use in the MDB is a case in point. The expanding publication program of the AALC is an illustration of the awareness of this. Secondly, proper decision-making depends on information, yet, so often, it is undertaken in an information vacuum, even in terms of what many would regard as very basic data. Also, wrong decisions can be made because information is ignored; this is the worst form of ignorance.

Inclusiveness

While few would argue with the statement that 'management learning and improvement require the inclusion and participation of those involved and affected', such inclusion has not only to be appropriate to the context, it should also be on merit. Where these qualifications are not satisfied, inclusiveness can be at the expense of purposefulness. Such an observation is not limited to community involvement. The GABCC, perhaps the most inclusive of the institutional arrangements, noted in its first annual report that one of the keys to its success thus far 'has been the breadth of effective representation by members' (GABCC 1998: 10).

More complex issues and larger areas being covered almost inevitably mean more complex arrangements and institutions. What are the advantages and disadvantages of a political layer, such as a Ministerial Council? It may be necessary where the issues are many, complex and cover large areas. Whether or not the various arrangements are inclusive is another issue. For example, in terms of aspects of certain trans-border water issues, Queensland has demonstrated a lack of inclusiveness and recognition of responsibilities (ones that are acknowledged internationally). This is in spite of the existence of the Border Rivers Commission. A lack of inclusiveness has been a major aspect of continuing problems relating to Snowy River water.

Though inclusiveness is by no means limited to community partici-pation, this is often the most difficult to put in place. To begin with, what is meant by 'the community'? In the context of this chapter, community involvement is rarely inclusive or representative, rather comprising a small number of committed individuals. Rarely is there true community involve-ment. Secondly, if the community can be defined, how should it be involved? Rarely is there a clear process. It should not be through undertaking tasks that are – and once were – properly the preserve of governments, tasks for which 'the community' does not have the time, money or other resources. Rather, community input should be as an equal participant in setting directions, determining values, at policy and decision making levels, and then maintaining a watching brief. The management of the Barmah-Millewa forests, especially their water allocation, provides a good illustration of government agencies and the community working together to achieve agreed outcomes (MDBC 2000: 40-41). Thirdly, if the community is to be involved, it should be provided with the resources to be so in a meaningful way. The major problems of community involvement are that its representatives are not elected and, through no fault of its own, it is often unable to deliver. One way of overcoming these and other problems would be the greater involvement of local government. For many, a key issue is the lack of formal involvement of local government in any of the arrangements, yet it is at this level that much of the implementation of programs takes place.

Striving for inclusiveness is clearly not without its difficulties. While it raises inevitable questions of accountability, most – in some cases, much – of the work of the various arrangements is largely undertaken by specialist bureaucrats (and others). The success of these arrangements suggests that there are situations where it is better to leave things to the committed specialists. With increasingly complex and difficult resource management issues to consider, it may be better to leave things to the specialists rather than endeavouring to facilitate wider inclusiveness. Such an observation can apply to a Murray-Darling Basin-wide issue such as dryland salinity and a more specific one such as the security of the Hume Dam. However, this may result in 'suspicion' of activities undertaken (in these instances by the MDBC), not just by members of the community but also by other government agencies. This can be the result of non-involvement of agency staff. The strong involvement of 'on the ground' people in the AALC and its activities, the use of staff on secondment for specific tasks rather than consultants, and the level of communication between those involved, i.e. its inclusiveness, give the Australian Alps arrangement a strength that some others do not have.

Inclusiveness can also be considered in terms of subject matter as well as people. Here there are often deficiencies, as a number of examples have already indicated, such as the arbitrary boundary lines of the Victoria-South Australia Groundwater Agreement, the absence of floodplain management from the current province of the BRC, and the over-emphasis on water in the MDB Initiative, in spite of the renewed emphasis on integrated catchment management and increased involvement with the dryland regions through the Landmark project (MDBC 2002). Of particular concern in the management of water and other natural resources is the frequent absence of or only limited concern for the social or human dimension. To seek sustainable natural resources management without a human dimension is pointless. Whether or not the MDB Initiative's Human Dimension Program is able to overcome such concerns remains to be seen.

Another aspect is the lack of clear interconnections between the various arrangements and the over-arching MDB Agreement, except through the involvement of many of the same people in various aspects of the arrangements.

Flexibility

The inter-governmental arrangements that have been discussed in this chapter were all put in place to deal with particular situations. In most cases, their specific nature has enabled them to be kept relatively simple. An independent review commended the minimal bureaucratic processes of the AALC (AACM 1997).[7] However, they have all demonstrated a capacity to grow and evolve, a necessary characteristic given that change is the only certainty. As noted earlier, nearly all of them pre-date requirements for sustainability as such, but there has been a natural evolution to embrace it. A number of the arrangements demonstrate the move from development to management, especially in terms of water resources, and now there is evidence of change in the agreements and institutions as a result of the COAG water industry and other reforms. The New South Wales-Queensland Border Rivers Agreement and the MDB Initiative provide illustrations of all of these changes.

The evolutionary and flexible nature of all of the arrangements is clearly evident. They have explored their mandates in order to meet changing situations. Changes can be made when needed, though perhaps none has been as radical as that from the RMWA to the MDB Initiative. As has already been noted, the arrangements can also be regarded as experimental and innovative, certainly at the times at which they were established, the GABCC being the most recent example. The Victoria-South Australia Groundwater

---

7   Commissioned by the AALC, this is probably the only *independent* review that has been undertaken of any of the arrangements and their associated institutions. It should be read by those involved in all of the other arrangements.

Agreement is kept under regular review by its Committee, while the new arrangements for the NSW-Queensland Border Catchments are clearly of an experimental nature. Of particular interest will be their impact on the management of the intersecting streams, where for a number of reasons, including a lack of inclusiveness on the part of Queensland, the previous arrangements did not work particularly well. The Snowy Mountains Authority, now Snowy Hydro, has experienced significant change. The mining of groundwater along the Victoria-South Australia border has significant implications for the aquifers' large salt store, a fact that may require a different form of management and decision-making body in the future.

The core principles of adaptive management are important charac-teristics of all of the inter-governmental resource management arrangements operating in the MDB. They are by no means free of the associated tensions, many of which will no doubt increase as the arrangements continue to change in order to meet new challenges. The arrangements and their institutions will also continue to be surrounded by uncertainty, because of their very nature, the political environments in which they operate, and the resources they have to manage. The uncertainty is heightened because they are inter-governmental arrangements, though this very fact brings benefits that are too great to be abandoned. The background to all of the arrangements is the recognition that resources which straddle boundaries cannot be adequately managed solely within the confines of those boundaries, be they within or between juris-dictions, a fact that is still not adequately acknowledged by too many people.

Some other issues

There are important issues that cannot easily be addressed within the context of the above key principles, though they are clearly relevant to an adaptive approach to resource and environmental management.

Work that is done and actions that are undertaken need to be intellectually rigorous, clearly based on the best available knowledge, such as the MDB Initiative's Salinity Audit (MDBMC 1999a). This eliminates many sources of disagreement. It requires input from people with specialist knowledge, such as from the MDB Initiative's special issue working groups.[8] In such situations, members must participate as true 'public servants', providing good technical advice and, if necessary, putting jurisdiction allegiances to one side. In spite of all its politicking, the Murray has a long history of decision-making based on technical knowledge, as with the Chowilla and Dartmouth Dams, when the South Australian Commissioner voted contrary to the view of his government. Taking such actions for the wider good are even more needed today. As was indicated earlier, it is critically important that the knowledge and technical understanding of issues are communicated to politicians and the community at large in a manner that can be understood. There must be a principled approach to addressing issues

---

8   These are selected on merit, but there is a problem with 'generalists' having replaced 'specialists' in some government agencies. Dovers has commented on the damage done by 'managerialism', 'where generic management skills are valued above specialist ones'. The anecdotal evidence of the consequences is considerable and significant.

based on technical understanding and out of this must come the solutions to problems. Otherwise, political opportunism reigns, especially with short-term issues, though long-term issues and responsibilities generally dispense with their political aspects. Specialists and specialist knowledge will be increasingly important if the various inter-governmental arrangements discussed in this chapter are to continue to be successful. At the same time, it has to be recognised that scientific advice is not unequivocal (and many of today's problems are consequences of acting on past best advice) and there are many 'political' considerations.

Increasingly, actions will have to strive for 'satisfaction' rather than 'win-win', as with the vital need for environmental flows and the Cap on water extractions in the MDB.[9] Given the intractable nature of many of the resource and environmental issues, it is inevitable that there will have to be more regulation and direct intervention. Currently, there is an inability to deal with some issues, especially those within State jurisdiction yet which have implications beyond State boundaries, such as land clearing, major tree plantations (given their water demands), and urban developments, and some that are regarded as being within the private domain, such as farming methods. Tackling such issues will require political action, such as by the MDB Ministerial Council. The principled approach to issues will also have to extend to the political decision-making.

Political backing is also required for a further task that needs to be undertaken by the arrangements – in the continuing absence of an alternative. They must value and care for the environmental infrastructure, the rivers, the aquatic environments, the land, the flora and fauna. Who or what else will? The environmental infrastructure is fundamental to the objectives of all of the arrangements that have been considered.

Conclusion

Apart from the MDB initiative, the inter-governmental arrangements discussed in this chapter are little known. By and large, they are successful experiments that have worked well and continue to do so. They are breaking down the barriers. In many respects, they are world-class, a fact that has to be placed alongside critical comment. It is valid to ask: 'What would things have been like without them?'

Some of the arrangements and their processes will be severely tested by emerging challenges and they may need to be changed to deal with them. Given the severity and long-term nature of such issues as salinity, tightening the Cap, and river health, there may have to be a much higher level of intervention and direction than has previously been experienced or required. Such issues will require a higher level of commitment and co-ordination of government agencies and others and they may well provide the catalyst for this. On the other hand, it has been suggested that the federal government

---

9   Yet more studies and more consultation rather than a decision on environmental flows for the River Murray and the continuing non-compliance with the Cap in parts of Queensland and New South Wales illustrate the problems (*Land and Water News*, April 2002, MDBMC 2001c).

should take over management of the MDB, or there could be another revival of the Inter-State Commission (Coper 1989). These are all issues about which decisions have to be made. They illustrate the urgent need to see the larger picture, the wider good, to dispense with parochial States' rights and sectional interests.

However, the problems that have been identified are very largely not with the arrangements and their processes *per se* but with some of the people involved with them; that is, the human element. Good arrangements need good people. In this context, 'good' certainly includes technical competence. The problems that stem from content-free managerialism have already been noted, while partial knowledge management can be little better (for example, concern has been expressed at the fact that there are no 'water people' in CEO positions in major agencies). But 'good' implies more than technical competence. There is a need for honesty and integrity, to tell it as it is, based on the best scientific and other information. If diverting more water to the Snowy River causes the water distributors and the irrigation industry to greatly increase the efficiency of their water use, that will be for the wider good. The president of the Environment Institute of Australia has described continued land clearing in Queensland and NSW as a selfish 'crime' against the environment; some years ago, the former Bishop of Bendigo said it was wrong for irrigators to let their saline drainage water pollute the River Murray. There is an on-going need for commitment, co-operation, openness and trust. For example, these qualities seemed to be more evident in the early days of the MDB Initiative than they do now. There has been a down-sizing of trust. The BRC has been told that the community wants a higher level of co-operation between NSW and Queensland on border issues (BRC 1999, 2). Some may regard such words as old fashioned, but the qualities they embrace are desperately needed.

References

AACM, 1997, *Evaluation of the Australian Alps Liaison Committee, final report*, 1997, Adelaide: AACM International Ltd.

AALC, (Australian Alps Liaison Committee) 1996, *Transborder protected area cooperation*, Canberra: Australian Alps Liaison Committee.

AALC, 2001, *The Australian Alps National Parks Co-operative Management: annual report 2000-2001*, Canberra: AALC.

APLC, (Australian Plague Locust Commission), 1999, *Australian Plague Locust Commission: Annual report 1997-98*, Canberra: APLC.

Barrie, D, 1992, *Environmental protection in Federal states: interjurisdictional co-operation in Canada and Australia*, Canberra: Federalism Research Centre, Australian National University.

BGA (Border Groundwaters Agreement), 1996, *Border Groundwaters Agreement Review Committee: five year management review 1991-1996*, Melbourne and Adelaide: Border Groundwaters Agreement Review Committee.

BGA, 2000, *Border Groundwaters Agreement Review Committee: fourteenth annual report to 30 June 1999*, Melbourne and Adelaide: Border Groundwaters Agreement Review Committee.

BGA, 2002, *Border Groundwaters Agreement Review Committee: sixteenth annual report to 30 June 2001*, Melbourne and Adelaide: Border Groundwaters Agreement Review Committee.

CC, (Constitutional Commission), 1988, *Final Report of the Constitutional Commission, vol 2*, Canberra: Australian Government Publishing Service.

Clark, SD, 1983, Inter-governmental quangos: the River Murray Commission, in Curnow, GR, and Saunders, CA, (eds), *Quangos: the Australian experience*, pp 154-172, Sydney: Hale & Iremonger.

Coper, M, 1989, *The second coming of the fourth arm: the present role and future potential of the Inter-State Commission*, Discussion Paper No 2, 1989-90, Canberra: Department of the Parliamentary Library.

Crabb, P, 1988, Managing the Murray-Darling Basin, *Australian Geographer* 19: 64-88.

Crabb, P, 1995, Managing water resources: seeking unity in the interests of diversity, in Bradstock, RA et al (eds), *Conserving biodiversity: threats and solutions*, pp 162-173, Sydney: Surrey Beatty & Sons.

Crabb, P, 1997, *Murray-Darling Basin resources*, Canberra: Murray-Darling Basin Commission.

DBBRC (Dumeresq-Barwon Border Rivers Commission), 1998, *Dumaresq-Barwon Border Rivers Commission annual Report 1997/98*, Sydney and Brisbane: DBBRC.

DBBRC, 2001, *Dumaresq-Barwon Border Rivers Commission annual report 2000/2001*, Sydney and Brisbane: DBBRC.

Fisher, T, 2000, Water torture: will the Snowy ever get a drink?, *Habitat Australia* 28(2); 8-10.

GABCC (Great Artesian Basin Consultative Council), 1998, *Great Artesian Basin Consultative Council annual report 1997-1998*, Brisbane: GABCC.

GABCC, 2000, *Great Artesian Basin Strategic Management Plan*, September, Canberra: GABCC.

GABCC, 2001, *Great Artesian Basin Consultative Council annual report 2000-2001*, Brisbane: GABCC.

ISR (Industry, Science and Resources), 2000, Corporatisation of the Snowy Mountains hydro-electric Authority: draft environmental impact assessment and Supplement, Canberra: Department of Industry, Science and Resources.

Mackay, J, 1996, The Australian Alps, in *Transborder protected area cooperation*, Canberra: Australian Alps Liaison Committee.

MDBC (Murray-Darling Basin Commission), 2000, *Murray-Darling Basin Commission: annual report 1999-2000*, Canberra: MDBC.

MDBC, 2002, *Policy discussion paper: how to encourage sustainable land use in dryland regions of the Murray-Darling Basin*, , Canberra: MDBC.

MDBMC (Murray-Darling Basin Ministerial Council),1999, *The salinity audit of the Murray-Darling Basin: a 100-year perspective 1999*, , Canberra: MDBMC,.

MDBMC, 2001a, *Basin Salinity Management Strategy 2001-2015*, Canberra: MDBMC.

MDBMC, 2001b, *Integrated Catchment Management in the Murray-Darling Basin 2001-2010: delivering a sustainable future*, Canberra: MDBMC.

MDBMC, 2001c, *Review of cap implementation 1999/00: report of the independent audit group*, Canberra: MDBMC.

Morwood, (nd), *Dumaresq-Barwon Border Rivers Commission: functions, role, institutional arrangements*, Brisbane: Dumaresq-Barwon Border Rivers Commission.

NSWDLWC, 2000, *The Lake Burley Griffin Catchment Protection Scheme 1965-1998*, Sydney: NSW Department of Land and Water Conservation.

Painter, M, 1998, *Collaborative federalism: economic reform in Australia in the 1990s*, Cambridge: Cambridge University Press.

Paterson, J, 1987, *The River Murray and Murray-Darling Basin Agreement: political economic and technical foundations*, DWR Staff paper 02/87, Melbourne: Department of Water Resources.

Pegrum, R, 1983, *The bush capital: how Australia chose Canberra as its federal city*, Sydney: Hale & Iremonger Ltd.

Powell, JM, 1993, *The emergence of bioregionalism in the Murray-Darling Basin*, Canberra: Murray-Darling Basin Commission.

SADME (South Australian Department of Mines and Energy), 1982, *A management proposal for the groundwater resources along the state border of South Australia and Victoria*, Adelaide: SADME.

Scanlon, J, 2000, Transcript of evidence to the Parliament of South Australia Select Committee on the River Murray, Adelaide.

SMA (Snowy Mountains Authority), 1986, The Snowy Mountains Hydro-Electric Authority, in *Australian Year Book 1986*, Canberra: Australian Bureau of Statistics.

SMA, 2001, *Snowy Mountains Hydro-Electric Authority: Annual report 2000-2001*, Cooma: Snowy Mountains Hydro-Electric Authority.

Snowy Water Inquiry, 1998, *Snowy Water Inquiry: final report*, 23rd October 1998, Sydney: Snowy Water Inquiry.

Starr, B, 1999, *Googong Dam catchment management: a review*, Prepared for ACTEW Corporation, Canberra: Barry Starr Ltd.

Walker, G, et al, 1999, *Effectiveness of current farming systems in the control of dryland salinity*, CSIRO Land and Water, Canberra.

WCED (World Commission on Environment and Development), 1987, *Our common future*, Oxford University Press, Oxford.

Wettenhall, RL, 1983, 'Quangos, quagos and the problems of non-ministerial organization' in: Curnow, GR, and Saunders, CA, (eds), *Quangos: the Australian experience*, pp 5-52, Sydney: Hale & Iremonger.

Wettenhall, RL, 1985, 'Intergovernmental agencies: lubricating a federal system', *Current Affairs Bulletin* 61(11): 28-35.

11

Legal Perspectives

Gerry Bates

Law School, University of Sydney

The purpose of this chapter is to review legal responses to natural resources management in Australia. In common with the other contributions to this book, it attempts to reflect the core themes around which the collective project is based; persistence, purposefulness, information richness and sensitivity, inclusiveness and flexibility. Because of the large number of statutes alone that relate to natural resources management, across the different legal jurisdictions (Commonwealth, six States and two Territories, not to mention a number of external territories), this chapter will concentrate upon identifying and discussing the common themes and approaches in the law that have developed over the past few decades. It will explain the structure and meaning of current approaches, analyse their limitations, and suggest measures for improving legal responses.

Summary

In analysing the response of the law against the criteria established by the key themes, this chapter will suggest that;

- Natural resources policies, and therefore natural resources law as a reflection of those policies, are undergoing constant change and refinement over time. New ways of tackling natural resources management problems have been and still are emerging, and these innovations are, eventually, likely to be supported in law. This reflects a capacity to adopt a *flexible approach* to natural resources management; however, the time taken to develop such changes, and thus the timing of the introduction of changes, invariably does not keep pace with the progress or enhanced understanding of the problem.

- The law as set down in legislation does not always reflect what happens in practice. The availability of legal rights and powers often does not reflect the reality of natural resources management. Although to some extent absence of legal power has restricted policy approaches to natural resources management, *persistence* and *purposefulness* in natural resources management is more likely to be constrained by political influences, which include social, cultural and economic considerations, than by absence of legal power.

- The law concentrates more upon processes and procedures, hoping that these will achieve outcomes, rather than proscribing those outcomes. To this extent *purposefulness* is not strong in legislation. Although modern natural resources law generally states its objects, those objects are not generally cast as duties on decision-makers. Ultimate control is often vested in ministers. Governments manipulate the purse strings of government agencies, and this affects the ability of managers to carry out programs authorised by law.

- The law invariably confers broad discretionary powers on natural resources managers; it does not confer duties. Although access to a wide range of management tools is essential in devising appropriate responses to natural resources management issues, criteria for measuring the success of decision-making against the objectives of legislation are markedly absent in legislative schemes. Requirements to monitor the effects of policies, programs and decisions are generally also lacking in legislation. On this score, natural resource legislation generally fails the tests of *purposefulness* and *information richness and sensitivity*.

- Development of natural resources management policy and law today generally makes provision for a large measure of public participation. There are also many, although often more restricted, opportunities for members of the public to enforce the law. *Inclusiveness* has thus been a welcome feature of the development of this area of the law.

Ownership and management of natural resources in Australia

In Australia, as throughout the rest of the world, the development of the law is inevitably shaped by the system of government adopted by the nation. Our western style of government – parliamentary democracy – was inherited from our British forbears, and consequently our legal system reflects our desire to protect the social values associated with this form of government. After settlement, Australia inherited the existing common law and legislation of the United Kingdom. The common law is that body of law declared and developed by the courts of law over centuries; legislation, also known as statute law, is the law embodied in an Act of Parliament. Both forms of law exist side-by-side, unless and until an Act of Parliament repeals or changes the common law.

The common law exists principally to protect the property rights and economic interests of the owners of land and other resources. Those who have the best possessory right (and the best of all is ownership) can control the utilisation and management of a resource. The common law recognised, however, that some natural resources could not, or should not, be owned by anyone. While acknowledging that an owner of land should be allowed to also own static natural resources found on that land, such as vegetation, forests, and minerals, the common law would not extend such rights to movable resources such as air, water and wildlife,[1] although the owner had a right to take such resources into possession. The reason why only static natural resources were capable of being owned by a landholder lies in the practical impossibilities inherent in 'owning' resources that, by their very nature, are going to pass naturally from one property to another. For example, if a landowner were to own the wildlife found at any particular point of time on the land, and that wildlife then passed onto an adjoining property, imagine the arguments that might ensue between neighbours, resulting in many possible acts of trespass onto land to regain lost resources. The impossibility of 'owning' air or water becomes even more pronounced. Nevertheless, because the landowner can exclude others from the land, the owner is in the best position to take such resources into possession. Once possessed, a person can then enforce this right of possession against the whole world because there is no one else with a better right of possession.

The common law also denied private ownership of certain static and movable resources because it was in the public interest to do so; the seashore,[2] and the sea for navigation and fisheries.[3] The common law, however, provided no regime of management for such resources; any of these resources could lawfully be taken into possession or used by anyone even to the extent of depleting or destroying the asset (the so-called 'tragedy of the commons').

The common law principle of unrestricted rights of access to natural resources, however, could not survive the pressures of both recreational and commercial exploitation. In the face of heightened public and governmental concern about the continuing depletion and degradation of natural resources, made possible by the technological advances brought on by the industrial revolution, governments everywhere were ultimately forced to step in to modify or overrule common law rights by legislation to ensure the sustainability of those resources.[4] As Brennan J remarked in *Harper v Minister for Sea Fisheries* (1989) 169 CLR 314 at 329, the public right of fishing in tidal waters is not limited by the need to preserve the capacity of a fishery to sustain itself. The management of a fishery to prevent its depletion by the public must be provided for, if at all, by statute. Government has therefore progressively moved to vest ownership of natural resources in the Crown. Water, fish and other wildlife, as well as mineral resources, are now owned by the Crown, and managed by government.

---

1   *Walden v Hensler* (1987) 163 CLR 561.
2   *Beckett v Lyons* [1967] 1 Ch 449.
3   *A-G (British Columbia) v A-G (Canada)* [1914] AC 153; *Ball v Consolidated Rutile Ltd* [1991] 1 Qd R 524.
4   The transition from 'common property' to 'public property' occurs at this time: see Yandle (1983). A right of common is one conferred upon members of a group who have common access to the exclusion of everyone else; a public right is available to any member of the public. Scarcity is the catalyst for government intervention, converting the right from one of common to a public right, which can be controlled by government on behalf of the public. The allocation of rights to use that public resource may then create rights in the licence holder analogous to rights of private property in that others may be excluded.

As the government, on behalf of the Crown, now allocates these public resources, the public only has common law rights to access these resources to the extent that government has not abrogated them. This allows government instrumentalities to manage these natural resources, to determine what shall be protected and what may be exploited, and the conditions on which utilisation will occur. Government draws up management plans for the use and protection of natural resources, and allocates access to resources generally through licensing arrangements.

The structure and content of natural resource law

The purpose of natural resources law

The purpose of law is to protect the social values enshrined in society and give legal effect to the policies of government. The dominant social value espoused by our system of government is capitalism; so it is no surprise to find that law and policy relating to natural resource management traditionally supports the economic utilisation of those resources. This concentration upon rights of economic utilisation, however, meant that the law developed with no sense of environmental values, and with little appreciation of the necessity for sustainable management of land and other natural resources. The law of natural resources in Australia is therefore primarily legislation that is designed to give expression to the policies of government in relation to the sustainable management of all forms of natural resources. Modern natural resources management legislation has the following priorities:

- to set up government regulatory structures for natural resource management that apply to both the private and the public sector. These include the creation of regulatory authorities, such as environment protection and resource management authorities; and the creation of specialist courts and tribunals to hear both merits appeals and enforce the law;

- to enable members of the public, in varying degrees, to take part in strategic planning and project evaluation that determines the use of resources and environmental effects of utilisation. Requirements and procedures for public consultation are often set out in legislation and accompanying regulations; though consultation may also occur as a result of political rather than legal influences;

- to invest government regulators with powers to determine how to manage natural resources and provide them with management tools to control environmentally significant activities and encourage best practice resources management. This toolkit commonly includes the ability to develop strategic policies and plans, determine standards, issue licences, and implement and enforce the law; supplemented, importantly, by the ability to offer economic incentives to encourage better performance 'beyond compliance' and to achieve the objectives of legislation and policy instruments. The implementation and extent of such powers may be to some extent guided by both the stated or implied objects of the legislation and by specific criteria for decision-making contained within it;

- to require persons proposing to carry on environmentally significant activities to seek permission from government regulators. Depending on the activity for which permission is sought, the permitting authority may be either central government (for example, permits to access public forests and fisheries) or local government (for example, development control). Often, a number of permits for an activity are required from different regulatory authorities for different aspects of a proposal;

- to require activities of potential environmental significance to be assessed before permission can be granted. This usually involves initial assessment to determine the environmental significance of a proposal; together with more detailed assessment of proposals declared or found to be of major environmental significance;

- to provide that non-compliance with the law will attract liability for a range of administrative, criminal and civil sanctions; and to enable regulators and, to a more limited extent, members of the public, to enforce the law. Regulators may issue compliance and remediation notices, as well as institute both civil and criminal enforcement proceedings. Members of the public may be empowered also to commence civil and sometimes criminal proceedings to enforce breaches or threatened breaches of the law; and

- to a limited extent, to enable the merits, rather than the legality, of decisions of government regulators to be challenged by members of the public. This right is generally restricted to the more significant proposals for development, though sometimes may extend to other activities of environmental significance, such as potential harm to endangered species.

The structure of natural resource legislation

The legislative scheme for natural resource management may be broadly described as generally prohibiting any potentially destructive activities that may have been permitted at common law, but then setting up an administrative scheme for the issue of licences to permit such activities under conditions. There are very few absolute prohibitions in natural resource law; although drift net fishing and the taking of whales are two examples. In general, however, any prohibited activity may be permitted by licence issued by a regulatory authority. Such a system inevitably confers significant discretion upon the regulatory authorities. Legislation governing the use and management of natural resources commonly incorporates all or a combination of the following:

- a definitions or interpretation section (sometimes called a 'dictionary') defining key terms or concepts in the legislation. This is important because legal terms often do not bear their normal, everyday meanings.[5] In the absence of any other assistance, however, reference to the Oxford English Dictionary is a recognised source of authority for the meaning of undefined terms;

- a statement signifying to what extent the legislation may affect or interact with other legislation;

- a statement that the Crown is bound by the legislation;

- a statement that the legislation is not to affect the availability of civil (common law) remedies;

- a statement of the objectives of the legislation;

- a statement of the objectives of the statutory authorities created by or operating under the legislation;

- a statement of the functions of those statutory authorities;

- provisions which empower the creation of instruments of management or control such as policies, plans, notices and conditional licensing by statutory authorities;

- provisions which identify relevant criteria which govern the exercise of specific functions;

- provisions which impose certain duties on statutory authorities, decision-makers and individuals to do certain things, such as a requirement that in the exercise of specific functions an authority is to have regard to stipulated instruments of management or stipulated criteria; and

- provisions for enforcement of the legislation. These include administrative orders issued by regulatory authorities, as well as court-based prosecutions and civil remedies.

Legislative tools for natural resources management

Some of the common management tools provided by legislation to natural resources managers to achieve the objectives of the legislation include the following.

- *State policies.*[6] State policies aim to ensure that consistent planning or environmental controls are imposed throughout a State; and that a co-ordinated and integrated approach is taken to development which might require the input of a number of permitting authorities. State

---

5   For example, under the *Catchment and Land Protection Act* 1994 (Vic) the term 'land' includes wildlife.

6   Policies are commonly introduced under environmental planning and pollution control legislation; for example, *Environmental Planning and Assessment Act* 1979 (NSW), Pt 3; *Environment Protection Act* 1970 (Vic), s 16.

policies generally introduce special procedures for assessing and permitting the utilisation or development of resources.

- *Resource assessment programs.*[7] These provide for the collection, analysis, monitoring and publication of information about the availability and uses of natural resources.

- *Management plans, strategies and programs.*[8] These are a central feature of resources management, and commonly provided for in national parks, wildlife, forests, water, land degradation and fisheries legislation. Plans usually focus on particular areas or particular resources in particular areas. They may also adopt a regional or local geographical approach, for example, under environmental planning legislation where plans generally coincide with local government boundaries.[9] Legislation may specify what the plan may contain, prescribe or be designed to achieve but such statements are not generally exhaustive. A plan, like a policy, may proscribe procedures and criteria for decision-making. Where management plans exist, it is usual to prohibit resource development or utilisation that is not in accordance with the plan.

- *Property and conservation agreements and covenants.*[10] These enable resource-based agencies to make legal agreements with private landowners, but also sometimes other public sector agencies, in order to pursue the objectives of legislation. Such agreements normally provide for financial or equivalent management incentives (for example, grants for fencing). They may be created as contracts between the landowner and responsible authority; but in terms of longer term management are more effective where the agreement 'runs with the land' so as to bind future owners and other successors in title (covenants).

- *Guidelines and priorities.*[11] These effectively indicate criteria that should or must be followed in applying for permits of various kinds, and in environmental assessment of proposals or in decision-making. When provided for by legislation rather than merely drawn up by agencies

---

7 For example, Crown Lands Act 1989 (NSW), s 30 (assessment of Crown lands); *Water Act 1989* (Vic), s 22 (water resources); *Pastoral Land Management and Conservation Act 1989* (SA), s 6 (assessment of condition of land); *Soil Conservation and Land Care Act 1989* (SA), s 35.

8 For example, *Fisheries Management Act 1991* (Cth), s 17; *Crown Lands Act 1989* (NSW), s 112; *Catchment Management Act 1989* (NSW), s 30 (corporate plans empower programs); *Pastoral Land Management and Conservation Act 1989* (SA) s 41; *Soil Conservation and Land Care Act 1989* (SA), s 36; *Catchment and Land Protection Act 1994* (Vic), ss 23-36; Native Vegetation Regulations 1991 (SA), reg 3(1)(l).; *Conservation and Land Management Act 1984* (WA), ss 53, 55.

9 For example, *Environmental Planning and Assessment Act 1979* (NSW), Pt 3.

10 For example, *Conservation and Land Management Act 1984* (WA), s 16; *Soil and Land Conservation Act 1945* (WA), s 30B; *Conservation, Forests and Lands Act 1987* (Vic), s 69, 70; *Native Vegetation Act 1991* (SA), s 23; *Soil Conservation and Land Care Act 1989* (SA), s 13; *Threatened Species Conservation Act 1995* (NSW), ss 121-126; *Environment Protection and Biodiversity Conservation Act 1999* (Cth), s 305.

11 *Threatened Species Act 1995* (NSW), ss 57-59, 75-77; *Environmental Protection Act 1993* (Qld), s 18; Sch 4 (standard criteria – best practice environmental management).

for guidance,[12] they are more likely to be regarded as mandatory. Guidelines may also support Codes of Practice.

- *Codes of practice.* Codes of Practice may be developed by particular industry sectors[13] or by the regulatory authorities.[14] They generally appear in the form of industry codes for best practice directed to particular industries or activities and may be supported by more detailed guidelines. Codes that are not legal instruments, and therefore not legally enforceable, are known as voluntary codes of practice. Sometimes, however, compliance with a code of practice may be made part of a legislative scheme[15] and in this event the code will effectively provide best practice environmental management standards that are legally binding.[16] Codes, standards and other documents published by specified bodies may also be incorporated or referred to in State policies[17] or environmental protection agreements.[18] The Industry Commission (1997) has argued that voluntary standards and codes provide greater flexibility than regulations and are more intelligible to resource managers. They are more adaptable to the individual situation and circumstances of particular localities and regions, are better able to handle changes to knowledge and technology, and can be used to promote best practice management. Such voluntary standards may further stimulate awareness and encourage innovation and commitment to best practice natural resources management. Finally, they allow mandated standards to be reserved for the areas where they are most needed and likely to be cost effective.

- *Economic incentives.* These may be offered as an inducement to the promotion of good resource management,[19] for example, grants and

---

12   For example, many guidelines on environmental impact assessment are drawn up by planning agencies for the assistance of proponents of projects and the public generally. In NSW, however, guidelines have been given enhanced legal status by being incorporated in the Environmental Planning and Assessment Regulation 2000, cls 51, 82, 84.

13   For example, the Australian Chemical Industry Council 'Responsible Care' program; Australian Tourism Industry Association 'Code of Environmental Practice'; and the Australian Minerals Industry 'Code for Environmental Management'. More generally note the Business Council of Australia's 'Principles of Environmental Management'; Institution of Engineers Australia's 'Environmental Principles for Engineers'; Australian Manufacturing Council 'Best Practice Environmental Regulation' 1993.

14   For example, the Victorian EPA has published Codes of Practice relating to septic tanks, small wastewater treatment plants, and VOC emissions from the printing industry, under the auspices of its 'Best Practice Environmental Management Series' of publications.

15   For example, in respect of ozone depleting substances; *Ozone Protection Act 1989* (NSW), s 9; Ozone Protection Regulation 1991 (NSW) regs 24, 25, 31, 41-43; *Ozone Protection Act 1990* (NT), s 11; Ozone Protection Regulations 1990 (NT), regs 4-8, 13, 14; Environmental Protection (Interim) Regulation 1995 (Qld) regs 17-19, 21, 24.

16   For example, to demonstrate compliance with the general environmental duty; *Environmental Protection Act 1994* (Qld), s 219; *Environment Protection Act 1997* (ACT), ss 31, 33.

17   *Protection of the Environment Operations Act 1997* (NSW), s 35(d); *Environment Protection Act 1970* (Vic) s 72.

18   *Environment Protection Act 1997* (ACT), s 39(c)(i).

19   For example, *Conservation, Forests and Lands Act 1987* (Vic), s 68; *Native Vegetation Act 1991* (SA), s 24.

rates relief in conjunction with property or conservation agreements (see above); or as an encouragement towards the achievement of better standards of resource management, for example, through the imposition of the polluter pays principle and load based licensing,[20] where polluters of natural resources will be levied in direct proportion to their impact on the environment. Credit trading schemes offer another form of economic incentive.[21]

- *Declarations of protected areas.*[22] This is a common device for conservation and management, which can be either permanent or temporary depending upon management imperatives. Such declarations normally cover only public land, unless agreement can be reached with a private landowner.[23] For privately owned land conservation or property agreements are likely to achieve a more satisfactory negotiated solution.

- *Conservation or land management notices and orders.*[24] These enable land management agencies to prohibit certain activities or compel private or public landowners to carry out conservation or land management works on their land; and may enable the agency to enter onto land and carry out such works and recover costs from the landowner. Such costs may often be secured against the property; and it is generally an offence to refuse to comply with such an order.

- *Conditional leases.*[25] Leases of crown land may only be issued subject to conditions of management.

- *Conditional licensing.*[26] It is common in all natural resources management and environmental protection legislation to allow a competent authority to permit by licence activities which otherwise would be illegal. Conditions under which activities may be carried out may then be imposed by the authority. Any breach of the licence, or carrying on an activity without a licence where one is required, is regarded as a criminal offence. The regulatory authorities generally also have powers to modify, suspend and cancel licences where the proper management of the resource makes that necessary.

---

20 For example, Protection of the Environment Operations (General) Regulation 1998 (NSW), Div 4.

21 For example, *Protection of the Environment Operations Act* 1997 (NSW), s 69; *Forestry Act* 1916 (NSW), s 33C; *Electricity (Pacific Power) Act* 1950 (NSW), s 9(2); *Energy Services Corporations Act* 1995 (NSW), s 9(3A).

22 For example, *National Parks and Wildlife Act* 1974 (NSW), s 33; *National Parks and Wildlife Act* 1970 (Tas), s 13; *Forests Act* 1958 (Vic), s 50; *Nature Conservation Act* 1992 (Qld), s 29.

23 For example, *Wildlife Act* 1975 (Vic) s 14; *National Parks and Wildlife Act* 1972 (SA), s 44.

24 For example, *Soil Conservation and Land Care Act* 1989 (SA), s 38; *Soil and Land Conservation Act* 1945 (WA), s 32; *Catchment and Land Protection Act* 1994 (Vic), ss 37-47; *Soil Conservation Act* 1938 (NSW), ss 15A, 18, 21CA, 22; *Threatened Species Conservation Act* 1995 (NSW), ss 114-120; *Environmental Protection Act* 1993 (Qld), Sch 4 (standard criteria).

25 *Pastoral Land Management and Conservation Act* 1989 (SA), ss 22, 26.

26 For example, *Native Vegetation Act* 1991 (SA), s 29; *Environment Protection Act* 1993 (SA), s 36; *Territory Parks and Wildlife Conservation Act* 1976 (NT), ss 42-44; *Nature Conservation Act* 1992 (Qld), s 81.

In practice it is essential that regulators have access to the widest possible range of management tools from which they can select the appropriate response to any particular problem. Older legislation does little more than adopt a regulatory regime based on prohibition, licensing and enforcement. Modern environmental and natural resources legislation, however, has been slowly introducing innovations such as new forms of property rights and economic incentives that are a welcome addition to the toolbox. But these and other possible reforms are yet to be widely accepted or efficiently utilised.

To what extent do the objects of legislation guide decision-making?

It has become increasingly common for modern environment protection and natural resources legislation to specify the objects of the legislation.[27] Even different parts of the legislation may specify the objectives of that part.[28]

Interpretation Acts throughout Australia commonly state that in the interpretation of a provision of legislation, a construction that would promote the purpose or object underlying the legislation shall be preferred to a construction that would not promote that purpose or object.[29] Defining the objects of legislation is therefore more than simply an object in expressing the intent of the policy embodied in the legislation; it may guide the parameters of the exercise of legal powers under the legislation. This is so whether or not the objects are expressed in an objects clause or simply divined from the content of the Act in general. For example, in *Woollahra MC v Minister for Environment* (1993) 23 NSWLR 710 a purported exercise of discretion under the *National Parks and Wildlife Act 1974* (NSW) by the Minister to allow 'development' in the Sydney Harbour National Park was held invalid by reference to the (implied) objects of the legislation.[30] The objects of legislation may therefore be a constraint upon the exercise of statutory powers, in so far as they assist in the interpretation of those statutory powers.[31]

It is common drafting technique now to specify the objects of legislation in an objects clause. Objects of legislation may be, and often are, expressed simply in terms which declare the objects of the legislation or statutory authorities created by the legislation,[32] but may go further and bind those authorities or individual decision-makers in some way to carrying out the principles expressed

---

27   See for example, *Catchment Management Act 1989* (NSW), s 5; *Crown Lands Act 1989* (NSW), s 10; *Fisheries Management Act 1994* (NSW), s 3; *Waste Minimisation and Management Act 1995* (NSW), s 3 (underlying principles and objects); *Threatened Species Conservation Act 1995* (NSW), s 3.

28   *Waste Minimisation and Management Act 1995* (NSW), ss 6, 9, 30.

29   For example, *Acts Interpretation Act 1901* (Cth), s 15aa; *Interpretation Act 1987* (NSW), s 33.

30   See also *Willoughby CC v Minister* (1992) 78 LGERA 19; *Packham v Minister* (1993) 80 LGERA 205.

31   *Woollahra MC v Minister for Environment* (1991) 23 NSWLR 710; *Packham v Minister for Environment* (1993) 80 LGERA 205. See also Rohde (1995).

32   *Waste Minimisation and Management Act 1995* (NSW), s 17 (waste boards); *Water Board (Corporatisation) Act 1994* (NSW), ss 21, 22 (Sydney Water); *Protection of the Environment Administration Act 1989* (NSW), s 6 (Environment Protection Authority).

in such clauses,[33] The specific functions under the legislation which further these objects may therefore be so intricately linked to or interrelated with the overarching principles embodied in an objects clause within the framework of the legislation, that a decision which does not pursue or seek to achieve those overall objectives may be declared legally invalid.

Where objects are specified in legislation, then the most common instruction to statutory authorities is that they should 'have regard' to them, or take them 'into consideration' or 'into account', in making decisions or exercising functions. Objects, however, sometimes go further than a mere statement of general intent to suggest some sort of responsibility to pursue or fulfil those objectives. For example, in South Australia, the requirement under the *Environment Protection Act* 1993 is that

> [t]he Minister, the Authority and all other bodies and persons involved in the administration of this Act must have regard to, and seek to further, the objects of this Act ...[34]

In Queensland, the statutory requirement appears slightly stronger: a person on whom functions or powers are conferred must perform those functions or exercise those powers 'in the way that best achieves the object of this Act'.[35] Tasmania's Resource Management and Planning System contains perhaps an even stronger direction:

> It is the obligation of any person on whom a function is imposed or a power is conferred under this Act to perform the function or exercise the power in such a manner as to further the objectives set out in Schedule 1 ...[36]

The objectives set out in Sch 1 include the promotion of sustainable development, as defined. The exact nature of this statutory obligation has not yet been legally confirmed. It would, however, seem to impose duties on decision-makers more onerous than the duty simply to 'have regard to' or 'seek to further' those statutory objectives.[37] Section 6(2)(a) of the *South Australian Water Resources Act* 1997 contains a clause requiring all administrators under the legislation to 'act consistently with' the object of the legislation. It has been commented that (Dyson 1997: 305):

> a requirement to 'act consistently with' the Object, coupled with civil remedies available to 'uninterested' third parties (s 141) could be seen as a limiting factor in the scope of administrative discretion, increasing the risk of challenge of administrative decisions, and possibly engendering a corresponding lethargy in the bureaucracy. However, such a provision contributes significantly to the degree of accountability and transparency in decision-making under the Act.

---

33 *Land Use Planning and Approvals Act* 1993 (Tas), s 5; *Environmental Management and Pollution Control Act* 1994 (Tas), s 8; *Catchment and Land Protection Act* 1994 (Vic), s 21, 22; *Water Resources Act* 1997 (SA), s 6; *Soil Conservation and Land Care Act* 1989 (SA), s 8.

34 *Environment Protection Act* 1993 (SA), s 10(2).

35 *Environmental Protection Act* 1994 (Qld), s 5.

36 *Land Use Planning and Approvals Act* 1993 (Tas), s 8.

37 An interpretation supported by the decision of the Tribunal in *Bates v Department of Transport and Works* [1994] TAZRMPAT 169.

Under s 3 of the *Fisheries Management Act* 1994 (Cth), 'the following objectives must be pursued by the Minister in the administration of this Act and by AFMA in the performance of its functions'. The emphasis of the objectives is on efficient and cost effective fisheries management and preserving the sustainability of fisheries resources.[38] In New South Wales perhaps the strongest provision in relation to the objects of legislation is contained in s 12 of the *Crown Lands Act* 1989 (NSW) which states that the Minister is 'responsible for achieving the objects of this Act'.

The difficulties in enforcing such statutory instructions as legally binding duties should not be underestimated; but it is at least arguable that instructions that require decision-makers to 'seek to further', 'pursue' or 'achieve' objectives may be regarded as imposing stricter or more focused duties of compliance or achievement than a mere instruction to 'have regard to' those objectives. Importantly, however, legislation rarely tells us how to measure achievement in pursuance of those objectives. Criteria by which success may be measured are rarely spelt out,[39] and criteria for decision-making are also often not indicated in the legislation. To the extent to which criteria for making particular decisions are spelt out in legislation (see below), then these may be referred broadly back to the objects of the legislation, though there is usually no formal link. However, since statutorily expressed criteria for decision-making are likely to be regarded as mandatory by the courts, then failure to properly consider the mandated criteria can result in a decision being declared illegal; and to this extent the objects of the legislation may be taken to have been indirectly enforced.

Duties cast upon individuals to do or refrain from doing specific things may also be generally referable back to the general objects of the legislation. For example, the *Catchment and Land Protection Act* 1994 (Vic) contains clearly defined duties on both landowners and the Secretary of the department to take all reasonable steps to avoid or to do specified things, which clearly, although not expressly stated, are referable back to the objects of the legislation contained in s 4.[40] Similar duties are cast on lessees under s 7 of the *Pastoral Land Management and Conservation Act* 1989 (SA); and landowners under s 8 of the *Soil Conservation and Land Care Act* 1989 (SA). The *Threatened Species Conservation Act* 1995 (NSW)[41] casts limited duties on ministers and public authorities to take appropriate action to implement recovery plans and threat abatement plans.

On the other hand, specific powers conferred on decision-makers by legislation may also be interpreted to override more broadly expressed objectives. For example, in *Rosemount Estates v Minister* (1996) 90 LGERA 1; (1996) 91 LGERA 31, the Land and Environment Court of NSW had held unlawful a declaration of a State environmental planning policy by the minister on the basis that it had not countenanced public opinion and had therefore not

---

38   The difficulties in interpreting the precise nature of these requirements were discussed in *Bannister Quest Pty Ltd v Australian Fisheries Management Authority* [1997] FCA 819 (14 August).
39   See later discussion.
40   Sections 20, 21.
41   Sections 69-73, 86-90.

complied with the objects of the *Environmental Planning and Assessment Act 1979* (NSW). The Court of Appeal reversed this decision because of the inclusion in the Act of specific powers that enabled the minister to effectively override the general object of public participation.

It is apparent therefore that the extent to which decision-making is guided or constrained by the objects of natural resource legislation varies enormously between different statutes and between jurisdictions. It is also apparent that legislation makes little attempt to incorporate performance standards for evaluating the success of policies, programs and decisions as measured against the objectives of the legislation; and fails generally to require monitoring of the effects of such decision-making.

Statutory functions defined in legislation generally encapsulate powers, authorities and duties.[42] Statements of the statutory functions of authorities created by the legislation,[43] like statements of objects, may indicate the boundaries of decision-making authority.

Mandatory or directory?

Statutory functions may be regarded as either mandatory or directory (discretionary). Statutory duties are commonly marked by such phrases in legislation as 'the authority must' or 'shall'; discretions are often granted by use of the term 'may'. For example, public authorities in NSW *must* have regard to the existence of critical habitat, and *must not* make decisions inconsistent with the provisions of a recovery plan.[44] Statutory instructions which indicate that authorities 'are' to do various things may also be taken to be duties imposed upon them. For example, public authorities in NSW *are* to take action to implement recovery plans.[45] On the other hand, the Director-General of National Parks and Wildlife in NSW *may* grant a licence to take threatened species,[46] thus indicating a clear statutory intent to confer discretion rather than a duty. The conferment of a duty imposes an obligation on an authority to perform that duty in accordance with any statutory instructions. These instructions may require certain factors to be taken into account, but within that framework usually give the authority discretion to determine how best to perform the particular duty. Powers give discretion to the authority to determine whether action needs to be taken, or how best to perform a duty; they do not impose a duty to take action.

Failure to exercise a power is not legally enforceable; although the necessity to consider whether the power should be exercised may be interpreted as a duty. Where a power has been exercised it may be subject to 'judicial review' to determine whether it has been exercised in a manner which is legally acceptable. Judicial review is a way of assessing the quality of an exercise of discretion; a sort of legal 'performance standard' for administrative decision-making. Effectively

---

42   For example, *Water Board (Corporatisation) Act 1994* (NSW), s 3.
43   *Water Act 1989* (Vic), s 213 (ministerial functions in relation to water management schemes); *Catchment Management Act 1989* (NSW), s 15 (Catchment Management Committees).
44   *Threatened Species Conservation Act 1995* (NSW), ss 50, 69.
45   *Threatened Species Conservation Act 1995* (NSW), s 69.
46   *Threatened Species Conservation Act 1995* (NSW), s 91.

the law presumes that when decision-makers are empowered by statute to exercise discretions, the legislature that has conferred those powers would not intend them to be exercised in an unreasonable manner. A decision-maker must therefore take into account all relevant considerations, exclude irrelevant ones and come to a decision that is defensibly reasonable on the evidence. Decisions that fail the scrutiny of judicial review may be declared invalid. In practice, of course, since judicial review is a legal challenge to decision-making, the ability of a complainant to initiate such a challenge will depend upon whether the complainant has 'standing' to initiate the challenge; the prospects of obtaining hard evidence; and the costs of, and resources needed to mount, such a challenge.

Criteria for the exercise of statutory functions

Criteria for decision-making under legislative powers are commonly expressed by way of directions to decision-makers contained in the legislation or accompanying regulations. Criteria may be of general application, in that they apply to all decision-making functions; or they may be specifically drawn up for particular purposes within the statutory scheme. One of the most common generic criteria for decision-making in natural resources law would be the requirement to have regard to the principles of ecologically sustainable development (ESD).[47]

It is also common for legislation to require decision-makers to apply specific criteria to the exercise of particular powers; for example, in relation to allocating rights,[48] the content of management plans[49], licensing,[50] and declaring protected areas.[51]

Legislation may also expressly (though unusually) prohibit the consideration of factors other than those indicated by the legislation: for example, decision-makers may be restricted to environmental or nature conservation matters when making certain determinations thus excluding economic, social or other factors.[52] Once again, however, as is the case with statements of objects, natural resource legislation rarely requires monitoring of the outcomes of decision-making or indicates performance standards for the exercise of statutory powers.

Criteria for evaluating success

Natural resources legislation rarely indicates what criteria are to be used for evaluating the success of legislative programs, plans, policies or decision-making. This is generally because, while broad objects are stipulated in legislation, policy and decision makers are rarely required to achieve those

---

47   See below.
48   *Water Act 1989* (Vic), s 40.
49   *Fisheries Act 1995* (Vic), s 28; *Catchment and Land Protection Act 1994* (Vic), s 24.
50   *Fisheries Act 1995* (Vic), s 42; *Water Resources Act 1989* (Qld), s4.46.
51   *Fisheries Act 1995* (Vic), ss 69-89.
52   *Endangered Species Protection Act 1992* (Cth), s 27; *World Heritage Properties Conservation Act 1983* (Cth), s 13; *Coastal Waters Alliance of Western Australia Inc v Environmental Protection Authority* (1996) 90 LGERA 136 (EPA restricted to consideration of environmental factors; not allowed to take into account economic and political considerations).

objects; and there is little in the way of infrastructure for monitoring success. Lack of legal requirements for measuring success may lead to lack of administrative accountability for the conduct of programs. The Commonwealth Auditor-General has commented, for example, that success rates of the Commonwealth's various natural resources grants programs, funded under the auspices of the Natural Heritage Trust, are impossible to evaluate because adequate records that indicate what was the purpose of the expenditure and monitor achievement, have not been kept (ANAO 1997). Introduction into recent legislation of, for example, state of the environment reporting[53] can at least be seen as an attempt to monitor environmental improvement or deterioration, and therefore indirectly the success or otherwise of policies, programs and regulatory activities. So may statutory instructions for periodic review of plans and policies.[54] These lack, however, any allocation of responsibility for lack of achievement or under-performance in program implementation and decision-making.

Requirements to state criteria for evaluating the success of biodiversity protection programs have also appeared recently in the Commonwealth's *Environment Protection and Biodiversity Conservation Act* 1999. The Act stipulates that criteria, against which achievement of the objectives of recovery plans, threat abatement plans, and wildlife conservation plans are to be measured, must be included in the plan.[55] The Act does not, however, indicate what might be the consequences of failure or under-achievement; though presumably since such plans can be amended one might expect that this would be the outcome of evaluation of the performance criteria. Legislation, however, is notoriously reluctant to prescribe responsibility for, or indicate what should be done to address, the under-performance or failure of plans, policies, programs and decision-making.

Have regard to

Legislation commonly provides that public authorities or individual decision-makers must 'have regard to', 'take into account' or 'take into consideration' stipulated objectives, criteria or general considerations, including ESD,[56] or that the objects of legislation or statutory authorities are, or are to be promoted 'having regard to', for example, the principles of ESD.[57] Naturally the matters to which regard must be had would be expected to influence decision-making. However, such a statutory instruction falls short of actually requiring the statutory functions to be implemented or command decision-making.[58]

---

53   For example, *Protection of the Environment Administration Act* 1991 (NSW), s 10.

54   For example, *Environment Protection and Biodiversity Conservation Act* 1999 (Cth), s 331.

55   Sections 270, 271, 287.

56   *Protection of the Environment Operations Act* 1997 (NSW), ss 13 (draft policies); s 45 (licensing); *Water Board (Corporatisation) Act* 1994 (NSW), s 22; *Contaminated Land Management Act* 1997 (NSW), s 10; *Environmental Protection Act* 1970 (Vic), ss 20C, 26B; *Environment Protection Act* 1993 (SA), ss 47, 57; *Environmental Protection Act* (Qld), ss 44, 89, 110, Sch 4 (standard criteria).

57   *Protection of the Environment Operations Act* 1997 (NSW), s 3(a); *Protection of the Environment Administration Act* 1991 (NSW) s 6(10)(a); *Waste Minimisation and Management Act* 1995 (NSW), ss 3(2), 17(c); *Environment Protection Act* 1993 (SA), s 10(1)(b).

58   *R v District Council of Berri* (1984) 51 LGRA 409.

The *Macquarie Dictionary* definition of 'regard' is to 'take into account or consider.' A statutory instruction to 'have regard to' means 'to take those matters into account and to give weight to them as a fundamental element' in making a decision,[59] but not to make it by reference to them exclusively.[60] The expression 'introduces a factor which is material to the function'.[61] Gummow J also remarked in *Turner v Minister for Immigration and Ethnic Affairs* (1981) 35 ALR 388 at 392, '[m]ere assertion that regard has been had will not suffice, if it is demonstrated that regard has not been paid in any real sense'. This 'real sense' is more fully developed in *Parramatta CC v Hale* (1982) 47 LGRA 319 which considered the obligation in s 90, as it then was, of the *Environmental Planning and Assessment Act* 1979 (NSW) to 'take into consideration' relevant matters. Moffitt P held that simply adverting to a matter and then rejecting it was not taking it into consideration. To do that a decision-maker had to acquaint itself with such relevant material as would enable it to consider whether such matters were indeed material to the decision. In other words regard must be adequate not cursorily given.

Due weight

Where a number of factors are mandated for consideration without any statutory indication as to the priority or weight to be accorded to the various factors, then the relevance of each of those factors is a question of fact for the decision-maker to determine.[62] For example, although application of the precautionary principle (see below) may be relevant to, even required of, decision-making, it is but one factor to be taken into account and does not outweigh all other considerations.[63] It is clear, however, that all statutorily mandated criteria must be given due weight, rather than no weight at all. Due weight may mean whatever weight is due as the focal point of the scheme of the legislation.[64] In the context of any particular determination that 'due weight' could in fact be nil.

Failure to have regard to or consider any statutorily mandated factors or give due weight to them may thus result in any consequent decision being declared invalid.[65] But while environmental or sustainability criteria may be mandated as relevant to decision-making, the practical effect of the 'have regard to' type formula is that in practice these criteria may not command decision-making. Legislation rarely makes such criteria the focal point of reference in natural resources management, although arguably it should.

---

59   *R v Toohey; ex parte Meneling Station Pty Ltd* (1982) 158 CLR 327 at 333 per Gibbs CJ.

60   *Minister for Immigration and Ethnic Affairs v Baker* (1997) 24 AAR 457 at 463-4.

61   *R v Toohey; ex parte Meneling Station Pty Ltd* (1982) 158 CLR 327 per Mason J at 337.

62   *Randwick MC v Manousaki* (1988) 66 LGRA 330; *Australian Postal Corporation v Botany MC* (1989) 69 LGRA 86; *Minister for Aboriginal Affairs v Peko Wallsend Pty Ltd* (1986) 162 CLR 24 at 41.

63   *Greenpeace Australia Ltd v Redbank Power Company Ltd* (1994) 86 LGERA 143.

64   *Town of Walkerville v Adelaide Clinic Holdings Pty Ltd* (1985) 55 LGRA 176 at 197.

65   *Parramatta CC v Hale* (1982) 47 LGRA 319; *King v Great Lakes Shire Council* (1986) 58 LGRA 366.

Conclusion

It is clear that natural resource legislation confers wide powers upon decision-makers to manage natural resources. On the one hand, the conferment of wide discretion assists managers to choose the right management tools and approaches to apply to a given situation or problem; but on the other failure to demand outcomes, proscribe performance standards, focus decision-making on stipulated objectives and criteria, or require monitoring of performance, can lead to failures in management regimes that would not accord with the expressed objects of the legislation. Failure to support the declared objectives of the management regime established by the legislation with stipulated performance requirements may suggest a certain lack of political commitment to those objectives. In this regard, the influence of competing political considerations becomes all too apparent. While it is inevitable that such considerations will shape natural resources management policies, arguably these influences should be applied more in policy development than in the implementation of legislation once enacted. The reality, however, is that by building into legislation a wide measure of discretion, decision-makers are not only allowed to choose the appropriate tools for the job, but may in effect decide, or be required by political direction, to minimise or abandon efforts directed towards the sustainable management of natural resources.

In analysing the strengths and weaknesses of natural resource legislation in Australia, it may be helpful to bear in mind the principles and guidelines endorsed in 1995 by the Council of Australian Governments (COAG) for the development of national standards and regulations. These principles and guidelines, which have relevance to the design of natural resources management legislation, stipulate that:

- an assessment of a proposed standard requires an adequate evaluation of its economic and social costs and benefits. Such an evaluation is best conducted prior to the design and implementation of the standard;

- mandated standards are most likely to be efficient where the management of the environmental risks does not vary greatly. If they do, the hazard is best tackled by a code of practice;

- there is a direct link between the achievement of the standard and the reduction in the risk of environmental damage;

- as far as practicable, mandated standards should be expressed in broad outcomes, in preference to processes, outputs or technical requirements; and

- measurable and audited standards are more easily enforced. Those that cannot be enforced discredit the regime.

It is clear that natural resources legislation in Australia does not always, or indeed often, reflect or promote these standards.

Public participation in natural resources management

If governments have learned anything over the years, it is that allowing the public to participate in policy making before decisions are taken can save a lot of political anguish later on. Consequently, Australian natural resources legislation is quite generous in the ability it gives for ordinary members of the public, as well as specific user and interest groups, to participate in strategic policy development for the use of natural resources. Today, virtually no important policies for natural resource management are put into place without wide distribution of policy proposals, extensive advertising for public submissions, and public hearings. Indeed, legislation often demands it.

The courts traditionally protect opportunities for public participation very strictly. Procedural irregularities of any significance are likely to lead to a decision being declared invalid. As early as 1973, the High Court stressed in *Scurr v Brisbane City Council* (1973) 133 CLR 242 that provisions enabling public participation not only avail the general public but importantly are a means of heightening the quality of decision-making by exposing decision-makers to additional information and viewpoints to which they might otherwise not have had regard.

As decision-making becomes increasingly focused, however, on particular proposals for development or utilisation of resources, so opportunities for public involvement become increasingly channelled towards a formal challenge of the licensing of such proposals in a court or tribunal setting. As this channelling takes place, so the opportunities for participation become more restricted. Sometimes legislation may justify restriction or removal of public rights to challenge decision-making on the basis that an opportunity for input into strategic planning has already been afforded.[66] Legislation commonly allows persons to settle disputes over the use or management of natural resources in three principal ways; by the issue of administrative orders by regulatory authorities, by legal action and by a merits appeal.

Administrative orders

Most regulatory authorities are generally empowered to enforce their requirements for managing resources through the issue of orders directed at licence holders who are in breach of conditions of their licence; and others who are infringing or likely to infringe the law, for example, by acting contrary to management plans, conditions of leases or regulations. The range of orders includes directions to stop work, directions for remediation and clean-up, and directions to undertake works. The power to issue such orders is constrained only by the legal principles that orders should reasonably relate to the particular activity in respect of which the order is issued; and that persons served with such orders should be able to understand what they have to do to comply with them. Failure to comply with such orders is generally a criminal offence;

---

66   See, for example, the *Forestry and National Parks Estate Act 1998* (NSW).

and ultimately a regulator may be able to undertake necessary work, recover the costs of that work against the offender and even secure the costs of work against other property owned by the offender. In practice therefore regulators generally have wide powers to enforce their requirements for best practice management of natural resources.

Legal action

Legal action may be categorised as civil enforcement, judicial review and criminal prosecution.

Civil enforcement

Modern natural resources management legislation generally preserves rights to undertake common law actions for damage to private resources. Such rights are commonly enforced through the law of nuisance, trespass and negligence. Modern statutory schemes also provide for civil enforcement of the legislation and instruments of management put in place under the legislation. Civil enforcement may often be undertaken by members of the public, as well as by regulatory authorities, pursuant to statutory rights conferred by the legislation. Common remedies sought by such civil action are an injunction or stop order to halt the activity being complained of; and a declaration that explains the respective legal rights and obligations of the parties. In practice, such civil enforcement is more often pursued by members of the public than regulatory authorities, which is curious considering that civil enforcement has distinct advantages over prosecutions, which is the form of legal action most likely to be relied on by regulatory authorities. Criminal prosecution is essentially reactive not anticipatory or preventive; and compensation for, or remediation of, environmental damage is not the purpose of criminal sanctions and thus penalties imposed are likely to be less than would be imposed if the object was to compensate for damage caused. The criminal standard of proof is also more demanding than the civil standard; proof beyond reasonable doubt rather than proof based on the balance of probabilities, which is the civil standard. Perhaps the failure to pursue civil remedies can be explained by the existence of the power vested in regulatory authorities to issue administrative orders, which are themselves a form of civil enforcement.

Judicial review

Judicial review is a form of civil enforcement, but directed at decision-makers rather than those undertaking questionable activities. The law presumes that when Parliament invests regulators with powers to make decisions it intends that those powers should be exercised for the purposes for which they were given, and in a reasonable manner. Any excess or misuse of power, or unreasonable use of power such as by failing to take into account all relevant considerations and excluding irrelevant ones before making a decision, may lead a court to invalidate an administrative decision. Judicial review of administrative decisions therefore sets a sort of judicial performance test for administrative decision-making. This review concentrates on the way the decision was reached, and whether it was lawful, not the merits of the decision itself. In that regard it is therefore fundamentally different to merits review (below). All natural resources management decision-making is potentially subject to judicial review; and indeed controversial decisions in respect of resources such as forests and fisheries often have been challenged by this form of legal action. However, because judicial review seeks to challenge how a decision was made, it is vitally dependent upon evidence as to how that decision was made; and gathering such evidence is not an easy task. It will be easier to scrutinise decisions for possible irregularities if decision-makers are required to give reasons for decisions when asked; but there is no general legal right to demand reasons and few statutes actually give such a right. At Commonwealth level reasons for natural resources decision-making may be sought,[67] but at State level this is generally not the case.

An application for judicial review may also be used to force administrators to carry out their statutory duties. An order of *mandamus* may issue to persons who have statutory duties to perform but are neglecting those duties. In natural resources management this form of review has potential but is rendered almost redundant because most statutory functions are conferred by way of powers rather than duties; criteria for evaluating the exercise of duties are generally absent in legislation; and in any case a court would be reluctant to tell a resource manager how to perform a particular function.[68] Until more specific obligations are imposed on resource managers this form of review will only rarely be possible.

Criminal prosecution

The threat of criminal prosecution has generally been the backbone of legal enforcement of requirements for natural resource management. It is usual for a statute to specify that breach of any of its provisions, as well as breaches of regulations and instruments of management issued under the legislation, and failure to obey the instructions and administrative orders, lawfully given, of authorised officers acting under the legislation, will be regarded as a criminal offence. Commonly, significant offences may be committed without any intention to commit the offence; the act constituting the breach will be enough to ground liability. Over the years, maximum fines for offences have increased; the liability of corporations and corporate officers for offences committed by themselves or by their employees and agents has significantly widened beyond the scope of the general law; and the range of penalties that may be imposed has significantly widened from fines and jail terms to include such things as community service orders and orders to publicise offences. It might be argued that significant deterrents against breaking the law are in place; but in general the deterrence factor is significantly lessened if courts do not impose realistic fines or other forms of punishment. It may be remarked

---

67   *Administrative Decisions (Judicial Review) Act 1977 Cth)*, s 13.
68   An example of a failed attempt to plead such an obligation is *Bridgetown/Greenbushes Friends of the Forest Inc v Executive Director of the Department of Conservation and Land Management* (1997) 94 LGERA 380.

that in general the courts have not traditionally regarded environmental offences as 'real' crime and therefore the range of penalties has tended to be fairly low. This has undoubtedly discouraged regulators from bringing criminal prosecutions. This situation improves markedly where offences are sent to a specialist environmental or resources court or tribunal for resolution; but not all such bodies are vested with the jurisdiction to hear criminal as well as civil cases. In practice regulators treat criminal prosecution as a last resort; partly because of the inevitably high commitment of human and financial resources to court action; partly because of the likelihood of penalties being imposed that the regulator considers unrealistic; and partly because it is usually more efficient to realise a solution to a problem through negotiation and use of administrative orders where necessary. Modern natural resources management undoubtedly depends more on negotiation about outcomes and introduces more flexibility into decision-making than used to be the case. But this makes it even more imperative that the regulatory system is underpinned by a clear statement of intent and imperatives, and the possibility of strong and realistic regulatory action should there be a breakdown.

Standing to take legal action

In order to maintain any form of court action, a person must establish 'standing' to bring the action; the right to be heard in court. It is said to be a means of ensuring that only those who have a legitimate interest in a matter are allowed access to the court. This begs the question of course what is a legitimate interest. Courts of common law deal with litigants seeking protection of their private interests; they are not used to dealing with matters of public concern where a litigant may have no private interests to protect. Consequently, at common law, only litigants who can show some private interest of theirs is at stake have the right to launch a court action.

The general approach of a court to interpretation of rights granted by statutes is to presume that a statute does not intend to affect the common law or private rights protected by the common law unless by express or necessary intendment those common law rights have been modified or displaced. Consequently legislation that gives rights to members of the public to challenge environmental decision-making through judicial review, to enforce the law by civil action, or indeed to bring a merits appeal (below) has often been restrictively interpreted so as to reflect the common law view that a person, to gain standing under the statutory scheme, must in fact have an interest that would be recognised at common law.[69] Since many statutes were not entirely clear about the range of interests intended to be recognised by the legislative scheme, empowering for example, 'persons aggrieved'[70] to undertake such actions, enforcement of much environmental law has been very severely restricted by this strict application of common law rules that were hardly appropriate in cases involving protection of public rather than private interests. Recently, however, the Federal Court in particular has begun to grant

---

69   For example, *Australian Conservation Foundation v Commonwealth* (1980) 146 CLR 493.
70   For example, *Administrative Decisions (Judicial Review) Act* 1977 (Cth), s 5.

standing to litigants who can effectively represent the public interest,[71] while some Commonwealth statutes[72] have begun to more precisely define who should have rights to enforce the law, such rights in fact being clearly more extensive than would be allowed at common law.

Nevertheless, for many potential litigants seeking to enforce the law, running the gauntlet of the standing requirements can effectively put paid to their action no matter how strong their case on the evidence. It is clear that breaches of the law may go unpunished simply because the person seeking to point out those breaches to the court may not be regarded as having the right to do so. Such a situation naturally leads public litigants to seriously question the commitment of government to compliance and enforcing compliance with the law, and lessens their resolve to participate any further in natural resources management. The development of such attitudes can seriously undermine the objects of legislative schemes for natural resource management, which more and more seek to involve the public in decision-making and enforcement, both as a means of information gathering prior to making decisions, and as aid to enforcement later.

New South Wales is the only State that has had the resolve to abolish rules of standing. In that State, any person may enforce the law by civil action or proceedings for judicial review,[73] while effectively any person may also launch a merits appeal against a restricted class of development applications so long as they were an original objector to the class of decisions subject to merits appeal. Since this has been the situation in NSW for some 20 years, there has been plenty of time to confirm that removing formal standing requirements in fact supports rather than detracts from legislative schemes for natural resources and environmental management. It is high time other jurisdictions followed suit.

Merits appeals

Sometimes decision-making, particularly in respect of the issue of licences to develop or use natural resources, may be challenged on the merits by persons to whom the legislation gives such rights. A merits appeal concentrates on the quality of the decision not its legality. It is common for applicants for licences to be afforded an opportunity for merits appeal to a specialised court or tribunal.[74] Sometimes some sort of internal reconsideration must take place before a formal appeal may be lodged. Opportunities for other objectors to have decisions reviewed are, however, much more limited. For objectors who are not applicants for licences, the most common form of merits appeal arises

---

71   For example, *North Coast Environment Council Inc v Minister for Resources* (1994) 127 ALR 617.
72   For example, s 487 of the *Environment Protection and Biodiversity Conservation Act 1999* (Cth) extends the test of 'person aggrieved' under the *Administrative Decisions (Judicial Review) Act 1977* (Cth) to persons and organisations that, in the two years preceding the decision under challenge, have engaged in a series of activities in Australia for protection or conservation of, or research into, the environment.
73   For example, *Environmental Planning and Assessment Act 1979* (NSW), s 123.
74   For example, *Environmental Planning and Assessment Act 1979* (NSW), s 97.

in respect of local authority approvals for development,[75] though other decision-making processes, for example, licensing of emissions of pollution, or the taking of threatened species,[76] may be appealable. Merits review is often resisted by regulatory authorities because it lengthens and increases the costs of the decision-making process; may produce decisions that do not accord with agency policy; and are generally made by persons not connected with either the issue or the objectives or culture of the agency making the decision. This latter of course may also be argued as an advantage. Merits review is generally undertaken by a specialist court or tribunal consisting of assessors with professional backgrounds appropriate to the subject matter of the appeal. Persons with legal qualifications may also hear such cases. The main advantage of a merits appeal is that it gives a person who is dissatisfied with the original decision a 'day in court' to test the suitability of that decision and the conditions applicable to the project. Generally speaking the final verdict will be accepted by all parties because of the perceived independence of the adjudicators. For objectors, the most common criticism is that merits appeals are not available except for a very limited number of significant proposals. Whether merits appeals actually deliver better decision-making is hard to assess; though they do often force original decision-makers to rethink and justify their approaches.

Costs of enforcement

The most common criticism of legal processes for resolution of disputes is the cost of taking action. In fact legal processes are treated differently to merits appeals. For merits appeals, the general rule is that, win or lose, each party bears their own costs. While such a rule undoubtedly assists objectors to proposals who, even if they lose, do not have to pay the costs of the other party, it undoubtedly disadvantages applicants who win or defend their appeals. The justification for this approach is that, for a limited number of significant issues, it is in the public interest that decision-making should be tested and it would be a disincentive to encouraging participation by the public if costs were payable to the applicant/proponent if the objector should lose. For the proponent/applicant the costs of a merits appeal are simply another cost of doing business.

Theoretically, the same justification could apply to the costs of legal action, where the normal rule is that the loser of the action pays the costs of the winner. Indeed the Land and Environment Court in NSW has for many years used such an argument to justify the exercise of its discretion, in appropriate 'public interest' cases, to refuse to award costs to the winner of a legal action.[77] This approach has recently been upheld, narrowly, by the High Court of Australia.[78] Nevertheless, in legal actions it is by no means certain that even if a case qualifies as a 'public interest' case that the court will exercise its

---

75   For example, *Environmental Planning and Assessment Act* 1979 (NSW), s 98.
76   For example, *Threatened Species Conservation Act* 1995 (NSW), s 106.
77   For example, *Oshlack v Richmond River Council* (unreported, LEC, 25 February 1994).
78   *Oshlack v Richmond River Council* [1998] HCA 111.

jurisdiction to refuse to award costs. Such a determination is not automatic; it very much depends upon an exercise of the court's discretion taking into account all the circumstances. The question of the cost of taking legal action therefore still looms very large in terms of disincentives to enforcing the law.

Establishment of specialist courts and tribunals

One welcome feature of modern natural resources law is the establishment of specialist environmental courts and tribunals to hear cases involving all types of legal action and merits appeals. The extent of jurisdiction of these bodies, however, varies greatly throughout Australia. In some jurisdictions specialist courts hear all forms of action,[79] others only have merits appeals functions,[80] while others hear both merits appeals and civil enforcement applications but have no criminal jurisdiction.[81] There seems little doubt that specialist courts and tribunals are generally willing to invest environmental cases with a greater degree of significance than non-specialist courts (eg, Stein 1996; Stewart 1999), if comparison of criminal penalties is any guide (Zapparoni 1997). On the civil side, these specialist courts and tribunals have also been prepared to take on judicial review of environmental decision-making as rigorously as other courts; and willingly enforced the law through the application of civil remedies. A large proportion of merits appeals are won by objectors, so that it could hardly be a general criticism of these bodies that they are captured by established developmental interests. All courts and tribunals exercising legal jurisdiction are, however, required to apply the law not make policy; although some measure of discretion does exist in determination of a penalty and awards of costs. And although with a merits jurisdiction, specialist courts and tribunals can actually make the final decision on an application for development or access to a resource, legislation restricts the circumstances in which such appeals can be lodged.[82]

Specialist courts, like any other court, also depend heavily on the evidence of experts in reaching conclusions, both in legal and merits proceedings. However, the courts rely on the parties to produce such 'experts', and naturally the parties will endeavour to produce experts who unequivocally support their particular point of view. The courts traditionally deal with conflicting evidence by looking to the credentials and experience of such experts. This process may well exclude from the evaluation process those independent experts who are perhaps most qualified to assist the court, because they have not been retained by the parties in dispute. There is a case to be made for empowering specialist environmental courts to call on the assistance of independent experts to assist in the resolution of cases where detailed scientific or technical evaluations are essential to the outcome.

---

79   For example, the NSW Land and Environment Court.
80   For example, the Administrative Appeals Tribunal in Victoria, a division of which hears planning and environment appeals.
81   For example, the Tasmanian Resource Management and Planning Appeal Tribunal
82   See earlier discussion.

Tensions inherent in legal responses to natural resources management

Over the decades it has become apparent that the development, implementation and enforcement of natural resources management policy has been heavily influenced by a number of key factors. For example, the development of natural resource policy, and hence natural resources law, is based upon scientific evaluation, but influenced heavily by prevailing economic, social and cultural expectations. The implementation of the law is determined by internal agency culture; the attitude of the responsible minister, who may in turn be influenced by cabinet government; the structure of government administration, and the resources allocated to implementation. Enforcement of the law is generally determined by agency culture, public pressure, the attitudes of courts and tribunals, and the costs, flexibility, simplicity and availability of legal processes for enforcement. Some of these considerations manifest themselves in the following ways.

Influence of the common law

The governmental approach to natural resources management has had to be applied in the context of a social system that hitherto placed few restrictions on the exploitation of natural resources by private owners. The common law effectively allowed landowners to do what they wished with their land and its resources, subject only to the right of other landowners not to be unreasonably interfered with by such use. So for example, although a neighbouring landowner could complain about pollution from a neighbour adversely affecting his property, he could not complain about his neighbour destroying vegetation or forests on the land or filling in the wetlands. The common law viewed pollution as devaluing the property values of a neighbour; but environmental destruction that did not affect the neighbour was no business of anyone other than the rightful owner of the resource. What natural resource legislation does is effectively make natural resources exploitation and management the business also of government, with a consequent potential to deny access and affect the economic development of those resources.

Naturally there were bound to be tensions between the previously unregulated private interests and the government regulators, tensions that often manifest themselves in demands for no regulation, deregulation or compensation. While some intrusions into these rights have been successfully made to protect public interests, most notably in the area of land use or environmental planning, it remains true that the most significant environmental problems facing Australia to-day have also proved to be the hardest for governments to tackle because they force regulators to confront the traditional rights of private landowners. Town and country or urban planning succeeded because it addressed significant social rather than environmental problems; reforms reflecting increased environmental concerns were grafted on later. Attempts to curb degradation and destruction of natural resources on private land however; for example, clearance of native vegetation and forests, land degradation, and loss of biodiversity in general, have historically proved difficult to introduce, and have been inadequate in their coverage, implementation and enforcement. Water and fisheries reforms have also had to grapple with the difficulties inherent in modifying or removing entitlements that over the years had come to be regarded as *de facto* property rights.

Although generally not required as a matter of law, the issue of compensation for restricting existing rights has also proved difficult for governments to resist. As a result much needed environmental controls have invariably been too long delayed; and even when finally introduced continuing agitation for compensation has often ensured a muted response to implementation and enforcement. Only in recent times has inescapable scientific evidence of the looming environmental, economic and social repercussions of doing nothing prompted governments to tackle head on the question of placing uncompensated restrictions on the managers of private land, particularly in rural areas where the most pressing environmental problems, such as native vegetation removal, dryland salinity and run-off from acid sulphate soils have been emerging.

Licences as private property

The licensing system is the backbone of natural resources law. Licences not only regulate the use of those resources that have always been regarded as public assets, such as sea fisheries; but also regulate activities on private land that at common law have always been regarded as within the province of the landowner to control, such as development on the land and exploitation of natural resources such as water and wildlife.

Licensees of course are apt to regard their entitlements under a statutory licence as in the nature of property rights, even though in law they are more in the nature of personal arrangements. For example, a licensee with a right to take water to irrigate land, naturally is likely to regard that water entitlement as something that gives value to the property and may therefore agitate to have it regarded as effectively annexed to the property, or even to be able to sell the entitlement to a neighbour separate from the property. Similarly a person granted a licence to take commercial quantities of fish may regard that entitlement as able to be traded quite separate from its attachment to any particular fishing boat or person. In the past, regulatory authorities responsible for allocating access to resources such as water and fisheries have in fact allowed the entitlements granted by licence to mature into de facto property rights with consequent rights of trade and claims for compensation for any modification or removal. This has meant that the regulators effectively often lost control of the management of those resources. However, a return to some form of private ownership of public resources, underpinned by strong statutory management requirements, is increasingly being seen as having the potential to give much needed incentives to the exploiters of natural resources to take more responsibility for, and interest in, the sustainable use of those resources.

Demands for compensation

The removal of unlimited rights of access to and control of natural resources from private landowners inevitably created tensions because such policies overrode existing common rights to exploitation and use of those resources. Landowners demanded compensation for loss of existing rights because government had effectively acquired those rights from them. The argument that since our society and our economy is effectively based on the economic value of property rights, including statutory entitlements, any adverse dealing with those rights should be compensated, carries a very strong political message, if not a legal one. So, for example, when the South Australian government in the 1980s wished to limit the clearing of native vegetation throughout the State it found that it could not do so politically, although it could do so legally, without paying out tens of millions of dollars in compensation for lost opportunities. The South Australian government spent around $70 million from 1985 to 1991 compensating landowners for refusing them permission to clear native vegetation from their properties.[83] Applications to clear were rejected at a staggering rate of 96 per cent. It is estimated that in that time up to half-a-million trees and 25 million plants were saved. This legislative entitlement was replaced in 1991 with an arrangement whereby incremental costs would be compensated only where this was judged to be over and above that expected of all South Australian farmers.

Compensation may be justified on grounds of equity and to encourage efficient investment. Federal and most State law therefore provides a right to compensation for the removal of an actual property right. However, where compensation is necessary, it may be argued that it should only be offered for a transitionary period as an equitable means of bringing about a rapid and irreversible transition from unacceptable to more preferred management practices. The South Australian example, given above, can be viewed in these terms; automatic compensation terminated with the repeal of the 1985 Act. Another important consideration is that if irreversible losses are to be avoided people need a positive incentive to reveal new findings. If, for example, farmers discover that remnant vegetation on their property contains an endangered species or, more seriously, one thought to be extinct, then unless there is a guarantee of compensation they have a strong financial incentive to fail to act to protect it (Bowers 1994: 13).

Where land management unreasonably interferes with others, then it is easier to resist calls for compensation. Many planning decisions taken in the broad public interest, for example, affect private rights without compensation; and restrictions on emissions of polluting effluent are not compensated under the law because the common law has never recognised any right of one private landowner to unreasonably interfere with the property rights of another. Where rights of natural resources management that do not affect other landowners are modified, restricted or removed, however, then claims for compensation are more difficult to resist. The public should be expected to pay

---

83   J Bradsen, Chairman of the South Australian Native Vegetation Authority, personal communication, February 1991.

for the future denial of existing rights currently being exercised in a lawful manner.

The corollary to this of course is that unless procedures for compensating a modification or removal of rights are included in a statute, then the courts will prefer a construction that does not allow those rights to be unduly interfered with. In other words, that legislative provisions that enable public authorities to invade or erode existing rights and privileges should be construed strictly in favour of the individual.[84] Obviously such an approach cannot survive against a clear statutory intent to allow the modification or removal of rights without compensation; but the expectation that neither common law nor statutory rights would or could be removed without compensation has been an expectation deeply embedded in the political psyche, an attitude strongly influenced of course by the common law, and an attitude that in fact has bedevilled and led to the failure of many governmental attempts to limit private rights in order to further environmental outcomes. Bonyhady (1992) has reviewed a number of these failures.

The real problem with creating expectations that any intrusion into common law or statutory rights in the pursuit of environmental policies will be compensated, is of course that governments will not be able to make sufficient money available to fund the environmental program and therefore the objectives will not be realised. As Bonyhady remarks 'because both ownership and property have such powerful rhetorical force, even if constitutionally entitled to do so, governments are reluctant to infringe them without paying full compensation which in turn constrains government action because of the limitations of the public purse'. Raff (1998) has pointed out for example, that in Victoria, although the provisions of the *Fauna and Flora Guarantee Act* 1988 enable Interim Conservation Orders to be made, compensation might be payable; and no such orders have in fact been made in the ten years of the operation of the legislation. This is why, if a co-operative effort between landowners and government can be negotiated, it is likely to be far more attractive politically than a compensatory approach.

There is clearly a difference, however, between taking away a right in its entirety and merely restricting certain aspects of the exercise of that right. The moral justification for compensation is much harder to resist in the former case than the latter.

The psychological and political attachment to compensation in fact appears to have been overcome as regards lost opportunities. For example, recent restrictions on clearance of native vegetation have been introduced without schemes for compensation; and restrictions on development of listed heritage properties do not attract compensation. In place of provision for compensation have come schemes for financial assistance for resource maintenance and works. So for example, property owners may now apply for government grants for undertaking land management and protection or heritage restoration; claim various forms of tax and rate relief, and enter into property agreements and covenants with financial benefits attached.[85] The

---

84   Per Gillard J in *Protean (Holdings) Ltd v Environment Protection Authority* [1977] VR 51 at 56.
85   See earlier discussion.

Commonwealth government has been keen to fuel the voluntary approach to natural heritage conservation by making millions of dollars available from the partial sale of Telstra to fund heritage restoration and management projects through the auspices of the Natural Heritage Trust.[86] However, removal, by contrast to restriction, of existing rights is still regarded by governments and the courts as legitimately raising an expectation that compensation will be available. Courts are likely therefore to strictly interpret legislative provisions that purport to take away property rights without compensation.[87]

This does not of course mean that a permitting authority must never take a decision that conflicts with existing private rights; only that the power to do so must be clearly expressed.[88] The right to compensation for removal of fishing entitlements consequent upon the declaration of marine parks or reserves has in fact been statutorily guaranteed in Western Australia to holders of leases, licences and permits,[89] illustrating once again the property-like status of a fishing entitlement that in theory amounts to no more than a mere permit or licence for access to a public resource.

Section 51(xxxi) of the Australian Constitution also requires that if the Commonwealth enacts a law providing for the acquisition of property for purposes for which the parliament has power to make laws, that the acquisition must be on 'just terms'; that is that compensation must be paid. In *Newcrest Mining (WA) Ltd v Commonwealth* (1997) 147 ALR 42 at 149 Kirby J, in the High Court, remarked that this provision was a protection against 'arbitrary and uncompensated deprivation of property'. It will be noted, however, that compensation is only payable if property is 'acquired'. Mere sterilisation of a particular land use does not necessarily amount to an acquisition. In *Commonwealth v Tasmania* (1983) 46 ALR 625 (the *Tasmanian Dams* case) Tasmania argued that because the Commonwealth had passed legislation forbidding the construction of a hydro-electric dam in an area of high conservation value in western Tasmania that the Commonwealth had thereby 'acquired' the property and compensation was therefore payable. The High Court, rejecting this argument, pointed out that sterilising this particular form of land use did not thereby prohibit other uses to which the property might be put and the Commonwealth had not effectively acquired the property. In *Newcrest*, however, the effective termination of a right to mine was considered to be an acquisition of property. The case concerned mining leases over crown land at Coronation Hill in the Northern Territory. Subsequent to the issue of the leases that land was added to the Kakadu National Park. Under the *National Parks and Wildlife Conservation Act* 1975 (Cth) mining was prohibited. The lessees claimed that the Commonwealth had therefore effectively acquired the leases, an argument that was accepted by a majority of the High Court. Although this case has been criticised on the basis

---

86   *Natural Heritage Trust of Australia Act* 1997 (Cth).
87   For example, *Springhall v Kirner* [1988] VR 159
88   Equally, of course, national parks legislation may be construed as not authorising the creation of private rights because this would be inconsistent with the purpose of the legislation: see *Woollahra MC v Minister* (1991) 23 NSWLR 710; *Packham v Minister* (1993) 80 LGERA 205.
89   *Fishing and Related Industries Compensation (Marine Reserves) Act* 1997 (WA).

that it fails to take account of the public interest in the sterilisation of the property interest, it is nevertheless consistent with the finding in the *Tasmanian Dams* case. In *Newcrest,* there was no other form of land use open to the plaintiff following the sterilisation of that particular form of land use; effectively therefore the Commonwealth had acquired the property, that is the unexpired term of the mining leases. *Newcrest* also arguably confirms that extinguishment or complete sterilisation of native title is an acquisition of property for which compensation must be paid.[90]

This requirement to pay compensation for acquisition of property in fact only applies to the Commonwealth; State constitutions do not contain similar provisions requiring compensation to be paid for acquisitions of property. This helps to explain why courts of law have adopted a fairly strict approach to interpretation of legislation that appears to enable interference with private property rights; and also underpins the nervousness with which politicians still approach the regulation of private property interests.

Roles of Commonwealth, State and local governments in natural resources management

It has been clearly established through a number of decisions of the High Court of Australia, over the past 25 years, that the Commonwealth governent has undoubted constitutional powers to override State decision-making on the use and management of natural resources. In practice, however, since the heady heyday of federal intervention in the 1980s, political constraints have influenced any decision to use these powers. The Commonwealth and States have now adopted a more co-operative approach to environment protection and natural resources management, marked by the signing of the Intergovernmental Agreement on the Environment 1992 and subsequent developments. The upshot of all this has been the recent passage of the Commonwealth's *Environment Protection and Biodiversity Conservation Act* 1999 under which the Commonwealth effectively declares which issues in natural resources management it regards as being of Commonwealth concern.[91] All other matters will be left to the states to manage; while the Commonwealth will even entrust the management of issues of national concern to the States if it can be confident, via a negotiated bilateral agreement accrediting, for example, environmental assessment processes or State management plans, that the resources will be satisfactorily managed. At least it should now be clear, in most circumstances, which level of government has primary management responsibility for particular resource issues. On the other hand, the negotiation of bilateral agreements that effectively transfer Commonwealth responsibilities to the States may themselves evoke new tensions in natural resource management.

---

90 *Western Australia v Commonwealth* (1995) 183 CLR 201.
91 These are world heritage properties, RAMSAR wetlands, listed threatened species and ecological communities, listed migratory species, nuclear activities, the Commonwealth marine environment, and any other matters prescribed by regulation after consultation with the States. The Commonwealth will also be responsible for activities on Commonwealth land, the actions of Commonwealth agencies, and the Regional Forestry Agreement process.

This 'co-operative federalism' has been reflected in recent years through the Commonwealth government basically adopting an initiation and co-ordinating role with respect to the development of national policies for resources management and environment protection. This role relies on the expectation that if the States and territories help to produce such strategies, they are more likely to regard themselves as having greater ownership of them and are therefore more likely to implement them. Not only that, but the Commonwealth in any case does not have the on-ground resources to manage natural resources in the States. It is one thing to intervene in a State land use or resource issue; but another to actually provide funds for management that might inevitably have to follow such an exercise of Commonwealth power. Consequently a great deal of effort has gone into the production of national strategies during the 1990s. Some of the more important initiatives relevant to natural resources management include the Oceans Policy, the National Forests Policy, the National Greenhouse Strategy, the National Strategy for Ecologically Sustainable Development, the National Strategy for the Conservation of Australia's Biological Diversity, and the National Strategy for the Conservation of Australian Species and Communities Threatened with Extinction (see Haward, Mobbs, Dovers, this volume).

The development of national strategies suffers from the expected criticisms that:

- they are slow to be developed;
- they are too much affected by political considerations;
- they represent a lowest common denominator approach to natural resources management; and
- they are strong on motherhood statements of concern but come up short on positive action.

On the other hand, the advantages are seen to be that:

- national, uniform approaches to national problems can be agreed upon;
- there is nothing to prevent any party introducing policies or legislation that seek to go further than the agreed strategy;
- all policy and legal initiatives are in any case subject to political influences at any level of government; and
- they form a strategic policy framework within which each party can take positive action that fully recognises the political, economic and social circumstances of that party.

The implementation of national strategies and policies is generally encouraged by the possibility of attracting funding through the auspices of the Natural Heritage Trust. Many existing Federal government natural resources management and environmental protection programs have been brought under the umbrella of this Trust. It is difficult, however, to evaluate whether the existence of national strategies and Federal government funded programs has fundamentally encouraged effective responses to natural resources management issues and problems. The Commonwealth Auditor-General has indicated that the Commonwealth is still unable to indicate in any detail the outcomes that have been achieved from natural resources management and environment programs such as Landcare, Save the Bush, One Billion Trees and other programs (ANAO 1997). This may suggest a general absence of requirements for monitoring the effects of such policies and projects, and lack of performance standards on which an evaluation of effectiveness may be based.

Local government

Legislation has only recently begun to recognise the potentially important role of local councils in natural resources management. This is surprising given that they are responsible for significant environmental responsibilities such as sewage and stormwater management, and waste disposal, as well as being significant landowners. Local government could in fact play a much more substantial role in natural resources management than it does now, but it lacks appropriate incentives to do so (Wild River, this volume). It is a common complaint of local government that it is being saddled with increasing environmental responsibilities without the financial capabilities to effectively carry them out. In fact current legislation often constrains local government from playing a more substantial role (Cripps et al 1999; Wild River, this volume). Examples of initiatives that could be introduced to provide the necessary incentives for local councils are:

- empowering councils to introduce environmental levies (charges which may be imposed on a household by the council) for environmental programs. This could be done by defining the environment as a service for which a local government can impose a charge; or by amending the definition of service within the relevant local government legislation to include the environment. Where the introduction of such levies is lawful, then local councils should be required to justify to rate-payers why it is not proposing to introduce such levies for environmental improvement programs;

- extending the ability of local government to enter into management agreements with landholders when planning approval is sought, which is the current situation, to empowering councils to enter into such agreements at any time;

- enabling local governments to enter into covenants with landholders and provide for registration on title; and

- correcting perverse ratings systems. Most land rating systems are based on 'unimproved capital value' or 'site value' which is market value less the value of built improvements. In deriving this value it is usually assumed, for example, that most agricultural land will be cleared and put to its most profitable agricultural use. This approach to valuation provides a perverse incentive for people to clear land that can be offset by offering rate and land tax rebates for land under a conservation covenant. The ratings system may also penalise those who wish to leave their land 'unimproved', in order to foster conservation of natural resources.

The immunity of the Commonwealth from State laws

The Crown

Executive government in Australia is generally referred to as the 'Crown'. Yet conceptually the Crown is not the same as government. The elected government administers, manages and controls Crown assets on behalf of the people of the Commonwealth or a State. Government authorities, as part of executive government, are thus instruments of the Crown. Local government authorities generally are not. Australia inherited a general presumption, implied in British law, that Parliament, when it legislates, does not intend to bind the Crown. As a presumption, this implication can be rebutted by clear evidence to the contrary, such as by a statement that the legislation does bind the Crown; or even in the absence of such a statement that by 'necessary implication'.[92] Parliament must have intended to bind the Crown. In practice it is obviously important that the Crown should be subject to its legislation, because the Crown is a significant owner of land and the impact of natural resources legislation would obviously be dramatically curtailed were the Crown to be exempt.[93] Fortunately modern environmental and natural resources law usually makes it clear that the Crown is in fact bound by the legislation,[94] although there may still be provision for exemption.

This legislation commonly asserts that 'This Act binds the Crown, not only in right of (New South Wales) but also, so far as the legislative power of Parliament permits, the Crown in all its other capacities'. This reference to the Crown in all its other capacities is an attempt to bind particularly Commonwealth agencies operating in or affecting the State law. While no doubt evincing an intention to bind the Commonwealth, the effectiveness of this clause of course depends on whether the Commonwealth can be bound in the first place. For various reasons, the Commonwealth is in fact considered immune from State environmental and planning laws; a situation that has caused a great deal of conflict between the States and the Commonwealth over the years. Political resolution of this unsatisfactory situation still does not appear to have been concluded.

Commonwealth places

Under s 52 of the Constitution of the Commonwealth of Australia the Commonwealth has exclusive power to legislate in respect of Commonwealth places; for example, airports; customs, police, and broadcasting facilities; lighthouses; post offices; hospitals; laboratories, reserves and defence

---

92   *Bropho v Western Australia* (1990) 93 ALR 207
93   For example, in *Forestry Commission (NSW) v Corkhill* (1991) 73 LGRA 247 the NSW Court of Appeal found that when the *National Parks and Wildlife Act* 1974 (NSW) had been enacted the Parliament had given detailed attention to the relationship between that Act and the Forestry Commission; and since it could have made special provision for the Commission but did not, the clear inference to be drawn was that the legislature intended the Act to apply to the Forestry Commission.
94   The usual formula is 'this Act binds the Crown in right of (the state)'.

facilities.[95] It is likely therefore that State environmental and planning laws do not apply to Commonwealth places unless Commonwealth legislation expressly provides for such application.[96] This also means that State laws will not necessarily automatically apply following disposal of Commonwealth property; some further action at State level, such as rezoning under State planning legislation, may be required to apply State laws to these places.[97] Subsequent purchasers, lessees or licensees of Commonwealth places may also enjoy the same immunities as the Commonwealth from application of State laws, until land is unequivocally brought under State control.[98] So, for example, the privileges and immunities of the Crown in right of the Commonwealth will extend to the activities of lessees on federal airport land.[99] This principle does not, however, affect the ability of the Commonwealth itself to control the future use and development of Commonwealth places through the terms (for example, covenants) on which a property is sold or otherwise transferred.

The High Court has recently confirmed that the only laws that may be validly enacted in respect of a Commonwealth place are federal laws.[100] The *Commonwealth Places (Application of Laws) Act 1970* (Cth), which makes provision for the application of some State laws to Commonwealth places,[101] is not generally regarded as including environment protection and planning laws. The effect of this Commonwealth immunity means that the effects of Commonwealth activities upon natural resources, for example, through pollution emanating from Commonwealth places, or as part of the provision of infrastructure for Commonwealth places, cannot be legally controlled by State environment protection and planning legislation, unless the Commonwealth voluntarily subjects itself to such control.

General immunity

The High Court has developed a doctrine of implied immunity of the Commonwealth from State laws.[102] Although this has arguably been narrowed

---

95   This remains the case even though the Commonwealth may transfer management to a non-government organisation. This does not affect the status of the place as a Commonwealth place.

96   Constitution, s 52; *Commonwealth Places (Application of Laws) Act 1970*, s 4(2)(a); *Botany MC v Federal Airports Corp* (1992) 175 CLR 453; *Ventana v FAC* (1997) 95 LGERA 58.

97   When the Commonwealth disposes of such land it ceases to be a Commonwealth place. This does not mean, however, that local planning schemes will automatically apply to the land. Because the State could not make laws with respect to Commonwealth places, it could not make a law purporting to apply to such a place once the Commonwealth had disposed of it. To apply to such a place, a planning scheme will need to be specifically amended to provide for compliance once the property has been disposed of; *AG (NSW) v Stocks & Holdings Pty Ltd* (1970) 45 ALJR 9.

98   *Brisbane CC v Group Projects Pty Ltd* (1979) 145 CLR 143; *BMG Resources Ltd v Beaconsfield MC* [1988] Tas R 142; *Kangaroo Point East Association Inc v Balkin* [1994] QPLR 6.

99   *Ventana v Federal Airports Corporation* (1997) 95 LGERA 58.

100   *Allders International Pty Ltd v Commissioner for State Revenue (Victoria)* (1996) 140 ALR 189. This is so even if the Commonwealth place is leased to another entity for commercial purposes.

101   This was enacted to overcome the effect of two High Court decisions which held that neither State criminal laws nor building regulations applied to Commonwealth places; *Worthing v Rowell and Muston Pty Ltd* (1970) 123 CLR 89; *R v Phillps* (1970) 125 CLR 93.

102   *Commonwealth v Bogle* (1953) 89 CLR 229; *Commonwealth v Cigamatic Pty Ltd* (1962) 108 CLR 372.

recently,[103] prompting the Australian Government Solicitor to remark that State laws imposing pollution controls on activities are probably capable of binding the Commonwealth.[104] there is still much uncertainty. The future relationship between the Commonwealth and the States in relation to adherence to State environmental laws is more likely to be constrained by the proposed COAG Agreement (below) than by legal authority.

Section 109 inconsistency

The Commonwealth can avoid the application of State laws by operation of s 109 of the Constitution, which provides that to the extent of any inconsistencies between federal and State legislation Commonwealth law will prevail. Australian Defence Industries Ltd (ADI) for example, is exempted from State laws that relate to the environmental consequences of the use of land or premises.[105] Similar exemptions have been given to the Australian Nuclear Science and Technology Organisation (ANSTO).[106] In *Botany MC v Federal Airports Corporation* (1992) 109 ALR 321 it was held that the environmental assessment provisions of the *Environmental Planning and Assessment Act* 1979 (NSW) did not apply to the Federal Airports Corporation, which was authorised by Commonwealth legislation and regulations to construct a third runway at Sydney Airport. The Federal Airports Regulations 1992 expressly authorised works associated with construction of the runway 'in spite of' any State laws relating to environmental assessment. Where, however, there is no expressed intent to override State laws then unless the Commonwealth law effectively 'covers the field' or constitutes a comprehensive code by which an activity may be regulated, then it may be interpreted as not having intended to affect State laws.[107]

Using this constitutional power, the Commonwealth may also effectively exempt private or statutory corporations from the effect of State laws. For example, s 116 of the *Australian and Overseas Telecommunications Corporations Act* 1991 (Cth) empowered the making of regulations to allow carriers to engage in specified exempt activities despite specified State laws.[108] These exemptions applied to non-government carriers as well as the Commonwealth carrier. Carriers were also empowered to access land and install facilities

---

103 *Residential Tenancies Tribunal of NSW v Henderson; ex parte Defence Housing Authority* (1997) 71 ALJR 1254. A majority of the court held that, while the Commonwealth is immune from State laws which purport to modify the nature of executive power vested in the Commonwealth Crown (its capacities), it was not immune from legislation which merely sought to regulate activities entered into by the Commonwealth in exercise of those capacities. In this case State legislation which purported to affect the Commonwealth as a landlord were held to apply to the Commonwealth. In the context of environmental regulation the distinction may be particularly elusive.

104 *Legal Briefing* 'The Commonwealth's Implied Constitutional Immunity from State Law' No 36, 30 August 1997; and see Bradbury (1998).

105 *Defence Act* 1903 (Cth), s 122A.

106 *Australian Nuclear Science and Technology Organisation Act* 1987 (Cth), s 7A.

107 *Botany MC v Federal Airports Corp* (1992) 175 CLR 453 at 252; *Commercial Radio Coffs Harbour v Fuller* (1986) 60 LGRA 68.

108 Commonwealth power to make laws concerning telecommunications is contained in s 51(v) of the Constitution

thereon, powers which included the clearing of vegetation.[109] Schedule 3 of the *Telecommunications Act* 1997 (Cth), which replaces the 1991 Act, continues to exempt activities from State planning, environmental assessment and heritage laws,[110] and the Australian Communications Authority from the Commonwealth *Environmental Assessment (Impact of Proposals) Act*[111] before issuing facility installation permits, and sets up its own regime for assessing and meeting environmental impacts. Although State laws have ostensibly been replaced by a Code and by explicit statutory instructions in the 1997 Act, the Environment and Natural Resources Committee of the Victorian Parliament, for example, identified numerous problems with the Code and the degree of compliance by carriers (Victoria 1994: 77). Excessive removal of vegetation has been identified as a common problem (Victoria 1994: 102).

The COAG Agreement

Not surprisingly, the immunity of the Commonwealth from State environmental laws has been a major source of conflict between the Commonwealth and States. In November 1997 the Council of Australian Governments drew up a draft Agreement which, besides defining the extent of Commonwealth responsibilities and interests in the environment, contained provisions for the recognition by the Commonwealth of the importance of complying with State environmental laws.

The Agreement contains a commitment by the Commonwealth to subject itself to State environmental laws. However, this commitment will apply only to those Commonwealth departments, agencies and statutory authorities which are required by the Commonwealth to comply, or elect to comply, with State environment and planning laws.[112] All non-Commonwealth tenants and persons undertaking activities on Commonwealth land; and all Commonwealth Government Business Enterprises, non GBE companies, statutory authorities whose primary functions are commercial, and business units, will be subject to State laws.[113] Certain matters will also be exempt from compliance on grounds of national interest: these include aircraft noise and emissions.[114] Where a Commonwealth department, agency or statutory authority is not bound to comply with State environment and planning laws, then the Commonwealth will ensure that at least they will operate, and secure approvals in accordance with, Commonwealth measures which are at least equivalent to the environment and planning laws of the State in which the Commonwealth activity or property is located; and that the Commonwealth will endeavour to adopt standards of 'best practice' in managing its environmental responsibilities.[115] Implementation of this Agreement may require

---

109   Sections 128-130, 134.
110   Section 37.
111   Section 28.
112   Council of Australian Governments, Heads of Agreement, November 1997, Attachment 3, cl 2 (c),(d).
113   Heads of Agreement Attachment 3, cl 2(a),(b)
114   Heads of Agreement Attachment 3, cl 4.
115   Heads of Agreement Attachment 3, cl 3. A similar commitment is made for exemptions; cl 5.

further legislative action; the parties have agreed to 'seek to legislate' within two years of the signing of the Agreement.[116] The practical status of this Agreement is, however, at time of writing, uncertain.

Lack of whole of government approaches to natural resource management

A major and perhaps the most significant difficulty faced by government managers of natural resources to-day is the tendency of governments still to react to perceived problems rather than plan ahead in a comprehensive and co-ordinated way. For example, when pollution was identified as a problem, governments responded by creating a regulator and giving it statutory powers to control pollution. The same reaction has been apparent in responses to protection of wildlife, and management of natural resources such as water, fisheries, minerals and forests. The result has been a plethora of legislation concentrating upon specific environmental problems and management of specific resources, coupled with the creation of numerous agencies of government responsible for administering that legislation. In reality, however, most environmental problems and resource management issues fall across, and sometimes outside, the jurisdictions of a number of government agencies, and solutions that call for whole of government responses have been traditionally difficult to achieve because of the splintered way in which government administration has allocated legal responsibilities, budgets and human and other resources. The result is that although an agency such as an environment protection authority is often viewed by the general public as having, because of its title, the ability to protect the environment, the reality is that no single government agency has that capacity. Yet modern natural resource management issues, such as catchment protection, water allocation and fisheries management, inevitably demand at least a co-ordinated response from government based on a recognition that many of the influences which impact upon the problem fall outside the jurisdiction of any one agency to manage. For example, commercial fisheries in coastal waters or estuaries may be managed by State fisheries authorities; but many of the influences that impact upon those fisheries lie outside the jurisdiction of those authorities to control. Estuaries are inevitably affected by activities that take place higher up the catchment; activities that are managed and controlled for example, by local authorities and by State authorities responsible for activities as diverse as road and bridge construction, forestry, public works, irrigation, sewerage, water allocation, agriculture, subdivision, and all forms of development. Effectively managing a catchment therefore demands at the very least a whole of government co-ordinated approach that has traditionally been lacking in our jurisdictional-based schemes for natural resource management. The New Zealand *Resource Management Act* 1989 is often hailed as a novel and successful approach to a more integrated and co-ordinated system of natural resources management, and it is; but this Act operates in the context of a unilateral

---

116   Heads of Agreement Attachment 3, cl 6.

system of government in which local authorities play a much more prominent role in resource management than is currently the case in Australia. Perhaps more pertinent to whole of government management of natural resources would be to consider the establishment of a Parliamentary Commissioner for the Environment along the lines of the New Zealand and ACT models.[117] The recent creation of a Sydney Catchment Authority,[118] invested with legal powers to control potentially damaging activities in the outer catchment that might impact upon the inner catchment under its control, however, may mark the birth at least of a more catchment based approach to natural resources management.

The greatest challenge facing governments in the years ahead will undoubtedly be to devise institutional arrangements that can deliver timely and effective whole of government natural resources management.

Ecologically sustainable development

In the 1960s and 1970s everyone talked of 'balanced' development; now it is fashionable to refer to 'ecologically sustainable development' (ESD). ESD, which carries the concept of balance between environmental and economic objectives, has become the most important policy criteria for natural resources management. Statutory requirements to 'have regard to' ESD appear not just in resource based legislation, but perhaps more importantly in legislation conferring discretionary powers to take or approve activities that might impact upon the environment and natural resources.

Although legal definitions of the concept of sustainability differ, most are fundamentally based upon the definition of ecologically sustainable development agreed to by the Commonwealth, States and local government and embodied in the *National Strategy on Ecologically Sustainable Development* 1992 and the *Inter-Governmental Agreement on the Environment* 1992. This definition states, in summary:

> Ecologically sustainable development requires the effective integration of economic and environmental considerations in decision-making processes. Ecologically sustainable development can be achieved through the implementation of the following principles and programs ... the precautionary principle; intergenerational equity; conservation of biological diversity and ecological integrity; and improved valuation, pricing and incentive mechanisms.

The focus on these four means of achieving ESD does not reflect all of the principles commonly referred to as the components of ESD at an international level. These principles, however, are clearly not intended to be exclusive and other principles may be required to be considered in order to meet defined statutory objectives; for example, the statement of objectives contained in ss 21 and 22 of the *Sydney Water Act* 1994 (NSW) may require Sydney Water to build into its processes public participation, access to

---

117   *Environment Act* 1986 (NZ); *Commissioner for the Environment Act* 1993 (ACT).
118   *Sydney Water Catchment Management Act* 1998 (NSW).

information and to justice, the polluter pays principle, and the application of environmental impact assessment, all of which are regarded as important components of sustainable development at an international level (Sands 1995).

Legal definitions of ecologically sustainable development, however, are problematic because:

- they tend to treat sustainability as part of a procedure for, rather than as a focus or an outcome of, decision-making;
- there tends to be little accountability for pursuing or achieving sustainable outcomes; and
- there are few requirements for actually monitoring the sustainability of outcomes.

A common drafting technique in legislation is to specify ESD as one of a number of objectives of the legislation; or as one of a number of features to which regard should be had by decision-makers. Such an approach clearly misses the point that ESD is not a factor to be balanced against other considerations; ESD *is* the balance between those other considerations; between developmental, social and environmental imperatives. As the definitions of ESD point out, ESD 'requires the effective integration of economic and environmental considerations in decision-making processes'.[119] In other words ESD is the objective of the management regime created by the legislation, not a factor that can be further balanced against other influences. This balancing process should be undertaken in order to reach or achieve ESD; not to assess the relative priority of ESD to other factors. For example, it could be argued that legislation which encompasses ESD as an objective of the legislation, but then requires decision-makers to have regard to social and economic factors in decision-making (for example, the *Threatened Species Conservation Act* 1995 (NSW)) effectively gives a 'double weighting' to social and economic factors. If ESD is to be pursued seriously then surely this should be the paramount object of the legislation; and decision-makers should be instructed to do more than simply 'have regard to' it.

Practical implementation of ESD

Clearly the principles of ESD are intended to influence governmental and corporate decision-making. However, the principles of ESD tell us little about how to translate the concepts into practical action. They do seem, however, to imply a preventative approach to environmental degradation in order to ensure the avoidance of environmental degradation or harm.

First, it is obvious that environmental and resource degradation is more often than not caused by decision-making carried out by statutory authorities whose mandated concerns traditionally contain no reference to such considerations. For example, legislation conferring statutory powers and duties upon roads and other public works authorities, fire brigades, and energy, drainage and irrigation authorities have rarely required them to exercise their functions

---

119   For example, *Protection of the Environment Administration Act* 1991 (NSW), s 6(2).

with due regard for the environment. The acceptance of ESD as a desirable feature or object of decision-making, however, really obliges governments to extend the consideration of environmental factors to all agencies of government. It is becoming increasingly common therefore to see statutory authorities that traditionally have had no mandated concern for the environment, to be required now to exercise their functions at least with due regard to the principles of ESD. New South Wales has been particularly active in this regard.[120] Imposing such a requirement could facilitate a more integrated or whole of government approach to natural resources management.

To date in Australia 'integration' has meant mainly the integration of approvals processes for development and pollution control licensing. Integrated assessment of proposals and activities is undoubtedly assisted by the integration of procedures for obtaining land use planning and pollution control approvals so that both aspects are dealt with as part of the one application, even if different aspects of the proposal are investigated by different regulatory authorities. Tasmania has introduced this approach in its Resource Management and Planning System, which encompasses a range of legislation spanning various aspects of environmental management all pursuing the same overall objective of ESD.[121] NSW has recently made special provision for 'integrated development', defined as development which requires development consent plus approvals under other legislation,[122] while South Australia also provides for reference of certain development activities to the EPA for approval.[123] Traditionally the types of developments which are required to obtain a pollution control license or environmental approval are also required to undergo environmental impact assessment through the development control process.[124]

There is, however, increasing recognition that integrating other environmental management functions will further the promotion of ecologically sustainable development. For example, national strategies with respect to coastal protection, fisheries management and water reforms stress the importance of integration. At State level such integration is beginning to occur in policy development, for example, in relation to water reforms in NSW and in relation to tackling the effects of dryland salinity; but in a legislative sense we are still a long way from adopting whole of government approaches to natural resources management.

---

120 See for example, *Fire Brigades Act* 1989 (NSW), s 10A; *Coastal Protection Act* 1979 (NSW), ss 27, 37A, 54A; *Sydney Harbour Foreshore Authority Act* 1998 (NSW), s 18.

121 For the purposes of this work, the major legislative components of this system are the *Environmental Management and Pollution Control Act* 1994, *Land Use Planning and Approvals Act* 1993, *State Policies and Projects Act* 1993, *Living Marine Resources Management Act* 1995.

122 *Environmental Planning and Assessment Act* 1979 (NSW), Pt 4, Div 5 introduced by the *Environmental Planning and Assessment Amendment Act* 1997 Sch 1; see also ss 44 (integration of works approvals and licensing covering all forms of pollution and all activities), ss 50-51 (timing of licensing of development requiring consent and integrated development under *Environmental Planning and Assessment Amendment Act*).

123 *Environment Protection Act* 1993 (SA) s 57; *Development Act* 1993 (SA), s 38; Development Regulations 1993 (SA) Schs 9, 22.

124 For example, as 'designated development' in NSW; *Environmental Planning and Assessment Act* 1979 (NSW), s 77A.

Innovations in policy approaches to natural resources management

Notwithstanding the quite wide range of instruments potentially available to policy-makers to manage natural resources, in practice, most governments, in most circumstances, have utilised only a very limited number of them. These have been principally subsidies and piecemeal regulation prohibiting particular acts.[125] The former have often proved environmentally counter-productive while the latter have commonly suffered from serious design faults (Gunningham and Grabosky 1998, Chapter 5).

To the extent that the success of existing regulatory regimes can be measured by results, current approaches, despite some successes, fall far short of achieving the objectives stipulated by the legislation. Many agricultural and other resource management practices remain unsustainable, both ecologically and economically. Species and populations of plants and animals continue to decline and be threatened with extinction. A significant proportion of natural resource degradation results from land clearing, causing salinity, soil erosion, and sedimentation of nearby waterways. Yet restricting land clearing has proved to be one of the most politically sensitive issues in natural resources management in Australia.

Current policies contribute to these problems in a variety of ways. First, rather than provide incentives for environmental stewardship, they often provide incentives for conduct harmful to the environment. There are insufficient incentives to compensate for the sacrifices, which the appropriate level of environmental stewardship might require on the part of landowners. Rural landowners maintain a traditional hostility to government intrusion in the management of natural resources. Second, poor regulatory design and a failure to harness the potential of third parties to act as surrogate regulators have compounded the ineffectiveness of regulation (Gunningham and Grabosky 1998). Coercion is a particularly blunt instrument; monitoring is extremely difficult and expensive, and sanctions lack political acceptability. Moreover, in circumstances where what is needed are positive measures to reverse degradation, in conjunction with the development of an ethic of environmental stewardship, then command-and-control has little to contribute. Even where command-and-control is practicable, it is not necessarily desirable. Such measures are commonly criticised by economists as being inefficient, unnecessarily intrusive, and unduly expensive to administer. Some regulations may inhibit innovation and discourage people from searching for new and more efficient ways to use a resource. On the other hand, some forms of command and control regulation may serve as an essential safety net, providing a backdrop of minimum standards without which other, less coercive strategies, cannot function successfully.

---

125 In the main, species specific measures (mostly the prohibition or limitation of taking) have dominated, but note the gradual emergence of a new type of instrument: the threatening process concept. See de Klemm 1997.

This section looks at some of the innovative approaches to natural resources management that have been introduced into some government policies but which are so far of limited application; and discusses other approaches that could and perhaps should be relied upon more heavily in the future.

A statutory duty of care

The Industry Commission's Report into natural resources management in Australia, *A Full Repairing Lease*, recommended as a fundamental concept of legislation that a general 'duty of care' for the environment should be imposed on managers and owners of natural resources and any others whose actions could significantly affect the environment. The duty would require them to take all reasonable and practical measures to prevent harm to the environment. Adoption of voluntary standards and codes of practice would be the practical means of fulfilling this duty. This recommendation was based upon the inclusion of such a duty in Queensland, South Australia and the ACT.[126]

The duty of care would require natural resources managers to meet the cost of protecting the environment where it is reasonable and practical to do so. This test, as the Commission points out, is widely understood and applied in many areas of regulation:

> the starting point for determining what needs to be done is the present state of the environment – not one that existed in the past or might be desired now. The extent and timing of what needs to be done is defined by applying the test of 'reasonable and practical'. There is likely to be more scope to act the longer the time horizon ... the consequences of the duty of care for most producers in an industry are not likely to be substantial – by definition any cost imposed by it cannot be unreasonable. Those whose environmental management is at best practice levels are unlikely to be affected by it. The only group of producers who can be significantly affected are the minority whose management is at the worst practice end of the spectrum (Industry Commission 1997: 172, 173).

A breach of the duty of care would not in itself be a breach of legislation for which prosecution would be possible; but it could trigger the possibility of civil enforcement to restrain threatened breaches. Failure to comply with the duty could also lead to a denial of defences to charges of breaches of legislation that rely on some form of due diligence or honest and reasonable mistake of fact. The duty of care, in conjunction with voluntary codes of practice, is seen as capable of providing broad guidance to natural resources managers as to what is required of them; is much more flexible and less prescriptive than many alternative approaches; would fill in the cracks in existing legislation where no specific duties are imposed but substantial harm to the environment is threatened; and would promote a wide range of 'no regrets' measures to protect the environment – that is, those which are low

---

126   *Environmental Protection Act* 1994 (Qld), s 36; *Environment Protection Act* 1993 (SA), s 25; *Environment Protection Act* 1997 (ACT), s 22

cost or reduce costs by increasing productivity. The introduction of a statutory duty of care would also complement introduction of criteria for measuring the success or otherwise of government policies, plans, programs and decision-making.[127]

Creation of new forms of property rights

Resource management policy appears to be moving in the direction of creating or recreating private rights of property in water and fisheries resources that are underpinned by a strong regulatory regime of management (Smith, McKay, this volume). The theory behind this is that if resource users enjoy some form of private ownership of a public resource, then they will have more incentive in making sure that the resource is properly managed. The *South Australian Water Resources Act* 1997 for example, is quite clear that the issue of water entitlement creates a right that can be dealt with as private property.

In relation to sea fisheries, the statutory licence has been described by Mason, Deane and Gaudron JJ in *Harper v Minister of Sea Fisheries* (1989) 88 ALR 38 as 'an entitlement of a new kind created as part of a system for preserving a limited public natural resource in a society which is coming to recognise that, in so far as such resources are concerned, to fail to protect may destroy, and to preserve the right of everyone to take what he or she will may eventually deprive that right of all content' (at 62). Modern fisheries management legislation is now going beyond this to creating privately trade-able shareholdings in certain fisheries, underpinned by a system of strong regulatory management and enforcement. Four Commonwealth fisheries are now managed using individual transferable quotas: the Southern Blue Fin Tuna Fishery, the South-east Trawl Fishery; the South-east Non-trawl Fishery and the Macquarie Island Fishery. NSW has also developed individual transferable quotas under the *Fisheries Management Act* 1994.

Creation of property rights may even occur as an inducement to take environmentally beneficial action without regulatory control. For example, in the absence of strict regulatory controls on industrial emissions of greenhouse gases, new species of property rights are being created to facilitate the management of emissions of greenhouse gases. In NSW a forestry right extends to the sequestration of carbon by trees and forests.[128] A carbon sequestration right may be conferred by agreement or otherwise to the legal, commercial or other benefits (present or future) of carbon sequestrated by any existing or future tree or forest on the subject land after 1990. The profit is the right to the benefit conferred by the carbon sequestration right. The Forestry Commission and electricity generators are empowered to deal with and trade in these rights.[129] In Victoria, a landowner may also enter into an

---

127 See earlier discussion.
128 *Conveyancing and Law of Property Act* 1919 (**NSW**), s 87A introduced by the *Carbon Rights Legislation Amendment Act* 1998 (NSW).
129 *Forestry Act* 1916 (NSW), s 33C; *Electricity (Pacific Power) Act* 1950 (NSW), s 9(2); *Energy Services Corporations Act* 1995 (NSW) s 9(3A).

agreement with others for the establishment and maintenance of trees on the land. That agreement will then create rights that may be registered so as to become a covenant binding on the land; in other words a property right separate from the ownership of the land.[130]

It is too early to say whether these initiatives in creating private entitlements, particularly out of or to protect public natural resources, will lead to better resources management.

Economic incentives

In modern approaches to natural resources management, both regulatory and voluntary schemes are usually underpinned by some form of economic incentives. The least interventionist and most popular economic approach is generally the introduction of positive incentives such as tax credits, tax deductions, rate relief, direct subsidies for fencing and technical support, and management agreements or covenants.

Although they violate user and polluter pays principles (see OECD 1989: 29-30; 1993a: 32-4, 59; 1993b: 33; 1994; 1995: 17-22), and are a drain on the public purse, positive incentives may have particular application to natural resources management. For example, where the producers come from low-income groups, then subsidies may be more attractive in social welfare terms than taxes or regulation. In addition, the substantial political influence of resource users may make it necessary to offset existing perverse incentives with positive incentives rather than attempt their immediate removal. In some circumstances the ability to offer positive incentives might render unnecessary the use of more coercive instruments which may be difficult to enforce in geographically isolated areas. For example, rural landowners who are forcibly constrained from clearing land are unlikely to become enthusiastic land managers. They may, however, be convinced by the provision of positive incentives for resource management. Similarly, it has been argued that: 'Without management, the vegetation will ultimately disappear as surely as if it had been cleared in the first place. Controlling clearing ... has to be seen as only the first step in what must become an ongoing process of native vegetation management' (Harris 1995). A number of incentive schemes working in Australia were identified by the ANZECC Working Group Report (1996) including Landcare, Bushcare, local government rebates, and land management agreements. But as the report notes, these forms of assistance are often limited and inconsistent.

Conclusions

Natural resources law in Australia is a reflection of government policy on natural resources management. The law cannot compel any particular approach; but it can and should provide appropriate tools to natural resources managers to implement and enforce government policy. It is clear, however,

---

130   *Forestry Rights Act 1996* (Vic).

that the expressed objectives of natural resources law may be manipulated for political reasons; that management on the ground may not reflect the objects of, or breadth of powers contained in, the legislation; and that legal accountability is restricted by a failure to specify prescribed outcomes measured against best practice management criteria. The law is media specific, jurisdiction based, and often lacks appropriate procedures for integration of decision-making. Governments are finding it difficult to introduce much-needed whole of government approaches to natural resources management. Some of the most serious impacts on natural resources are authorised by laws that require little in the way of consideration of those impacts. On the other hand, recent legislation is taking a more innovative approach to the provision of management tools; and there is a strong focus on public participation in planning and decision-making, although this may be adversely affected by lack of funding for participation, particularly where Indigenous communities are concerned. The law often enables natural resources decision-making to be effectively challenged; but the complex procedures and costs of legal action are prohibitive.

Some specific recommendations are:

- There should be a whole of government and community approach to natural resources management that encompasses all public sector policy development, planning and decision-making.

- Mechanisms for financial and other resourcing to support community, including Indigenous, involvement should be introduced.

- Where significant impacts on natural resources may occur from a development or activity requiring approval, then procedures for public and agency consultation, and requirements for concurrence, should be clearly set out.

- Criteria for evaluating the success of government policies, plans, programs and decision-making should be introduced; monitoring for effectiveness should be required; and the consequences of failure or under-performance indicated.

- Criteria and procedures for adjudging the potential for significant impacts on natural resources should be clearly set out.

- Criteria and procedures for making decisions about potentially significant impacts on natural resources should be clearly set out. These decisions should be subject to merits appeals.

- Where a potential impact on natural resources would trigger the precautionary principle, then decision-making should be guided by that principle.

- Conflicts between government authorities over approaches to natural resources management should be referred initially to the respective ministers and ultimately to the Premier or Prime Minister for resolution. Public statements of reasons should be provided for decisions taken following such referrals.

- Merits appeals should be able to challenge all decision-making where potentially significant impacts on natural resources have been identified; have been considered but rejected; or have not been considered but an applicant contends that such impacts are possible.

- 'Any person' enforcement provisions should be introduced into all legislation.

- Specialist environmental courts should be able to appoint independent experts to assist the court in evaluating conflicting scientific or technical evidence.

- An effective quality assurance process should be introduced for consultants advising consent and determining authorities in relation to natural resources management issues.

- A user pays system should be introduced that reflects the real costs of agency assessment of proposals.

- Further consideration needs to be given to balancing the mix between regulation and economic and educational incentives.

References

ANAO (Australian National Audit Office), 1997, *Commonwealth natural resource management programs*, Performance audit 36, Canberra: Australian Government Publishing Service.

Bonyhady, T (ed), 1992, Property rights, in Bonyhady, T (ed), *Environmental protection and legal change*, Sydney: Federation Press.

Bowers, J, 1994, *Incentives and mechanisms for conserving biodiversity: observation and issues*, Canberra: CSIRO Division of Wildlife and Ecology.

Bradbury, A, 1998, Federal immunity and compliance, Paper delivered to the National Environmental Law Association Annual Conference, May, Canberra.

Cripps, E, Binning, C, and Young, M, 1999, *Opportunity denied: review of the legislative ability of local government to conserve native vegetation*, Canberra: CSIRO Division of Wildlife and Ecology,

De Klemm, C, 1997, Regulation and management of destructive processes, *Environmental Law and Policy* 27: 350

Dyson, M, 1997, The Water Resources Bill 1996, *Environmental and Planning Law Journal* 14: 305,

Gunningham, N, and Grabosky, P, 1998, *Smart regulation*, Oxford: Oxford University Press.

Harris, C, 1995, Native vegetation clearance controls – the South Australian experience, Paper delivered to *From Conflict to Conservation* seminar, November, South Australian Department of Environment and Natural Resources, Adelaide.

Industry Commission, 1997, *A full repairing lease: inquiry into ecologically sustainable land management*, Report no 60, Canberra: Australian Government Publishing Service.

OECD (Organisation for Economic Cooperation and Development), 1989, *Agricultural and environmental policies: opportunities for integration*, OECD, Paris.

OECD, 1993a, *Agriculture and the environment in the transition to a market economy*, Paris: OECD.

OECD, 1993b, *Agricultural and environmental policy integration: recent progress and new directions*, Paris: OECD.

OECD, 1994, *Environmental externalities and public goods in agricultural policy reform: new approaches, The role of direct income payments*, Paris: OECD.

OECD, 1995, *Sustainable agriculture: concepts, issues and policies*, Paris: OECD.

Raff, M, 1998, Environmental obligations and the Western liberal property concept, *Melbourne University Law Review* 22: 657-359.

Rohde, J, 1995, The objects clause in environmental legislation, *Environmental and Planning Law Journal* 12: 80.

Sands, P, 1995, International law in the field of sustainable development: emerging legal principles, in Lang, W (ed), *Sustainable development and international law*, London: Graham and Trotman.

Stein, P, 1996, The role of the NSW Land and Environment Court in the emergence of public interest environmental law, *Environmental and Planning Law Journal* 13: 179.

Stewart, A, 1999, Effects of the Land and Environment Court, *Environmental and Planning Law Journal* 16: 482.

Victoria, Environment and Natural Resources Committee, 1994, *The environmental impact of Commonwealth activities and places in Victoria*, Melbourne: Government Printer.

Yandle, B, 'Resource economics: a property rights perspective', (1983) 5 *Journal of Environmental and Planning Law* 1.

Zapparoni, C, 1997, *Environmental regulation: do we need a bigger stick?* Paper delivered to the National Environmental Law Association Annual Conference, Adelaide.

12

EPAs – Orphan Agencies of Environmental Protection

Dr Peter Christoff

School of Anthropology, Geography and Environmental Studies,
University of Melbourne

Even after 200 years of European colonisation, Australia's rural landscapes are rapidly changing – transformed by the industrial intensification of farming and by market pressures on land use, leading to inappropriate cropping or stocking practices and to land clearing which proceeds largely unrestrained in Queensland and by neglect elsewhere. As a consequence, as the latest national State of the Environment report shows, profound problems – dryland salinity, erosion, declining water quality, and loss of biodiversity – are intensifying across much of the Australian countryside. Similarly, Australia's urban land-scapes – both the built environment and its remnant natural components – also are being reshaped by the incremental pressures of population growth and the forces of globalisation, through suburban expansion and under the influence of capital investment in central business districts and industrial suburbs. While agricultural, industrial and domestic resource use and pollu-tants affect the quality and condition of local environments, the large ecological footprint of Australian consumers contributes to profound global and environmental changes and the sizable ecological shadow of Australian industrial activity falls across the Pacific region and beyond.

How we now respond to these environmental pressures, changes and outcomes is conditioned by the interaction, and sometimes conflict, between a range of historically determined institutional developments.[1] For instance, Australia's long-established administrative boundaries remain largely insensi-tive to ecological considerations and until the last decade of the 20th century, significant instances of cooperation and coordination in matters of resource policy or environmental protection between the States, or between local governments, were rare. In addition, many environmental issues have achieved only fragmented institutional recognition, with resultant problems for policy coordination and associated turf war between agencies: for example, water quality could be simultaneously the regulatory concern of water supply and sewerage authorities, health departments, environmental protection agencies (EPAs) and local government.

---

1   By institutions, I mean rules, laws, codes and informal cultural practices rather than the organisations (including broadly described public agencies and private enterprises) which realise them.

The evolution of Australia's environmental institutions and agencies has been substantially influenced by three transnational waves of environmental concern. These occurred at the end of the 19th century, during the 1970s, and then during the late 1980s and early 1990s. During the late 19th century and early in the 20th century, Australian colonies and then States looked mainly to British regulatory innovations to ameliorate the impacts of industrialisation and urbanisation on human health and welfare and to counter local public concerns about sanitation and disease. Public authorities were created in most capital cities to limit urban pollution, manage urban open space, parks and gardens, and to provide or supervise the development of infrastructure providing clean drinking water, sewerage, and the disposal of domestic and industrial waste (Dingle and Rasmussen 1991; Dunstan 1984; Henry 1939; Powell 1976, 1989). At the same time, influenced by American as well as Imperial models, departments and statutory bodies to facilitate the 'wise use' of natural resources were established in all colonies, or, later, States. Only during the past three decades have the practices of these agriculture, water, timber, minerals and energy departments come under scrutiny for their specifically *ecological* impacts. Their practices have been over-written by a range of newly articulated global environmental regimes and their activities have been increasingly circumscribed by new domestic laws that define broader environmental responsibilities. Cultural and political changes have meant that these bodies have grappled with and internalised – to some extent – responsibility for aspects of ecological management. However, the activities of these bodies have rarely been well-coordinated and this has left significant gaps in ecological governance.

The historical workings of Australia's federal system further complicate this legacy, as different States and the Commonwealth produced different solutions to similar environmental concerns (Grabosky and Braithwaite 1986: 30-31). They created a wide range of laws, standards and agencies – a problem of regulatory dissonance only relatively recently and partially addressed through the National Environment Protection Council with its attempts to facilitate the creation of uniform standards for air and water quality, waste materials and so on. For instance, when the first wave of truly global public concern over environmental degradation, during the late 1960s and early 1970s, profoundly reshaped domestic attitudes and opinions about environmental degradation, only three Australian States – New South Wales, Victoria and Western Australia – established environment protection agencies[2] intended to rationalise and focus environmental powers drawn from the plethora of laws and departments which had been partially responsible for environmental matters to this point, and to increase the capacity to regulate and manage urban pollution. These new agencies were styled largely on the legislative and organisational initiatives of United States administrators and specifically employed the United States' *National Environmental Policy Act* (1969) as their template. Similarly, departments of conservation were established to aggregate

---

2   Including here the NSW State Pollution Control Commission (SPCC) which was established in
     1970 and was, in effect, comparable to the Victorian and WA EPAs. It was replaced by the
     NSW EPA in 1992.

responsibility for the management and preservation of wildlife, and of nature conservation reserves on public land. These too mirrored overseas developments and rationalised agencies created in the 1950s to take responsibility for the implementation of nature conservation legislation and to manage national parks. At the same time, national government undertook the first round of environmental institutional innovation, with the establishment of a national Department of Environment, laws to enable environmental impact assessment, and agencies to manage the environmental values of Commonwealth land, and to oversee the 'national estate'.

International recognition, in the late 1980s, of problems such as climate change, biodiversity loss and ozone depletion led to resurgent environmental awareness and international public pressure and provoked a third wave of institutional innovation in Australia in the early 1990s. The most significant and persistent national developments during this period included that Intergovernmental Agreement on the Environment (IGAE), the National Environment Protection Council (NEPC), mentioned earlier, as well as a National Biodiversity Strategy. Meanwhile, newly elected governments in 'laggard States' such as Queensland, South Australia and Tasmania undertook a process of administrative modernisation and rationalisation in the environmental domain, creating autonomous Departments of Environment and environment protection agencies in order to bring themselves 'into line' with other States. At the same time, the 'lead States' – New South Wales and Victoria – revised long-established structures and practices of environmental governance in order to reflect overseas developments which were moving away from an emphasis on direct regulation towards a more nuanced mix of cooperative and coercive measures. At State level, one also notes attempts in several States (particularly in Victoria and Western Australia) to draw resource management and environment protection responsibilities together into 'mega-departments', partly with the aim of forcing greater administrative contact between these functions and to enhance the effectiveness of environmental protection over State-based resource-extraction functions such as forestry (Christoff 1998).

In all, this very general introduction should emphasise that, in a chapter of this length, the scope of any discussion of the institutional dimensions of environmental protection must be confined if it is to be of much value. Nevertheless some observations may be made about the broad characteristics of the developments described above.

First, Australian environmental institutional innovation – the development of Australian environmental agencies and their enabling laws and regulations – has followed a pattern common to most countries in the industrialised world. It has been shaped by a long-established transnational discourse about ecological governance. Increasingly, the direct and indirect influence of international environmental regimes (such as the Montreal Protocol, Climate Change Convention, Biodiversity Convention and Basel Convention) on the one hand, and regular contact between bureaucrats and policy makers in State and national departments with their counterparts in OECD countries on the other, have served to guide and discipline domestic environmental policy. It is therefore possible, overall, to identify a degree of convergence between Australian and OECD environmental policies and practices, broadly defined. However, innovations in Australian environmental protection policies, standards and modes of implementation – especially with regard to pollution management – have generally lagged behind and been dependent on the example of overseas policy implementations and demands.

Second, until the 1990s, constitutional responsibility for environmental protection and natural resource management was seen to rest with the States. Therefore the interaction between these historical waves of institutional innovation and Australia's federal system has resulted in an assemblage of environmental agencies, laws and standards which remains uneven and dissonant across States and leaves the Commonwealth's role ill-defined. Within States, even following the establishment of departments dedicated to environmental management, and agencies to regulate environmental pollution, the jurisdiction of the lead agencies over all public and private actors in the field remains incomplete and often responsibilities remain fragmented between several bodies. Nationally, the influence of Environment Australia and other Commonwealth departments over actual or potential areas of national environmental responsibility has been limited as successive national governments have preferred to support forms of 'cooperative federalism' in order to minimise political conflict with the States when addressing environmental issues. Nevertheless, the unevenness which exists as a result of historical circumstance has been reduced but not overcome through the creation of a set of national agencies and intergovernmental processes which facilitated the development of national benchmarks and standards. Recent national and intergovernmental developments (including the IGAE, subsequent Council of Australian Government [COAG] arrangements and the NEPC) have attempted to address these problems. In other words, the trend over the past decade has been towards integration of environmental institutions and convergence of environmental regulatory practices *within* the federation. Nevertheless, entrepreneur agencies in Victoria and New South Wales still tend to have disproportionate influence over policy developments in the environmental domain. Partly for this reason, the remainder of this chapter elaborates on these points by concentrating on recent developments in pollution regulation on Victoria.

Victoria's Environment Protection Authority – an 'orphan agency'?

Victoria's Environment Protection Authority (VEPA) was established some three decades ago, in 1971, with statutory responsibility for 'protecting Victoria's environment from pollution'. Despite amendment, its founding legislation, the *Environment Protection Act 1970 (Vic)* (the EP Act), still reflects the circumstances of the VEPA's creation. It retains a strong emphasis on curbing industrial and ambient pollution with impacts on urban conditions and human health, and on rationalising the administration of regulations governing and limiting air, water and noise pollution.[3] The VEPA remains poorly equipped to regulate the full range of current ecological pressures – such as non-point source pollution, or energy consumption, as this relates to induced climate change, or threats to biodiversity caused by agricultural and forestry practices.

Regulatory style and policy instruments

Under a system established in 1973, waste discharge licences are set by the EPA in relation to State Environmental Protection Policies (SEPPs) established pursuant to the requirements of the EP Act. By the early 1980s, SEPPs had been declared for air, water and noise for most of the State. They define the 'beneficial uses' of the environments and media to which they apply, and provide environmental quality objectives based on technical assessments of the limits on pollution necessary to protect beneficial uses in the specified areas or media (VEPA 1994a).

The VEPA has claimed that it relies upon direct enforcement (via its licensing powers and capacity to prosecute breaches of licence conditions) for its effectiveness, and that this was responsible for the improvements in environmental conditions which occurred over the period from 1971 to 1985 (Grabosky and Braithwaite 1985: 38). However, prosecution has remained an action of 'last resort', used when voluntary compliance and negotiated resolution of perceived problems failed.

More recently, it has been suggested that the VEPA's current policy is to avoid prosecution and to encourage a negotiated settlement, and that justification of this policy is on the grounds of the expense of litigation and failure to achieve desired outcomes in the courts (Masterson 1993). While there are recognised ambiguities, complexities and inadequacies in using measures such prosecutions and the issuing of infringements notices as agency performance indicators, it is evident that the ratio of VEPA prosecutions to infringement notices, breaches and complaints remains low. The number of industry infringement notices issued peaked at 641 in 1989-90 and in 2000-01 were a quarter of that number (146) (VEPA 1986 onwards). Although the number of prosecutions for industrial pollution related offences increased over the period from 1982 to 1989, this number remained small, peaked at 79 industrial cases in 1986-87, and has since fallen back to approximately half that level in 2001 (VEPA 1986 onwards). There is no suggestion, however, that these declines necessarily reflect a corresponding resolution of Victoria's pollution problems; the total annual number of public environmental complaints has begun to rebound towards a level achieved only during the last surge of public environmental awareness, between 1988 and 1990.

The VEPA's use of the courts as a mechanism for enforcing environmental protection in Victoria is, in reality, also influenced by its perception of its chances of winning cases in a legal system which, unlike in NSW, does not

---

3   When the Act was passed, it replaced statutory provisions found in more than 25 existing Acts.

have a court dedicated to environmental matters nor a judiciary which is scientifically literate or especially sensitive to ecological concerns. Recourse to the courts will inevitably also be influenced by the resources the VEPA can devote to legal pursuit and consideration of the strength of its potential defendants.

More generally, restrictions on access to the legal system with regard to environmental breaches – including financial limits to legal action by ordinary citizens; the absence of an effective Environmental Defender's Office; and the public's very limited standing before the courts and the Administrative Appeals Tribunal (AAT) – and the capacity of the AAT to override the findings or proposals of the EPA in licencing and other matters – have all served to discourage the development of a litigious approach to environmental problem-solving (particularly compared with the United States, but also with NSW). Planning ministers may also veto, accede to, or 'fast-track' proposed developments in the face of assessments made under the *Environmental Effects Act 1978* (Vic). The discretionary nature of the environmental enforcement regime in Victoria has always allowed substantial flexibility in the interpretation of environmental policy as stated in legislation.

Indeed during the first five years of the 1990s, the regulatory style and focus of the VEPA's activities changed significantly. The information bulletin, *Protecting Victoria's Environment* (VEPA 1994a: 2) captured the key themes of this shift:

> Today the Environment Protection Act reflects the following key principles: the precautionary principle, the protection of intergenerational equity, the polluter pays principle, and the protection of biodiversity.
>
> In particular, it puts the responsibility for sound environmental management on all Victorians – businesses, communities and individuals – where it belongs. The emphasis is shifting to market mechanisms, collaboration and co-regulation, rather than just the traditional 'command and control' approach, to achieve environmental performance.
>
> At present EPA maintains standards of environmental quality through works approvals, licences, inspections, pollution abatement notices and land use planning referrals. The EPA is investigating the usefulness of different economic instruments to control pollution in the future, such as environmental taxes and levies.
>
> The EPA is shifting the regulatory emphasis to target polluting industries more efficiently. New approaches to environmental management are being developed to increase the operational flexibility of industry without compromising environmental standards. This would allow industry to select the most cost-effective measures to manage its total waste output, without being constrained by detailed licence conditions.
>
> The EPA's long-term measures to minimise wastes, prevent pollution and address community concerns are complemented by inspection and enforcement activities. EPA also conducts out-of-hours and unannounced visits and concentrated inspections.

Increased organisational emphasis was placed on preventative measures – 'clean production' – rather than end-of-pipe-solutions to pollution, an approach underpinned by the VEPA's perception that during the 1970s and 1980s it had 'eliminated the major point sources of pollution in Victoria' and that 'by the mid-1980s it was already clear that relying on end-of-pipe waste controls was not achieving enough (VEPA 1994a: 1). This development was reinforced by the debate over sustainable development following the publication of the Brundtland Report (WCED 1987); the general change in the climate of public concern over deteriorating environmental conditions which occurred internationally during 1988-1990; the response of overseas environment protection agencies to increasing environmental 'deregulation'; and interest in 'ecological modernisation' and the establishment of a culture of environmentally responsible industry behaviour and 'willing compliance' (Vig and Kraft 1990; Weale 1992).

Correspondingly, the VEPA Industrial Waste Management Policy, proposed in 1985, finalised in 1990, and revised in 1998 (VEPA 1998a) became the EPA's main tool for effecting 'cradle to grave' industrial waste management, with an emphasis on waste minimisation. The *Environment Protection (Resource Recovery) Act* 1992 (Vic) enabled the VEPA and industry to enter into voluntary partnership agreements to develop waste reduction plans such as the one concluded with Alcoa in 1993. And the VEPA's enhanced its advisory role to consumers and industry, for example, through its involvement in the Australian Centre for Cleaner Production.

During the same period, organisational rhetoric shifted from an adversarial to a co-operative approach to managing compliance both in VEPA-industry relations and in its public stance. The VEPA began to propose a broad range of voluntary non-regulatory instruments for encouraging compliance and providing incentives for improving the environmental performance of industry and the general community. A Clean Technologies Incentives Scheme (1989), voluntary Environment Improvement Plans (EIP) (first drawn up by Petroleum Refineries of Australia as part of joint company/ VEPA/community initiative in 1991), voluntary self-monitoring and reporting by industry under its accredited licencee scheme (introduced in 1994), and incentives such as grants, subsidies and prizes, were each used alongside the VEPA's more traditional legal and economic regulatory mechanisms.

The use of economic instruments for environmental management was also debated strongly by Australian environmental agencies, including the VEPA and Environment Australia, during this time (Christoff 1995, James 1997). In 1985, Grabosky and Braithwaite (1985: 184) had reported that 'with every Australian environmental protection agency ... the incentives model had been firmly rejected. A variety of reasons were given for this, but the most fundamental one was that it was simply impracticable with present regulatory resources'. The change in attitude that occurred in the early 1990s was largely the product of the international and local revalorisation of the market as an instrument for public choice and self-management, particularly in the United States but also throughout the OECD (Rabe 1991; Weale 1992). There was a corresponding increase in interest in non-legal and market-based instruments to influence industry and consumer environmental behaviour (OECD 1989).

Victorian examples of such developments included: the NREC Report on *Waste in Melbourne*, which recommends the application of 'user pays' as an economic incentive to minimise domestic waste production; attempts to increase fees for irrigation water to full cost; similar changes in tariffs and methods of charging domestic energy and water rates; and through the system of program accounting adopted across much of the Victorian public sector during the period 1985-90. In 1993, the VEPA established a small (two person) unit to investigate the possible use of new economic instruments, including tradeable waste permits, in Victoria.

The VEPA's resources remained largely static during the 1990s (they were not savaged, as were those of other government departments and agencies during the time of the Kennett Coalition Government) and this may account for its failure to proceed along this path despite local and overseas evidence for the usefulness of certain economic environmental incentives such as subsidies, resource fees and taxes, and a growing body of theoretical and practical examples of other measures, such as creation of a market for tradeable permits for specific pollutants or groups of pollutants (Dietz and Vollebergh 1988; Eckersley 1995).

The move from an overt emphasis on 'strong' regulatory instruments to 'soft' or 'weak' ones was also evident in the change in VEPA's formal perception and handling of VEPA-community relations, and its increased involvement in a variety of consultative bodies, advisory councils and bipartite and tripartite bodies with community, industry and government (eg, Australian Centre for Cleaner Production; Waste Minimisation Consultative Committee; Recycling and Resource Recovery Council). The last two were disbanded by Environment Minister Tehan in 1996, during the second Kennett Government (Christoff 1998).

The transformation is also mirrored in language now used to define relationship between the VEPA, industry and other groups – now referred to as its 'clients'. Such terminology and the creation of 'client support units' with dedicated staff to liaise with clients such as Shell, ICI and the Tasman Institute, confirm the tendency away from an adversarial to a co-operative approach to managing compliance and also reflects a greater sophistication in managing agency-public relations. The notion of 'client' relationships suggests that priority will be given to servicing and accommodating client needs ahead of statutory requirements to effect regulatory outcomes, and often is a clear indication of some degree of 'agency capture'. It also masks the contradictory requirements of the VEPA's different 'clients' – government, industry and the public – and obscures the inherently conflicting roles for the VEPA in seeking to co-operatively assist government agencies and industry to improve environmental performance, while simultaneously being expected to police and bring them to heel for breaches.

Finally, as noted above, a number of fora and councils linking the EPA to the community were closed during the period of the Kennett Government (1992-99). However, the EPA's public consultation processes, for instance, with regard to reviewing State Environment Policy Plans (SEPPs) and its Industrial Waste Strategy, remained intact.

The strongest justification for altering an existing policy is the detailed recognition that the policy, or its instruments, has not succeeded or can be surpassed. Has the EPA adopted a new regulatory approach because of evidence of the failure or relative weakness of the 'traditional' means of regulation, or clear evidence of the added benefits of the new instruments? VEPA management is unable to justify the new policy directions, at least insofar as the shifts in direction or policy emphasis relate to detailed evaluations of past performance. In Victoria – as in New South Wales – there has been no detailed performance audit of the State's principal environmental regulatory agency.

Agency funding and staffing

The Victorian EPA experienced overall growth in both staff and budget during the 1970s and 1980s. Although total staff numbers initially fell from 240 in June 1982 to 209 in 1984, they then rose to a peak of 346 in June 1992, an increase of 44 per cent during the period of the Cain-Kirner Labor Government. Upon assuming power, the Kennett Government immediately cut staff levels by 15 per cent (to 294) in 1993. These levels have since increased from that level to almost equal their peak in 1992. Over the past five years – but especially since the election of the Bracks Labor Government – total expenditure and budget allocations to the agency have grown markedly, the latter to $44.9 million in 2000-01, almost double the allocation under Labor in 1992.

Nevertheless, the EPA remains unable to fulfil its mandate because of chronic staff shortages – a situation exacerbated by the first Kennett Government between 1992 and 1996. For instance, it is unable to conduct *timely* strategy and policy reviews and therefore to update environmental standards to reflect international best practice. Assuming standards need revision at least once a decade, it is alarming that the draft Port Phillip Bay SEPP has taken over eight years to review, and at mid-2001 the review remained incomplete and therefore Victorians are still governed by the original version, completed in 1975. Similarly in 2001, revision of the 1981 Air SEPP remained incomplete, although the standards of the initial SEPP were resoundingly criticised by Dr Jonathan Streeton, consultant to the EPA, as inadequate and therefore unnecessarily endangering human health. The Air SEPP was divided into two parts in 1999. The SEPP on Air Quality – based on the National Environmental Protection Measure (NEPM) for Air concluded in 1998 – was released in 1999, after almost a decade's review (VEPA 2000a). The second part, the SEPP (Air Quality Management), was only released as a draft in December 2000. Meanwhile, data on compliance with licence requirements are only checked 'periodically by EPA, backed up by spot checks and investigation of community complaints', while the number of vehicles reported by the public to the EPA for apparent pollution was 8520, while the number of prosecutions – probably reflecting the level of effective follow-up – was 25 (VEPA 2001).

Agency organisation and co-ordination

A decade ago, the VEPA was reorganised to enable it to deal with pollution in an integrated manner, rather than employing – as it had – isolated departments concerned with isolated media (air, water, noise, etc). This enables more effective handling of large industrial operators, via consolidated licences and related negotiations, as well as a better overview of environmental conditions.

The VEPA also participates in a range of State interdepartmental committees and Commonwealth intergovernmental committees relating to environmental performance, policy and standard formulation (eg, NEPC processes). These contacts have encouraged more elaborate policy networks which assist in the communication of environmental concerns to departments and agencies otherwise isolated by the traditional vertical and horizontal compartmentalisation of (federal) government.

Agency performance measures and audit

Environmental policy analysts point to the need for reflexivity in policy development and implementation. Effective performance reviews are essential to such reflexivity. The VEPA has never undergone such a performance review or audit in its 30 year history. It is worth considering who should undertake the audit of the VEPA. Several possibilities suggest themselves, including the Victorian Auditor General; a statutorily independent Commissioner for Ecologically Sustainable Development; an independent consultant; the EPA itself; or a Commonwealth agency (such as Environment Australia).

To date, the only assessments of the VEPA's performance are found in its Annual Reports (VEPA 1971-2001), in the 1988 Victorian State of the Environment (SoE) Report on *Victoria's Inland Waters* (OCE 1989) and in the Auditor-General's *Report on Ministerial Portfolios*, April 1991 (AGV 1991). The summary findings of the Auditor-General's Report are worth quoting briefly, particularly as the report reflects upon aspects of the VEPA's reorientation towards self-monitoring and confirms assessments made in the 1988 SoE Report with regard to industrial waste and emissions to water. Overall the audit review disclosed that:

- there is limited assurance that the information held by the EPA on industrial processes, volumes, rates and composition of discharges, emissions etc. is accurate and incorporates significant changes in industrial and other processes that have occurred since the granting of a licence to discharge;
- the self monitoring strategy reflects an 'honour system' approach which could be seen to be subject to deception and manipulation by licensees in the timing of samples;
- the EPA has not developed a formalised environmental risk management strategy to justify the allocation of resources towards particular individuals, forms or industries;

- the application of pollution offences under the Act had, on the basis of fines' magnitude alone, been of limited success in deterring polluters; and

- although it has been in a position to do so, the EPA had not obtained details of discharges to sewers, under trade waste agreements between dischargers and sewerage authorities, and therefore was not in a position to assess the risk to the environment from industrial waste (AGV 1991: 55).

This assessment is all the more disturbing if one sees that the VEPA's move away from use of strong enforcement measures (effective licence monitoring and prosecution) has been accompanied by staffing levels which seem to have always been insufficient to the task of deploying and employing those measures in the first place.

Metaphorically speaking, most regulatory agencies are unloved. But some are loved less, have less influence and are therefore more vulnerable than others, and the VEPA is one of these. It is an 'orphan agency' – that is to say, it is constantly seeking approval from and always 'disliked' by at least one of the three groups it is meant to serve (industry; government and the community). This occurs in part because of the way it is required structurally to fulfil contradictory roles, to meet both the legitimation and accumulation functions of the state. As there is always at least one of its three 'client groups' which disapproves of its actions, it always needs to adjust its behaviour to reassert the legitimacy of its functions in order to maintain its budget, staff and powers. The problem of 'organisational location' in the State explains a great deal about EPA actions and internal culture, not just in Victoria but wherever such agencies have been established. All government agencies, and especially regulatory bodies, are driven and challenged by a set of underlying organisational aims, which include to maintain or increase their political capital, staffing and budget; to gain acceptance of outputs and outcomes; and to generate positive perceptions of their performance. It is obvious, in the case for the VEPA, that these aims may not necessarily be synonymous with improved environmental protection and may simply involve careful reinvention of the wheel or the packaging of appeasement measures as novel improvements in environmental management.

Conclusions – institutional over-reach?

It is beyond the capacity of this paper to offer a comparable summary of the history and performance of comparable agencies in other States. These histories vary insofar as there are in fact two generations of Australian EPAs – those established in Victoria, New South Wales[4] and Western Australia during the early 1970s, and then the newer EPAs created in all other States in the early 1990s. Nevertheless, a brief examination of the performance of these

---

4   The NSW State Pollution Control Commission, established in 1970, was in effect comparable to the Victorian EPA. It was replaced by the NSW EPA, which began operations in 1992.

agencies indicates that the themes suggested above are common to most of them. Some of the issues which they face in common are discussed below. These shifts may now be reviewed and summarised, as follows, under some of the headings which have been used throughout this book.

Persistence

The EPAs established in Australia were created in two waves – the first wave in the early 1970s and the second in the early 1990s. The three agencies created in the early 1970s have displayed a remarkably high degree of organisational persistence and resilience to political manipulation and occasional pressure for their closure. They are now embedded features of the environmental regulatory landscape and are buffered by entrenched, if somewhat qualified, public support.

One outcome of this persistence, and therefore stability, has been the creation of a significant institutional memory within the longer-established agencies. Because of this perception of security and because of the organisation's 'ecological mission', there is also a tendency for staff – including senior staff – to be dedicated to their tasks and to remain there for long periods. For example, VEPA Chairman, Brian Robinson retired in 2002 after over 15 years in that position and longer in the organisation. Most senior staff in the VEPA have served for over a decade, usually in senior positions. As a result, strategic capacity has not been significantly affected by funding pressures, or by staff turnover and some losses lower in the organisation during the politically turbulent past decade. While this stability may lead to reduced internal impetus for innovation, such continuity enhances the capacity to refine policy over time.

The Commonwealth EPA (now dismantled) and, more importantly, the intergovernmental National Environment Protection Council (NEPC) have involved State environmental agencies in a process of national integration of environmental standards across a limited number of areas of regulatory concern, including (it is argued) the development and management of a National Pollutant Inventory, State of the Environment reporting (Harding and Traynor, this volume), and management of chemicals and hazardous wastes policy. The persistence of these attempts at national guidance in the face of changes in government at both State and federal levels is uncommon in many other policy domains.

Purposefulness

All State EPAs have their core goals well defined both in legislation and regulation. In general, these goals have been systematically revised and adjusted over time, just as legal and regulatory standards have been reviewed over time in all agencies, and the environmental targets often tightened over time in the light of new scientific information and public pressure. However, their capacity to respond to environmental issues and concerns has not improved over this time, despite the ways in which the first-wave agencies have been reorganised internally.

A mixture of impetuses has driven goal development. Sources of change are sometimes domestic, but more often transnational and international in origin. In particular, one can see the rhetoric and certain practices of the leading Australian EPAs (in particular Victoria and NSW) shifting to accommodate the new discourse of environmental governance which emerges in the late 1980s in the United States and among key OECD nations. Accordingly, the mix of certain policy instruments has been revised over the past decade.

However, the incapacity of EPAs to actually command their regulatory field – to offer environmental protection 'in the round' – is increasingly evident. In general, these agencies have focused on regulating urban environmental conditions and trends, where they have had inadequate control over impacts on biodiversity, energy use, transport emissions, etc. Their responsibilities for managing non-point source pollution (particularly of surface and groundwater) in rural landscapes has been only weakly met and they have had almost no influence over rural issues of biodiversity conservation, land degradation, energy use, emissions, etc.

In addition, State-based EPAs are decreasingly able to regulate or control many of the influences over which they were established to hold sway. In Australia, this loss of control has been disguised by trends which show some improvement in environmental conditions. For instance, during the past two decades, Australia, like most developed countries, has experienced a shift towards a city-based information economy and a growth in service sector industries in the inner city areas of major capital cities: 'the fastest area of job growth [1985-95] has been in the cafes, accommodation and restaurant sector' (Bell 1997). At the same time, manufacturing firms have either relocated to 'green field sites' in the outer metropolitan suburbs, 'emigrated' to the near-Asian region or disappeared in the face of intensified trade competition following trade deregulation and tariff reductions (Fagan and Webber 1994; Bell 1997). There has been a concomitant decrease in gross levels of point source pollutant emissions from the manufacturing sector in the inner city. The resultant trends and improvements in Australian urban environmental conditions have been claimed, incorrectly, by State environmental regulatory agencies as evidence of their performance, for instance, in fostering 'cleaner production'.

In addition, Australian industries and consumers have grown increasingly dependent on imported elaborately-transformed manufactures, including capital machinery and consumer durables. Consider certain consumer goods, such as ecologically-efficient Swedish washing machines or fridges from New Zealand, as examples of ongoing technological innovation overseas, including towards increased resource efficiency and pollution minimisation characteristics. The 'renovation' of the domestic car fleet with more fuel efficient and less polluting imported cars is merely another example of a trend that has offered an illusion of domestic ecological modernisation based on local regulatory practice. This has meant that a growing proportion of environmental improvements in Australia's cities is 'externally sourced'. These changes also have had an impact on urban-based resource use, waste output and pollution, thereby reducing the intensity and rate of per capita contributions to – but always not the total increase in – aggregate urban environmental impacts. In reality, Australian State-based regulators have had almost no control over the environmental impacts of imported producer and consumer technologies, and national regulations governing the environmental impacts of imported goods are ineffectual, in part because of the over-whelming influence of the States in their articulation and implementation. In all, these changes highlight the increasingly global dimensions of ecological management and environmental policy, a central problems for 'local' EPAs.

Information-richness and information-sensitivity

Australian EPAs have employed direct monitoring across the range of environmental media and sinks to register environmental trends and guide future policy. Networks have been established to monitor air and freshwater and marine water quality. The data from these networks have been supplemented by information from other government agencies (such as rural water authorities, local governments and other departments) as well as from industry sources. The Victorian and NSW EPAs have also had internal facilities for scientific research, and have commissioned work to supplement their capacities in these areas as required. The adequacy of these monitoring efforts to provide EPAs with a firm basis for interpreting the activities of individual enterprises and the impacts of diffuse (non-point-source) pollution has been criticised by community bodies.

Weaknesses in information availability and in the capacity to interpret data are increasingly evident. Retreating from an initial phase of politically constrained, under-funded and therefore only partially effective direct monitoring, the Victorian EPA has tended towards co-operative regulation, reliance on data provided by compliant companies and a winding back (or refusal to increase the intensity) of the VEPA's own monitoring effort. In other words, the relatively high degree of direct control over monitoring by the Victorian EPA during the 1970s and 1980s has been diminished in favour of partnership agreements with major industrial enterprises, that entail self-monitoring, and a contraction of the general monitoring network on grounds of cost and relative effort. In addition, the corporatisation of various pre-viously public sector resource-management agencies (such as the former Victorian Rural Water Commission) has led to the dismantling of well-established monitoring networks without adequate replacement. The sensitivity and richness of the data available to the regulatory agency has diminished accordingly. Goals for environmental regulation are not always based on realistic estimates of ecological trends, in part because of a paucity of appropriate monitoring and data.

There has been no systematic external performance audit of any Aust-ralian EPA. The performance criteria and indicators against which they report are weak, providing some insight into organisational changes but few measures of trends which can be causally related to the agency's work. Indeed, it is difficult to disaggregate the impacts of EPAs on ecological governance and conditions in many instances. Confounding factors include changes in industrial practices, externally-driven change in industrial, commercial and domestic technologies (eg, cars, fridges, etc), changes in cultural practices. As a consequence, it is not surprising that these agencies are more sensitive to political change and public pressure than to trends in environmental performance data.

The integration of State of Environment reporting processes with the operations of EPAs has not occurred, in Victoria or elsewhere. Indeed, in November 2002, Victoria has yet to re-establish its SoE reporting program, which was closed by the Kennett Government a decade earlier.

Overall, these observations highlight a series of problems that can be summarised as follows. Australian EPAs lack the capacity – and often the will – to fulfil their mandate. Increasing their resources and public profile would certainly enable them to do more. Yet it is also obvious that there are fundamental limits to what such 'localised' agencies can achieve. The widely-held expectation that EPAs can, given their present resources and regulatory scope and culture, guide complex economies towards ecological sustainability is manifestly unrealistic. The task is one of both enhancing these capacities and redefining and extending the limits of such regulation, avoiding institutional over-reach while developing complementary programs for ecological governance.

References

AGV (Auditor-General, Victoria), 1991, Report on Ministerial Portfolios, April 1991, Melbourne: Government of Victoria.

Bell, S, 1997, Ungoverning the economy: the political economy of Australian economic policy, Melbourne: Oxford University Press.

Bennett, J, and Block, W (eds), 1991, Reconciling economics and the environment, Melbourne: Australian Institute for Public Policy.

Bonyhady, T, 1993, Places worth keeping, Sydney: Allen and Unwin.

Christoff, P, 1995, 'Market-based instruments: the Australian experience' in Eckersley, R (ed), Markets, the state and the environment: towards integration, Sydney/London/New York: Macmillan.

Christoff, P, 1998, Degreening government in the Garden State: environment policy under the Kennett Government, Environment and Planning Law Journal 15: 10-32.

Christoff, P, 1999, 'Regulating the urban environment', in Troy, P (ed), Serving the city: the crisis in Australia's urban services, Sydney: Pluto Press.

Department of Environment, Sports and Territories (DEST), 1993, Environmental economics – moving to sustainability, Papers of the 1993 Environmental Economics Conference, Canberra.

Dietz, F,J, and Vollebergh, HRJ, 1988, 'Wishful thinking about the effects of market incentives in environmental policy', in Dietz, FJ and Heijman, WJM (eds), Environmental policy in a market economy, Wageningen: Pudoc.

Dingle, T and Rasmussen, C, 1991, Vital connections –Melbourne and its Board of Works 1891-1991, Melbourne: Penguin/Viking.

Dunstan, D, 1984, Governing the metropolis: politics, technology and social change in a Victorian city: Melbourne 1850-1891, Melbourne: Melbourne University Press.

Eckersley, R (ed), 1995, Markets, the state and the environment: towards integration, Sydney/London/New York: Macmillan.

Fagan, RH and Webber, M, 1994, Global restructuring: the Australian experience, Melbourne: Oxford University Press.

Grabosky, PN, 1993, Rewards and incentives as regulatory instruments, unpublished paper.

Grabosky, P and Braithwaite, J, 1986, *Of manners gentle: enforcement strategies of Australian business regulatory agencies*, Oxford and Melbourne: Oxford University Press.

Henry FJJ, 1939, *The water supply and sewerage of Sydney*, Sydney: Halstead Press.

James, D, 1997, *Environmental incentives: Australian experience with instruments for environmental management*, Environmental Economics Research paper No 5, Canberra: Environment Australia.

Janicke, M, 1990, *State failure*, London: Polity Press.

Janicke, M, Monch, H, Ranneberg, T and Simonis, U, 1988, *Economic structure and environmental impact: empirical evidence on thirty-one countries in East and West*, Berlin: Berlin fur Sozialforschung gGmbH (WZB), Wissenschaftszentrum.

Janicke, M, Monch H, and Binder, M, (eds), 1992, *Umweltentlastung durch industriell Strukturwandel? Eine Explorative Studie uber 32 Industrielander (1970 bis 1990)*, Berlin: Edition Sigma, Rainer Bohn Verlag, Berlin.

Kraft, ME, and Vig, NJ, 1990, 'Environmental policy from the Seventies to the Nineties: continuity and change', in Vig, NJ, and Kraft, ME (eds), *Environmental policy in the 1990s*, Washington, DC: Congressional Quarterly.

Masterson, V, (1993), *Economic and environmental performance in water markets*, Thesis, Masters of Environmental Science, Monash University, Melbourne.

Moran, A, Chisholm, A, and Porter, M (eds), 1991, *Markets, resources and the environment*, Sydney: Allen and Unwin.

OCE (Office of the Commissioner for the Environment, Victoria), 1989, *Victoria's inland waters*, Melbourne: Victorian Government Printing Office.

OECD, 1989, *Economic instruments for environmental improvement*, Paris: Organisation for Economic Co-operation and Development.

Powell, JM, 1976, *Environmental management in Australia, 1788-1914*, Melbourne: Oxford University Press.

Powell, JM, 1989, *Watering the Garden State: water, land and community in Victoria 1834-1988*, Sydney: Allen and Unwin.

Rabe, BG, 1991, From pollution control to pollution prevention: the gradual transformation of American environmental regulatory policy, *Environmental and Planning Law Journal* 8: 226-231.

VEPA (Victoria, Environment Protection Authority), 1971-2001, *EPA Annual Reports*, Melbourne: VEPA.

VEPA (Victoria, Environment Protection Authority), 1991a, *EPA Review*, Summer.

VEPA (Victoria, Environment Protection Authority), 1993a, *A question of trust: accredited licensee concept: a discussion paper*, Publication No 385, July 1993, Melbourne: VEPA.

VEPA (Victoria, Environment Protection Authority), 1993b, *EPA Review*, Winter.

VEPA (Victoria, Environment Protection Authority), 1994a, *Protecting Victoria's environment, EPA Information Bulletin*, Publication 273, January, Melbourne: VEPA.

VEPA (Victoria, Environment Protection Authority), 1998a, Zeroing in on waste: pathways to cleaner production for Victorian industries, Publication 537, Melbourne: VEPA.

VEPA (Victoria, Environment Protection Authority), 2000a, *Protecting Victoria's Air Environment: Draft variation to State Environment Protection Policy (Air Quality Management) and State Environment Protection Policy (Ambient Air Quality) and Draft Policy Assessment*, December, <http://www.epa.gov.au>

Vig, NJ and Kraft, ME (eds), *Environmental policy in the 1990s*, Washington DC: Congressional Quarterly.

Weale, A, 1992, *The new politics of pollution*, Manchester and New York: Manchester University Press.

WCED (World Commission on Environment and Development), 1987, *Our common future*, (The 'Brundtland Report'), Oxford: Oxford University Press.

13

Parliamentary and Intergovernmental Processes

Brett Odgers

Consultant, Canberra

This component study provides a brief description of contemporary changes in the Australian Constitution, which are proving significant for resource and environmental policies. The second section is an account of the role, procedures and performance of Australian parliaments and political parties in the natural resources and environment field. Further observations on the relationship between parliaments and the executive branch of government together with pertinent trends in government bureaucracies comprise the third section, and then the role of the Australian Senate is discussed.

Intergovernmental institutions and processes are assessed in section five, using the Australian and New Zealand Environment and Conservation Council as a case study. Section six highlights the interaction between parliaments and intergovernmental processes, on the one hand, and national bodies representing the industry sector and the environment movement, on the other.

The overall focus of the analysis is on policies relevant to the national strategy for ecologically sustainable development, pollution control, and land conservation and water management. The final section draws conclusions against the criteria of persistence, purposefulness, information-richness, inclusiveness, flexibility and institutional integration.

The Constitution

As an institution itself, the Australian Federal Constitution has undergone many changes. The small number of amendments to the formal Constitution has been far from meeting the manifold demands over the years, so informal arrangements of the Constitution have been continuously subject to significant changes. Federalism has exhibited the following swings in emphasis over the past 30 years in Australia: centralist coercive, cooperative, concurrent, competitive, coordinate (strict separation of powers) and decentralist. Given this experience (or experimentation), Australia has positioned itself to capitalise on the advantages and minimise the disadvantages of federalism, or face instability.

The Commonwealth, on the one hand, and States and Territories on the other, enjoy respective sovereignties under the Constitution, and together with the local government sphere, stand in direct relationships with their respective populations. The three spheres have generally different sorts of political objectives with respect to natural resource and environmental management. Despite the more recent experiments with coordinate and decentralist federalism, the Constitution, with respect to natural resource and environmental issues, is mainly about concurrent powers (Galligan 1996). Intergovernmental arrangements and procedures are therefore particularly important.

More recently, the term 'national' has gained new currency denoting the policies being developed in abundance and adopted by all Commonwealth, State and Territory governments after consensual processes. Intergovernmental institutions and processes support the facility of the federation to persist in its century-old form and produce agreed national, as distinct from Commonwealth, policies. The Constitution shows in this respect continuity, purposefulness and flexibility. Its performance against the criteria of monitoring, information-richness and inclusiveness is, however, increasingly questionable due in large part to its formal and antiquated rigidity.

Nowadays, citizen involvement is becoming increasingly important with respect to the formation, implementation, monitoring and effectiveness of resource and environmental policies. This phenomenon has been paralleled over the past decade by the collective efforts of the Commonwealth and the States and Territories to agree upon 'new federalism', mostly in the form of 'efficiencies' such as avoiding overlap or duplication, national micro-economic reform, uniform legislation and mutual recognition of standards. The prospective reforms of intergovernmental finance accompanying the introduction of the GST in July 2000 offered more 'balance of power' – rather than 'checks and balances' – between the two principal spheres. At the same time, there are persistent tensions between all three spheres and particularly unresolved stresses of resources, responsibilities and relations with respect to the local government sphere. Amongst the Constitution's grave deficiencies are no provision at all for Local Government and very little provision for intergovernmental bodies. Rising expectations and demands from the Australian population over basic concerns and the steady growth in globalisation pressures and international obligations, are powerful forces affecting mainly the Commonwealth's responsibilities.

Parliaments and political parties

Australia has a strong parliamentary tradition of responsible, representative government. The States all preceded the Commonwealth with this system and the Northern Territory and Australian Capital Territory have emulated them in recent times as they acceded to self-government. In character with the federation, each jurisdiction exhibits basic differences as well as similarities. Queensland, the Northern Territory and the ACT do not have a second chamber. The committee systems all vary in terms of their functions and influence. The Tasmanian Lower Chamber (albeit since 1998 with a quota for election of 16.5%) and the NSW, SA and WA Upper Houses are elected by proportional representation. The extent of devolution, or rather delegation, to the local government sphere varies considerably, with Queensland and New South Wales tending to go the furthest.

The major similarities are the institutions of cabinet government and political parties. Responsible or cabinet government requires that Governments be made and unmade in the Lower House or Assembly. It is common for ministers to be members of upper chambers but the Prime Minister and premiers and the bulk of their cabinets are from the House of Representatives and Legislative Assemblies. Most important of all, the parliaments have, especially over the past 30 years, been dominated by the executive, more particularly the Prime Minister or premier, and cabinet. To a degree, parliaments give the appearance of being incessantly in electoral mode, particularly given the average span between Commonwealth elections since federation of two years and four months. As well as forming governments and oppositions (alternative governments), the main function of parliaments is to examine, initiate and pass laws, as the representatives of the people to raise and debate issues, question and criticise government, examine proposed new laws and review or monitor the implementation of legislation. Through these latter functions, parliaments can regain influence in policymaking (Uhr 1998).

Procedural reform to loosen executives' control over parliaments has made little progress. However, there is an increasing readiness on the part of the larger parliaments to make wider use of parliamentary committees and extra-parliamentary bodies to assist them in policy formation, scrutiny and monitoring, in addition to the growth of administrative and freedom-of-information laws and tribunals. Many of these developments have been in order to expose maladministration and corruption in the executive and the bureaucracy. All the 'accountability' advances have not restored 'responsible' government, nor tackled the broader issues of macro policy and social and ethical responsibility.

Executives resist accountability measures and the establishment of independent public bodies. In the Commonwealth sphere, the Productivity Commission, Auditor-General and administrative review bodies are influential. Proposals for a Parliamentary Commissioner for the Environment (Molesworth 1998) were rejected by both the Commonwealth Government and Parliament, despite the strong precedents set in Canada and New Zealand. In recent years the Commonwealth Government has supported 'summits' or assemblies of people's representatives, from vested interest through to youth, on major and complex issues such as taxation, constitutional reform, drugs, genetically modified foods and even 'national strategies', which have attracted media and public endorsement. This could be seen as filling a vacuum left by the decline of parliaments as representative, deliberative institutions. At the same time, parliaments seem to be working harder, longer and more productively. The volume, range, complexity and selectiveness of legislation grow inexorably. The main problem is the paucity of national goals, strategic thinking and consistently applied criteria of public interest. Historically, there is hardly any record, except in wartime, of parliaments and executives dealing comprehensively with issues of great magnitude or wholesale restructuring; or of choosing to address the need to change underlying economic and social norms (although some examples in the public health field provide precedents).

Under conventional assumptions by governments (allied to abject weakness on taxation increases) about the role of the state, the public sector has been contracting. Parliaments, however, have to respond to the people's concerns, to the forces of new technologies and of globalisation, to the steady accumulation by private corporations of power over production, consumption and human well-being and to changing values in the community.

There is an increasingly diverse system of democratic mechanisms, social movements, interest group activity and constituency expectations (Marsh 1999). As a consequence, the statute book and subordinate legislation expand relentlessly. In order to satisfy differing demands, some of the more complex Commonwealth legislation purports to streamline the regulatory state or facilitate the handing back of powers to the States, the community or the private sector.

Parliamentary committees have assumed an increasingly important role. Their responsibilities are comprehensive and there is a strong tradition now of particular reports being responsive to community concerns, of enduring value and having a salutary impact on policy and administration. Compared with their parent chambers, they resist the constraints of short-termism, bounded rationality and oppressive timetables. The fourth section of this chapter appraises the committee system of the federal parliament.

Parliaments in both the Commonwealth and State/Territory spheres are displaying persistence and learning, with monitoring improving as mandatory reporting to parliament by government agencies continues to expand and improve. Potentially, they are making progress towards the inclusiveness of the processes and structures by raising the awareness and participation of citizens; and heading towards information-richness and sensitivity, given their powers of inquiry and access to prime sources of information.

These attributes remain subject to the related parliamentary short-comings on purposefulness and flexibility. Parliaments have little control over agenda- and priorities-setting and policy time frames; they entertain only superficial aspirations to formulate overarching goals, values and guiding principles. The continuing procedural rigidities and imperatives of legislating, general business and closure reduce the scope for debate over issues, ideas and goals in the policymaking process. Purpose and flexibility are conditioned to a great extent by the functioning of political parties.

The functioning of political parties

The role of political parties is not so much evolving as changing in fundamental and less predictable respects than the other aspects of parliaments. For most of the Commonwealth's history, they have been assumed to make parliaments and cabinet government workable. They are the principal agents of policy and state power. They have a vital role therefore in elevating processes and debates to the commanding heights where goals may be set and criteria of national interest and priority applied rigorously. In fact, the major political parties have in the past 20 years converged in assuming a primacy of select economic objectives along with reacting *ad hoc* on other issues and to the more insistent lobbying of particular interest groups. Their preference for rhetoric obscures reality. The interdependencies, linkages and longer time frames of competing policy issues tend to be ignored. Only recently have there been shifts to acknowledge, for example, social impacts of economics orthodoxy and reconciliation implications of native title law and Indigenous peoples' policy.

Political parties in Australia are primarily State-based, organisationally and in terms of political and policy commitments. The major parties are for the most part preoccupied with sectoral or generic issues, not intersectoral or even cross-sectoral policy. In the Commonwealth sphere especially, there is a trend for the major parties to be influenced unduly by facile opinion polls and media.

Currently both major parties are generally weak on natural resource and environmental issues, which have, since around 1996, been subsumed and marginalised under other subjects. The Democrats and the Greens are much better focused and each of these two parties plays a potentially crucial role. Improved organisational structures, wider participation by party members, policy professionalism and access to dedicated think tanks (Evatt Foundation, Menzies Centre) and other expert advisers are raising the capacity for policy development by the major parties. Caucus committees of the major parties are important and are proving more amenable to being engaged in briefings or consultations on background information and longer run issues. Of particular significance is the National Party which, in struggling to maintain its rural constituency, is contending with the manifest social and economic aspects of natural resource and environmental issues.

This evolving configuration of power and policy formation is especially relevant where the anticipated outcomes of research into sustainable development involve shifts in basic concepts, values, perceptions and understanding of complex issues. All political parties are apprised of the need to arrest the alienation and decline in trust and credibility accorded them by the community. This is a strong incentive to achieve greater learning, purposefulness, information wealth, inclusiveness and adaptation. Yet, political parties at present are slow and cumbersome in pursuing these themes. Nevertheless, proponents of policy change need to take an opportunistic and risk analysis approach towards realising the political potential, as indeed practised routinely by professional pressure groups.

A major drawback for members of parliament, as indeed for governments, is that ESD has lost the political force and momentum it had during 1991-93 when the wide range of interests represented in the ESD process had achieved integrated principles and proposals and were collectively committed to their achievement.

The Executive and Administration

The executive is created by and directly responsible to parliament: ministerial responsibility entails individual responsibility for the administration of respective departments and collective Cabinet responsibility to parliament (and the public) for the whole conduct of administration. With the decline in this responsibility in practice, albeit with indications of parliamentary resurgence, described above, the location of policymaking is mainly with the executive, their party and advisers, and the public service. The further concentration of power in the hands of Prime Minister (PM) and premiers turns attention to their respective predilections, processes and departments.

Coincident with the period of the ESD process in 1991-93 were radical reforms of Commonwealth and State bureaucracies and centralisation of power in the PM's and premiers departments. The objectives were leadership, control, coordination and efficiency, giving rise to the precept of 'whole of government' positions. In parallel, consideration was being given to 'new federalisms' and distinctions between 'core' government functions and those that could be divested, privatised or contracted out.

Public interest and policy integration

These developments were an opportunity to define 'the public interest' in ways that could clarify criteria, methods of assessment and policy priorities, together with procedures for consistent application. The prevailing view has, however, been that cabinet and ministers, the elected representatives, are the founts of the public interest along with statutes, policy statements and the like. This 'retrospective' view ignores a number of factors: first, ministers have choices, power and discretion; they often need advice on prospective outcomes, impacts and ramifications for other portfolios (whole of government). Secondly, policies emanate from negotiations and the weighting of competing interests, some of whom (eg, future generations) may not be represented. Ministers are not omnipotent in assessing their political risks and, accordingly, they have a need for information about stakeholders, or prospective winners and losers.

The opportunity for fundamental policy integration based on criteria of 'public interest' (or 'common good') remains to be taken. Public administrations, however, have been losing capacity to contribute or be involved. The new Public Service Acts promote efficiency, probity, service delivery, contractual employment, narrow 'anti-corruption' ethics and duty of care, and impartiality, but no traditional duty to serve the public or to advise Ministers on the public interest. Citizens are seen as customers or clients, giving rise to a 'democracy deficit' or 'lack of citizen inclusion' (Curtin 2000). Managerial skills and private sector experience are recruited while the store of intelligentsia, professionals and experts is discounted (Yates, Institution of Engineers 2000). Consequently, the scope, the time and the incentives for public servants to convey to the executive analysis of the public interest or, say, priorities for sustainable development, are scarce.

As the lead Department on ESD, Environment Australia suffers the more traditional handicap of not being a central or senior department, when the latter more powerful institutions have not yet accepted that economic and ecological sustainability are interdependent. Greater advocacy on the part of the Environment Minister and Environment Australia would help, requiring strong research and intellectual support. A Bureau of Environmental

Economics or Evaluation is needed to link with the research capabilities in the Treasury, Transport, Industry, Resources and Agriculture, Forests and Fisheries portfolios.

The OECD Environment Committee conducted a major program on 'policy integration' in the 1980s, addressing the paradox of Environment Departments that struggled to uphold environmental objectives amongst Departments that declined to accept the environmental significance of their functions. The recommendations, now widely applied in Europe, included strategic or policy environmental assessment, priority targets in the state budget, agriculture, energy and transport areas, policy tools such as economic instruments (notably taxation), natural resource accounting and annual reporting, and a stronger role for the Environment Minister in Cabinet Committees. Commonwealth structures and processes for institutionalising policy integration are poorly developed, with notable current exceptions such as the Australian Greenhouse Office and the primary industries, resources and energy portfolios, which are subject to collegial Ministerial direction and show a genuine and consistent, if slowly evolving, commitment to ESD.

In the State and Territory sphere there has been very little horizontal integration of administrations, apart from the strong coordination and centralist functions of premiers and chief ministers' departments. State governments labour under certain disadvantages: limited financial resources and rather fragile or unstable political situations; severe loss of technical expertise under 'downsizing' and 'new managerialism'; problems in matching ecological, social and regional exigencies with appropriate governing bodies, notably in water management; and declining research, development and extension capacity. The States and Territories have strong and well-integrated statutory laws for natural resource and environmental management, but their implementation suffers from lack of policy and institutional integration across the bureaucracy.

New South Wales and Western Australia have taken the crucial step of establishing ESD units in their respective Premier's Departments and recruited leading practitioners. The Victorian Government is seeking to achieve similar ends with the establishment of a parliamentary commissioner for sustainable development. Some States are more advanced than the others and the Commonwealth in developing partnerships with leading private sector corporations on sustainability initiatives, notably in the energy sector, but serious inconsistencies persist over the whole economy.

By comparison, local governments have been generally more effective than the other two spheres of government with procedures and organisations to integrate economic, social and environmental management, and to monitor performance (see Wild River, this volume). They have displayed the advantages of being closer to communities, information-sensitivity and institutional flexibility. With respect to natural resources and environmental management, the 'subsidiarity' principle – that policy and administration should be at the lowest appropriate level of government, that is, where information-richness and inclusiveness flourish – applies particularly to local government.

The committees of the Commonwealth Cabinet have from time-to-time, with the support of the PM's office and department, but depending largely on the time frame allowed for preparation of policy options, taken an integrative approach to their whole-of-government prescription. Cabinet procedures, however, mandate late rather than early coordination checkpoints in the policy cycle and there is not yet a manual for assessing the public interest. The bureaucracy failed to design an appropriate vehicle for the ESD strategy or to assimilate the Resource Assessment Commission as a promising ESD mediating, integrating and research agency. Similarly, the Economic Planning Advisory Council was abolished in 1996 after a short yet very productive period.

Cross-sectoral initiatives have, over the years, been taken by scientific and research bureaux in the transport, primary industries, environment and immigration portfolios, but these have (with the notable exception of primary industries) been largely dismantled. The public service is definitely making progress towards information-richness, but not yet with sensitivity and whole system understanding, despite notable efforts by the 1996 State of the Environment report and CSIRO in its modelling of strategic priorities and *Ecumene* project.

Consequently, in the ESD, resource and environmental field, the Commonwealth bureaucracy for its part has not been able to convey to the government the scale, complexity, urgency and significance of resource and environmental issues, nor has it yet grasped the potential leverage of the ESD strategy for these purposes. The bureaucracy has been weakened in persistence, learning and purposefulness. The situation nevertheless offers greater prospects of effectiveness through:

- consolidating the impressive progress towards information-richness;

- quantitative modelling the ESD framework to illustrate the key system linkages and to serve as public or national interest templates (for which there are valuable examples with European and American research and advisory centres) in order to enhance governmental sensitivity to the big picture insights;

- conveying potential constituencies and alliances for policy formation through identifying and involving stakeholders in the research; and

- maintaining contacts with relevant parliamentary and executive authorities in order to generate discussion and flexibility around goals, uncertainties and opportunities.

The Senate

The Senate is a feature of the Australian Constitution and represents in many ways the system's upholding of democratic processes and resistance to the decline in responsible government. Persistence and resilience have maintained its parity in lawmaking powers with the House of Representatives (except that it cannot introduce or amend proposed laws that authorise budget expenditure or impose taxes). It can initiate non-financial legislation. Its composition of 12 senators from each of the States and two from each of the mainland Territories (always one-half the number in the House of Representatives), elected for six years with half the Senate retiring every three years, consolidates its multiple functions of legislature, States' house, house of review, regulatory scrutiny and deliberative assembly.

Further, it is elected by a system of proportional representation (PR) (unlike the House of Representatives' first-past-the-post preferential) that enshrines representation of minorities and inhibits the dominance of the two major political parties and the Lower House. In addition to a general decline in voter identification with the major parties, many voters now cast their Senate votes with a view to the review, checks, balances and deliberative role of the Senate. Since 1974 it has become almost impossible for the government party to be the majority in the Upper House. In the past 30 years the Opposition party in the House of Representatives has never had a majority in the Senate. The trend in recent elections has been for up to 25 per cent of Senate primary votes to be cast for minority parties and independents.

PR expands the scope for the Senate, compared with the House, for representation beyond major parties and territorial constituencies to reflect community diversity, significant groups, social movements and issues or values that are ignored or neglected by the major parties (Sawer and Miskin 1999). The powers of the Senate and the holding of the balance of power in the Senate confer immense political power on minor parties with sufficient numbers. The recent experiences of the Democrats, who presently hold the balance of power in their own right, indicate that procedures for negotiations with the government of the day are not well developed and have favoured the latter. The minor parties have yet to realise their own strengths. Amongst their strengths is they have already adopted valuable networks and consultation processes commensurate with both the specialised and wider constituencies they purport to represent.

Senate committees

The practice and procedures of the Senate can facilitate purposefulness in its expanding role. While many of the changes pertain to the maintenance of its constitutional status, a key area of progress is the Committees. The modern, extensive committee system dates from 1970 and the recent changes are intended particularly to strengthen further the powers of inquiries, over government for the production of documents and witnesses, and for facilitating the participation of citizens and interest groups. Parliament House is very well served by media, information and research services.

The Senate has made provisions for the committee structures to be representative of its overall membership. The House of Representatives also has effective investigative committees, in particular the Standing Committee on Environment and Heritage. In 1998 the House reduced the membership of its general purpose standing committees to ten members, six government and four non-government, mainly on the grounds that smaller committees operate more effectively and many Members were too widely committed (House of Representatives Standing Committee on Procedure 1998). During the crucial GST tax debate, when the Senate had three committees inquiring and reporting in concert, it demonstrated its potential for strategic community opinion formation and interest group integration. This illustrated its more general capacity to raise awareness about macro issues, promote public debate, mobilise a range of expert opinion, attract publicity and secure community and interest group involvement.

Both the Departments of the Senate and the House of Representatives are working to expand community involvement in their procedures and practices. They arrange frequent lecture series, seminars and briefings on a wide range of policy and institutional topics, often with the support of the Parliamentary Library. These represent substantial opportunities to inform and discuss with Senators, Members and their support staff. Committees are empowered to undertake activities to inform themselves on issues without the necessity for a formal reference from the chamber or a Minister.

The Senate's performance

Most pertinent to ESD, resource and environmental research and policy are the legislative and general purpose 'reference' standing committees. The more important currently are the Standing Reference Committees on:

- Environment, Recreation and the Arts
- Rural and Regional Affairs and Transport

The counterpart Standing Legislation Committees become important when legislation is pending. All Committees inquire into and report on matters referred by the Senate. The *Consolidated Register of Senate Committee Reports 1970-99* shows that the Senate and its committees have been abundantly productive. The bulk of subjects has been other than legislation references, indicating a readiness to investigate issues proactively. '*Environmental issues*' have been accorded a great deal of attention over the whole period, but the scope of water, land and ocean *resource management* topics has been smaller and more specialised. However, the number of natural resource management topics has declined in the past five years.

It is interesting that the changing structures and nomenclature of the committees over this period show an awareness of cross-sectoral issues. The committee responsible for health has on a number of occasions cross-referenced its work with the environment committee. The industry, science and technology committee and resources and energy committee produced several reports in the early 1990s that were connected explicitly with land and water management. The foreign affairs and trade committee has from time-to-time looked at environmental and agricultural issues. There could be opportunities, particularly nowadays, to insert resource, environmental and sustainability issues into the deliberations of economics and finance and transport and infrastructure committees. No such opportunity has been taken in the past, with the outstanding exception of the Senate committee inquiries into the GST in early 1999, when submissions and witnesses from environmental groups were taken into account. No committees appear to have given much attention to wider or more fundamental issues of sustainability, such as the deliberations of the House of Representatives committee on long term futures and the Australian population.

In quite recent times, the standard of performance individually and collectively has been very uneven across the committees and amongst Senators in general. The most significant example, affecting both the committee system and the Senate as a whole, would probably be the Environment Protection and Biodiversity Conservation Bill of 1999. The Bill consolidated existing Commonwealth legislation, strengthened Australia's capacity to protect its biodiversity and replaced the *Environment Protection (Impact of Proposals) Act 1974* (Cth) that was hitherto the most potent instrument available to the Commonwealth for integrating environmental goals with other national economic and social policies. The Senate Environment, Communications, Information Technology and the Arts Legislation Committee had called for submissions in late 1998 and their report drew attention to basic issues still requiring consideration. The precipitate last round negotiations, covering a host of amendments, was between the Government and the Democrats, with the latter consulting very selectively with some peak environmental groups, dismissing those with fundamental concerns about the legislation. The fast-tracking of this legislation, with its major gains and major flaws, was met with dismay by key interest groups, representing the industry sector as well as the environment movement. The *Environmental Protection and Biodiversity Conservation Act 1999* (Cth) (EPBC Act) lacked mechanisms for the implementation of ESD and relinquished a great deal of the concurrent powers, which the Commonwealth could exercise over ESD.

The style of committee reports from both Houses is consensual and bipartisan, although recently Senators of the two major parties have broken this pattern. This development raises again the question of whether Senators and Members should be bound by a code of ethical behaviour. Government responses to committee reports are very uneven. Given their wider representation, Senate committee reports cover a wider range of issues and influence policy formation in more diverse ways. The Senate committee system in particular is evolving positively on the criteria of persistence, information resources, inclusiveness and adaptability, while the strategic planning elements of the 'purposefulness' criterion still tend to be undermined by the Government's agenda.

Intergovernmental institutions and processes

Whereas the institutions discussed above are amply documented, researched and debated, there is a dearth of studies on intergovernmental relations in Australia, especially regarding the developments and practices over the past fifteen years. Even the fundamental issue of vertical fiscal imbalance has attracted meagre attention, partly because centres for the study of federal financial relations have lost funding. Rare are books on the subject, or publications by participants. Government communiques and papers are generally unrevealing. A survey by the *Australian Journal of Public Administration* (Althaus 1997) of the journal's coverage in the period 1970-95 found a gap in intergovernmental relations – only 4 per cent of article content focused on 'federalism and intergovernmental relations'. It has been even less in the other main journal of the Australian public administration discipline, the *Canberra Bulletin of Public Administration.*

The Council of Australian Governments (COAG) is of prime importance as it is the main forum for policy development by the heads of government from the three spheres (local government has a seat) on fundamental issues of national and strategic significance other than fiscal relations, which is the agenda of the equivalent (less the President of the Australian Local Government Association) Premiers Conferences. COAG was established in 1992 as the result of pressures from the States and the complementary aim of the Commonwealth to achieve greater efficiency in the allocation of roles and responsibilities between the spheres of government. All governments had been concerned at the modest productivity of intergovernmental ministerial councils in general. More significantly, COAG was seen as necessary to address issues on a whole-of-government basis, that is, where major national issues could be resolved on the basis of full policy integration.

During the formative period 1990-92, environmental issues and the ESD national strategy were prominent in the short list of COAG agenda items. Water resources in particular were connected with micro-economic reforms, another leading agenda item; greenhouse policy assumed added importance with the prospect of an international treaty with major economic and political significance; and the States were concerned about continued Commonwealth takeover of environmental matters.

Criteria for inclusion on the COAG agenda included: most governments and the PM have to agree; the issue must be widely known and the subject of authoritative reports, with a 'champion' amongst the heads of government; political and economic imperatives; a perception of mutual benefits from policy change; prospects of early progress and political feasibility; and COAG as the appropriate vehicle, in combination with, or rather than, another process (Weller 1996). A further COAG requirement is the achievement of whole-of-government (WOG) positions, which is a step towards policy integration but not subject to a 'national interest' framework of principles and criteria. For example, COAG participants subsumed the ESD strategy under environmental issues and micro-economic reform generally, with the result that more fundamental, system-wide sustainability issues have not been raised. Water and land issues were not treated as the imperative challenge to restore and expand Australia's natural resource production base.

The performance of COAG is mixed and not impressive by the criteria of persistence, information-sensitivity and inclusiveness. It has significant potential in the areas of both purposefulness and flexibility. It met annually and was very productive to 1996. It has improved coordination and demarcation of roles and responsibilities. The WOG mandate was translated to ministerial councils to good effect, resulting in particular in collaborative initiatives by the environment and resources councils. COAG's water reforms have been beneficial; COAG gave support to the Intergovernmental Agreement on the Environment (IGAE) and to the establishment of the National Environment Protection Council (NEPC). It has tended to influence government and legislation generally in ways that represent a shift of powers away from the Commonwealth.

COAG has met rarely and briefly since November 1997 – the meeting on drugs policy in April 1999 was more like a single-issue Special Premiers' Conference. COAG depends on a supply of high-profile national issues, individual champions among heads of government and concerted initiatives by governments on pressing common problems. The arrangements for Ministerial Councils, the IGAE, NEPC and EPBC Act are not commensurate with some of the wider and prospective issues of sustainability, social welfare, long run structural reforms and resource allocation which should warrant a revitalised COAG. The Australian Labor Party is committed to it as a forum for cooperative national policies, involving local government and including regional development and natural resources investment. Without COAG, intergovernmental Ministerial Councils assume more importance.

The Australian and New Zealand Environment and Conservation Council

From 1972, ANZECC provided a forum for its members to exchange information and develop coordinated policies on national and international issues. Members were the Commonwealth Ministers for the Environment and Science, and the ministers responsible for the environment and conservation in each State and Territory, New Zealand and Papua New Guinea. The chair was rotated annually and members exercised equal rights,[1] Memoranda of understanding for coordination and collaboration operated with related ministerial councils. Environment Australia provided the secretariat.

ANZECC operated through its council, two standing committees of officials (on environment protection and conservation, respectively) and numerous taskforces, working groups and networks. The work was shared fairly evenly amongst the members. A perennial problem was agenda overload as upward flow of reports from sub-committees and emergence of new environmental problems showed no sign of flagging. Attempts to set priorities rested normally on simple comparisons and negotiations over current concerns of respective jurisdictions and the resource constraints of smaller States. The National Strategy for ESD has not been used as a framework for quantitative assessment of agenda priorities. The design of sustainability indicators was on ANZECC's agenda for many years with little progress being made.

Council met twice a year and the subordinate committees and taskforces worked intensively on a wide range of issues requiring coordination across member governments or demanding national consideration. Council had the advantage of being able to combine the pollution control and conservation perspectives, thereby assessing the relative significance of land, air, inland waters and oceans issues. Liaison with COAG and other ministerial councils allowed an ESD perspective to apply in respect of economic significance, for example, with salinity, greenhouse strategy, water reforms, native vegetation and marine protection. ANZECC had a very close relationship with the National Environment Protection Council. They both had obligations under

---

1   In 2000, following a threatened withdrawal of Commonwealth funding for ANZECC, the chair was permanently vested with the Commonwealth.

the Intergovernmental Agreement on the Environment (1992), which aims to improve environment protection, heritage and nature conservation through a cooperative national approach and clearer definition of responsibilities, policymaking procedures and uniform standards. Established in 1996, the NEPC is a powerful statutory body that determines mandatory national standards for Australia for air, water, noise, vehicle emissions, waste management, hazardous wastes and contaminated sites. Its charter is explicitly ESD and protocols ensure public and stakeholder consultation. Like ANZECC it has liaison agreements with intergovernmental councils in the transport and health sectors.

Both ANZECC and NEPC sought to achieve 'best practice' environmental regulation through streamlined procedures and careful choice of policy instruments. The processes of policy and standards formulation, however, were cumbersome and resource-intensive, due to the need for a sound scientific basis for draft standards, consultation protocols and the varying exigencies of the member jurisdictions. There was a risk of piecemeal or parochial compromises on overall strategy and standards. However, the senior officials involved with both bodies were experienced, knowledgeable and skilled negotiators, with excellent working relationships and well versed in their respective regional interests. The records of both bodies tend to show that concurrent federalism is at work in positive and efficient ways: the jurisdictions learn from one another, more readily adopting innovations and progressive policy outcomes through their regular exchanges. As a consequence, the NEPC is very productive and ANZECC made steady progress across many fronts, both overcoming potential conflicts and incorporating ESD-oriented whole-of-government positions.

In August 2001 the environment protection functions of ANZECC were assigned to NEPC, who also took over the secretariat responsibilities at their office in Adelaide. This arrangement represented the maturing of pollution control policies, as well as considerable efficiency gains. ANZECC ceased to exist. Its conservation functions were taken over by the new intergovernmental Natural Resources Management Ministerial Council. Committed to 'conservation and sustainable use', the NRMMC is an amalgamation of ministerial councils for agriculture, forestry, fisheries, aquaculture and conservation. The Primary Industries Ministerial Council continues. NRMMC is focused in particular on the National Action Plan for Salinity and Water Quality and the Natural Heritage Trust; there are advisory committees also on land, water and biodiversity, marine and coastal, and forestry. Both NRMMC and NEPC are chaired by the Commonwealth, rather than rotation amongst members. The Australian Local Government Association has only observer status.

The challenges ahead continue to lie with the need to influence the resource development, transport and economics agencies in the respective jurisdictions and, of equal importance, to achieve policy integration with related intergovernmental ministerial councils, notably in the policy areas of minerals, energy, transport, health and economic management. Protocols for the operation of ministerial councils have been urging closer liaison and exchange but have not led to many successes. The Productivity Commission has urged ministerial councils to engage in partnerships, effective coordination and public participation (Productivity Commission 1999).

ANZECC demonstrated persistence and learning; inherent expertise, sensitivity to information resources and risk management; rigorous monitoring technologies and procedures; and adaptability. It was not strong on strategic planning and purposefulness: its successes were largely within its own field – air and water quality, solid waste management, conservation of fauna and flora – and not the cross-sectoral challenges, with the exception of unleaded petrol and motor vehicle pollution. Its inclusiveness occasionally extended to the local government sphere but otherwise, in common with most intergovernmental bodies, was a major failing. The NEPC shows a real commitment to general inclusiveness, participation and accountability, based on an ESD charter.

Non-government organisations

A central theme in the history of natural resource and environmental issues over recent decades has been the growth in influence of non-government institutions (NGOs) on government institutions and policymaking. In the first place, there is increasing awareness, knowledge and ownership of, and growing sophistication towards, the environment on the part of the general community, and even the media. More particularly, the business sector and the environment movement have raised considerably their respective levels of interaction with government. The following brief appraisal relates to the previous sections regarding the Commonwealth sphere and intergovernmental institutions.

The model for this note is furnished by Ian Marsh in his book *Beyond the two party system* (1995) and articles on the policymaking process and the pluralisation of Australian society. He argues that the proliferation of interest groups, the advent of think tanks and strengthening of minor parties have taken power away from the major parties and established a new pattern of democratic governance. The new pattern is more suited to the incorporation of fundamental and complex social and environmental issues; it influences public agenda setting and opinion formation; and assists in interest integration and in the groundwork for policy implementation. The Senate and some intergovernmental bodies such as the Murray Darling Basin Commission and the NEPC are well placed to mobilise this interest group and community involvement.

Confrontations like the Franklin Dam, Wesley Vale, Wet Tropics rainforest world heritage and 1990 federal election (with the ACF supporting Labor) have been supplanted by a mixed array of organisations and mechanisms. The problems and the stakes are of greater magnitude while the community-wide resources being brought to bear have grown commensurately. There are abundant examples of various interest groups acting in concert or contributing to debate on issues of ESD and environment, including public health associations, overseas aid groups, industry councils, consumer associations, trade unions, churches and welfare councils. Environment and business groups have participated jointly and collaborated on joint initiatives: Landcare, ACF-Business Council and the ESD working groups of ten years ago. Governments have been compelled, at least, to become increasingly open and accessible to NGOs and the public. Formal protocols to render this involvement purposeful and efficient have become common; financial assistance was made but has been cut.

The environment movement achieved considerable success in the 1980s and early 1990s, yielding a legacy of strong organisation, membership, expertise and experience in dealing with governments at a level of strategic policy integration (across a wide range of issues and including the ESD strategy). The basic values of the movement generally represented reformist views about the structures of institutions, production and consumption being causes of environmental problems. While cooperating with government as opportunities arose, the movement lost ground in the 1990s in face of changing government leadership and priorities, withdrawal of government funding and counter-movement forces. It still has extensive lobbying capability and employs information technology most effectively. Many activists have moved into influential private sector positions. It has lost some confidence in government process, partly because of forestry, land clearing, salinity and greenhouse, but remains persistent in its lobbying and manages to avoid incorporation into government. It has a better appreciation of the limits to governments' capability and is redirecting energies to regional and community-based projects. However, the movement became fragmented in the wake of the deals over the *Environment Protection and Biodiversity Conservation Act 1999* and is concerned over potential conflicts of interest and narrowing of the environmental agenda with partnerships between business groups and key NGOs.

The business sector does not have the same long history as the environment movement of community-based, concerted and militant campaigning. Along with most of the environment groups, however, industry groups especially appreciated the importance of ESD and collaborated in the formulation of the national strategy. At the same time, in the wake of the environment movement's successes in the 1980s, industry established highly competent networks to manage their responses, in particular, to the national greenhouse response strategy, ESD implementation and the NEPC. They established parity, at least, with the environment groups in terms of cooperation with government, expertise, scientific backing and promotion of their worldview. At the same time, there are signs of shifts in values and culture in the business community towards sustainability and the incorporation of environmental factors. Industry and the environment movement have both displayed persistence, purposefulness, resourcefulness, policy integration and inclusiveness. They have thereby helped parliaments and intergovernmental institutions to develop these attributes and to extend their strategic thinking. The main challenge they both still face is flexibility in a world where grave social and environmental problems, rapid changes, complexity, adaptation and uncertainty flourish.

Conclusions

Institutions for policy development in natural resources and environmental management are faced with formidable barriers in order to attain persistence and learning, purposefulness, information-richness and -sensitivity, inclusiveness and flexibility. Australia is at a point in time where efforts must be redoubled to overcome these barriers and this chapter concludes generally that the potential exists to make progress on the scale that is needed. A rigid and antiquated constitution presents major problems, but the basic federal structure confers many advantages. Natural resources management is suitable for a mix of centralised and decentralised government. Given the three spheres – Commonwealth, State and Territory and local government – the appropriate model is concurrent powers, with substantial measures of intergovernmental competition and cooperation. Contemporary moves toward coordinate separation of powers are likely to be counter productive.

There will be in the near future main chances to exploit the advantages as one of the longstanding disadvantages – vertical fiscal imbalance – is diminished, if only temporarily. The proceeds of the GST should relieve many of the pressures on the States, with possibly some spillover to local government. It becomes crucial in this scenario to strengthen intergovernmental institutions. They are vital to the functioning of a federation and Australia has in recent times developed an abundance of such bodies. Their performance has been unsatisfactory to many a government and stakeholder. With notable exceptions, including the National Environment Protection Council, they lack status, resources, purposefulness, flexibility and inclusiveness.

These weaknesses, and hence imperatives for change, are shared to a certain extent by the Commonwealth, State and Territory bureaucracies. The basic problems are twofold: first, the dearth of over-arching national goals and strategic visions, translated in turn into principles and codes of ethical conduct; and secondly, the feebleness of policy integration, whereby policy-making and institutional arrangements effectively combine and synergise related sectors. Policy integration involves, in particular, collaboration across departmental lines and dismantling the hegemony or primacy of the narrower efficiency and small government features of 'new public management'.

There are signs that policy integration is on the agenda, for example, in the form of more frequent combinations of ministers taking concerted actions and agencies such as the Australian Greenhouse Office. More generally, however, there persists the 'muddling along ... accumulating change and responding pragmatically to issues as they arise; a strategy, which might not allow society to learn quickly enough.' (Cocks 1999: 84) The crucial body in the intergovernmental context is the Council of Australian Governments, its potential demonstrated already in the fields of water reforms and ESD institutions.

Governments tend to discount the role of parliaments in policy formation and to evade their responsibility to parliament. Parliaments are on the path of resurgence in this respect through accountability mechanisms and the empowerment of committee systems. The performance of the Senate exemplifies this capacity, augmented in its case by the proportional representation voting method, its distinctive democratic mandate and its federalist functions. It meets very well the criteria of persistence, information-richness, inclusiveness and flexibility. The principal problem across the parliaments, the executives and the public services, remains the lack of purposefulness in their activities and the persistent vagueness, even neglect, of what is the 'public interest'. The setting of priorities and formation of policies warrants a coherent framework, consistently applied. Frameworks such as the ESD national strategy, for example, define relevant goals and principles, including intergenerational equity, which should be elements in an overarching and binding expression of public or national interest.

Responses have been slow and wayward in answering the persistent calls from authorities for partnerships to be formed between governments, the private sector and communities. Precedents are being set but not resolutely followed for new and successful means of enhanced democratic governance, such as summits, citizens and youth forums, deliberative assemblies on complex and controversial topics. Governments are inconsistent in their support of non-government organisations and citizen empowerment, but the latter are manifest engines of change where change is needed. They have a growing influence over the recognition of big issues, public agenda setting, opinion formation, interest integration, as well as laying the groundwork for policy implementation. People are tending to be alienated from established institutions and vested interests, concerned at uncertainty and the complexity of major issues, yet sensing that Australia is at a turning point and seeking a more directed, overall framework for society (Mackay 1999).

The opening of public debate and pluralism of participants is mainstreaming environmental and natural resource issues, in effect, into the system-wide issues of ESD. They bolster participatory inclusiveness by governmental institutions and draw attention to the basic connections and interdependence between competing policy priorities. The corollary for parliaments, executives and intergovernmental institutions is the need to reflect these perspectives and aspirations of the community in their own thinking and procedures. Current trends in political parties and public services have been regrettably tending in the reverse direction.

References

Althaus, C, 1997, What do we talk about? Publications in AJPA 1970-95, *Australian Journal of Public Administration* 56: 141-146.

Beale, R, 1995, Turf protection: conflict between authorities, *Australian Journal of Public Administration*, 54: 143-147.

Cocks D, 1999 *Future makers, future takers – life in Australia 2050*, Sydney: University of New South Wales Press.

Curtin J, 1999, New public management meets civic discontent? The Australian Public Service in 1999, *Australian Journal of Public Administration*, 59: 115-124.

Canberra Bulletin of Public Administration, 1992, *Sustainable economic growth and development – implications for governance in the Asia-Pacific Region*, Includes articles by Harris, S, and Eckersley, R, A joint publication of RIPAA (ACT Division) and the

Canadian Institute for Research on Public Policy, *Canberra Bulletin of Public Administration*, Vol, 69.

Cullen, P, Whittington J, and Fraser, G, 2000, *Likely ecological outcomes of the COAG Water Reforms*, Technical Report, Canberra: Cooperative Research Centre for Freshwater Ecology,

Department of the Senate Committee Office, 1998, *Consolidated Register of Senate Committee reports (1970-1998)*, Canberra: Commonwealth of Australia,

Department of the Senate, 1997, *Work of the Committees (January-June 1997)*, Canberra: Commonwealth of Australia.

Ecologically Sustainable Development Steering Committee, 1992, *National Strategy for Ecologically Sustainable Development*, Canberra: AGPS.

Ecologically Sustainable Development Working Group Chairs, 1993, *Intersectoral Issues Report*, Canberra: AGPS,

Fenner Conference on the Environment, 1994, *Sustainability: Principles to Practice – Outcomes*, Commonwealth of Australia.

Fenner Conference on the Environment 1994, *Sustainability: Principles to Practice – Proceedings*, Commonwealth of Australia.

Galligan, B, 1996, What is the future of the federation? *Australian Journal of Public Administration* 55(3): 74-82.

Galligan, B, and Fletcher, C, 1993, *New federalism: intergovernmental relations and environment policy*, Consultancy report to the Resource Assessment Commission, Canberra: Commonwealth of Australia.

Heads of Government in Australia, 1992, *Intergovernmental agreement on the environment*, Heads of Government in Australia.

Hundloe, T, 1992, The Industry Commission and the environment, *Australian Journal of Public Administration* 51: 476-489.

Kellow, A, 1997, Problems in international environmental governance, *Journal of Environmental Management* 56: 54-64.

House of Representatives Standing Committee on Procedure, 1999, *It's your House: community involvement in the procedures and practices of the House and its committees*, Canberra: Commonwealth of Australia.

House of Representatives Standing Committee on Procedure, 1998, *Ten years on: A review of the House of Representatives committee system*, Canberra: Commonwealth of Australia.

Lindsay, AD, 1955, *The modern democratic state*, Oxford: Oxford University Press.

Lothian, A, 1997, ESD in state government decision-making, In: Hamilton, C and Throsby, D (eds), *The ESD Process: evaluating a policy experiment*, pp 53-67, Canberra: Academy of the Social Sciences in Australia.

Mackay, H, 1999, *Turning point – Australians choosing their future*, Melbourne: Macmillan.

Marsh, I, 1995, *Beyond the two party system*, Melbourne: Cambridge University Press.

Marsh, I, *The Senate, policy making and community consultation*, Australian Senate Occasional Lecture Series, Canberra: Senate Procedure Office.

May, P, and Handmer, J, 1992, Regulatory policy design: cooperative versus deterrent mandates, *Australian Journal of Public Administration* 51(1): 43-53.

Molesworth, S, 1998, The compelling case for an Environmental Commissioner, *Newsletter of the Environment Institute of Australia*, Melbourne.

Mulgan, R, 2000, Perspectives on 'the public interest', *Canberra Bulletin of Public Administration* 95: 5-12.

National Environment Protection Council, 1999, *Annual Report 1998-99*, Canberra: National Environment Protection Council.

Organisation for Economic Cooperation and Development (OECD), 1991, *Policy integration*, Background paper Number 3 for the Environment Committee Meeting at Ministerial Level, Paris: OECD.

Parkin, A,(ed), 1996, *South Australia, federalism and public policy*, Canberra: Federalism Research Centre.

Preston, N, 1999, Ethics and government – preliminary considerations, *Australian Journal of Public Administration* 58: 16-18.

Productivity Commission, 1999, *Implementation of ecologically sustainable development by Commonwealth departments and agencies*, Final Report, Canberra: Productivity Commission.

Resource Assessment Commission, 1992, *Methods for analysing development and conservation issues: the Resource Assessment Commission's experience*, Research Paper Number 7, Canberra, Commonwealth of Australia.

Sawer, M, and Miskin, M, 1999, *Representation and institutional change: 50 years of proportional representation in the Senate*, Canberra: Department of the Senate.

Uhr, J, 1998, *Deliberative democracy in Australia: The Changing Place of Parliament, Reshaping Australian Institutions*, Melbourne: Cambridge University Press.

Weller, P, 1996, Commonwealth-State reform processes: a policy management review, *Australian Journal of Public Administration* 55: 95-110.

Yates, A, 2000, *Government as an informed buyer*, Canberra: Institution of Engineers Australia.

Yencken, D, *Sustainable Australia: refocusing government*, Australian Conservation Foundation and Nature & Society Forum, Tela Series, Melbourne: Australian Conservation Foundation.

14

Local Government

Su Wild River

Centre for Resource and Environmental Studies,
The Australian National University

In many ways, Local Government (LG) cuts across all other sectors considered in these collected studies of institutions for natural resource and environmental management (NREM). For one thing, all NREM issues have a local manifestation, even when those issues impact on many LGs within a region, State or country. And in most cases, the LG will have a profound and enduring engagement with the issues that is worthy of consideration by other institutions. LGs are involved in a multitude of processes and institutions involving consultation, regional cooperation and debates on, and action for, ecologically sustainable development. They are managers, regulators and leaders, working directly with environments and communities, face-to-face, every day, in the public interest. They represent and include many Indigenous peoples, both through formal and informal channels. They are involved in statutory management and in environmental planning and protection, and in these and other roles they liase with most departments in the other spheres of government, both individually and through their LG associations. They have had long-standing experience with marketisation, and are arguably the most efficient and effective sphere of government in Australia. Further, they are fascinating and complex institutions in their own right. And importantly, there is much still to learn about and from the complex workings of these changing institutions, which carry such significant responsibilities in the fields of NREM.

This chapter is structured around the key research question of the capacity for Australian LG adaptation in dealing with policy and institutional challenges for NREM. In addressing this, it first provides a conventional 'outside-in' picture of LGs in Australia, focusing on State and federal government laws, policies, and perceptions, and those of other outsiders to LG. The second section describes key aspects of the institution of LG in Australia. The third section gives more detail on the NREM aspects of LG work. The fourth section contrasts with the previous sections by presenting 'inside-out' viewpoints, where case studies of LG work towards NREM goals are presented from LG perspectives. The fifth section summarises the case studies, then discusses them in relation to five core principles of adaptation, namely persistence, purposefulness, information-richness and sensitivity, inclusiveness and flexibility. The conclusion pulls together key themes and lessons, and proposes some legal, scientific and policy questions worthy of further investigation.

The institution of LG in Australia

Formal LG in Australia dates back to 1838. In July 2000, there were 627 LGs, and over 100 Community Councils and other organisations, servicing predominantly Indigenous communities (Information Australia 2000). In the 1999-2000 financial year, LG expenditure totaled $13 billion, which was 4.5 per cent of total government spending. Recent estimates suggest that around 27 per cent of LG expenditure at this time was on NREM purposes – an expenditure of over $3400 million (Trewin 2000). In contrast, SGs spent nearly $2,400 million on NREM issues (2 per cent of their total spending), and the Federal Government (FG) spent $650 million on NREM (0.4 per cent of their total spending) (Trewin 2001; Commonwealth of Australia 1999; Searle 2000). In other words, LG environmental expenditure is significantly higher than the other spheres, both in comparative and absolute terms.

LGs cover most of Australia's landmass, and as they are locked into local areas and communities, LG has both an inherent stability, and diversity. LG has also been the subject of broadly-based and intense reform agendas over recent decades, which have been driven from both within and outside of LG ranks. Understanding the institution of Australian LG requires a familiarity with both their stable and changing features.

Stable local government features

Many features of LG are as old as the institution itself. A very brief discussion of several key points is all that can be provided here. LG is a fundamental tier of government. Throughout Australia's history, State and Territory governments have constituted LGs to provide basic services at small scales in dispersed communities, and to meet community demand for democratic representation at the local level. LG responsibilities were not passed on to the federal government in Australia's Constitution at Federation, and since then, numerous campaigns, and a referendum in 1988 have failed to result in such constitutional recognition. Because of this, LGs remain statutory 'creatures of the State', and the federal government has no direct powers over them. However LGs are also emergent institutions, and throughout all of Australia's history local democratic representation has been demanded by local communities (Maiden 1966; Power 1981).

Australian LGs have distinctive, but highly varied geographic and demographic features both within and between States. The commonly-used terminology to compare LGs can be confusing, since the terms 'large' and 'small' are used without definition, while LG populations tend to be inversely related to their land area. The exact geographic size is relative to the size of the State. For example, Victoria and Tasmania are geographically smaller than some of the largest LGs in Queensland and Western Australia, but even within those compact States, LGs with comparatively extensive land areas have relatively few residents. For most authors on LG, 'size' refers to the population of residents or rate-payers and this is the case for the remainder of this chapter.

LG has distinctive powers, structures and functions. LGs lack judicial powers, and rely on State courts for legal rulings. LG legislative functions are undertaken by elected Councillors, including a senior Councillor (referred to as 'Mayor' in this paper). Voting in LG elections is only compulsory in Queensland, Victoria, New South Wales and the Northern Territory. Executive powers in LG are overseen by an appointed Chief Executive Officer (although the title differs between States). This is the only executive position in many of the smallest LGs, but larger ones employ managers and officers for policy development and a mix of officers and contractors for direct service delivery. These are usually grouped within departments including finance and administration, engineering, planning, environmental health, and many more in larger LGs. Direct contact between individuals in each of the legislative and executive roles is common throughout LG, but in no other tier of government. Each manager and officer is also usually involved in administering several (sometimes over a hundred) separate statutes, and in associated liaison with relevant State or federal government departments.

LGs are politically complex and distinctive. The issues that matter most to different LGs relate to their population and geographic size, main economic activities, location (for example, remoteness), environmental quality, and a range of other unique features. Active commitment to these issues of local importance tends to be the motivator for community members to stand for local elections. This means that elected councillors tend to be committed to positions on key local issues, rather than being attached to any formal political party. It is only in Australia's capital and other large cities that party politics are explicit at the local level (Chapman 1997).

Each Australian LG is represented at the political level by at least two Local Government Associations (LGA). These peak bodies include the Australian Local Government Association (ALGA) and at least one Statewide LGA. Many States also have district LGAs. There are also peak bodies representing each of the common professions within LG. ALGA and the State LGAs each hold annual conferences of about three days duration, with some form of proportional representation from all member councils. Delegates vote on hundreds of practical, policy and other issues, sourced from any member council, or any of the LGAs. This process provides LG with a united voice in its negotiations with State and federal governments and other LG stakeholders. LGA conferences are the LG equivalent of a parliament, but they operate very differently. Because highly varied local issues, rather than party politics underlie the political representation, voting blocs are issue specific, and alliances shift with the issues. This makes for quite congenial relationships across political, geographic and other spectrums, compared to State or federal parliaments.

Local government roles vary considerably within and between States, and have increased over recent decades. Some roles are undertaken as statutory requirements. Others are optional, and undertaken through adoption of local laws, or as voluntary initiatives. Roles that LGs generally take on include:

- public works and services such as road and bridge construction;
- community services such as street lighting, public toilets, car parks and campsites;

- community development;
- public order and safety such as fire prevention, animal protection and beach patrol;
- health services such as immunisation and infectious disease control;
- welfare services including meals-on-wheels, child care and emergency care centres;
- housing and community amenities for people with special needs;
- recreation and cultural facilities including swimming pools, parks, reserves, cultural heritage sites and pathways; and
- trading systems and other involvement in fuel, energy, transport and communications (Power, Wettenall et al 1981; McNeill 1997).

Australian LG functions are also internationally distinctive in what they do not cover, such as police, school and hospital services that are provided by LGs in other countries such as Britain and the United States, but by State governments in Australia.

Finally, it is worth noting that many of the challenges facing LGs are also consistent throughout most of the institution. Key among these are the chronic resource shortages facing most LGs, and especially the smaller ones. Over 50 per cent of LG funds are gathered through land taxes, or rates (ABS 1992-98). These are notoriously unpopular taxes, and community outrage usually follows any attempt to raise rates, to pay for improved or new services. Rate capping by state governments is also increasingly occurring, has not helped LGs, and has the capacity to cause long-term problems (Wensing 1997). LGs are often also constrained due to inadequate statutory powers, lack of technical expertise or knowledge about problems, and lack of time to adequately address them. LGAs have strong policy platforms of ensuring that new LG requirements are fully funded, but this is rarely achieved, and in many cases the continual increase in LG roles and responsibilities is placing considerable strain on LGs (ALGA 1998a).

LG as a changing institution

Despite an inherent stability, change rather than continuity has defined the institution of Australian LG in recent years. Changes have often been imposed by State governments, frequently with instigation from the Commonwealth, but input and even drive from LGs and LGAs has also regularly occurred. This section deals with some of the externally-driven changes to the institution of Australian LG over the last decades, also discussing LG views on and responses to these and some of the limitations of the reform processes.

Since 1989, all States have developed new Local Government Acts, providing wider general competence powers, setting accountability mechanisms, reducing detailed prescriptions, and providing the framework for microeconomic and other reforms (Wensing 1997: 90-1). The changes reflect and encourage a more strategic and responsible approach to local governance compared to the traditional, relatively rudimentary administration of infrastructure and services. For instance, the Western Australian *Local Government*

Act 1995 states that the general function of LG is to provide for the good government of persons in its district, also indicating that a liberal approach is to be taken in interpreting this function (Pt 3, Div 1, s 3.1). LGs throughout Australia are now also required to develop strategic and holistic visions for their local areas through corporate planning processes, involving consultation, review and accountability mechanisms.

Each State has now also increased LG accountability by embarking on programs to define, measure and report on LG performance, based mostly on micro-economic indicators such as the cost of delivery of various services (WADLG 1997, for example). Many other statutes implemented by LGs also involve specific reporting and accountability requirements (such as numbers and timing of decisions made under Planning Acts, and of licences issued under Environmental Protection Acts). The Commonwealth government has attempted to determine whether and how these programs could be made compatible to allow for national comparisons of LG performance, but has concluded that practical difficulties mean that such an approach is not warranted at this time (NOLG 1996-97: 135-138).

The advent of National Competition Policy has impacted heavily on LG, since each State has passed legislation ensuring that LGs, along with other public agencies, identify and avoid anti-competitive behaviour (CofA 1996: 36-7). Different States have embarked on the reforms with varying verve. In Victoria for instance, the Kennett Government established tough annual targets for proportions of Council expenditure to be subject to compulsory competitive tendering, and most achieved the 1996-97 target of 50 per cent (NOLG 1996-97: 150-3). In contrast, Queensland has taken a gradual and consultative approach, initially requiring only the 17 largest councils to conduct a public benefit assessment into the possible corporatisation and commercialisation of their significant business activities. Definitions of types of activities that could require such assessments were suggested, with transparent and accountable decision-making processes providing the safeguard to ensure that the LGs followed up their assessments with appropriate decisions about whether to proceed with competitive tendering. Most Queensland LGs are essentially required simply to identify activities that compete with the private sector, and then decide whether these should be subject to a Code of Competitive Conduct (QG 1996).

Changes aiming at enhancing the competitive efficiency of LGs have encouraged them to reconsider both the functions they perform and the ways they perform them. As a result, many LGs have used contractors to divest themselves of some basic operational service delivery. State governments have also provided statutory opportunities for private operators to become certified and compete to perform many traditional LG roles, such as building approval. Debates about the types and importance of values that are saved and lost in these process are ongoing, and issues such as job opportunities for locals and the quality of the work performed are not resolved to the satisfaction of all stakeholders (Phillips 1998). However, in Victoria, where the changes have been most extensive, many report an increased flexibility with opportunities to determine and achieve policy outcomes that were previously not even considered. Publications such as *Attending to the environment: a manual for contract specifications* have provided models to help LGs ensure that desired local values are maintained through the competitive tendering process (Osmond and Ray 1996).

The reduction in some direct service delivery by LGs through competitive reforms has not reduced LG roles overall, since this rarely removes LG responsibility for issues, and has also been coupled with increasing roles in other areas. Some, such as the responsibility for issuing environmental licences for over 10,000 potentially polluting activities in Queensland, are essentially new government functions, since before this devolution in 1995 there were no enforceable environmental requirements facing those businesses (Wild River, Hahn et al 1998: 10). Others, such as achieving waste minimisation targets, or effectively managing prescribed wastes, require improvements to the way activities are conducted (NSWSWAC 1997). Many are also entirely voluntary, relying on enthusiasm from within council or the community for their initiation and drive. These include efforts towards *Local Agenda 21*, a United Nations initiative aiming to promote ecological sustainability through LG efforts. In any case, a key problem for LG remains, in that their increased roles are rarely supported by sufficient, long-term and reliable funding options that ensure that both old and new roles can be undertaken effectively over time (LGAQ 1997).

Last century also saw a significant reduction in the number of LGs in Australia, with a particularly sharp decline in the final decade, as shown in Table 14.1. These reforms have stemmed from State governments, and often also LG pursuit of values such as improving economies of scale, achieving transparency, better distributing resources and power, enhancing capacity to deal with modern social issues, and decreasing tyrannies of geographic boundaries. Other options for advancing these goals without the financial, personal and practical costs of forced amalgamations have not been tackled with such vigour (Vince 1997).

Table 14.1. Australian Local Governments, 1910-2000

	1910	1991	2000
New South Wales	324	176	176 (1)
Victoria	206	210	78
Queensland	164	134	125 (31)
South Australia	175	122	69 (6)
Western Australia	147	138	142
Tasmania	51	46	29
Northern Territory	1	8	8 (61)
Total	1067	826	627 (727)

Note: Aboriginal and Torres Straight Islander and other Local Governing Bodies are indicated in brackets, only for 1997. Sources: NOLG 1996-97: 40, LGANT 1998, Information Australia 2000.

Reduction of LG numbers was particularly severe in Victoria, and offers insights into institutional reform and adaptation that are worthy of particular attention. The reductions were forced on LG between 1992-94 by the (radical Liberal) Kennett government. This also involved the dismissal of virtually all democratically-elected councillors, and their replacement for up to two years by appointed Commissioners. The realisation that this move was soon to occur sparked the inception of a new institution, the Victorian Local Governance Association (VLGA), with a mandate to protect local democracy and progress the cause of responsible local governance. Having been sacked, many ex-councillors from all political persuasions joined the VLGA, which also held a great many well-attended public meetings throughout Victoria, on issues of democracy and good governance. Membership has now increased to include many Victorian LGs, and some surprising outsiders including a former New South Wales Minister for LG. In contrast to Kennett's autocratic approach, the intentionally inclusive Bracks (Labor) government has welcomed VLGA as a valuable partner in the development and delivery of many new programs in Victoria (Hill 1999).

An increasingly popular approach to improving intergovernmental relations for LG effectiveness, has been the signing of non-statutory agreements across spheres of government. These have sought to clarify roles and responsibilities of all spheres of government in relation to powers and responsibilities, funding and financial obligations, consultation, policy development, program implementation, and a range of other issues. LGA's have signed such agreements on behalf of their member councils. Some, such as the *Commonwealth-LG Accord* (CofA/ALGA 1995), or the *Protocol Establishing Roles and Responsibilities of the State Government and LG in the Queensland System of LG* (QG/LGAQ 1997), cover general issues in intergovernmental relations. Others, such as the *Intergovernmental Agreement on the Environment* (HoG 1992), or *The Newcastle Declaration* (Pathways 1997), target specific issues. The documents certainly highlight key areas of concern for LGs and the other spheres, but by no means guarantee solutions.

Reforms to the transparency and perceived integrity of LG operations have been approached in several ways. Statutory changes for instance have clarified roles within LGs, placing limits on what powers might be delegated to and beyond CEOs, and establishing mechanisms for dealing with conflicts of interest and other potential problems (LGTCQ 1994; QDLGP 1996 provide examples). LG officials themselves have clearly demonstrated their commitment to such improvements through such actions as the adoption of 'codes of ethics' to guide responsible local governance (IMM 1995).

A brief overview of challenges to the LG reform process concludes this section. First, the pace and extent of reforms beg the question as to whether sufficient time has elapsed to evaluate changes and justify a continuation or extension of the processes. New amalgamated or grouped institutions require time to establish, it will take some years before any costs and benefits can be adequately judged. This is especially since changes of government at State and federal (let alone local) levels have frequently resulted in major policy shifts prior to complete implementation of key elements of previous reforms. Second, the increased flexibility in decision-making that is typical of the reforms may be in conflict with clear State government intentions to enhance consistency in LG functions. Third, the degree of integration and professionalism that is now required of LGs may be critically compromised by increasing pressure on their financial and other resources. It is not clear whether the plethora of strategic and operational plans, agreements, and annual reports now involving LGs are any more than words on paper in response to such fundamental tensions. Finally, fundamental resource shortages also mean that the potential of many initiatives has not been adequately tested. These sorts of issues suggest that a policy of slowing and coordinating the reforms, ensuring that they have received adequate financial support, and thoughtfully considering their outcomes may be a better next step than major new institutional reform agendas.

Indigenous local governance

Local governance with respect to NREM has been present in Australia for tens of thousands of years. Indigenous Australians arranged themselves into widely recognised and distinct local authorities that actively and diligently described and maintained environmental and other values throughout the local areas that they were responsible for. The enduring and significant nature of these responsibilities has been demonstrated in numerous texts, and recognised in High Court judgments in recent years (see for example Berndt and Berndt 1977; *Mabo v Queensland (No 1)*; *Wik Peoples v Queensland*). Despite numerous and ongoing attempts by colonists to extract Indigenous Australians from their lands, waters and traditions, most remain closely tied to their country, and retain a sense of personal responsibility for land and cultural management there. Australia can rightly be seen to have had two overlapping and often conflicting systems of environmental local authority ever since the commencement of formal LG.

Formal governance by Indigenous peoples is currently most dominant at the local level. There is currently only one Indigenous federal parliamentarian, few in State governments, and about a thousand in LG. Naturally, it is those areas with predominantly Indigenous populations that enjoy Indigenous local governance. Debate is ongoing about the appropriateness and effectiveness of the Indigenous LG systems (Fletcher 1998). There are also several programs, such as the Remote Area Management Project in the Northern Territory (NT), providing training and other assistance to address the challenges facing Indigenous LGs.

NT has by far the most extensive system of Indigenous LG. 634 of the 762 of Councillors in the NT were Aboriginal in 1998 (LGANT 1998). The NT is also the most unusual system of local governance in Australia. For instance, it is the only jurisdiction where LG boundaries are not contiguous, and instead often cover little more than the town or community area. It is also only NT LGs that have no planning powers, as discussed below. There are four legal forms of local governance in the Northern Territory. The six Municipal Governments cover each major population centre (Darwin, Alice Springs and others), and are a lot like small town councils in other States. A second type of LG in the NT are the Special Purpose Towns (Jabiru and Nhulunbuy) which service remote mining communities. Although constituted under separate Acts of Parliament, these most closely resemble the Municipal Governments, in the scope of their powers and their predominantly non-Indigenous populations.

The 32 Community Governments are a third form of LG constituted under the NT *Local Government Act* 1993. These have predominantly Aboriginal populations ranging from 155 to nearly 1,500 people (NT Govt 2000). The Community Governments are the only government agents in most remote communities. Because of this, Community Governments accept statutory responsibilities for far more roles than LGs elsewhere. In addition to all of the usual LG powers, these Councils are also responsible for functions such as policing, aged care, airstrips, banking, building, domestic violence response, education, post office, tourism, women's centres, and many others (RAMP 1997). Incorporated Associations are the fourth form of LG in the NT, and are constituted under the Commonwealth *Aboriginal Councils and Associations Act* 1976. The Incorporated Associations carry out many of the functions of the Community Councils, but cannot make by-laws. Their decision-making powers are also more limited, extending only to the Association, and not to the whole community (RAMP 1997).

Queensland also has separate statutory systems for Indigenous Community Councils in remote areas. Eleven Aboriginal Councils are constituted under the *Community Services (Aborigines) Act* 1984 and 20 Island local governments are constituted under the *Community Services (Torres Strait) Act* 1984. These councils have jurisdiction over similarly small land areas to the NT Community Councils, and are excised from other LG boundaries. The excisions are predominantly from the two most northern Queensland shires of Torres and Cook. The powers of Aboriginal and Islander Community councils are more limited than those of the remainder of Queensland LGs. For instance, the Community Councils cannot charge rates, and are therefore almost entirely dependent on the State and federal governments for revenue.

The remaining States do not have such formalised systems of Indigenous LG, although many have significant Indigenous populations. In recent decades, many such LGs have been criticised for failing to provide adequate infrastructure and services to local Indigenous communities (Rumley and Rumley 1987). Various attempts have been made to improve processes and outcomes for local service delivery to Indigenous communities, and several have, or seem likely to deliver significant improvements (ALGA 1998b). There is certainly still a long way to go however, and many Indigenous communities still lack very basic services. (Other Indigenous institutional issues and structures are discussed by Orchard et al, this volume.)

Natural resource and environmental management by Australian LGs

This section gives a very brief overview of some important dimensions of NREM by LGs. For ease of discussion, issues are grouped into three broad areas of environmental planning, management and protection. In essence, environmental planning is the process of deciding what activities will occur in an area, management is the operation of those activities and protection involves minimising the waste or pollution associated with the activities.

Environmental planning is a highly purposeful activity, aiming to ensure that land is available to meet a range of identified objectives, which may be compatible, multiple or incompatible when co-located. Planning is essential for NREM, since it determines long-term land uses and thus defines which NREM values are eroded or protected over time. LG environmental planning roles are established through the State Planning Acts and every Australian State has completely replaced or substantially updated its Planning Act since the late 1980s. The new Acts describe formal processes for ensuring that all stakeholders can contribute to planning decisions, as well as establishing sustainability principles and practices to support them. Essential elements of modern planning regimes include:

- a strategic plan, establishing patterns for development and retention of desired values;
- a planning scheme, including a record of actual land uses, indicating land ownership and activities that may or may not be carried out on specific land parcels, and conditions governing such activities;
- processes for referring development applications to interested agencies;
- development control mechanisms that restrict certain activities, in order to protect other desired values;
- systems for affecting land use changes, which recognise strategic planning goals and provide for review, appeal and enforcement of decisions; and
- public input to the planning process, including consultation on strategic plans, public access to information on planning schemes, and opportunities to object to land use changes (for detailed discussions on land use and environmental planning in Australian contexts see Conacher and Conacher 2000, Bruce 1988 and Sulman 1921).

LGs are recognised planning stakeholders in every jurisdiction although their level of involvement and capacity to make decisions varies widely. Two jurisdictions that contrast strongly in this way are Queensland and the Northern Territory. The Northern Territory *Planning Act* 1999 replaced a planning regime in which LGs had virtually no planning powers, but the new Act is only a small improvement. The Territory Government (TG) develops regional strategic plans, and while LGs are invited to comment on these, there is no obligation for the TG to involve them in any final decisions. The TG also develops any local strategic plans, although few of these have been produced. Development applications go through the TG, and although LGs can suggest conditions, there is no obligation for the TG to accept them. LG officials report that sound recommendations to ensure adequate infrastructure are often rejected, leaving LGs to wear the long-term costs of service provision in difficult circumstances (Wood 1998). Until recently, appeals against planning decisions were decided by the NT planning Minister, but the new planning Act now directs these to the Land and Mining Tribunal.

In contrast, in Queensland, under the *Integrated Planning Act* 1997 LGs develop the strategic plans for their local areas, and can also produce development control plans, although both of these are submitted to the SG for approval. LGs also have played central roles in developing each of the regional strategic plans in the State. As well as playing these key roles in strategic planning, Queensland LGs are highly empowered in decision making for individual developments, receiving development applications and coordinating the Integrated Development Assessment System for most planning decisions. LGs decide the conditions on most approvals, and can also require that basic infrastructure be provided by developers. Appeals against LG decisions go through the Planning and Environment Court, and not to the relevant State government minister.

More broadly, groups of LGs throughout Australia have cooperated to develop regional strategic plans. The federal government, ALGA and others have assisted this process through their support for the formation of Voluntary Regional Organisations of Councils (VROCs), which have often had a planning focus. The VROCs provide united voice for groups of LGs, and can strongly influence State government development decisions, in favour of regional environmental values (RCC 1995). In the recent *Regional environmental indicators project*, ALGA worked with the Commonwealth Department of Environment, Sport and Territories and with LGs from six regions across Australia. The projects made progress in establishing regional indicators, and ways of linking the needs of different tiers of government, for state of environment reporting (ALGA 1997). As such, these projects dealt with both environmental planning and management issues.

Environmental management is potentially the core of LG environmental business in the long-term. After all, effective planning processes should result in environments that need day-to-day management rather than repeated planning, and state-of-the-art environmental protection systems should reduce waste and pollution problems so that they are largely addressed during activities, rather than as an add-on. LG and their advocates identify a broad range of inherent environmental management roles for LGs. They include:

- biodiversity and native ecosystem conservation;
- parks and open space;
- weed and feral animal control, fire, flood and other disaster risks;
- transport and service corridors;
- energy and water supply;
- environmental and visual amenity;
- physical and natural resources;
- avenues for community involvement; and
- environmental legislation and policy (see LGTCQ 1989; Brown 1997; Berwick and Thorman 1999; Williams 1989; Environs 1996; MCA 1989; LSP 1996; CPDP 1997; AHC 1998)

LG environmental management roles differ from those in planning partly in their scattered statutory and non-statutory bases, rather than their definition in a single Planning Act. And LGs undertake environmental management as both regulators and operators of activities. For instance, functions such as water supply, sewage treatment and waste management, are required of LGs in most jurisdictions. As an example, in Queensland, the *Sewerage and Water Supply Act* 1949 states specifically that it is to be administered by LGs (ss 5-6). In meeting its sewage treatment responsibilities however, LGs must comply with the *Environmental Protection Act* 1994, and the Environmental Protection (Water) Policy 1996, and associated licence conditions. These require that the standards in the *Australian Water Quality Guidelines* be met (ANZECC 1992). In addition, Queensland LGs regulate non-point source water pollution by local businesses. These operational and regulatory roles are usually undertaken by different departments, so the complex, information-rich statutory systems need to be understood by many officers and managers. LG workers rarely have the time to become experts in each relevant statute, so they instead become most sensitive to those elements that are likely to cause problems if overlooked, such as those where complaints or prosecutions may follow.

The adoption of formal Environmental Management Systems (EMSs) by LGs, has gained momentum since EMS certification became available with the publication of *ISO14001: 1996 – Environmental management systems – specifications with guidance for use* (Standards Australia). Despite there being no statutory requirement for LGs or any other organisations to strive for ISO14001 certification, several proactive LGs have embarked on ISO14001 processes and a few have completed their certification. ALGA is supporting this development with its ISO 14001 guide to assist LGs through the meticulous process. The ALGA model argues that benefits for LGs include achieving more structured approaches to managing and delivering on environmental policies, defining tasks and responsibilities, helping to achieve beneficial environmental outcomes, greater operational control and potential efficiencies through forward planning and budgeting. ALGA suggests that an EMS can also improve relations with regulatory authorities, local communities, staff and other agencies (Sheldon (ed) 1996).

Besides formal EMSs, other non-statutory, or optional LG environmental management roles are promoted by publications such as the *National local government biodiversity strategy* (Berwick and Thorman 1999); *Protecting local heritage places* (AHC 1998); *Choosing and using environmental indicators* (Heath 1999) and *Turning the tide: integrated local area management for Australia's coastal zone* (Brown 1994).

As well as these nationally-based non-statutory roles, LGs are the key players in an international initiative focused on environmental planning and management. Local Agenda 21 (LA21) was initiated at the 1992 United Nations conference on environment and development (the Rio Earth Summit). Among the conference outcomes was the challenge for LGs to produce a LA21 for their local area, to 'provide a framework for bringing together disparate actions into a coherent strategy which is focused on making the operations of the council and community more sustainable' (Whittaker 1996: 15). The official Australian LG guide to developing a LA21 (sponsored by Environs Australia and Environment Australia) suggests five action areas comprising: preparing the ground; building partnerships; determining vision, goals, targets and indicators; creating a local action planning document; and implementing, reporting, monitoring and review (Cotter and Hannon 1999). However, few of the initiatives that are promoted as LA21s in Australia have addressed all of these action areas, and in practice, the term can refer to any integrated, strategic environmental initiative.

Environmental protection includes both waste management and pollution prevention activities. Links between these activities have increased in recent years, as contemporary environmental protection legislation has highlighted the risk of pollution from traditional landfills. LGs long-standing role in waste collection and disposal has also been extended into comprehensive recycling and waste avoidance measures, a shift that has strong community support. LG formal roles as pollution prevention regulators are also increasing, although there is considerable variation in these roles between States. FG targets for competitive reforms, waste avoidance and pollution prevention have driven many of these changes from the outside, while diminishing availability of landfill sites and increased understanding of waste issues have led LGs to reconsider their waste systems from within.

Traditional approaches to waste management by LGs involved unsorted waste collection and disposal of mixed wastes to landfill sites, which were usually simply holes in the ground. Over time, the availability of areas for such holes has reduced, especially in cities where land is most costly and where most waste is generated. Scientific knowledge about groundwater and other pollution risks from landfills has also increased, and SGs and the FG have encouraged LG understanding of these issues while pollution prevention laws have increased LG liability for any pollution incidents. Such statutory shifts have some origins in Australia's National Strategy for Ecologically Sustainable Development which inspired more holistic and integrated environmental protection legislation in many States (ESDSC 1992).

Australia's National Waste Minimisation and Recycling Strategy (CEPA 1992) was also highly influential in shifting waste management thinking and practices in Australia. The strategy identified a hierarchy of waste management priorities (the waste hierarchy) which in order of importance are waste:

- avoidance;
- reduction;
- reuse;
- recycling/reclamation;
- treatment; and
- disposal.

The other main influence on LGs of this strategy was its adoption of a national target of a 50 per cent reduction of waste to landfill by the year 2000. The strategy did not clearly state a baseline for this reduction, and most States adopted 1994 as the base year in establishing their targets since this was when the SG responses were formalised. SGs typically adopted these targets into their statutory framework for waste management, and passed on the responsibility for the waste reduction to LGs (Healey 1996: 28-30). This courageously substantive goal has been achieved by some LGs with many others attempting it, but the overall failure to achieve the target is most likely behind the lack of Statewide and national reporting of outcomes.

New waste management and pollution prevention laws have also increased the focus on the disposal of hazardous wastes. These have links to the National Pollutant Inventory, which indicates the relative toxicity of various wastes and sets thresholds for reporting and managing these. Wastes listed on the Inventory are commonly identified as 'regulated wastes' in State government environmental protection legislation, and the movement of large quantities is controlled by 'waste tracking systems', while their disposal in approved waste facilities is required.

LGs have traditionally contracted out many waste management roles, especially kerbside waste pickups and other waste transport. But the combined changes to regulated waste management, waste reduction targets, waste tracking systems, and competitive reforms have brought in new opportunities and incentives for LGs to increase the roles of private operators in waste management. LGs now increasingly contract private companies to design, build, own and operate many waste systems. However, the development of waste management as a viable competitive industry is still hampered by many factors including:

- very low profit margins and unstable markets for recyclable or reusable waste (waste after all, is rubbish),
- refusal by many waste producers to pay adequately for waste disposal, which is exacerbated in this large country, by the ready availability of spaces for illegal waste dumping,
- challenges of ensuring that waste producers sort wastes to avoid contamination, which is difficult since it involves time and effort by waste producers, for no direct benefit, while failure to sort is often undetectable during waste pickups, and
- the cost, effort and inherent difficulties of complying with justifiably strict pollution prevention requirements for regulated wastes.

This section has highlighted some major NREM areas in which LGs play large, and increasingly important roles. Key trends are the increasing suite of statutory responsibilities, which are sometimes accompanied by sufficient powers and budgets to adequately tackle the new work areas. Regional cooperation and coordination is increasingly being achieved, often as a statutory requirement. As with LG roles in general, the rate of change, and scope of the new responsibilities often make it difficult for LGs to deliver effectively in the new areas, while maintaining previous responsibilities.

Case studies of resource and environmental management by LG

This section steps away from conventional perspective on LG, which relates it to State government or federal government initiatives. This discussion is of LG experiences of NREM from LG perspectives. These case studies are drawn from a set of 34, collected by the author during several years of research in this area[1]. They represent a good spread of contexts for environmental local governance. The LGs involved cover four Australian States and the Northern Territory, capital cities, regional and remote areas. The case studies are similarly varied, covering a range of different issues. Despite this variation, several patterns emerge from the set and these are discussed, along with the lessons from previous sections, below.

It is worth noting that each of the case studies reported here are from LGs with strong environmental commitments, policies and programs. Not all LGs are like these, and many do not make explicit efforts to protect their local environments. This research did not explore why LGs do or do not attempt to deliver environmental outcomes, but instead focuses on the types of issues facing those LGs that do. In seeking to address those issues, researchers and policy-makers may encourage more such attempts, by many more LGs in the future.

Douglas in Queensland's Far North and Noosa on the Sunshine Coast are two Queensland shires whose local economies have flourished by way of environmental gains. They have much in common. Both have enjoyed several successive terms of office with mayors whose strong environmental commitments have been balanced by visions for dynamic private sector and community development. Both have variety in their strong local economies, and are leading tourist destinations. Both are gateways to world heritage areas, and have significant areas of national park within their boundaries, which have increased in recent years. In both shires, population caps and other constraints on development have helped retain distinctive local characters, while adding to property values, and drawing visitors to places whose special environmental values are widely recognised. This has engendered ongoing business and residential support for environmental initiatives (GHD 1997 for example).

In Noosa, the expansion of national park areas was driven in the early 1980s by a local community group, called the Noosa Parks Association. Council initially resisted the transfer of land to national parks. The election of a comparatively 'green' council in 1988 led to council support for, and acceleration of national park expansion. Although economic benefits have followed these trends, current councils are now questioning the need to continue the primacy of environmental policies (Playford 1997).

According to people involved in such initiatives, this type of outcome is distinctive of LG. It is in this sphere that tangible environmental values are perceived, and where people care about them the most. Visions for desirable, balanced futures also emerge locally, along with community commitments to retain and improve them. The balancing of environmental and economic outcomes occurs, and benefits can be perceived locally. Although other government agencies have sometimes expressed concern that environmental gains in Douglas and Noosa might be at the expense of other areas, these councils disagree. They argue that the transferable model involves visioning

---

1   Case studies are available from the author, or on the website of the Centre for Resource and Environmental Studies, Australian National University <www.cres.anu.edu.au/lgcases/>.

and enhancing distinctive local values, while recognising the regional context and maintaining a long-term vision. Working from local assets towards regional gains in this way has also allowed the shires to drive broader environmental policy agendas, and effectively draw other players in as partners for regional initiatives, that have benefited neighboring areas (Berwick 1997; Playford 1997).

Regional strategic planning in Australia's South West contrasts with these experiences, having been frustrated by inconsistent approaches between agencies, and challenges in maintaining funding and momentum for locally-driven efforts. The *South West Environmental Strategy* (Bradby and Pearce 1997), was a product of the VROC Regional Environmental Indicators Project (discussed above). The process in Western Australia was managed and driven by the recently disbanded South West (Western Australian) LG Association. The strategy used and advocated a 'ground-up' approach to coordinating efforts for future environmental preservation and restoration on a regional planning, rather than ad hoc basis. Specific recommendations ranged from strategies to identify, protect and utilise environmental values, to ensuring coordination and cooperation between a wide range of public, private and traditional aboriginal stakeholders.

The consensus approach used in developing the strategy, with membership of seven non-government, and seven government agencies, generated significant momentum and enthusiasm amongst participants, but this was difficult to maintain once the funding for the project ran out. Momentum was further lost when the National Heritage Trust provided funding for a second strategy, with a larger, overlapping area, but coordinated by a State agency. After this, even the LGs who had been the strongest drivers became disillusioned or distracted and failed to effectively implement key parts of the strategy. Eventually, even the VROC disbanded (Sherwood 1998).

Kogarah City Council, on the shores of Botany Bay in Sydney's south, has effectively maintained momentum in environmental achievements by gradually building capacity and commitment. Strong environmental agendas of key staff are again balanced by a recognition that sustainable outcomes need solid economic and community foundations. The opportunity recently arose to redevelop an old service-station site at Kogarah. After much debate, council decided to sacrifice some potential profits from the project to turn it into an environmental landmark. Kogarah Council wrote the development controls from the principles of sustainability, incorporating stormwater reuse, cross-ventilation, photovoltaic solar cells, and natural lighting for energy efficiency. The final outcome was compromised by the reluctance, or inability of the developer to fully deliver on the sustainability principles that were built into the plan. However, the groundwork that was done for that project provided information to cost-effectively incorporate sustainability principles into the redevelopment of Kogarah's city centre.

The city centre project is ongoing, but Council is optimistic that this will be a powerful showcase of the potential for optimising environmental values in a potentially dynamic urban setting. Meanwhile, other successful projects have fostered community and Council trust in and commitment to enhancing local environmental sustainability. The construction of an artificial wetland as part of an integrated project to help improve stormwater quality was initially met with some local distrust. But careful and committed community consultation programs have resulted in strong support for the project. Momentum for learning about and protecting local environmental values was also injected through the community when Kogarah hosted an international art exhibition for world environment day, and local children from all backgrounds took part in the event (Kogarah 1998; Taper 1999). Environmental strategists in key positions at Kogarah have argued that perhaps the most important outcome from these initiatives has been the learning that has accompanied them both within and outside Council. They point to the importance of ensuring that real successes are achieved, so that benefits are realised, and can then be demonstrated to others in the local area and beyond (Taper 1999).

Moreland City Council in inner-North Melbourne has had similar successes in showcasing ecological sustainability. Moreland renovated and expanded previous municipal offices, following its inception after the Victorian LG amalgamations. Sustainability principles were incorporated into the project from the start, with the new offices aiming to double the floor space, while reducing energy use. Recycled or environmentally-friendly building materials were also used when feasible. In addition, Council saw the project as providing leadership opportunities through collaborative and responsible processes during design and construction. The building is now complete, and intended energy savings and most of the design and construction goals were achieved. Sustainable behaviour amongst staff is encouraged through induction programs, encouragement to use public transport or cycling for work trips, and other measures. Public attention is focused onto the sustainability principles by the entry to the building through a 'solar pergola', which feeds electricity to the offices and the electricity grid. Even the Councillors are constantly reminded of local environmental values, by the 'environmental watch-ducks', that overlook the glass-walled council chambers. These are a statue of a local, threatened cormorant species, and Councillors have sometimes reported shifting to environmental votes on issues, having glanced up at the watch-ducks (Hill and Kyle 1999).

But such positive outcomes commonly elude many less empowered LGs. Litchfield Shire, situated at the gateway to Kakadu National Park in the Northern Territory, has a rapidly growing population, with rural residential subdivisions predominating. Applications for and decisions about these are made by the Territory government, which is strongly encouraging development in this outer Darwin region. The Territory government has repeatedly ignored requests by Litchfield Mayor Gerry Wood and others, to account for environmental values and ongoing management costs in its subdivision design. The complex local drainage system of interlinked billabongs, and tropical weather patterns with regular summer flooding, make road and stormwater system maintenance a costly nightmare for Council. Litchfield has lobbied for sensible subdivisions, sufficient road widths for vegetation retention and adequate, safe drainage, but the government has rarely delivered. Even the most fundamental NREM principles are carefully restated by Council with each new application, often to no avail.

Councillor Wood adopts brave and creative strategies to make Council's case. On a moderate front, he works constantly with local communities on low-cost projects to encourage people to take personal responsibility for pollution and litter management, waterway preservation and other local environmental initiatives. His more colourful approaches have included an article in the local newspaper, where he posed as a fictional wealthy sheik, claiming to have bought all outer Darwin from the Territory government. Wood himself was also quoted in the article, saying 'the government probably consulted with us like they usually do, but forgot to tell us about it' (Times 1998; Wood 1998).

Each of these cases of NREM initiatives driven by LGs offer broader institutional lessons. Table 14.2 summarises these in relation to core principles of institutional adaptation. Lessons from the outside-in perspectives that were presented earlier are also included. Each principle is then discussed separately in the next section.

Institutional adaptiveness by LGs in resource and environmental management

The discussions above have described features and processes of LG institutional arrangements that influence their NREM functions. Table 14.2 summarises elements of LG NREM, in relation to the five criteria for institutional adaptiveness. It is worth noting that all Australian LGs have committed themselves to ongoing adaptation by way of the Australian LG Accord (ALGA 1998a).

Persistence

Two main themes emerge from the expressions of persistence within the NREM case studies. First, most of their successes are characterised by a striking balance of ecological with economic and social values. Second, this is compromised by reductions in capacity, which can occur for many reasons.

Balancing of ecological, social and economic values is attempted as both an outside-in and an inside-out initiative for LG. The creative integration of these values can have a physical presence for the local initiatives, since it is at the local level that a sense of place informs actors' responses to policy initiatives. For example, in placing its solar-energy array above the entrance to the new Moreland City offices, the LG has ensured that energy-efficiency issues will be considered by its clients for decades. It borders on redundant to say that persistent initiatives are established over time, but gradual, careful progress, with tangible benefits over the long-term, certainly features strongly.

The outside-in initiatives reported here have tended to use processes, rather than physical features, as strategies to achieve persistent outcomes. These have included funding, statutory powers and responsibilities, reporting require-ments and provision other resources, as well as guidance or prescriptions for consultative efforts. Again, some of the most effective initiatives involve the bedding down of efforts through investment in physical assets. These include

Table 14.2 Elements of Local Government Institutional Adaptiveness in Natural Resource and Environmental Management

	Persistence	Purpose-fulness	Info-richness and sensitivity	Inclusiveness	Flexibility
Challenges	Need to maintain momentum, retain environmental strategists, build community empowerment	Election cycles, constant changes and narrow perspectives, undermine long-term processes.	Most sensitive and responsive to local needs. Challenge to integrate local knowledge with wider issues.	Challenge to ensure that all stakeholders are treated fairly, and their views considered and respected.	Flexible modern NREM roles can be resource intensive, and uncertainty in decisions remains.
Drivers	Perpetual LG responsibility for land and infrastructure management.	Environmental strategists in key positions. Strategic plans balancing broad values.	Broad community involvement in early stages of decision making. LG openness to community views.	Closeness to community. Models and processes for considering broad stakeholder views in decisions.	Communities and emerging environmental issues demand flexible responses.
Constraints	Shortage of essential resources: money, time, expertise, statutory powers, political will.	Lack of resources restricts the content, quality and quantity of long-term, strategic environmental plans.	Lack of data, info and knowledge. Small LGs have poor access to technical expertise.	Poor consultation and historical exclusion of stakeholders brings on conflict, and discourages inclusiveness.	Lack of coherent environmental powers or the means to support them restricts options.
Oppor-tunities	Environmental strategists with local commitments. Special local and regional environmental values. Histories of success.	New Planning and LG Acts require strategic planning for long term management of environmental values and other resources.	State of environment reports, and other annual reporting requirements provide data in accessible forms.	Successful consultation and other inclusive processes lead to trust between community and LG, encouraging more inclusiveness.	New LG Acts provide greater flexibility and autonomy in decision making, with greater accountability and scrutiny.
Threats	Electoral cycles, loss of environmental strategists and conflicting processes can take momentum from long-term processes.	Systems identifying and protecting known environmental qualities and values can fail to protect newly recognised values. Known values at risk under weaker systems.	Risk that poorly integrated reports, policies, plans etc become words on paper, rather than resources in constant and effective use.	Unsuccessful consultation and poor or unclear environmental outcomes can erode community support.	Time required to prepare plans etc can be prohibitive.

regional waste facilities, which are likely to be maintained by regional players for the life of the facility, partly because any alternative will be less cost-effective than using an established, accessible system. Persistent outcomes are threatened by the loss of funding, as in the removal of environmental licence fees by many Queensland LGs, in response to complaints by local industry.

The capacity to balance different values for persistent outcomes is clearly compromised when resources or momentum are inadequate or lost. A greater commitment from State governments and the federal government, to ensuring that new initiatives are adequately supported throughout their intended life-span would help. This would have to include provision of both financial and other practical resources, as well as sufficient powers to undertake tasks effectively. The plethora of new plans, policies, agreements and other written expressions of persistent policy goals may well be little more than words on paper if these essential elements are omitted.

Purposefulness

The purposeful achievement of economic, environmental and community issues is a feature of many LG NREM efforts described above. The defensive avoidance of future costs in Litchfield Shire's lobbying for sufficient space for infrastructure is one example of an agency seeking to provide for its own long-term needs. Using contract specifications, market development strategies, or direct involvement of developers, to drive outsourced environmental innovations are another.

Both flexible and inflexible statutory systems pose threats to LG purposefulness in NREM. Inflexible systems can only protect those environmental values that are explicitly recognised in planning schemes or other policy statements. These fail to deliver environmental outcomes when-ever specific values are not explicitly protected. Emerging scientific knowledge about environmental threats are hard to build into such anticipatory frameworks. Flexible systems, which rely on general statements to protect environmental values can lack the detail needed for firm rulings in favour of environmental outcomes. LG purposefulness is further undermined when other agencies fail to abide by the strategic plans, and other articulations of local visions and issues. There are many examples of State and federal governments failing to comply with LG strategic plans in their development of Crown land.

Information-richness and sensitivity

Information-richness appears to have been increased by the many recent reforms to LG and their NREM roles. This is in part due to new statutory arrangements that require broad-based consultation and scientific information in plans and assessments. LG sensitivity to issues that are perceived as important by locals, remains higher than for information contained in plans and other documents. Risks and limitations of this tendency have sometimes been effectively addressed by the intentional inclusion of broadly-based stake-holders in committees and other policy development and implementation forums. Although generally unpopular, the compulsory competitive tendering of LG services in Victoria had the valuable benefit of increasing information richness. In preparing tender specifications, LGs systematically assessed why and how they performed each of their functions. In the process, many were able to improve efficiency and effectiveness of much of their work. Unfortunately, the same process has also led to some loss of knowledge, as contractors can lack the long-term local commitment that LGs have.

There is great diversity in LG capacity to acquire and use additional information. For instance, the capacity to gather and use environmental information is compromised throughout the Northern Territory, by LG poverty, combined with limited statutory powers. Litchfield Shire's lobbying of the Territory Government therefore remains constrained, since council lacks sufficient funds to initiate research into fundamental issues, such as the determination of drainage patterns affecting developments. And even when councils are well-informed, the SGs sensitivity to their demands is very low, and the institutional arrangements enable consistent favouring of developmental over environmental goals.

Inclusiveness

Inclusiveness of LG stakeholders in environmental decision making occurs with various levels of intensity and integrity. At times, LGs take steps to include a broad range of local and regional stakeholders in decision making. LGs views and issues are also variably included in the decisions made by other spheres of government. Inclusion of outsiders in LG processes enables both teaching and learning for all parties.

Learning about the issues that matter to other stakeholders, and incorporating them into the policy process perhaps has more integrity than any other form of inclusiveness. This was demonstrated in the South West Regional Planning process, in many regional waste management strategies, and in aspects of the implementation of the Queensland *Environmental Protection Act* 1994. Considerable time and effort is required to establish effective representative groups, and continue to involve them throughout policy development and implementation. A risk with these inclusive processes is that subsequent decisions, that fail to address the issues expressed by participants, can erode both trust and willingness to cooperate in future processes.

Inclusiveness that provides stakeholders with the understanding needed to accept legitimate reforms needs to be undertaken carefully. This is because intended outcomes can be elusive if pursued too quickly, or without sufficient respect. An example is provided by the initial solar building project at Kogarah, which failed to fully deliver on outcomes, because the developers were uncommitted to Council's environmental vision for the site. Kogarah learned from the experience, and has invested more time and effort into successive environmental initiatives, with better, although slower, outcomes.

Flexibility

Flexibility is demonstrated in most of the case studies, and is certainly a strong feature of LG NREM work. The resilience of key elements of the institution despite intense reform agendas is notable throughout the discussions in this paper. The reforms have tested LG flexibility, and in many cases have specifically aimed to increase it. There is certainly the chance that this aim runs counter to the simultaneous goals of other spheres, to increase consistency in Australian local governance.

Conclusions

LGs are key players in NREM in many ways, and their work cuts across most of the other institutional issues discussed in this volume. LGs proactively tackle many NREM issues, continue to be confronted with strong reform agendas, and are formally committed to adaptive responses. Fundamental resource shortages, the constant changes and outside influences and a range of other constraints, limit LG capacity to consistently and effectively deliver NREM outcomes. Yet there are many cases where LG initiatives have been visionary in reaching beyond statutory requirements in their NREM goals.

Further attempts to encourage LG adaptation for NREM purposes must be considered in relation to the stresses of the already changing setting of this institution. Institutional changes to improve LG delivery of NREM goals have the greatest chance of success if they win the support of ALGA and the State LGAs, provide clear local benefits over the long-and short-term, and reinforce rather than undermine existing successful programs. Such initiatives would necessarily provide LGs with the necessary statutory, financial and other resources necessary to get the job done.

References

AHC (Australian Heritage Commission), 1998, *Protecting local heritage places: a guide for communities*, Canberra: AHC.

ALGA (Australian Local Government Association), 1997, *Regional environmental indicators project: environmental indicators for reporting at local, state and national levels*, Canberra: ALGA.

ALGA (Australian Local Government Association), 1998a, *1998 National agenda for Australian local government*, Canberra: ALGA.

ALGA (Australian Local Government Association), 1998b, *Working out agreements with Indigenous Australians*, Canberra: ALGA.

ANZECC (Australian and New Zealand Environment and Conservation Council) (1992), *Australian water quality guidelines*, Canberra: ANZECC.

Berndt, RM, and Berndt, CH, 1977, The world of the first Australians (first published in 1964), Sydney: Ure Smith.

Berwick, M, (1997), Mike Berwick, Mayor of Douglas Shire Council, Interviewed by Su Wild River, unpublished, 9 September 1997.

Berwick, M, and Thorman, R, 1999, *National local government biodiversity strategy*, Canberra: ALGA in conjunction with Biological Diversity Council.

Bradby, K, and Pearce, D, 1997, *South west environmental strategy*: South West Western Australian Local Government Association, Bunbury.

Brown, V, 1994, *Turning the tide: integrated local area management for Australia's coastal zone*, Canberra: Department of the Environment, Sport and Territories,

Bruce, J, 1988, *The new planning system in Victoria*, Melbourne: The Law Book Company.

CEPA (Commonwealth Environmental Protection Agency), 1992, *National waste minimisation and recycling strategy*, Canberra: AGPS.

Chapman, R, 1997, 'Intergovernmental relations', in Marshall, N, and Dollery, B, *Australian local government: reform and renewal*, pp, 40-68, Melbourne: Macmillan Education Australia.

CofA (Commonwealth of Australia) (1996), *Commonwealth competitive neutrality policy statement*, Canberra: AGPS.

C of A, 1999, *Environment Australia Annual Report, 1998-99*, Canberra: AGPS.

CofA/ALGA (Commonwealth of Australia/Australian Local Government Association), 1995, *Commonwealth-local government accord*, Canberra: CofA.

Conacher, A and Conacher, J, 2000, *Environmental planning and management in Australia*, Oxford University Press: Melbourne.

Cotter, B and Hannan, K, 1999, *Our community our future: a guide to Local Agenda 21*, Melbourne: Environs Australia.

CPDP (Cleaner Production Demonstration Project, by Dames and Moore) (1997), *Cleaner production manual: environment and business profiting from cleaner production*, Canberra: Environment Australia.

Cripps, E, Binning, C, and Young, M, 1999, *Opportunity denied: review of the ability of local governments to conserve native vegetation*, Canberra: CSIRO Wildlife and Ecology.

Osmond and Ray, 1996, *Attending to the environment: a manual for contract specifications*, Melbourne: Environs Australia.

Environs (Environs Australia) (1999), *Our community our future: a guide to Local Agenda 21*, Melbourne: Environs Australia and Environment Australia.

ESDSC (Ecological Sustainable Development Steering Committee) (1992), *National strategy for ecologically sustainable development*, Canberra: AGPS.

Fletcher, C, 1998, *Grounds for agreement: evaluating responses of Northern Territory governments to the Aboriginal Land Rights (NT) Act 1976*, Canberra and Darwin: Australian National University.

GHD (Gutteridge Haskins & Davey Pty Ltd), 1997, *Douglas Shire draft tourism strategy*, Cairns: Gutteridge Haskins & Davey Pty Ltd, Douglas Shire Council.

Healey, K (ed), 1996, *Waste management: managing waste disposal, exporting toxic waste, packaging and pollution, recycling and minimising waste*, Sydney: The Spinney Press.

Heath, I, 1999, *Choosing and using environmental indicators*, Canberra: Australian Local Government Association.

Hill, A, and Kyle, L, 1999, *A documentation of the environmentally sustainable principles and practices used in the Moreland Civic Centre Redevelopment Project: Stage 1 – Coburg Offices*, Melbourne: Moreland City Council.

Hill, M, (1999), Mike Hill, Victorian Local Governance Association, Interview by Su Wild River, Unpublished, Melbourne: November 1998.

HoG (Heads of Government), 1992, *Intergovernmental agreement on the environment*, Canberra: Heads of Governments of Australia.

IMM (Institute of Municipal Management), 1995, *Code of ethics*, Melbourne: IMM.

Information Australia (2000), *Australian local government guide, 28th Edition, July 2000-November 2000*, Melbourne: Information Australia.

Kogarah (Kogarah Municipal Council), 1998, *1998 State of the environment report*, Sydney: KMC.

LGANT (Local Government Association of the Northern Territory), 1998, *Fact sheet: local government in the Northern Territory: a summary*, Darwin: LGANT.

LGAQ (Local Government Association of Queensland), 1997, *Local government development program – optimising the provision of local government infrastructure and services*, Brisbane: LGAQ.

LGTCQ (Local Government Training Council of Queensland), 1994, *The councillor handbook: a guide to local government in Queensland*, Brisbane: Terry Coman & Associates Pty Ltd.

Litchfield Times, 1998, 'Wealthy sheik buys all outer Darwin', August 6, pp 1, 3.

LSP (Local Sustainability Project), 1996, *Getting ahead of the game*, Canberra: Centre for Resource and Environmental Studies.

Mabo v Queensland (No 1) (1988) 166 CLR 186.

Maiden, H,E, 1966, *The history of local government in New South Wales*, Sydney: Angus and Robertson.

MCA (Municipal Conservation Association of Victoria), 1989, *How to save energy in local government*, Melbourne: MCA.

McNeill, J, (1997), 'Local government in the Australian federal system', in Dollery, B, and Neil, M, (eds), *Australian local government: reform and renewal*, pp 17-39, Melbourne: Macmillan Education Australia.

NOLG (National Office of Local Government, Commonwealth of Australia), 1996-97, *Local government national report: report on the operation of the Local Government (Financial Assistance Act) 1995*, Canberra: NOLG.

NSWSWAC (New South Wales State Waste Advisory Council), 1997, *State Waste Advisory Council 1996-97 Report*, Sydney: NSWSWAC.

NT Govt (Northern Territory Government) (2000), *Community information about the local government directory, Northern Territory government*, Darwin: NT Govt.

Pathways 1997, *The Newcastle declaration*, World Executive Committee, ICLEI (International Committee for Local Environmental Initiatives), Australian Local Government Association, Lord Mayor of Newcastle, Newcastle: Pathways to sustainability conference, June 1997.

Phillips, B, 1998, *Building controls – the role of local government: maintaining standards – the role of local government, in building controls, the role of local government*, pp 17-26, VLGA, 6 April 1998, Melbourne: Victorian Local Governance Association,

Playford, N, (1997), Councillor Noel Playford, ex-Mayor, Noosa Shire Council, interviewed by Su Wild River, Unpublished, Melbourne: May 1997,

Power, J, Wettenall, R, and Halligan, J, 1981, Overview of local government in Australia, In: Power, J, Wettenall, R, and Halligan, J (eds), *Local government systems of Australia*, pp,1-121, Brisbane: Australian Government Publishing Service.

QDLGP (Queensland Department of Local Government and Planning, Incorporating Rural Communities), 1996, *Material personal interests: guidelines for councillors*, Brisbane: QDEH.

QG (Queensland Government), 1996, *National competition policy and Queensland local government*, Brisbane: QG.

QG/LGAQ (Queensland Department of Local Government and Planning, Incorporating Rural Communities; Local Government Association of Queensland), 1997, *A protocol establishing roles and responsibilities of the state government and local government in the Queensland system of local government*, Brisbane: QG.

RAMP (Remote Area Management Project), 1997, *Remote area management project*, Darwin: RAMP.

RCC (Regional Coordination Committee, South East Queensland 2001), 1995, *South East Queensland regional framework for growth management 1995*, Brisbane: SEQ2001.

Rumley, H, and Rumley, D, 1987, *Aborigines and local government in the East Kimberley*, Canberra: Centre for Resource and Environmental Studies.

Searle, R, 2000, *Australian Bureau of Statistics taxation revenue Australia 1999-2000*, Canberra: Commonwealth Grants Commission.

Sherwood, J, 1998, John Sherwood, previous Executive Officer, South West (WA) Local Government Association, interviewed by Su Wild River, unpublished: December 1998.

Standards Australia, 1996, *ISO 14001: 1996 – Environmental management systems – specifications with guidance for use*, Sydney: Standards Australia.

Stirling (Stirling City Council). 1998, *'Case' for the 1998 recycling and waste reduction awards*, Perth.

Sulman, JJ, 1921, Town planning in Australia, Cited in Conacher, A, and Conacher, J, 2000, *Environmental planning and management in Australia*, Melbourne: Oxford University Press, p 111.

Taper, B, 1999, Bruce Taper, Kogarah Municipal Council, Interviewed by Su Wild River, unpublished, Sydney: December 1999.

Trewin, D, 2000, *Environmental expenditure: local government Australia 1998-1999*, Canberra: Australian Bureau of Statistics.

Trewin, D, 2001, *Australia's environment: issues and trends*, Canberra: Australian Bureau of Statistics.

Vince, A, 1997, 'Amalgamations', in Dollery, B, and Marshall, N (eds), *Australian local government: reform and renewal*, pp 151-171, Melbourne: Macmillan Education Australia.

WADLG (Western Australian Department of Local Government), 1997, *Comparative indicators for Western Australian local governments*, Perth: WADLG.

Wensing, E, 1997), 'The process of local government reform: legislative change in the states', in Marshall, N and Dollery, B, *Australian local government, reform and renewal*, pp,89-102, Melbourne: Macmillan Education Australia.

Whittaker, S, 1996, 'Are local councils 'willing and able' to implement Local Agenda 21?' Keynote paper at *Sustainability & Local Environments: Myths, Models & Milestones*, Environs Australia National Conference, Sydney: November 28-29.

Wik Peoples v Queensland (1996) 187 CLR 1.

Wild River, S, Hahn, L,, Cunningham, R, Miller, G, Renouf, G, Brown, T, Donnelly, C, McNevin, B, Stanmore, E and Dickson, M, 1998, *Statewide benchmarking study into environmental and other impacts of the Queensland Environmental Protection Act 1994 for environmentally relevant activities: technical report on benchmarking issues for administering authorities*, Report to Queensland Department of Environment, Canberra/Brisbane: Australian National University/Mary Maher & Associates.

Williams, S, 1989, How to save energy in local government, Melbourne: Municipal Conservation Association.

Wood, G, 1998, Gerry Wood, President Litchfield Shire Council, interview by Su Wild River, unpublished: October 1998.

15

Marketisation in Australian Freshwater and Fisheries Management Regimes

Jennifer McKay[1]

Professor of Business Law, School of International Business, Director, Water Policy and Law Group, University of South Australia

Since 1788, water and other resources in Australia have been viewed as a subset of the economy and those inputs have been exploited in pursuit of economic growth and social objectives such as settlement. Indeed, water was seen as the *Magic Pudding* (Lindsay 1918), the agent to exploit the land and develop it. However, we now know that the land could not sustain the application of the water and annual supply was also extremely variable. Many State and federal governments and major NGOs such as the Australian Conservation Foundation and National Farmers Federation have spent the past two decades actively reviewing this and looking at ways to improve land and water resources management regimes. This has been prompted by mounting evidence of unsustainable resource use regimes, community pressure, poor returns on labour and investment in rural communities, expanding cities, and international obligations. The community has been alerted to problems such as salinity, algal blooms and depletion of fish stocks. A recent solution promoted has been the use of the market to give incentives to rural and urban communities to value land and water resources by imposing a regime which at least in name attempts 'full cost recovery' and involves the private sector in the provision of some services. These marketisation policies in water and fisheries aim to encourage greater economic efficiency in water use to move water to higher value uses and to encourage better management of the resources by fishers (eg, Parliament of Victoria 2001).

Australia has thus moved from a simple but flawed scheme where each State allocated water, often at no cost and with no regard for the environmental impact, to a more sophisticated a water property rights allocation regime. On the spectrum below there has been movement from the first to the later schemes (after Rolf 1993):

- Unregulated exploitation leading to the tragedy of the commons;
- Single purpose economic development projects from public resources under regimes granting user rights based on very poor information;
- Once user rights were possessed, then to control externalities when either user groups or the public call for regulation;

---

1   This work is dedicated to Karen Stediford, 1956-2000.

- To moderate market shifts, when market pressure requires one group to be protected, this can be producer protection, consumer protection, industry protection or environmental protection; and

- Evolve a sustainable allocation policy based on a comprehensive inventory of natural resources with perhaps some withdrawal of pre-existing rights from groups in some areas or at least an assessment of the land capability.

Some progress is being made toward the final stage as a fully-evolved scheme which looks at economic, environmental and social issues. The progress has been to enact laws which require the triple-bottom line view but there is a great need to improve the institutional arrangements which are impeding the implementation (Jones et al 2001). The last section of this chapter proposes an improved regulatory model for water management. Many of the present impediments are related to the ethos of the institutions and the lack of cooperation over State borders, the lack of broad community consultation in decisions, the susceptibility of local polities to groups with vested interests derived from past allocation policies, and the anachronistic focus on short term issues with no consideration of inter-generational equity. A way to progress water management in Australia would be to insist that States create template water legislation and share data.

Australian water and fisheries policies in relation to marketisation will be reviewed in this chapter. The focus is the period since 1995 for freshwater and since 1990 for fisheries. The lessons learnt show that there is still a dearth of *ex ante* and *ex post facto* studies on the functioning and costs of markets as incorporated in the regulatory changes. There is still considerable uncertainty as to how to weigh up ideals in laws, which now demand a complex array of issues (see Figure 15.1) be considered and which also now place some groups in direct conflict. Most past water resource development projects were uni-dimensional: such as power supply or irrigation. However, these projects must become multi-purpose and the community has – for example, in the campaign to return environmental flows to the Snowy River – demonstrated that it will not necessarily support only singular uses of water resources. There are additional issues of definitions of key concepts in markets and in law, and the application of trade practices law to these new markets. Finally, there are some special elements of community resources such as fisheries and water, which are looming as issues for the future especially with regard to Indigenous rights and climate change.

Hence, marketisation is only one element of the ultimate movement from the unsustainable practices of the initial allocation of these resources (the first dot point above) into the other phases. Market models impose their own level of regulatory complexity, and past experience with corporate regulation in Australia has demonstrated a weakness in compliance monitoring (Grabosky and Braithwaite 1986). Full regulatory monitoring (the *ex post facto* studies) must be commissioned and implemented to inform the development of the best possible system given the complexities and uncertainties above.

Rural and urban water resource institutions and management approaches pre-CoAG and Hilmer

From 1788 to the present, Australian States created water bodies each of which became very powerful (eg, Powell 2000). The bodies held a prime position in the development of each State as the body which allocated water. The bodies were, in the earliest days, granted powers under the common law of England but eventually these were added to by licensing powers to grant water to non-riparians and powers over the drilling of wells. Colonial governments were not obliged to consider Indigenous rights to the land or water as Australia was deemed to be settled with no pre-existing system of law; *terra nullius*. This was despite the fact that there was evidence of water holes being managed and protected by tribes as increase sites and that complicated ecological wedges were created in rivers to share the bounty (Callicott 1994).

Figure 15.1 provides a summary visual representation of the relative complexity of Australian water resource policy and law over time, derived from the literature on water policy regimes in Australia and research on this topic over the last 20 years. From fine-scale Indigenous management regimes, through various colonial and post-Federation consolidations and decay of regimes defined by singular goals, we are now in a position where Australian water resources management regimes are the most complex they have ever been.

Figure 15.1. Relative complexity of SE Australian water resource development policies

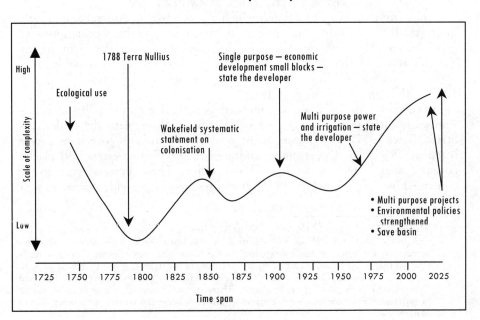

This is a result of the wider and more openly competing interests currently active in the sector. In particular, environment, social and cultural (ie, non-economic) issues are now much more relevant than at any time in the past. That increasing complexity demands sophisticated and sustained attention to ongoing policy monitoring and improvement, which in turn can benefit from an appreciation of past trajectories of policy change.

The common law was relied on from the time of Caucasian settlement to Federation and up to 1992 when the *Mabo* case[2] overturned the notion of *terra nullius*. The common law of England applied to water and this had three different types of rules. There were rules for the use of water flowing in a watercourse (Riparian doctrine), rules for the use and collection of water falling on private land, and very underdeveloped common law rules for groundwater. The riparian system required that the downstream user of water in a water course was entitled to receive water sensibly undiminished in quantity or quality. The upstream user has the right to use water for ordinary stock purposes and for domestic purposes. As irrigation developed after 1900 and Australia entered a drier phase, the riparian doctrine was superseded by statutory schemes, which gave non-riparians access to water. In each State there has been litigation to determine if the schemes superseded the riparian doctrine. Nevertheless, the statutory schemes and the body administering them became the order of the day. In relation to water falling on land, persons were free to confine it both under the common law and under the schemes. It is only recently that laws attempt to impose State control and ownership over such water, for example, the Victorian *Water Act* 1989 and the South Australian *Water Resources Act* 1997. In SA, the landowner can only build a dam in a surface water prescribed area with a licence.

The common law of England, which was received in Australia, had little understanding of aridity and hence the need to use the vast amount of groundwater. The common law gave the overlying owner the right to use groundwater and this was unlimited with no concept of 'reasonable user' applied.[3] Australia led England in requiring the doctrine of reasonable user in 1962[4] with England following in 1994.[5]

Federation in 1901 was a contested issue and eventual political compromises resulted in the power over water still remaining with the underlying States (Bates 1987). The powers of the new Commonwealth government were listed in s 51 of the Constitution and are broad with numerous (39) placita covering such topics as trade and commerce. These powers were to be construed liberally (Crawford 1991). It was because of the wide powers in s 51

---

2   *Mabo v State of Queensland* (1992) 107 ALR 1. This case overturned the notion that the indigenous inhabitants did not have a settled law and hence the land was *terra nullius*. Upon settlement, the common law was applied to the territory as was relevant. The case really decided that native title was part of the common law of Australia as it had been held to be in other jurisdictions ie, Canada. Native title rights to fisheries and freshwater as well as land were covered in the subsequent legislation. There is much evidence to suggest native use of fisheries and water courses and the question will be if these can co-exist with other uses of those resources.

3   *Ballard v Tomlinson* [1884] 2 ChD 194.

4   *Gartner v Kidman* (1962) 108 CLR 12.

5   *Cambridge Water Co Ltd v Eastern Counties PLC* [1994] 1 All ER 53.

that a prohibition over Commonwealth power was inserted to protect the rights of the residents of the States to the reasonable use of rivers for conservation or irrigation. Section 100 was inserted because NSW, Victoria and South Australia feared Commonwealth laws under s 51 may affect their common interest in water for irrigation.[6] After Federation, each State went its separate way in developing water resources.

Over the next 90 years, a competitive and certainly introspective system of allocating water for rural use evolved, in which each State has a complex pattern involving a history of partisan political negotiations and interest groups (Hallows and Thompson 1999). Each State created its own agencies, often dividing it into rural and urban and each agency evolved a unique allocation, pricing, sharing and administrative system. For example, in NSW it is still possible to carry forward unused water from an irrigation allocation into another year. In Victoria this is not possible, the rule being 'use it or lose it' (Bjornlund and McKay 1998). Indeed, water was regarded as the meta-phorical 'Magic Pudding', a children's story character Albert created by Norman Lindsay in 1918.[7] Water was first seen on the eastern seaboard to be in abundance and when exploration revealed the drier inland regions, dams were built to render it in abundance. This was driven by the single focus policy of economic development with little appreciation of the impact of irrigation on the soils. Hence, the water pudding could always be augmented and it was believed the pudding would never deteriorate no matter how much was used.

Dam construction is in many ways an index of water resources institutions and management techniques in Australia. 'The first large dam in Australia was built in 1858 to supply Sydney. It is now honoured as an Engineering landmark dam and as a ... monument to the origins of water resources development in Australia' (Broughton 1999: iii). In 1900 the combined storage capacity of all large dams was $0.25km^3$; by 1950 this was $9.51km^3$ and by 1990 the total was $78.92km^3$. Almost 90 per cent of that capacity were constructed since 1950 and between 1960 to 1989 saw 75 per cent of construction, with the real peak between 1970-79 (Broughton 1999). The water industry in 1990 was thus one of Australia's largest with assets valued at over $90 billion in replacement cost terms with about half of this in rural areas (Productivity Commission 1999). The Commission stated that water has been often poorly managed, misused and overexploited and, drawing on the National Competition Council Annual Report, went on to say that environmental degradation and its associated economic and social costs are particular problems in this sector. The National Land and Water Resources Audit estimated that the loss of production due to salinity is $137 billion annually and the loss of capital value of land is $700 million annually (NLWRA 2001: 122). At present 2.5 million acres or 4.5 per cent of

---

6   Lane's Commentary on the Australian Constitution, 1986, LBC, p 853.
7   The Magic Pudding was inexhaustible and enjoyed being eaten – 'eat away, chew away, munch and bolt and guzzle, Never leave the table 'til you're full up to the muzzle'. The pudding was prone to run away but also was likely to be stolen. The custodians had to keep careful watch over it. The changes to water allocation policies provoked by the environmental aspects of the COAG reforms are seen by some as stealing the magic pudding.

cultivated land is affected and up to 15 million acres could be affected. The impacts on native vegetation and wildlife are profound.

Up to the 1970s, water resource laws of each State promoted irrigation developments in inland Australia to develop and populate the land. The settlers were commonly migrants from Europe or soldier settlers from both world wars. Hence, the State governments were purposeful in developing the water resources and schemes and all the planning decisions as to location were left to them. The Commonwealth funded works to help some of these schemes, such as the hydro-power scheme in the Snowy Mountains in the 1940s. In 1978 the tide had turned and the Commonwealth, under the *National Water Resources Financial Assistance Act*, provided funding to conserve water, manage water quality, and promote desalination and flood mitigation. The *Natural Resources Management Act 1992* widened the range of eligible activities to include an integrated approach to management of land, water, soil and vegetation. However, powerful State government departments had continued to divert rivers and go far afield to build dams to ensure water supply. This process was stable and created a water resource history in Australia which until recently was not marred by major water quality issues. However, in the 1970s, the Senate noted that large scale irrigation can result in major salinity problems as on the Murray River which was then identified as 'one of the biggest water pollution problems facing Australia' (Senate Select Committee 1970).

The development of Australian water resources has never been a steady process, but one marked by failures and successes of a physical, environmental, technological, institutional or political kind (Johnson and Rix 1993). These authors described the post war to 1990 experience in water resource management agencies in three phases (p 182):

- extensive capital development;
- confusion, or 'muddling through'; and
- intensive capital development.

In the past two decades community attitudes have changed, as evidenced in the Landcare movement with 4200 groups forming and undertaking actions such as fencing off river banks to reduce erosion and improve water quality. Indeed, community involvement and partnership in the various Natural Heritage Trust funding schemes set the agenda for natural resources management not only in rural Australia, but urban Australia as well in programs such as Coastcare. However, it must be recognised that there is a huge information and knowledge deficit in understanding of natural systems such as of the effects on rivers of agricultural and pastoral activities, or urban activities such as watering gardens with potable water. So actions by individuals are based on mistaken or incomplete understanding of their effects and government policies were cited as having perverse effects (Industry Commission 1997: 98).

Core theme analysis of pre-COAG arrangements — freshwater

Persistence of the institutions

A State government who has sole power in this arena created each water body above. Each water authority was a major instrument of social change through allocation of irrigated farmlands to settlers. A prime argument for the substantial post-1995 reforms described above was that the monolithic 'statutory authority' model was rigid and had not responded to emerging imperatives of environment and economic efficiency. Institutions can be too persistent.

Information richness and sensitivity

The information available to State water resources bodies has never been particularly rich and they have not always been sensitive to it. Part of the reason lies with the inexact nature of riparian and groundwater hydrology and of meteorology, and the short duration and patchiness of records. In drought years when attention became highly focused, monitoring stations were set up but later abolished (see Smith, this volume). In addition, in the early soldier settler schemes it was perceived that there was plenty of rainfall, and there was competition between the States for the spoils of Commonwealth sponsored schemes. The Commonwealth established the Australian Water Resources Council (AWRC) in 1962 to make a comprehensive assessment and to extend measurement and research to provide a sound basis for planning of developments. AWRC created a system of national indicators for drainage basins and stream gauging stations.

It is hard to have information richness when there are multiple government departments involved in management of resources. For example, until recently in NSW the department responsible for operating stream gauging stations was different to the main developer departments. Water quantity gauging, however inadequate, has taken place since 1880 but water quality only since 1960. In Victoria, by World War II, stream gauging was still under-developed with problems in ensuring long term continuity of data – a problem still noted in the late 20th century (Powell 1999: 62). After the war, automatic gauging stations resulted in improved quantity data. In Victoria, like NSW the monitoring of water quality came much later with the rise of environmental concern in the 1970s.

Inclusiveness

The water institutions had a great deal of power but the health departments in each State had the power over water quality. This was despite there being considerable power in the Australian Constitution, at least since 1970, over issues of water pollution, enough to devise a national standard (Moeller and McKay 2000). So each State agency was not, and still is not, regulated on its quality assurance testing schemes and it different standards of water quality apply in different regions of the nation and notably poorer water quality is provided to some Aboriginal communities (HREOC 1997). This has been called environmental racism (see McKay and Moeller 2000). This has not been addressed in the market reforms and hence is a latent social justice issue for drinking water. This is despite support from water industry officials in Victoria for mandatory regulation (Moeller 2002). The irrigation authorities are obliged to provide water fit for the purpose under the common law and the *Trade Practices Act* 1974 (Cth). In NSW, the Water Administration Corporation was sued in 1999 for selling contaminated water to a potato farmer.[8]

Water resources institutions (with the exception of South Australia) did not invite much community consultation and there has always been some type of divide be it rural-urban, irrigation-town, local-central. In relation to environmental monitoring, in all States environmental protection regimes are a recent initiative (1960s or more often 1970s) and they have taken on the role of environmental protector. Victoria provides a good example. Groundwater was within the ambit of the powers of the State Rivers and Water Supply Commission (SRWSC), but in practice was governed by the Mines Department. Public anxiety over the disjointedness of water resources planning focused on the entrenched urban/rural divide of the Melbourne and Metropolitan Board of Works (MMBW) and the SRWSC. The unifying statute was the *Water Act* 1975 (Vic), which aimed to diminish administrative fragmentation and the reported chronic failure to ensure more direct forms of political accountability. The MMBW was brought under the control of the Minister of Water Supply, as was the case with the SRWSC. However, despite this, the legislation had no direct effect on the duties or functions of the two lead agencies or upon their long-standing power bases in the State. After a change of government, water reform in Victoria was achieved by the *Water Act* 1989 (Vic) which abolished the SRWSC and created the Rural Water Commission. In 1991, the RWC was replaced by five regional organisations and MMBW became Melbourne Water.

Flexibility

In all the States, the government departments have been flexible in producing rural development policies aimed at putting settlers on the land, and when farm sizes were shown to be too small, new policies and processes allowing consolidation were developed. These resulted in 'home maintenance areas' with farms of 200-250 hectares. Policies were changed: for example, in 1925 new construction in the Murrumbidgee Irrigation Area was curtailed and farmers could buy rather than lease the land. So there was flexibility within this predominant purpose but the time lags involved were considerable. Generally, in the pre-1970s, there was not the flexibility to consider other issues in relation to the development of water such as environmental concerns.

---

8   *Punteriero v Water Administration Ministerial Corporation NSW* [1999] HCA 45.

The Council of Australian Governments' marketisation reforms in the global context

Australia has been part of a global trend in the past two decades, which has seen over 75,000 former State-owned companies in 100 countries privatised or corporatised (Nellis 1999: 16-19). This trend has often been supported by rhetoric rather than considered study (eg, Havrylyshyn and McGettigan 1999). The casual empirical observations – that is, rarely based on reported studies – of the IMF suggest that in industrial and middle income countries, privatisation leads to improved performance of divested companies and that privately owned firms outperform State owned enterprises. However, the costs of corporatising a natural monopoly such as water are those of market failure. Market failure in water may take these forms:

- competition failure, price abuse and unfair practices;
- monopolism and abuse of market dominance;
- risk to public health by changes to performance standards and by the requirement of third party access to pipes;
- environmental failure in not promoting ecologically sustainable development;
- scant consideration of social welfare and equity considerations; and
- regulatory and monitoring failure through inadequate funding and/or corruption.

Hence, the key to success of natural resources regulation is sound administrative policy-making and enforcement capacities of government. Where these do not exist, privatisation leads to stagnation and decapitalisation, through capture of the resources in the hands of a few. With natural resources laws, the same problems could arise in relation to monitoring of volumetric allocations and use of water if the system proposed by the States requires it (discussed below).

The *Trade Practices Act* 1974 (Cth) heralded a new era in the development of competition reform in Australia (National Competition Council 1999). A Commonwealth statute, it provided for the first time that Australia is one market, rather than a series of markets delineated by State borders. At that time it was a hotly contested piece of legislation, especially the consumer protection provisions which provided rules to limit the abuse of market power by businesses. Despite this innovation, by the late 1980s and early 1990s it had become clear that a more coordinated and balanced approach to government reform was required.[9]

After a series of inquiries, including those by the Industry Commission in 1990 and 1992, the Council of Australian Governments (COAG) agreed to implement the National Competition Policy Package. This requires some form of water market to be developed in each State and offers payments to the

---

9   The earliest government micro-economic reforms took place in the agricultural sector where the government abolished a number of support measures in 1973 and manufacturing and trade reform took place in the same year with a 25 per cent cut in tariffs

States in the form of incentives. For Victoria, the payment in 1999-2000 totals $152.2 million (Marsden Jacobs 2000: 6). One of the impetuses for the reforms was the finding by the Industry Commission (1990) that water industries had rate of return on capital invested as low as 1.5 per cent per annum in 1987-88. The Commission called for major institutional change and pricing reform, tradable water entitlements, and permanent and inter-sectoral water transfers between groundwater and surface water in all irrigation systems. Shortly thereafter, the Industry Commission (1992) repeated this call, and recommended the introduction of Tradable Water Entitlements in particular permanent and intersectoral transfers for ground-water and surface water in all irrigation systems.

The reforms in the National Competition Policy (NCP) below apply to the water industry, and changed every aspect of the operations of the various bodies. The reforms on government owned enterprises were to prompt:

- independent oversight of prices;[10]
- competitive neutrality;
- structural reform; and
- third party access to infrastructure.[11]

The actions were targeted to achieve an efficient and sustainable water industry were incorporated in the NCP agenda (National Competition Council 1998: 103-9). These were to corporatise the sector; that is, create Government Business Enterprises and create these policies:

- introduce consumption-based pricing and full cost recovery;
- implement a Conduct Code Agreement so that water businesses adhere to the Competition laws Pt IV of the *Trade Practices Act* 1974.
- separate the roles of service provision from water resource management, standard setting and regulatory enforcement;
- provide that future investment in new rural schemes or extensions to existing schemes being undertaken only after appraisal suggests it is economically viable and ecologically sustainable;
- the development of a comprehensive system of water entitlements backed by separation of water property rights from land and clear specification in terms of volume, reliability and transferability;
- the implementation of integrated catchment management and water supply guidelines; and
- educating Australians about the need for water reform and consulting about the way reforms will be implemented.

In the first five years, the jurisdictions took some time to adopt the measures (McKay 2002b). By the end of 2001, all were compliant, but some had not exercised elements such as water markets in Western Australia. The Acts are still introspective with only Queensland stating that the aim is to manage

---

10   This incorporated extending the reach of the anti-competitive conduct provisions of Pt IV of the TPA to all public and private sector businesses.

11   The *Competition Reform Act* 1995 (Cth) inserts a new Pt IIIA into the *Trade Practices Act* 1974.

water for the benefit of the people of Australia, and only Queensland, NSW and Victoria consider Indigenous issues. The objects in each Act are broad, for example, in SA the objects provide the Minister must ensure that 'The physical, economic and social well being of the State and facilitate economic development of the State while protecting the entitlements of future genera-tions and ecosystems dependent on those resources'.[12] This onerous obligation is to be achieved through community-based water management plans being drafted by selected individuals and advising the Minister. The processes for the selection of representatives is open to the usual problems of local partici-patory democracy such as cynical manipulations of results to gain political legitimacy and lack of breadth of issues covered (Swanson 2001). In order the achieve the COAG aims it may prove necessary to add, to the all the Water Acts, procedures to ensure reliable hydrological, environmental, sociological and economic data are provided, training on the use of the data and a transparent process for appointments and review of the plans. In order to progress implementation, template legislation in every State would allow dialogue on more constructive topics than working out the different meanings across the Acts.

Case study of tradeable rural water entitlements

Three southern States had allowed trade in water rights for a few years before compulsion by COAG. South Australia introduced it in 1983, NSW in 1989 and Victoria in 1991. SA grafted this initiative onto conservative water allo-cation policies, Victoria on to less conservative policies and NSW into a situation were water has been grossly over-allocated. The reactions to the markets are summarised below:

- trading in rural water entitlements policy has resulted in huge quantities of sleeper (never used) and dozer (sometimes used) water licences being activated. This has negative environmental effects (McKay and Bjornlund 2001; personal communications, various water industry officials). Hence it appears that allocations will need to be reduced and existing irrigators will need to buy water. Many irrigators see this as an unfair income redistribution as they have to buy unused water from their neighbours. The cotton industry is aggrieved by this and has called for compensation (Land and Water News et al 2001);
- water trade has had the positive benefit of moving water away from some areas of poor soil and allowed growers to retire on the farm thus preserving rural communities; and
- the long-term social justice aspects of this trade are also poorly researched and it seems that water is being stockpiled[13] and the ACCC have launched a research project into this.

---

12   Section 5 of *Water Resources Act 1997* (SA).
13   Pers comm various water industry officials.

Case study: allocation of water for the environment

In SA, most water has been sold upstream and this has negative environmental effects as it reduces stream flows in the lower river thus increasing saline intrusion – the land upstream also has higher groundwater salinity levels. The State government has had in place a policy of requiring irrigation and drainage management plans. However, only 30 per cent of growers used these plans in their ongoing management,[14] a clear example of regulatory failure. In 2001 Environment Australia and the Natural Heritage Trust commissioned an independent report on environmental aspects of COAG reform in all States, especially their implementation, by Jones et al (2001). The results showed that implementation was patchy, slow and sometimes absent, there were poorly developed tools for ecological outcomes, and programs were underfunded. Other studies reported that progress was uneven across water use categories and between jurisdictions (Productivity Commission 1999: 134). Recently the public has become concerned about the issue of salinity to the point that there is a movement by Premiers in three States to accede to a National Water Policy on this issue (reported in *Australian Financial Review*, 4 April 2002: 4).

Case study: urban reform

Urban reform was well advanced with consumption-based charging, corporatisation of functions and contracting out. The Productivity Commission especially noted the contracting out of the management and operation of Adelaide's water supply to United Water. The Agreement for water reform set target dates of 1998 for the completion of the first group of reforms including structural separation of water supply functions, adoption of two-part tariffs for urban water and the implementation of a comprehensive system of water allocation. The NCP process did not require privatisation or contracting out and each State is taking a different path in reform – some may still privatise significant segments. For example, the Sydney Water Board was corporatised and its wholesale, retail and trading businesses separated. Melbourne Water was corporatised and divided into a headworks section, and three retail businesses. There has been a change in government in Victoria, with a new Labor Government reasserting in February 2000 that the State will remain the owner of all water businesses (The Hon S Garbutt, cited in Marsden Jacobs 2000). The ACT combined its electricity and water functions to gain economies of scale in administration maintenance and some capital. South Australia corporatised a body with statewide responsibility for its water resources and outsourced the management of its supply function for Adelaide (Fels 1999).

The average urban Australian household uses five swimming pools of potable water per year or about 250kl and in the nation 84 per cent of all water is from surface water, 15 per cent groundwater (mainly Perth) and less than 1 per cent desalination (SA Department of Water Resources 1999: 4). Only five utilities reported using recycled water and then only for non-potable

---

14   This judgment is based on data collected from a current Land & Water Australia-funded research project.

uses. Clearly, there is scope for demand management policies which are presently still not coordinated or pushed to the public. In Melbourne the three utilities all have good schemes in place but the competition between them seems to limit cooperation.

In relation to the urban sector, the Brotherhood of St Lawrence in Victoria noted impacts of the COAG reforms on lower income urban consumers (Don Siemon 2000). Siemon has noted that the price changes in Victoria to achieve marginal cost pricing since COAG are regressive, with the losers being tenants and larger lower income households, that there is no income support system available and such groups are more at risk of the cut-off of supply. Proposals have been floated to cap price rises to below CPI, to direct capital subsidies to particular localities and to restructure concessions, but no government response in Victoria has been noted.

Case study of a new utility and its regulatory model

The reforms have created hybrid bodies which are empowered under an Act to look like businesses but are subject to Ministerial control; a good example is Goulburn-Murray Water (GMW). This is a Statutory Authority with powers defined by the *Water Act* 1989 (Vic) and empowered by a Ministerial order under the Act (Goulburn-Murray Water 2000: 1). The duties of the all Victorian bodies are set out in the objects of the Act which are demanding in requiring functions to be performed in an environmentally sound way to plan for State and local community, for future needs and to educate the public. In doing so, GMW has nevertheless adopted commercial approaches of governance derived from Australian corporate law as it strives 'to manage its business in a way which is consistent with best practice in the private sector.' GMW has adopted the term Directors instead of the term members as listed in the *Water Act* and uses 'Board' rather than 'Authority'. This may be confusing to customers and the wider community as the whole concept of corporate governance in Australia is unclear. Even in the corporate sector it is unclear if it means shareholders and managers or all stakeholders (Hill 1999). Clearly, the Act requires the broadest possible interpretation. One issue is enforcement and the extent to which managers are liable. Clearly it will be hard to fine managers when the objects of the organisation are so wide and the means to achieve these objectives are poorly defined.

The Directors do have some comfort in an immunity for acts done in good faith under s 90. The GMW has been given other powers under the *Murray Darling Basin Act* 1993 (Vic) and is answerable to the Murray Darling Basin Commission on these powers and to the State government under s 40 of the *Water Act* on the other powers. GMW is obliged to exercise its functions within the framework of s 40 which is subject to preferred allocation policies and Ministerial direction. This scenario creates a potential conflict, yet the marketisation model requiring full cost recovery encourages the addition of extra lines of business to the portfolio of these organisations. To address the issue of conflict the Corporate Governance Manual requires the Board to be aware of such conflict and to deal with it with great care. Corporate planning is regulated by the *Water Act* which requires a plan for the next year to be submitted by 30 April setting out charges and tariffs. GMW has established a set of committees and delegated powers to them. Some of these have community representation.

Clearly a new model is needed rather than grafting new requirements onto an old model, and this is addressed in the next section.

Figure 15.2 Water government business enterprises as green enterprises

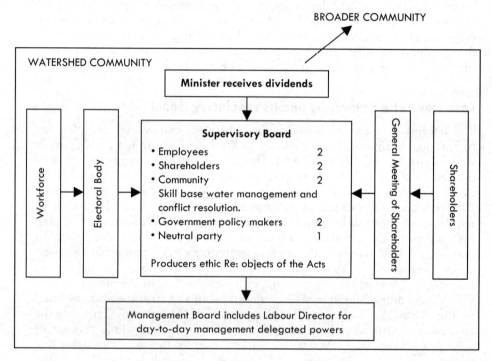

Adapted from Australia Reconstructed, 1997, Janicke & Weidner, Political Systems Capacity for Environmental Policy 1997.

Overall the COAG reforms have created hybrid bodies with inherent conflicts; for example, between encouraging demand management measures and revenue lost from such. The bodies at the present time do not have broad community representation as would be expected when trying to achieve the broad objectives. The regulatory model proposed Figure 15.2 may aid implementation of the reforms, including a nine member, representative board.

Issues in marketisation in Australian fisheries

Government involvement in regulating the fishing industry is commonplace in Australia, Canada and the US and is done to prevent overexploitation which has occurred in situations of unfettered access. Fisheries have a dimension of the tragedy of the commons problem. In Australia the reason for government intervention in the 'community fishing resource'[15] was to stop overcapitalisation and economic inefficiency and to promote sustainable practices. The current practices for Commonwealth fisheries management are found in the *Fisheries Management Act* 1991 (Cth) and *Fisheries Administration Act* 1991 (Cth) which recite three key objectives of optimum resource utilisation, maximum efficiency and ecologically sustainable development. These objectives are not mutually exclusive and hence subject to conflict.

Australian governments have employed various effort and output regulations, with effort controls giving way to output controls in recent years (Kaufman et al 1999: 9). In theory it has been regarded that regulating access by tradable property rights through individual transferable quotas provide the greatest likelihood for an efficient allocation assuming that the total allowable catch (TAC) is set optimally in relation to maximum economic yield (Kaufman et al 1999: 8). This system is well regarded and AFMA has been buying fishing permits because in the past policies have encouraged too many fishers and it is considered that the demand for fish could be met with fewer operators (F Meare, cited in Da Silva 1999). Individual transferable quota (ITQ) are a component of output controls where a share of the TAC is allocated to individual fishers. Hence, the incentive is for the fishers to harvest their quota as cost effectively as possible. If the quota is tradable then it is considered that there are further incentives to reduce over-capacity as less profitable fishers sell quota to more profitable ones. Potential problems with ITQ are: quota monitoring, data corruption, TAC setting, socio-economic impacts, highgrading and management costs (Kaufman et al 1999). With ITQ fishers have an incentive to not report catch and therefore it is important to have an effective regulation system in place or it degenerates into open access fishing. If this is the case, then fishers more likely to misrepresent catch and effort and costs and earnings data which impacts on stock assessments and socio-economic data. It has been stated that regulation is a device to transfer income to well-organised groups (Joskow and Noll 1981: 36). Transferability may be seen as unfair, as quota allocations only go to vessel owners and not crew. Transferability may also lead to the concentration of quota in a few large corporations and current fishers may capture all the gains with no long-run improvement in incomes of future fishers. In the South East trawl fishery, a recent study concluded that concentration of market power is not likely to be an impediment to trade but the potential still exists in other fisheries with different characteristics (Kaufman et al 1999: 9). Ecological, economic and social variability in context across different fisheries demand a context-sensitive regulatory and market design.

Governments use policies to allocate property rights and the method of allocation and the nature of the rights can create environmentally unsustainable practices and economic inefficiencies (Rolph 1983). This has been the case in fisheries in Australia under effort regulation in the past and now under ITQ because of the incentive for fishers to maximise the value of their catch within their quota by discarding small, damaged or low value fish.

---

15   The Australian Fisheries Management Authority uses this term to describe fisheries.

Discarding is a waste and if not accounted for can increase uncertainty surrounding stock and catch assessments.

The ITQ system in Commonwealth fisheries are administered by the Australian Fisheries Management Authority which does require that the full costs of information gathering on stock, and compliance programs be borne by the applicant (Cox and Kemp 1999). This is a good policy but open to the issues mentioned above. Despite this endorsement, when ITQs were introduced there was much controversy and litigation over the initial allocation of quota and this created uncertainty and a mistrust of government (Kaufman et al 1999: 159). ITQs operate in 20 fisheries in total in both Commonwealth and State managed areas, accounting for about one quarter of total landed tonnage in 1997-98.

The final issue with the marketisation in the South East trawl fishery is whether the quota market operates efficiently (Kaufman et al 1999). Leaving aside the TAC considerations, the market will probably be thin as there will be few operators in Australia and so fishers may need to rely on their own networks to get information. The fisheries authorities can remove some impediments to the market and it has been suggested that they publish information about quota holders and develop an electronic trading system. In short, it has been stated that trading of quota will not alone mitigate or eliminate discarding problems because fishers may over-catch their quota. Further policies, which introduce flexibility into the quota system, will be needed (Kaufman et al 1999: 138). Such policies could include options to lease or purchase additional quota, time to lease in quota, carry-over or carry-under provisions, quota substitution, deemed values (government pays a certain price) and surrender provisions.

Finally in the ITQ allocation process, periodic reviews were recommended to overcome ecological surprises, new technology and new information and to ensure efficient and equitable adaptation of existing conditions and management strategies (Young 1995).

Future issues and the core themes applied to post-COAG regulatory models in the water industry

The water reform process is only seven years old, but is a radical departure from the old processes. It has taken some time to adjust to the new factors, bodies and issues in water management of which the market reforms are but one component. Unfortunately the political process set the few goals in very broad terms and thus the legacy of the past is relevant. The past processes have been to divide up the resource; what is needed now is an integrative body (see Figure 15.2) which incorporates many stakeholders and aggregates decisions and makes transparent any conflicts. Neither social nor environmental justice are served in the allocation, nor the quality of drinking water and irrigation water, while each State implements its own complex patch work. States need to adopt a genuinely integrative model and some federal assistance must be given to balance the richer States that is, NSW, who are better able to aid their growers to adjust (McKay and Bjornlund 2001).

Perhaps the need for balance will eventually be reflected in template legislation to make the playing field level. There are other issues:

- the dearth of empirical evaluation studies of the reforms especially the adoption of community participation in local level water allocation plans;
- the potential misuse of market power by water buyers;
- the question of political will to regulate markets;
- the question of the will of the utility to instigate water recycling and support water efficient housing which ultimately reduce its own revenue base;
- customer pricing issues fairness and equity; and
- Indigenous issues.

On the issue of patchy evaluations it is still early days in the regulation of these former public utilities in Australia. The cooperative Utilities Regulators Forum made up of regulators operating in industries where former public monopolies existed published its first discussion paper in July 1999. The forum aims to share information working toward best practice in principle, processes and organisation of these utilities (Commonwealth of Australia 1999). The whole system is in evolution and thus deserves close monitoring.

In relation to misuse of market power, the head of the Australian Competition and Consumer Commission is on the public record as saying that any proposed mergers or acquisitions in the water industry will be examined closely under s 50 of the *Trade Practices Act* to determine if such an action would substantially lessen competition (Fels 1999: 5). In order to assess a merger then the ACCC needs to draw a boundary around the market and assess the level of competition. Presently, water markets are relatively small and fragmented and are very thin in the initial stages. New processes to consider in the water industry will include horizontal mergers between suppliers of the same goods and vertical mergers between successive activities within one production process. These have indeed happened already as discussed above. Vertical integration is a concern if concentration at one level of production can be utilised as market power in a successive level of production. The original architect of competition policy, Professor Fred Hilmer, wanted to separate out components of vertical production without natural monopoly characteristics and to encourage new entry. Hilmer assumed that competitive gains from keeping sequential activities separate outweigh the efficiency gains of vertical integration (*Hilmer Report* 1993). While this may work in most utility markets, for some water markets the efficiency losses of keeping activities separate may outweigh the gains. The question needs to be asked whether there much potential for competition, especially where the State based regimes differ.

The natural monopoly characteristics of water markets may continue to provide water suppliers with the discretion to achieve commercial objectives by exploiting pricing power. Hence, reform processes must adopt a pragmatic combination of pro-competitive measures and regulatory measures.

The third issue is the impact of political processes in the different States. For any of the water market regimes to work to provide for long-run economic and environmentally sound outcomes, regulations will need to be enforceable and enforced. So regimes requiring prudential checks on the buyers, the creation and implementation of whole farm management plans, and the evolution of water management plans in each State (through water allocation management plans) need to be monitored. Sometimes political perceptions can get in the way; for example, interstate trade has been going on between Victoria, NSW and SA for some time. In May 2000, the Victorian Minister terminated interstate trade in water between Victoria and SA and NSW because of the different ways each State has for managing water allocations. Victoria was concerned that the policy in NSW, which allows water to be carried forward from one season to the next, would put NSW irrigators in a position to make windfall gains. It was suggested that the NSW irrigators might acquire water cheaply from Victoria at the end of the season and carry it forward and make a windfall gain by selling the water in the next season (University of New England 2000: 17).

Finally Indigenous issues and native title rights to freshwater and to marine fisheries remain to be considered by the courts now that the pathway has opened up for co-existence of rights.

Core theme analysis of post-COAG arrangements-freshwater

Despite the rubric in all the Acts regarding triple bottom line management of water, this seems to be tasked to be achieved by a constrained set of organisations and not an overarching green enterprise as set out in Figure 15.2.

Persistence

The objects of the *Water Act 1989* as amended in Victoria refer to the COAG requirements specifically and the words sustainable and integrated management are used in the 'Purposes' section.[16] The Act looks to promote better management and an integrated approach to eliminate inconsistencies in the treatment of surface and groundwater and to involve the community in decision regarding the making, use and conservation of water modify existing bulk entitlement procedures. The other major Acts predate the COAG reforms, being the *Water Industry Act 1994*, the *Melbourne and Metropolitan Board of Works Act 1958* and the *Melbourne Water Corporation Act 1992*. The *Water Industry Act* disaggregated the previously integrated Melbourne Water, which had inherited some of the roles of the former and all powerful Melbourne and Metropolitan Board of Works (MMBW). Hence, there was has been a sense of persistence of an organisation in Melbourne and Melbourne Water inherited a unique closed catchment system set up in the early days of the State and has fewer problems than its counterparts in other

---

16   Section I of the *Water Act 1989* as amended.

States (Bartley 2000). Since 1995 there has been a change in government and a major review was completed in June 2000. The report specifically looks at water markets and the restrictions to trade – a lack of clear property rights with homogeneity as to title (Marsden Jacobs 2000: 55). The review highlights three issues. First, the bulk transfer rules which restrict the persons or bodies who can hold bulk entitlements. Second, the restraint on the rights of individuals to purchase water unless they hold land on which the water can be applied. Finally, the provisions in Regulations defining procedures to be followed for the approval of water trades which create an overall net cap on transfers between irrigation districts.[17] The review document makes the points that the water industry has natural monopoly characteristics, which prompt a role for central governments (Marsden Jacobs 2000). Hence it is expected that a strong body will emerge with perhaps some of the strength and persistence of its predecessors. The review invited public comment on these and other issues in 2000 and the Victorian Government will presumably consider these in constructing a new model. This rather narrow review does not address the other major issues, especially environmental sustainability.

The Queensland Water Reform Unit produced a five volume draft policy paper in October 1999 which reviewed the current legislative framework of the *Water Resources Act* 1989. It states that 'the present Act has narrow organisational and administrative arrangements' and is silent on any role for the private sector in the development and provision of water services (Queensland Office of Water Reform 1999: ii). In its place there is proposed a powerful body administering a wide remit including unbundling of water allocations and transfer independently from land. Transfers, which under the definition can be permanent or a lease, would need to comply with plans and may be limited in volume, geographical area and between sectors. Public comment is proposed on transfers and a water transfer register will be set up.

New South Wales has divided it rivers into categories of stress and has classified the security of water holdings for the market process. NSW has always had the aim to consolidate water management legislation and has attempted to create a new body with a wider power base. If all aspects are fully operational then water management in NSW will be by a radically different, not persistent set of institutions.

South Australia has a persistent and well-developed system of water allocation plans for prescribed areas, which have facilitated trading of water over the last 17 years. The *Water Resources Act* 1997 provides the power for the water allocation plans to be reviewed in accordance with the State Water Plan. So it is surmised that what ever happens politically this process will tend to continue creating a persistent regulatory presence.

Purposefulness

The purposefulness of regulation will be best examined over time. At present, all policies present a scheme involving the government as a central figure although only Victoria makes this explicit, with the review document stating

---

17   Water (Permanent Transfer of Water Rights) Regulations 1991.

that the State remains the owner of the water business. The long run will require an examination of the enforceability and the laws and the funding to ensure enforcement and therefore achievement of the environmental goals of any Acts .

The Queensland Act is purposeful in making water allocation decisions on the basis of basin-wide assessments, and through licences being converted into transferable water allocations. The allocations will be expressed volumetrically, specifying the location of the water and purpose of use. Water allocations will be transferable within the constraints set in the transfer rules, which will be in the broader plans and will not attach to land. A public register will be set up detailing encumbrances as it is aimed to facilitate financial institutions using these as collateral.

The Minister, in his statement as the preface of the New South Wales water reform White Paper, specifically mentions the need to clearly define and strengthen water rights, separate water from land title to facilitate trade and create more streamlined and transparent administrative processes

In Victoria, power at present remains fragmented between two major Acts. The first is the *Water Act* 1989 which provides for allocation of water and to create authorities to deliver services. The second is the *Water Industry Act* 1994 which creates a licensing regime for the delivery of water and sewage subject to oversight form the Office of the Regulator General. The *Water Act* has been amended many times since 1989 and, after COAG especially in the areas of interstate trade and the bulk entitlement rules. The bulk entitlement rules (s 34) are comprehensive and must be made on a prescribed form. The application must be advertised and a panel may be appointed to review it and advise the Minister. The panel has a wide remit to protect the environment and also to consider factors such as existing and projected availability and quality of water in the area and purpose for which the water will be used (s 40). The panel must consider submissions made to it and the conservation policy of the government – all in all, a series of conflicting considerations with heavy political overtones. Decisions are subject to appeals by a tribunal and the Supreme Court (s 64e). An application may be refused or approved subject to conditions including the volume of water being specified and accounted for. An authority holding a bulk entitlement may sell it with the approval of the Minister in whole or part by a variety of means, by auction, tender or any other manner it thinks fit (s 46). This is a broad provision, and on its face may create a shield behind which unconscionable dealings may occur.

South Australia, through the State Water Plan process, evidences purpose through attempting a balance between the COAG environmental and economic objectives in a way that involves the community in the plan. The hierarchy is the State Water Plan providing an overall policy framework for water allocation, and catchment water plans and water allocation plans providing regional and local foci. The plan must be updated every five years. In relation to trading, the State Water Plan has noted a number of issues in relation to trading and through the process above will examine and consult on these. The issues are pricing of water, secure property rights, cost-recovery mechanisms (including catchment levies), maximising use of infrastructure, and re-use of non traditional sources of water. In relation to pricing of water, the State Plan states that prices are considered to 'not reflect the true costs associated with water resources management and to not provide adequate signals and incentives to encourage efficient water use' (South Australia 1999: 66).

Information richness and sensitivity

Regarding the information base to support water allocations for the environment, it has been noted in 2001 that 'these are difficult and contentious issues, with many different interests and fairly poor information' (Jones et al 2001). This reflects the long-standing deficiencies in basic information streams in the water sector (see also Smith, this volume).

In Queensland, the information on water resources still suffers from a shortage of time series data and is inhibited by lack of records prior to 1945. The situation has, however, improved. For example, in Queensland the Office of Water Reform has identified the need to 'establish a transparent system of information collection and management to facilitate planning co-ordination' (Queensland Office of Water Reform 1999: ii).

Through its proposed water reforms, NSW aims to create a system where water planning will form a part of a broader natural resources planning framework, and to provide a one-stop shop for water use approvals. However, nowhere in the White Paper nor in the Act is there reference to the sources of supply of information vital to meet such aims. The operations of the system at present also suggest that information is still scarce (*Sydney Morning Herald* 2002). The Victorian Act requires information on environmental factors and prospective use to be considered, but seems to rely on other agencies to provide that information.

The SA State Water Plan recognises that information on who has water, how much they are using and the market price for transfer is essential to effective marketing. The government proposes to make information on water allocations and use readily accessible and encourage the emergence of water brokers and public water auctions. The State Water Plan addresses the need to gather environmental information and proposes that South Australia become a model for the collection of effective water resources information, knowledge gathering and synthesis, communication of information and application of knowledge (South Australia 1999: 72). This was started in 1998 under a multi-agency program, via a formal agreement to share collection and reporting of data. The information gathered looks at present and future issues, encompassing surface and ground water, quality, quantity, ecosystem health, and land-use planning. The government plans to make the information available to the broader community on the internet and to involve the public in the development of monitoring programs through the catchment water plans.

Inclusiveness

In modern Australia, an inclusive water marketing management institutional framework would need to be adaptive and to incorporate these factors:

- Indigenous representation – only three States do this Queensland, NSW and Victoria (McKay 2002a) and a definition of Indigenous rights (see ATSIC Lingairi Foundation 2002);

- environmental issues such as salinity, blue green algae and diffuse pollution from agricultural runoff, with methods to measure and evaluate the impacts of land use changes adequately funded;

- cost recovery but making trade-offs transparent and funding community service obligations;

- incorporation of private sector providers with the appropriate attention to corporate governance regimes to address the concerns in the community since the corporate excesses of the 1980s;

- consideration of intergenerational equity and sustainable livelihoods for the rural sector; and

- compensation when the past flawed allocation policies are changed to better reflect the above with explicit, transparent and equitable policies to provide compensation.

Most States in their new Acts cover most of these ideals in the objects clauses collectively. It is early days yet in the implementation of these difficult issues but clearly all these issues need to be considered to make the policies inclusive and much attention must be paid to the means to develop the institutions (see Figure 15.2) in order to achieve this.

All agencies in the four States are not inclusively run as the most senior Board in each case does not have a wide representation. In concert with COAG requirements, the Queensland Office of Water Reform policy paper cites that legislative provision needs to be made to (1999: ii):

Allow for the effective involvement of the private sector in the development of water infrastructure, particularly to provide reasonable investment certainty and in relation to the entry to private land to undertake feasibility studies and the acquisition of land for the development of infrastructure.

In NSW, the Minister for Land and Water is also the Minister for Agriculture. This is a common model throughout the history of the Australian States but such a conjunction of interests may not always be profitable for the concept of sustainable water management, as the Minister may be captured by the concept that water only has an agricultural value. If two Ministers were present – as in SA – any negotiations may proceed on a different basis. The NSW Act attempts to account for environmental flows, unlike the *Water Act* 1912 (NSW), however, the early implementation suggests that information is still poor (Jones et al 2001). Rivers and aquifers will be classified to prioritise action according to their level of environmental health and conservation value. The new system will incorporate community members to advise on water management and contribute to the making and amending of plans. All other works by other bodies, such as local government wanting to extract gravel, must be consistent with the water management plan (New South Wales 2000: 26). The EPA will oversee the auditing program to determine if the plans meet agreed environmental objectives. The plans will recite the present requirement that anyone wanting to transfer water for more than five years must have a property-based plan integrating water, soil and vegetation capabilities. Such plans will be required for any application and this approach will allow the cumulative aspects of proposals to be considered in the decision making process. Two rights to water will exist. One is a 'basic right' analogous to riparian rights, which will not require an approval. The volume can be limited to two megalitres per year for domestic consumption with an additional amount for stock based on land area and location. Existing dam owners subject to conditions will still be able to harvest 10 per cent of run-off. The 'privileged entitlement' will be subject to approval and will specify how much water can be taken where, when and at what rate. These are divisible and tradeable but will be divided into high, medium and low flow access in unregulated rivers, and general and high access for regulated rivers and ground-water. A water use approval will need to be obtained if the use is to be consistent with the sustainable capacity. These will be site specific and not tradeable.

Historically in Victoria, the three bodies involved in water resource planning have not had a harmonious relationship, with delays and Councils failing to refer subdivision applications to water authorities and allowing development in contravention of water policy as expressed in planning schemes such as buffer zones for water catchments (Bartley 2000: 199). In South Australia, the State Water Plan described earlier is more inclusive of public, private and community sectors.

Flexibility

The Queensland model requires the production of plans to establish a water supply framework. There are to be various types of plans depending on whether water is fully allocated in a catchment. The plans would aim to look into the future to consider 'possible developments over time'. Stewardship of the water resource including provisions for environmental requirements and the release of new allocations will remain a function of State government but administratively will include involvement of the public and private sector. All developments whether initiated by government or the private sector will need to show that they satisfy a genuine need and are economically viable and ecologically sustainable (Queensland Office of Water Reform 1999: iv).

The New South Wales Act was heralded as 'robust, but flexible' (New South Wales 2000: 5), as water management needs to be adaptive to address new issues, changing community expectations and have the ability to adapt to new technology. Different components of water entitlements will be able to be owned and traded separately and from one physical location to another. Transfer applications will be reviewed for potential environmental impacts and impacts on other water users. It will be possible to trade across different water sources within a unit (eg, groundwater and riverine). The government will also own and trade water.

In the *Water Act* 1989 (as amended) in Victoria, the Schedule to the *Act* lists the bulk entitlements of each water user. This is not a flexible way to provide information. The components of the decision making process in

Victoria incorporate flexibility, as there are many bases on which to support a decision. Such flexibility may be seen in the early days to create a 'kangaroo court' and until there are court determinations uncertainty may prevail. With regard to the bulk entitlement rules there are restrictions on persons or bodies as described in s 34 and restrictions on the rights of individuals to purchase water unless they hold land. These last restrictions are cited by Marsden Jacobs (2000) to exist in the administrative application of the legislation rather than in the Acts, and have been raised for comment in the review.

The SA State Water Plan proposed an adaptive management framework. The government has set in place a reporting cycle of performance of the policies, which provides a feedback loop to enable continuous improvement. It is still early days in the administration of the plan in SA so there has been no published review of performance.

Summary and conclusions

There are currently a number of unresolved and complicated policy ideas on the topic of Australian marketisation models in freshwater resources and also fisheries. The main thread of all of these is the lack of inclusiveness of policy that varies regionally (the States are still sovereign) or over issues such water quality or subsidies to promote structural adjustment.

The history of policy and legal development prior to the onset of marketisation in 1995 is crucial to understanding the present deficiencies with the marketisation models. That period included dramatic examples of resource over-exploitation, algal blooms, salinity and the ignoring of Indigenous interests in resources. To date, the four jurisdictions discussed have made different levels of progress in their rural and urban sectors. Clearly, ongoing, intensive policy monitoring and evaluation will be required.

From the data available it is possible to reach some conclusions. Allocation systems as existed in water and fisheries have created many negative externalities, especially over exploitation of the resource. This was partly because issues such as environmental sustainability were not on the agenda until many decades into the life of these regimes. Hence, in any new natural resource management policy the allocation mechanism could be useful but only if sustainabilty is built into the allocation of the quantum. The major problem with that as a policy is the scarcity of data and, as the fisheries case study shows, reporting to the resource manager by resource users can be negligently or deliberately misleading. In the water sector the problem is that the records of rainfall and streamflow and the behaviour of aquifers is still poorly understood. The Commonwealth and the States have made some moves and these will improve the situation in the long term. In this context, policies need to communicate the uncertainties to users and importantly have provisions to allow rebating of water or fish allocations. Tradable rights in water or fish are only partially *market* policy regimes, being utterly dependent in sustainability terms on, firstly, the setting of outer limits of exploitation (TAC limits in fisheries, total water extraction limits), which in turn is dependent on quality data and monitoring and, secondly, on the regulatory (legal) framework within which the market operates.

This raises the spectre of administrative law remedies (compensation) to changes in allocations or quotas. Maybe the judiciary needs to be educated in this regard, to temper the normal bias of judges to promote equity and the rights of users without due consideration of the condition of the resource. The clarity of expression of social and policy goals in statute law is important in this sense (see Bates, this volume). This needs to be improved and the methods to be used to achieve the triple bottom line goals of social, ecological and economic sustainability need to be examined. These requirements will generate a series of conflicts between sectors of the community that have hitherto been dormant.

There is considerable evidence from programs such as Landcare that the rural and urban community recognises the fragility of the environment and the interactions between uses of water. However, these reforms will probably reduce water allocations in some areas rather than giving money to support conservation works, hence the disputes will become focused on real choices between, say, ecotourism in the Snowy River and farmers (Bonyhady 2002). The four States discussed here have all grafted on to old ways of thinking the new requirements of economic, social and environmental sustainability. As yet there is little judicial guidance in how to balance these in a case situation where prior rights are affected.

Subject to the above, the elements of emerging water markets will need to be defined clearly, and especially the property right regimes. The inherent problems with Australian market schemes and their early implementation have been shown in the fisheries and the water context to be lack of information about market participants, thin markets and the erroneous belief that the pre-existing scheme gave users of the resources some rights. Many jurisdictions propose a public register system which may overcome the problem of poor information about market participants and monitor market behaviour. The monitoring needs to take place on a number of dimensions – environmental, social and economic – and this will require significant funding. The risks are too high in the modern world of natural resource management to allow for any regime to not be closely monitored and assessed. That is a clear lesson of the past water and fisheries regimes.

Acknowledgements

I am grateful for the assistance given to me by Paul Martin, Dr Anthony Moeller, Dr John Pisaniello, Goulburn Murray Water, Associate Professor Rick Sarre, Janet Matheson and Shelly Murphy. I also acknowledge the support of Land & Water Australia.

References

Aboriginal and Torres Strait Islander Commission and Lingairi Foundation ,2002, On shore water rights discussion booklet 1, Lingiari Foundation, Broome WA, PO BOX 1375.

Bartley, M, 2000, Interagency cooperation for the achievement of policy outcomes: integrated catchment management in Victoria, In: Vince, A, and Moin, G, (eds), *Proceedings, 1st Australian Natural Resources Law and Policy Conference: Focus on Water*, March, Canberra.

Bates, G, 1987, *Environmental law in Australia*, 2nd edn, Sydney: Butterworths.

Bjornlund, H, and McKay, J, 1998, Overcoming the introspective legacy of tradeable water entitlement policies in South Eastern Australia, In: Just, R, and Netanyahu, S (eds), *Conflict and cooperation in transboundary water resources*, pp 316-30, Dordrecht: Kluwer.

Bonyhady, T, 2002, *Sydney Morning Herald*, 20 May.

Broughton, W (ed), 1999, *A century of water resources development in Australia, 1900-1999*, Canberra: Institution of Engineers Australia.

Callicott, JB, 1994, *A multicultural survey of ecological ethics from the Mediterranean to the Australian outback*, Berkeley: University of California Press.

Commonwealth of Australia, 1999, *Best practice utility regulation: discussion paper*, Canberra.

Cox, A, and Kemp, A, 1999, *Efficient access right regimes for exploratory and developmental fisheries*, ABARE Conference paper 99:35, Canberra: Australian Bureau of Agricultural and Resource Economics.

Crawford, J, 1991, The Constitution and the environment, 13 *Sydney Law Review* 13-15.

Da Silva, D, 1999, Net loss, *Australian Financial Review*, 26 November: 62.

Don Siemon, 2000, Consumer aspects of water utility privatisation, Paper to workshop session, Xth World Water Congress, Melbourne.

Fels, A, 1999, Recent developments in competition policy: the impact on water and wastewater industries, Speech, 8 October, <www.accc.gov.au>.

Goulburn-Murray Water, 2000, *Corporate governance manual*, Tatura Victoria: GMW.

Grabosky, P, and Braithwaite, J, 1986, *Of manners gentle: enforcement strategies of Australia business regulatory agencies*, Melbourne: Oxford University Press.

Hallows, P,J, and Thompson, D,G, 1999, *The history of irrigation in Australia*, First Mildura Irrigation Trust,: Australian National Committee on Irrigation and Drainage.

Havrylyshyn, O, and McGettigan, D, 1999, *Privatisation in transition economies: lessons from the first decade*, Geneva: International Monetary Fund.

Hill, J, 1999, Deconstructing Sunbeam: contemporary issues in corporate governance, *Company and Security Law Journal*, 17: 288-302.

Hilmer Report 1993, Independent Committee of Inquiry into Competition Policy in Australia, *National Competition Policy*, Australian Government Publishing Service, Canberra.

Human Rights and Equal Opportunity Commission, 1997, *Face the facts: some questions and answers about immigration, refugees and indigenous affairs*, Canberra: Dept of Immigration.

Industry Commission, 1990, *Measuring the performance of selected government enterprises*, Canberra: Australian Government Publishing Service.

Industry Commission, 1992, *Water resources and waste water disposal*, Canberra: Australian Government Publishing Service.

Industry Commission, 1998, A full repairing lease: inquiry into ecologically sustainable land management, Canberra: Australian Government Publishing Service.

Johnson, M, and Rix, S (eds), 1993, Water in Australia: managing economic, environmental and community reform, Sydney: Pluto Press.

Joskow, PL and Noll, RG, 1981, Regulation in theory and practice: an overview, In: Fromm, G (ed), Studies in public regulation, Cambridge MA: MIT Press.

Jones, G, Whittington, J, McKay, J, Arthington, A, Lawrence, I, Cartwright, S, and Cullen, P, 2001, Independent jurisdictional reports on the achievements of the COAG water reforms, Canberra: Cooperative Research Centre for Freshwater Ecology.

Kaufman, B, Geen, G, and Sen, S, 1999, Fisheries futures: individual transferable quotas in fisheries, Canberra: Fisheries Research and Development Corporation.

Land and Water News and Whyatt, S, and Murphy, K, 2001, Liquid gold, Australian Financial Review, 28 August: 2.

Lindsay, N, 1918 The magic pudding; being the adventures of Bunyip Bluegum and his friends Bill Barnacle and Sam Sawnoff, Sydney: Angus and Robertson.

Marsden Jacobs, 2000, NCP review of legislation: issues paper, Canberra: Australian Government Publishing Service.

McKay, J, 2002a, Legal issues in water resources planning regimes – lessons from Australia, In: Brennan, D, (ed), Water policy reform: lessons from Asia and Australia, Australian Centre for International Agricultural Research Proceedings no 106, pp 48-62, Canberra: ACIAR.

McKay J, 2002b, Onshore water rights briefing paper, Background briefing papers indigenous rights to waters, Lingairi Foundation, Broome ,WA.

McKay, J and Bjornlund, H, 2001, Market mechanisms as a component of environmetal policy that can make choices between sustainability and social justice, Social Justice Research, 14, 304-317.

McKay, JM and Moeller, A, 2000, Statutory regulation of water quality in modern Australia: has it been forgotten by the regulators? Water International, 25: 595-609.

Moeller, A and McKay, J,M, 2000, Is there power in the Australian Constitution to make federal laws for water quality? Environmental and Planning Law Journal, 17: 294-307.

Moeller A, 2002, Thesis PhD University of SA Best Practice in drinking water quality regulation- elements of an Australian model.

National Competition Council, 1998, Compendium of national competition policy agreements, Canberra: NCC.

National Competition Council, 1999, National Competition Council: some impacts on society and the economy, Canberra: NCC.

National Land and Water Resources Audit, 2001, Agricultural assessment 2001, Natural Heritage Trust, Land & Water Australia on behalf of the Commonwealth of Australia, Canberra, Atlas at <www.nlwra.gov.au/atlas>.

Nellis, J, 1999, Time to rethink privatisation in transition economies? Geneva: International Monetary Fund.

New South Wales, 2000, Water reform: a proposal for updated and consolidated water management legislation for NSW, Government of NSW.

Parliament of Victoria, Environment and Natural Resources Committee, 2001, Inquiry into the allocation of water resources, Melbourne: Government Printer.

Powell, JM, 1999,Victoria chapter in Broughton (ed)1999, A century of water resources development in Australia, 1900-1999, Canberra: Institution of Engineers Australia.

Powell, JM, 2000, Snakes and cannons: water management and the geographical imagination in Australia, In: Dovers, S (ed), Environmental history and policy: still settling Australia, Melbourne: Oxford University Press.

Productivity Commission, 1999, The impact of competition policy reforms on rural and regional Australia, Canberra: Australian Government Publishing Service.

Queensland Office of Water Reform, 1999, Water reform consultation papers various volumes, Brisbane.

Rolph, E, 1983, Government allocation of property rights: who gets what? *Journal of Policy Analysis and Management*, 3: 45-61.

Senate Select Committee on Water Pollution, 1970, *Water pollution in Australia*, Canberra: Australian Government Publishing Service.

South Australia, 1999, *Water Plan of South Australia: policies for a sustainable future, Draft for discussion*, Department for water Resources, Government of SA

South Australia, Department of Water Resources, 1999, *Water pricing in SA: discussion paper*, Adelaide: The Department, For water Resources

Sydney Morning Herald, 2002, Ten years on Mabo gets wet, 3 June, <http://www.smh.com.au/articles/2002/06/02 1022982650280.html>

Swanson, LE, 2001, Rural policy and direct local participatory democracy: inclusiveness, collection action and locality based policy, *Rural Sociology*, 86: 1-21.

University of New England, 2000, *Water Policy Newsletter*, vol 10: 17.

Young, MD, 1995, The design of fishing rights systems: the NSW experience, *Ocean and Coastal Management*, 28: 45-61.

PART V

PEOPLE, POLICY AND PROGRAMS

16

Catchment Management Arrangements

Sarah Ewing

Centre for Environmental Applied Hydrology, Department of Civil and Environmental Engineering, University of Melbourne

Each month in Victoria, the Board of the North-Central Catchment Management Authority (NCCMA) meets to coordinate the implementation of its regional catchment strategy. The Board is made up of nine community members, with skills and experience in land protection, water resource management, primary industry, conservation, local government and industry. Since its formation in 1997, the CMA has had two main roles: the development of strategic objectives and priorities for catchment management; and the management of all waterways, floodplains and regional drainage in the area. The example of the NCCMA is repeated in eight other CMAs across the State which, together, encompass all of rural Victoria. In turn, these CMAs are just one example of a range of regional frameworks in place for integrated catchment management in Australia.

Integrated catchment management (ICM) is one of several terms describing regional, holistic approaches to environmental decision-making; similar terms include integrated environmental management and integrated resource management (Margerum 1999; Born and Sonzogni 1995). These concepts have emerged in response to three major concerns: first, for a more holistic model of how the resource system works and is sustained; second, for greater 'bottom up' participation in resource decisions; and third, for greater diversity in participation in decision-making and in the range of outputs sought (Burch 1999).

ICM is being advocated in many countries throughout the world. In Canada, regional bodies have had a long history of involvement in catchment planning and management (Shrubsole 1990). In Ontario, for example, there are 38 catchment-based conservation authorities, which have been in place since 1946, involving partnerships between the provincial and municipal governments (Shrubsole 1996). More recently, in Europe, initiatives in the UK and France have laid the basis for integrated catchment planning (Buller 1996; Edwards-Jones 1997; Gardiner 1997). In Australia, New South Wales, Victoria, Queensland and Western Australia have explicit policies or legislation in place to integrate management across catchments. And, in the Murray-Darling Basin, the Ministerial Council has now committed member states to ICM (MDBMC 2001).

What is ICM ?

Integrated catchment management can be contemplated in several ways. Syme et al (1994), for example, refer to it variously as a philosophy, a process and a product. ICM as *philosophy* refers to the need to foster an organisational culture, in which cooperation and collaboration are central; as *process*, it refers to cooperation between government and community; and as *product*, it refers to the development of catchment plans and their implementation. Fitzpatrick (1992) describes it as 'a method of managing the interaction of a range of forces', of which there are never less than three: nature, land users and government agencies. And the Australian Water Resources Council (AWRC) (1988: xii, 30) refers to ICM as a tool which allows for 'consideration of diverse interests and values', the proper achievement of which is favoured by devolution of power 'from higher organisation to competent lower organisation'.

This chapter sketches the institutional arrangements and processes in place for ICM in Australia, and considers the extent to which they support long-term, adaptive capacities. The imperative of this review derives from two observations. First, while there has been considerable discussion about the substance of ICM (what it is), there has been rather less on the matter of how it is put into effect. As Mitchell and Hollick (1993: 737) observe, 'Intuitively, most people can relate to the basic idea, but it is difficult to translate it into operational terms'. Secondly, we have limited understanding of the extent to which the institutional arrangements in place have served to make collective action possible. Their influence on problem solving is critical to an understanding of the barriers to adaptive change (Aley et al 1999; Miller 1999). In designing institutional arrangements for ICM it is not enough to consider just our knowledge of biology or hydrology. The promise of ICM embodied in the various strategies and processes described here cannot be realised unless we also consider the science of human organisation and the conditions best suited to adaptive environmental learning. This requires considerations of persistence, flexibility, information-sharing and a need for inclusive and participatory approaches (Lee 1992; Lee 1993).

ICM in Australia

In Australia, catchment management, particularly the control of erosion and the retention of forest cover, has been a topic of considerable discussion for more than a century (Burton 1992). Through the latter half of the 19th century, there was substantial public concern about the possibilities of severe erosion from the frantic timber clearing and excavation proceeding on the goldfields. During the first half of the 20th century, broader issues of land use control and catchment management came to the fore and in several States, specific entities were established to address problems such as flooding, drainage and water supply. The Hunter Valley Conservation Trust, established in 1950, is the first example of an authority established, specifically, to coordinate the management of land and water resources across an entire catchment (Burton 1992). Enthusiasm for the concept of integrated catchment management emerged in the early 1980s (AWRC 1988) and stemmed broadly from concern about: the continuing and increasing degradation of land and water resources; the lack of an integrated and coordinated approach to the problem; and increasing public expectations for involvement in decision making (Syme et al 1994). Nowadays, the rhetoric of ICM places great emphasis on the building of 'partnerships' between community and government.

In June 1999, the House of Representatives Standing Committee on Environment and Heritage initiated an inquiry into catchment management, prompted by continuing concern for the management of Australia's water resources. One element of the inquiry addressed the role of different levels of government in catchment management (HRSCEH 2000). In addition, several States have recently undertaken, or are planning reviews of, institutional arrangements and processes in ICM. For the purpose here, discussion is confined to a brief account of arrangements in Victoria, New South Wales, Queensland and Western Australia.

ICM in Victoria

Historically, in Victoria, the timing of initiatives to tackle catchment management issues has reflected the priorities of the day; for example, the *Thistle Act* 1856 was followed by the *Rabbit Suppression Act* in the 1870s and a Sand Drift Committee in the 1930s (Thompson 1981). By the 1960s, the development of cooperative projects with groups of farmers, rather than individuals, was becoming an important feature of Victoria's effort to tackle land degradation. The State's Soil Conservation Authority had a number of group projects in place, some long enough to demonstrate a community benefit beyond that enjoyed by the participating landholders.

The advent of Landcare in 1986 is arguably the most significant development in catchment management in Victoria in recent times. It heralded a significant shift in Victoria's approach to land and water management, marked by an increasing emphasis on the community and government working together to solve problems, using an integrated, whole-of-system approach (Ewing 1999). There was concern, however, that land and water management was still inadequately linked, that community consultative processes were inefficient and that the regulatory framework was inconsistent, narrow and inflexible. A case was put for legislative reform which led, finally, to the passage of the *Catchment and Land Protection Act* 1994 (Vic). Under the Act, a regional Catchment and Land Protection Board (CALP Board) was established, in each of ten Catchment and Land Protection Regions covering the State.

One of two specific functions of the CALP Boards was to develop a Regional Catchment Strategy, building on extensive planning already under-taken for Landcare, salinity and water quality. Over a period of two years, ten Regional Catchment Strategies were developed and these are now recognised as the over-arching strategy for development, management and conservation of land and water resources in each region. The other key function of each Board was to provide advice on federal funding programs and State priorities for action in its region. The Act also provided for the appointment of a statewide

Council to advise Government on matters relating to catchment management and land protection, on the condition of the State's land and water resources and on the statewide priorities to be given to catchment and land protection programs.

In 1997, the nine non-metropolitan CALP Boards were replaced by nine Catchment Management Authorities (CMAs) and the statewide Council was replaced by a slimmer Catchment Management Council. This was prompted by concern that in order for regional strategies to be implemented, regional bodies with effective decision-making powers were needed (Catchment Management Structures Working Party 1996). Unlike their predecessors, the CMAs have a role in service delivery, particularly through the direct provision of waterway and floodplain-related activities and in the negotiation of works programs with government agencies (Table 16.1). To provide for continuity of pre-existing waterway, water quality, salinity and regional development bodies, each Authority has established 'Implementation Committees'. These committees, organised on the basis of sub-catchment or issue, are responsible for the development and implementation of detailed works programs and the overseeing of on-ground delivery. They are appointed by, and report to, the Authority Boards.

Table 16.1. Summary of ICM arrangements in Victoria

Key ICM policy tools	Objective	ICM structures	Functions
Victoria Catchment and Land Protection Act 1994; Catchment and Land Protection (Amendment) Act 1998.	The stated goal of catchment management in Victoria is 'to ensure the sustainable development of natural resource-based industries, the protection of land and water resources and the conservation of natural and cultural heritage' (Department of Natural Resources and Environment 1997).	State: Victorian Catchment Management Council (VCMC) (10 community members, 1 agency representative; skill-based; appointed by the relevant Minister). Regional: Catchment Management Authorities (CMAs) (x 9) in non-metropolitan areas (nine members; skill-based, though between them, Board members are expected to have experience and knowledge of land, waterway and floodplain management; primary production; conservation; finance; and local government; appointed by the relevant Minister); Catchment and Land Protection Board for the Port Phillip metropolitan area (status as a CMA yet to be resolved).	The VCMC advises the Minister(s) on matters relating to catchment management and land protection; the condition of land and water in the State; and statewide priorities for catchment management and land protection programs.

In partnership with government, CMAs are responsible for further development and implementation of regional catchment strategies. They also have a role in service delivery, particularly through the direct provision of waterway and floodplain-related activities and in the negotiation of works programs with government agencies |

ICM in New South Wales (NSW)

Not unlike Victoria, catchment management in NSW has developed progressively from the single discipline, single agency approach of 50 years ago. Catchment management principles were institutionalised in the Hunter Valley Conservation Trust in 1950 and were also evident in the charter of other organisations, such as the Ministry of Conservation (established 1944), which had responsibility for coordination of the State's soil, water and forest resources (Martin et al 1992; Verhoeven 1997a). In 1987, a State policy for Total Catchment Management (TCM) was released. In general, it required the NSW government to 'ensure the coordinated use and management of land, water, vegetation and other natural resources on a catchment basis' (Soil Conservation Service of NSW 1987: 6). TCM was to be achieved by:

- establishing better coordinating mechanisms;
- facilitating the development of TCM strategies;
- requiring consideration of TCM and its strategies in the environmental planning processes of the State; and
- fostering the involvement and participation of the community (Martin et al 1992: 188).

TCM was formalised with the introduction of the *Catchment Management Act* 1989, to 'implement total catchment management of natural resources'. The Act provided for the establishment of a State Catchment Management Coordinating Committee (SCMCC) and a network of regional Catchment Management Committees (CMCs) and Trusts to coordinate TCM at the catchment level. This involved the bringing together of authorities, groups or individuals to ensure effective total catchment management; it did not, however, include *control* or *direction* of same.

By 1996, considerable effort and financial resources had been invested in TCM by the community and Government, and a stocktake was called for. A review found that strategies prepared by CMCs had been valuable but often unable to address the causes of major natural resource problems. In addition, CMCs had been limited in their capacity to ensure that the strategies were implemented (Department of Land and Water Conservation, 1997; Verhoeven 1997b). About this time, there was also growing concern about the plethora of community-led natural resource committees around the State which, in combination, were placing considerable strain on the limited number of skilled people, available and willing to contribute to them. During 1999, the SCMCC led a review on the number of committees and their functions, the upshot of which was that 43 Catchment Management Committees (CMCs) and five Regional Catchment Committees (RCCs) were replaced with 18 new Catchment Management Boards (Department of Land and Water Conservation 1999) (Table 16.2). The new Boards, which came into effect in May 2000, are established under the both the *Catchment Management Act* and the Catchment Management Regulation 1999. Like their predecessors, they have no legislated powers. The new Boards do, however, have a more focused role to develop plans for catchments and to strengthen links to local groups, such as Landcare groups (Bellamy et al 2002).

Table 16.2. Summary of ICM arrangements in NSW

Key ICM policy tools	Objective	ICM structures	Functions
New South Wales *Catchment Management Act 1989; Catchment Management Regulation 1999.*	The *Act* seeks to implement 'total catchment management of natural resources'. Total Catchment Management is defined as 'the coordinated and sustainable use and management of land, water, vegetation and other natural resources on a water catchment basis so as to balance resource utilisation and conservation' (Verhoeven 1997a).	*State:* State Catchment Management Coordinating Committee (SCMCC) (20 representative members; including representatives of CMBs, 'rural interests', local government, environment and government agencies. Chairperson nominated by the relevant Minister; no statutory power). *Regional:* Catchment Management Boards (CMBs) (x 18); Members of CMBs are appointed by the Minister, from nominations provided by relevant groups. The new Board structure (effective 2000), adds Indigenous interests to the previous membership of government agencies, business interests, local government and environmental interests (Bellamy *et al.* 2002). Catchment Management Trusts (CMTs) (x 3), authorised by CMT-specific regulations under the *Act.* Membership is as for CMCs. Regional Catchment Committees (RCCs) (x5) are not constituted under the *Act* but operate under the direction of the SCMCC.	The SCMCC provides Ministerial advice on policy issues and manages programs and the establishment of State priorities. It provides a central coordinating mechanism for the purpose of TCM throughout NSW (Bellamy et al 2002). CMBs oversee and coordinate natural resource management activities at a regional or catchment level. In their first year, each Board was to produce the 'key components' of a draft Catchment Management Plan. CMTs differ from Boards in having fund raising and financial administration capacities (Bellamy *et al.* 2002). RCCs were first established by the SCMCC to operate for the 98/99 funding year for the purpose of developing regional NREM strategies and submitting regional funding proposals for 99/00 to the State Assessment Panel (Dore 1999). They are now subcommittees of the SCMCC (Bellamy *et al.* 2002). Also, specific natural resources are being managed through 70 floodplain and coastal management committees, 22 water management committees and 15 regional vegetation committees (Department of Land and Water Conservation 1999).

ICM in Queensland

According to Reeve (1988), land degradation did not become a popular concern in Queensland until the early 1940s. The government made its first legislative response in 1941, in the enactment of the Burdekin River Trust Bill, which was designed to reduce river erosion with river improvement works. By the mid-1950s, following similar moves in Victoria and NSW, planning at group and catchment levels was occurring (Hocking 1960). During the 1970s, community-based District Advisory Committees were formed in declared areas of Soil Erosion Hazard to advise the Government on matters of planning and implementation and to provide local leadership in coordination of activities. However, with much of their energy expended on unsuccessful policy recommendations, the Committees gradually lost impetus and were disbanded in 1986 (Keith and Roberts 1992).

The Queensland government initiated an ICM program in 1990, apparently in response to renewed community interest in a catchment-based approach (Department of Primary Industries 1993). The following year, an ICM Strategy was released with the purpose of integrating the management of 'land, water and related biological resources in order to achieve the sustainable and balanced use of these resources' (Queensland Government 1991). According to Rowland and Begbie (1997), the strategy was a mix of the approaches then being taken in Western Australia and NSW. Initially, the ICM program focused on five pilot study areas, each of which involved the establishment of a Catchment Coordinating Committee (CCC), supported by a catchment coordinator employed by the (then) Department of Primary Industries. The pilot studies differed in the way in which their committees formed and operated, but the approaches used were consistent with the overall framework proposed in the strategy. Experience gained in the pilot studies has helped inform the implementation of ICM in other catchments (see for example, Johnson et al 1996).

The strategy provided for the establishment of Catchment Coordinating Committees (CCC). CCCs do not have statutory decision-making powers and their decisions are not legally binding, but formation and membership of CCCs are subject to approval by the relevant Minister. Typically, CCCs include representatives of the main sectors of the community and government; however, the nature of CCC membership is not prescribed and this is reflected in the different make-up of these groups across the State. Their key roles are 'to provide a forum for community input and discussion, to identify and prioritise complex land and water resource issues in the catchment and to develop catchment management strategies' (Queensland Government 1991) (Table 16.3). There are now over 30 CCCs (now called Catchment Management Associations) operating in Queensland. In addition, there are 13 Regional Strategy groups, which develop regional natural resource management strategies (HRSCEH 2000). These groups have formed in response to Natural Heritage Trust federal/ State partnership agreements.

Table 16.3. Summary of ICM arrangements in Queensland

Key ICM policy tools	Objective	ICM structures	Functions
Queensland ICM strategy 1991 (Queensland Government 1991).	The purpose of the Strategy is 'to integrate the management of land, water and related biological resources in order to achieve the sustainable and balanced use of these resources' (Queensland Government 1991).	*State:* Landcare and Catchment Management Council (LCMC); is approved by, and reports directly to, the Minister. Comprised of representatives of peak industry, government and community sectors, with an interest in the management and use of natural resources (Queensland Government 1991). *Regional:* Catchment Management Associations (CMAs) (formerly known as Catchment Coordinating Committees, CCCs) (x ~ 30); membership is not prescribed but formation and make-up is subject to approval by the relevant Minister; formed only when strong Government and community support; no statutory decision-making powers and decisions not legally binding; as a condition of their formation, CMAs are assisted by a catchment coordinator. Regional Strategy Groups (RSGs) (x ~13); comprised of key stakeholder interests; community-led; formally endorsed by the Queensland Government on the recommendation of the LCMC (Dore 1999).	The LCMC provides advice to Government on the development and coordination of the ICM program, Landcare and Natural Heritage Trust (NHT) initiatives in Queensland. The CMAs' key roles are to provide a forum for community input and discussion and to develop and implement catchment management strategies (supported by DNRM) (Department of Natural Resources and Mines 2001a). RSGs have formed primarily to facilitate development of regional approaches to natural resources management as per NHT Federal/State partnership agreements (Dore 1999).

The strategy also provided for the establishment of a State Catchment Management Coordinating Committee (CMCC) to oversee and guide the whole ICM program. One of the Committee's early tasks was to address confusion over the relative roles of catchment care groups and Landcare groups in the new framework. The CMCC was, itself, subject to the same confusion and later merged with the Queensland Landcare Council, to form the Landcare and Catchment Management Council (LCMC). The new Council advises not only on ICM but also Landcare and the direction and operation of Natural Heritage Trust (NHT) initiatives in Queensland.

Specifically, the LCMC has the task of advising government on the merit of strategies developed by Regional Strategy Groups (Dore 1999).

There remains no direct legislative base for the ICM framework in Queensland though, at the time of writing, the State government has been investigating this possibility.

ICM in Western Australia

In Western Australia, land management at the regional level has, for many years, been facilitated through designated Land Conservation Districts, of which there are roughly 150 covering most of the State. An amendment to the *Soil and Land Conservation Act* 1945, provides for a District to be established where a group of land users make such a request of the Minister for Agriculture. The applicants determine the boundary and, as a result, Districts range vastly in size, from small areas addressing acute problems to whole shires. When a District is formed, the Minister appoints a Committee (LCDC) to represent the interests of landholders, producer groups, local government and conservation groups. LCDCs are active in sharing information and perform an administrative function for Landcare (Robertson 1989).

Western Australia established its first State government policy to guide ICM in 1987; entitled *Working Together*, it was published in 1989 (Government of Western Australia 1989). The policy's emphasis was not on the establishment of new institutions but, rather, on the more effective coordination and strengthening of existing State authorities and legal arrangements. ICM was described as an 'umbrella' policy, 'pulling together and streamlining activities carried out by local government and a number of State government agencies' and providing opportunity for community involvement. Unlike other States, WA chose to adopt a less structured approach, preferring instead to allow for the development of 'flexible community-based structures suitable for regional and local circumstances' (Thurlow and Hamilton 1997). A review of ICM in 1991 concluded that ICM as a State policy must be given legitimacy and credibility through explicit political, administrative and financial commitment. Specifically, it was recommended that the State government should publicly endorse ICM, release a revised ICM policy and direct CEOs of State agencies to include ICM as a key component in their corporate plans and programs (Mitchell 1991).

Now, rather than ICM, the preferred policy framework in WA is regional and sub-regional natural resource management (NRM) (Government of Western Australia nd). Within this, the concept and principles of ICM have been endorsed as the primary means of NRM. The Western Australian government defines ICM as 'the co-ordinated planning, use and management of water, land, vegetation and other natural resources on a river or groundwater catchment basis'. The aim of Western Australian ICM is to 'bring all stakeholders together to form a plan of action that addresses social, economic and ecologic concerns within a catchment' (HRSCEH 2000: 33). No single group or agency has overall responsibility for catchment management and there is no legislation that provides a total framework.

The WA government is developing a State natural resource management framework policy that will include as a key element, the development and implementation of regional strategic plans (State Salinity Council 2000: 26). It is underpinned by a wide range of Acts and a range of government agencies, statutory bodies, policies and regional structures. These include non-statutory advisory boards such as the State Salinity Council; strategies such as the Salinity Strategy and the State Planning Strategy; and five regional NRM bodies (Table 16.4).

Table 16.4. Summary of ICM arrangements in Western Australia

Key ICM policy tools	Objective	ICM structures	Functions
Western Australia ICM policy document *Working Together* 1989 (Government of Western Australia 1989).	*Working Together* suggests that ICM be seen as an 'umbrella' policy, pulling together and streamlining activities carried out by local government and a number of State government agencies and providing opportunity for community involvement (Government of Western Australia 1989).	*State:* State Salinity Council (non-statutory); Soil and Land Conservation Council, peak Landcare body for WA, established under the *Soil and Land Conservation Act* 1945. Regional NRM Chairs group (non-statutory). *Regional:* Regional NRM organisations (non-statutory) eg, South Coast Regional Initiative Planning Team. Members are nominated by relevant interest groups and organisations, such as sub-regional groups, local government and State agencies. *Sub-regional:* Sub-regional NRM organisations (non-statutory) eg, Blackwood Basin Group. Land Conservation District Committees (LCDCs). Established under a 1982 Amendment to the *Soil and Land Conservation Act* 1945.	SSC coordinates advice and recommendations to a Cabinet Standing Committee on policy development and priorities for salinity management and on implementation and performance of the salinity strategy. SLCC provides policy and advice to government on the conservation, sustainability and improvement of soil and land resources. Regional NRM organisations coordinate efforts between smaller, more localised sub-regional groups, develop priorities and secure resources. LCDCs variously define problems, plan and implement projects, encourage land conservation and establish standards for land management.

Discussion

As the previous discussion has showed, there exist several different models for ICM arrangements in Australia, though familiar themes such as participation, coordination, and decentralisation are common to all. The tradition of adaptive management (AM) suggests the imperative of policy-as-experiment, or learning-by-doing. In this sense, we might be encouraged by the range of ICM experiments in place; indeed, as Goodin (1996: 42) has argued, 'we ought embrace as a central principle of design a desire for variability in our institutional arrangements'. This is a necessary but not sufficient condition for AM. We need also to be disciplined in seeking to learn from the experience of different arrangements. In the sections which follow, attention turns to an analysis of the adaptive capacities of existing arrangements for ICM in Australia.

Inclusiveness

ICM in Australia is dependent upon the coordinated activity of a variety of groups with particular values and motives. It is critical, therefore, that institutions designed to support ICM are sensitive to this motivational complexity. Typically, the response has been to establish regional advisory bodies, with the objective of involving local people with local knowledge and experience in land and water management. Ideas of inclusiveness and community participation mobilised in ICM policy, suggest that finding a social and spatially-based catchment community is unproblematic and that a boundary can be drawn to mark its beginning and end. But, experience has shown that the definition of catchments in purely physical terms, may work against effective ICM (Syme et al 1994). If landholders do not identify with a 'catchment community', the collaboration and support that is required for ICM will be difficult to get. Even the physical logic of a catchment comes unstuck where there is no coordinated drainage. Across much of the rangelands, for example, where water flows are infrequent and episodic, planning and management may be better related to land systems or socio-economically-defined systems. For this reason, in Queensland, it is envisaged that, rather than a uniform blanket of catchment-defined regions, there may be a 'patchwork' of different arrangements in different parts of the State to suit varying levels of community capacity and different biophysical characteristics (Government of Queensland 1999).

There is also the matter of scale. Typically, regional ICM bodies have two primary tasks: first, to integrate decision-making across issues and second, to provide increased community autonomy and responsibility in decision-making. In this there exists an inevitable tension. On the one hand, they must be large enough to effect integrated management; on the other, they need to be small enough to retain genuine community participation. If a group is too small, its ability to deal strategically with catchment issues, across disciplines and communities, will be compromised. If it is too big, then it runs the risk of being 'irrelevant' and of disenfranchising voluntary support (such as Landcare groups) (Ewing 2000). This is important, because under partnership agreements between the federal and State Governments,

ICM groups and the strategies they develop, are assumed to represent the 'grass roots' community view.

When legislative reform was first proposed in Victoria, the issue of how community interests might best be represented on the CMAs was the issue which, more than any other, prompted widespread debate. In the final event, the government resolved that members would be appointed, not to represent a particular interest, but rather on the basis of skill. A strong case can be made for such an approach. As one community leader put it recently:

> As an individual punter out there, I want to have the confidence that there are the skills on that board that can make decisions. You need science skills, economic skills, farmers' skills and environmental interests – you need all of those. [1]

Nevertheless, it remains a vexed issue. Conservation groups in Victoria, for example, argue that the CMAs are dominated by the interests of primary producers (indeed, the legislation requires this) and are, therefore, designed to protect and preserve traditional economies. Inevitably too, there have been charges of political bias and of processes being distorted to the extent that community participation functions largely within constraints determined by, and in the interests of, government. In NSW, for example, Margerum (1999: 157) found that political interference had significantly undermined the efforts, and credibility, of several CMCs:

> elected ministers from both parties have excluded certain groups, weighted committees in favour of certain political affiliations and even rejected individuals nominated by organisations as their representative.

In Victoria, the incoming Labor Government, keen to distance itself from the cronyism of the previous (Kennett) Government, vowed to restructure CMAs, 'to make them more representative, skills-based and accountable' (ALP Victoria 1999: 11).

Whether elected or appointed, on the basis of skills or interest, catchment management bodies are vulnerable to charges of elitism, not in the least because certain groups and individuals have a greater capacity to participate in participatory politics and planning. Those with political experience, who know how to work with the bureaucracy or who can leave the farm work to someone else, are the ones most likely to be involved. And if, as Curtis (this volume) suggests, we are approaching the limits to voluntarism, the issue is amplified. The point is that if there are indeed catchment 'communities', they are fractured and differently empowered. The consultative practices of ICM need to be sensitive to this and work to facilitate meaningful participation across the diverse range of participants.

---

1   Leith Boully, in House of Representatives Standing Committee on Environment and Heritage, Official Committee Hansard, Inquiry into catchment management, 13 October 1999, Canberra, p EH61.

Persistence and purposefulness

Experience suggests that a statutory basis offers the most enduring support to ICM (Mitchell 1991). This was the conclusion of the Parliamentary Inquiry, which recommended that national catchment management principles be developed and enacted in comprehensive, national catchment management legislation (HRSCEH 2000). The Inquiry further recommended that the government work to create catchment management authorities (CMAs) in legislation and that these authorities form the basic administrative element of each catchment system in the country and, overall, of a national catchment authority. At present, it is only in Victoria that catchment authorities enjoy formal structures, power and funding.

One of the arguments often raised against formalising or expanding the role of catchment groups, is concern about creating a fourth tier of government. Thurlow and Hamilton (1997), for example, refer to the 'threat' of new legislation or structures, compromising WA's hitherto 'evolutionary' approach to ICM support. And, in a submission to the Industry Commission, the NSW government expressed concern about potential overlap in responsibilities and an absence of community support (Industry Commission 1988). In their capacity to scrutinise central agencies and call them to account, locally-based community organisations can be unsettling for bureaucratic agencies accustomed to centralised power and process. That there exists continued resistance to new, devolved arrangements is, therefore, hardly surprising; but nor is it helpful.

In Queensland, while ICM has no legislative backing, an ICM policy has been in place for over ten years. Indeed, the ICM program has been surprisingly robust, with its philosophy and implementation remaining relatively constant (Bellamy et al 2002). Nevertheless, the CMAs have been increasingly frustrated in their lack of authority to legislate or pass laws to regulate resource use. They are only able to influence resource use through other organisations, such as local government, which does have this authority. Legislation would likely provide stronger recognition and status for community groups and help give effect to their plans and strategies (Bellamy et al 2002; Department of Natural Resources and Mines 2001b). In the meantime, groups remain highly dependent on the support of prominent community leaders and resource agencies. Johnson et al (1996: 313), for example, in a review of a successful ICM program in the Johnstone River catchment (JRC) note that:

> The JRC enjoyed the personal interest and favour of the Minister for Primary Industries. His influence had a significant impact on the agency responsible for administering the ICM program. In this regard, it is likely that the experience of the JRC will be atypical of other initiatives in Queensland.

Given the extent of degradation in Australia's catchments, it is clear that considerable levels of funding will be required for a long period of time, if ICM programs, and the institutions which support them, are to be effective. In this respect, the States remain highly dependent on the Commonwealth for financial support, through programs such as the Natural Heritage Trust and, more recently, the National Action Plan for Salinity and Water Quality (NAP). The NAP is the latest in a number of proposals to promote the ecologically sustainable use of Australia's catchment systems. It proposes to deliver programs via catchment (or regional bodies), a condition of which is that programs first be accredited. The success of the NAP is, therefore, highly contingent upon catchment management bodies first having sufficient capacity, and resources, to satisfy the Commonwealth's conditions.

With the exception of Catchment Management Trusts (CMTs) in NSW (such as the Hunter CMT) which have the capacity to raise their own funds through a levy system, funding for catchment management bodies is typically managed by State agencies. When the Labor Government came into power in Victoria in 1999, one of its first actions was to fulfil an election promise to rescind the levying powers of the State's CMAs. The 'catchment tax', as it became known, gave CMAs the capacity to raise and manage their own funds for on-ground works. The previous (Kennett) Government had introduced these new rating powers with little explanation, for which it was widely criticised. (In a rear guard, action, it called on the services of Denise Drysdale, a television personality, to sell the idea to aggrieved ratepayers). However, the notion of locally-raised funds being spent on *local* catchment projects, with *local* accountability, did gradually win support and even the Victorian Farmers' Federation expressed the view that the tariffs should remain. But the Labor Government argues that 'community ownership ... comes from consultation, not from paying $25 a year' and that the levy was 'unfair and anti-country'.[2] On that basis, the State budget now includes an additional allocation to CMAs in lieu of locally-raised funds. Publicly, issues of equity have driven this agenda; in practice, it means that CMAs remain highly dependent on central State agencies for funds.

This leads to the issue of the often sharp separation of responsibilities *between* State agencies. In ICM, the contemporary mode of government agencies is 'coordination' and integrated delivery of programs. However, rather than coordination, 'turf warfare' has often arisen between administrative departments competing for standing and authority in environmental matters. Robinson and Humphries (1997) conclude that this sort of activity has typified the institutional response to ICM in WA. At the time of first implementing ICM, the WA government decided that no new legislation or agencies would be established. The rationale was that institutional arrangements in the State were not complex and that the public service was relatively small; cooperation and coordination should, therefore, be achievable within the existing system (Mitchell and Hollick 1993). In practice, ICM has proved difficult because of the disposition of power among several government agencies (Wallis and Robinson 1991). No single group or agency has overall responsibility for catchment management; those six agencies most involved, are together responsible for 77 legislative Acts, many of which have both a direct and indirect effect on catchment management (HRSCEH 2000). A Machinery of Government Taskforce has recently proposed significant changes

---

2   Victoria, Legislative Assembly, 14 December 1999, *Debates*, p 1099.

to the Environment and Heritage portfolio, to address this problem of an excessive number of overlapping agencies (Machinery of Government Taskforce 2001).

Unlike WA, Queensland, Victoria and NSW have brought together previously separate functions into a single department, but this is also not without its problems. In Queensland, for example, under the *Vegetation Management Act* 1999, the Minister for Natural Resources and Mines must prepare Regional Vegetation Management Plans. These plans state outcomes for management of vegetation in the landscape and set down voluntary and statutory actions to achieve them. But this planning process is undertaken completely independently of catchment management planning and water resource planning (Bellamy et al 2002).

It remains that a fundamental weakness with the present arrangements is the limited devolution of natural resource management to regional bodies and the lack of capacity for them to effectively handle such devolution. This applies not only to catchment bodies but also to others such as local government (Wild River, this volume). In most instances, local government is poorly equipped to respond to land and water issues, and integration between regional catchment plans and the statutory and strategic planning responsibilities of local government is poor. In Queensland, this has been addressed through 'Integrated Planning Guidelines' consistent with the requirements of Queensland's *Integrated Planning Act* 1987. These will help local governments identify and implement planning provisions, for catchment issues, within their planning schemes. In Victoria, there are explicit linkages between the *Planning and Environment Act* 1997 and the *Catchment and Land Protection Act*; these require that all planning be strategically based (Government of Victoria 1997). However, in most parts of the State, the complexities of these linkages, and the implications for CMAs and local government, remain unclear.

Information-richness

Adaptive Management is an approach which has the potential to transform organisations and decision-making processes and make them more willing to experiment and learn. This requires not just the acquisition of knowledge but also a purposeful response to new understandings. McLain and Lee (1996) observe that the ability of institutions to respond to new knowledge depends on whether they have access to new information and whether they have the will and capacity to act on that information.

Several recent reviews have concluded that one of the greatest difficulties facing natural resource managers in Australia is the absence of necessary data. Of those data collection systems that do exist, few provide sufficient detail for management decisions at a regional or local level (Bellamy et al 2002; HRSCEH 2000; AFFA 1999; Margerum 1999; Industry Commission 1998). In Queensland, for example, the National Land and Water Resources Audit's recent dryland salinity assessment identified that current monitoring frameworks do not provide a suitable framework for the assessment of dryland salinity and its impact. The lack of available data limits the capacity to provide a statewide risk assessment to underpin regional catchment planning processes for vegetation management (NLWRA 2001).

State of the Environment (SoE) reporting is the most recent and widely-used mechanism in Australia for monitoring the physical environment (Harding and Traynor, this volume). But, as ICAM (1999) observes, the links between those working on SoE reporting and catchment monitoring programs are often poor. The result is that information collected in the field is not assured of inclusion in indicator information, resulting in significant data gaps within SoE reports at the regional level. Often, too, SoE does not provide for an evaluation loop between the problems and programs being carried out to address them, a problem enforced by a lack of structural accountability within those organisations conducting the reporting. This makes informed debate about the current state of catchments and the priority of real (as opposed to perceived) problems, very difficult. In Victoria, at least some headway has been made, with the development of a suite of 30 catchment indicators to meet the upward reporting requirements of the Department of Natural Resources and Environment, the Catchment Management Council (VCMC) and the regional CMAs (Department of Natural Resources and Environment 2001). Most of the indicators contribute information that (i) reflects on the condition of the State's land, water or socio-economic resources and (ii) has the potential to reflect on the impact of catchment management programs and provide feedback to planning cycles. The primary means of reporting will be through the indicators' web site, *Victorian Catchment Condition Indicators Online* <www.nre.vic.gov.au/vcio>.

Clearly, without detailed data to enable appropriate monitoring, the effectiveness or otherwise of programs designed to address catchment management issues cannot be known with certainty. Nor can it be known whether changes to programs are required to make them more effective. Adaptive management requires continual feedback between the development of scientific understanding about the environment and its problems, and the response of human institutions to those problems. Cullen (1998) suggests that a critical first step should be the development of *knowledge strategies* which identify the knowledge needs necessary to achieve ICM.

Conclusions

In the 1970s and '80s, Australia experienced a crisis in natural resources management which lead to a search for a better way. Change occurred and ICM programs were created. And now, by virtue of our federal system, States have responded to the challenge of supporting ICM in several different ways. In effect, we have in place many valuable 'experiments'.

To what extent existing arrangements will be robust and capable of adapting to new situations, remains to be seen. Significant tensions remain. For example, asymmetries persist in the power and knowledge structures framing ICM; there is often a mismatch of powers and funds and difficulty in accessing relevant information and skills. There are also the problems of representation; of limits to the supply of volunteer effort; and of the need for cooperation and coordination across different tiers of government and across diverse groups such as river management committees, regional strategy groups and NRM groups.

Many of the features of institutions that can support an adaptive approach are absent from ICM arrangements in Australia: there is often not a statutory base from which transparent and accountable processes and a degree of persistence can ensue; there is insufficient longevity and continuity, to experiment, adapt and learn; there are insufficient human, financial and informational resources; and there is no mandate for regional bodies, or State agencies, to experiment with different approaches. If adaptive management is to achieve its promise in the policy and practice of ICM, it is critical that attention be given to innovations in the institutions and decision-making processes which frame it.

References

Aley, J, Burch, WR, Conover B and Field D, (eds), 1999, *Ecosystem management: adaptive strategies for natural resources organizations in the 21st century*, Philadelphia, PA, USA: Taylor and Francis.

AFFA (Agriculture, Fisheries and Forestry Australia), 1999, *Managing natural resources: a discussion paper for developing a national policy*, Canberra: Commonwealth of Australia.

ALP Victoria, 1999, *Our natural assets: valuing Victoria's natural environment*, Melbourne: Australian Labor Party.

Australian Water Resources Council, 1988, *Proceedings of the National Workshop on Integrated Catchment Management*, National Workshop on Integrated Catchment Management, Newman College, University of Melbourne, Department of Water Resources, Melbourne: Victoria.

Bellamy, J, Ross, H, Ewing, S, and Meppem, T, 2002, *Integrated catchment management: learning from the Australian experience for the Murray-Darling Basin*, Overview report, Canberra: CSIRO Sustainable Ecosystems.

Born, SM and Sonzogni, WC, 1995, Integrated environmental management: strengthening the conceptualization, *Environmental Management*, 19(2): 167-181.

Buller, H, 1996, Towards sustainable water management: catchment planning in France and Britain, *Land Use Policy*, 14(4): 289-302.

Burch, WR, 1999, Introduction, In: Aley, J, Burch, WR, Conover B and Field, D (eds), *Ecosystem management: adaptive strategies for natural resources organizations in the 21st century*, Philadelphia PA: Taylor and Francis; pp vii-xi.

Burton, J, 1992, Catchment management in Australia – an historical review, In: *Catchments of green: a national conference on vegetation and water management*, Adelaide, Greening Australia, pp 1-8.

Catchment Management Structures Working Party, 1996, *Review of catchment management structures in Victoria: discussion paper*, Melbourne: Department of Natural Resources and Environment.

Cullen, P, 1998, *A knowledge strategy for water and catchment agencies*, CRC for Freshwater Ecology Discussion Paper, Canberra: CRCFE.

Department of Land and Water Conservation, 1997, *Outcomes of the review of total catchment management in New South Wales*, Sydney: Department of Land and Water Conservation.

Department of Land and Water Conservation, 1999, *Strengthening catchment management tin New South Wales*, Sydney: Department of Land and Water Conservation.

Department of Natural Resources and Environment, 1997, *Managing Victoria's catchments: partnership in action*, Melbourne: Department of Natural Resources and Environment.

Department of Natural Resources and Environment, 2001, *Victorian catchment indicators 2001 our commitment to reporting on catchment condition*, Bendigo: Department of Natural Resources and Environment.

Department of Natural Resources and Mines, 2001a, *A framework for NRM in Queensland, Draft Discussion Paper*, Regional Partnership Agreements, Brisbane: Department of Natural Resources and Mines.

Department of Natural Resources and Mines, 2001b, Workshop on Queensland implementation of National Action Plan for Salinity and Water Quality, Workshop Notes, Gatton, 12 April 2001.

Department of Primary Industries, 1993, *A guide to ICM in Queensland*, Brisbane: Queensland Department of Primary Industries.

Dore, J, 1999, Regional natural resources management (NRM) and integrated catchment management (ICM), Unpublished discussion paper, Canberra: Griffin nrm.

Edwards-Jones, E, S, 1997, The river valleys project: a participatory approach to integrated catchment planning and management in Scotland, *Journal of Environmental Planning and Management* 40(1): 125-141.

Ewing, S, 1999, Landcare and community-led watershed management in Victoria, Australia, *Journal of the American Water Resources Association*, 35(3): 663-673.

Ewing, S, 2000, The place of Landcare in catchment structures, Proceedings of International Landcare 2000 conference: *Changing landscapes, shaping futures*, Melbourne: Victoria.

Fitzpatrick, N, 1992, Integrated catchment management workshop, *5th Australian soil conservation conference*, Perth: Department of Agriculture, Western Australia.

Gardiner, J, 1997, ICM in the UK – an overview of progress: *Advancing Integrated Resource Management: Processes and Policies*, Proceedings of Second National Workshop on Integrated Catchment Management, Australian National University, Canberra: River Basin Management Society.

Goodin, RE, 1996, Institutions and their design, In: Goodin, RE (ed), *The theory of institutional design*, pp 1-53, Cambridge: Cambridge University Press.

Government of Queensland, 1999, Submission to House of Representatives Standing Committee on Environment and Heritage Inquiry into Catchment Management, Canberra: Parliament of Australia.

Government of Victoria, 1997, *Working together in catchment management: local government and catchment management authorities*, Melbourne: Victoria, Department of Infrastructure and Department of Natural Resources and Environment.

Government of Western Australia, nd, *Western Australian Government framework to assist in achieving sustainable natural resource management in Western Australia*, Perth: Water and Rivers Commission, Department of Conservation and Land Management, Agriculture Western Australia and Department of Environmental Protection.

Government of Western Australia, 1989, *Working together: integrated management of Western Australia's lands and waters*, Perth: Western Australian Government.

Hocking, ET, 1960, They saved farms from being washed into the sea, *Queensland Agricultural Journal*, 8: 23-27.

HRSCEH (House of Representatives Standing Committee on Environment and Heritage), 2000, *Co-ordinating catchment management: report of the inquiry into catchment management*, Canberra: Parliament of Australia.

ICAM (Integrated Catchment Assessment and Management Centre),1999, Submission to House of Representatives Standing Committee on Environment and Heritage Inquiry into Catchment Management, Canberra: Parliament of Australia.

Industry Commission, 1998, A full repairing lease: inquiry into ecologically sustainable land management, Canberra: Australian Government Publishing Service.

Johnson, AKL, Shrubsole, D and Merrin, M, 1996, Integrated catchment management in northern Australia: from concept to implementation, Land Use Policy, 13(4): 303-316.

Keith, K and Roberts, B, 1992, The development of group extension in Queensland, Proceedings of 5th Australian soil conservation conference, Perth: Western Australian Department of Agriculture.

Lee, KN, 1993, Compass and gyroscope: integrating science and politics for the environment, Washington, DC: Island Press.

Lee, RG, 1992, Ecologically effective social organization as a requirement for sustaining watershed ecosystems, In: Naiman, RJ, Watershed management: balancing sustainability and environmental change, pp 73-90, New York: Springer-Verlag.

Machinery of Government Taskforce, 2001, Government structures for better results: the report of the taskforce established to review the machinery of Western Australia's government, Perth: Ministry of Premier and Cabinet.

McLain, RJ and, Lee, RG, 1996, Adaptive management: promises and pitfalls, Environmental Management, 20(4): 437-448.

Margerum, RD, 1999, Integrated environmental management: the foundations for successful practice, Environmental Management, 24(2): 151-166.

Martin, P, Tarr, S, and Lockie, S, 1992, Participatory environmental management in New South Wales: policy and practice, In: Lawrence, G, Vanclay, F, and Furze, B, Agriculture, environment and society: contemporary issues for Australia, pp 184-207, Sydney: Macmillan.

MDBMC (Murray-Darling Basin Ministerial Council), 2001, Integrated catchment management in the Murray-Darling Basin 2001-2010, Delivering a sustainable future, Canberra: Murray-Darling Basin Ministerial Council.

Miller, A, 1999, Environmental problem solving: psychosocial barriers to adaptive change, New York: Springer-Verlag.

Mitchell, B, 1991, Integrated catchment management in Western Australia: progress and opportunities, Perth: Centre for Water Research, University of Western Australia.

Mitchell, B and, Hollick, M, 1993, Integrated catchment management in Western Australia: transition from concept to implementation, Environmental Management, 17(6): 735-743.

NLWRA (National Land and Water Resources Audit) 2001, Australian dryland salinity assessment 2000, Canberra, NLWRA.

Queensland Government 1991, Integrated catchment management: a strategy for achieving the sustainable and balanced use of land, water and related biological resources, Brisbane: Department of Primary Industries.

Reeve, IJ, 1988, A squandered land: 200 years of land degradation in Australia, Armidale: NSW, Rural Development Centre, University of New England.

Robertson, G, 1989, Community involvement in land conservation: the Western Australian experience, Australian Journal of Soil and Water Conservation, 2(3): 19-23.

Robinson, S and Humphries, R, 1997, Towards best practice: observations on Western Australia legal and institutional arrangements for ICM 1987-1997, Proceedings of Second National Workshop on Integrated Catchment Management, Advancing Integrated Resource Management: Processes and Policies, Australian National University, Canberra: River Basin Management Society.

Rowland, P and Begbie, D, 1997, Integrated catchment management in Queensland – an overview and review, Proceedings of Second National Workshop on Integrated

Catchment Management, Advancing Integrated Resource Management: Processes and Policies, Australian National University, Canberra: River Basin Management Society.

Shrubsole, D, 1996, Ontario conservation authorities: principles, practice and challenges 50 years later, *Applied Geography,* 16(4): 319-335.

Shrubsole, DA, 1990, Integrated water management strategies in Canada, In: Mitchell, B, *Integrated water management: international experiences and perspectives,* pp 88-118, London: Belhaven Press.

Soil Conservation Service of NSW 1987, *Total catchment management: a state policy,* Sydney: Soil Conservation Service of NSW.

State Salinity Council 2000, *Natural resource management in Western Australia: salinity,* Perth: State Salinity Council.

Syme, GJ, Butterworth, JE and Nancarrow, BE, 1994, *National whole catchment management: a review and analysis of processes,* Canberra: Land and Water Resources Research and Development Corporation.

Thompson, GT, 1981, *A brief history of soil conservation in Victoria: 1834-1961,* Melbourne: Victoria, Soil Conservation Authority.

Thurlow, B and, Hamilton, B, 1997, Integrated catchment management in Western Australia, Proceedings of: *Second National Workshop on Integrated Catchment Management, Advancing Integrated Resource Management: Processes and Policies,* Canberra: Australian National University, River Basin Management Society.

Verhoeven, J, 1997a, Total Catchment Management: a case study of institutional and legal arrangements, Proceedings of: *Second National Workshop on Integrated Catchment Management, Advancing Integrated Resource Management: Processes and Policies,* Canberra: Australian National University, River Basin Management Society.

Verhoeven, J, 1997b, Status report of ICM in New South Wales, Proceedings of: *Second National Workshop on Integrated Catchment Management, Advancing Integrated Resource Management: Processes and Policies,* Canberra: Australian National University, River Basin Management Society.

Wallis, RL and Robinson, SJ, 1991, Integrated catchment management: the Western Australian experience, *Environment,* 33(10): 31-33.

17

Institutions and Processes for Resource and Environmental Management in the Indigenous Domain

Kim Orchard

Orchard's Innovative Consultancy Service

Helen Ross

*School of Natural and Rural Systems Management,
The University of Queensland, Gatton*

Elspeth Young

National Centre for Development Studies, The Australian National University

Traditional Indigenous institutional arrangements command that when one clan group enters another's country, respect must be given to the traditional owners of that country by acknowledging them and their ancestors. The visitors must identify who they are, where they have come from (by acknowledging their ancestral lines), why they are visiting another clan's country and where they are going. We respect this protocol in the new medium of writing, by acknowledging Australia's extensive network of Indigenous clans and nations, and particularly thanking those on whose particular ideas and experiences we draw (see acknowledgments).

Institutions and processes, reflecting structures and functions of Australian Indigenous and non-Indigenous society, are fundamental to understanding the contemporary challenges facing Indigenous resource and environmental managers. This chapter explores how, historically, Indigenous Australians and governments have addressed the question of Indigenous natural and cultural resource management needs; how this background has shaped the institutional arrangements and processes of the past three decades; and how these are affecting current practices. We then look to the future, using lessons from the successes and failures of the past to lay a new foundation for future resource and environmental management institutions. In our outline of the evolution of these institutional arrangements, we particularly stress how they have developed through a series of opportunities that reinforce each other; how institutional arrangements set up under Indigenous customary law interact with government initiated approaches designed specifically to cater for Indigenous needs; and the extent to which Indigenous people participate in the so-called 'mainstream' institutional arrangements for natural resource management (NRM). While all those involved in Australian NRM are used to navigating the interactions among Commonwealth, State and local government responsibilities, and to linking these formally and informally with community-based NRM activities, the challenge for Indigenous people is arguably more complex. For them 'community-based' NRM activities are founded in a different set of property rights, needs and processes of decision-making to those of non-Indigenous Australians.

After overviewing basic institutional arrangements, we focus on a number of key areas, illustrating these through selected case studies. Key issues include:

- Ways of organising government support programs, and Indigenous access to them, including Indigenous input into policy and program development and delivery;
- NRM partnerships between Indigenous and other organisations; and
- Indigenous initiatives in NRM, and how institutional arrangements can help them to flourish.

Our analysis of contemporary institutional arrangements and processes for Indigenous NRM is based primarily on secondary information. However it also draws significantly on our collective experience as former public servants, advocates for community interests and academics. Recent information was obtained through interviews with key Commonwealth government departments and a selection of Indigenous participants in NRM. Case studies, partly based on some limited field visits, were selected partly because of some of our recent research and also through the advice of our contacts in Indigenous NRM. They are inevitably limited in number and, as we acknowledge, offer only a flavour of the important issues and innovations now arising in this key element of Australian NRM.

The chapter concludes by relating our findings to the broader issues of inclusiveness, persistence, purposefulness, information and flexibility that form the overall framework of this national study of NRM institutional arrangements. Key definitions fundamental to the discussion are as follows:

- We use the term 'Indigenous peoples' to refer generically to all Aboriginal and Torres Strait Islander peoples of Australia.
- 'Community-based' activities include all non-government activities, including those incorporating private landholders. While 'community' is a problematic concept, generally 'community-based' activities involve some form of organisation of individuals into collective decision-making and subsequent action.
- In using the term 'natural resource management' we acknowledge that, from an Indigenous perspective, cultural heritage protection and management are an integral part of a holistic system consisting of economic, ecological, cultural and social inputs.

Overview of institutional arrangements

Contemporary institutional arrangements affecting Indigenous interests in NRM are exceedingly complex. They include customary bases of resource decision-making, the organisational infrastructure specifically developed to serve Indigenous people's needs, and the 'mainstream' Australia-wide set of institutional arrangements that, because they do not acknowledge particular Indigenous interests, may well restrict Indigenous resource managers from acting as they wish. Many aspects of these institutional arrangements reflect the persistence of the concept of the Australian continent as *terra nullius*, an unowned territory whose first peoples lacked the capacity to manage the fragile environment and its resources. Policies of extermination, protection, assimilation, integration and now reconciliation, have dramatically impacted on the relationship and trust between Indigenous people and governments over the past two centuries.

Customary bases of resource decision-making are founded in Aboriginal customary law, commonly referred to as 'The Law' or 'Dreaming'. Indigenous customary law provides a set of institutional arrangements governing people's affiliations with land and natural resources; people's affiliations with one another through kinship and land; their rights to knowledge; rights to resource use and responsibilities for maintaining healthy ecosystems; decision-making rights and norms for consensus decision-making; and rules for sharing resources, and seeking permission for their use. While these arrangements differ in detail from one land-holding group to another, they share general philosophies and principles among all Indigenous groups.

Indigenous people's strong and intensely personalised relationship with land and natural resources accord with Maslow's (1954) hierarchy of fundamental human needs – achieving survival; feeling safe and secure; being socially accepted; achieving self-esteem; and achieving self-actualisation, the basis for strong identity. That relationship is today commonly referred to as the inseparable linkage between people and 'country', a 'multidimensional (concept consisting) ... of people, animals, plants, Dreamings; underground, earth, soils, minerals and waters, surface water and air' (Rose 1996:8). As we have already acknowledged, customary law commands an ethical and moral approach to the protocols and practices utilised in consultation and decision making. Showing respect to traditional owners and custodians by acknowledging their country and ancestry ensures that the information provided by them will also be respected and not used to take their country or its resources away from them. Following these practices will go a long way towards amending past practices and developing more cooperative arrangements for the future.

Prior to 1967, Indigenous affairs were administered largely by the State governments, which managed reserves and Indigenous welfare systems and created legal provisions both suppressing and preserving some of the people's customary legal rights. Following the successful referendum which gave the Commonwealth decision-making powers with respect to Indigenous peoples, the concept of Indigenous organisational infrastructure, within which natural resource management is included, became more widely recognised. Today's

Indigenous organisational infrastructure includes both governments acting on behalf of Indigenous needs; and also the structures established by a wide range of Indigenous organisations involved in service delivery. The main specialised *organisations* (statutory and non-statutory) participating in this set of resource management arrangements are:

- The Aboriginal and Torres Strait Islander Commission (ATSIC), established 1989 (see Figure 17.1). ATSIC, an elected body of Indigenous people representing constituencies throughout the country, administers and manages the decisions made by its Commissioners, and maintains many of the roles formerly conducted by the Department of Aboriginal Affairs. ATSIC is linked directly to the national parliament through the Minister for Aboriginal Affairs. Initially ATSIC's NRM role focused on programs to assist in the acquisition of lands for Indigenous groups, and the provision of funding to manage such lands for their legal purpose. In 1994-95 that direct responsibility was transferred to the Indigenous Land Corporation (ILC) (see below). ATSIC's contemporary role in NRM focuses primarily on policy development and coordination with relevant resource and environmental management agencies; administering key pieces of legislation and, to a limited extent, program delivery.

- The ILC, a statutory body identified under the *ATSIC Act* (1989), was established as part of the third stage of the Commonwealth government's response to the High Court *Mabo* (Native Title) decision. The ILC has primary responsibility for administering the Indigenous Land Fund as well as the former ATSIC Land Acquisition and Land Management Programs.

- Aboriginal Land Councils, such as the Northern and Central Land Councils, were initially statutory organisations set up under the *Aboriginal Land Rights (Northern Territory) Act* 1976 (Cth) to administer land claim processes and provide administrative services relating to the land granted to Indigenous people under the Act. Subsequent 'statutory' land councils have been formed under various State land rights legislations (eg, in New South Wales and Queensland). Other land councils, often small-scale but also including larger organisations such as the Kimberley Land Council, were set up independently of government as 'non-statutory' bodies. While, in order to attract support for their resource and environmental management activities, they have incorporated under legislation such as the *Aboriginal and Torres Strait Islander Councils and Association Act* 1976 (Cth), many of these non-statutory land councils have always had to struggle for adequate funding. Depending on finance and the legislative frameworks in each State and Territory, the statutory and non-statutory land councils now have much the same functions – they represent their constituents in seeking land and providing administrative services with respect to land. Liaison with prospective developers of land, to ensure Indigenous interests are represented and the statutory obligations such as heritage protection are met, is a key function of all of these organisations. A number have become Native Title Representative Bodies, administering native title claims processes on behalf of their Indigenous constituents under the *Native Title Act* 1993 (Cth).

- Indigenous resource agencies, formed to facilitate the overall day-to-day administration for groups of small outstation communities, have in addition to dealing with service delivery, often focused on supporting Indigenous aspirations for NRM. Some, such as Dhimurru in Arnhem land, the Kowanyama Land and Sea Management Agency and the Quandamooka Aboriginal Land and Sea Management Agency (see Boxes), focus specifically on environmental management. These agencies are often linked to other Indigenous organisations, such as a land council (Quandamooka) or a group of communities (eg, Kalano Association in the Katherine area, Balanggari in the East Kimberley); some, such as Tangentyere Council (Alice Springs) principally deliver services, including environmental management, to town camps and small groups of people living on areas excised from pastoral leases.

- Other Indigenous organisations, such as incorporated Community Councils, and service organisations concerned with providing medical services, legal services, housing associations, and education may be peripherally involved in resource management.

All of these types of Indigenous organisation have to maintain a precarious balance between the requirements of their Indigenous constituents, and the external institutional arrangements in which they are enmeshed (Sullivan 1989). As the example of the Quandamooka Aboriginal Land Council shows (Box 17.2), these include their relationships with their funding bodies, the terms of funding, and the legal and organisational frameworks governing every issue they deal with. These relationships often involve tussles between Indigenous wishes and government policies, programs and priorities, and proposals may need to be tailored to fit the rules and regulations applied by government assistance programs. This can lead to problems. For example, in the absence of land rights legislation, the only way that Indigenous groups in States such as Western Australia could regain their traditional 'country' was through government-funded purchase of pastoral leases under the Commonwealth Aboriginal Affairs portfolio. Funding applications were assessed primarily on the basis of the commercial viability of the pastoral enterprise but, as both government staff and Indigenous applicants well knew, the main reason for buying back the land was cultural. Not surprisingly, given the degraded status of these marginal properties, commercial viability was never realised. Instead of admitting that this was inevitable, government authorities then usually refused to give these groups recurrent maintenance funding, blaming them for their lack of entrepreneurial commitment. The real problem was the initial incompatibility of the institutional structure and Indigenous needs (Young 1988).

Until the 1990s little was known about the effectiveness with which 'mainstream' institutional arrangements catered for the needs of Indigenous land managers. Government departments such as Primary Industry commonly

Figure 17.1. Structures and Processes in the Aboriginal and Torres Straight Islander Commission

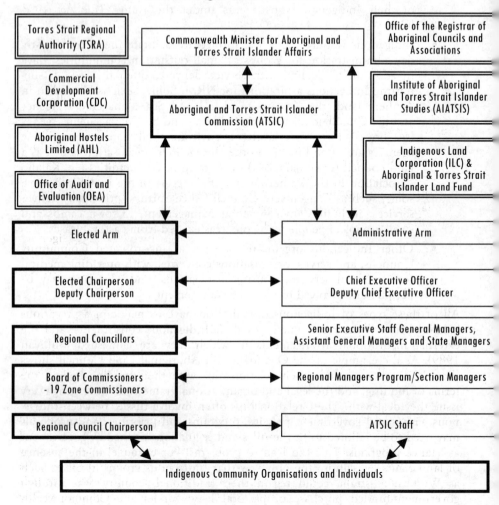

Legend
In accordance with the Aboriginal and Torres Strait Islander Commission Act (1989), the institutional arrangements and processes are addressed through a considerable number of sections. While their funding comes from the Aboriginal and Torres Strait Islander Portfolio Allocation, the Authorities and agencies bordered by double lines have a relationship with ATSIC through the ATSIC Act and through their Aboriginal and Torres Strait Islander clientele.

Source: ATSIC Act (1989) and amendments

saw ATSIC and related organisations as responsible for all Indigenous needs, including environmental and resource management; at the same time ATSIC, generally lacking in skills and expertise in environmental matters, insisted that mainstream agencies had to serve Indigenous needs in this field. In 1991 an Australian National Parks and Wildlife Service initiated report, *Caring for country* (Young et al 1991), documented these deficiencies and identified many unacknowledged barriers to Indigenous access to Commonwealth level funding programs. Many of these persist. For example, as Young et al (1991) identified, only about 4.2 per cent of mainstream NRM funding was allocated to Indigenous organisations in 1990-91. Although, through the efforts of the CEPANCRM[1] program, this had increased to some 12.8 per cent of the Environment Australia biodiversity program funding in 1996-97, this declined once more following the introduction of the Natural Heritage Trust in 1996-97. In 1999, Indigenous projects received some 2 per cent of NHT funding, a proportion commensurate with the national Indigenous population but which falls far short of the land areas owned by Indigenous people (around 17% of Australia) and the vast additional areas they participate in managing.

The main 'mainstream' government agencies involved in Indigenous environmental management are:

- Environment Australia, the Commonwealth agency that caters for conservation of biodiversity, environmental protection and heritage protection (see below).

- Agriculture, Fisheries and Forestry Australia (AFFA) (the former Department of Primary Industries and Energy) which supports a number of relevant programs. The Natural Heritage Trust (NHT), operating through AFFA is the main financial program currently supporting Landcare.

- State agencies under portfolios dealing with conservation and protected area management, mining, land matters, agriculture, pastoral development, and tourism. In response to Native Title and Land Rights legislative processes State governments have begun to review their existing legislation in order to achieve accreditation under the Commonwealth legislation. They are also currently reviewing their cultural heritage protection legislation pending the passage of the Commonwealth Aboriginal and Torres Strait Islander Heritage Protection Bill 1998. States also have to deal with the High Court's decision that Murandoo Yanner, in 1997 Chair of the Carpentaria Land Council in central north Queensland, did not violate the Queensland *Fauna Conservation Act* 1974 when he used a traditional form of harpoon to kill two juvenile estuarine crocodiles for food, on land over which he claims Native Title.

- Local governments, which are becoming increasingly important to Indigenous interests. While some Indigenous communities are now in the conventional sense registered as local government councils (eg,

---

1   The Contract Employment Program in Aboriginal Natural and Cultural Resource Management, a program in the Environment portfolio.

Deed of Grant in Trust (DOGIT) communities in Queensland, and some NT councils), most local government institutions occur within 'mainstream' society. Local government inclusion or exclusion of Indigenous interests in environmental and other decision-making can significantly support or frustrate Indigenous planning. Some local governments have become principal parties in native title claims. This has occurred through the Rubibi Working Group/The Shire of Broome Interim Agreement in Broome, WA (Smith 1998: Padgett 1999); the Minjerribah/North Stradbroke Island Native Title Process Agreement between Redlands Shire Council; and Quandamooka Land Council, and the Dhungutti agreement in northern NSW.

Both Indigenous and non-Indigenous resource management organisations and institutions are subject to some form of legislation, sets of policies, and funding programs, all of which enable them to pursue their own goals. In addition to identifying mismatch between Indigenous needs and the institutional frameworks that affect them, it is also vital to identify their shared interests. The establishment of partnerships between government agencies and Indigenous bodies, such as the joint management of national parks, and regional agreements approaches (see below), is a relatively new initiative that greatly strengthens Indigenous participation in environmental decision-making. Regional authorities, such as the Torres Strait Regional Authority, empower Indigenous people in determining their own priorities in resource and environmental management and can play key roles both in negotiating what activities to encourage and in allocating appropriate funding to them.

Linkages between government agencies and Indigenous organisations have changed subtly over the last three decades. In the early 1970s, the approach was predominantly consultation, which implied that government would seek, but not necessarily heed, Indigenous wishes (Coombs et al 1989). Decision-making through negotiation, implying mutual accommodation of interests, expanded following a series of influential reports on failures in the implementation of Indigenous development policies (eg, Coombs et al 1989; House of Representatives Standing Committee on Aboriginal Affairs 1990). Such landmarks, coupled with increased Indigenous political power through the recognition of land rights and native title claims, and the national reconciliation movement have established a fascinating historical sequence of events in the development of contemporary institutional arrangements for Indigenous NRM support.

Together these have created unique pathways that have resulted in contemporary institutional arrangements in specific agencies such as Environment Australia, the Commonwealth Government's key environmental agency (Fig.17.2). This Figure traces the connections between 'mainstream' legislation (NPWC Act) and Indigenous specific legislation (*Aboriginal Land Rights (Northern Territory) Act 1976 (Cth) (ALR Act)*), the role of this in fostering the agency's role in establishing joint management in Kakadu National Park, and the subsequent establishment of joint management over Uluru-Kata Tjuta NP in 1985 and Booderee NP in 1995. This has been coupled with the development of NRM training programs that recognise Indigenous knowledge and practices and the establishment of key activities such as CEPANCRM and the Indigenous Protected Area Program.

Figure 17.2. Environment Australia – Institutional Arrangements and Processes related to Indigenous Issues

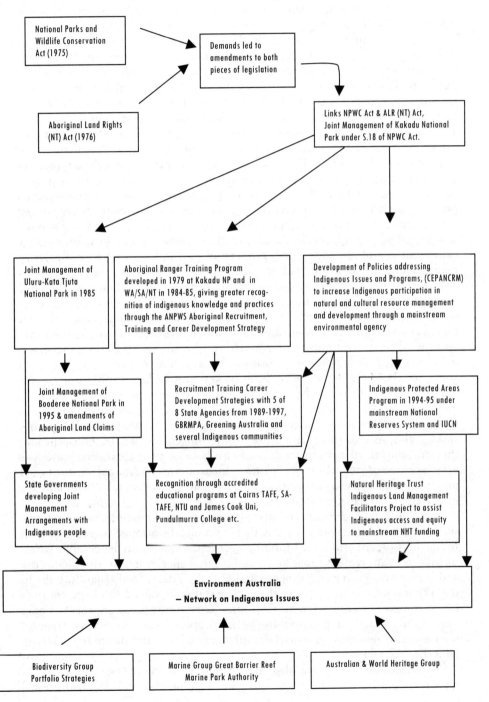

Indigenous peoples as resource managers

While, as discussed above, many institutional arrangements for the support of NRM have proved inadequate for meeting the needs of Indigenous resource managers, significant changes in recent decades offer some grounds for optimism. One important change is the broader and more overt recognition of Indigenous people as resource managers, not only in a traditional sense but increasingly also in the development of natural resources for commercial purposes. Traditional ecological knowledge, and the conviction that resources should be managed sustainably in a way that is compatible with such a knowledge system underlies both approaches. Customary behaviour, including a range of socially-applied rules and regulations provides institutional frameworks for both of these elements. Although such institutional structures are well recognised within Indigenous communities they are poorly understood and often ignored by non-Indigenous society.

As Rose (1996) explains, traditional Indigenous resource management provides a vital link that binds people to their country. Subsistence use of both plant and animal resources remains a major priority for any Indigenous communities with appropriate access to these elements and in many smaller communities still provides a high proportion of people's sustenance. Resource management, in terms of monitoring natural resources and taking steps to ensure that they are maintained, has always formed part of these activities and many institutional rules, such as unspoken agreements to limit harvesting to immediate subsistence needs, are still in place. But the importance of such practices has perhaps now become more widely discussed as productivity has declined through the impact of population growth, redistribution and externally imposed development pressures. It is common now for people to comment about the depletion of 'bush tucker' around larger Indigenous settlements; and in many of the former pastoral leases now under Indigenous ownership people have deliberately fostered the regeneration of such foods in paddocks suffering from decades of over-grazing by cattle. Many wildlife species also receive direct attention from Indigenous people, both because they are still valued as bush foods, and also because their increasing scarcity is now acknowledged. Hunting regimes incorporate traditional institutional practices, such as ensuring that, as far as possible, hunters take male animals in preference to females with young.

Wildlife management has now also become a community-based activity, supported both by community members and also by a range of external non-Indigenous organisations and funding agencies. Community based approaches to wildlife management range from endangered species monitoring (eg, turtle and dugong in north-east Arnhem Land and the Torres Strait Islands, bilby in the Tanami desert) to ensuring the sustainability of valued food species such as magpie geese (Davies et al 1999). Some community-based approaches have been fundamental in the establishment of specialised community resource management agencies, such as Dhimurru, based at Yirrkala in NE Arnhem land (Box 17.1 below).

Indigenous people are also increasingly involved in managing natural resources partly or wholly within the commercial world. Institutional arrangements here tend to combine customary rules and regulations along with those established by non-Indigenous resource management structures. Pastoralism and tourism are two of the principal forms of commercial resource development with significant Indigenous involvement. Indigenous tourist enterprises, primarily ecotourism, offer tourists opportunities to learn about Indigenous NRM at first-hand, and at the same time provide comfortable venues for forays into remote and physically beautiful landscapes such as northern Queensland or parts of the Kimberley. Indigenous pastoralism ranges from fully operational cattle enterprises to the management of small 'killer' herds designed to meet the needs of the local community. Non-Indigenous institutional arrangements, such as those applying to disease control and the marketing of stock, dominate the former; but killer herds generally operate along with the maintenance of bush tucker, and hence Indigenous institutional arrangements play a very important part in their management (Young 1995). Nevertheless, the management of both small and larger scale Indigenous pastoral enterprises is distinctly different from conventional non-Indigenous pastoral management, a factor that has led some regionally based Indigenous groups to establish their own institutional structures for the industry. Such initiatives have included the Central Australian Aboriginal Pastoralists Association (CAAPA), established in 1985 with funding from the Aboriginal Development Commission; and the Kimberley Aboriginal Pastoralists Association, established in the 1990s. The fortunes of such organisations have been mixed – CAAPA, for example, was wound up in 1989 because of large-scale financial problems. But their very establishment provides clear evidence that conventional institutional structures have not, as far as Indigenous pastoralists are concerned, been meeting the needs of these types of enterprise. Other Indigenous institutions, such as the Central Land Council, the Institute for Aboriginal Development in Alice Springs and also the ILC, now play important roles in working along with these types of organisation.

Indigenous resource management institutions

The spectacular growth of Indigenous resource management institutions is the other major development of recent decades. Some of these organisations aim to fill yawning gaps in existing institutional structures, particularly at local community levels; others reflect the fact that the services and support offered by 'mainstream' institutions were not appropriate, either culturally or economically, for Indigenous needs.

Community-based Indigenous resource management institutions

Community-based resource management institutions have generally been established to meet direct pressures arising from perceived threats to Indigenous community needs. While some have focused on broad needs and strategies others have been much more specific. For example, in the 1980s and 1990s, Kowanyama Aboriginal community, in the south-west of Cape York peninsula, formed a regional planning strategy to establish co-management of fisheries in the Mitchell River, in the framework of an integrated catchment management plan for the river and its tributaries. That strategy included fostering cooperation with neighbouring non-Indigenous land-holders, and obtaining support from both State and federal government agencies. The Yirrkala community's Dhimurru Land Management Aboriginal Corporation, at least in its earlier phases, focused specifically on managing coastal areas affected by non-Indigenous recreational use from residents in Nhulunbuy, the nearby Arnhem land mining town (Box 17.1). These efforts have subsequently been extended to research and management of threatened wildlife species such as turtle.

Box 17.1. Dhimurru Land Management Aboriginal Corporation

Dhimurru, established in 1992 by Yolngu living in and around Yirrkala, has focused primarily on dealing with increased coastal degradation resulting from uncontrolled use of traditional lands and resources by non-Indigenous residents of the nearby mining town of Nhulunbuy. It aims to integrate Yolngu and non-Indigenous resource management knowledge and skills within a system of cross-cultural cooperation that, amongst other things, promotes Yolngu employment and training; educates non-Indigenous people about Yolngu resource management approaches; develops environmental management plans for the region; rehabilitates degraded areas; controls visitor access to specific areas; and provides a formal contact point with external individuals and government agencies that support resource management. Marine turtle monitoring and fire management are prime targets of some of Dhimurru's work. However, while Dhimurru has been generally assessed as one of the most successful Indigenous resource management agencies (Davies et al. 1999), the organisation continues to face grave problems in ensuring ongoing funding. Dhimurru administrators and Board of Management have had to spend a great deal of time applying for government support funds and lobbying possible donors. Dhimurru Community Rangers have primarily been funded through programs such as ATSIC's Community Development Employment Program (CDEP), DETYA's former Training for Aboriginals Program and CEPANCRM (see below).

Despite Dhimurru's impressive achievements the viability of the organisation is still threatened by funding inadequacies. This experience is typical of other community-based Indigenous resource management agencies. The problem of funding is a fundamental theme arising throughout our analysis.

Community-based Indigenous resource management institutions may also co-operate with local, largely non-Indigenous organisations such as Landcare groups. Such interactions may also take place through larger regional Indigenous organisations, such as land councils, that are charged with representing their interests in broader arenas.

Indigenous resource management institutions: land councils

Generally, Indigenous land councils, originally established to meet a number of demands such as representation of their constituents' claims for recognition of traditional rights, and coordination of administrative needs in a range of different spheres, have become increasingly involved in the management of land and sea resources. Land councils vary according to scale and organisational complexity; the legislative framework within which they were established; and the socio-demographic and economic structures of the groups that they represent. The resource management activities of these councils also vary, because of the complexity of needs in the region covered, because of differences in access to funding and also because of the priorities of the Indigenous groups concerned. We here comment on the activities of only three land councils: two that operate on a local level, but under different State jurisdictions – Quandamooka, (Queensland), and Toomelah-Boggabilla (NSW); and one large regional land council, the Central Land Council (NT).

While Quandamooka Aboriginal Land Council (QALC) and Toomelah-Bogabilla Local Aboriginal Land Council (TBLALC) operate similarly to conventional local government councils they also overtly subscribe to the philosophy of *Caring for country* (see Fig.17.3). As Box 17.2 summarises, QALC's resource management activities are conducted by the Quandamooka Aboriginal Land and Sea Management Agency (QALSMA). In contrast, TBLALC resource management activities form part of the organisation's own brief (Box 17.3). QALC is an incorporated body registered under the *Aboriginal Councils and Associations Act* while TBLALC is established as a statutory body under the NSW *Aboriginal Land Rights Act* (1978).

Box 17.2. Quandamooka Aboriginal Land Council and the Quandamooka Aboriginal Land and Sea Management Agency.

While QALC and QALSMA have primarily aimed to advance the Common Law Rights of the Nughi, Koenpul and Nunuccal people in the Moreton Bay area of south east Queensland, they now focus more specifically on providing Indigenous response to developments proposed by the Redlands Shire Council (with which they are negotiating the working detail of native title arrangements), and seeking funding to enable them to cover their costs. Residential, commercial and recreational interests in the Moreton Bay area, because of its location in close proximity to Brisbane, are expanding extremely rapidly, and hence pressures on Indigenous resource interests and use are growing strongly. While QALC was incorporated in 1991 QALSMA was only set up in 1998. It primarily addresses Indigenous concerns over problems with the management of fisheries and marine habitats in Moreton Bay. Other concerns are sand-mining, fire management and tourism development on North Stradbroke Island – Minjerribah. QALCs funding has relied heavily on government agencies – ATSIC, DETYA, EA – and, as with Dhimmuru, the council is forced to spend a significant amount of effort in dealing with unwieldy bureaucratic procedures. Co-operation with non-Indigenous local government, including a Native Title Process Agreement with Redlands Shire is occurring and this has fed into a comprehensive regional planning study addressing issues concerning environmental and cultural conservation, local economic development and service provision on the island. This study was financed by the Redlands Shire Council and Native Title funding. All of these interactions have had a significant impact on members of the QALC, many of whom are low income earners dependent on CDEP or pensions, or, because of the limited job opportunities on the island, unemployed. In addition to securing funding, these voluntary members have had to grapple with understanding Native Title legislation, as well as rules and regulations relating to environment protection, water resources, marine and fisheries, cultural heritage protection, intellectual property rights, and workplace relations.

Figure 17.3 demonstrates the range of institutional arrangements QALC and QALSMA work within.

Figure 17.3. Institutional Arrangements and Processes of the Quandamooka Land Council, and Quandamooka Land and Sea Management Agency

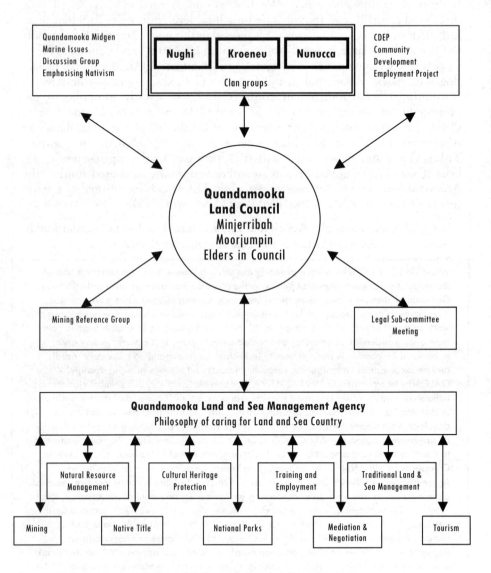

Source of Information: Dale Ruska and Sallyann Gudge on 7 December 1999.

Box 17.3. Toomelah-Boggabilla Local Aboriginal Land Council

TBLALC, representing Kamilaroi/Gamilaraay people in the Moree Plains Shire Council region of north central NSW, is concerned with land acquisition and management, native title rights and the protection of sites of significance, including Boobera Lagoon and Pungbougal Lagoon. Its area covers part of the most important cotton-producing region of Australia. It also negotiates with State and local government agencies operating within the region, and must seek funding to cover its costs. Boobera Lagoon, a place of great cultural significance for the local Gamilaaray people, has so far been the key issue. Protracted negotiations finally resulted in the placement of a limited term Heritage Protection Declaration on Boobera site from July 2000, prohibiting controversial use of the lagoon for motor boating and water-skiing. Further negotiations on these issues are, however, also likely to be contentious because Pungbougal Lagoon, also identified as culturally significant as well as being an environmentally sensitive waterway that is a breeding ground for the Jabiru (a water bird) which migrate annually from Northern Territory, has been suggested as an alternative water-skiing site.

Community volunteers who oversee the administration and operations of TBLALC, like QALC, have limited formal educational experience, high levels of unemployment and limited resources, and face many challenges in understanding legal and institutional frameworks that affect them. They have had some success. In December 1998 under a Federal Court order the Minister for Aboriginal and Torres Strait Islander Affairs was instructed to make a decision under the *Aboriginal and Torres Strait Islander Heritage Protection Act* 1984 on the 1994 Boobera Lagoon Section 10. Although not a legal requirement, this decision has encouraged an agreement between TBLALC and the Warialda Rural Pastoral Protection Board to fence the Travel Stock Reserve, thus limiting access by stock to the shoreline of Boobera Lagoon. These gains in general fall well below the levels of protection desired by TBLAC. But they have still encouraged the Kamilaroi/Gamilaraay people because their priorities have at least been recognised nationally.

As both of these case-studies suggest, land councils continually face funding uncertainties in dealing with their resource management needs. This demands great expenditure of effort in writing proposals, and in cobbling together funding from a number of different sources. Dealing with the bureaucratic procedures and institutional rules and regulations that characterise government funding agencies is another major, time consuming difficulty. In addition such organisations have to seek a two-way relationship of trust with non-Indigenous stakeholders.

The Northern Territory's Central Land Council (CLC), established as a statutory body under the ALR Act, serves a constituency of more than 15,000 Indigenous people living in a large number of rural and urban communities throughout the southern half of the NT. While initially charged largely with the coordination, lodgement and conduct of claims under the Act it has, as the area of Indigenous freehold land increased following successful claims, faced the challenge of managing these returned areas. Lack of appropriate support/extension services, coupled with determination to develop Indigenous approaches to NRM and to make moves towards political and cultural autonomy, led to the growth of CLC's land management activities. These have expanded from data collection and a GIS mapping unit, and providing community environmental management advice and technical support, to the present land management section. This includes a specialist pastoral management unit, an enterprise support unit and a land assessment unit. Broadly-based planning, using technical and professional skills available through these different sections, has become progressively more important. CLC's particular contribution to such planning is its emphasis on Indigenous participation, through innovative methods that fully acknowledge Indigenous land and resource valuation, and rely heavily on Indigenous traditional ecological knowledge and Indigenous perceptions of resource use priorities. Participatory methods developed through CLC's program are now being applied by other Indigenous resource management agencies and innovations arising from this work are increasingly recognised within Australia and internationally.

CLC land assessment and planning includes cooperation with a range of external government agencies such as Commonwealth and NT conservation and primary industry agencies and CSIRO. CLC also cooperates with other Indigenous agencies in central Australia, notably Tangentyere Council and Anangu Pitjantjatjara. Such cooperation has been a highly positive outcome, both for Indigenous NRM and also for NRM in the arid/semiarid regions. Accessing adequate and guaranteed funding remains the prime challenge for CLC. Like the smaller land councils described above CLC staff have had to spend an inordinate amount of time in submitting funding applications, usually to a range of mainstream bodies. While they have had significant success, particularly in project funding through programs such as Land & Water Australia and the NHT-supported Landcare, they still need more broadly-based support. Discrete project funding is too restrictive, and cannot hope to cover the range and depth of needs for CLC's constituents (Walsh 1996).

Government Indigenous resource management institutions: ATSIC and ILC

ATSIC, as discussed earlier, has conventionally been perceived as responsible for dealing at Commonwealth government level with all Indigenous needs. Indigenous land acquisition was formerly part of its portfolio. However, as recognised at least a decade ago (Young et al. 1991), ATSIC has generally lacked the technical and professional expertise to cater for diverse land management needs; and the recognition of the significance of this issue in relation to land acquisition has been very belated. Since 1995 the ILC has been responsible for Indigenous land acquisition, coupled with the goal of managing that land according to sustainability principles that foster social, economic and ecological benefits. Most of its land management efforts are, however, conducted indirectly, through other Indigenous agencies that are granted ILC project funding. Despite the holistic aims of sustainable land management, ILC's financial support appears to strongly emphasise economic benefits, on the principle that land that has been purchased on the market should be used for commercial enterprises such as pastoralism, agriculture or tourism. ILC also has to balance its funding allocation between land purchase and meeting the costs of managing land already purchased. Not surprisingly it emphasises that the institution should be seen as a last resort for grants/loans for land management – people should try to raise their own resources first. However ILC, in conjunction with ATSIC, does play a key role in planning for Indigenous NRM, through implementation of the national and regional Indigenous Land Strategies; and it works closely with other Commonwealth agencies such as Environment Australia in programs such as the IPA (see below).

Community level Indigenous institutions, such as QALC or TBLALC, have identified problems in dealing with the bureaucratic procedures of national level Indigenous institutions such as ATSIC and ILC, as well as with 'mainstream' agencies such as EA. Procedures such as developing local land management plans, contributing to the subregional overview of land needs to establish ILC's regional and national plans and commenting on ATSIC or Environment Australia's regional development processes pose a number of challenges. For example, lack of procedural coordination may undermine success in land acquisition because, by the time ILC decides to fund a purchase, the land may well have been sold to someone else. Either ATSIC or ILC could assume the important role of coordinating Indigenous NRM funding support and land management planning using line departments such as AFFA or EA along with Indigenous organisations. Perhaps a 'one plan fits all' approach could be negotiated with relevant agencies so that when ATSIC Regional Councils review their plans these issues could be addressed. It remains to be seen whether that occurs. The 'mainstream' programs still need to be monitored to ensure Indigenous people have equality of access, and other portfolios need to be advised by these national Indigenous organisations to ensure that unintended barriers are not placed in the way of potential Indigenous applicants.

Partnerships

Formal partnerships between two or more parties, typically a government organisation (or whole government) and an Indigenous community-based party, are a relatively new form of institutional arrangement in NRM. Indigenous people are parties to wildlife and fisheries 'co-management agreements' in Canada (Osherenko 1988; Pinkerton 1989) and timber and water resources management in USA (Ross 1999). In Australia, joint management of national parks, for example, Kakadu, Uluru Kata Tjuta and Nitmiluk in the NT, provides the most widely recognised example of such partnerships (Woenne-Greene et al 1994; de Lacy 1994). More recent joint-management agreements have been applied in Jervis Bay Capital Territory (Booderee) and also in New South Wales (eg, Mutawintji, Jervis Bay National Parks), and other participatory arrangements are now in place in South Australia (Witjara NP). Partnerships can also be less formal, perhaps involving agreements between local Indigenous land management agencies and non-Indigenous stakeholder groups to manage a particular resource where interests come into conflict (eg, Toomelah, above). They may also involve agreements with research organisations willing to share their scientific and technical expertise with Indigenous resource managers (eg, Dhimurru, Central Land Council, above).

Some newer types of partnerships are now emerging, reflecting recognition of the need for additional approaches that enhance Indigenous involvement in making decisions about NRM. It is possible that Indigenous Land Use Agreements negotiated or registered under native title provisions will add further scope for new partnership developments (Smith 1998; Padgett 1999). Here we review one of these initiatives, the Indigenous Protected Area Program. This program aims to provide a 'win-win' solution that addresses the under-representation of certain ecosystems in the National Reserve System, and at the same time meets Indigenous landowners' needs for financing conservation if they desire to pursue such an approach on their own lands.

Indigenous protected areas

The Indigenous Protected Areas (IPA) Program is a component of the National Reserve System Program. As the Interim Biogeographic Regional Assessment (Thackway and Cresswell 1995) showed, many of the gaps in the National Reserve System coincide with Indigenous-owned land. The IPA Program supports Indigenous landowners to declare their own reserve on such land, or have one declared on their land under State conservation legislation. It also provides funds for Indigenous people to plan and negotiate joint management of existing conservation areas, an opportunity that broadens the idea to Indigenous groups who may lack formal land ownership.

The IPA concept was first explored through a consultancy commissioned by Environment Australia, which examined legal implications and also identified Indigenous perceptions about the approach (Smyth and Sutherland 1996). Proposals were then elaborated with advice offered during two consultative conferences with Indigenous people and twelve pilot studies, distributed throughout the country, were then used to test the concept at local levels. Funding for these early activities came from the transfer of a proportion of CEPANCRM funding. Subsequent funding has come from the National Reserve System program funds, approximately 10 per cent of which are available to support IPAs, a source that comes under the National Heritage Trust (NHT). Since NHT has a finite life, IPAs will have to find another source of funding if they are to continue after the Trust is wound up in 2001-2002. This insecurity could destroy this promising institutional arrangement, a story that, given the demise of earlier effective Indigenous NRM programs such as the Aboriginal Rural Resources Initiative (ARRI) and CEPANCRM (see below, Davies et al. 1999; Orchard 2000), is all too familiar. IPAs will continue to be funded under the new Natural Heritage Trust. Funding covers preparatory steps for either IPAs or joint management, including consultations among Indigenous landholders and access to technical advice; and the development of a plan of management. After formal declaration, IPAs are funded for management. Six IPAs, two of which are described in greater detail below (Boxes 17.4 and 17.5) had been declared by 2000. IPA management, as illustrated in the Nantawarrina example (see Box 17.4) is based on zoning for different conservation purposes according to the IUCN guidelines.

Box 17.4. Nantawarrina IPA, South Australia

In August 1998 Nantawarrina, a former cattle station owned by the Adnyamathanha people living at Nepabunna, was the first IPA to be declared. It adjoins the Gammon Ranges National Park in the Flinders Ranges, and has an area of 570 square kilometres. The land includes areas of high conservation status and wilderness, as well as areas degraded by former pastoral management and mining activities. The parties to the agreement are the Nepabunna community, the Aboriginal Lands Trust of South Australia (formal owner of the land) and Environment Australia. The goals of the IPA are to achieve an acceptable level of ecological sustainability for Nantawarrina; to maintain and protect the interests of the Nepabunna community in cultural heritage and traditional beliefs for present and future generations; and to promote economic sustainability for present and future generations. Key elements of the management plan include weed and feral animal control, restoration of the habitat of native animals such as the *Andu* (Yellow-footed rock wallaby), tourism development in ways which are compatible with cultural values, and managing visitor access. IUCN designated conservation purposes, identified in Nantawarrina's zoning system include one region to be managed mainly for conservation, by maintaining habitats to meet the needs of specific species; and another area that will be managed mainly for landscape conservation and recreation.

Box 17.5. Deen Maar IPA, Victoria

Deen Maar, a small IPA on the Victorian coast, was founded and declared an IPA by the Framlingham community, under State-supported 'self-declaration' rather than through a formal agreement with another party. This strategy allows the Indigenous owners to maintain a high degree of control over the IPA process. Funding has enabled the Framlingham community to develop an Environmental Management Plan and to undertake rabbit and weed control, tourism development and management of visitor impacts. The IPA has had considerable success in land restoration, for instance by restoring natural levees, and especially in protecting the critically endangered Orange Bellied Parrot. Twenty parrots, a fifth of the known population, have now been identified in the area.

Environment Australia, in accordance with IUCN Protected Areas guidelines, maintains that a property is defined as a protected area not by its current condition but rather by the management intent of the land holders. Indigenous people's aspirations and long-tem commitment to protect and restore the natural and cultural values of 'country' have been supported through the IPA Program even when the current biodiversity values did not appear high. Deen Maar IPA (see Box 17.5), declared in July 1999, illustrates this point. Prior to the community's efforts, the land was not noted for its conservation status, although Victoria was interested in the proposal because the State was short of reserves protecting coastal ecosystems.

The IPA Program lays particular stress on the importance of cultural heritage to Indigenous people, and is sensitive to the management of these aspects. Environment Australia's handling of intellectual property, a fundamental issue in such a situation, has been innovative. The formal IPA agreements include clauses which vest intellectual property rights arising from the

IPA in the Indigenous party, protect pre-existing intellectual property, and give the Commonwealth a licence to use, but not to pass on, the material. If the Commonwealth wants to disclose any sensitive information it must consult with the Indigenous party, and must obey any request that denies disclosure.

As an example of a partnership, the IPA Program appears to be especially responsive to the wishes of Indigenous parties, both in the development of the program concept and in the planning of particular IPAs. This contrasts with joint-managed national parks, each of which has developed relatively independently, rather than as elements of an explicit policy or program. Indigenous parties hold considerable control and management responsibility in IPAs, and the government commits resources to make the conservation purposes possible. As Szabo (1999) observes, the program accepts Indigenous people's legitimacy and capacities as land managers in their own right, puts them on a more equal footing with government, and resources them to manage their land. Advantages for EA and other government conservation agencies include the opportunity to improve the ecological representativeness of the national reserve system, and to devote funding directly to managing for biodiversity, rather than first having to spend money on purchasing the land. Further, the IPA partnerships promote the sharing of Indigenous and non-Indigenous ecological expertise and human resources, and force greater mutual understanding of shared and differing goals.

A partnership model for consultation/negotiation

In developing partnerships between Indigenous people and natural and cultural resource management agencies, Indigenous land and sea managers have recommended institutional arrangements and processes that will improve their inclusion in the decision making process. In 1993, the House of Representatives Standing Committee on the Environment, Recreation and the Arts supported a model for protected areas which had been developed through a succession of consultative processes (HRSCERA 1993; Breckwoldt et al 1997). The model proposes a national Aboriginal and Torres Strait Islander National Natural and Cultural Resource Management Body, to interface with regional equivalents. Each would be composed of half Indigenous people and half representatives of national or regional agencies respectively (see Figure 17.4).

Funding

One of the most striking messages coming from our case-studies and other literature (Young et al 1991, Davies et al 1999) is the universal problem with funding – there is never enough of it; what there is may only be available for one component of a project; alternatively the formal focus of the funding may be completely inappropriate for Indigenous needs, and, finally, accessing funds demands traversing a bureaucratic maze of application forms, rules and regulations. An additional issue, implied by concerns over the longer-term

Figure 17.4. A Model for Indigenous/non-Indigenous Consultation and Negotiation over Protected Areas

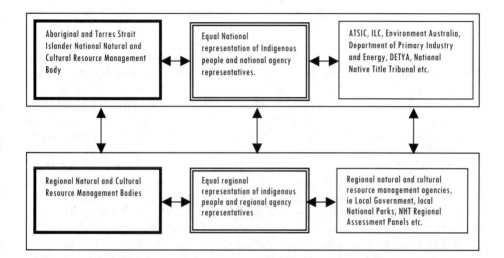

prospects of the IPA Program, is the history of abandoning special Indigenous support programs, even when they have had a positive impact. We here explore only a few examples of the complex question of funding.

Commonwealth government departments have so far provided the principal funding for Indigenous NRM. Such funding has come from conventional 'mainstream' programs, and also from programs that specifically focus on Indigenous needs. In 1990-91 the allocation of mainstream Commonwealth funding for NRM to Indigenous groups amounted to approximately $1.6 million, 4.2 per cent of the total. Indigenous land then accounted for about 12 per cent of the continent (Young et al 1991). Although it must be acknowledged that this comparison is somewhat simplistic, it nevertheless focuses attention on issues concerning the Commonwealth's commitment to enhancing sustainable development in the most remote and fragile parts of the continent. This figure was, however, enhanced by the financing of specifically focused finite-term programs, and it is here that some measure of success can be identified.

Specific programs for Indigenous resource management have been stimulated by key reports into Indigenous social issues. The cross-portfolio Aboriginal Employment Development Program (AEDP) was developed from a national consultation process on employment led by the late Mick Miller (Miller 1985), an Aboriginal man from northern Queensland. A similar process of extensive consultation also occurred with the Royal Commission into Aboriginal Deaths in Custody and the Commonwealth Government's response to the Report. We now have a third such process on the political agenda, *The Report into the Removal of Aboriginal and Torres Strait Islander People from their Family*, better known as the 'Stolen Generations'. Government has responded by developing a policy, and has repackaged ATSIC programs to address the recommendations of the report. As has happened with the AEDP and initiatives arising from the Deaths in Custody report, we suspect there will continue to be varying degrees of success and failure in implementing policies and delivering programs to Aboriginal and Torres Strait Islander people, primarily because of some misinterpretation of the intentions of the originating policies.

The Contract Employment Program for Aborigines in Natural and Cultural Resource Management (CEPANCRM) was created by the former Australian National Parks and Wildlife Service in 1990 under the ATSIC co-ordinated Aboriginal Employment Development Program (AEDP) with initial funding of $1.5 million. For the next seven years CEPANCRM, with its provision of funds for employing people in a great diversity of conservation and NRM projects, was the cornerstone of Indigenous NRM financial support. ANPWS and its successor body the Australian Nature Conservation Agency used CEPANCRM as a catalyst to develop more appropriate funding arrangements for Indigenous resource management. By 1996-97 around 13 per cent of EA's NRM funding (excluding CEPANCRM) and 34 per cent with CEPANCRM, was provided to Indigenous land-holders (Taylor 1998). An independent review of CEPANCRM in 1997 recommended that the program be continued, extended by additional efforts to improve the involvement of State conservation agencies in Indigenous NRM, and a shift in focus from basic employment generation (often short-term) to broader environmental and cultural management. Despite that assessment CEPANCRM was wound up in 1997-98, and no equivalent program has subsequently been put in place.

The CEPANCRM story is not an isolated case. The Bureau of Rural Resources' Aboriginal Rural Resources Initiative (ARRI) program aimed at assisting Indigenous people in dealing with wildlife harvesting and management issues, including commercial enterprise development, also achieved considerable success during its short lifetime. Like CEPANCRM it was funded under the banner of the AEDP and formed part of the Commonwealth Government's response to the Royal Commission into Aboriginal Deaths in Custody. Though the AEDP Review in 1994 identified little success from the implementation of the AEDP, ARRI and CEPANCRM stood out as achieving a high level of success.

Programs such as CEPANCRM and ARRI have to some extent been complemented by Indigenous NRM support provided through other programs such as the management component of ATSIC's Land Acquisition scheme and its contemporary ILC land purchase scheme. However, as discussed earlier, the NRM component of such funding has generally been geared towards business funding and the realisation of commercial viability of resource use. Funding for non-commercial resource management, including conservation has been much harder to secure. ATSIC's Heritage Protection Program, specifically designed to deal with regional land management needs, theoretically also offers funding opportunities. However, since allocation of these funds depends also on Regional Councils or the Board of Commissioners' assessment of all their priorities, such as housing, infrastructure, economic development activities or addressing social justice issues, the amount left over for NRM may be very small.

Future prospects for the financial support of Indigenous NRM are very uncertain. Indigenous groups will have to increase their ability to tap into the bureaucratic mainstream; and at the same time they will have to find other avenues, perhaps through agreements outside the government sector. The Natural Heritage Trust Indigenous Land Management Facilitators Project, established through a Memorandum of Understanding between Environment Australia and AFFA to help Indigenous communities involved in land management activities, is probably a useful initiative. Through the Bushcare and National Landcare programs twelve facilitators have been supported to advise communities on any land management issue including how to seek funding, and also to provide feedback to policy makers on issues of concern to Indigenous communities. However, like the IPA program, this project also receives its support through the NHT, and therefore the fundamental lack of security remains.

Education for resource management

Education and training are vital if Indigenous resource management agencies are to function effectively. As the above discussion shows, effectiveness relates not only to these agencies being able to devise their own approaches to resource management and to obtain financial support to carry these out, but also to the extent to which those agencies, and their workers/directors etc, can communicate and understand vital elements of the mainstream system. Formal education and training for Indigenous resource managers has now operated for at least two decades in universities (eg, Charles Sturt University, and more recently Northern Territory University) and other colleges such as Batchelor. In 1979 Kakadu National Park introduced the first Ranger Training Program in Australia, not only to develop the traditional owners' capacity in scientific and technical skills but to also seek accreditation for their traditional knowledge practices. Important issues in education have included the need for full accreditation, so that Indigenous resource managers are fully recognised in the mainstream system; and at the same time catering for the needs of people who may not be formally employed by Indigenous land councils or government sponsored agencies, but who are responsible for day-to-day activities within their own community. The experiences of Cairns TAFE (Box 17.6) provide an example of how some of these issues have been tackled.

Lessons learned

The development of institutional arrangements for the support of Indigenous NRM has, like that of Australian Indigenous affairs in general, been complex and highly political and, for everyone involved, both non-Indigenous and Indigenous, has produced much frustration along with some degree of success.

Box 17.6. Cairns TAFE

Cairns TAFE established training for Community Rangers, individuals identified by their communities as suitable for undertaking the diverse tasks related to resource management within their own communities, in 1989. Courses have been delivered both by non-Indigenous professionally and technically qualified staff and also by Traditional Owners with unique traditional ecological knowledge. Despite funding uncertainties the program was maintained and from 1995 became involved with the development of a National Curriculum framework for Indigenous resource management – *Caring for Country*. The program received accreditation from Education Queensland in December 1998 and national accreditation for this program is under consideration by the Australian National Training Authority (ANTA). The development of the program was coordinated by the Indigenous Productivity Unit (IPU) of the Tropical North Qld Institute of TAFE under the advice of the National Curriculum Framework Steering Committee and Industry Reference Group and the Caring for Country Curriculum Advisory Committee. The IPU looks broadly to improve and increase Indigenous participation in education, and hence increase Indigenous competitiveness for employment. Links have also been established with resource management training elsewhere, including Batchelor College and Kakadu ranger training. Initial funding came directly through DETYA, as part of the Commonwealth government's Aboriginal Employment Development Policy. It now comes under the Queensland TAFE within the Department of Employment, Training and Industrial Relations. However, despite progress in accrediting this program, community ranger graduates are still required to have extra skills if they are to be employed as Rangers with the QPWS.

It reflects the interaction between Indigenous custom in NRM, institutional arrangements for Indigenous NRM that are part of structures specifically designed for Indigenous affairs administration, and 'mainstream' arrangements open to all Australians. Key positive characteristics, many of which have been identified throughout the last three decades, include the following:

- A new institutional arrangement in one field, such as the development of joint management for national parks, stimulates initiatives in other areas. Joint management led to a demand for training for Indigenous rangers, which over time stimulated important changes in the education sector, and in community initiatives in natural resource management (the concept of community rangers, analogous to park rangers).

- Community consultation, and identification of major community concerns, has influenced the existence or form of policies and programs in both mainstream and Indigenous-specific institutional arrangements for NRM. Consultation has increasingly become part of a negotiation process, in which Indigenous and non-Indigenous inputs and power are more evenly shared, and there is a commitment to incorporate Indigenous priorities into the final agreement. The need to cater for Indigenous protocols in intellectual property is a major example. Many other programs, such as CEPANCRM and IPAs have used consultation and negotiation processes with considerable success; and negotiation is central to the establishment of joint management plans for national parks such as Kakadu and Uluru Kata Tjuta.

- National and international *networking*, eventually fostered by DETYA's and ATSIC's financial assistance for Indigenous people to travel, is increasingly important. Examples include spin-offs from the Kowanyama community's establishment of a natural resource management office, based on learning from USA Native Americans, with interest in such an approach now being taken up by other community organisations including Quandamooka Land Council. Academics and non-Indigenous community staff, many of whom have examined initiatives from elsewhere, contribute to these learning processes. CLCs innovative approaches to Participatory Land Assessment and Planning owe much to international experience developed particularly in Africa, and lessons from this are now being taken up by Indigenous resource management agencies in other parts of Australia.

- Key events, including public inquiries (not necessarily in the NRM field), and commissioned studies, have exposed problems and provided recommendations which have given major impetus to new institutional arrangements. The cross-portfolio Aboriginal Economic Development Program, formed as a result of the Miller Report (Miller 1985) brought the Commonwealth environment and primary industries portfolios strongly into Indigenous NRM through special programs. *Caring for country* (Young et al 1991) exposed the barriers to Indigenous access to mainstream programs, challenging the relevant portfolios to adapt their programs to Indigenous needs. It also challenged ATSIC to recognise NRM as a fundamental element in its Indigenous land acquisition program, and provided a useful overview of Indigenous NRM activities to assist policy-makers. The Deaths in Custody and Stolen Generations Inquiry reports have each encompassed land and NRM issues in their recommendations, and have proved instrumental in the allocation of financial support to programs such as CEPANCRM and ARRI.

Nevertheless, despite these positive signs, significant problems still remain. These include, importantly, the problems of financial support for Indigenous natural resource management. As identified above, funding mechanisms for Indigenous NRM remain inadequate and often inappropriate. The situation has changed little over the last decade (Young et al 1991). Major deficiencies include:

- the provision of short-term programs to meet what are essentially long-term needs;
- failure to recognise that applicants, and particularly Indigenous applicants have to devote significant human and technical resources both to successfully obtaining funding, and to meeting the stringent terms and conditions that are applied in the wake of funding;
- failure to acknowledge that, because of the lack of funding continuity, individual Indigenous people's careers in NRM are very insecure;
- failure to provide adequate funding to cover heavy training costs;

- continuing mismatch between the purposes of funding bodies and the needs and aspirations of Indigenous resource managers; and
- a persistent scarcity of resources to provide professional and technical support for Indigenous natural resource management.

As a result many Indigenous NRM activities are financially supported through disparate sources. Indirect funding, such as funding for employing Indigenous resource managers and rangers through the community-controlled Community Development Employment Program funds (analogous to 'work for the dole') and DETYA employment and training funds probably still provide the vital security for much Indigenous NRM.

- Despite the excellent initiatives of Cairns TAFE, Batchelor College, Charles Sturt University and the Northern Territory University Faculty of Aboriginal and Torres Strait Islander Studies, much remains to be done nationally to provide educational programs geared to Indigenous needs, and where appropriate providing Indigenous resource managers with accredited training.
- Indigenous NRM continues to survive by fitting square pegs into round holes. Mainstream institutional frameworks generally take sectoral approaches, addressing the needs of NRM in agriculture or fisheries rather than seeing these needs in a holistic framework that encompasses many other elements essential to community development. For Indigenous people, NRM is intertwined with cultural heritage and is part of a broader community planning structure that also includes services such as education, health, infrastructure provision and economic development. Indigenous natural resource managers thus have to conform, at least on the surface, to guidelines that cannot be maintained and are inappropriate for their purposes. They may become 'foragers in the bureaucracy' (Young 1994).
- The contribution of Indigenous ecological knowledge to NRM needs must not be tokenistic. It should be overtly recognised as complementary and equally important as that of scientific knowledge to NRM. This must be an underlying principle of partnerships.
- NRM partnerships need to be based on mutual respect – the fact that Indigenous and non-Indigenous partners can have different goals needs to be accepted and accommodated.

Institutional adaptiveness

In terms of this book's overarching themes, we can make the following comments on characteristics of the sector of Indigenous resource management:

- Persistence. Funding uncertainties are a very significant constraint on successful Indigenous NRM. This should be a national concern, given that the management of *some 17 per cent* of the country – and many other areas under non-Indigenous ownership – is at stake. In contrast, numerous Indigenous communities and organisations have shown themselves to be very persistent indeed in their efforts to realise their aspirations towards effective environmental management.

- Purposefulness. Indigenous initiators of NRM projects have shown themselves very dedicated to their aims and programs, despite considerable odds. The rooting of NRM in customary law and cultural heritage may help to explain the strength and persistence of Indigenous intent. Different purposes in NRM, between Indigenous groups and their funding bodies, are still often not acknowledged.

- Information. A two-way approach to the handling of knowledge in NRM is developing, with increasing mutual recognition and interface between the paradigms of traditional ecological knowledge and western science. The recognition of intellectual property in traditional ecological knowledge, and the protocols for access to and dissemination of traditional knowledge, are important dimensions of NRM (egs in IPAs, and CLC participatory mapping);

- Inclusiveness. There remains a need to improve the inclusion of Indigenous people and their perspectives in NRM (eg, Toomelah, Quandamooka) although progress is noticeable particularly in the last decade or so.

- Flexibility. Flexibility is needed wherever partnerships are formed, to accommodate the interests of both parties. The negotiation of Indigenous Land Use Agreements under native title legislation is likely to prove an important arena for negotiated arrangement in NRM.

We are at a stage of rapid development of institutional arrangements in Indigenous NRM, thanks to the combined influences of native title legislation and its negotiation provisions, and the reconciliation movement. Indigenous Land Use Agreements, a term for agreements negotiated or ratified through native title provisions, are emerging as an important and flexible instrument for combining Indigenous and non-Indigenous aspirations in NRM. We are seeing the emergence of greater Indigenous involvement in planning, at regional and local levels, for a variety of reasons including the opportunities native title presents and particularly its emphasis on negotiated settlements. Specialised NRM programs for Indigenous groups are still required, in addition to fostering smoother access to mainstream programs. Australia needs to re-create support programs similar to CEPANCRM and ARRI, with longer life-spans, as a vital foundation for Indigenous NRM.

Acknowledgements

Elspeth Young died shortly before final publication of this book. Her co-authors wish to acknowledge the important contribution she has made to Australian Indigenous peoples' lives through her research and her strong personal commitment to Indigenous land management. She respected Indigenous peoples' perspectives, empathised with the diverse circumstances of each of the communities she worked with, and was able to work flexibly with each towards meeting their needs. She consistently provided benefits for the communities in which she conducted research, and gave credit to the people who supplied information. Through her research and educational roles she increased awareness of the important policy issues in Indigenous development, and inspired many others to devote their research opportunities to assisting Indigenous people. We will miss our friend and colleague, but her influence lives on.

We thank the following people and their organisations for participating interviews and providing information towards this study: Bruce Rose, Kevin McLeod, Dennis Rose, Steve Szabo, Alison Russell-French, *Environment Australia*; Chrissy Grant, Kieran Hotchin, *Australian Heritage Commission*; Barry Hunter, *Australian Conservation Foundation*; Ros Sultan, Pam Bigelow, Tom Collis, Andrew Robert, Wendy Ludwick, *Tropical North Queensland Institute of TAFE*; Dale Ruska, Sallyann Gudge, *Quandamooka Land and Sea Management Agency*; Albert Dennison, *Toomelah-Boggabilla Local Aboriginal Land Council*; Wieslaw Lichacz, Brian Stacey, Mark Sullivan, Joann Schmider, *ATSIC*; and Marcia Langton, *University of Melbourne*.

References

Breckwoldt, R, Boden, R, and Williams, R, 1997, *Contract Employment Program for Aboriginals in Natural and Cultural Resource Management, CEPANCRM: evaluation for Biodiversity Group, Environment Australia*, Canberra: Indigenous Programs Section, Environment Australia.

Coombs, HC, McCann, H, Ross, H, and Williams, N, 1989, *Land of promises: Aborigines and development in the East Kimberley*, Canberra: Aboriginal Studies Press.

Davies, J, Higginbottom, K, Noack, D, Ross H, and Young E, 1999, *Indigenous community wildlife management in Australia: Sustaining Eden*, London: International Institute for Environment and Development.

De Lacy, T, 1994, The Uluru/Kakadu Model – Anangu Tjukurrpa, 50,000 years of Aboriginal law and land management changing the concept of national parks in Australia, *Society and Natural Resources* 7: 479-498.

House of Representatives Standing Committee on Aboriginal Affairs, 1990, *Our future our selves*, Canberra: Australian Government Publishing Service.

House of Representatives Standing Committee on Environment, Recreation and the Arts (HRSCERA) 1993, *Biodiversity: the role of protected areas*, Canberra: AGPS.

Maslow, A, 1954, *Motivation and personality*, New York: Harper.

Miller, M, 1985, *Report of the Committee of Review of Aboriginal Employment and training Programs*, Canberra: AGPS.

Orchard, K, 2000, CEPANCRM case study, In Buchy, M, Ross H and Proctor, W, *Enhancing the information base in Australian natural resource management*, Report to Land and Water Resources Research and Development Corporation, Australian National University, Canberra.

Osherenko, G, 1988, *Sharing the power with native users: co-management regimes for Arctic wildlife*, Canadian Arctic Policy Paper 5, Ottawa: Canadian Arctic Resources Committee.

Padgett, A, 1999, Native title and associated resource use issues, Paper presented at the Australian Agricultural and Resource Economics Society 43rd Annual Conference, Christchurch, New Zealand, January 20-22.

Pinkerton, E (ed), 1989, *Cooperative management of local fisheries: new directions for improved management and community development*, Vancouver: University of British Columbia Press.

Rose, DB, 1996, *Nourishing terrains: Australian Aboriginal views of landscape and wilderness*, Canberra: Australian Heritage Commission.

Ross, H, 1999, New ethos, new solutions: lessons from Washington's co-operative environmental management agreements, *Australian Indigenous Law Reporter*, 4 (2): 1-28.

Smith, DE, 1998, *Indigenous Land Use Agreements: the opportunities, challenges and policy implications of the amended Native Title Act*, Research Discussion Paper 163/1998, Canberra: Centre for Aboriginal Economic Policy.

Smyth, D and Sutherland, J, 1996, *Indigenous Protected Areas: conservation partnerships with Indigenous landholders*, Canberra: Indigenous Protected Areas Unit, Biodiversity Group, Environment Australia.

Sullivan, P, 1989, *Aboriginal community representative organisations: intermediate cultural processes in the Kimberley region, Western Australia*, East Kimberley Impact Assessment Project working paper no 22, Canberra: Centre for Resource and Environmental Studies, Australian National University.

Szabo, S, 1999, Indigenous Protected Areas: a new approach to Biodiversity Conservation in Land and Sea Country, Unpublished paper, Biodiversity Group, Environment Australia, Canberra.

Taylor, J, 1998, Indigenous Participation in Conservation and Land Management Programs in Gillespie D and Cooke, P, *Improving the Capacity of Indigenous People to contribute to the conservation of Biodiversity in Australia*, Report commissioned by Environment Australia for the Biological Diversity Advisory Council.

Thackway, R, and Cresswell, ID, 1995, *An interim biogeographic regionalisation of Australia: a framework for establishing the national system of reserves*, Canberra: Australian Nature Conservation Agency.

Walsh, F, 1996, Interactions between land management agencies and Australian Aboriginal people: rationale, problems and some lessons, in Saunders, DA, Craig JL and Mattiske, EM (eds), *The role of networks*, pp 88-106, Chipping Norton, NSW: Surrey Beatty and Sons Pty Ltd.

Woenne-Green, S, Johnston, R, Sultan, R and Wallis, A, 1994, *Competing interests: Aboriginal participation in national parks and conservation reserves in Australia – A review*, Melbourne: Australian Conservation Foundation.

Young, E, 1988, Land use and resources: a black and white dichotomy, In: Heathcote, RL and Mabbutt, J (eds), *Land, water and people: geographical essays on resource management and the organisation of space in Australia*, pp 102-124, Sydney: Academy of Social Sciences of Australia/George Allen and Unwin.

Young, E, 1994, Foraging in the Bureaucracy: issues in land management and Aboriginal development, In: Jull, P, Mulrennan, M, Sullivan, M, Crough, G, and Lea, D (eds), *Surviving Columbus*, Darwin: NARU, ANU.

Young, EA, 1995: *Third world in the first: development and Indigenous peoples*, London/New York: Routledge.

Young, E, Ross, H, Johnson, J, and Kesteven, J, 1991, *Caring for country: Aborigines and land management*, Canberra: Australian National Parks and Wildlife Service.

18

The Landcare Experience

Allan Curtis

Bureau of Rural Sciences, Canberra

Australia has relied heavily on voluntary approaches, including Landcare, to managing a range of difficult, long-term environmental problems (Curtis and Lockwood 2000). Landcare means different things to different people. Campbell (1994) believed that most landholders see Landcare as a way of coming together and working with government to solve problems in their local area.

Landcare groups are autonomous in that they are not formally linked to government and members usually determine group structures, processes and priorities. Nevertheless, State agency staff and government funding priorities have played critical roles in Landcare group development and activity (Lockie 1992; Curtis 1998). Groups have also been dependent upon government for inter-group communications (Edgar and Patterson 1992). Uphoff (1991) referred to the paradox of participation, where 'top-down' efforts were required to promote 'bottom-up' development. Midgley (1986) concluded that there was little evidence that State support can lead to independent, effective community organisations. Landcare therefore appeals as an important international example to explore the potential of State-sponsored community participation to contribute to rural development (Curtis 1998).

This chapter draws upon the author's research and experience with Landcare in Victoria, including five statewide surveys between 1991 and 1998; case studies in the North East region during 1993 and 1997; and interviews and survey work in the Corangamite, Glenelg and Goulburn Broken regions during 1999. This research has investigated:

- Landcare program logic and effectiveness (Curtis et al 1995; Curtis and De Lacy 1996a; Curtis and De Lacy 1996b; Curtis and De Lacy 1998; Curtis 1999);
- agency-community partnerships in Landcare (Curtis and De Lacy 1995; Curtis 1998);
- factors affecting Landcare group effectiveness (Curtis et al 2000);
- women's participation and experience in Landcare (Curtis et al 1997);
- Landcare participation as volunteer activity (Curtis and Van Nouhuys 1999; Curtis 2000);
- the impact of Landcare networks (Curtis et al 1999); and
- burnout amongst Landcare participants (Byron and Curtis 2000).

Research undertaken in other Australian States is not discussed in this chapter. The author has also been a Landcare group member for over ten years and until recently, had been a ministerial appointee to regional catchment committees, regional assessment panels and to the Murray-Darling Basin Ministerial Council's Community Advisory Committee.

Reflecting on this research and experience the author explores the strengths and limitations of Landcare to identify some of the key principles and management approaches needed to underpin the work of effective local organisations and volunteers.

Landcare begins in Victoria

Landcare can be viewed as part of a lengthy process where Australians have adapted emerging theories of rural development to an Australian context. A small vanguard of Australian soil conservationists, extension agents and farmers were attracted by the core elements of rural development theory that emphasised self-help supported by change agents; human resource development rather than technology transfer; public participation; cooperative efforts at the local community scale; and the challenging of social and economic structures (Curtis 1998). Early experience with groups in Australia confirmed overseas evidence, including from the United States, that participation through local organisations could accomplish broad-based rural development (Jones and Rolls 1982; Chambers 1983; Esman and Uphoff 1984; Roling 1987).

Key players in the Victorian agencies responsible for Landcare nominated the development of over 100 Group Conservation Area projects (GCAs) between 1960 and 1980, as the most useful place to begin exploring the origins of Landcare (Edgar and Patterson 1992; O'Brien et al 1992; Poussard 1992; Pennicuik 1992). GCAs had legislative backing and distinguished between the government's responsibility to fund non-productive work and landholder responsibility to fund productive works. GCA projects were catchment based with strong agency input into planning and implementation. Participating landholders were required to enter into formal agreements to complete and maintain work carried out by agency staff. Despite widespread acceptance of these projects, they were 'top-down' and failed to generate a sense of community responsibility for tackling issues or maintaining project infrastructure after projects had been completed.

Drawing upon their experience with GCAs, agency staff worked with local landholders to establish Land Protection Groups that provided increased local participation and community control of projects. Farm Tree groups were also appearing in rural Victoria in the early 1980s. The first of these groups was established in 1981 through a partnership between the Victorian Farmers and Graziers Association (now the Victorian Farmers Federation) and the Garden State Committee (now Greening Australia, Victoria). Farm Tree groups represented an important development in Landcare by explicitly linking the conservation of biodiversity and agricultural production, and by establishing formal links between the conservation movement and the farming community.

These approaches were brought together under the Victorian Landcare program launched by the Department of Conservation and Environment and the Victorian Farmers Federation in 1986 (DCE 1992a; Kirner 2000). Poussard (1992: 233) summed up the essence of Landcare as being about 'landholders working in their own local social group to solve their own local land conservation problems in their own way.' The Landcare program was controlled by the Minister with advice from a steering committee with membership drawn from key stakeholders, including a Landcare group representative; and supported by a full-time statewide coordinator and agency staff in the regions (O'Brien et al 1992).

Edgar and Patterson (1992) suggested the Victorian Landcare program emerging in 1986 incorporated four elements: information exchange; financial assistance; community involvement; and enforcement or prosecution. They highlighted the efficacy of information transfer in achieving behaviour changes when individuals were highly motivated and where management changes were relatively straightforward and demonstrated to be profitable. These authors acknowledged this 'was often not the case with soil conservation, salinity or vermin and noxious weed control.' Under these circumstance incentives 'may be provided to farmers to encourage them to adopt a new practice. This can be justified where there is a significant off-site benefit to the community or to initiate the adoption of a practice which has significant benefit to the individuals but the adoption rate has been slow.' (1992: 199). The obligation of government to provide limited financial support for Landcare work where there was a community benefit was incorporated into the Victorian 'Decade of Landcare Plan' (DCE 1992a). Edgar and Patterson (1992) suggested enforcement and prosecution was a last resort. Indeed, the Victorian 'Decade of Landcare Plan' explicitly stated that 'The Landcare Program departs from a regulatory approach ...' (DCE 1992b: 20).

Most Landcare groups have developed in rural areas, membership being voluntary and open to any local person. Groups frequently operate at catchment or subcatchment scales and are encouraged to view their activities holistically, using a systems approach. Groups have no legislative backing and are only informally linked to local government and regional planning bodies such as Catchment Management Committees (CMC). While the focus of group activity is usually on privately owned or leased land managed by group members, groups also work on roadsides, reserves and other public lands. Groups are involved in a variety of rural development activities, including:

- meetings held to discuss issues, identify priorities, liaise with agency staff, prepare funding submissions and debate resource management issues;
- workshops conducted to develop property and catchment plans and enhance skills;
- field days, farm walks and demonstration sites used to identify best practices;

- educational and promotional activities such as tours, conferences, workshops, newsletters and field guides to facilitate information exchange; and

- onground work such as tree planting and seed collection, building salinity and erosion control structures, pest plant and animal control, and erecting fencing.

The benefits of Landcare membership for landholders were seen as being:

- sharing problems and ideas;

- working more effectively to address common problems;

- learning about land management;

- planning at the property and catchment scale so that resource management is based upon a shared understanding of important physical, social and economic processes operating within and beyond the farm gate;

- accessing financial and technical assistance from government; and

- having greater opportunities for social interaction (Campbell 1989; Curtis and De Lacy 1995).

Recognising the success of Landcare groups as a potent force for improved natural resource management, the National Soil Conservation Program (NSCP) was re-organised in 1988 to incorporate Community Landcare Support (Campbell 1991). The NSCP had been established in 1983 to provide national leadership in the management of land degradation issues (Roberts 1989; Chamala and Mortiss 1990). During 1988, the Australian Conservation Foundation (ACF) and the National Farmers Federation (NFF) joined forces to develop a joint proposal for a National Land Management Program (Farley and Toyne 1989). After lobbying from major farmer and conservation groups, the Commonwealth government committed spending of $360 million in the *Decade of Landcare* program (Hawke 1989). Landcare was now a national program.

Landcare evaluation

Program evaluation is an important but challenging undertaking. Cook and Shadish (1986: 193-194) explained that program evaluators seek 'knowledge about the value of social programs and their constituent parts, knowledge that can be used in the short term to make the programs more responsive to the social problems they are meant to ameliorate.' While consideration of program effectiveness might involve assessment of the achievement of goals assigned by program managers, Scriven (1993) argued this should only occur to the extent goals overlapped stakeholder needs. Prosavac and Carey (1992) raised the issue of the appropriateness of programs and emphasised the importance of identifying the theoretical framework underlying a program. Unravelling program logic is also seen as an important step in identifying intermediate objectives used to assess program effectiveness (Chen 1990; Rossi and

Freeman 1985). It is also important to distinguish the program as implemented from the program as planned (Patton 1990).

Evaluation of Landcare offered particular challenges in that there were a large number of stakeholders, considerable regional variation in program implementation and little detail in program documentation about program logic. There was also the issue of what could reasonably be expected of volunteer groups working with limited resources to address very difficult issues. As might be expected, there has been considerable debate about these issues and a variety of approaches adopted. Most Australians approaching the evaluation of Landcare have agreed that it is unreasonable to assess group effectiveness by measuring changes in the biophysical condition of watersheds.

Campbell (1992) and later, Alexander (1995) reported their observations as National Landcare Facilitators working with groups and other stakeholders across Australia. Woodhill (1990) interviewed a large number of Landcare participants in the early stages of Landcare in the State of New South Wales to investigate program implementation and stakeholder concerns. Black and Reeve (1993) and Mues et al (1994; 1998) employed quasi-experimental designs using surveys to explore the impact of Landcare on the adoption of best practice and identify correlates of adoption. Carr (1993), Ewing (1995), Lockie (1995) and Morrisey and Lawrence (1995) completed qualitative studies of small numbers of Landcare groups to explore, amongst other things, stakeholder perspectives of Landcare, group effectiveness, and the impact of Landcare on social relationships. The federal government completed a comprehensive review of the Decade of Landcare Plan (Commonwealth of Australia 1997) and used the Australian National Audit Office to review the effectiveness and efficiency of natural resource management programs, including Landcare (ANAO 1997). Consultants engaged by the federal government in 1999 to evaluate NHT programs, including Landcare, were asked to examine the achievement of program objectives.

Examination of program documents (ASCC 1991) and discussions with program managers suggested that from a government perspective, community Landcare was a catalytic program attempting to engage a large proportion of the rural population and produce more aware, informed, skilled and adaptive resource managers with a stronger stewardship ethic. It was expected that this process would contribute to the adoption of more sustainable practices (Curtis and De Lacy 1995). Landcare therefore involved limited government funding of education and demonstration activities as opposed to large scale, onground work. This changed in the lead up to the 1996 Federal election, when both major political parties committed to increased Landcare funding, including onground work on private land where there were identifiable conservation benefits.

With proceeds from the partial sale of Telstra, the national communications carrier, the incoming Liberal Government established a five-year, $1.25 billion Natural Heritage Trust (NHT) (Commonwealth of Australia 1998). The NHT employs cost-sharing principles that enable community and private benefits from specific works to be identified. The National Landcare Program is one of the programs funded under the NHT. In 1999-2000, the NHT funded 870 NLP projects, worth $71 million of the $200 million spent through the NHT (Wonder 2000). Landcare groups are often involved in other NHT programs and have become an important part of the delivery mechanism for NHT.

Landcare achievements

Landcare offers a powerful example of how to establish effective local organisations across a range of jurisdictions and issues. Landcare has mobilised a large cross-section of the rural population. There are now over 4,000 Landcare groups with around 120,000 volunteer members or just over 30 per cent of the farming community (Mues et al 1998) or about 50 per cent of households in areas with a Landcare group (Curtis 1998). Groups provide opportunities to learn by doing and through interaction with peers (Chamala 1995; Millar and Curtis 1997). Group processes enable participants to discuss conflicting views in a reasonable fashion and have generally enhanced social cohesion, increased the capacity of rural communities to attract resources from governments and better equipped them to respond to change (Alexander 1995; Curtis and De Lacy 1995). With strong agency commitment to participatory processes, agency staff and Landcare members have established robust, productive partnerships and avoided many of the perils of co-option (Curtis 1998). Landcare participation has also increased awareness of issues, enhanced landholder skills and knowledge and contributed to increased adoption of best management practices (Mues et al 1994, 1998; Curtis and De Lacy 1996a). There are also examples where group activity has had substantial impacts on land and water degradation at the local or subcatchment scale (Campbell 1994; Commonwealth of Australia 1997). Recent evaluations of NHT suggest that government investment through Landcare has been more than matched by community contributions (Hill 2000). Landcare participants are represented on regional Catchment Management Committees (CMC) and other important fora and are contributing to important natural resource management decision-making (Curtis et al 1995; Ewing 2000). By enhancing citizen competency, providing continuity of community representation and acting as a place of retained knowledge, Landcare groups and their emerging networks appear likely to bridge the gap between the demands of adaptive management and the limitations of stakeholder participation (Curtis et al 1999).

In drawing lessons from the Australian experience with Landcare it is important to explore some of the key reasons Landcare has been successful. Support for Landcare has been linked to increased community awareness of the social and environmental costs of land degradation. It also seems reasonable to argue that part of the reason for such widespread acceptance of Landcare was increased awareness of the extent of social and economic decline in rural areas and of the need to address these issues. Australia has a tradition of strong government intervention in economic and social affairs and this may explain why a program such as Landcare might take hold easier in Australia than in other countries, for example in the United States. With hindsight, the apparent failure to articulate a detailed program structure also appears to have been a strength: one reason Landcare has such broad appeal is because different stakeholders have been able to attach their own meaning to Landcare. Previous discussion of the beginnings of Landcare in Victoria suggested that much of the early success of Landcare was due to the energies, commitment and expertise of agency staff. There were also important community leaders who embraced Landcare and its precursor organisations and worked tirelessly to establish local groups and build the political coalition necessary to support Landcare.

Landcare emerged as part of an iterative process of applying sound rural development theory and practice in Australian contexts over a considerable time frame. Amongst other things, Landcare embraced:

- the local scale as the most appropriate for mobilising community participation;
- the use of groups as a strategy for learning by doing, drawing on local knowledge, invoking peer pressure to encourage adoption of improved practices and overcome the problem of free-riders, increasing the capacity of local people to pull down resources and shape decisions, and to plan for and take onground action;
- a high degree of group autonomy as a way of empowering landholders; and
- the use of change agents as important catalyst for the emergence and development of groups.

Landcare success can also be attributed to its implementation as part of total catchment management (TCM) as the planning framework for achieving ecologically sustainable development in Australia (see Ewing, this volume for discussion of catchment management in Australia and of Landcare/CMC links). The Landcare package therefore included:

- a systems approach to resource management based on catchments as the planning unit;
- integration of economic, social and environmental values;
- recognition that stakeholder participation is an essential component of legitimate, successful resource management;
- use of an adaptive approach to planning and management;
- recognition of the need to address long term and incremental change; and
- establishment of catchment-based regional planning units and clearly differentiating the roles of these regional flora and Landcare groups (Curtis and Lockwood 2000).

Despite the rhetoric of Landcare as a 'grass roots' development, government (and bipartisan) support has been critical to Landcare success. Amongst other things, government support has enhanced Landcare credibility; funded facilitation and coordination by agency staff; provided important communication links between groups; and through cost-sharing arrangements under NLP/NHT, funded much of the community education and onground work of groups. Community groups were initially able to attract funds on the basis of a two dollar government contribution for each community dollar invested. Community contributions could be of an 'in-kind' nature, that is, in labour and materials. State and federal government support for arrangements establishing regional CMCs has also facilitated regional planning and improved linkages between Landcare groups.

Landcare limitations

Despite impressive achievements, there have been concerns about Landcare program logic and implementation (Lawrence 2000). Landcare has been criticised as an exercise in shifting responsibility for action from government to local communities (Martin et al 1992). Rural communities are aware that successive Victorian governments have cut extension support and other programs in rural areas (Curtis 1998). Landcare participants know they are being asked to undertake work that has community benefits in terms of bio-diversity conservation, improved public health and protecting export income (agriculture and tourism). They also understand that many of the problems they are being asked to address have resulted from previous government policies. Establishment of the NHT with federal government funding for large-scale onground work was in part an acknowledgment of the legitimacy of these arguments. Successive federal governments have also expressed concern that State governments were using federal Landcare/NHT funds to cover for reduced State government funding on natural resource management (Hill 2000).

There are concerns about government co-opting Landcare. Midgley (1986: 41) defined co-option as 'a process by which the State seeks to gain control over grass-roots movements and to manipulate them for its own ends.' State agency staff shape the decision making of many Landcare groups (Curtis 1999). Governments can also control groups through their funding priorities (Lockie 1992) and group work is significantly related to government funding (Curtis 1999). There is also evidence that State agencies have captured a large part of the Landcare funds provided by the federal government (Curtis 1998).

Much of the Landcare program logic was sound in that Landcare participation could reasonably be expected to contribute to increased awareness of issues, enhanced landholder skills and knowledge and increased adoption of best management practices. The Landcare program also assumed that attitudinal change, particularly the development of a stewardship ethic, would be a cost-effective lever for effecting behavioural change. Australian research suggests that this approach was misguided in that most farmers had a strong stewardship ethic and stewardship is not strongly linked to adoption of best-practice (Curtis and De Lacy 1998). This research suggests it is more important to address the economic constraints affecting the capacity of landholders to adopt best practice or move to more profitable enterprises.

Conservationists are alarmed by continued loss of critical habitats and believe Landcare has not adequately addressed biodiversity conservation. In part, these concerns reflect unrealistic expectations of Landcare. Landholders are most concerned about the economic impacts of land degradation.

However, landholders are concerned about the environmental impacts of land degradation and it appears that much of the appeal of Landcare is that it reflects values already widely held in the rural community, including a strong stewardship ethic (Curtis and De Lacy 1998). Conservationists must appreciate the limited capacity of landholders to adopt costly or unproven conservation measures when most are struggling financially. CMC members are usually Ministerial appointees (Ewing 2000) and conservationists, including the ACF, have been excluded from most regional CMCs and RAPs on the basis that membership of these bodies should be skills and not stakeholder based. This approach has constrained the capacity of Landcare to deliver on biodiversity conservation (Curtis and Lockwood 2000).

Unfortunately, efforts to develop comprehensive cost-sharing guidelines for the NHT have foundered within the federal natural resource management bureaucracy. Campbell (1997: 144), as Assistant Secretary in Environment Australia, highlighted this issue when he stated: 'we need better ways of identifying and evaluating the public good to justify investment of public funds on individual properties, and to work out equitable cost-sharing arrangements.' In the absence of rigorous, transparent cost-sharing guidelines there is considerable risk that public benefits flowing from NHT expenditure will not be maximised and that the NHT process will become politicised (Curtis and Lockwood 2000).

Concerns with NHT administrative processes go beyond the normal teething problems that might accompany the start-up of a large program. Separate regional, State and federal assessment panels assess NHT project applications by Landcare groups. As the Australian National Audit Office (ANAO 1997) indicated, there should be no need for three separate assessments of projects. Curtis and Lockwood (2000) argued for the devolution of greater power to regional communities, suggesting that each CMC be given a budget to manage to achieve outcomes identified in their regional catchment plan and negotiated with State and federal agencies. Landcare groups would then simply apply to their regional CMC for funding. Boully (2000) emphasised that the targets identified through such a process would need to be backed up by sanctions implemented by government. This debate has been advanced considerably by the recently released discussion paper addressing the sustainable management of natural resources in rural Australia (Commonwealth of Australia 1999).

Landcare groups also complain that NHT application forms are too complex. The 1999 application form was still over nine pages in length with 46 pages of background questions to be addressed. By comparison, Victorian government weed and rabbit programs have delivered substantial sums of money in a short period based on a simple two-page application form. The potential of poor program management to affect Landcare outcomes was highlighted by the decline in onground work in Victoria in 1997-98 that followed delays of up to nine months in funding NHT projects (Curtis 1999). Failure by government to deliver NHT funds on time was perceived as a breach of trust that contributed to growing disillusionment about government commitment to a Landcare partnership (Curtis 1999).

The capacity of landholders to give their time and energy to Landcare is being tested by recent attempts to use Landcare as a vehicle for delivering substantial proportions of NHT funds. Landcare group activity is at historically high levels (Curtis 2000). For example, in the 1999 regional studies in Victoria, significantly higher proportions of respondents indicated that 1997-98 was the most active year compared to 1995-96. Almost three-quarters of the respondents in the 1999 regional studies said that starting or completing a project was an important reason for changes in Landcare activity levels. This explanation scored the highest or second highest rating. Increased levels of Landcare activity in recent years correspond with significantly increased funding to groups under the NHT, Victorian government rabbit and weed control programs and from levies imposed on property owners by CMCs (Victoria's Catchment Management Authorities). For example, the mean value of government funding has risen significantly from $8,232 in 1994-95 to $13,966 in 1997-98 (Curtis 1999). A stepwise multiple regression of selected variables from the 1997-98 survey found a significant positive relationship between group ranking on an activity index combining onground and community education activities and government funding; frequency of contact with government officers; and the age of the group (Curtis et al 2000).

Data from the 1999 Goulburn Broken survey emphasised the heavy commitments of rural people to paid employment, their families and volunteer work, including Landcare (Curtis 2000). When on-farm and off-farm work was combined, 76 per cent of respondents worked more than 40 hours per week, with a median of 59 hours per week. Just under half the respondents indicated that they contributed to the care of children under the age of 18, with 75 per cent of these individuals contributing to the care of more than one child. Eighty per cent of respondents were a member of at least one other voluntary group (mean 3) and 88 per cent of these respondents said they attend activities quarterly for at least one other group. Work, family and other volunteer commitments were rated very highly as factors contributing to changes over time in the level of respondent's Landcare activity. Changed workload had the number one rating and changed family commitment was rated number two. Group leaders and members are devoting considerable time to Landcare group activity. Group leaders recalled spending a mean of four hours per week and members just over two hours per week on group activities over a three month period. In another study leaders were asked to keep a diary of their administrative work in the previous month (April 1999). April is a month of moderate levels of activity for most groups. Combining the time spent by the three leaders of each group produced a mean of 17.2 hours spent on administrative activity per group, per week. This represents close to half of a full-time employed person (Curtis 2000). It seems we are fast approaching the limits of volunteers to contribute to Landcare. Lack of time to carry out Landcare work was rated as a major constraint affecting Victorian groups by 32 per cent of respondents in 1997-98, up significantly from 21 per cent in 1994-95 (Curtis 2000).

There are critical, ongoing Landcare group management issues. Many groups need assistance with leadership succession planning, with priority setting and catchment planning, and with member recruitment and retention

(Curtis 2000). Leadership is considered a critical factor in organisational success (Waddock and Bannister 1991). A majority of respondents in the 1997-98 Victorian survey said that support for leadership and management training was inadequate. Over half of the respondents in the 1999 regional studies said that usually there is not someone willing to take on the leadership roles in their group. Leadership issues were rated as an important factor affecting group activity levels by about half the respondents. Most groups did not have an established process for leadership succession (Curtis 2000).

Priority setting is also linked with more effective voluntary groups (Selin and Myers 1995). In the 1997-98 Victorian survey there was a significant positive correlation between catchment planning and group activity. About half of the respondents in the 1999 regional studies said their group was not involved in catchment planning. Perhaps of greater concern was the finding that most respondents thought catchment planning was not important in getting onground work under way. Part of the explanation seemed to be that there was often no documented outcome of planning processes (Curtis 2000).

The most successful volunteer organisations are those with strong induction programs and management styles that reinforce the worth of volunteer contributions (Pearce 1993). Volunteer literature emphasises that it is more efficient to devote resources to retention than to attracting and inducting recruits (Curtis and Van Nouhuys 1999). Around 40 per cent of groups in the 1999 regional studies had not adopted approaches likely to enhance membership retention. For example, groups did not follow up with members when there was a pattern of absence and had not publicly acknowledged the contribution of individual members to projects or administration (Curtis 2000). Pearce (1993) suggested the benefits of social interaction are an important factor motivating people to volunteer and the most important reason volunteers remained with an organisation. About half the respondents in the 1999 regional studies said their group had not been involved in social activities in the past year and social activity rated very low in terms of the proportion of group energy devoted to a range of group activities (Curtis 2000).

Landcare participants say they receive inadequate support in terms of training to improve the competencies of group leaders; government funding for onground Landcare work; and support with group administration, particularly in terms of funding to employ coordinators. Fifty-five per cent of the 1997-98 Victorian respondents said support with leadership and management training for leaders was inadequate. While the mean value of funding per Landcare group has increased significantly under the NHT, 33 per cent of Victorian groups received less than $2,000 in 1997-98 and a majority of groups said the funds they received were inadequate to address problems in their area. The proportion of Victorian groups reporting inadequate government support increased significantly between 1991-92 and 1997-98 for group administration (from 18% to 46%); and for coordination of onground work (from 22% to 35%). Reduced State government extension support for groups (around 40% in the 1990s) was highlighted by a significant increase in groups reporting no or rare contact with agency staff (up from 8% in 1994-95 to 15% in 1997-98) (Curtis 2000).

Most Victorian Landcare groups do not have a funded coordinator (62%, 1997-98). Some groups have members with the skills, commitment and time to undertake group administration, but many groups want ongoing funding of a coordinator (usually part-time and often in partnership with other groups). The assumption was that groups could be 'kick-started' by government funding of a coordinator, but over time they would become largely independent of funded coordination. At present there is no provision under the NHT to fund coordinator positions that are not project based. This approach fails to acknowledge the growing weight of Australian (Campbell 1992; Rush 1992; Curtis 1999) and overseas (Brudney 1990; Pearce 1993) evidence highlighting the critical role of group coordination in volunteer programs. Given the heavy work, family, Landcare and other community responsibilities of Landcare volunteers it seems the Landcare/NHT reflects an outdated view of the reality of life for most rural people. Individual landholders should not be expected to take leading roles in administering government funded Landcare projects. If the minimum standard of administrative support available under the NHT was a coordinator shared between four or five groups, then there would be about 1000 Landcare group coordinator positions across Australia. This might cost around sixty million dollars per year. One way of looking at this investment is that there are about one thousand park ranger positions across Australia managing the relatively small area of State and national parks.

Campbell (1992) and Curtis (1999) identified the potential for burnout in Landcare. Maslach and Jackson (1981) defined burnout as a syndrome with three core dimensions – emotional exhaustion, depersonalisation and reduced personal accomplishment – that can occur among individuals who do 'people work' of some kind. In response to community and agency concerns about burnout, a pilot study was undertaken in the Goulburn Broken in 1999 to trial a burnout measure, assess the extent of burnout and identify factors contributing to higher burnout (Byron et al 1999). This research used a modified version of the Maslach Burnout Inventory (MBI), the most widely used and validated burnout measure (Schaufeli et al 1993). Analysis of Goulburn Broken survey data indicated that a small proportion of individuals were experiencing high levels of burnout, but that burnout was an issue for many respondents. By comparison with norms from previous studies overseas:

- 30 per cent per cent of leaders and 12 per cent of members were above the norm for emotional exhaustion;
- 9 per cent per cent of leaders and 15 per cent of members were above the norm for depersonalisation; and
- 80 per cent of leaders and 90 per cent of members had scores on personal accomplishment below the norm but indicating higher burnout (Byron et al 1999).

Multivariate analyses showed that increased levels of emotional exhaustion (higher burnout) were significantly associated with respondents who had negative evaluations of group leadership; attendance at a higher proportion of Landcare activities; and indicated that in their group some important things just do not get done. Men were significantly more likely to have high levels of depersonalisation. Lower scores on the personal accomplishment sub-scale (higher burnout) were significantly associated with respondents who had attended a smaller proportion of all group activities; spent fewer hours on Landcare activity; spent more hours per week on farming related activity; and felt that their group did not prioritise their Landcare activities. To the extent that many of these correlates of higher burnout are ongoing issues it seems there is considerable potential for burnout to increase over time (Byron and Curtis 2000). One approach to the management of burnout is to hold burnout workshops to raise the awareness of burnout and explore management strategies in a constructive manner. It would be unreasonable to expect groups to develop and undertake such complex management practices without substantial assistance from trained support staff.

These program management deficiencies reflect the absence of a coherent and determined approach to the management of Landcare as a volunteer organisation. The reality is that community Landcare has been run with small budgets and limited numbers of personnel; has very few senior staff directly involved in program management; and a limited number of managers with specific knowledge of volunteer management. The literature on volunteerism provides a useful place to start for those attempting to address these issues (Curtis and Van Nouhuys 1999).

Conclusions

As a program that involved only limited funding of a community development process, Landcare has probably exceeded any realistic goals established at the start of the Decade of Landcare in 1989. Landcare group activity has mobilised a large cross-section of the rural community, increased awareness of issues, enhanced the knowledge and skills of resource managers, increased adoption of best practice and contributed to improved environmental conditions in some smaller catchments. The rapidly increasing number of Landcare networks provide another tier of local organisation likely to enhance the capacity of groups to address regional problems, pull down resources for Landcare and shape natural resource management policy. Landcare therefore offers a powerful example of how to establish effective local organisations across a range of jurisdictions and issues.

Support for Landcare has been linked to increased community awareness of the social and environmental costs of land degradation. It also seems reasonable to argue that part of the reason for such widespread acceptance of Landcare was increased awareness of the extent of social and economic decline in rural areas and of the need to address these issues. Australia has a tradition of strong government intervention in economic and social affairs and this may explain why a program such as Landcare might take hold easier in Australia than in other countries. The apparent failure to articulate a detailed program structure also appears to have been a strength. One of the reasons Landcare has such broad appeal is because different stakeholders have been able to attach their own meaning to Landcare. Much of the early success of Landcare in Victoria was due to the energies and commitment of agency staff. There were also important community leaders who embraced Landcare and its precursor organisations and worked tirelessly to establish local groups and build the political coalition necessary to support Landcare. Despite the rhetoric of Landcare 'grass roots' development, government support has been critical to Landcare success. It is also important to remember that Landcare emerged over time as part of an iterative process in which sound rural development theory and practice was adapted to Australian contexts.

There are a number of critiques of Landcare, but it seems to me that poor program management at State and federal levels has had greatest impact on Landcare outcomes. Landcare participants say they need more support in terms of government funding for onground work; better support for group administration, particularly in terms of funding of coordinators; and training for group leaders. In part, these program management deficiencies reflect the absence of a coherent and determined approach to the management of Landcare as a volunteer organisation. Many groups are not effectively managing leadership succession planning, priority setting and catchment planning, or member recruitment and retention. Landcare is only loosely coordinated at State and regional levels and there are few staff dedicated to providing that support. The dismantling of State government funded agency extension services and the deliberate gearing up of Landcare group activity under the NHT has exacerbated these deficiencies in support to groups and raised questions about government commitment to Landcare. These issues are contributing to growing disillusionment with Landcare and undermining public trust in government. Given their work, family, Landcare and other community responsibilities, most rural people have very little discretionary time to devote to Landcare activity. Given the low profitability of key farming enterprises it is difficult to afford labour that is critical for fencing and tree planting. Rural land managers also understand that public benefits exceed the private benefits for much of the onground Landcare work they are being exhorted to undertake and that government policies have often contributed to current problems. There is also evidence that these issues are contributing to burnout amongst Landcare participants and there is considerable potential for burnout to increase over time.

It seems that without improved support that we are approaching the limits of what Landcare participants can accomplish. In part, the rhetoric of support for Landcare has not been matched by resources because increased federal government commitment of resources has often only substituted for cuts made by State governments, particularly in Victoria. Given the apparent limits of voluntary action and evidence that environmental conditions continue to deteriorate, Australians need to re-evaluate their reliance on voluntary approaches to improved natural resource management (see also Ewing, Orchard et al, Dore et al, this volume). However, Landcare should remain as one of the preferred approaches to improving resource management. One way of supporting Landcare is to augment the work of rural land managers with the employment of professional organisations, such as the Australian Trust for Conservation Volunteers (ATCV) that are paid to implement onground work. For large regional projects the onerous tasks of project management should pass from Landcare groups to regional CMCs.

The Australian experience with Landcare suggests that some of the key principles and the types of support that might underpin a more effective approach to supporting these local organisations include:

- establishing institutional arrangements that facilitate the transfer of decision making to local and regional stakeholder representatives;
- clearly articulating and separating the roles of regional planning bodies (aggregating and articulating regional needs, setting regional priorities for allocating government funds, providing accountability for expenditure of public moneys, linking and supporting independent local groups, managing the implementation of large regional projects) and local community groups (mobilising participation, initiating social learning, undertaking onground work at the local scale with adequate support);
- acknowledging that the most important roles for most landholders are participating in group activities, articulating community values and establishing community priorities and undertaking work on their properties as opposed to administering government funded projects;
- developing rigorous and transparent cost sharing principles that can be used to allocate public money for work on private land where there are community benefits;
- provision of sufficient government funding to support priority setting, group coordination, and onground work on private property to the extent activities match regional priorities and have identifiable community benefits;
- fostering an agency culture that supports community participation;
- acknowledging that community organisations cannot be sustained without professional management that addresses critical group management issues, enhances the skills of group coordinators and leaders, and facilitates feedback to program managers;
- facilitating and resourcing the development of independent networks of community groups;
- accepting that interest in group establishment and the intensity of individual participation will vary between communities, individuals, and over time, and that people must be encouraged to 'come when they are ready'; and
- identifying flexible policy packages to accommodate the diversity of landholders' circumstances and motivations, including incentives for landholders to maintain the supply of public benefits, particularly for biodiversity conservation.

Greater devolution of power and responsibility to local and regional organisations must be matched by the commitment of sufficient resources, particularly in those areas where agriculture is unprofitable or community benefits of work exceed private benefits. We cannot assume that Landcare activity will be sustainable without ongoing and substantial investment by government.

References

Alexander, H, 1995, A framework for change: The state of the community Landcare movement in Australia, The National Landcare Facilitator Project Annual Report, Canberra: National Landcare Program.

Australian National Audit Office, 1997, *Commonwealth Natural Resource Management and Environment Programs: Australia's land, water and vegetation resources*, The Auditor-General performance audit, Report No, 36: 1996-97, Canberra: Australian Government Publishing Service.

Australian Soil Conservation Council, 1991, *Decade of Landcare plan*, ASCC: Canberra.

Black, AW and I, Reeve, 1993, Participation in Landcare groups: the relative importance of attitudinal and situational factors, *Journal of Environmental Management* 39:51-57.

Boully, L, 2000, Relationships and a learning culture, pp 44-48 in Proceedings of the International Landcare 2000 Conference: Changing Landscapes – Shaping Futures, 2-5 March 2000, Melbourne.

Brudney, JL, 1990, *Fostering volunteer programs in the public sector: planning, initiating and managing voluntary activities*, San Francisco: Jossey-Bass.

Byron, I and A, Curtis, 2000, Landcare in Australia: burned out and browned off, *Local Environment* 6: 313-328.

Byron, I, Curtis, A and Lockwood, M, 1999, *Providing improved support for Landcare in the Shepparton Irrigation Region*, Albury: The Johnstone Centre, Charles Sturt University.

Campbell, A, 1997, Facilitating Landcare: Conceptual and Practical Dilemmas, pp 143-153 in Lockie, S and Vanclay, F (eds), *Critical Landcare*, Wagga Wagga: Centre for Rural Social Research, Charles Sturt University.

Campbell, A, 1994, *Landcare: Communities shaping the land and the future*, Allen & Unwin, Sydney, Australia.

Campbell, A, 1992, Taking the long view in tough times, National Landcare facilitator 3rd annual report, To Department of Primary Industries and Energy, Canberra: National Soil Conservation Program.

Campbell, A, 1991, Landcare-testing times, National Landcare facilitator 2nd annual report to Department of Primary Industries and Energy, Canberra: National Soil Conservation Program.

Campbell, A, 1989, Landcare in Australia: an overview, *Australian Journal of Soil and Water Conservation* 2(4): 18-20.

Carr, A, 1993, Community involvement in landcare: The case of Downside, Report No, 93/2, Canberra: Centre for Resource and Environmental Studies, Australian National University.

Chamala, S, 1995, Group effectiveness: from group extension methods to participative community Landcare groups, pp 5-43 in *Participative approaches to Landcare: policies and programs*, Chamala, S and Keith, K (eds), Brisbane: Academic Press.

Chamala, S, and Mortiss, P, 1990, *Working together for land care*, Brisbane: Australian Academic Press.

Chambers, R, 1983, Rural development: putting the last first, New York: Longman.

Chen, HT, 1990, *Theory-driven evaluations*, Newbury Park, California: Sage.

Commonwealth of Australia, 1998, *Natural Heritage Trust-guide to new applications 1998-1999*, Canberra: Commonwealth of Australia.

Commonwealth of Australia, 1999, Managing natural resources in rural Australia for a sustainable future, a discussion paper for developing national policy, Canberra: Commonwealth of Australia.

Commonwealth of Australia, 1997, *Evaluation report of the Decade of Landcare Plan-National Overview*, Canberra: Commonwealth of Australia.

Cook, TD and Shadish, WR, 1986, Program evaluation: the worldly science, *Annual Review of Psychology* 37: 193-232.

Curtis, A, 2000, Landcare: approaching the limits of volunteer action, *Australian Journal of Environmental Management*, 7: 19-27.

Curtis, A, 1999, Landcare: beyond onground work, *Natural Resources Management*, 2(2): 4-9.

Curtis, A, 1998, The agency/community partnership in Landcare: lessons for state-sponsored citizen resource management, *Environmental Management*, 22(4): 563-574.

Curtis, A, and Lockwood, M, 2000, Landcare and catchment management in Australia: lessons for state-sponsored community participation, *Society and Natural Resources*, 13: 61-73.

Curtis, A, and Van Nouhuys, M, 1999, Landcare participation in Australia: the volunteer perspective, *Sustainable Development*, 7(2): 98-111.

Curtis, A and De Lacy, T, 1998, Landcare, stewardship and sustainable agriculture in Australia, *Environmental Values* 7: 59-78.

Curtis, A and De Lacy, T, 1996a, Landcare in Australia: beyond the expert farmer, *Agriculture and Human Values* 13(1): 20-31.

Curtis, A and De Lacy, T, 1996b, Landcare in Australia: does it make a difference, *Journal of Environmental Management* 46: 119-137.

Curtis, A and De Lacy, T, 1995, Landcare evaluation in Australia: towards an effective partnership between agencies, community groups and researchers, *Journal of Soil and Water Conservation* 50(1): 15-20.

Curtis, A, Van Nouhuys, M, Robinson, W and MacKay, J, 2000, Exploring Landcare effectiveness using organisational theory, *Australian Geographer* 31: 349-366.

Curtis, A, Britton, A and Sobels, J, 1999, Landcare networks as local organisations contributing to state-sponsored community participation, *Journal of Environmental Planning and Management*, 42(1): 5-21.

Curtis, A, Davidson, P, and De Lacy, T, 1997, The participation and experience of women in landcare, *Journal of Sustainable Agriculture*, 10(2/3): 37-55.

Curtis, A, Birckhead, J and De Lacy, T, 1995, Community participation in landcare policy in Australia: The Victorian experience with regional landcare plans, *Society and Natural Resources* 8: 415-430.

Department of Conservation and Environment, 1992a, Victoria's decade of Landcare plan, Melbourne: Australia, DCE.

Department of Conservation and Environment, 1992b, Decade of landcare guidelines regional landcare action plans, Melbourne: Australia, DCE.

Edgar, RV, and Patterson, D, 1992, The evolution continues – Victorian Landcare groups, pp 198-203 in Proceedings Volume 1 of the 7th International Soil Conservation Organisation conference – people protecting their land, 27-30 September, Sydney.

Esman, MJ and Uphoff, NT, 1984, *Local organisations: intermediaries in rural development*, New York: Cornell University Press.

Ewing, S, 2000, The place of Landcare in catchment management structures, pp 113-118 in Proceedings of the International Landcare 2000 Conference: Changing Landscapes – Shaping Futures, 2-5 March 2000, Melbourne.

Ewing, S, 1995, Small is beautiful: the place of the case study in Landcare evaluation, *Rural Society* 5(2/3): 38-43.

Farley, R, and P, Toyne, 1989, A national land management programme, *Australian Journal of Soil and Water Conservation* 11(2): 6-9.

Hawke, RJL, 1989, *Our country: Our future*, Statement – on the environment by the Prime Minister of Australia, Canberra: Australian Government Publishing Service.

Hill, R, 2000, 2000, Address to the International Landcare 2000 Conference: Changing Landscapes – Shaping Futures, 2-5 March, Melbourne.

Jones, G, and M, Rolls, 1982, Extension and relative advantage in rural development: an introduction, pp 1-11 in Jones G and M, Rolls, M (eds), *Progress in rural extension and community development*, vol 1, New York: Wiley.

Lawrence, G, 2000, Global perspectives on rural communities – trends and patterns, pp 144-151 in Proceedings of the International Landcare 2000 Conference: Changing Landscapes – Shaping Futures, 2-5 March, Melbourne.

Lockie, S, 1995, Rural Gender Relations and Landcare, pp 71-82 in Lockie, S, and Vanclay, F (eds), *Critical Landcare*, Key Papers Series, No 5, Wagga Wagga: Centre for Rural Social Research, Charles Sturt University.

Lockie, S, 1992, Landcare – before the flood, *Rural Society* 2(2): 7-9.

Martin, P, Tarr, S, and Lockie, S, 1992, Participatory environmental management in New South Wales: Policy and practice, pp 184-208 in Lawrence, G, Vanclay, F and Furze, B (eds), *Agriculture, environment and society*, Melbourne: Macmillan.

Maslach, C and Jackson, SE, 1981, *Maslach burnout inventory manual*, Palo Alto, California: Consulting Psychologists Press.

Midgley, J, 1986, Introduction: social development, the state and participation, pp 1-11 in Midgley J (ed), *Community participation, social development and the state*, London: Methuen.

Morrissey, P and Lawrence, G, 1995, A critical assessment of Landcare in a region of central Queensland, pp 63-75 in Vanclay, F (ed), *With a rural focus*, Wagga Wagga: Centre for Rural Social Research, Charles Sturt University.

Mues, C, Chapman, L and Van Hilst, R, 1998, Landcare: *Promoting improved land management practices on Australian farms; A survey of landcare and land management related programs*, Canberra: Australian Bureau of Agricultural and Resource Economics.

Mues, C, Roper, H and Ockerby, J, 1994, Survey of Landcare and land management practices: 1992-93, Report No, 94/6, Canberra: Australian Bureau of Agricultural and Resource Economics.

Millar, J and Curtis, A, 1997, Moving farmer knowledge beyond the farm gate: An Australian study of farmer knowledge in group learning, *European Journal of Agriculture Education and Extension*, 42: 133-142.

O'Brien, B, Pennicuik, M, and Edgar, R, 1992, A description of group action in Victoria, in Hamilton, GJ, Howes, KM and Attwater R (eds,) Proceedings of the 5th Australian Soil Conservation Conference vol 8, Perth: Department of Agriculture.

Patton, MQ, 1990, *Qualitative evaluation methods*, Newbury Park, California: Sage.

Pearce, JL, 1993, *Volunteers: The organizational behavior of unpaid workers*, Routledge, New York.

Pennicuik, ML, 1992, Victoria: the landcare success story, in Hamilton, GJ, Howes, KM and Attwater R (eds), Proceedings of the 5th Australian Soil Conservation Conference vol 8, Perth: Department of Agriculture.

Poussard, H, 1992, Community landcare to test government policies and programs, Pages 233-236 in Proceedings Volume 1 of the 7th International Soil Conservation Organisation conference – people protecting their land, 27-30 September, Sydney.

Prosavac, EJ and Carey, RG, 1992, *Program evaluation: methods and case studies*, Prentice Hall, New Jersey.

Roberts, B, 1989, The land care movement: a new challenge to advisers, *Australian Journal of Soil and Water Conservation* 2(4): 4-8.

Roling, N, 1988, *Extension science: information systems in agricultural development*, Cambridge: Cambridge University Press.

Rossi, PH and Freeman, HE, 1985, *Evaluation: a systematic approach*, Sage, Beverly Hills, California.

Rush, J, and Associates, 1992, A review of the efficiency of landcare facilitator projects, Report prepared for the Land and Resources Division, Department of Primary Industries and Energy, Canberra.

Schaufeli, WB, Enzmannand, D, Girault, N, 1993, Measurement of burnout: A review, pp 199-212 in *Professional burnout: recent developments in theory and research*, Schaufeli, WB, Maslachm C, and Marek, T (eds), Washington DC: Taylor and Francis.

Scriven, M, 1993, *Hard-won lessons in program evaluation*, San Francisco: Jossey-Bass.

Selin, SW, and Myers, N, 1995, Correlates of partnership effectiveness: the coalition for unified recreation in the Eastern Sierra, *Journal of Park and Recreation Administration* 13(4): 37-46.

Uphoff, N, 1991, Fitting projects to people, pp 467-511 in Cernea, M (ed), *Putting people first*, 2nd edn, New York: Oxford University Press.

Waddock, S, and Bannister, B, 1991, Correlates of effectiveness and partner satisfaction in social partnerships, *Journal of Organizational Change Management* 19(2): 74-89.

Wonder, B, 2000, Sustainable agriculture: dream or reality? The challenges ahead, pp 265-269 in Proceedings of the International Landcare 2000 Conference: Changing Landscapes – Shaping Futures, 2-5 March, Melbourne.

Woodhill, J, Wilson, A and McKenzie, J, 1992, Land conservation and social change: Exension to community development – a necessary shift in thinking, pp 263-271 in Proceedings Volume 1 of the 7th International Soil Conservation Organisation conference – people protecting their land, 27-30 September, Sydney.

PART VI

PERSPECTIVES AND SYNTHESIS

19

The Disappointment of the Law

Tim Bonyhady

Australian National University

The law lies low in most accounts of Australian environmental policy and decision-making. Most geographers, even many political scientists, who consider environmental issues, have little eye for legal issues. Most practitioners of environmental studies are the same, for all their claims to inter-disciplinarity. Yet the enduring power, and constraints, of established academic disciplines are not the only reason that the law has such a poor profile in most environmental analyses not written by lawyers. The relative insignificance of the law is another factor. While rarely irrelevant, the law generally provides little more than a loose framework for how policies are formulated and decisions are made. The stronger the law, the more likely it is to go unenforced or be amended.

The legislation which governs the rangelands of western New South Wales is one example. This *Western Lands Act* 1901 (NSW) is the oldest major piece of natural resource or environmental legislation in Australia. Within the framework of this report, it is the most 'persistent' Act, a remarkable example of the endurance of law through very changing circumstances. Except for the New South Wales *Water Act* of 1912, which appears set for immediate repeal, and Western Australia's *Rights in Water and Irrigation Act* of 1914, which remains in force, no other resource legislation of any consequence has come close to celebrating a centenary.

Yet as so often, the endurance of legislation is not what it superficially seems. As a result of repeated amendment, the Act which survives in name is a very different creature to that first introduced 100 years ago. Originally less than 14 pages long, embodying 36 sections and one appendix, it now sprawls to 85 pages containing 77 sections and 4 schedules as well as another 13 pages of notes. When last reprinted in March 1997, covering amendments prior to June 1996, it had been amended 75 times. Since then it has been altered three more times. Just six of the Act's original sections remain more or less intact and none of them are of much consequence.

Like many other pieces of environmental legislation, the *Western Lands Act* started as a product of crisis, both biophysical and political. Its immediate trigger was the Long Drought which started in the mid-1890s and ran into the early 1900s. But the Act was also both an expression of increasing European understanding of the environment of semi-arid Australia, acquired gradually through the second half of the 19th century, and a manifestation of the settlers' unwillingness to make the most of this understanding. While the Royal Commission which reported on the administration of the Western Division in 1901 recognised the environmental devastation caused by just 40 years of pastoralism west of the Darling, the new legislation accommodated vested interests by seeking to ensure the continuation of pastoralism in the west, starting with its reduction of the rents paid by pastoralists. As Michael Quinn has noted, it failed to address 'the incompatibilities between pastoralism and the environment' (Quinn 2000: 253).

The legislation now in force is stronger than the original. Pastoral lessees are obliged not to overstock their land. The Commissioner for Western Lands is also empowered to order them 'to prevent the use by stock of any part of their land for such periods as the Commissioner considers necessary and to erect fencing for that purpose'. (Section 18D) Yet as noted by Mark Stafford-Smith and Nick Abel (this volume), the amendments to the Act have all been piecemeal. Particular problems have excited *ad hoc* solutions but 'without fundamental reform'. At the same time, the Act has become increasingly complex, creating 'a legislative tangle barely intelligible to the agencies that apply it, let alone the landholders who become ensnared in it'.

Such unintelligibility never provides a good basis for law enforcement. Yet even if the Act had been more lucid, experience elsewhere in Australia's rangelands suggests that it would not have been enforced. The common experience across the continent through the 20th century was one of a profound gulf between the letter of legislation and its implementation however modest the environmental and economic aspirations of the statutory regimes. As described by John Holmes:

> Administrative inertia, coupled with the political power of the lessees (with no countervailing interest groups) led to a progressive decline in annual rents, and a de facto transfer of beneficial ownership of the pastoral resource from lessor to lessees, with miniscule market differentials between comparable leasehold and freehold land. Tenure security was progressively enhanced through longer terms and rollover provisions well ahead of expiry, and with the disuse of resumption provisions. (Holmes 2000: 230)

Perhaps most significantly, the environmental impact of pastoralism went ignored, despite already being clearly understood in 1901 (Quinn 2000: 253).

This gulf between law and practice endures, as Stafford-Smith and Abel discuss. Enforcement remains exceptional – confined to extreme cases. A key problem is the requirement that land be managed 'sustainably'. As with so much of the larger concern with environmentally sustainable development, this obligation is inherently imprecise, so prosecutions generally occur only where there have been 'such blatant abuses that most of the industry was already appalled by the actions of the accused and there was a neglible chance of the pseudo-scientific justification being challenged in court'. Even worse, the law is not be invoked until damage is more or less irrevocable (Stafford-Smith and Abel, this volume).

This experience could be attributed to the age of the legislation and the limitations of patchwork amendments, so what of 'environmental law' which has emerged over the last 30 years as an explicit arena of legislation, litigation, professional practice and academic study? Already in 1970 the Liberal-Country Party Government of Henry Bolte introduced Australia's first *Environment Protection Act* in Victoria. In 1971 the Labor Government of John Tonkin followed with an *Environmental Protection Act* in Western Australia. By 1973 the first environmental law course was being offered within a Law Faculty at the Australian National University and environmental law had entered the *Australian Digest* (Bonyhady 1993: 329).

Implementation of these laws has also proved notoriously weak. While the number of prosecutions is only a crude measure of enforcement as an increase in the number of convictions may, for example, simply be a result of officers targeting easier cases, Peter Grabosky and John Braithwaite revealed in the mid-1980s that New South Wales and Victoria were the only States with any commitment to prosecution as a means of securing pollution control. Queensland was more or less typical of the remainder. Its Air Pollution Council had initiated seven prosecutions in a decade; its Noise Abatement Authority had reported one; its Water Quality Council had launched none (Grabosky and Braithwaite 1986: 43).

The readiness of government to curtail environmental legislation, where it could not ignore its provisions, is at least as significant. A key example is the *Environmental Planning and Assessment Act* introduced in New South Wales in 1979 by Paul Landa, the first Minister for Planning and Environment in the Wran Labor Government. Perhaps no other Australian resource or environmental legislation has had such reach – applicable to almost every aspect of both city and bush. The *Act's* new framework for environmental decision-making was at least as ambitious. As Landa explained in parliament, Labor wanted to increase State and regional planning. It aspired to demarcate the responsibilities of State and local government so that the State would not be involved 'unnecessarily in local planning issues'. It intended to give members of the public a 'meaningful opportunity to participate in planning' (NSWPD 1978-79 151: 3351).

The Labor Government – perhaps for the first time in an Australian environmental Act – sought to articulate these goals in the legislation. While statements of purpose had been almost unknown in any legislation prior to the 1970s because it was feared that a vague statement would 'obscure what is otherwise precise', if it did not 'degenerate into pious incantations', such statements began to come into favour after a British inquiry in 1975 recommended their adoption as a 'convenient method of delimiting or otherwise clarifying the scope and effect of legislation'. (Rohde: 81) The *Environmental Planning and Assessment Act's* objects included not just 'the promotion and co-ordination of the orderly and economic use and development of land' and 'the proper management, development and conservation of natural and man-made resources' but also 'the protection of the environment', the 'sharing of responsibility for environmental planning between the different levels of Government in the State' and 'increased opportunity for public involvement in environmental planning and assessment' (s 5).

Bob Carr – then a journalist with the *Bulletin*, soon to be Labor member for Maroubra – conveyed the excitement engendered by the Act in an extended account of Landa's achievements and failings. Carr observed that 'previous State planning law was just a rewrite of the 1932 English *Town and Country Planning Act*, enacted in NSW in 1945'. While most Australian States had begun trying to overhaul their planning legislation in the early 1970s, New South Wales was the first to succeed in doing so. Landa's Act, Carr declared with manifest approval, 'broadened the whole scope of planning to encompass ecological and social factors and, in addition, gave citizens the right for the first time to object to developments' (Carr 1980: 23).

The Sydney solicitor, Michael Mobbs, who doubled as an Independent member of the Sydney City Council, made even more of the 1979 legislation a few years later. Rather than casting the Act's ecological goals as separate from its participatory provisions, as Carr had done, Mobbs saw that the involvement of local government and ordinary members of the public was vital to achievement of the Act's ambitions. As Mobbs put it, the Act 'attempted to take as much politics as possible out of planning. The prime beneficiary was intended to be the environment and open and shared decision-making was thought to be the best way there' (Mobbs 1986: 47).

Yet the separation of local from regional and State issues, which was integral to the Act's scheme for local, regional and State environmental plans, was always easier said than done. As noted by the *Local Government, Planning and Environment Service* (par 10021), '[m]atters which are seen by a council to raise only local issues sometimes have implications for State or regional environmental planning. Matters which are seen by the government as being of State or regional significance will very often also have implications for local environmental planning.' Already when the legislation was being debated in parliament, there were concerns at the extent of the State government's power to override local government and exclude the public without being subject to any appeal (NSWPD 1978-79 150: 3120-9).

The substantive provisions of the Act also only partially realized its goal of increasing public participation. The Act made substantial provision for public participation involvement in plan-making – creating rights to comment on both the environmental studies and draft plans which were meant to precede final plans. It also gave members of the public an unprecedented right to enforce its provisions – overcoming the common law's restrictive rules of 'standing'. But it was relatively parsimonious in relation to development applications. Far from enjoying a general right to object and appeal as had existed in Victoria since the early 1960s, members of the public were limited to contesting 28 categories of 'designated development' – principally different forms of industry such as abattoirs and pulp and paper works notorious for their pollution.

By 1981, the Wran Government was retreating from this scheme – enacting a series of special Acts to approve particular developments which, in almost every case, were being challenged in the courts for flouting the *Environmental Planning and Assessment Act*. The result, at least initially, was uproar. The press accused the government of treating the Act 'with contempt' (*Sydney Morning Herald*, 13 December 1982: 2). Jim McClelland, the former Whitlam Minister and first Chief Judge of the Land and Environment Court, warned that environmental planning law was an arena in which 'the cherished democratic principle of the independence of the judiciary' looked as if it might 'face one of its sternest tests'. (*National Times*, 20-26 February 1983: 22) But because there was no electoral backlash, the government persisted. As McClelland noted, 'Wran taught his successors that they could get away with brushing any court aside' (*Sydney Morning Herald*, 11 November 1987).

Bob Carr played a key role in the next major regression from Landa's scheme as Wran's third Minister for Planning and Environment when he introduced the first major amendments to the Act itself in 1985. Instead of retaining or expanding the provisions for public objection and appeal, Carr reduced them. Far from maintaining some demarcation between State and local government, the amendments significantly enhanced the State's own decision-making powers. Not least, the new legislation empowered the Minister for Planning to approved developments which contravened planning instruments made under the Act. Each change was contrary to what the original legislation had aspired to achieve. Yet, as Patricia Ryan was quick to point out, the government lacked the 'honesty' to change its objects (Ryan 1986: 146).

The Liberal-National Party Government of Nick Greiner would have liked to take this process much further. Vexed by the success enjoyed by conservationists in the courts when exercising the open standing provisions to challenge the Forestry Commission's repeated failure to prepare environmental impact statements for its operations (Bonyhady 1993: ch 5), it sought to initiate 'an era of development never before seen' in New South Wales by exempting the Commission from this obligation. Had the government succeeded, the Commission would have become the only statutory authority in New South Wales to enjoy this immunity. But Labor declared it would 'not agree with any backdoor dismantling of the *Environmental Planning and Assessment Act*'. After lambasting the Greiner Government for trying to 'circumvent' the Act, it joined with the Democrats and Independents in rejecting this legislation in the Legislative Council (NSWPD 1988-89 205: 4127, 4130; Bates 1989: 1-2).

Since Labor returned to government in 1995 with Carr as Premier, it has been much more successful in undermining the Environmental Planning and Assessment Act with the Liberals' and National Party's support. The Bengalla open cut coal mine near Muswellbrook was the first beneficiary, despite international recognition of the need to reduce fossil fuel consumption and Australia's ratification of the Climate Change Convention (Pearson and Lipman 1996: 416). When the government intervened, Rosemount Wines had twice challenged the mine successfully in the Land and Environment Court. Bengalla had also taken the second case on appeal and the Court of Appeal had heard both sides' argument. But without waiting for the Court to hand down its judgment, the government introduced a special Act which not only approved the mine but also validated a much more general policy directed at facilitating mining.

Over the next two years, the government legislated to approve two other major development projects – the upgrading and expansion of the copper smelter and refinery at Port Kembla and the construction of a coal terminal at Kooragang – which were being challenged in the Land and Environment Court (Norton 1999: 10). It also twice amended the *Environmental Planning and Assessment Act* itself. Each time, as in 1984, it extended the State government's powers, while curtailing environmental protections, the power of local councils and the public's rights (Pearson 1996: 346). Far from repealing the Act's original objects to increase the power of local councils and the public, which appeared even more nonsensical than in 1984, it added a new object – to encourage ecologically sustainable development – while providing no new mechanisms for achieving this goal.

The Carr Government amended the Act even more fundamentally in 1998 – achieving even more than what Labor had lambasted the Liberal-National Parties for attempting a decade previously. As part of its *Forestry and National Park*

Estate Act, the government not only exempted integrated forestry operations from the environmental impact assessment requirements of the *Environmental Planning and Assessment Act* 1998 but also barred members of the public from taking legal action in relation to breaches of either the new Act or of forestry agreements made under it (see Mobbs, this volume). In doing so, the 1998 Act freed the Australian statutory agency most notorious for ignoring environmental laws from the obligation of having to consider them. As noted by Aiden Ricketts and Nicole Rogers, the small group of ministers responsible for forest agreements and integrated forestry operations can now breach the law with impunity (Ricketts and Rogers 1999: 162).

The cumulative result of all these special Acts and amendments has been profound. According to Justice Paul Stein, who was both a significant actor within, and keen observer of, the State's environmental planning system during 12 years on the Land and Environment Court, almost everything Landa set out to achieve has been eroded. As a result of Labor's legislation in the second half of the 1990s, 'the last vestiges of traditional planning and genuine public partici-pation have been largely abandoned'. Despite all the political rhetoric about ecologically sustainable development, and even its legislative embrace as an object of the *Environmental Planning and Assessment Act*, ecological sustainability is 'seldom applied in practice'. The norm is now '*ad hoc* decision-making, often at the behest of individual entrepreneurs who court State or local governments politicians' (Stein 1999: 145, 146, 150).

This contradiction of the 1979 Act is all the more striking because of the pivotal role played by Bob Carr. More than any other Labor or Liberal politician, State or Federal through the 1980s or 1990s, Carr has made much of his environmental concerns. His image has combined the bushwalker conservationist, keen to experience the Blue Mountains or Buddawangs in the company of the late Milo Dunphy, with the armchair conservationist, quick to show off his book learning. No other Premier or Prime Minister would have thought to start the millennium by triggering a debate in the *Sydney Morning Herald* with a gloomy prognosis for the planet because of population growth (*Sydney Morning Herald*, 6 January 2000: 9). Yet New South Wales's prime piece of environmental legislation has more or less been undone while he has been Minister for the Environment and Planning and then Premier.

This retreat is also all the more significant because it is far from confined to the 1979 Act. Instead a range of legislation, State and federal, has suffered much the same fate. Even the common law has moved at least partly in the same direction. The High Court's decision in 1994 to overturn the rule in *Rylands v Fletcher* (1868) LR 3 HL 330 is one example. This rule imposed what was generally thought to be 'strict liability' – or liability without negligence – for the escape of dangerous substances from land occupied by the defendant. Its premise was that those responsible for especially hazardous activities on land should be subject to special liability. Without considering the merits of this premise, the High Court decided that liability in these cases should be determined according to the more general but much more relaxed standard of negligence (Trindade and Cane 1999: 424).

A handful of these changes can be explained away on the basis that the original laws were too ambitious. One example is Victoria's *Environment Protection*

Act which initially provided that all emissions – however, great or small, hazardous or benign – had to be licensed. According to the High Court of Australia, the Act also precluded Victoria's Environment Protection Authority from weighing economic considerations against environmental ones when deciding whether or not to grant a licence. Instead, the Authority was simply to ensure that the environment was not compromised. As noted by Michael Barker, the Act was 'premised on the belief that environmental quality should be achieved regardless or cost; that pollution should be *prevented*, not merely controlled' (Barker 1984: 226).

The first of these provisions for universal licensing was probably impracticable and was never properly implemented. In 1984 the State Labor government of John Cain abandoned it, opting instead for a more focussed scheme of works approval and licensing of a narrow band of 'scheduled premises' which were likely to be responsible for substantial pollution (Brunton 1994: 49). The focus on environmental protection in licensing was arguably also unrealistic, albeit of limited practical significance because it applied only where the Environment Protection Authority had failed to finalise a State Environment Protection Policy. Most likely, it was also overturned in 1984 as a result of another new provision requiring the Authority to have regard not just 'to the ability of the environment to absorb waste without detriment to its quality' but also 'to the social and economic development of Victoria' (s 13(1)(g)).

Yet the regression of some environmental laws has also been a result of the enduring developmentalist ethos of government – both fuelled and masked by the rise of economic rationalism, and the associated vogue for deregulation, privatisation, contracting out and market mechanisms. Even the language of 'planning' and 'environment' – so prevalent in the titles of Australian legislation since the 1970s – has gone into at least occasional retreat. From 1982 until 1993 South Australia had a *Planning Act* – a deliberate statement of the significance of public co-ordination and control of land use in the collective interest. Now, at least partly prompted by the State's need for investment in the wake of the State bank crash, South Australia has a *Development Act* (1993).

Just as with the amendments to the New South Wales *Environmental Planning and Assessment Act*, local government has rarely benefited from these measures because of the deep-seated reluctance of State governments to give local councils substantial power, let alone the means to exercise it. Queensland's *Environmental Protection Act* discussed by Su Wild River (this volume) is one example. This Act imposed a significant administrative burden on councils. In its first three years, they issued over 10,000 licences. But because the Queensland government empowered councils to set their own licence fees, many opted to charge little or nothing to avoid electoral opprobrium. The result has not just been that Councils have been left 'without their required environmental protection budget'; the new legislation has also been undermined by a dearth of enforcement. In the first two years of the Act councils initiated just two prosecutions. (Brody and Prenzler 1998: 68).

Members of the public have equally gained little from recent environmental legislation, while often losing rights of real significance. Although some legislation has extended the opportunities for public submissions and comments on draft plans or agreements, government has been loathe to increase the public's much more significant rights to allow members of the public to object against specific licence and lease applications, let alone challenge the merits of particular approvals before independent tribunals. Where these rights have been created, they have also been the target of more than usual attack. The standard claim is that members of the public exercise these rights obstructively, delaying and hence adding to the cost of development without any corresponding public benefit. Yet there is not just a dearth of empirical evidence which clearly supports this claim; the few existing analyses of third-party appeals suggest that they cause little delay while enhancing decision-making (Bonyhady, 1993: 27-9; Hodgson 1996: 15, 27; Raff 1995: 73-5).

The Victorian Liberal Government of Jeff Kennett was responsible for one of the most significant reductions in the public's rights in 1993. These amendments to the *Planning and Environment Act* 1987 – the Victorian counterpart to the New South Wales *Environmental Planning and Assessment Act* – reduced the provision for public participation to levels not seen since at least the 1950s. In addition to confining the right of appeal to objectors, they introduced a filing fee for appeals for the first time. At least as significantly, they provided that planning schemes could exempt broad classes of development from public notice so that members of the public had no opportunity to contest them. They equally provided that planning schemes could exempt broad classes of development from appeal (Raff 1995: 73-9; Eccles 1995: 238-9).

The provisions for public appeal against the grant of new water rights have proved equally vulnerable not only in New South Wales (Pearson 1995: 347) but also in Queensland where increasing competition over water has resulted in unprecedented litigation, particularly on the Balonne River. In 1995 the State's Court of Appeal favoured public participation – holding that the right of anyone 'aggrieved' to appeal against the licensing of new dams 'should be given its natural meaning' rather than read restrictively (*Stevenson* v *Wenck* [1996] 2 Qd R 84 at 89). But a year later, the State parliament legislated to confine the right to objectors against the original licence application, who in turn had to live within eight kilometres upstream or 24 kilometres downstream of the property containing proposed dam.

This trajectory of the law has failed to receive adequate acknowledgement. Instead the common assumption of lawyers writing through the 1970s into the 1980s was that environmental law was set for enduring improvement – as if the ideal of progress was just as applicable to environmental protection as resource development. The same optimism infused most writing about environmental law in the 1990s. In the preface to the fourth edition of his *Environmental Law in Australia*, Gerry Bates enthused about how environmental law continued 'to change and expand rapidly' as legislation which, in many cases, had stood for more than two decades, was 'being replaced by more modern thinking'. (Bates 1995: vi)

This appetite for the new ignores the value of much of the old. While there is now much more environmental law than thirty years ago, there have been significant losses as well as gains. As much as government may have discovered more effective mechanisms for environmental protection, it has displayed a powerful preference for the *ad hoc* over the planned and the concentration of power over its distribution. These dimensions of the law provide little reason to set much store in the possibilities of adaptive policy learning.

References

Barker, ML, 1984, Environmental quality control: regulation or incentives? *Environmental and Planning Law Journal*, 1: 222-32.

Bates, G, 1989, Forestry (Commission) protection in New South Wales, *Environmental and Planning Law Journal*, 6: 1-2.

Bates, G, 1995, *Environmental law in Australia*, 4th edn, Sydney: Butterworths.

Bonyhady, T, 1993, *Places worth keeping: conservationists, politics and law*, Sydney: Allen & Unwin.

Bonyhady, T, 1995, A usable past: the public trust in Australia, *Environmental and Planning Law Journal*, 12: 329-38.

Brody, M, and Prenzler, T, 1998, The enforcement of environmental protection laws in Queensland: a case of regulatory capture, *Environmental and Planning Law Journal*, 15: 54-71.

Brunton, N, 1994, Water pollution in New South Wales and Victoria: current status and future trends, *Environmental and Planning Law Journal*, 11: 39-70.

Carr, B, 1980, Landa treads on corns in his march to power, *Bulletin*, 27 May 1980, 22-8.

Eccles, D, 1999, The impact of Victoria's new planning schemes on third party rights, *Urban Policy and Research*, 17: 235-43.

Grabosky, P, and Braithwaite, J, 1986, *Of manners gentle: enforcement strategies of Australian business regulatory agencies*, Melbourne: Oxford University Press.

Hodgson, J, 1996, Third party-appeals in South Australia 1972-1993, *Environmental and Planning Law Journal* 13: 8-28.

Holmes, J, 2000, Pastoral lease tenures as policy instruments, 1847-1997, in Dovers, S, (ed,), *Environmental history and policy: still settling Australia*, Melbourne: Oxford University Press,, 212-42.

Local Government, Planning and Environment Service (New South Wales), *Volume C*, Butterworths, Sydney: May 1985.

Mobbs, M, 1986, The powers of the Minister under Section 101 of the Environmental Planning and Assessment Act 1979, In: *Environmental law: update in development control legislation*, Sydney: College of Law, 45-68.

Norton, C, 1999, Subverting the rule of law? Retrospective legislation in New South Wales Environmental Planning, *Impact* 55: 10-12.

Pearson, L, 1996, Amendments to the Environmental Planning and Assessment Act, *Environmental and Planning Law Journal*, 13: 343-7.

Pearson, L, and Lipman, Z, 1996, Fast-tracking mining projects in New South Wales: State Environmental Planning (Permissible Mining) Act 1996, *Environmental and Planning Law Journal* 13: 402-16.

Quinn, M, 2000, Past and present: managing the western division of New South Wales, in Dovers, S, (ed), *Environmental History and Policy: Still Settling Australia*, Melbourne: Oxford University Press, 243-57.

Raff, M, 1995, Pragmatic curtailment of participation in Victoria, *Environmental and Planning Law Journal* 12: 73-8.

Ricketts, A, and Rogers, N, 1999, Third party rights in New South Wales environmental legislation: the backlash, *Environmental and Planning Law Journal*, 16: 157-63.

Rohde, J, 1995, The objects clause in environmental legislation – *The Nature Conservation Act 1992* (Qld) exemplified, *Environmental and Planning Law Journal*, 12: 80-96.

Ryan, P, 1986, Environmental Planning and Assessment Act amendments – The last word? *Environmental and Planning Law Journal*, 3: 137-52.

Stein, P, 1999, The use of land at a metropolitan and local level: the retreat from planning, in Troy, P, (ed,) *Serving the City*, pp, 144-53, Sydney: Pluto Press.

Trindade, F, and Cane, P, 1999, *The law of torts in Australia*, 3rd edn, Melbourne: Oxford University Press.

20

Science, Research and Policy

Ian Lowe

Griffith University

There is an increasing expectation that policies affecting natural resources or the environment will be based on sound knowledge. There are many recent examples. The science predicting that CFCs would deplete the ozone layer, when later confirmed by actual measurement, became the basis of policies to phase out release of the chemicals. The emerging understanding that human actions are discernibly influencing the changing global climate has driven the policy debate and led to the establishment of some broad targets for national emissions. The developing understanding of the need for environmental flows in river systems and the causes of salinity are driving policy decisions about water allocation and land repair.

So sustainability requires more basic data about local species, a better understanding of the complex systems by which they interact, and an improved decision-making framework. That framework needs to incorporate both better scientific knowledge and other knowings, as well as a shift in values from the prevailing emphasis on short-term economic goals. There is a clear need for improved understanding of complex natural systems and the way we disrupt their functioning, but a better understanding will not by itself bring about sustainability unless it is accompanied by a shift away from current values. Knowledge that motor vehicles are the principal cause of urban air pollution has not stopped construction of more urban arterial roads. Understanding the consequences of large-scale land clearing has not halted the destruction of huge areas of Queensland bush. Above all else, achieving the declared goal of sustainable development requires a new social ethic which gives the welfare of future generations and the survival of other species a higher priority than economic growth.

Detailed agreement is not necessary to obtain support for a policy direction. At the time of the 1996 election, the Coalition proposed selling 49 per cent of Telstra and using a small fraction of the proceeds to fund environmental programs under the Natural Heritage Trust. Some, like the leader of the Liberal Party and subsequent Prime Minister, were mainly driven by their ideological desire to sell the publicly owned utility and regarded the environmental repair scheme as sugar to coat the pill. Some members of environmental groups were so worried about land degradation they were prepared to live with the selling of a fraction of the public stake in Telstra, even when this was seen as possibly leading to the complete loss of the public asset. There were some environmentally-concerned members of the Liberal Party who saw the strategy as win-win, achieving both environmental goals and the sale of Telstra. Those groups did not agree with each other, but they found common cause in the policy they could all support. To achieve the goal of sustainable use of the environment and our natural resources, the most urgent political task is to find a policy framework that unites disparate interest groups and provides a solid basis of support.

Improving our understanding

Basic knowledge

We urgently need a better understanding of the local biota. It has been estimated (SoEAC 1996: 4-4) that we have only identified about ten to 15 per cent of the million or so species found in Australia. Even at higher levels of organisation such as vascular plants and vertebrates, we are still encountering species that were previously unknown such as the Wollemi pine, a tree growing to 35 metres in height within 100 kilometres of Sydney (SoEAC 1996: ES-9). As taxonomy is not seen either as an exciting area of science or as a high priority for research resources, the rate of progress is alarmingly slow. It is estimated that it will take hundreds of years to identify all the plant and animal species of the continent if we continue to proceed at current rates (SoEAC 1996: ES-9). There is no prospect, even in principle, of understanding the impacts of our actions on those species we have not yet even identified.

While 85 to 90 per cent of the species living here are unknown, many of the others are not well understood; they have simply been identified and described in enough detail to allow recognition. Again, there is no realistic prospect of understanding all the impacts of our actions on species whose characteristics and behaviour remain largely a mystery. Without an improved understanding of the basic building blocks of the natural systems of Australia, we cannot hope to achieve sustainability.

Understanding systems

We also urgently need a better understanding of complex systems. It is now clear that many of today's environmental problems stem from past well-intentioned advice, whether to irrigate arable land or to clear vegetation or to introduce exotic species. While each research project extends our knowledge base or clarifies our understanding of some parts of the system, it also invariably raises new questions. Sometimes research or the emergence of new evidence casts doubt on what was previously regarded as solid knowledge, such as the value of irrigating the soils of arid regions, or the sustainability of logging old growth forests. Since it seems almost certain that advancing knowledge will reveal some current practices to be unsound, that advancement of knowledge should be a high priority. A small investment in R&D now may avoid irreparable damage later.

There is a more fundamental limitation on our ability to know the impacts of our actions on natural systems. Most of our modelling assumes we are making small, reversible changes to systems that are in equilibrium. The caution expressed by the Inter-governmental Panel on Climate Change (IPCC, 1996) applies more generally to non-linear systems.

> Future climate changes may involve 'surprises'. In particular, these arise from the non-linear nature of the climate system. When rapidly forced, non-linear systems are especially subject to unexpected behaviour.

This is an important warning. When we change the conditions applying to complex systems, we produce changes which will not be expected; some of these will be counter-intuitive. We can now see some of the consequences of past actions; in some cases, we wonder why those consequences were not anticipated. It does not require detailed understanding of river systems to see that removing 99 per cent of normal water flow will produce significant changes to the riverine ecosystem, nor does it take much understanding of biodiversity to see that clear felling of forests will put pressure on forest-dwelling species by destroying their habitat.

One recent piece of research illustrates the complexity of the interactions between species in natural systems. A study of truffles, the fruiting bodies of fungi, in the eucalyptus forests of south-eastern New South Wales showed the crucial role of the long-footed potoroo in the health of the overall ecosystem (Claridge and May 1994). The potoroo unearths and eats the truffles, then excretes the spores of the fungus, thereby making it available to other trees. The fungus becomes attached to roots of trees in a mutually beneficial symbiotic arrangement. So we now know that even a forestry economist who was interested only in the production of saw-logs should recognise the value of the long-footed potoroo to the health of the growing timber. This relationship has only been understood in the last few years. There are undoubtedly many similar stories yet to be uncovered of the importance of apparently minor species to the health of ecological systems such as forests, grasslands or estuaries. What we now know, in general, is that the loss of any one species from a complex system will usually have flow-on consequences, and in some cases those effects will not have been predictable from our previous knowledge. So we need to invest more research effort into inter-disciplinary studies of complex systems, integrating the disparate relevant fields of knowledge. As a recent international workshop concluded, 'we now urgently need a better general understanding of the complex dynamic interactions between society and nature. That will require major advances in our ability to assess such issues as the behaviour of complex self-organising systems, irreversible impacts of interacting stresses, various scales of organisation and social actors with different agenda.' (Friibergh Workshop 2000)

Research capacity

The political changes of the last decade have gradually reduced the capacity of our research institutions to achieve the needed advances in knowledge. The national capacity for basic research has been undermined by the increasing dependence of CSIRO on non-government funding and the steady reduction in the core funding of universities. Increasingly, our research effort is driven by short-term economic priorities, as more researchers are forced to seek commercial support. This determines what sorts of research projects will be put forward; they will mainly be those that researchers think are likely to attract resources. A process of funding universities according to their research expenditure puts a premium on expensive applied work, rather than advancing of theoretical understanding. There are obvious risks in this approach. As a salutary example, the two crucial pieces of research that showed the depletion of the ozone layer by CFCs were both refused funding through the normal peer-review process; the work was only done because both James Lovelock and later Sherwood Rowland had access to discretionary funds (Lowe 1989: 22-27). There can be genuine differences about the right balance between basic and applied research, so that the present policies are seen by some as a reaction to an earlier over-emphasis on basic or theoretical studies (Moore 1998). However, there is a real risk that the advances in fundamental understanding we need won't be achieved by the existing system of research support. There is little chance that unconventional or unpopular theories will be properly tested in the present climate. The process of funding research and the procedures for refining knowledge need to be explicitly pluralistic and recognise different legitimate approaches. This does not justify a populist relativism in which any crackpot theory is equally valid. The test of any scientific theory is its ability to explain the observable and make predictions which can be tested against the real world. Some complex environmental problems have different possible explanations; we need to ensure that the research support process does not preclude study of the alternatives. Thus it is a high priority if our policy framework is to be information-rich for our research system to be explicitly and practically pluralistic.

Other knowings

We also need to develop a process that recognises and values Indigenous ecological knowledge. Most decision-making implicitly assumes that Western scientific knowledge is inevitably superior to Indigenous knowledge. Of course, there are many examples of scientific understanding underpinning modern use of natural resources, and there are many complex effects we now understand in ways that Indigenous Australians did not. This should not blind us to acknowledging that Indigenous people also have an understanding of remote parts of Australia that has allowed them to live and reproduce there, while non-indigenous people regularly perish in those places or require multi-million dollar rescue operations. In some national parks, Indigenous understanding of natural systems is now used as part of the management process. This is a useful model for the future, valuing and incorporating relevant Indigenous knowledge. Just as scientific knowledge embodies theories and models which are at least as important as facts, so Indigenous knowledge incorporates metaphors and images which are also important. We need to acknowledge and respect those metaphors and images as well as the extensive factual knowledge about individual species or the location of water. This is an important dimension of the principle of inclusiveness, ensuring that the decision-making process recognises and values different knowings.

Applying our understanding

Decisions about the natural resources and environment need to use a longer time frame than has been usual in recent thinking, need an appropriate structure that allows an integrated or holistic approach, and need to recognise the primacy of ecological considerations rather than seeing them as an optional extra.

Time scales

We should base our choices on a much longer time horizon than is the norm in political discourse. We need to use time-scales of decades or centuries rather than weeks or months. The damage done to Australian natural systems by inappropriate practices has taken decades or centuries to reach the point at which action is demanded, and will take decades or centuries to repair. This conclusion is not unique to Australia, but quite general (US National Research Council 1999). So the use of natural resources and the way we treat the environment need to be decoupled from the day-to-day adversary system of party politics, almost ensuring *ad hoc* decision-making, and put on a secure long-term footing. In other words, the framework for policy should have the quality of persistence.

This argument suggests that decisions should rest on the secure foundation of scientific knowledge. Crabb (this volume) argues that we should aim for 'a principled approach to issues based on technical understanding'. While this approach has an obvious appeal, its usefulness is limited by two fundamental problems. First, technical understanding is rarely clear and unambiguous. Secondly, even when our understanding is definite, values will always have a role in determining the response.

Technical understanding

While we should try to ensure that research is not consciously biased, there is no prospect of research being independent of theories or underlying values. Our mental models or prevailing theories determine which data we collect, how we assess the results, which research programs we set up, which projects we fund and which researchers we see as credible. As Albury (1983) argues, the process of advancing knowledge is inevitably value-laden, as is its assessment. So there are always social and political dimensions to the decisions about which science is supported. Changes to the membership of research funding bodies can influence the balance of support between broad areas, while some Ministers have been known to put their own personal stamps on the program of research. Deciding to ask a question does not guarantee that it will be answered, but we are less likely to find answers to questions we decline to ask. In an atmosphere of limited funding for research, a decision to fund one project always precludes the support of others.

Even when there is agreement to study a particular problem, if it is a complex issue there can be alternative explanations. While the data do not allow the issue to be resolved, different scientists will legitimately come to different conclusions, as in the debate about the source of the phosphorus in inland streams (Wasson et al 1996: 7-17). The debate about whether there is a discernible human influence in the observed changes to the global climate is another example. While atmospheric scientists warned in 1985 that human actions seemed to be changing the climate (Pearman 1988), it took another decade for the wider scientific community to accept that conclusion (IPCC 1996) and there are still some scientists who do not accept the dominant view (Lindzen 1996). Again, values play a role in assessment of the data and the validity of models. Natural systems often do not allow controlled experiments, while the lack of baseline data and the long time-scales involved make it unlikely we will achieve the goal of certain technical knowledge. It is now 35 years since Weinberg (1968) warned that there is a class of problems which can be framed in scientific terms, which sound like scientific questions, but cannot be answered in terms which are acceptable to the scientific community. The two specific examples he gave were the operating safety of nuclear reactors and the biological effects of low doses of ionising radiation. Many ecological problems are equally intractable. In the absence of full scientific certainty, Weinberg warned, values inevitably play a role in assessing the data. We do not know whether there is a safe level of ionising radiation, below which there is no damage to humans. In the absence of certainty, most scientists who work in the nuclear industry believe there is a threshold level below which no damage is done, while most scientists who work for environmental groups believe that the probability of damage remains a linear function of dose at very low levels. There is no prospect of resolving that disagreement by careful evaluation of epidemiological evidence or by controlled experiments.

While we need to recognise these fundamental limitations, we should also recognise that the level of understanding can be improved by developing better approaches. As the Friibergh Workshop (2000) concluded:

> By structure and by content, sustainability science differs fundamentally from science as we know it. What were essentially sequential phases of scientific inquiry such as conceptualising the problem, collecting data, developing theories and applying the results become parallel functions of social learning, additionally incorporating the element of action. Familiar forms of developing and testing hypotheses run into difficulties because of non-linearity, complexity and long time lags between actions and their consequences. All these problems are complicated further by our inability to stand outside the nature-society system. We therefore need new methodologies such as the semi-quantitative modelling of qualitative data and case studies, and inverse approaches that work backwards from undesirable consequences to identify pathways to avoid those outcomes. Scientists and practitioners need to work together to produce trustworthy knowledge that combines scientific excellence with social relevance.

This is not a minor criticism, but a major challenge to the whole process of producing scientific knowledge. It argues that a radically different approach will be needed to develop the knowledge base we need if we are to interact sustainably with natural systems.

Applying the knowledge

Finally, even if the technical knowledge is clear and unambiguous, the response usually involves some balance between ecological needs and desired outcomes in other areas: economic, social or political. It has been understood for decades that the diversion of water from the Snowy River has affected its ecological values. Restoring even a small fraction of the previous flow of the Snowy has economic, social and political implications, so the issue was on the political agenda for years until its recent resolution. Similar comments could be made about the extraction of water from the Murray-Darling river system, the use of the Great Artesian Basin, the stocking of some rangelands, clearing of vegetation from agricultural land and traditional irrigation practices, all issues of such complexity that they remain unresolved. Though Smith (this volume) laments the absence of 'an acceptable code of practice' for inland waterways, Bates (this volume) argues that the failure to manage natural systems when a problem is recognised is usually due to 'political realities'; in other words, social or economic or political considerations usually outweigh the known ecological needs. As Hamilton (this volume) argues, 'the best use of a resource cannot be decided by technical knowledge by experts'. Since differences about resource or environmental issues are usually based on differences in values, we need to recognise the role of values in the analysis of complex issues. Since there are legitimately (and inevitably) different acceptable values in a pluralistic democratic society, there will always be some degree of disagreement or conflict about environmental or resource issues. The principle of inclusiveness means that the process for resolving these disagreements needs to explicitly recognise and focus attention on the role of the underlying values.

This is simply an extension of a general argument advanced by the Ranger inquiry over 20 years ago, that the role of experts should be to provide technical information that allows the general public (or their elected representatives) to make decisions based on that information (Fox et al 1976). The Resource Assessment Commission made a similar case in their report on the proposal to mine Coronation Hill (RAC 1991). The proposal was evaluated in economic terms, giving the range of estimates of the economic benefits to the mining company and to the broader community. It was evaluated in environmental terms, giving various assessments of the risk to the Kakadu wetlands of the proposed extraction process. It was also evaluated in social terms, assessing the possible costs and benefits for both the local Indigenous people and the broader community. Striking the balance between these considerations, deciding whether the economic benefits were worth the environmental risks and the social effects, was (as the RAC said) inevitably a value judgement. There is no prospect even in principle of some sort of modernised felicific calculus which tells decision-makers the 'right' choice to make. It is history that the Hawke Government decided not to approve the project, but many people disagreed with that decision; indeed, there is evidence that many members of Hawke's Cabinet did not agree with the Prime Minister, and the disagreement was one of the factors involved in Keating's subsequent successful challenge to Hawke's leadership (Kelly 1992:

536-542). So it needs to be recognised that a secure and universally accepted technical understanding does not of itself ensure sound use of natural resources or environmental assets. In the final analysis, there will always be political factors influencing the way the technical understanding is used.

While there can be no simple algorithm for deciding what level of environmental risk is justified by a given social or economic benefit, there is a broad general approach that provides guidance. We have a National Strategy for Ecologically Sustainable Development (COAG 1992). The ESD approach is based on sound general principles for balancing social, economic and environmental considerations. Those principles have now also been embodied in a wide range of State and Commonwealth laws. This specifies a purposeful approach, but one that also requires flexibility in its application to a variety of local problems.

Present structures

Present administrative structures might almost have been designed to prevent a coherent and integrated approach (SoEAC 1996). We routinely use waterways as the boundaries between jurisdictions, making it almost impossible to apply a holistic approach to catchments. Environmental regulations differ between adjoining States, even though plant and animal species clearly do not recognise and react to the arbitrary lines drawn on the map of Australia by imperial bureaucrats in London in the 19th century. Division of government responsibilities between different departments and agencies makes a rational and integrated approach very unlikely, especially as agencies charged with economic development are often reluctant to consider the environmental consequences of their decisions to promote mining, agricultural development, industrial production, transport corridors or the general goal of rapid economic growth. There is a need for greater reciprocity of approach. Environmental ministers and bureaucrats usually feel obliged to strike a balance between environmental goals and other priorities, especially economic considerations; it is very rare for ministers and officials in economic development agencies to feel the same need to compromise their economic goals to accommodate environmental priorities.

Balancing social, economic and environmental factors

Policies must draw on best available knowledge, but must also recognise the values embedded in that knowledge (or those knowings) and the limitations of that knowledge. Policies should also legitimately consider social and economic dimensions, hopefully in better balance than has been recent practice. Many of the serious problems in the areas of environment and natural resources stem from an indefensible over-emphasis on short-term economic outcomes to the exclusion even of longer-term economic effects. The profit-and-loss accounts which are used for economic management need to be augmented by a balance sheet which includes the state of the natural assets used for productive enterprise; there is strong evidence that the appearance of economic success in the last 50 years has been achieved by systematic liquidation of natural assets. While the Australian Bureau of Statistics is working on parallel accounts which incorporate natural assets, the project is not near the point of allowing the broader approach to become part of routine decision-making. In its absence, natural assets are treated as income rather than capital stock. This approach is not even economically sustainable.

The 1996 State of the Environment Report argued that most decision-making is based on the implicit assumption that the economy is paramount, so that social or environmental problems can always be solved if the economy is sufficiently healthy (SoEAC 1996). We now know that this approach has produced environmental effects which cannot simply be solved by a healthy economy. No amount of dollars can bring back an extinct species, while the costs of saving one which is critically endangered may well be out of reach – as is the cost of repairing saline agricultural land, degraded grazing land or polluted estuaries. As the Brundtland commission observed, unless our economic and social decisions are *ecologically* rational, we will be unable even to maintain living standards, let alone achieve the improvements which are sought (WCED 1987). Thus the ESD approach demands a balancing of social, economic and environmental considerations, while the Brundtland caveat suggests that the primacy of environmental issues should also be recognised.

Implementing wise choices

The very notion of 'managing' the environment involves unjustifiable hubris. We have great difficulty managing a small well-defined system, such as a farm, to allow genuinely sustainable production with no loss of natural values. As discussed above, the present knowledge base is nowhere near being adequate to understand all the interactions between species in the natural systems of Australia. There is a more basic problem. As a general rule, complex systems can't be managed. They can be perturbed and their responses can be studied, but our predictive capacity is still poor. While general systems theory has not fulfilled the hopes of its proponents in the 1970s, there may still be some value in the idea of encouraging basic study of the behaviour of complex systems, rather than hoping that general laws will emerge from a series of specific case studies. The power of the metabolism model for human settlements flows from the observation that complex systems can be modelled in terms of flows of nutrients and other resources, use of energy and other inputs, and production of wastes. So an improved understanding of the general behaviour of systems will increase the chances of knowing how a particular system will react to human changes.

A second important complication of decision-making is a recognition of redistributive effects. It should now be understood that change always has costs as well as benefits, losers as well as winners. These effects should be explicitly recognised, rather than persisting with the delusion that magic-pudding policies can be devised which benefit everybody concerned. We should probably accept that there is some responsibility for those who benefit from policy changes to compensate those who lose, as in the example of noise imposed on Sydney residents by the new second runway. In that case, air travellers pay a hypothecated levy on top of the scheduled air fare, and the proceeds of the levy are used to compensate the residents affected by the resulting noise. While that system of losers being compensated by bene-ficiaries was a hasty response to an urgent political problem for the government of the day, it has established an important precedent. There is an obvious dimension of social justice in the principle that those who benefit from public policy should compensate those who are disadvantaged by that policy. Historically, there has been a tendency for policy formulation to reflect and reinforce existing power relations. It is difficult to justify that within a limited time frame, but it is almost impossible to defend when the inequity is inter-generational (Flannery 1994). Many of the choices made about natural resources or the environment have effectively disadvantaged all future genera-tions for the benefit of the present generation (or, more frequently, a small privileged minority of this generation). This is the moral equivalent of stealing from our own children to benefit some of the present generation. In those terms, it is morally indefensible.

An extreme form of institutionalised inequity is the prevailing fashion of trusting market forces. Market demand represents the collective wishes of present-day consumers. As such, it is a reasonable basis for the allocation of essentially trivial items, such as tickets to opera or football matches. It is inappropriate when used as the basis for allocating educational opportunities or access to health care, because of the obvious equity considerations; those who are sufficiently wealthy will always get what they want, whereas those with more limited resources will have fewer choices. It becomes a fundamental issue when applied to choices in environmental management or use of natural resources. There are two important interest groups who cannot even in prin-ciple express their wishes in the present market: all other species and all future generations. So a proposal to leave these choices 'to the market' is effectively a political proposition to put the wishes of the present generation of consumers above the needs of all other species and all future generations. Couched in those terms, it is morally reprehensible.

Policies for use of natural resources or management of environmental problems need to recognise the enormous diversity of Australia. Extending from the wet tropics to the Southern Ocean, from the Indian Ocean to the Pacific, with annual rainfall varying from a few centimetres to more than ten metres and with ecological systems extending from marine to Alpine, it is impossible to prescribe general rules that apply equally to all parts of Australia. As Smith and Abel (this volume) argue, broad general principles which can be adapted to suit local conditions are more likely to be useful than any attempt to prescribe a universal solution to the diverse problems of Australia. While this approach can be seen as 'fragmented and generally uncoordinated' (Haward, this volume), it is an inevitable consequence of the diversity of the continent. General laws have an appealing administrative simplicity, but they would inevitably form a Procrustean bed into which every regional problem would be uncomfortably compressed. Flexible responses to suit local conditions are necessary.

Thus the principle of flexibility will remain vital in determining responses to different situations. It also has a wider implication. We should recognise that decision-making will always involve uncertainty and retain the flexibility to change our approach when unexpected problems emerge. A persistent political problem is that an admission of past error is seen as a sign of weakness, so elected politicians continue to embrace old policies long after they have proved useless or counter-productive. Dams are still being proposed, new irrigation schemes are being seriously considered, land is being cleared and urban arterial roads are being constructed long after the problems of these activities have become apparent. To some extent these activities represent a problem discussed above, the over-emphasis on short-term economic priorities at the expense of all other considerations. They also reflect the reluctance of decision-makers to abandon their old ways, even in the face of overwhelming evidence.

Creating the preferred future

The future is not somewhere we are going, but something we are creating. It will be the product of our decisions and actions, just as the Australia of today has been shaped by past choices. Strategic choices open up some opportunities and close off others. There is no reason to suppose that the current fad of leaving our fate to the forces of global markets will bring about the desired goal of sustainability.

Since environmental assets are generally not priced by today's markets, they will inevitably continue to be consumed at rates that exceed the optimum. The usual response of environmental economics is to argue for the inclusion into prices of a component reflecting the value of the environmental assets used. This approach would be an obvious improvement on the usual alternative, which effectively puts no value on those assets. The obvious objection is the lack of an intellectually defensible framework for calculating those environmental costs; estimates of the appropriate addition to the price of coal-fired electricity which would reflect the cost to future generations of climate change now vary by two orders of magnitude (Sorensen, 1997). In the absence of agreed prices, any attempt to include a component reflecting environmental costs will meet political resistance. When one Minister in the Keating Government canvassed the possibility of a very modest carbon tax, the response from Australian industry bordered on the hysterical, mainly because it was seen as an arbitrary levy. Other Ministers joined the chorus in an extraordinary process of pre-Budget decision-making, and the government as a whole backed away from the idea. There was no rational basis for the argument against the tax; it was simply political opportunism. There is no objective rationality in a tax system that imposes large levies on petroleum fuels while exempting gas, coal and electricity, but that was the Australian system at the time of writing. As any change produces losers as well as winners, the losers are certain to object. They are always likely to carry the day because the indignation of those who feel disadvantaged is often more politically effective than the guilty smugness of those who gain a windfall advantage from a policy change. Governments are usually only able to achieve major tax reform if they can convince a significant minority that nobody will be significantly worse off; this unlikely claim was the key to the Howard Government's imposition of its Goods and Services Tax on the Australian community. The GST makes sustainability less likely by a series of perverse incentives, such as increasing the subsidy of diesel fuels, reducing the price of gas-guzzler luxury cars and increasing the cost of investing in efficiency improvements. A carbon tax or similar environmental levy could be used to provide economic incentives for desirable behaviour, but the GST encourages practices that reduce the prospects of sustainable resource use. While economic signals alone will not achieve a sustainable future, they can influence behaviour at the margin for good or ill. In the current absence of a preferred vision of a sustainable future, there is no rational basis for using price signals to promote that future.

Developing a vision of a desired future may not achieve the political momentum that would implement that vision. It is at least as important to devise viable pathways from where we are to where we want to go. Articulating those viable pathways is the key to gathering support from a broad coalition of interests for the substantial changes that are needed. Without such viable paths, there is no real prospect of developing the political commitment to change. Political leadership is improbable; as Kennedy (1993: 310) observes, those who prosper in diverse democratic systems are those who are careful to avoid antagonising powerful interests. Such leaders, Kennedy argues, will always be reluctant to embrace change as long as they can argue that experts are divided or more study is needed. In the case of complex environmental problems, that will always be true. The transition to sustainable use of our environment and natural resources requires a coalition of interests broad enough to demand political support.

References

Albury, R, 1983, *The politics of objectivity*, Waurn Ponds: Deakin University Press.

Claridge, AW and May, TW, 1994, Mycophagy among Australian mammals, *Australian Journal of Ecology* 19: 251-275.

Council of Australian Governments, 1992, *National Strategy for Ecologically Sustainable Development*, Canberra: AGPS.

Flannery, T, 1994, *The future eaters*, Sydney: Reed Books.

Fox, A et al, 1976, *Ranger Environmental Inquiry*, Canberra: AGPS.

Friibergh Workshop Report, 2000, <http://www.sustainabilityscience.org>.

Inter-governmental Panel on Climate Change (1996), Second Assessment Report, IPCC, Geneva.

Kelly, P, 1992, *The end of certainty*, Sydney: Allen and Unwin.

Kennedy, P, 1993, *Preparing for the Twenty-first Century*, London: Harper-Collins.

Lindzen, R, 1996, Global warming: the origins and nature of the alleged scientific consensus, <www.cato.org/pubs/regulation/reg15n2g.html>.

Lowe, I, 1989, *Living in the greenhouse*, Newham, Victoria: Scribe Books.

Pearman G, 1988, Greenhouse gases: evidence for atmospheric changes and anthropogenic causes, In: Pearman, G (ed), *Greenhouse: planning for climate change*, Leiden: CSIRO/EJ Brill.

Resources Assessment Commission, 1991, *Kakadu Conservation Zone: draft report*, Canberra: AGPS.

Moore, J, 1998, *Investing for growth: competitive science*, Canberra: Department of Industry, Science and Tourism.

State of the Environment Advisory Council, 1996, *State of the Environment Australia 1996*, Melbourne: CSIRO Publishing,

Sorensen, B, 1997, The cost of carbon emissions, In: *Proceedings of Conference: Responses to Global Warming*, Paris: International Energy Agency,

Wasson, R, et al, 1996, Inland waters, In: State of Environmental Advisory Council, *State of the environment Australia 1996*, Melbourne: CSIRO Publishing,

World Commission on Environment and Development, 1987, *Our common future*, Oxford: Oxford University Press.

Weinberg, A, 1968, Science and trans-science, *Minerva* 9: 220-232.

21

Politics and Policy

Robyn Eckersley

Department of Political Science, University of Melbourne

What are the key political and policy lessons to be learned from a review of the processes, organisations and institutional arrangements for natural resource and environmental management in Australia over the last three decades? In this synthesis of the work of the other contributors to this project, I shall reflect on how the processes of policy making may themselves become more reflective in this particular policy domain. Given that the broader goal of this project is 'to overcome *ad hockery* and policy amnesia' and explore how we might move towards 'adaptive policy learning', then greater reflectiveness – by which I mean greater *critical* reflection on past experience and as well as new research – is clearly an essential prerequisite to adaptive policy learning. In this respect, my approach will seek to move beyond a narrow 'problem-solving approach' to policy learning, which takes the institutional framework of action, including the configuration of knowledge and power, as given.

As Robert Cox explains, 'whereas the problem-solving approach leads to further analytical sub-division and limitation of the issue dealt with, the critical approach leads towards the construction of a larger picture of the whole of which the initially contemplated part is just one component, and seeks to understand the processes of change in which both parts and whole are involved' (1981: 129). Such an approach necessarily entails a critical examination of not only the processes, organisations and institutional arrangements for natural resource and environmental management in Australia but also the broader political and economic institutional context, including the changing global context, in which they are situated. Critically reflecting on this broader institutional context (rather than simply bracketing it away) is likely to deliver a keener appreciation of the parameters and possibilities of policy learning while also suggesting what kinds of deeper transformations may be required to the democratic processes of the state. Enlisting this 'outside-in' critical approach, I shall seek to:

- explore different *levels* of adaptive policy learning, in order to provide a framework for assessing the lessons from the case studies;

- sketch the changing global and national context in which natural resource and environmental policy processes takes place in Australia;

- draw out the salient political lessons from the case studies in this volume, pointing to both the democratic barriers and opportunities for innovative policy learning, and relating these to the broader institutional context in which policy making takes place; and

- looking to the future, remind the pessimists that innovative learning can still take place in the face of obdurate and inhospitable economic and political contexts.

While there are many political and policy lessons to be highlighted in this synthesis, I have marshalled the material around the guiding theme of democracy, or the quality of the 'communicative context' of politics and policy making, in order to bring into sharper relief both the democratic innovations and democratic deficits associated with natural resource management and environmental policy making in Australia.

Adaptive policy learning: the 'simple' versus the 'paradigmatic'

Adaptive policy learning approaches are typically offered as a corrective to ad hoc, incremental or 'muddling through' approaches to policy formulation and implementation (Lindblom 1959), on the one hand, and rigid, technocratic, 'grand social engineering', on the other hand. Dovers in the opening chapter has defined adaptive learning as an approach that is characterised by persistence, purposefulness, information-richness and sensitivity, inclusiveness and flexibility. While unavoidable and challenging tensions are likely to arise between some of these characteristics (most notably between persistence and purposefulness, on the one hand, and information-richness and sensitivity, inclusiveness and flexibility, on the other hand), the overriding emphasis on *adaptive* policy learning ought to favour, where practicable, the periodic adjustment of policy goals and tools in response to feedback over rigid, centralised and technocratic policy making. Indeed, such informed, reflexive adjustment in response to feedback is the very essence of adaptive policy learning.

However, there are narrow and broad ways of understanding adaptive policy learning, ranging from a simple adjustment of policy tools (which may uncritically accommodate deeper contradictions in the broader policy environment) to an innovative transformation of policy direction in response to a critical analysis of existing structures, past failures, new circumstances and new knowledge/information. Seen in this light, different levels of adaptive learning may improve policy outcomes by differing degrees. To understand why this might be so, it is useful to distinguish at least three different levels of learning or adaptation (following Hall 1993: 278):

- change in the application of policy instruments (first order/instruments)
- change in both the instruments of policy and the policy setting in which they are applied (second order/policy goals)
- changes in policy paradigm, that is, 'the hierarchy of goals' behind the policy settings (third order/policy paradigm)

According to Norman Vig, changing the suite of policy instruments may contribute to policy learning, but not necessarily *policy innovation* 'unless the use of these instruments is accompanied by changes in higher order principles' (Vig 1997: 11). We might therefore call the former 'simple policy learning' and the latter 'paradigmatic policy learning'. The latter kind of learning cannot take place in the absence of sustained critical reflection on the broader institutional context in which policies are made and implemented. We might also expect that the introduction of new policy tools (for example, the replacement of prescriptive regulation with market-based policy instruments), without a systematic critical analysis of the reasons for regulatory failure, will not necessarily lead to improvements in environmental outcomes (although they may lead to greater economic efficiencies). One simple explanation for regulatory failure may be lack of adequate resourcing, staffing and monitoring by the relevant regulatory agencies rather than any inherent defect in prescriptive regulation. However, these are ultimately empirical questions that have not yet been the subject of sufficiently rigorous and detailed investigation. Moreover, the case for new market-based instruments has been defended by a range of different advocacy coalitions for vastly different reasons to promote both conservative and radical (including green) social purposes (Eckersley 1995: 12). We can therefore only make sense of these developments by linking the case for new instruments with broader policy strategies and the more fundamental normative and cognitive frameworks in which they are embedded.

In a recent comparison of environmental policy developments in the United States and the European Union, Norman Vig has identified what he calls a paradigm shift in the regulatory principles involving a combination of 'an array of neoliberal strategies and instruments with the general philosophy of sustainable development' (Vig 1997: 4). A similar shift is also evident in Australia. However, this peculiar mix of new market-based strategies (which can be traced to broader shifts in national and global economic policy directions) with new philosophical discourses in environmentalism, incorporates both potential synergies *and* tensions. Moreover, there is room to argue that the higher order ideological shifts in government economic policy (which must also be located in the context of the intensification of economic globalisation) are exerting stronger pressure on the direction of environmental policy than the new philosophical discourses in environmentalism. Either way, however, these developments vindicate the insights of 'the new institutionalism' in political science, which has emphasised the centrality of ideas and values as *independent* variables in policy analysis (thus policy changes cannot simply be reduced to 'power-based' or 'interest-based' explanations, or to the impersonal dynamics of the economy).

Whether new environmental policies can be successfully implemented in the absence of shifts in the overarching hierarchy of policy goals is an interesting question, and probably ultimately an empirical question, that will vary according to the environmental problem, time frame and region under study. However, it would seem a reasonable hypothesis that new environmental policy goals are more likely to be achieved when accompanied by deeper ideological realignments that accord greater weight and priority to environmental goals vis-a-vis economic goals (with corresponding shifts in the ways in which these goals are linked).

The Australian and international experience reveals that such broader ideological realignments have taken place, but they have been mostly rhetorical and aspirational rather than substantive and binding. That is, while one can point to a proliferation of formal overarching or meta-policy commitments to sustainable development at the local, national and supranational levels, for the most part they remain vague, are usually not legally binding and can therefore be easily ignored or overridden by an executive and/or legislature preoccupied with other policy goals. This can be said for the 1992 Rio Declaration, Australia's National Strategy for Ecologically Sustainable Development 1992, the European Union's Fifth Environmental Action Plan and *Sustainable America* (PCSD 1996), the first report of the US President's Council on Sustainable Development (established in 1993).

For example, a particular government might launch a new set of policy tools (replacing prescriptive regulation with market-based policy instruments) as part of a new or more concerted commitment to particular environmental goals (to improve, say, water quality) which in turn forms part of a new overarching environmental meta-policy (a commitment to sustainable development). However, if the overarching meta-policy remains mostly aspirational and rhetorical, and especially if it is contradicted by economic and industry policy and practices, then we might expect that the environmental policy goals and related tools will not be wholly effective within their stated terms. While it is fair to say that the sustainable development debate has prompted increasing reflection upon not only instruments and policy settings but also a certain degree of (modest) realignment in the hierarchy of economic and ecological goals away from the rhetoric of balance and trade-off and towards the rhetoric of integration, genuine integration has, in most cases, remained elusive for a host of complex reasons. To the extent to which the principles of Ecologically Sustainable Development (ESD) formulated in the 1992 National ESD Strategy have found their way into *general* policy making, as distinct from subsidiary environmental policy making, they have mostly served as 'factors to be balanced with others' rather than the central overarching framework for government across all policy domains (eg, Bates, this volume).

The formal and final responsibility for resolving economic and ecological contradictions principally lies with the political system – essentially the governments of nation-states. However, for reasons explained below, in the Australian context this is not usually the place where we might expect to find any significant motivation to reorder the hierarchy of economic and environmental policy goals, including corresponding bureaucratic and ministerial hierarchies. The source of normative-cognitive innovation is more typically traced to local, national and transnational environmental organisations and other advocacy coalitions, policy professionals and scientists, universities and think tanks, local networks and communities, progressive business, and international organisations and multilateral arrangements. In this respect, such normative-cognitive shifts are more likely to *culminate* in, rather than *originate*, with the Commonwealth and State governments. To begin to understand why, we need to locate environmental policy in a broader political and economic context.

The global and national context

A central insight of the new institutionalism in political science is that institutions shape and constrain ideas, choices, interests and policy outcomes (eg, Koelbe 1995).[1] It follows that institutional change can open up new horizons for policy innovation, while institutional inertia can constrain innovation and mostly permit only policy incrementalism. This insight can apply as much to local institutions such as local government, to global economic or environmental governance regimes and to more fundamental constitutional structures, such as the constitutional framework of particular states or indeed the underlying structure of the state system. The purpose of this section is to locate the case studies on resource and environmental management in Australia in their broader national and global setting in order to direct attention to the general ways in which Australia's particular political and economic institutions operate to constrain environmental policy innovation.

The intensification of economic globalisation, a process that has been actively constructed by states, multinational corporations and international organisations such as the World Trade Organisation, has been widely interpreted as narrowing the political autonomy or policy parameters of states. For example, within the discipline of international political economy, increasing attention has been focused on the ways in which state policies (including defence and trade policy, fiscal and monetary policy, education, and legal regulation – not to mention environmental policy) are increasingly defined in the context of comparative international competitiveness. In place of social democracy and the welfare state we now see the ideological ascendancy of neoliberalism and 'the competition state', the primacy task of which is to make economic activities located within the state more competitive in global terms (Cerny 1997: 259). While this notion of competition is not necessarily new, what is new is the character and intensity of the competitive game (Porter 1990; Strange 1995; Cerny 1997; Palan and Abbott 1996). The new game is for states to pursue a now familiar repertoire of measures: reducing government spending, deregulating economic activities and financial markets, privatising state-owned enterprises, dismantling protection and other trade restrictive measures, controlling inflation and sidelining macro-economic demand management in favour of a micro-economic reform designed to improve international competitiveness. As Robert Cox explains, 'Neoliberalism is transforming states from being protective buffers between external economic forces and the domestic economy into agencies for adapting domestic economies to the exigencies of the global economy (1995: 39). Similarly, Palan and Abbott have described the competition state as being 'in the grip of a "beauty contest", trying to outbid other states by offering more attractive incentives to capital' (1996: 38).

---

1   Institutions are not intentional actors, they are a social phenomena embodying a particular rationality. According to Robert Goodin, institutions might be defined as 'organised patterns of socially constructed norms and roles, and socially prescribed behaviours expected of occupants of those roles, which are created and recreated over time' (Goodin 1996b: 19).

The upshot is that while nation states still arguably constitute the principal form of political rule throughout the world, the idea that they occupy the 'commanding heights' of governance, effectively and legitimately regulating and insulating social and economic life within their borders, has fallen by the wayside. These developments have been widely interpreted by critical political theorists and activists as constituting a crisis of democracy insofar as markets are increasingly taking over from politics as steering mecha-nisms and states are enforcing or otherwise being constrained by decisions and rules made in multilateral fora or in world markets. According to Cerny (1997: 258), 'As international and transnational constraints limit the things that state and market actors believe the state can do, this shift is leading to a potential crisis of liberal democracy as we have known it – and therefore of the things people can expect from even the best-run government'.

These developments have significant implications for successful adaptive policy learning, which presupposes a vibrant and flourishing democracy. Moreover, examining this broader context also helps to explain the Common-wealth government's increasing endeavours 'to streamline the regulatory state' and hand back environmental management responsibility to the states, the private sector and the community (see Odgers, this volume). This is one of the central objectives of the new *Environmental Protection and Biodiversity Conser-vation Act* 1999 (Cth) and it also informs numerous other environmental policy initiatives (such as Landcare). This is broadly consistent with the increasingly influential idea that governments should 'steer and not row' (Osborne and Gaebler 1992), a notion that provides one neoliberal recasting of the rationale of government to that of co-ordinator rather than provider of social services, a shift that has also ushered in profound changes in public sector management.

The changed expectations and understandings of the role and character of government in OECD countries are reflected in the mostly bi-partisan consensus of the major political parties in Australia on the need to foster 'a more competitive nation' along broadly neoliberal lines (albeit in subtly different ways). To the extent to which there is ideological polarisation on the question of the issue of the pace, direction and consequences of national economic policy, it is more usually found between the major parties (the Liberal-National Coalition and Labor) and minor parties (notably, the Democrats, the Greens, One Nation), rather than *between* the major parties. These trends do not point to any immediate sea change in the overarching hierarchy of goals framing national economic and environmental policy, although it is possible to point to a range of promising developments at the margins.

However, while the general lesson seems to be that the sustainable development debate has not succeeded in bringing about any fundamental reframing of economic policy in Australia, it cannot be dismissed as entirely ineffectual. Indeed, some OECD countries with strong, diversified economies (eg, Sweden, Germany, the Netherlands) have pursued green competitive strategies which have brought together economic and environmental goals into a virtuous relationship, particularly in the domain of industry policy. However, Australia has yet to exploit the technical, economic and environmental benefits of what has become known as 'ecological modernisation' (Christoff 1996; Hajer 1996; Moll 1996). According to this new green competitive strategy, it makes both economic and ecological sense for firms and farms to reduce resource and energy inputs and minimise pollution. Moreover, the new discourse has pointed to the longer term limitations of 'end-of-pipe' solutions to environmental problems on the basis of a longer term assessment of costs and benefits and a more cautious approach to risk assessment and scientific uncertainty (Weale 1992). A key insight of this new discourse is that the balance sheet of costs and benefits of new environmental initiatives and expenditure (whether taken from the perspective of firms or states) changes in favour of the environment the more the time frame of analysis is lengthened. Seen in this light, the traditional discourse of balancing environment and development considerations, which typically pulled back from charging producers and consumers the full environmental costs of their activities, has come under challenge for not avoiding costs but rather merely passing them on in space and time. Moreover, such costs can mount dramatically over time, with an increasing proportion being required for restoration or damage limitation rather than problem prevention. There are obvious lessons here for Australia's agricultural and other rural industries.

However, Australia's heavy dependence on energy intensive and resource extractive industries, which includes reliance on the export of primary commodities, has been traditionally taken by successive governments as a warrant for limiting the horizons of strategic environmental planning to a more short-sighted and narrowly conceived understanding of the 'national interest' that remains wedded to continuing past investment patterns. This is especially evident in relation to greenhouse policy, but the same might be said of many other environmental policy domains. To date, the federal and State governments have not made any concerted attempt to link the vulnerabilities in the Australian economy (such as heavy reliance on commodity exports and balance of payments problems) with persistent and/or looming ecological problems (such as land degradation and global warming), least of all address these vulnerabilities and problems in a positive, synergistic way.

Moreover, the political opportunities for synergistic economic and ecological restructuring are somewhat limited in the context of Australia's federal political system. In broad-brush terms, under the Westminster political system the development of disciplined parties in the lower house has served to concentrate political power in the hands of the political executive. In recent times, this concentration of power has been intensified with profound changes in the public service, which is less able to provide the traditional 'fearless and independent advice' to government. Moreover, the increasing reliance on politically appointed staff, and the general contraction of the public service, has arguably contributed to the ascendancy of 'policy amnesia' over 'policy learning'.

Executive power has traditionally been wielded by one or other of the major parties (the Liberal Party, in coalition with the National Party, or Labor), which have been historically dominated by what might be loosely called 'productivist interests' (industry/business, agriculture, unions) that have generally been slow to absorb new ecological values, ideas and practices. Accounting for and internalising environmental costs invariably entails a redistribution of benefits and burdens in society, which is typically resisted by those who stand to incur the burdens. These developments conspire with short election cycles to restrict rather than lengthen the horizons of policy planning. However, there are now new challenges to this consensus in the form of new minor parties in the Senate, various environmental advocacy organisations and movements, new research (in universities and think tanks) and new treaty obligations. Herein lies the impetus for potential institutional renewal and policy innovation.

The federal character of Australia's political system also provides plenty of opportunities for policy gridlock in cases of overlapping jurisdiction, where governments of different political persuasions typically find it difficult to reach agreement over regional and national policy questions. The primary intergovernmental coordinating mechanisms (ministerial councils, COAG) tend to drive decision making to a lowest common denominator, although the new National Environmental Protection Council provides a bold new experiment in intergovernmental law making (insofar as it enables decisions to be made by a two-thirds majority of ministers rather than by consensus and Environmental Protection Measures approved by the Council can automatically become law, subject to Parliamentary disallowance). Moreover, the division of fiscal responsibilities between the Commonwealth and the States has generated the problem of 'vertical fiscal imbalance', which has left the States with a narrow fiscal base relative to their legislative powers and political responsibilities. This has made many States reluctant to take on many new environmental initiatives in the absence of Commonwealth financial assistance (a recent example is the refusal by Queensland to proclaim its new legislation restricting land clearing until the Commonwealth offers financial assistance). However, recent shifts in Commonwealth taxation policy, notably the introduction of a Goods and Services Tax (GST), is expected to boost State revenues and place the States in a better financial position to tackle major environmental problems such as land and water degradation. In this respect, national environmental organisations may find themselves having to pay more attention to the States (relative to the Commonwealth) in their lobbying efforts. In this respect, the environment movement must learn to exploit the benefits (rather than lament the costs) of the States taking over greater areas of environmental management, which provide many opportunities for local policy diversity and experimentation.

Political lessons from the case studies

From a political perspective, ecological problems represent a major disjuncture in democratic accountability and control. This arises because there is no necessary connection between those who create ecological problems, those who have the expertise to understand them, those who suffer their negative consequences and those who must take political responsibility for them. If there is a general lesson from the eco-political literature, it is that many of these 'democratic deficits' in relation to political accountability and control may be remedied by new forms and styles of political communication which bring together as many disparate players as practicable (including culprits and beneficiaries, experts and laypeople, indigenous and 'settler' communities) into an open and constructive dialogue aimed at reaching a broad social consensus.

One of the central political lessons to arise from the environmental policy literature in general, which is also confirmed in the case studies in this volume, is that policy learning of the innovative kind presupposes a vibrant democracy or 'free communicative context' in which informed and reflective policy dialogue can flourish (Dryzek 1987, 1990, 1992; Eckersley 2000; Goodin 1996a; Lafferty and Meadowcroft 1996; Torgerson 1995, 1997). That is, innovative policy learning presupposes not only the full range of civil and political rights, including freedom of information and freedom of speech, and but also inclusive representation and participation in policy making. Inclusive representation and participation together enable the continuing public testing of claims from different social perspectives and standpoints (including those of specialists and laypeople), a process which facilitates 'inclusive thinking' and enables the ascendancy of public reason over private reason. That is, the discursive democratic requirement that, if collective agreement is to be reached, policy stakeholders must defend their proposed norms in terms that may be acceptable to differently situated others, is the very mechanism which steers policy deliberation away from the merely selfish or 'vested' interests of particular stakeholder towards public, generalisable ones (relatively speaking). Given that the protection of natural resources and the environment are public or generalisable interests, then this mode of dialogue would seem to be especially conducive to natural resource and environmental policy making. Such deliberative modes of democratic dialogue have been widely defended in the political studies literature as especially suitable candidates for a post-positivist, socially and ecologically inclusive model of environmental decision making and risk assessment at the local, regional and global level. In parti-cular, this dialogic model is considered superior to merely aggregative models of democracy, which simply add up individual preferences, but do not encourage or enable any critical reflection, self-correction, communication, or collective learning among the community of preference holders (herein lies the limitations of contingent valuation, cost-benefit analysis and opinion polling as tools of environmental policy). Unlike aggregative models of democracy, the dialogic model is explicitly *educative*.

Moreover, a dialogical approach necessarily requires a greater degree of diversification in the chains of policy formulation, implementation and monitoring than is usually found in more traditional policy making (e.g. the party room, Cabinet and senior political and bureaucratic advisers, and professional policy networks), and with that, a certain degree of relinquish-ment of central executive control over policy formulation. Against this back-ground, the case studies confirm and refine two, interrelated political insights.

The first is that the success of alternative policy making initiatives – like any policy making initiative – is a function of the quality of the 'communi-cative context'. That is, innovative policy making demands meaningful infor-mation, sufficient time, adequate resourcing, inclusive representation and participation, continuing publicity and strong political receptivity and com-mitment from all spheres of government to be both effective and legitimate.

The second insight is that while the political executive has supported a range of alternative policy initiatives in the environmental domain (outside the formal 'Green Paper/White Paper' process), its preparedness to relinquish some control of the policy process and/or fully support and resource new initiatives has been limited. That is, despite the emergence of 'new discursive designs' such as advisory panels, community planning initiatives, stakeholder groups, public inquiries, regional management regimes and even consensus conferences, the executive typically retains considerable discretion in deciding whether and to what extent it will follow any decisions or recommendations emerging from such bodies. Viewed from the conventional perspective of Westminster parliamentary democracy, this retention of executive discretion must be considered appropriate and in accordance with the doctrine of responsible government. However, when set against the requirements of deliberative or 'educative' democracy, the retention of executive discretion may be seen as a constraint on innovative policy learning in those circumstances where Parliament functions as a 'rubber stamp' of the executive rather than as a genuine deliberative forum.

Since I do not have the space to systematically explore the full political implications of these two insights I shall merely offer a number of general observations which relate to the quality of the communicative context of environmental policy making. I interpret this phrase broadly to include not only the more obvious requirements of democracy (such as a free flow of information) but also the relationship between power, knowledge and critical discourse, and the social and cultural context of policy making.

In terms of the democratic requirement of a free flow of infomation, it appears that extensive environmental data gathering programs are not always helpful to policy makers unless the thinking behind the social construction of data categories and processes is rendered transparent and the data categories made meaningful. As Harding and Traynor (this volume) make clear, state of environment reporting in Australia is still in its infancy and raises many unresolved political questions, including how far such reports should go in *evaluating* the information that is gathered. Moreover, policy makers face a paucity of systematic reviews of whether particular environmental policies are achieving their objectives over given periods (Dingle Smith, this volume) – knowledge that is an essential prerequisite to policy learning. Yet the release of meaningful public data can lead to greater citizen engagement. A good overseas example is the establishment of the Toxic Release Inventory in the US, which brought considerably public pressure to bear upon polluters, with consequent reductions in pollution (Vig 1997: 13). Australia's new National Pollutant Inventory is less comprehensive, but a step in the right direction.

As we have seen, the case studies demonstrate that many of the new and widely-heralded experiments in community participation in natural resource management have not achieved their full potential owing to the failure on the part of the political executive to relinquish sufficient control to, or to adequately empower, fund and resource/support and publicise or continue, these new initiatives. This lesson applies, in different ways, to the Resource Assessment Commission, to the National Conservation Strategy for Australia, the National Strategy for Ecologically Sustainable Development 1992, the consultation mechanisms under the Regional Forest Agreement process, local catchment management authorities, and, above all, the Landcare movement, which seems to have reached the limits of its potential. Indeed, a more cynical view of the Landcare initiative is that it reflects, in part, a relinquishment or dereliction of government responsibility in the form of cost-shifting, manifested in the exploitation of voluntary rural labour as part of an overriding concern to reduce government expenditure. While this is perhaps too cynical, it is clear that the Landcare movement needs more political support, in the form of funds, publicity and professional expertise (Curtis, this volume). Similar lessons apply to local governments, which, by virtue of their status as a creature of State governments, lack the legislative powers and fiscal resources to realise their yet to be fully tapped potential to enact innovative environmental policy (Wild River, this volume)

However, it is necessary to look critically as well as sympathetically at the potential of place-based community initiatives, including those of local governments. On the one hand, community-based initiatives (including local government) offer great opportunities for diverse experimentation in ways that are especially sensitive to local conditions, particularly in rural areas. On the other hand, the small or local scale of a particular local community or local government may make it an inappropriate, *sole* locus of management responsibilities in those circumstances where the geographical reach of the natural resource or ecological problem is too large and complex for the local community to track, comprehend and control. Moreover, place-based communities are rarely homogenous social structures and insofar as there are shared community norms, they may sometimes be part of the problem rather than the solution when viewed from an ecological perspective (for example, 'good' land is cleared land to the Queensland farmer). More generally, analysis of local level behaviour is often insufficient to explain interaction at the local level. That is, it is usually necessary to locate local interactions in the contexts of larger economic forces and institutions. These insights are consistent with the dialogical approach to environmental policy formation which seeks an understanding of complex interdependencies by linking together the multiplicity of actors, interest and institutions (at different sites) which shape the pattern of resource use in particular places and to critically deliberate on the implications of these linkages in a representative forum. As Agarwal (2000) has pointed out, it is always necessary to ask: who possesses and/or shares the authority to make, manage, monitor and enforce the rules and structures which shape and constrain the use of natural resource and the environment?

It is also often the case that the involvement of representatives from local communities typically takes place within an asymmetical power and knowledge structure. For example, particular local catchment management authorities typically enjoy a much reduced access to resources, knowledge and influence than State agencies, officials or university researchers. Moreover, the capacities of local catchment management authorities varies across different districts, and not all districts are at the same stage of 'readiness' to avail themselves of new policy initiatives and funding opportunities such as that provided by the Natural Heritage Trust scheme (Ewing, this volume).

However, the limitations of local community initiatives do not provide a warrant for more centralised bureaucratic control. In any event, local communities can sometimes thwart or delegitimise centralised policy directives in circumstances where they have not been included in policy negotiations. The general point to emerge from the case studies is that the involvement of local place-based communities and local government must be seen as a necessary though not always sufficient condition for successful policy innovation. Among other things, they provide one of many possible checks on the accountability and responsiveness of central agencies. This is especially important when it is remembered that, historically, many natural resource based agencies in Australia (such as Forestry Commissions) have been 'captured' by the industry they are meant to regulate and have been prone to treat those firms exploiting natural resources as 'clients' rather than regulatory subjects. Such bureaucratic agencies (the personnel of which typically share the education and worldview of their 'clients') have often stifled new initiatives, resisted criticisms and provided a conservative influence on policy development. Such arrangements are part of a broader history of 'statist developmentalism' in Australia (Walker 1999).

However, other environmental regulatory agencies have often been saddled with competing mandates which cannot be effectively integrated. As Christoff (this volume) shows, the Victorian EPA has a conflicting mandate to work cooperatively with industry, to act as a public watchdog and to discharge its functions efficiently. These contradictions raise broader questions concerning the possibilities of effective agency integration, insofar as they suggest the need, at least in some circumstances, for a separation of environmental advocacy roles and enforcement roles on the one hand, and industry development roles on the other. Alternatively, this might merely serve as a warning that integration between development and environmental protection agencies may be premature until such time as environmental agencies acquire more status, funding, and political salience – a development that itself would be indicative of a more fundamental normative and cognitive reordering in the hierarchy of economic and ecological goals.

Finally, there are deeply entrenched cultural understandings and boundaries which constrain the reach of environmental policy, such as the boundary between what is 'public' (the proper business of politics) and 'private' (not the business of politics). For example, it needs to be emphasised that most land in Australia is privately owned and/or managed by private holders, not community or public bodies. Moreover, most of this land is exploited for private profit, and only a small subset of private land is exploited in a manner that is wholly consistent with the principles of ESD (eg, organic farms, ecotourist operations such as Earth Sanctuaries, private land held in trust as biodiversity reserves – this list is not exhaustive). This may seem an obvious point but it is worth emphasising the political limits facing governments when considering how far to regulate activities on private land in the name of environmental protection. Essentially, the decision as to whether and how to utilise private land is generally understood to be a *private* one; at best, governments can qualify the way the land is utilised by means of incentives and sanctions, but except in atypical cases of compulsory acquisition, they cannot wholly dictate the use of land. This explains why regulations which generate actual or potential economic losses on the part of private holders must usually be accompanied by compensation (eg, the Victorian *Flora and Fauna Guarantee Act* 1988). Culturally, private property rights are considered 'sacrosanct' and new environmental laws and the traditional responsibilities imposed by the common law (negligence, nuisance) stop a long way short of the general idea that the holders of land are 'trustees' or 'custodians' of land on the behalf of, say, 'the public environmental good' or present and future generations. Against this background, the creation of a new species of property right in public environmental goods, such as tradable licenses to use water, carries potential dangers. While tradeable license schemes promise new incentives and greater efficiencies, the ecological success of such schemes is a function of the total *aggregate* levels of resource use or waste permitted in particular watersheds/airsheds/regions, levels that usually need to be reduced over time. Yet once the right to draw water or emit waste acquires the status of private property, there is always the risk that governments may find it increasingly difficult or costly to 'take back' or otherwise infringe upon the right.

Looking to the future

In this synthesis I have sought to emphasise the relationship between different levels of environmental policy learning (first order instruments, second order policy goals and third order policy paradigms) in order to show how problems encountered in the application of particular instruments or the pursuit of particular policy goals can often be explained in terms of conflicting policy paradigms, that is, conflicts in the hierarchy of goals underlying different policy settings, including deep seated normative-cognitive understandings. Moreover, I have sought to show how policy paradigms are shaped not only by the ideological disposition of particular governments but also by national political institutions and economic contexts, local cultural dispositions (such as public/private boundaries) as well as new global dynamics.

Although I have sought to show how institutions shape and constrain ideas, choices, interests and policy outcomes, institutions can, over time, also be reshaped by innovative ideas and practices on the part of individuals and organisations. Many of the new processes and strategies in natural resource and environmental management implemented in the last three decades may be seen as innovative when set against the longer history of natural resource and environmental management in Australia. Moreover, many of these initiatives conform to what Lafferty and Meadowcroft refer to as '*cooperative management regimes*: a type of formation which involves a number of social partners in a collaborative attempt to resolve specific environmental difficulties' (1996: 257). The hallmark of such regimes is that they seek to cultivate processes of discursive consensus formation and involve each participant assuming some degree of responsibility for the implementation of the agreed solution (1996: 257-258). Lafferty and Meadowcroft argue that the great advantage of such regimes is 'that they modify the institutional context of environmental policy making, without necessarily requiring formal institutional change' (1996: 263). In terms of cost-effectiveness it is cheaper to modify conceptual paradigms operating within marginally adjusted governmental structures than it is to engage in a whole-sale reorganisation of such structures. Nonetheless, in the longer run, such conceptual modifications can gradually lead to deeper institutional transformations.

Notwithstanding the somewhat inhospitable context, then, there is still room for creative engagement with existing institutions. Drawing from the case studies, I offer four concluding general recommendations towards improving the policy learning context for natural resource and environmental management in Australia:

- Continue and enhance extensive environmental data gathering programs but devote more effort to rendering the information meaningful to both the public and policy makers;
- Conduct more systemmatic reviews of whether, to what extent and how particular natural resource and environmental policies are achieving their objectives;
- Continue to develop and enhance community participation and cooperative management regimes in natural resource and environmental management and ensure that such initiatives are properly funded, technically supported, publicised and empowered by the relevant State and federal agencies and political executives; and
- In the longer term, work towards developing alternative, 'green competitive strategies', or 'ecological modernisation' strategies, in industry and agriculture.

Although the fourth recommendation is perhaps the most crucial, since it entails a re-arrangement in the hierarchy of environmental and economic goals at the State and Commonwealth levels, it is also the most difficult to achieve. However, I have suggested that the initial impetus for unsettling established policy paradigms typically comes from above and below the state rather than from within. That is, normative-cognitive shifts are more likely to culminate in, rather than originate, with the Commonwealth and State governments (provided, of course, there is sufficient receptivity to new thinking within government and bureaucratic circles). We might therefore understand many of the new community-based and regional initiatives in natural resource management and environmental protection as already contributing to the necessary realignment of normative-cognitive thinking that may lead in the longer run to, say, a green taxation policy, an ESD coordinating office in the Prime Minister and Premiers' departments, the greening of Australia's energy industries, and the creation of a Parliamentary Commissioner for the environment (to name but a few of the measures that would be indicative of a major realignment in the hierarchy of ecological and economic goals in Australia).

However, in the medium to longer term, a resolution of the deeper structural contradictions between ecological and environmental policy in Australia is unlikely for so long as 'distortions' in the communicative context of policy making persist. Nonetheless, I have suggested that a greater diversification in the chains of policy formulation, implementation and monitoring is one way of creating a more favourable climate for a deliberative 'stakeholder democracy' in the absence of more deep seated structural reforms to our Westminster system of parliamentary democracy.

References

Argawal, A, 2000, 'Community' and natural resource conservation, In: Gale, Fred P and M'Gonigle, R Michael, (eds), *Nature, production, power*, Cheltenham, UK: Edward Elgar.

Cerny, P, 1997, Paradoxes of the competition state: the dynamics of political globalisation, *Government and Opposition* 36(2): 251-274.

Christoff, P, 1996, Ecological modernisation, ecological modernities, *Environmental Politics* 5(3): 476-500.

Cox, RW, 1981, Social forces, states and world orders: beyond international relations theory, *Millennium: Journal of International Studies* 10(2): 126-55.

Cox, R, 1995, Critical Political Economy, In: Cox, R, Gill, S, Hettne, B, van der Pijl, K, Rosenau, J and Sakamoto, Y (eds), *International political economy: understanding global disorder*, Halifax, Novia Scotia: Fernwood Publishing.

Dryzek, J, 1987, *Rational ecology: environment and political economy*, Oxford: Basil Blackwell.

Dryzek, J, 1990, Green reason: communicative ethics for the biosphere *Environmental Ethics* 12: 195-210.

Dryzek, J, 1992, Ecology and discursive democracy: beyond liberal capitalism and the administrative state, *Capitalism, Nature, Socialism* 3(2): 18-42.

Eckersley, R, 1995, *Markets, the state and the environment: towards integration*, Melbourne: Macmillan.

Eckersley, R, 2000, Deliberative democracy, ecological representation and risk: towards a democracy of the affected, In Saward, M (ed), *Democratic innovation: deliberation, association and representation*, London: Routledge.

Goodin, R, 1996a, Enfranchising the earth, and its alternatives, *Political Studies* 44: 835-49.

Goodin, R, 1996b, Institutions and their design, In: Goodin R (ed), *The theory of institutional design*, Cambridge: Cambridge University Press.

Hajer, M, 1996, Ecological modernisation as cultural politics, In: Lash, S, Szerszynski, B and Wynne, B (eds), *Risk, Environment and modernity: towards a new ecology*, London: Sage Publications.

Hall, PA, 1993, Policy paradigms, social learning and the state, *Comparative Politics* 25(3): 275-296.

Koelbe, TA, 1995, The new institutionalism in political science and sociology, *Comparative Politics* 27(2): 231-243.

Lafferty, WM, and Meadowcroft, J (eds), 1996, *Democracy and the environment: problems and prospects*, Cheltenham, UK: Edward Elgar.

Lindblom, CE, 1959, The science of muddling through, *Public Administration Review* 19: 79-88.

Moll, A, 1996, Ecological modernisation and institutional reflexivity: environmental reform in the late modern age, *Environmental Politics* 5(2): 302-323.

Osborne, D, and Gaebler, T, 1992, *Reinventing government: how the entrepreneurial spirit is transforming the public sector, from schoolhouse to statehouse, city hall to pentagon*, Reading, Mass: Addison-Wesley.

Paehlke, R, and Torgerson, D (eds), 1990, *Managing leviathan: environmental politics and the administrative state*, Broadview Press: Peterborough, Ontario.

Palan, R, and Abbott, J (with Deans, P), 1996, *State strategies in the global political economy*, London: Pinter.

Porter, M, 1990, *The competitive advantage of nations*, London: Macmillan.

Strange, S, 1995, The defective state, *Daedalus: Journal of the American Academy of Arts* 124(2).

Torgerson, D, 1995, The uncertain quest for sustainability: public discourse and the politics of environmentalism, In: Fischer, F, and Black, M (eds), *Greening environmental policy: the politics of a sustainable future*, Paul Chapman Publishing Ltd.

Torgerson, D, 1997, Policy professionalism and the voices of dissent: the case of environmentalism, *Polity* 29: 358.

Vig, N, 1997, Toward common learning: trends in US and EU environmental policy, *Lecture for summer symposium, the innovation of environmental policy*, Bologna: Italy, 22 July .

Vig, NJ and Kraft, ME, 1997, *Environmental policy in the 1990s*, Washington, DC: Congressional Quarterly Press.

Walker, KJ, 1999, Statist development in Australia, In: Walker, KJ and Crowley, K (eds), *Australian Environmental policy 2: studies in decline and devolution*, Sydney: University of New South Wales Press.

Walker, KJ and Crowley, K, 1999, Introduction, In: Walker, KJ and Crowley, K (eds), *Australian environmental policy 2: studies in decline and devolution*, Sydney: University of New South Wales Press.

Weale, A, 1992, *The new politics of pollution*, Manchester: Manchester University Press.

22

Economic Policy and Sustainable Use of Natural Resources

Onko Kingma
Capital Agricultural Consultants, Canberra

Warren Musgrave
WF Musgrave Consulting, Mittagong; Emeritus Professor of Agricultural Economics, University of New England

In preparing this book, the framework of our present mixed capitalist system was always understood to form part of the context of the analysis in all chapters. Many address economic issues either implicitly or explicitly. However, as the book and its themes were discussed the need became apparent that some explicit discussion of such issues was necessary, at least at the level of synthesis and identification of lessons to be learned.

The economic framework, with its central feature the market as a mechanism for equating the demand for and supply of goods, services and resources, influences decision making at all levels. Where markets, and their attendant institutions of clearly defined property rights and tradeability, function well, little regulatory intervention is required to ensure optimal (sustainable) use of natural resources. The reality is, however, that only a proportion of our economic activity concerning natural resources can be conducted within such 'efficient' markets. For this reason, resource allocation is often 'second best' with, sometimes, disastrous long term consequences for sustainability and, indeed, resource allocation well beyond the natural resources sector (Haward; Christoff; Bates; Dingle Smith; this volume).

Amelioration of such adverse consequences typically requires regulatory action to correct for this market failure. Sometimes such regulatory action is intended to improve the performance of the market, sometimes it is intended to substitute for it. Which route is taken depends on perceptions of the efficiency and effectiveness of the regulatory alternatives facing policy makers.

The purpose of this chapter is to elaborate upon this point, to illustrate the relevance of economic policy, market arrangements, systems of common property governance, and to explore the way we think about the economic, environmental and social policy nexus to sustainable resource management. The pervasive and fundamental nature of these phenomena in underpinning our society is so important that, if our institutions are not sufficiently tuned to the role of market institutions and systems of common property governance in achieving sustainability, any amount of effort to elicit better reactions from those who use or make policy for natural resources will fail.

The pervasiveness of economic institutions

Whether in the chapters on sectoral studies, the discussions on arrangements for management, regulating and motivating, or in the people and program chapters, the underlying economic system can be seen to have an impact on:

- expression of the values of our resources;
- determining the profitability of natural resources using enterprises and the use of natural resources;
- regulating the demand for and supply of natural resources in concert with other resources; and
- providing cornerstones for broader policies for natural resource management.

Examples of this from the book are: pricing and tradeability of water within the context of well-defined property rights (Smith; Crabb; McKay, this volume); rangelands values, tenure and access (Stafford Smith and Abel, this volume); instruments to handle common property and the use of tradeable quotas in the case of the oceans and fisheries (Haward, this volume); regulatory and motivational policy where the central mechanisms are economic signals to guide, for example, waste disposal and recycling in local government (Christoff, this volume); environmental protection and pricing (McKay, this volume); management of services by state authorities (Christoff, this volume); and so on. An inescapable conclusion is that economic signals must be accurate, sophisticated and appropriately packaged to facilitate a socially optimal outcome from use of natural resources.

There is no doubt the significant policy and program efforts documented in the earlier chapters have, in large measure, been successful in shifting us towards better awareness, attitude change and sounder economic behaviour (eg, Ewing; Stafford Smith and Abel; Crabb, this volume). There is, however, other regulatory arrangements aside, widespread and increasing concern that traditional economic policies, market arrangements and institutional settings may not be enough. Degradation of the natural resources base persists throughout Australia. The extent of recent degradation, loss of biodiversity, ecosystem ill-health, salinity etc has been documented in the Agriculture, Fisheries and Forestry – Australia Policy Discussion Paper, which argues (AFFA 1999: 4-5):

> the scientific evidence suggests ... degradation problems will probably become more serious ... we know that the decline in the condition of our natural resources in some areas is outstripping our efforts to counteract it using current approaches. The community, including most landholders, now has a higher expectation that the natural resource base will be better managed. There is a sharper consumer focus on environmental performance in production and on food safety, and international forums are now making connections between natural resource management and trade.

An implication is that economic policies must be better focussed and targeted to provide the right signals, institutions which lower transaction costs identified, and appropriate regulatory arrangements established to manage resources where high transaction costs prohibit efficient and effective market solutions.

Within the present policy framework, disillusionment is expressed with the usefulness of the economic measures and instruments that have served us in the past. The picture is complicated by the fact that, with economic growth, the demand for many natural resources is increasing. The range and number of natural resources users also appears to be growing, as are the possible uses to which society wishes to put natural resources. At the same time, some natural resources are becoming more scarce or the availability of some natural resources of a given quality is declining. In the latter case, this may be due to emergence of environmental problems following increasingly intensive use. Such problems necessitate the creation and implementation of novel economic and related regulatory instruments to replace those which may have served us well enough in the past, but are not adequate for the new realities.

Definition by biophysical scientists of the ecological and environmental problems which beset us has stimulated economists to pay greater attention to the implications of the limits to substitution between different classes of capital (most broadly, human and natural), of the limits to the application of economic concepts of allocative efficiency when inequitable outcomes for distant future generations threaten, of the existence of unpriced values, and of the limits transaction costs impose on the appropriateness of private owner- ship of resources. In this context, it is important to recognize that regulation and technology underpin market performance. Economists look to scientists and engineers to provide advice on technology in order to assess the impact of alternative arrangements for resource ownership and trade. In the absence of such advice their analysis can be based on excessively simplistic or just plain wrong technological assumptions. The ramifications of many developments in economic thinking for resources policy and management have yet to manifest themselves fully at the policy level.

The AFFA Discussion Paper goes on to argue that 'a new policy approach to natural resource management will be required'. Significant changes in land use and management practices are seen to be central to achieving sustainability (AFFA 1999: 6) and problems will not be able to be handled in isolation. 'We need to look beyond individual problems ... and take account of the links within and between natural systems and the inter play of economic, social and biophysical factors that influence natural resource decision making. An integrated approach is needed.' (p 7).

Underlying this shift in policy approach is the issue of relationships – and relationships are crucially influenced by economic settings. Ways in which individuals and groups consult, communicate and share understanding of each others' concerns are now central to the solution of Australia's natural resource management problems. In the words of the Discussion Paper, 'The way forward ... should involve close partnerships and cooperation between governments, regional communities and individuals. The partnership frame- work should reflect the respective roles and responsibilities of participants and the inter-relationships between them.' (p 13). Appropriate economic sig- nals will be central to achieving this, as well as the attendant issues of adequacy of technical, economic and social information flows for sound risk management decision making for natural resources use. New ways will have to be found of engaging, communicating between, and skilling stakeholders for effective natural resource management. This is all about stakeholder behaviour and economic settings play an important role in the determination of this.

These economic policy settings must be supportive of and facilitate the development of a learning society and be conducive to the building of social capital (Eckersley, this volume). The mix of economic instruments, couched within appropriately tuned property rights (Bates, this volume), becomes important here. These issues are discussed below.

Markets, property rights and incentives

Institutions

Institutions are broadly defined as the set of acceptable behavioural rules that govern action and relationships – social norms, ways of doing things and ways in which individuals and groups interact to achieve ends. By giving access to income streams and power, institutions largely determine the distributional characteristics of society. Who benefits and loses from institutional arrangements, who seeks to acquire property rights and who does not have access to property rights, are all important questions which condition important features of society and how members of it behave.

The economic model underpinning society has the capacity to bring forth an infinite array of technically efficient sets of relative prices – only one set will be consistent with prevailing institutions. The nature of these prices and the social sanctions they possess derive from the institutional base. Different behaviour and sets of prices will emerge with different institutional arrangements. 'Free market' prices generated by private enterprise are generally sanctioned as they are thought to reflect the preferences of individuals. They do, but only to the extent to which they are channelled and constrained by the existing institutional arrangements. Prices simply reflect the outcome of entrepreneurial decisions conditioned by present property arrangements. If sustainable natural resource management calls for institutional change, then a wider analysis is needed than simply a behavioural response to relative price changes. Institutions are moulded by history, values, beliefs, norms governing behaviour, power and so forth. Where institutional change is required, these (value-based) factors must, therefore, be taken into account – an experience which is novel for many disciplines.

Strictly speaking there is no such thing as a free market. In order to work, markets rely on an extensive apparatus of rights, supervision, enforcements and guarantees provided by the state. The important feature of such regulation is that it delineates what people cannot do, rather than what they can do, as in a 'command and control' system. Broad assumptions underlying the efficient use of markets have been discussed by Godden (1997). The key assumptions are: a sufficiently large number of buyers and sellers, all of whom are sufficiently small so that they cannot influence the market price;

commodities/resources are assumed to be homogeneous, allowing aggregation across different classes or qualities; time and place of transaction are assumed to be constant with no variation between regions; perfect knowledge/ information and hence certainty with regard to characteristics of commodities/resources and their use; only (measurable) transactions carried out within markets are assumed relevant; property rights must be clearly defined as well as transferability of the commodity/resource; excludability and rivalry must be present, meaning, broadly, that payment for the commodity/resource by one agent will preclude its consumption by another agent; and, related to property rights, externalities should not be present in commodities/resources transactions, meaning there are no (unpriced) side effects involved in transactions; and so on. For the economist, this ideal market is the starting point for exploration of the costs and benefits of less 'perfect' arrangements.

Markets

Where markets do not fail, an efficient price formation process and the resultant expression (ie, through prices) of the full cost of using natural resources and the true value of natural resources to society, will result in ecologically sustainable resource use or optimal rates of resource depletion. In this situation, potential problems of imbalance between supply and demand, both spatially (across resources and geographically) and inter-temporally (future generations), can be corrected through use of prices – as scarcity and demand increase, so prices will rise signalling to resource users that change in the pattern of resource use is required. The result is that incentives for management and maintenance of quality of natural resources increase. Assuming the above conditions for efficient markets hold, resource users will re-assess their requirements and substitute away from the threatened resources or use these resources differently (McKay, this volume).

Markets rely on secure and clearly defined property rights (ownership of natural resources and duties, privileges, rights, obligations associated with natural resources) and prevailing institutions (norms, regulations, ways of doing things, behavioural rules etc). Property rights (and other institutions) determine the bargaining position of natural resources users, which benefits and costs will be counted and who has access to income streams from natural resources use. Thus the search for more efficient mechanisms for pricing of natural resources must be accompanied by a review of property rights arrangements.

Where markets fail, then transaction costs, equity or ethical considerations may mean that institutions such as administrative pricing and regulations (Crabb, this volume) are preferable instruments. In this case, price signals to natural resources users are the result of judgments by regulators about what is optimal natural resources use (Christoff, McKay, this volume).

Key policy issue

The key policy issue is to assess to what extent imbalance between demand and supply and attendant degradation of natural resources, is a problem warranting policy action to improve pricing and/or property rights. Such action would involve either correction for external benefits and costs of some natural resources users' actions, or improvement of existing institutional arrangements which discourage sensible pricing and use of some natural resources, or modifying/introducing resource taxation arrangements for sharing of rents from natural resources use. Such reform can, at times, be made difficult in Australia due to, for example, Commonwealth-State Constitutional arrangements, vested interests in present property arrangements and the complexity of the trade-offs required. Such issues will no doubt continue to be a constraint on development of national policies for natural resource management, requiring special emphasis on consultation and cooperation at all levels of government and the community. An illustrative example of a framework within which this could occur is presented below.

Assessing benefits and costs

A well specified equation of direct and indirect benefits and costs will give an indication of the net benefits to society of a policy change. However, introduction of policies to correct for externalities is often undertaken by policy makers without fully addressing wider benefits and costs of the policy change or fully understanding the ways in which policies work out in practice. This can add to resource misuse. Examples from the book where such situations have occurred are: property rights changes which may not have reflected a socially optimal outcome because of the weak bargaining position of a significant proportion of stakeholders (Stafford Smith, Hamilton, this volume); changes in values and knowledge which may have created externalities, requiring further reform of private or common property rights (Hamilton, Haward, this volume); instances where power, technology and institutions may, in some circumstances, have acted in a mutually reinforcing way, creating inertia which may have supported existing, possibly obsolete, institutions (Eckersley, Lowe, this volume); instances where institutions have not been tailored to local needs thus imposing high costs on groups such as rural communities, and resulting in misallocation of resources by favouring groups outside the particular localities (Orchard et al, this volume); and so on. In such circumstances, existing institutional structures have become suboptimal from the viewpoint of society as a whole and the challenge is to define the desired new rights structure and the extent of compensation, if any, to be made to the losers.

Economic policy instruments

Clearly, from the above, in many instances, use and management of natural resources cannot be left to competitive market processes if efficient allocation of resources, and sustainability, are the objective (Bates, this volume). Consequently, while, on one hand, we see some natural resources problems dealt with by reforms which strengthen or create markets, on the other, we see others dealt with by the strengthening or creation of command and control mechanisms, such as covenants, licences, regulations, the setting of standards, and so on. A range of policy measures is potentially available to address these situations. Invariably a mix of measures will be most appropriate (Dovers 1995; Industry Commission 1998).

Policy measures for natural resource management generally involve opportunities to build institutional capacity and/or appropriate and effective incentive mixes. Dovers (1995) has outlined a range of instrument options while Young et al (1996) have identified similar incentives in five categories of: motivational, educational and information based instruments; voluntary instruments; property rights based instruments; regulatory instruments; and price based or financial instruments. Price or financially based mechanisms are generally looked to first from a policy viewpoint as potentially the most effective forms of intervention. Table 22.1 provides a broad summary of measures within each category. Within the pricing category, correction of market failures generally means introduction of pricing mechanisms. Examples are in water resources and fisheries (McKay, this volume) where institutional arrangements such as tradeable property rights have been introduced. Where there is clarity in these rights, pricing of resources and trading of them has been possible. Other examples are investment allowances under the taxation system to encourage activities such as conservation of water to combat drought, and levies such as in agricultural industries to encourage R&D.

Policies to change behaviour patterns are generally first directed to correction of causes within privately run production systems using economic measures. Issues here (within the context of markets which are already present) relate to availability of information, finance, technology, R&D results and resource assessment as a means of ensuring that natural resources users are aware of all the repercussions of their actions. For private sector activities to work, capital and human capital markets must be operating effectively. If resource degradation still persists, then the causes must be sought in outdated property rights and other institutions, pricing policies and/or market structure – there will be divergence between social and private benefits and costs (externalities) which will make the solution of degradation problems (perceived to be a problem from society's point of view) uneconomic for private natural resources users. Pricing in this context includes income taxation measures, user pays and resource rent taxes and subsidies. Finally, as already indicated, if efficient markets cannot be established/restructured to provide the incentives for improved management, then some form of regulation, typically involving government, may be the most cost effective solution (Industry Commission 1998). In the latter case, the efficiency of government enterprise and agencies, and their structure and accountability for effective delivery, should be an important consideration. The various case studies in this report provide explorations of all these situations.

As noted in the AFFA (1999) Discussion Paper and by Young et al (1996: 105), a policy approach is now required which both incorporates and goes beyond the conventional mechanisms, and which makes greater use of incentives and other economic instruments to close the gap between private actions and social objectives. Arriving at this new and innovative policy mix requires consistent and rigorous evaluation of measures. In this context, policy makers might take another look at the policy instruments and 'smart

Table 22.1. Some Policy Instruments to Encourage Natural Resource Management

Measure or Instrument Category	List of Instruments	Brief Comment
Motivational, Educational, Information	Information supply Research Education Advertising, awards, devolution of responsibility Audits	Centered on information provision for decision making, attitude change, awareness; research and extension; use of the media and campaigns; audits; reviews etc.
Voluntary incentives	Voluntary, incentive and community based programs Voluntary standard based initiatives	Relies on the good will of stakeholders; non-interventionist; opportunities for joint activities; grants may be useful; build community attitudes; low cost; incentives may be: standards based, grants, concessions, groups support etc.
Property rights	Exclusive use rights Contracts Individually transferable property right mechanisms Covenants Management agreements Offset arrangements Leasing, licensing	Appropriate where markets are not working properly – aim is to alter private costs and benefits so that any unaccounted social costs and benefits can be taken into account. This will change the incentives for particular individual and group behaviour.
Pricing	Performance bonds Charges, levies, use fees Hypothecation Tax instruments Correcting market failures Land taxes and rebates Cross compliance Conditional grants and payments	Work directly through markets (provided property rights are clear). Pricing instruments have a direct role in changing attitudes and behaviour.
Regulatory etc	Regulations restricting resource use Precautionary mechanisms	Seek to restrict or control certain activities or behaviour. Best known examples are zoning, land use restrictions (covenants), standards and bans. Regulations tend not to be motivational and often have high compliance costs etc.

regulation' alternatives suggested by Dovers (1995), the Industry Commission (1998, Ch. 8) and Young et al (1996).

Young et al (1996) and Dovers (1995) have summarised the literature aimed at developing the most useful set of criteria against which to evaluate the success of policy measures to achieve natural resource management. Their criteria are relevant to the issues in this book. Examples are:

- Economic efficiency – the chosen tradeoff between production and other goals is achieved at least cost (productive efficiency) and so that no re-assignment of property rights would improve the situation without making some-one worse off (allocative efficiency);
- Dynamic and continuing incentive – the (mix of) mechanism(s) continues to encourage technical innovation, natural resource management goals and adaptation to changing technology, prices and physical conditions;
- Equity – no group, including future generations, is unfairly treated by the use of the policy measure(s);
- Dependability or certainty – the measure(s) will deliver the desired natural resource management outcomes even when knowledge about likely responses is uncertain;
- Precaution – the measure(s) avoids the chance of serious or irreversible consequences especially if there is limited knowledge about outcomes;
- Administrative feasibility and cost – the measure(s) is easily understood and used, monitoring and information costs are minimal, government enforcement is cost effective, can be financed from available revenue and encourages self enforcement, and so on; and
- Community and political acceptability – the measures motivate the community to ensure natural resource management objectives are met, are perceived as being legitimately formulated and delivered and are consistent with the community's and government views.

Young et al have supplemented these criteria by guidelines for designing policy mixes that promote active natural resource management (Young et al 1996: 140). Examples of such guidelines are:

- preference should be given to policy mixes that motivate communities and industry to achieve natural resource management objectives;
- less interventionist instruments should be preferred to instruments which involve increased action by governments;
- financially attractive instrument mixes should be preferred to ones that reduce the net welfare of those asked to conserve natural resources; and
- policy changes should seek to reduce underlying causes and threats to sustainability of natural resources use, such as institutional failure, market failure, or incompletely specified property right structures, as well as the direct threats themselves.

While incomplete, the above serves to illustrate the considerations which must be taken into account in developing policies in the complex area of natural resource management. Assessment and implementation of the mix of most appropriate policies is a difficult task which must involve a systems approach and attention to both the physical and human responses to policy changes.

Some public administration issues

Many of the chapters in this book refer to experience with organisations developed to tackle natural resource management problems on the ground. Particular mention is made of community-based initiatives, often in partnership with government. To an economist, community-based activities such as Landcare represent attempts to cope with the common property issues characteristic of so many of our land and water management problems. More than ten years of experience with such activities leads to the conclusion that, while laudable in a number of respects, they have lacked certain characteristics needed if further progress is to be made in ameliorating the problems confronting us. These characteristics are now discussed, in the context of the core themes of this book. A concrete policy proposal, reflecting experiences of the authors of this chapter and the thrust of the rest of this book, is presented as a contribution to debate on the arrangements needed to be put on place if future natural resource management is to be efficient and effective.

Persistence

Many of our natural resources problems have major physical, social and financial dimensions. Much of the Australian landscape is affected, numerous communities and many people are confronted, and suggestions are emerging that adequate amelioration will cost substantial sums of money (ACF and NFF 2000). Such amelioration will require innovative action[1] regarding natural resource investment planning calling for long-term commitment of resources by all parties[2], and changes in administrative structures and responsibilities, particularly at regional and local levels (Stafford Smith and Abel, Dore et al, this volume).

Purposefulness

The innovative action referred to above could be embodied in a National Natural Resource Investment Strategy (NNRIS) possessing many of the desirable attributes listed by Young et al (1996). Building on experience to date, an NNRIS should be based on partnership arrangements between the expected beneficiaries in communities, government and the private sector. Its efficiency and effectiveness will require it to be planned, monitored, audited, reviewed and adapted in a decentralised and devolved way. This calls for an hierarchy of 'nested' targets, incentives and accountabilities. Monitoring and auditing will be essential to enable feedback and adaptation, assessment of compliance and application of agreed sanctions.

---

1   That such significant effort is necessary is assumed in what follows. Its precise extent, however, should be the result of more detailed analysis and debate than we have had so far. Financial commitment of this nature also assumes the political commitment necessary to make it possible.

2   This may be more difficult for government than for communities. Time horizons of several decades are involved. This will require those responsible for the formulation of government budgets to accept the principle of contractual commitment to long term funding of natural resource investment.

Successful examples of co-operative federalism provide precedents for the organisation of an NNRIS, particularly for the links between the Commonwealth and the States. Particularly relevant examples include COAG; the Murray-Darling Basin Initiative, and its Salinity and Drainage and Business Sustainability Strategies; and the National Competition Policy. Precedent for links between the States and regions and communities are fewer but elements of Landcare and related programs, the various institutions for catchment management that have evolved, and arrangements with local government, would be helpful. The essential features of a possible NNRIS would be:

- The establishment of a National Ministerial Natural Resources Council, which would set National targets for natural resource outcomes (as with the MDBS&D Strategy). The States and Territories would sign off on these targets.

- Agreement to fund the investment necessary to achieve these targets through partnership arrangements between the Commonwealth, the States, local governments and relevant communities (including the private sector).

- Agreement between the Commonwealth and the States that Commonwealth payments to the States should be periodic and conditional on attainment of targets (as with the NCP).

- A National Natural Resources Audit Commission (analogous to the NCC) should review the status of the Nation's natural resources and advise the Commonwealth on State progress in relation to targets, and the Ministerial Council on the need to revise targets and adjust the investment program, in the light of growth in knowledge.

- The Commission would also audit the partnership arrangements between the States and the communities to establish that they conform to the agreed partnership principles.

- The States should be free to establish their own programs to make their contribution to the national targets, but they should revolve around the pursuit of regional targets (deduced from those at the national level) through the implementation of community driven Natural Resource Investment Plans (NRIPs).

- The NRIPs would be partnership *contracts* between the State Government and appropriately constituted Community Implementing Entities. The partnership arrangement would be based on negotiated cost sharing agreements (reflecting the principles agreed by the Council) and provide for accountabilities based on practicable monitoring, auditing and review.

The above is merely an outline of the possible nature of an NNRIS. Considerable discussion and refinement is needed if a practicable structure is to emerge. The point, for the moment, is that experience to date, and the magnitude of the problems we are told we confront, are such as to require the development of something like the proposed Strategy. Such an initiative is a quantum leap relative to what is proposed in the draft Policy Discussion Paper on natural resource management released by the Comonwealth (AFFA 1999).

While an NNRIS has been suggested here for natural resources management only, there is considerable potential in broadening the concept to encompass wider aspects of resource use. Dominance of cross-cutting issues, principles of inclusiveness and the need for the integrated and holistic approach underlying ecologically sustainable development, suggest the NNRIS could be extended to environmental protection, biodiversity, greenhouse policy and much of rural policy. Such an approach to sustainable resource use is discussed in the final chapter of this book.

Information richness and sensitivity

Good planning is data hungry (Harding and Traynor, this volume), and an NNRIS would not be exceptional in this respect. Evaluations will be always regarded as being inadequate for decision-making but the precautionary principle (and the precepts of planning practicability) mean that methodological ideals must be compromised and decisions must be made on the basis of 'best bet' assumptions. Experience with the land and water management plans in NSW, and elsewhere, is that there is a temptation to over-invest in biophysical knowledge generation, and under-invest in socio-economic knowledge (Ewing, Curtis, Harding and Traynor, this volume). This temptation should be resisted in the interest of financially and socially sound planning.

Inclusiveness

In contrast to Landcare, all parties must pay greater attention to the acceptance of obligations and accountability, along with sanctions for non-performance, in partnerships between them (Curtis, this volume). Cost sharing must be negotiated[3], and resulting agreements embodied in a formal contract between the government and the community implementing entity. This means that the implementing entity must have the legal standing to enter into such a contract. The establishment of such entities will become one of the core challenges of natural resources management.

Experience suggests that selection of appropriate entities will be a matter of 'horses for courses'. In the case of the NSW Land and Water Management Plans, the implementing entities are the relevant irrigation companies, sometimes in association with local government. In dryland situations, any one of a range of possible organisations might be appropriate. Regardless of their nature, they must be able to accept the responsibility and demonstrate the capability to implement the relevant NRIP. They must also have the standing to enter into contracts with other parties concerning cost sharing. In the irrigation case, contract enforcement is enabled by the requirements of the legislation for the privatisation of the irrigation areas and districts, and by the irrigation and drainage licences. Such institutions typically do not exist in dryland situations. Equivalent arrangements suggest themselves, however.

---

3   Practicable generic formulae for cost sharing are almost impossible to develop because the difficulty in measuring all costs and benefits means that cost shares cannot be established on an objective basis. Negotiation between the contracting parties is unavoidable.

Flexibility

For a number of reasons, the NNRIS and the NRIPs must contain provisions for careful monitoring and for review and adaptation. There are a number of reasons for this, as mentioned above. In particular, the long life of most plans and their necessarily inadequate knowledge base will call for their modification from time to time in the light of improved knowledge, experience and changing attitudes (Dore et al. this volume).

Achieving sustainable use of natural resources

This paper has argued economic policy settings play a crucial role in addressing issues of sustainability in the use of natural resources. Market based solutions are central to this. However, as noted, there are valid reasons why markets may not be appropriate in all circumstances. Correction of this situation requires policy intervention to ensure outcomes from the actions of natural resources users coincide with social objectives; that is, to correct for market imperfections. Because such correction relies upon a comparison between market outcomes and social preferences, specification of these social objectives and values, and the preferred distribution of benefits and costs, is important. Little attention has been paid to this in planning for natural resource use.

The variety of instruments available to help in achieving socially optimal use of natural resources is discussed above and in previous chapters of this book. What is relevant here is that, invariably, a mix of instruments will be required to meet natural resource management objectives and that the best mix will vary with the circumstances. This requires evaluation and analysis of, and knowledge about, responses to change in physical production and environmental systems and by natural resources users. It also requires attention to consultation and communication arrangements and management approaches, appropriate to multi-stakeholder processes aimed at creating learning communities. This chapter contains an explicit proposal of the possible form of a National Strategy for natural resource management as an illustration of the broad policy direction which is needed at that level.

Innovative, new approaches to solving natural resource management problems and resolution of issues around externalities and common property (which dominate natural resource management) will require much greater attention to developing sound relationships between stakeholders. The structure of relationships and factors which influence these are crucial to good natural resource management outcomes. Major payoffs will, therefore, come from attention given to the institutional questions of how relationships, and values and norms and ways of doing things, can influence natural resource management outcomes. Modification of these subtle institutions, and the associated arrangements for consultation and communication between stakeholders, provide a powerful long-term tool to improve production and management systems. (eg, Ewing, Curtis this volume).

In this context, the Commonwealth position on natural resource management policy seems to have shifted from support for capital works up to the late 80s, to strong support for community processes, planning, awareness and the acquisition of skills in the 1990s, to now, greater emphasis on the development of partnerships which allow investment in natural resource management outcomes. This prompts a warning. Many chapters of this book have stressed the stretched nature of resources for community processes and leadership. Regardless of the precise nature of this new policy direction, in the absence of adequate support, this shift in government emphasis will have a detrimental effect on the progressiveness of groups, effectiveness of consultation and communication arrangements; and on the evolution of institutions associated with community development and the building of social capital. These factors are crucial to the efficient operation of markets and to bringing about truly community based solutions to the increasingly urgent problems in the use, conservation, protection and management of natural resources in Australia.

References

Australian Conservation Foundation and National Farmers' Federation (ACF–NFF), 2000, *National investment in rural landscapes: a national scenario for strategic investment*, Canberra, July, <www.acfonline.org.au>

Agriculture, Fisheries and Forestry-Australia (AFFA), 1999, *Managing natural resources in rural Australia for a sustainable future*, Draft Policy Discussion Paper, Canberra: AFFA.

Dovers, S, 1995, Information, sustainability and policy, *Australian Journal of Environmental Management* 2: 142-56.

Godden, D, 1997, *Agricultural and resource policy*, Melbourne: Oxford University Press.

Industry Commission, 1998, *A full repairing lease: inquiry into ecologically sustainable land management*, Canberra: Australian Government Publishing Service,

Young, MD, Gunningham, N, Elix, J, Lambert, J, Howard, B, Grabosky, P and McCrone, E, 1996, *Reimbursing the future: an evaluation of motivational, price-based, property right, and regulatory incentives for the conservation of biodiversity*, Biodiversity Series, Paper No 9, Canberra: Commonwealth Department of Environment, Sport and Territories.

23

Reflecting on Three Decades: A Synthesis

Stephen Dovers

Centre for Resource and Environmental Studies,
The Australian National University

Synthesis of this collection is difficult. That is not the fault of the contri-butors but rather of the breadth and depth of the field and of their work. One easy way is to draw out a few, big messages and leave it at that. The 'broad coalition' needed and noted by Lowe, Eckersley and others is one, and important. The implications of the dominance of one political ideology, source of information or 'rationality' discussed by Mobbs, Lowe and others is another. Some of those big messages will come across in the next few pages and are important both as context and topics of research and policy debate. The other easy way to go is to repeat a sample of more specific issues and recommendations, but individual chapters do that already, and better than I could. Instead, this chapter draws out some of what lies between – matters big enough to be of generic import, small enough to be practical.

A qualification is necessary before proceeding. A collection of this breadth and depth cannot be neatly summarised and readers should turn to each contribution for greater insight and detail. Nevertheless, some core messages do emerge and even some concrete suggestions. However, this distil-lation is that of one person, and contributors are not liable for any misinter-pretation of their material.

The common themes, and definitional issues

The efficacy of the five core principles

As set out in Chapter 1, this book utilises some core principles and common themes to maintain consistency and enable later synthesis. The core principles proposed for adaptive institutions, policy processes and management regimes were: *persistence; purposefulness, information-richness and sensitivity, inclusiveness, and flexibility*. Some contributors were able to easily fit at least part of their analysis or conclusions into the frame of the five principles; others found this more difficult. However, this would probably be the case for any mechanism used to draw together analyses of different phenomena, across different sectors and from the perspective of different disciplines and methodological approaches.

One of the difficulties, recognised from the start, was that there is considerable overlap and interaction between these principles, either as criteria or properties. Discussion of one without reference to the others is rarely possible. Also, the principles can be at times in tension – for example, flexibility is an antidote for excessive persistence and/or purposefulness, and purpose may be diluted, at least in the short term, by inclusiveness. The challenge is to balance or integrate these, not to maximise or optimise each separately. And, of course, they are qualitative and subjective as criteria, so exact evaluation is rarely possible and relative evaluations are required. Again, such problems would arise with any other construction of common themes or principles.

There are two, related yet distinct grounds upon which to assess the efficacy of the five principles: as themes around which to organise research, and as desirable properties of processes, institutions and organisations. As desirable properties of policy processes and institutional arrangements they tend to attract little criticism except for their generality and lack of operational usefulness at finer resolutions of analysis or prescription, and that they are subjective and qualitative. Taking the last criticism first, there are those who would elevate quantification as the more rigorous approach to analysing and prescribing policy and institutions, and in some cases it may be. But the subjective and qualitative nature of the field of policy and institutions is unavoidable – assuming away the complexity of institutional arrangements for the sake of mathematical feasibility is not wise. Institutions, politics, policy and the contested values of a diverse community cannot, I believe, be reduced to a few good numbers, and must remain the realm of consistent, qualitative reasoning, drawing on good, quantitative analysis as necessary and appropriate. Let us not mistake numbers for rigour. Ensuring rigour in qualitative analysis is eminently possible; so is the reaching of valid and applicable conclusions. The contributions in this book demonstrate that well. They also demonstrate that the theoretical and methodological treasury of the qualitative social sciences and the potential for sustained, empirical analyses of past and current experiences have scarcely been tapped.

On generality, there is scope to work such principles into greater detail. However, as we proceed from generality to prescriptive and analytical detail, we can expect greater contestation over each institutional attribute or analytical device. As with Australia's ESD principles, in vagueness lies the possibility of agreement. Initial ventures into the construction of more detailed iterations of the attributes of adaptive institutions are provided in Dore et al (this volume), Dovers and Dore (1999) and Dovers (2001b).

It is as themes around which to organise research that the five principles are more problematic. This indicates a need to explore more fully possible common bases for joint analyses of policy and institutional setting in natural resource management. While many disciplines can offer particular theoretical propositions and methodologies, the evident need for interdisciplinary approaches suggests that no specific approach will serve to satisfy or integrate different disciplines without significant revision. Wider discussion and comparative assessment of the track record and integrative potential of various 'synthetic frameworks' and interdisciplinary ventures – such as complex adaptive systems modelling, less formal constructions of systems properties, work in resilience and vulnerability, ecological economics and environmental history, among others – would assist in this regard.

Definitional issues

Both in preparation for this book and throughout this collection, there are implicit and explicit inconsistencies in the way in which key terms and concepts are used and applied. Unbending definitions were not imposed on the contributors, in part due to the potential inflexibility of doing so and in part the likelihood that these would be abandoned anyway. There is also the difficulty of reconciling the meaning of key terms as used in specific disciplines, and as used in policy debates and everyday language.

'Institution' is a prime example. Theory defines institutions as underlying patterns, and organisations as the more obvious manifestations of these (see Henningham 1995; Goodin 1996). Yet in NRM policy debates and in the language of stakeholders the meaning differs; institutions as bricks and mortar or as obvious organisations. Who is 'correct' on this, or at least whose preference should prevail? Here, the two have been generally conflated for convenience and for communication, with the proviso that organisations require sufficient longevity and social recognition and acceptance to be discussed in similar terms as institutions. In some of the chapters, such as those by Christoff and Eckersley, distinctions are drawn. 'Policy' is another term that is given or is assumed to have widely different meanings, evidenced through different emphases on policy *outcomes* (the common tendency for scientists and advocates) and on policy *processes* (the tendency of those from law, public policy or political science). Such definitional issues will always be a problem, and most especially for reviews that span sectors and disciplines. Making explicit the definitions used and recognising the convenience or other reason for that definition is a minimum requirement.

Another definitional issue concerns the use of the term 'economic rationalism', a peculiarly Australian usage. It has become a derogatory term, and too often the meaning is vague. It is better to identify the political philosophy of neoliberalism, and then to identify and analyse the practical manifestations that can be gathered under the rather ugly but more precise term 'marketisation'. Marketisation is discussed as an emerging issue later. 'Economic rationalism' only has meaning in a relative sense, when held against other rationalities. Indeed, the identification and analysis of underlying 'rationalities', as in the chapters by Mobbs and Eckersley, suggests a more analytical and less confrontational way forward.

For the future, these issues reinforce the suggestion above regarding development of joint or at least not inconsistent theory and method for interdisciplinary discussion of policy and institutional settings. Construction of the basic elements of a common lexicon will need to precede the development of shared theory or joint methodologies.

Some core findings

The above qualifications aside, the five principles do allow the identification of some core findings. The format following is a summary judgment, followed by identification of selected key issues illustrated by reference to particular analyses contained in this book.

Persistence

Have policy processes and institutional arrangements for resource and environmental management been maintained sufficiently over time to allow results to emerge, be evaluated and learned from? The answer from this study is equivocal, although tending closer to no than yes. What factors encourage or enable persistence? Prime factors would be legal status or some other equivalent means of ensuring efforts are maintained, good and widely accessible information flows, political will, and patience.

It must be remembered that there is a downside to persistence, where institutions outlive their usefulness and become impositions of defunct understanding; the rangelands study here makes that observation (Stafford Smith and Abel). Opposed to that is the tendency for changes of minister or government, or of policy fashion for that matter, to break the continuity of process that *might* have produced results: Mobbs points this out in the RFA case, and the 1992 Hawke-Keating transfer of leadership that contributed to the diminishing of the ESD process (Dovers). Creating and maintaining political support under such circumstances is not easy. Dore et al indicate a long history of change in regional policy, and most is less easily explained by changing imperatives as by changing governments. Rapid program change, such as the 1996 decision that REDOs (Regional Economic Development Organisations) no longer existed, are too often followed by resurrection and imitation. That does not help the relationship between stakeholders and government or the evolution of policy. Persistence is critical to the slow task of evolving political and institutional capacity. The WA linkage created in the late 1990s between state of environment reporting and the policy system was, potentially, an internationally remarkable case, but is now on hold following a change of government (Harding and Traynor).

On a more positive note, Crabb identifies some workable interjurisdictional arrangements that have stood the test of time. These are worthy of close analysis, although I am terrified that (unnecessary) scrutiny may politicise them and cause them to unravel! Among others, I have suggested that a statutory basis is critical to persistence (Dovers 1999). But the RAC had such status and is defunct (Hamilton). So that is too simple a prescription, perhaps, and the message should be that a solid legal and administrative basis is important. Crabb's positive examples fulfil that requirement, in a variety of ways. They also show the value of what he terms 'committed specialists', traditional principles of public administration, and *appropriate and effective* community involvement. Information flows are direct between the responsible officers and agencies rather than diluted through complex overlays of committee after committee. Some 'old-fashioned' ideas from public administration retain their value even in an age of managerialist fashions. Ewing is guardedly optimistic about catchment management, recognising the long evolution (fractured persistence) and the difficulty of the task. In the catchment realm, and in the Landcare case (Curtis), greater continuity of funding and staff would contribute to persistence.

Finally, persistence is retarded by a lack of monitoring – environmental and of policy interventions. Smith's judgment of the quality of basic monitoring in the water sector is sobering and is supported by both Christoff and Ewing. Christoff's note that no Australian environmental protection regime has ever been properly reviewed is frightening. Bates notes deficiencies in our knowledge of regulatory implementation. We cannot persist if we do not know what is happening.

Some possible policy and research directions that arise are:

- Exploration of mechanisms to encourage policy continuity but not stasis across changes of minister and government. One measure is greater use of representative policy bodies mandated by statute and with actual powers and roles: for example, a national council on ESD to match similar bodies in many other countries.

- Provision of continuity in resources and staffing of non-traditional scale resource management initiatives, at local, regional and catchment scale.

- Provision of longer term and strict mandates for information gathering, dissemination and use. Better a half-decent time series than a collection of latest-method data sets with no continuity. And better some empirical data on the performance of policy and management interventions than best or half guesses every few years (see 'Information-richness', below).

Purposefulness

Have policy processes and institutional arrangements for resource and environmental management evidenced the development and pursuit of widely agreed principles, goals or standards? In this case the answer is – overall, rather than in specific policies or programs – largely no. But there are encouraging signs. As well, recognising purpose may really be possible only in hindsight. As Eckersley notes, what seems inadequate now may be part of a deeper change. Davis (1993: 15) put it well, noting that, in public policy, 'apparent volatility can become, in retrospect, the stately march of consistent underlying change'.

So some care is needed. However, this study intentionally took a view back over time, and has described policy and institutional change not just in the last few years. We can look for some clues at least. Of course, purpose is a relative thing, it depends on what particular political rationality is at issue. Smith sees tensions between market reform and participation in the water sector: there has certainly been sustained purpose behind 20 years of economic reform, much more so than behind participation or environment. Yet the development and expression of ESD principles is somewhat encouraging, even if the expression is not operational yet in term of guiding decisions (Bates, Dovers). That situation may evolve positively, such as with the hoped-for but not yet realised transition from state of *environment* reporting to state of ESD (Harding and Traynor). At present, ESD principles are the most viable and accepted basis for purposefulness we have (for a list of the 120+ statutes that express them, see Stein 2000). As distasteful as it may seem, it is in the body of law – common or statute, with the latter by far the most significant – that purpose will be expressed and enforced. Agreement on basic criteria and principles is a major advance in any policy formulation process, as with the setting of the JANIS criteria and the CAR reserve system targets in the RFA process (Mobbs).

At a more pragmatic level, purposefulness can be enhanced by greater clarity of mandate for new endeavours, at whatever level. Curtis stresses the importance of program logic, to provide direction and to allow evaluation. This has been a criticism of many programs by those later tasked with evaluation. At such finer resolutions, simple continuity of programs, intent and funding comes across as a serious issue (eg, with Indigenous programs, Orchard et al).

Some possible policy and research directions that arise are:

- Sensitivity to historical context in both research and policy may assist in either recognising unappreciated persistence, identifying the preconditions for persistence, or tempering unrealistic expectations of current efforts. It may also empower those involved to understand that their seemingly futile efforts are part of a longer endeavour (for a discussion of the potential of engaging and empowering community through historical investigation, see Roberts 2000). The time depth of that perspective will vary with context and in some cases it would appear that anything more than a few years would help.

- Exploration of how to further evolve ESD principles, in two ways. First, as statutory objects and requirements on decision makers – they are too vague as yet. Second; as decision support techniques and research methods to assist the operationalisation of the principles. For example, applications of the precautionary principle may be informed by various techniques (risk assessment, safe minimum standards, mediation, etc) but many such techniques are still imperfect and we are not skilled at choosing the right technique in varying circumstances.

- Exploration of other legal bases and decision making guidelines, such as a statutory duty of care (eg, Industry Commission 1998; Bates, this volume) or the public trust doctrine rediscovered in Australia law by Bonyhady (2000).

- Development of standards and procedures for program and policy development to ensure clear statements of logic and intent, so that the direction is clear and more importantly that the program or policy can be monitored, evaluated and learned from.

Information richness and sensitivity

Have policy processes and institutional arrangements for resource and environmental management evidenced recognition of uncertainty, the importance of quality information and the wide ownership and application of this information, and consistency in monitoring and evaluation of environmental conditions and policy and management experiences? This is a more difficult question to answer, as it has multiple components, particular situations vary enormously, and the kinds and degrees of uncertainty and thus of information needs continue to change. Initially, this principle is discussed under two separate heads: information and monitoring of the environment; and of policy and management interventions.

Regarding basic environmental monitoring, it is unclear whether we progressing or regressing. In the water sector, Smith describes the collection and analysis of basic data as a story of 'long-standing and sorrowful neglect'. If that is the story with water, an issue of perennial and deep concern in this nation, what hope for newer issues where the basic monitoring tasks are less well understood (eg, biodiversity, or environmental weeds). Crabb confirms the lack of basic data, but also observes that when available it may be ignored. Often we see sharp, intensive phases of data gathering, such as through the RAC inquiries and the regional forest agreements process (Hamilton, Mobbs). But such attention may not last, and making such information gathering routine remains a challenge. The ESD working group reports of 1991 were, mostly, unprecedented reviews and consolidations of knowledge in their sectors, but were not widely available and in many cases have not been repeated (Dovers).

Regarding policy and management interventions, much as what is reported in this study is discouraging. Clarity is rare in this area – as Bates says, legislation rarely instructs how to measure the achievement of statutory objects. That is a pity, and could be redressed in many cases. Christoff's statement that no Australian environmental protection regime has been subject to systematic, external review is alarming for any institutional area, but doubly so for a central and longstanding part of environmental management. What hope of learning when such is the case? Ewing describes a paucity of information and a lack of feedbacks as core problems for catchment management organisations. Mechanisms such as state of environment reporting aim to utilise basic data, but very often find that such data are scarce indeed (SEAC 1996; Harding and Traynor). Harding and Traynor also point out that there is a lack of linkage between SoE reporting and policy making. Without such links, the fundamental purpose of SoE cannot be fulfilled. Communication and use of the information from extant policy experiences can be difficult also. The lack of empirical analysis of the operation of specific policy instruments is unfortunate, if McKay's conclusion from rights markets in the water sector holds more broadly (which I think it does). Dore et al state that we have the full range of regional organisational experiences, and perhaps even of what they define as the positive attributes of these, but they are scattered and the common basis of knowledge is thin (the Greening Australia project they draw on addressed this and is a useful model for consolidation of scattered experiences). Some very good reviews of issues and policy have little impact: the parliamentary committee reports discussed by Odgers are examples. Why do they not have an impact when they are useful? Lowe raises the deeper prospect of a fundamental run down, in recent years, of intellectual capacity and of the purchase of R&D on longer term issues.

Questioning the availability of information may seem strange, in the face of an avalanche of reports and audits and the rise of the indicator industry. But therein lies the problem perhaps. More attention is being paid to the 'middle' of the informing process – summary reports, periodic audits, consolidations – and not enough to either the basic monitoring that they depend on, or the monitoring and evaluation of policy and management interventions that enables improvement (Dovers 2001a). There is ongoing lack of clarity as to the basis and derivation of indicators and their ability to connect data and decisions (eg, Neimeijer 2002).

Some possible policy and research directions that arise are:

- It is clear that basic monitoring is essential, and that its value cannot be defined solely by what seems relevant right now. Uncertainty as an attribute of NRM problems does not permit certainty about what to monitor. It is also unclear exactly how inadequate our basic monitoring is, and it is imperative that we find out.

- Proper policy monitoring is rare, but should not be. The common, minimal clause in policy statements that 'the policy will be reviewed in x years time' is insufficient in an adaptive sense, but also from a standard public administration stance. In particular, there is a need to better define the data needed to test the efficacy of the policy or management intervention (eg, volume, locations and number of trades under a rights market regime, number and kind of prosecutions, number and content of management plans, etc) and to make its collection routine.

- Ways of connecting intensive, short term information gathering spasms (reviews, reporting, inquiries, etc) to longer term information needs and processes is important. This involves the gathering of information so that it links to previous or ongoing data sets (to establish time series), and institutional arrangements to link short and long term strategies.

- Linking basic monitoring and policy monitoring is a challenge – or, rather, the challenge is to create a state where policy monitoring is considered basic and routine, and is closely linked to environmental monitoring. This will require clarity as to *why* we collect data (and the 'why' may include a very pure monitoring approach that admits uncertainty and the fact that many crucial discoveries owe much to serendipity), *who* will collect and *who* will use it. These are all too often missing.

- Institutions and processes to enable policy learning across agencies and sectors are largely absent. Professional societies in the resource and environmental arena are generally small and divided, as are the policy and management agencies, and reliance on random conferences and personal contact between responsible officers is insufficient.

* The impact of marketisation is potentially of great significance and an under-explored area (see below).

Inclusiveness

Have policy processes and institutional arrangements for resource and environmental management been characterised by genuine and sustained community participation, sensitive to the demands of different situations? There are two answers to this and they are in tension. On the one hand, there has been an internationally remarkable increase in community based management and monitoring programs in this country – EverythingCare and EverythingWatch (that is a glib line, but is a compliment and a convenient abbreviation, not derogatory). On the other, there are disturbing signs that modern political trends devalue some important forms of community participation.

On the positive side, Curtis and Ewing show the potential and the actual advances in the areas of Landcare and catchment management. Orchard et al propose Indigenous Protected Areas as a win-win, participatory program, and in fact the Indigenous domain is the site of some of Australia's most interesting processes of inclusion. As Orchard et al show, that is a classic example of the need for participatory strategies to be sensitive to cultural and other contexts. We have had some good experiences with policy formulation when representative processes are used (Dovers, Haward, Hamilton). However, these analyses point out weaknesses as well, such as where representative stakeholders were, collectively, prepared to go much further than governments would permit (eg, rangelands and ESD strategies).

On the less positive side, inclusive policy discourse has become less evident, contrary to the recommendation of Eckersley. At the local scale, Curtis notes cost shifting and decreased traditional extension services. Ewing sees catchment communities as differentially empowered. The representativeness of many of our new community based organisations is a sensitive topic. Strangely, the democratic basis of local government (proper elections, accountability) and its nearness to the community noted by Wild River are overlooked by people who seem unwittingly more enamoured of boards and committees hand-picked by a Minister. Ewing asks whether participation is a 'disguised form of privatisation of state responsibilities'. Dore et al identify a lack of definition of roles, power and responsibilities at the regional scale. Smith asks whether marketisation and participation are consistent policy goals, and Eckersley deals with this issue also at a broader level. Shortages of human, financial and informational resources are commonly identified.

The most disturbing message comes from the lawyers. Bates states that public participation is often encouraged through law, but less often is the public granted power to enforce laws. Bonyhady is sharper, and records a diminishing of public standing in environmental law. Bates adds an interesting justification for standing: regulatory enforcement is expensive, but standing empowers citizens as surrogate regulators. Despite the cheapness of that, governments may like the notion less than citizens.

In most cases, criticisms of participatory processes identify poor design or a lack of genuine commitment on the part of governments. 'Participants' are not always blameless victims or universally desirable policy inputs, however. In the RFA case, Mobbs shows the common enough tendency for good, stated intent to be unfulfilled in the design and implementation of participatory strategies. She also highlights the temptation of stakeholders to leave a process for strategic, political reasons – as Hamilton records with the RAC. In his largely positive case studies, Crabb records a variable degree of participation and no observable correlation with effectiveness. This (probably unfashionable) finding is important – strong participation should be sought and enabled *when appropriate*. Given the sharp caution on the limits of volunteerism from Curtis, community time should be treated as a scarce resource and spent wisely. Overall, it seems that we are not too skilled at clearly defining and understanding the many kinds of participatory strategies available (including very little), and selecting these to match particular contexts.

Some possible policy and research directions that arise are:

- The status of community participation is unclear. Despite an increased reliance on community based programs, community input through law and higher level policy formulation, in many cases, has been diminished. Are we fair dinkum about it? If so, then clarification is required.

- If we are serious about community-based approaches, then they should be 'institutionalised' – not to control, but to empower through, for example, longer term funding, clearer mandates, and legal and administrative status. Similarly, more sustained engagement of representatives of key community interests in higher level policy debate is required.

- Again, the impacts of marketisation are likely to be significant, and need to be identified and analysed (see below).

Flexibility

Have policy processes and institutional arrangements for resource and environmental management exhibited a willingness and capacity to change and adapt in the face of accrued experience and the emergence of new information? Yes, but not always in a reasoned fashion rather than an *ad hoc* one.

The pattern of legal and policy development at the broader level often follows what Cristoff describes with environmental protection, with lead or innovator jurisdictions. However, it is not clear that the same jurisdictions are always innovators across all sectors, or laggards always laggards. That is worthy of investigation across sectors. Bates confirms the law as flexible, but observes that it has trouble keeping up. Institutions change slowly – their inertia is problematic in the rangelands (Stafford Smith and Abel). Given that, it is more specific and less 'institutionalised' areas where flexibility and experimentation might be more likely to be found. Odgers notes that the flexibility in our broadest structure of governance – the Constitution – is possible at the margins, whereas formal Constitutional change has proved hard. Crabb shows good things happening away from the political limelight in the Murray Darling Basin, but is less kind to the macro-settings there. To be fair, how long is long enough for institutional change – after all, we have only been at it for a century in the Basin.

Smith and McKay show the changes in the water sector over the years, and the massive shift in the 1990s, but ask whether that shift was undertaken with our eyes open. Ewing describes the steady learning and organisational development in catchment management, and the rapid rise of the Landcare movement shows flexibility and ability to change (Curtis). But it is not clear that these phenomena lift our capacities sufficiently above what has been lost (eg, extension, basic monitoring) for them to be regarded as significant improvements. Flexibility and adaptation demands consolidation, keeping the good of the old while adding new value. Not unthinking cuts, shifts and inventions. Wild River records the constant evolution and updating of the agenda of local government, and the good and bad of that.

Eckersley recommends experimentation and a diversity of channels of policy debate and formulation. Inclusiveness and flexibility are irretrievably linked. However, this depends also on the existence of structures and processes that enable discourse. These must not only exist, but be open and allow diversity. A number of studies in this report – Dovers, Mobbs, Haward, Stafford Smith and Abel – discuss short term but significant policy processes. These provide flexibility, indeed that is their point, but there is too often a disjunction between them, what happened before, and what comes after. Some possible policy and research directions that arise are:

- Generally, the provision of structures and processes that encourage communication, policy debate and the accrual of experience – see 'Inclusiveness' above.
- Better connections between short term policy processes and long term goals and implementation.

Other, emergent issues

The preceding discussion organised under the headings of the five core principles does not capture some further issues that emerge from preceding chapters. The following identifies and comments on seven of these. While these could be discussed under the headings of the principles that would have been awkward, and besides these issues are sufficiently important to warrant clear identification. While they are interrelated, the need for brevity does not permit exploration of that.

Resources (of various kinds)

Not surprisingly, a common finding is that of insufficient resources to undertake NRM tasks properly or even to fulfil modest, stated objectives. Financial, human and informational resources follow political profile and relative priorities in policy – a chicken-and-egg situation. Without profile, no resources; without resources, no profile. Stafford Smith and Abel observe in the rangelands that responsibilities are transferred under regionalisation, but without the necessary resources. Wild River reports on the inadequacy of resources – financial, informational and human – for local government to do what it could, and the issue emerges with Landcare (Curtis), catchment management organisations (Ewing) and in the Indigenous realm (Orchard et al). Christoff suggests that even long standing public agencies like EPAs never had sufficient wherewithal to do other than the basic regulatory functions – unfortunately, the 'extras' are where the adaptive capacity lies, such as monitoring, evaluating and developing better procedures.

Putting all these together indicates a policy and management field where debates about resources are about marginal improvements when they should be more honest about chronic human, informational, administrative and financial under-capacity.

While no one will ever have enough resources, the area of most concern to the bulk of the NRM policy community would be the resourcing of the newer, local and regional initiatives in which we have invested so much faith. For these local and regional arrangements, it helps to recognise two separate issues of resources. There are the resources needed for discrete 'projects', and those needed for longer term support of administrative and monitoring functions. Project funding has been better treated, most recently under the Natural Heritage Trust. The NHT epitomises the issue of project based funding, where getting particular things done is possible, but the longer term presence of groups remains shaky. On the basis of a significant body of empirical evidence, Curtis identifies a looming crisis of persistence. Having the administrative wherewithal for a Landcare or other group to still be around, doing and adapting in ten years should not be viewed as a short term project. If community based or regional (or any other) organisations are to be given a firmer footing over time, then some form of ongoing base funding is needed. Some contractual arrangement will be necessary, too. That implies the legal status to enter into and acquit such a contract and the administrative resources to maintain it, as recognised by Musgrave and Kingma. Many bodies do not have that status. The emerging policy of seven year support for plans under the National Salinity and Water Quality Action Plan *may* serve to clarify this.

There is also the overarching question of the public finance status of NRM, especially in terms of supporting new initiatives. Ewing describes the Victorian 'catchment levy' and its abolition. On one hand this was a regressive move. But a counter argument is valid – that NRM should be no differently treated than other demands on public finance and indeed that there are risks in differential treatment. There may be limits to community tolerance of many, small levies, and if used this should be done sparingly and carefully. Also involved here are issues of trust, that the money raised will be spent appropriately. There have been unfortunate experiences in the past, in this and other policy fields, and the loss of trust that has resulted is hard to rebuild. At a broader level, the reliance on windfall privatisation proceeds to fund NRM projects via the Natural Heritage Trust is problematic, despite the value of many specific programs and of the total expenditure. It is arguably not sustainable. Occasional arguments for a broader system of environmental taxes require close scrutiny, too. Hypothecation of tax revenue is not as much a part of the Westminster tradition of public finance as it is, say, within the USA system. We do not undertake systematic hypothecation very often (eg, the Medicare levy), and any tendency to rely on repeated one-off hypothecations may leave NRM vulnerable in the longer term. And, as with the catchment and other examples, there is the possibility of cost shifting behind any special or short term financial arrangements, especially where these involve more than one level of government.

While financial resources are a major constraint on human resources, there are other dimensions. Managerialism and public sector cuts have eroded professional and intellectual capital in some areas, and the implications of the concomitant increase in out-sourcing and the rise of the consultocracy require investigation. Traditional NRM arrangements had some good features as well as deficiencies, as demonstrated by Smith and by Crabb. In the community based and regional realm, a relatively short period has seen new jobs and new tasks defined, such as Landcare conveners. It is not clear how well existing training programs equip people for these new jobs. Definition of core competencies for the various new NRM jobs may be a way to clarify this question.

Power

Resources are one factor defining the relative influence of different ideas and groups. But the broader issue of power comes out of several of the studies here as well. Policy decisions are political and politics is very much about power. Not recognising the political nature of decisions is a confusion and a mistake; the demise of the RAC evidences the importance (Hamilton). Several other studies observe the devolution of responsibilities and tasks to regional and local bodies, unmatched by devolution of power and status (Ewing, Dore et al, Stafford Smith and Abel). Wild River points to this issue for local governments as statutory and financial creatures of the States. State governments are jealous of giving away power, and to expect them not to be is unrealistic. In the broader public interest there are limits to how much rein local groups can be given, but advances can be made in detailed definition of rights and responsibilities and the devolution of power and rights carefully matched to particular responsibilities. An accurate translation of the European concept of subsidiarity – to place responsibilities at the lowest *appropriate* level – might take us beyond the first step that was the Intergovernmental Agreement on the Environment (which, incidentally, is probably ripe for formal review after a decade).

Within government there are issues of power also. Odgers describes the changing loci of power, away from the parliament and the professional bureaucracy and toward the executive and ministerial offices. There is scope for further investigation of this phenomenon, and of other public administration issues such as the location of responsibilities for natural resources and environment within the portfolio and departmental structures of government. As Lowe points out, scattered and fractured responsibilities are a real problem. Australia has experimented with more than enough variations – environment departments, mega-departments, statutory authorities – to provide the basis of research into the efficacy of different arrangements.

Political (and community) will

Without sufficient political will, things will not get better. This applies to community groups and the private sector as much as to politicians and government. Among others in this volume Mobbs, Dovers, Hamilton, Bates and Odgers explore some issues of will. The earlier discussions of persistence *versus* flexibility are relevant here. On balance, though, this is too slippery a notion to handle properly here, or perhaps at all. More tractable and more consistent with the aims of this research is to concentrate on those factors that might generate political will – persistence, information richness, inclusiveness, and the development of stronger institutions.

Scale and variability

The rangeland analysis here by Stafford Smith and Abel deals most explicitly with environmental heterogeneity and issues of scale (not surprisingly, the authors are ecologists). That policy and management prescriptions should match the regional context is obvious, but the knowledge and delivery mechanisms for this may not be adequate. But the issue is strongly implicit elsewhere, both from an ecological perspective and from political, administrative and cultural ones. The 'Indigenous domain' is clearly not homogenous, either in geographic or cultural terms (Orchard et al). Curtis, Ewing, and Dore et al raise the issue of poor connections between different scales of organisation and management – local, catchment, region, State. The dismal match between historical political boundaries and natural processes – and even many social processes – is the logic behind catchment and regional initiatives. We should beware, though, of adding levels of governance without benefit. 'Natural' boundaries may not be good for managing human systems, as Ewing warns with catchments. Hydrological determinism can go too far.

At the macro political scale, the mismatch between State and Commonwealth processes that defines Federation is still with us; Crabb and Odgers explore the good and less good of that. The utility of local government for local scale NRM remains insufficiently explored (Wild River). The heterogeneity of the Australian environment, of the substantive issues to do with it, and of information availability and human capacities should be obvious, but it has not prevented simple models being foisted inappropriately at times. Development of more 'ecological' scales of data gathering and management – such as the Interim Biogeographical Regionalisation of Australia (IBRA) – attend this and may eventually offer tractable interjurisdictional information pathways. But the harsh and unavoidable reality of administrative and statutory settings will always constrain such moves, and should remain a check on more fanciful prescriptions of NRM enthusiasts such as abolition of the States or redefinition of local government by 'bioregions'.

Initial conditions and preconditions

Success and failures can often be traced to the initial conditions that shape policy formulation and influence implementation. If this is true, then more attention to the preconditions of policy success, and perhaps even creation of those, might be rewarding. Haward's analysis of the recent and moderately hopeful case of oceans policy reveals the precedents of many inquiries, but more importantly the harder legal resolution that was the Offshore Constitutional Settlement: ground rules had been worked out. The National Forests Policy and the interim forest assessments set the basic parameters for the Regional Forests Agreements process discussed by Mobbs, and in this case the setting of some (however arbitrary) ecological principles, the JANIS criteria, was especially important. In the creation and maintenance of regional initiatives (Dore et al), we might think of a staged process, where empowering and non-threatening capacity building from the ground up precedes the harder task of creating lasting institutional settings and delineation of rights and responsibilities. How many regions and catchments are ready for that second stage? In the National Strategy for ESD case (Dovers), the working groups in some sectors went further in terms of consensus and policy recommendations than others. They tended to be those where there was a history of more fruitful discourse, or at least a relative lack of bitter contest, and a shared admission of uncertainty (eg, fisheries).

If a discursive turn in policy formulation is desirable, as Eckersley suggests, then the preconditions of respectful, mutually informing discourse may be pivotal. Stakeholders plunged without preparation into compressed discussion of a highly contested allocation issue are unlikely to get on famously. In a study of attachment to place in the Barmah-Millewa forest undertaken during the heat of a native title case, Ellemor (1998) suggested joint oral history projects as a mechanism for enhancing mutual understanding, but that these would need to be a precondition, undertaken away from the heat of the political moment. Stability in the organisational arenas of discourse would also be desirable – a warning against unthinking change of the boundaries and membership of regional or catchment organisations, for example.

Integration of environmental, social and economic policy

A core element of ecologically sustainable development is the requirement to integrate environmental, social and economic policy. Eckersley discusses the importance and the difficulty of this goal. Sometimes, policy says 'balance' rather than integrate, but balance is the lowest common denominator alternative to integration. There are two elements to this: the integration in policy, and in research.

It is the unfortunate case, as Bates mentions, that 'environment' in this equation too often goes through a double dilution in decision making processes: environmental agencies trade the three off, and then environment gets traded off again when Cabinet or core economic agencies get their turn. In part, this is due to the seniority and power of government portfolios that answer to economic and (to a lesser extent) social imperatives. But it is also a function of the newness and novelty, in public policy terms, of the environment and of ESD principles. Further development of policy formulation and decision making procedures to integrate the three imperatives is an area for profitable investigation. There are some interesting cases and leads in this volume. Odgers points out that local government has arguably been more successful at integration of functions than State or Commonwealth governments. Is this simply due to the smaller size and propinquity of departments, or are there other factors? He also indicates the increasing cross-sectoral nature of Senate committee references. It is a pity that the potential of parliamentary committees and their reports is not more widely recognized. The administrative difficulties of integration are very real, though, and this can be observed when we create 'integrated' approaches that then must be integrated with other agencies and scales, such as in the catchment management case (Ewing). Clear negotiation of who is to do what is essential, as Curtis notes for Landcare and its relationship with other arenas of policy and management.

There are various policy and decision-support possibilities, all with various merits and applications, such as multi-criteria analysis, integrated regional planning, and strategic environmental assessment. There are also various institutional possibilities, such as offices of ESD in first ministers departments or representative national councils or commissioners for ESD (for discussions, see Victoria Public Accounts and Estimates Committee 2000; Dovers 2001b). These possibilities deserve wide debate.

In the contest of research, while 'interdisciplinary' and 'integrated' have become requisite slogans at workshops, we are not well advanced in understanding how to do such research. This issue has not been explored in this study, but is crucially important. Better documentation of 'interdisciplinary' projects and their success/failure would be a start, as would communication between the various interdisciplinary ventures such as ecological economics, environmental history, complex adaptive systems modeling, and so on. Are there common challenges and themes?

More relevant here is the integration of research and policy. Hamilton's portrayal of the Resource Assessment Commission shows an internationally remarkable experiment in integration – not only of research and policy but of environmental, social and economic considerations. The RAC was an ESD institution, with integration as a statutory mandate. It didn't last long. One key lesson there is that such integration will not last in close proximity to hot, current issues, but is better placed deeper in the policy process as a longer term strategy.

Finally, there is the question of integration of experiences across sectors. This study has shown the potential of viewing policy and institutions across the whole resource and environmental field rather than locating analysis and learning within one subset of that field. The common issues and thus potential for increasing the body of experience available to any individual manager or agency demonstrates that. McKay's discussion of rights markets in water and fisheries show common issues and challenges in two sectors that, in terms of both research and practical policy learning, have very little to do with each other. How to create a more coherent policy field than currently exists is a worthy question.

Marketisation

Marketisation refers to the manifestations of the neo-liberal political philosophy that has been greatly influential over the past two decades in Australia and world wide. Marketisation takes two general forms: the advocacy and to lesser extent use of market mechanisms (taxes, tradeable rights, etc); and the reform of public institutions to adhere to 'market principles' (privatisation, corporatisation, contracting out, etc). The trend to managerialism, where place or sector specific knowledge is deemed of lower priority than generic management principles, is related. In this volume, Smith, Hamilton, McKay, Eckersley and Lowe deal with the nature and impacts of marketisation in various ways. However, this topic has not been an explicit focus of the study, so only a few general comments can be made (for further perspectives generally, see Bell 1997; Orchard 1998, and specifically see Eckersley 1995; Dovers and Gullett 1999; Productivity Commission 2000).

Overall, 'economic rationalism' has become a complaint rather than a useful analytical label, and neoclassical economics is often blamed for things inappropriately. Greater and more sophisticated exposure of the strengths and weaknesses of economic theory and method is certainly desirable (for a review, see Common 1995). We are currently stronger on criticisms of economics and its ways than we are on policy prescriptions to redress the situation. The nascent field of ecological economic is the prime location of research on this.

On specific instruments, the label 'market mechanisms' is actually a mistake – as Bates points out, property rights-based policy instruments are as much legal as they are economic. Indeed, a mix of policy instruments is generally required, and no one category – be it economic, regulatory, educative, whatever – is better or worse but rather all are valid in different contexts (Dovers 1995). Also, the category 'market mechanisms' contains a richness and variety of possible instruments that renders advocacy of the general class meaningless. This applies to other broad categories such as statutory or educative as well. Second, what market mechanisms we have in place remain strangely under analysed. For examples, rights markets in water and fish (tradable water rights and individual transferable quota) have been established with little analysis, either *ex ante* or *ex poste* (McKay). Emerging work on the operation of such markets reveals a complex reality that often defies the predictions of both advocates and critics (eg, Connor 2001; Connor and Alden 2001). We need more such detailed, empirical evaluation of the performance of market and other policy instruments.

More profound than particular market mechanisms has been the marketisation of public institutions and policy processes. Natural resource management has been as affected (if not more) by this trend as any policy sector. The COAG water reforms are the most well known (see Fisher 2000), but other resource sectors such as forestry, fisheries and others have been fundamentally altered. At a more subtle level, the implications of such changes as contracting out of functions, increasing use of consultants and cuts to traditional extension services are generally unknown. Anecdotal evidence is that there have been implications, for integration across catchments and landscapes and across portfolios and agencies, for public participation as citizens become consumers, for access to information as commercial-in-confidence doctrines apply, and for long term monitoring. But we know little detail. That is a situation of gross policy ignorance that should not be tolerated. While there are limits to changing marketised arrangements – the horse has bolted, so to speak – adjusting the regulatory framework and creating countervailing policy measures, if necessary, should be possible. And we doubtless will implement more market based policies – there are good reasons why we should in some cases – and learning from the experience so far would be sensible.

There is a case for a new test and threshold of proof in such cases: that of *irreversibility*. Some policy interventions and institutional changes are irreversible, at least on any practical grounds or within any realistic time frame, and the strictures of demonstrating their efficacy and predicting their impacts should be far stronger than those that are reversible. The legacy of their failure or unintended impact is worse, after all. For example, privati-sation of an institution, process or resource will in most cases be irreversible; contracting out is not as it can be revisited. There is considerable scope for translating the legal doctrines of proof – beyond reasonable doubt, the balance of probabilities, and the lower evidentiary threshold – into the realms of science and especially into procedures for *ex ante* policy evaluation. At present, in applying the promising precautionary principle, the burden of proof regarding critical notions of 'serious' or 'irreversible' impact is focused on the environment rather than on our policy and management interventions. In adaptive terms, more scrutiny of social and economic policy proposals is required. While potentially a radical notion, it simply mirrors what we (in theory at least) increasingly require of developers in environmental impact assessment: why not the 'developers' of policy proposals that will determine the state of the environment? This raises the issue of the proper implemen-tation of strategic environmental assessment, to force attention on the ESD implications of government policy (Marsden and Dovers 2002).

Finally, Christoff raises the issue of the 'ecological modernisation' of production and consumption in Australia. The prospect of such a process of increasing efficiency in resource and waste systems is a comforting one. But Christoff questions whether environmental efficiency gains in this country has been due to local regulation and improvement, or whether they have in fact been 'externally sourced' through imports of elaborate manufactures. Clever country?

In conclusion

Many of the issues and imperatives raised in this study and summarised in this book are, to put it bluntly, bloody obvious. Given that many of the sectors and topics explored have been the subject of a deal of analysis already, that expectable conclusions are reached should not be a surprise. That policy *ad hockery* and amnesia is ongoing, and that the institutional and organisational foundations of policy and management are still imperfect, are not startling findings, and doubtless suit the cynical. The environment is still a marginal concern and there is insufficient evidence that we take sustainability seriously.

However, on the other hand there are issues and situations identified that are less expected or more recent. Some of these are problems, such as the current lack of forethought and expertise in implementing market-based policies or the diminishment of legal rights of citizens in planning law. Others are encouraging, such as the largely unnoticed existence of quite sound inter-jurisdictional resource management arrangements or the presence of good regional ventures.

One thing that does emerge, though, is that it is not at all clear whether the more encouraging ventures will survive - and hopefully improve - over time. Nor is it clear that the less desirable features of how we have managed resources and the environment are diminishing as we learn their weaknesses. One strength of this study is its recalling of memory over a few decades, rather than the (at most) few years that is the normal memory of policy debates. It is easy at any given point in time to refer to a few current initiatives and to believe that things are going to improve. Two decades of resource and environmental policy in NSW since the epochal *Environmental Planning and Assessment Act* 1979 shows the danger of such convenient forgetfulness (Farrier 1999; Bonyhady, this volume).

The other, obvious point is that there are not single policy answers or institutional or organisational models. For example, a successful regional organisational model in one place may be ill suited elsewhere. And there are almost always more than one or two causes behind any situation, be it failure or success or the much more usual mixture of the two. For example, declines in basic monitoring result from public sector cuts, but are also connected to the incentives (internally and externally imposed) that drive scientists, and to comforting beliefs that remote sensing, information technology and community monitoring can fill any gaps. So, in both analysis and prescription we need the capacity to interpret at a fine resolution, to pick and choose wisely, and to continue evaluating and learning. That we have not 'learned to learn' or shown evidence of sufficient improvement suggests the importance of structures and processes to establish resource and environmental management - or 'ESD' in the broadest sense - as an accepted, high profile and well informed feature of the policy landscape. The Productivity Commission's (1999) finding that implementation of ESD at the Commonwealth level failed to meet normal standards of good policy practice is as mundane as it is profoundly important and disturbing. An important social goal and policy agenda gets diluted and lost in an inadequate organisational and institutional setting.

Returning to the opening of this chapter, it is certainly true that a 'broad coalition' of support and intent around sustainability issues is required, but that does not yet exist in an overall sense (although it has emerged, for short periods, over particular issues). There are those who would say that, despite the remarkable developments of the past decade, we are further rather than closer to that than we were. Therein lies the chicken-and-egg dimension of institutional arrangements: without a strong presence in the field of public policy - which is what sound institutions can provide, over time - a clear and purposeful coalition is less likely to emerge. But, without that coalition, significant reform of policy processes and institutional arrangements is unlikely. Short term considerations and the simplicity of increasingly populist politics stands at odds against the need for bipartisan, long term approaches that deal properly with the particular complexity of sustainability issues.

That suggests an impasse, where a move needs to be made by someone. Loosely, the players are firms, governments, community and scientists. Who should make the move? Some firms are innovative, but profit constraints are real. A reasonable segment of the community, at least in non-metropolitan areas, has evidenced considerable if guarded commitment to longer term efforts and a preparedness to entertain significant change to the way they do things. Scientists and other researchers are beginning to respond to the need for different approaches – participatory, interdisciplinary and so on. But they have a way to go still, and the focus of research is still being instructed by short term imperatives imposed by government policy as well as traditional disciplinary divides.

On the basis of evidence in this book, it is governments who need to make the crucial moves (remembering that governments do, to some extent, reflect the community). Governments have done some fine things, or at least tried to; it is often in the realms of consistency, persistence and imple-mentation where the problems lie. But stop-start policy, inconsistent goals, populism, lack of clear purpose over time, patchy inclusion of stakeholders and short term resourcing do not the suit the task of addressing sustainability. If that sounds too much like the classic Australian whinge about government, it is tempered by the fact that the whinge is not for governments to 'do' some unspecified things, but rather and more often to create *the conditions* under which many things can be done, by those in government and outside, with purpose, over time. 'Political will' and prevailing political ideologies are easy, obvious targets, but they are hugely important. This study has examined the evolution of policy processes and institutions over the past few decades, and – while accepting that processes and institutions will always be still evolving – there are not enough cases yet where the improvement matches the potential.

References

Bell, S, 1997, Globalisation, neoliberalism and the transformation of the Australian state, *Australian Journal of Political Science* 32: 345-367.

Bonyhady, T, 2000, An Australian public trust, In: Dovers, S (ed), *Environmental history and policy: still settling Australia*, Melbourne: Oxford University Press.

Common, M, 1995, *Sustainability and policy: limits to economics*, Melbourne: Cambridge University Press.

Connor, R, 2001, Changes in fleet capacity and ownership of harvesting rights in New Zealand fisheries, In: Shotten R (ed), *Case studies on the effects of transferable fishing rights on fleet capacity and concentration of quota ownership*, FAO Fisheries Technical Report 412, Food and Agriculture Organization of the United Nations.

Connor, R and Alden, D, 2001, Indicators of the effectiveness of quota markets: the South East Trawl Fishery, *Marine and Fresh Water Research* 57: 387-397.

Davis, G, 1993, Introduction: public policy in the 1990s, In: Hede, A, and Prasser, S, (eds), *Policy making in volatile times*, Sydney: Hale and Iremonger.

Dovers, S, 1995, Information, sustainability and policy, *Australian Journal of Environmental Management* 2: 142-156.

Dovers, S, 1999, Adaptive policy, institutions and management: challenges for lawyers and others, *Griffith Law Review* 8: 374-393.

Dovers, S, 2001a, Informing institutions and policies, In: Venning, J, and Higgins, J, (eds), *Towards sustainability: emerging systems for informing sustainable development*, Sydney: University of NSW Press.

Dovers, S, 2001b, *Institutions for sustainability*, Tela paper 7, Melbourne: Australian Conservation Foundation.

Dovers, S, and Dore, J, 1999, Adaptive institutions, organisations and policy processes for river basin and catchment management, 2nd International River Management Symposium, Brisbane, 29 September-2 October.

Dovers, S, and Gullett, W, 1999, Policy choice for sustainability: marketisation, law and institutions, In: Bosselman, K, and Richardson, B, (eds), *Environmental justice and market mechanisms*, London: Kluwer Law International.

Eckersley, R (ed), 1995, *Markets, the state and the environment: towards integration*, Melbourne: Macmillan.

Ellemor, H, 1998, Place and natural resource management: the case of the Barmah-Millewa Forest, Australia, PhD Thesis, Australian National University.

Farrier, D, 1999, Dis-integrated resource management in NSW, 18th National Environmental Law Association Conference, Sydney, 8-10 September.

Fisher, T, 2000, Lessons from Australia's first practical experiment in integrated microeconomic and environmental reform, In: Productivity Commission, *Microeconomic reform and the environment: workshop proceedings, Melbourne, 8 September 2000*, Melbourne: PC.

Goodin, RE, (ed), 1996, *The theory of institutional design*, Cambridge: Cambridge University Press.

Henningham, J, 1995, *Institutions in Australian society*, Melbourne: Oxford University Press.

Industry Commission, 1998, *A full repairing lease: inquiry into ecologically sustainable land management*, Canberra: AGPS.

Marsden, S, and Dovers, S, (eds), 2002, *Strategic environmental assessment in Australasia*, Sydney: Federation Press.

Neimeijer, D, 2002, Developing indicators for environmental policy: data-driven and theory-driven approaches examined by example, *Environmental Science and Policy* 5: 91-103.

Orchard, L, 1998, Managerialism, economic rationalism and public sector reform, *Australian Journal of Public Administration*, 57: 19-32.

Productivity Commission, 1999, *Implementation of ecologically sustainable development by Commonwealth departments and agencies*, Canberra: Ausinfo.

Productivity Commission, 2000, *Microeconomic reform and the environment: workshop proceedings, Melbourne, 8 September*, Melbourne: PC.

Roberts, J, 2000, Oral history, ecological knowledge, and river management, In: Dovers, S, (ed), *Environmental history and policy: still settling Australia*, Melbourne: Oxford University Press.

SEAC (State of Environment Advisory Committee), 1996, *Australia: state of environment 1996*, Melbourne: CSIRO Publishing.

Stein, P, 2000, Are decision-makers too cautious with the precautionary principle? *Environmental and Planning Law Journal*, 18: 3-23.

Victoria, Public Accounts and Estimates Committee, 2000, *Follow-up inquiry into environmental accounting and reporting*, Issues paper 4, Victoria: The Parliament.

Table of Cases

Table of Statutes

Index